I Came Home and There Was No One There

Conversations and Stories about the Uprising in the Warsaw Ghetto

Jews of Poland

Series Editor
Antony Polonsky (Brandeis University, Waltham, Massachusetts)

Other Titles in this Series

Bolesław Prus and the Jews
Agnieszka Friedrich
Translated by Ben Koschalka

Palestine for the Third Time
Ksawery Pruszyński
Translated and with an introduction by Wiesiek Powaga

Blooming Spaces: The Collected Poetry, Prose, Critical Writing, and Letters of Debora Vogel
Debora Vogel
Edited by Anastasiya Lyubas

Macht Arbeit Frei?: German Economic Policy and Forced Labor of Jews in the General Government, 1939–1943
Witold W. Medykowski

New Directions in the History of the Jews in the Polish Lands
Edited by Antony Polonsky, Hanna Węgrzynek and Andrzej Żbikowski

Warsaw is My Country: The Story of Krystyna Bierzynska, 1928–1945
Beth Holmgren

For the Good of the Nation: Institutions for Jewish Children in Interwar Poland. A Documentary History
Edited and Translated by Sean Martin

Shadows of Survival: A Child's Memoir of the Warsaw Ghetto
Kristine Keese

I Came Home and There Was No One There

Conversations and Stories about the Uprising in the Warsaw Ghetto

Hanka Grupińska

Translated from Polish by
Jessica Taylor-Kucia

BOSTON
2023

The publication of this book has been supported by the Taube Foundation for Jewish Life & Culture

Library of Congress Cataloging-in-Publication Data

Names: Grupińska, Anka, author. | Taylor-Kucia, Jessica, translator.
Title: I came home and there was no one there: conversations and stories about the uprising in the Warsaw Ghetto / Hanka Grupińska; translated by Jessica Taylor-Kucia
Other titles: Conversations and stories about the uprising in the Warsaw Ghetto
Description: Boston: Academic Studies Press, 2023. | Series: Jews of Poland | Translation of: "Ciągle po kole" and "Odczytanie Listy."--Publisher | Includes bibliographical references.
Identifiers: LCCN 2023014905 (print) | LCCN 2023014906 (ebook) | ISBN 9798887192598 (hardback) | ISBN 9798887192680 (paperback) | ISBN 9798887192604 (adobe pdf) | ISBN 9798887192611 (epub)
Subjects: LCSH: Warsaw (Poland)--History--Warsaw Ghetto Uprising, 1943--Personal narratives. | Jews--Persecutions--Poland--Warsaw. | Holocaust, Jewish (1939–1945)--Poland--Warsaw--Personal narratives. | World War, 1939–1945--Registers of dead--Poland--Warsaw. | Żydowska Organizacja Bojowa (Poland)--History.
Classification: LCC D765.2.W3 G765 2023 (print) | LCC D765.2.W3 (ebook) | DDC 940.53/1853841--dc23/eng/20230407
LC record available at https://lccn.loc.gov/2023014905
LC ebook record available at https://lccn.loc.gov/2023014906

Copyright © 2023, Academic Studies Press
All rights reserved.

ISBN 9798887192598 (hardback)
ISBN 9798887192680 (paperback)
ISBN 9798887192604 (adobe pdf)
ISBN 9798887192611 (epub)

Cover design by Ivan Grave
Book design by PHi Business Solutions

Published by Academic Studies Press
1577 Beacon Street
Brookline, MA 02446, USA

press@academicstudiespress.com
www.academicstudiespress.com

Contents

Acknowledgments   vii

Part One   **Still Circling: Conversations with Soldiers of the Jewish Fighting Organization**

Recording the Holocaust	3
What Was of Importance in the Ghetto? Nothing! Nothing! Don't Be Ridiculous!	13
Back Then, There Were Many Legends …	41
Someone Must Have Pushed That Closet up Flush from Outside …	53
I'm Telling You so Superficially Because I Don't Remember	85
We Were Just Rank-And-File Soldiers	115
Well, I'm Here, Aren't I?!	163
Truth Be Told, I Left My House in 1942 and Never Went Back	177
And That's All My Life Story	225
I Know What I Know, And I Remember What I Remember	233
None of It Is of Any Significance	287

Part Two   **Rereading the List: Stories about the Soldiers of the Jewish Fighting Organization**

List of Those Who Fell in the Defense of the Warsaw Ghetto	475
A Rereading of the List	479
A Cemetery of Letters, a Cemetery of Words	489

Glossary	491
Bibliography	523
Index	529

Acknowledgments

The English-language edition of this book has been translated and published thanks to the generosity of:

The Kronhill Pletka Foundation (with the cooperation of Mr. Edward Serotta)

Mr. Zigmunt Rolat and Mr. Alan Silberstein (with the cooperation of Mr. Piotr Koral and Mr. Douglas Ades)

Taube Philanthropies

Stowarzyszenie Żydowski Instytut Historyczny w Polsce

Polish Cultural Institute, New York

The portraits of the author's interlocutors were taken by Adam Rozenman; other pictures in the first section of the book belong to the Collection of Łukasz Biedka.

The author expresses her gratitude to Professor Antony Polonsky for all his support.

Part One

STILL CIRCLING: CONVERSATIONS WITH SOLDIERS OF THE JEWISH FIGHTING ORGANIZATION

Recording the Holocaust

This book was created from the memories of people who are no longer.

I originally took my "circling" around the history of the Warsaw ghetto uprising into the public domain almost forty years ago. My first conversation with Marek Edelman—which is also the first in this book—was conducted in 1985 for the Polish underground periodical *Czas*. Before long, that conversation had been translated into several languages, and it rapidly became important, for in those days (too), the world was deeply divided, and in America or France, Marek Edelman's words from Poland sounded like a message from another world. In 1988 and 1989, I spoke with Warsaw ghetto insurrectionists living in Israel; in 1990, with Inka—Adina Blady-Szwajgier—in Warsaw.

The first edition of these conversations with soldiers from the Warsaw ghetto came out in 1991, thanks to Hanna Krall, who said: "This needs publishing" and called a publisher. "You need to talk to Stasia," Marek said to me in 1999. I was a few weeks too late. I listened to Chajka Bełchatowska too late, too; she was already very sick by then. In 1999, I managed to persuade Kazik Ratajzer that his story should be added to what was by then *Ciągle po kole* [Still Circling]. In 2000, I closed that circle around the uprising with a second conversation with Marek Edelman.

All of my interlocutors were talking to me years after the events. Some of them for the first time. Many of them for the first time using Polish words. Masza, Luba, Aron, Pnina, Kazik, and Szmuel had all managed to "assimilate" the Holocaust in Hebrew in one way or another. In any case, a different narrative was expected of them over there. Their conversations with me were more about unlocking their memories than naming events. The Polish words cleaved more nearly to the past than Hebrew ones; they were closer to the quick and made more painful meanings. My conversations with Inka and Marek were automatically filtered through our Polish experience. (In our communication, the Poland that was so irksome in both space and word had been present throughout the intervening years.) The language triggered nothing; it was an invisible tool wielded by the meanings that surfaced.

They remembered differently, for each of them was speaking about their own experience, stored in their own memory. (Their stories are not chapters in a history textbook. Their stories are the sort of material that is flattened by textbook history.) They used many words for the same meanings because their memory had registered itself in many languages—Yiddish, Polish, and Hebrew. Marek always said "Jurek Wilner," because Jurek was from Warsaw, but Szmulik Ron called Wilner by his Hebrew name, "Arie," because they were both Zionists. They all pronounced Rozowski's first name in different ways, because some of them preserved the "dark l" from Yiddish and called him "Welwł," while others Polonized it, as Welwel. Their own names have been recorded in a variety of ways as well: using German spelling, or a transliteration from the Hebrew, or a Polonized version. There are a lot of proper names here because they used so many. The mass deportation of residents of the Warsaw ghetto in July, August, and September 1942 is variously the "campaign" (Ger. "*Aktion,*" Pol. "*akcja,*" lit. "action"), the "deportation," the "*große Aktion,*" the "deportation campaign." But the same words mean different things in different places: "the deportation campaign" might elsewhere refer to the final liquidation of a ghetto in another city. "The campaign" was also the term used by Masza and Pnina for the uprising in the ghetto because they were translating the German word "*Aktion,*" and Anielewicz spoke of "self-defense." The word "uprising" came from another, later world.

Over thirty years have passed since the first edition of these conversations with the insurrectionists. The book has run into four editions in Polish and is considered one of the most fundamental titles on the subject. Today, we know differently about the uprising, the ghetto, and the Holocaust—we know less. The heroes of their stories are gone from the world of the living. And we are forgetting, because time, because events, because the further the past recedes, the weaker its influence is on our perception of the world. So, I explain more with both extensive notes and period photographs of everyday life.

The photographs supplementing the conversations, most of them never previously published, are from the extraordinary Collection of Łukasz Biedka. This is not ordinary, because the world captured in it is not ordinary; it is *extraordinary* because eighty years on, we are able to look into the eyes of those who were there. Photographs in ghettos were mostly taken by Germans (soldiers had cameras and were exempt from prohibitions), rarely by Jews (sometimes people employed in the Judenrat might take photographs covertly for propaganda purposes), and very rarely by Poles (we know, for instance, of a dozen or so photographs snapped in secret in the ghetto during the uprising by a Polish fireman). These from the Collection of Łukasz Biedka have not been attributed to any identifiable author; it is likely that all of them, or the vast majority, were taken by German soldiers.

I propose that these conversations be read—even more so today, as the hydra of nationalism once again rears its threatening head in Poland and all over the world—with a dual understanding: as a documentary record of a cruel time and also as a record of ways of thinking and stances that are present in every age.

***

Depositions, testimonies, paradocumentaries, fictionalized forms: much has been and still is being written on the Holocaust. And though the Holocaust seems like an impossible experience to record, we are constantly recording it. We cannot extricate ourselves from the recording of it. We seek a non-existent form for content that is too much to bear. To rediscover someone's death, re-decipher a fragment of a stranger's fate—in the tatters and scraps of memories. To jot them down, on another scrap of processed memory. To find a detail that will be ours: a red sweater, a girl with a piece of bread roll on Walicόw Street, a polka-dot dress, coupons cut out . . . We scour yet another text for a detail to take for our own. And in between is space for silence. Without silence there can be no recording of the Holocaust. And a moment later, we can comprehend, for a moment, that non-conveyable reality, and once again we understand that mute space, for beyond it is concealed a detail that will enable us to touch, for a second, that imagined world.

Marek Edelman says: there were two hundred twenty of us insurrectionists. Some historian writes: the ŻOB numbered four hundred fifty to five hundred people. There is no knowing how many soldiers made up the Jewish Fighting Organization—how many there were in January 1943 or how many in April 1943. We do know that in the night of April 18/19, twenty-two ŻOB groups stood ready to fight. Each group is assumed to have numbered around twelve fighters. And then the couriers, men and women, Jews and Poles, inside the ghetto and outside its walls. We know that there cannot have been fewer than two hundred twenty ŻOB fighters, and that there were not more of them than four hundred.

There were also others that fought in the uprising. Those known as "wildcats" (lit. "wild ones"), for instance. Armed after a fashion, they operated alone or in small groups, defending themselves in bunkers and ruins. There were also small groups along party lines that did not join the ŻOB, but perhaps had some form of contact with it. And then there was the other armed formation: the Jewish Military Union (ŻZW)—the soldiers who fought the battle on Muranowski

Square. I do not write about any of these in this book. I have set out to talk about the soldiers of the Jewish Fighting Organization: to reconstruct this army that was never written down anywhere.

In June, or perhaps it was July 1943, Celina Lubetkin, Antek Cukierman, and Marek Edelman were living in hiding at 4 Komitetowa Street (in the home of Mrs. Stasia Kopikowa, who successfully kept her true Jewish identity under wraps, and played the role of captain's wife in front of her neighbors). Celina, Antek, and Marek decided to write down the names of the ŻOB soldiers who had been murdered in the Warsaw ghetto uprising. They reproduced those names from memory. "After all, we all knew each other," Marek said. And they signed it off with the sentence: "This list is not complete owing to a lack of information on the other members of the ŻOB." Marek Edelman remembered that they wrote down two hundred twenty names. The list was probably taken to the apartment shared by Józef Sak and Tadek Borzykowski for safekeeping. It was probably Sak who took it to Żurawia Street, to Ignacy Samsonowicz. And it was most likely in November 1943 that Leon Feiner sent the list in microfilm form to London. It is possible that the addressees were Emanuel Sherer and Ignacy Schwarzbart.

I reread the "London list" of the soldiers who made up the Jewish Fighting Organization. Two hundred twenty-two names (there is a mistake in the numbering), each one with a letter representing the organization to which they belonged: D for Dror, B for the Bund, Sz for Haszomer Hacair. In January 1945, Melekh Neustadt came to Warsaw from Palestine. He, Marek, Antek, and Kazik sat together in the Polonia Hotel. Neustadt had the London list with him. He asked all about the ones who had been killed. In 1946, he wrote his book *Hurban begetto varsha*, and in it he noted down what he had heard in Warsaw and what he had found out in Palestine about the April insurrectionists.

After that, the London list was forgotten. It was probably in 2001 that I asked Marek Edelman whether anybody had ever written down the names of the April ŻOB fighters, the Warsaw ghetto insurrectionists. And it was then that Edelman remembered that they had sent the list they had written down on Komitetowa Street to London. A few weeks later, I was looking through papers that had been stored for nearly sixty years in a cardboard box that someone had labelled "Jews." I brought a copy of the London list back with me to Warsaw.

I am trying to reread it once again. In 2022, one more time. Because I am still receiving letters, handwritten and typewritten, telephone calls from Poland and abroad, and in them minor corrections, additions, adjustments, scraps of new detail. Lodzia Hamersztajn, for instance, asked me to be sure to correct the address of the postwar kibbutz at Poznańska Street: they lived at no. 38, not at no. 58. Majus Nowogrodzki wrote that in the new edition I must stress that Michał Klepfisz was awarded the Virtuti Militari, and that a copy of the certificate confirming his decoration is held in YIVO, in New York. And Gienia Pocalun wrote that Niuta Tajtelbaum loved animals.

The London list is in all certainty incomplete. It does not include the names of so many insurrectionists: those who survived are not on it, and those who perished but whom no one remembered are not on it. It is also, in a sense, erroneous: it does include the names of people who by April, or even by January 1943, were no longer in the ghetto. (There is the group of twelve Halutzim who were killed in Hrubieszów in 1942. There are also the names of three Krakow ŻOB members on it.)

My list is also incomplete, perhaps incorrect, and likewise erroneous. I recorded the names of 246 April insurgents, as well as twenty-nine Jewish and thirteen Polish ŻOB couriers. I found twenty names of ŻOB members who were murdered in January 1943. I counted 308 Warsaw ŻOB members who were alive in January 1943. 275 of them fought in the April uprising. Twenty of them were killed in the January operation. (This book does not contain the stories of ŻOB members who were arrested, or of ŻOB members murdered before January 1943.) I established that thirty-one of the insurgents survived the uprising and the war. I am unable—in any case, it is probably impossible by now—to create a full list of those names.

I collect scraps and snippets of all manner of notes and use them to discern stories of friendships, of longing for Eretz Israel, of unfinished lovings; I write down stories about dying. I seek out the detail through which I can come to an imagination of that world. I want to preserve as much as possible. Sometimes, I find nothing; all that remains is a name from the List. I write a little in others' words, a little in my own. In the Jewish texts, a boy was light-haired—not blond, but exactly that: light-haired. So, in my book Jurek Błones is light-haired, and so is Zygmunt Frydrych. Some expressions sound unnatural, clunky, or awkward: that during a raid, people were found, that someone looked "too dangerous" or had "safe looks," that a boy was "in a pair with" a girl. I didn't want to smooth those expressions out.

It's too late for a book like that, Marek Edelman said in 2001. Because although he was adamant that the detail was of no consequence—the historical, not the narrative detail—he did want things to be true, real, "without embroidery." But it wouldn't have been possible to write it all down any more realistically before, either. Because people's accounts, both the first and the most recent, are full of their own rememberings, full of distortions and non-memory. Sometimes unintentionally, though sometimes deliberately, a text by a participant or witness will create a new reality. Marek Edelman claimed that there are no true accounts because they are all "colored up." Facts and legends intermingle; crooked memories become tangled.

And this is the way our memory of history is constructed. And this is the way our memory of history is falsified. I came across a story about an insurrectionist called Aleksander. His surname had not been remembered. Some historian wrote that Aleksander was probably Efraim Fondamiński. In one book, Fondamiński was given the codename Aleksander. In the next, that name isn't even mentioned; all that remains was Efraim Fondamiński, the PPR leader in the ŻOB command. He was nothing to do with Aleksander. Fondamiński was no longer in existence in October 1942; he must have been killed in the *große Aktion*. But Aleksander perished in the uprising, on Miła, Marek Edelman claimed. This is how history is falsified: with forgotten facts, invented stories, imagined feelings. A myth emerges which sometimes, for a moment is stripped of its archeology.

The uprising in the ghetto ended on May 8, or maybe 10, Marek Edelman said. The active uprising went on until April 23 or 24, Antek Cukierman claimed. The uprising ended on April 28, Kazik Ratajzer told me. A different memory because of a different experience, a different way of seeing, and consequently—a different story.

Or a different example: in 1951, Bronisław Mirski (formerly Sławek Friedman) talked about his experiences as an insurrectionist with Bernard Mark, who was a historian, the director of the JHI, an activist in the ruling Polish United Workers' Party, and wrote his own version of those events from the past. Bronisław Mirski said that he had been in contact with Sara Żagiel in the ghetto. As Żagiel had left-wing sympathies, Mark wrote that Mirski had belonged to a communist youth group. Many years later, another historian repeated that record. But Sławek Mirski told me sadly in 2014 that he had never been a communist. This is how history is falsified.

The "List of those who fell in the defense of the Warsaw ghetto"—what I call the London list—is a primary source for these stories about the April insurgents in the ghetto. I reproduce that list and copy it out carefully. Then I impose my order on it: I add more names of January and April insurrectionists, mark the names of those whose names were on the list erroneously, and record the names of Jewish and Polish ŻOB couriers. I count the insurrectionists and talk about them. I give their forenames, the various versions, their variant spellings: many forenames, and a brief story. Sometimes it is no more than a formula: the name was recorded, and I found no further information.

In 2014, Aleksander Edelman asked me why Chawka Folman's biography is not in the book. Because Chawka wasn't in the uprising, I answered. (She was arrested in December 1942). Someone asked about Reginka Justman. (Reginka was in Krakow, not in Warsaw.) This, my rereading of the list of ŻOB members who took part in the Warsaw ghetto uprising, was authorized by Marek Edelman. And although it is not without hidden errors, this is how it will remain.

I wrote "Rereading the List" with the words I heard, and hear, these stories. (Because language, like image, can sometimes show, rather than explain). I hear that "Marek Edelman has a straight backbone" and that "such was the power of Abrasza's words," that "Masza was in a pair with Jakubek," "someone was given an assurance in the 'shop," and someone else "had safe looks." And if I write that "he was proud, so he was well suited to being a courier," it means that many Jews were not suited for the role of courier because they were afraid—outside the ghetto even more so than inside it. "Leon Feiner died in his bed": in his bed, and not on a heap of garbage, not in a gas chamber, and not even on the street. Quite simply: he died in his bed. Cukierman wrote that Artsztajn spoke "in a Jewish [Yiddish] full of pathos and exclamation marks, but it was a genuine language." So, I write that Artsztajn spoke in a genuine language, whatever that might mean or have meant, whatever we might be able to decipher from that. Let those listening to my stories of others decide.

In these insurrectionists' stories there is no fact, no event, no information, no adjective used out of a need for invention, supplementation, or beautification. All of them are taken from *somewhere*. (From written texts or my conversations. Once, Ala Margolis introduced me to a friend as: Hanka, who for twenty years has been talking to Jews who are still alive.) And that "somewhere" is important here because it means that this information has a source, but it is not the source that is important. In a sense it is even unimportant. Unimportant because no one can know how credible it is. And unimportant because memory and remembering are not about sources. Memory rapidly distances itself from its source, becoming autonomous, so that stories about that past likewise become autonomous.

I write: "recorded," "remembered," "written down somewhere"; sometimes I write "a historian mentioned." This is a way of saying that the information that I give exists beyond the source document, that some fact, on this occasion recounted (recorded) by me, is now beyond verification, that the authority of the source is no longer important. When I heard Marek Edelman's words that "Masza remembers it well," I called Masza Putermilch. As I record her memory, I use her name. I often use the names of those whom I talked to over several years. I wanted to "talk their memory out of them" as much as I could. Hear it and record it. Phrases and scraps of their stories that I took away from those conversations resounded in my head afterwards. I recorded the stories and the recounting of others. My book is a retelling of others' stories (which are also a little bit mine).

I Came Home and There Was No One There is a composition of two titles in a single volume for readers in English. We—the author, the translator, and the publisher—propose this composition because the two books supplement each other, are mutually complementary, form a single whole. The volume is a collection of the salvaged vestiges of memory of hundreds of the people who experienced that time and place: the Warsaw ghetto.

The preface addresses both parts of the book. The first part is a collection of the transcripts of ten conversations with former ŻOB soldiers, entitled "Recording the Holocaust." The core of the second section is composed of the pieced-together stories of those individuals, which commemorate that army in this lapidarium of words. This is followed by a reproduction of the London list of the ŻOB members and my own rereading of how the organization was divided into the various fighting groups, and the positions they defended in the ghetto. And finally, the extensive third part: the glossary, composed of the notes on names, terms, and concepts. (This part could, in fact, be read as an introduction to that world and that time.) My first guide to this past, Marek Edelman, in his afterword concludes the book.

Translation is always a challenge. In this case doubly so. In the Polish, I attempted to reproduce the uneven, characteristic, sometimes difficult language of my interlocutors, so as to retain their description of their world. Together, we decided to leave all proper names in the form in which they were used in that dual, Polish-Jewish world. We therefore deliberately did not transliterate press titles, school names, or organizations as an English-language reader of translations direct from Yiddish or Hebrew might expect to see them; likewise, given names and surnames are preserved as they functioned in their Polish context and featured in written sources from school registers to contemporary newspaper articles. We nonetheless—or, perhaps, even precisely in this way—hope to have created in this translation images that are immediate and comprehensible, though the world they describe is so distant and alien.

Hanka Grupińska
Warsaw, October 2, 2022

What Was of Importance in the Ghetto? Nothing! Nothing! Don't Be Ridiculous!

A conversation with Marek Edelman conducted with Włodzimierz Filipek for the Poznań-based underground quarterly *Czas* in 1985.

We'd like to ask what you did before the war. Society knows you as a soldier of the ŻOB,[1] as an insurrectionist in the Warsaw ghetto,[2] but we're interested in your genealogy, your family. Where did you live? What schools did you go to? Those are all things that nobody knows.
Ah, yes, those are all things that nobody knows, and above all the courts don't want to recognize ... but that's of no importance. I lived in Warsaw.

Were you born in Warsaw?
Let's say that. That's what it says in my papers. My mother was a repatriate from Russia, my father was a repatriate, also from Russia—from Belarus, to be precise, because he came from Minsk, Gomel. I was born in Warsaw. Before that, somewhere on the journey, my brother died. And if my brother had survived, I wouldn't have been born at all. My parents died very shortly afterwards.

Why did your parents leave Gomel and emigrate from Russia to Poland?
In all honesty, I can't tell you, because of course I wasn't born at that point. I can't imagine it was anti-communism. It might have been, but I can't tell you.

Was it for political reasons?
It may have been. After all, all the Poles who had Polish citizenship were leaving Russia at that point.

Did your parents have Polish citizenship?
I don't think my mother did, but my father did, so my mother was automatically entitled to it.

---

1 p. 500 Glossary—Jewish Fighting Organization.
2 p. 519 Glossary.

How old were you when you were left alone?
Now that's something I don't exactly know. My father died when I was maybe four or five, in 1924, or maybe in 1926, and I was born in 1922.[3] I remember him from sitting on his knee, but nothing more than that.

And your mom?
And my mom died in 1934, I think. So, I was twelve, maybe thirteen. But I don't know exactly because the cemetery where she was buried was bombed twice. Once in 1939, and later in the Warsaw rising.[4] There is no trace of her memorial. When I took my high school finals in 1939, I decided I ought to go to my mother's grave and tell her that I passed my exams. Back then, you could still make out where her grave was, but they were building roads, or something, and by 1940 the grave was no longer there.

What did your father do?
The very interesting thing is that nobody knows. Nobody in my house knows. I mean, maybe they did know, but I was too small for them to tell me. My mother worked in the administrative department of a children's hospital, always on the late shift. She came home at four in the morning, when I was asleep, and there was only Frania at home.

Who was Frania?
Frania was just Frania. I had no family. My parents came from Russia. Mom had twelve brothers, all SRs.[5] I don't know whether it was in 1918 or in what year it was that the Bolsheviks came to Gomel and took all twelve brothers out of the house. (The reason that Grandfather had so many children was because he was waiting for a daughter—don't laugh, it's important!) And when they had all twelve of the brothers lined up in front of the Poniatowski monument to shoot them, along she comes, this *malenkaia devochka*, and walks into the midst of them.[6] And this Russkii *chubarik* says: "Devushka, udirai!"[7] They shot all twelve brothers, and she was left alone. After the war, I think, the daughter of the eldest brother turned up here. Tania, her name was, but she's not here anymore. I mean, maybe she is; in any case, I had no other family than that. If they could shoot twelve brothers for being

---

3 Marek Edelman was born on January 1, 1919. Here he gave his year of birth as 1922 to avoid the danger of being subjected to forced retirement. (This was one of the methods of repression employed by the authorities of the People's Republic of Poland.)
4 p. 520 Glossary.
5 p. 516 Glossary—Socialist Revolutionary Party.
6 Rus.: little girl.
7 *Chubarik* (Rus.)—word historically used in Russian and Ukrainian to refer to a soldier of the lowest rank, a private; Rus.: Girl, scarper!

SRs in front of the Poniatowski monument in the Paskevich gardens in Gomel, who else could there have been? As Lenin said: "We'll do politics like the SRs, but we'll put the SRs in jail. And if need be, instead of putting them in jail, we'll shoot them, because in jails they have to be fed."

Did the SR tradition inspire your father in any way, too?
I don't know, I don't know. I can't say. My mother was a normal socialist. She was the chairwoman or secretary of some women's socialist organization.[8] In those years, that was a hugely revolutionary thing—in theory legal, but a huge revolution, because they were women, they were socialists, and they were Jews on top.

Do you mean that your mother belonged to the PPS?[9]
No. It was the Bund.[10] I remember she took me to a rally where she was speaking once, in Warsaw. The Bund was a Jewish socialist party like the PPS, and it argued that there would be socialism here, and that regardless of whether you were a Ukrainian, a Belarusian, a Jew, or a Pole, this would be a normal country.

Was your attitude toward communism unequivocal in the 30s?
Of course. I was taught that communism is a regular dictatorship, which kills people to stay in power. I was taught that from childhood—it's nothing I did; my mom taught me. She said: "Marek, you want to see socialism for the last time in your life? Come to Vienna with me,"—this was in 1934 or 1933, I can't remember now—"because this is the last time you'll see socialism." It was an international sporting meet for the working class, but I wanted to go camping with some girls, and I did.

What school did you graduate from?
Oh, I was thrown out of school after school.

Tell us about it.
But it's shameful. I was a poor student. I had tuberculosis and I didn't start school until the fourth grade of public school. After that, I went to high school. I think I lasted two years in my first high school. You weren't allowed to go to the May 1 parades, but I went and I ran into the principal as I was coming back. Being a polite boy, I bowed to him. The next day, he called my guardian in and said: "I have to throw him out of school because he goes to these parades, but I'm not throwing him out for being in the parade, only because he's stupid. Because if he hadn't bowed to me, I wouldn't have seen him." For the last two years, I was at

---

8   Jewish Working Women (Yid.: Yidishe Arbeter Froy). See p. 493 Glossary—"Bund."
9   p. 511 Glossary—Polish Socialist Party.
10 p. 493 Glossary.

the Merchants' Congregation. I had it really tough there, because it was a school where the ONR held sway.[11] Mosdorf's brother was at school with me.[12] It was horrible in that school. It was constantly closed, because they used to beat Jews there. But as a school it was excellent.

How many years did you spend at that school?
Two. From sixth to eighth grade. I left in 1939.

From what you say, I surmise that you never had any religious education.
No, no. I never had anything to do with God. The only thing I want is for God to protect me from my friends; I can defend myself from my enemies alone. But he doesn't even want to defend me from my friends.

It seems not, indeed...
My home was very secular, very progressive. In any case, the Church in Poland before the war was the Black Hundreds.[13] All the major anti-Jewish and anti-Ukrainian incidents started with churches.[14] In Warsaw, Father Trzeciak had a church on Teatralny Square, and that's where all the pogroms started.[15] "Don't buy from Jews," "Beat Jews," and so on. I was beaten up on Nowy Świat Street—I think it was during my high school finals.[16] You couldn't go down there, that was

---

11 p. 509 Glossary—National-Radical Camp.
12 Jan Mosdorf (1904–1943)—journalist and political activist from 1926 linked to the National Democracy (ND, "Endek") movement in Poland, one of the founders and leaders of the ONR, and initiator of many anti-Jewish riots. Arrested by the Germans for underground activity in 1940, he was later moved from Warsaw's Pawiak prison to the concentration camp Auschwitz I, where he collaborated with the international resistance movement. In the camp, he changed his attitude toward Jews: he is said to have "shown them considerable charity and assistance" (he worked in the camp administrative offices). Mosdorf is held up as a striking example—not the only one during the war—of a complete change of heart in a prewar anti-Semite. He was executed by firing squad with other prisoners in Auschwitz I on October 11, 1943.
13 The Black Hundreds—historically, a nationalist, conservative movement that emerged in the Russian Empire after the 1905 revolution. They opposed any kind of social change and advocated the Russification of other national groups and the expansion of Eastern Orthodoxy. They formed paramilitary gangs that attacked working-class institutions and activists and staged pogroms of Jews and Armenians. Colloquially, the term "Black Hundreds" is a synonym for far-right, fascist, antisemitic movements and paramilitary gangs in Europe.
14 p. 513 Glossary—Prewar antisemitism in Poland.
15 Fr. Stanisław Trzeciak (1873–1944)—Roman Catholic priest considered a specialist on Jewish issues between the wars. In numerous speeches and publications throughout the 1920s and 1930s, he stressed that the Jews pursued activities that were economically, politically, and morally detrimental to Poland. He called for legal opposition to them on an economic level, without violence or beatings, and for the "deyiddification" of Poland.
16 Nowy Świat—a fashionable street in downtown Warsaw.

ONR Falanga territory; it belonged to all the gangs that were scared of the Bank Square Jews, who beat them up with waggon shafts. You won't remember the waggoners. They had these waggons with shafts. I suspect they disappeared after the war. For any Jews walking down Nowy Świat—it was a disaster. And I don't remember exactly how it was, but that was the only time they beat me up so badly. I managed my high school finals somehow. I knew nothing, but I passed.

What was the source of your identity? I mean, what moved you?
I don't know what that means. You speak in such clever sentences.

Why didn't you become a Zionist?
Well, you're brought up in this or that kind of home, aren't you? My mom believed—and that's how she brought me up—that everything would be alright here, that everyone is equal and good, and so on. Zionism's a losing game in any case. Then and now.

Could you expand on that?
I'm not talking about the ideology. I'm saying that you can't go back to how things were two thousand years ago, because it's impossible. In a sea of a hundred million Arabs, you can't make a state that's against them, because sooner or later they'll annihilate those Jews just like Hitler annihilated them. I'm not saying it'll be today, but the Arabs will learn to shoot just like them. They're a far larger nation. It's a purely political matter. The Arabs say: "OK, why does there have to be a state of Israel here? It was the Germans who killed the Jews: why isn't it in Munich? Why aren't those three million Jews somewhere outside Hannover? It's the Germans who should be paying for it." And they're right! Just like people say that the Western Territories are Polish.[17] Really! For seven hundred years, there were Germans living there. Is Kyiv Polish today, even though Poland ruled there sometime in the past?

But ultimately the state of Israel was founded, and it exists.
Yes, well the Russians set up a political state for them. And then the Jews screwed the Russians over and went over to the Americans, but either way, they're doomed. A three-million-strong state in a sea of a hundred million Arabs can't exist. There's no chance. They'll be annihilated all over again and pushed back

---

17 Western Territories—a western and northern swathe of present-day Poland annexed to the country pursuant to the Potsdam Treaty of 1945. In parallel to this, the same treaty also recognized the annexation of parts of eastern Poland by the USSR in 1939.

into the sea. America will keep on giving them planes as long as it's got an aircraft carrier there. If the Americans start cozying up not to Mubarak but to some other Farak,[18] they'll drop those three million people like they never knew them. The state of Israel is a purely political thing. First the Russians wanted to throw the English out of there. Then the Americans wanted to throw the English out, and they did, and now they have their own outpost there. Of course, the only rock that holds that long is Gibraltar, but that is a rock. There's not much chance of a Jewish state existing in the Middle East.

But the state has been in existence for forty years now. And every state exists within certain political constellations. Did you use the same arguments on your Zionist friends in 1939?
I couldn't use the same arguments, because today my experience is different. But the situation was the same. There were three and a half million Jews in Poland, and three million of them wanted to live and work here and earn a living. But there were forty or fifty thousand people who were mystics and wanted to go to Israel. Zionism was a rejection of the Diaspora. It was a marginal political movement. It could only be marginal, because it was impractical, it had no chance. I mean, those fifty thousand Jews were a drop in the ocean. It was a mystical religious and nationalist thing. Above all, Jewish religiosity and Jewish mysticism ceased to exist after the war. They all ceased to exist during the war: religiosity, mysticism, faith. The Lord God turned away from them, and they turned their backs on God. "Kiss my ass!", they said to God.

What was of importance in the ghetto?
Nothing! Nothing! Don't be ridiculous. You think that what you see in the movies is true.

Do you remember any Hasidim in the ghetto?
Yes, of course, there were a lot of them, but all that ceased to exist in 1941. The only social movement that left no trace, nothing but abandoned prayer houses. The religious Jews left all those holy books of theirs behind and disappeared. In 1939, I was living on Dzielna Street, and in the house opposite there were these Jews who called themselves *toyte Hasidim*.[19]

---

18 Hosni Muhammad Mubarak (1928–2012)—Egyptian air force officer and politician from October 1981, following the murder of President Anwar Saddat, military dictator; sentenced to life imprisonment for pacification of anti-regime demonstrations, he died in a prison hospital.
19 *Toyte Hasidim* (Yid.: Dead Hasidim)—followers of Rabbi Nachman of Breslov, who after their tzaddik's death did not choose a successor. There was a group of Breslover Hasidim living in the ghetto, on Nowolipie Street.

Enclosure

They were from the East. Their rabbi had died, and they were his successors. A steadfast, serene, mystical Ukrainian group. Three months later, they were gone, leaving everything wide open, and that was the last of them. Any Jewish mementoes that were left, the Germans took from the burned-out houses and put them all on a train to Prague.[20] Their movement ceased to exist. Nothing existed. The Lord God had let them down. Because he had punished them for nothing. And so, they turned their backs on God: they shaved off their beards, took off their long coats, and left the synagogues. It's a terrible thing to be saying something like that in Poland today. It's because of the political Catholicism that has grown up here; these days, everyone believes in the Lord God to stick one up at the Reds. People go to church and make all this show, but between you and me, Poland was never really a religious country. The Church was always political, always sided with the state. And the Jewish religion was the same: it was political. If the Lord God turns his back on the Poles, if they start to massacre people in the churches—not beat people up with baseball bats, that's small beer—but if they take a hundred thousand people from outside the churches and gas them, you'll see that the churches will be empty and only their parade standards will be left. It was the same in the ghetto. Religion departed...

All that hogwash that they spout, that when the uprising began, the Jews were praying—it's all fancy literary devices. They were killing people for nothing! You happened to be walking down the street, dressed in black with gray hair? They'd kill you. So how could someone like that believe in God? He'd done nothing wrong. He would have even been willing to clean that German's boots, or whatever. He bent down; the guy shot him. What do you think? Christ orders twenty million Poles to be killed: will all the Poles believe in God then?

Well, fair enough. But is there any sort of order?
The order of things is that there need to be fewer people in the world.

I mean a bigger order. An order of values that, I agree, need not necessarily be represented by the Church.
Of course! And those values are represented by different people entirely, who know who needs to be beaten up. But the beatings have to be on the left and on the right—any totalitarianism. Because totalitarianism kills people. Like

---

20 During the war, the Germans stockpiled property looted from the Jews in Czechoslovakia and other occupied countries in Prague. This included some five thousand four hundred objects of cult, twenty-four thousand five hundred religious books, and six thousand artworks of historical value. The occupying authorities tasked a group of Jewish scholars with cataloguing the hoard. The collections were to have been used after the war in a planned "Central Museum of the Extinct Jewish Race." They now form part of the collections of the Jewish Museum in Prague.

Jaruzelski,[21] just like Stalin and Hitler. Why did the Blacks get equal rights? Not because Luther King went around with his hands up, but because the Black Panthers started burning cities down. People aren't angels.

Yes, but not being angels doesn't make them devils.
Of course not. People are like lions in a pride, throwing the weaker ones out to be devoured by the circling jackals. It's the same with people. There's no difference. It's philo-genetic.

Yes, but there are situations when people overcome their fear.
Yes, only in hunger and sores you aren't clever, you can't think.

What about Korczak?[22] Or Kolbe?[23]
I know twenty girls, young, healthy, beautiful ones, who did the same thing, far more beautifully than Korczak. But he had a big name, wrote books, and so on.

So, stances like that are possible?
No, no. It was a situation of duress. The stance of those two people who became symbols is just not what it is.

We understand that stances like those of Kolbe and Korczak weren't the only ones. You mentioned those twenty girls...
There were no "stances."

What was there?
Duty.

A sense of duty arises out of certain stances.
Maternal duty does, but as instinct. After all, in movies you see mothers in Auschwitz kicking their children to save themselves. And of course, things like that did happen. But in 90 percent of cases, mothers went with their children and daughters went with their mothers. You're wanting to fit today's morality to those times.

---

21 Jaruzelski, Wojciech (1923–2014), military commander, the last political leader in the Polish People's Republic. Remembered above all as the executor of Martial Law, imposed in the night of December 12/13, 1981, as a measure targeting the civil society movement Solidarity.
22 p. 507 Glossary.
23 Fr. Maksymilian Maria Kolbe, real name Rajmund Kolbe (1894–1941)—Franciscan friar, canonized in 1982. Founder and editor of several Catholic press titles, including *Rycerz Niepokalanej*, known for its anti-Semitic articles. Deported to Auschwitz concentration camp in 1941; volunteered to die in place of another prisoner.

No! No! We believe there was some sort of morality there, and we want to understand it.
An entirely different sort.

Fine, but what sort? It wasn't just instinct.
Of course, it was instinct! Kill the guy who's killing you—that was the only sort of morality. Kill him!

Yes, but up until the uprising,[24] it wasn't like that.
You're talking garbage! What do you mean, up until the uprising? It's the wherewithal that counts.

Do you mean to say that everyone had the same idea, that everyone would have wanted to kill them?
Of course. It's purely and simply about having the wherewithal. Killing is no big deal, you just have to have the means and the opportunity. And to know that if I kill them, they won't kill nine thousand defenseless others. It's also about taking the responsibility.

I'd like to go back a little. The war breaks out. Was the Holocaust obvious to you at that point?
Not in 1939. But after 1941 it was.

What happened to you after the outbreak of the war?
Nothing in particular happened to me.

Did you keep up your connections with the Bund?
Of course.

Could you tell us what it was like back then?
The practicalities are irrelevant. In 1939, nobody dreamed that they would massacre three and a half million Jews in Poland.

But there were rumors about the "Crystal Night" in the Reich,[25] and about the fate of the Zbąszyń Jews?[26]

---

24 p. 518 Glossary—Uprising in the Warsaw ghetto.
25 "Crystal Night" (Ger. *Kristallnacht*)—a pogrom perpetrated against the German Jews on the night of November 9/10, 1938, by Nazis from the SA, the SS, and the Hitlerjugend, which marked the beginning of a period of mass emigration of Jews from Germany. On that night, 91 people were murdered, 267 synagogues set alight, Jewish property destroyed, and cemeteries desecrated. Some twenty-six thousand Jews were deported to concentration camps.
26 p. 496 Glossary—Jews expelled from Germany.

No one was killed in Zbąszyń. Of course, there were persecutions, this and that. But I'm sorry, people were killed in pogroms before the war in Poland, too, just like in the "Crystal Night." In Przytyk and Radom, and so on. If you counted them up, it would be just as many.

So, people were less vigilant . . . ?
No, it's not that they were less vigilant. It simply didn't occur to us, my child, that they would kill three million people out of stupidity. After all, until 1939 there had never been any mass murders involving everybody being gassed. And even when reports reached us that they were gassing people,[27] everybody just laughed at them, and said: "What are they talking about?"

People didn't believe it?
Well, how can you believe that you're such a pretty girl, and just because you're so beautiful they're going to kill you?

How would you say the Bundists saw their mission after 1939?
No differently. The same as before. Their work was the same on the Aryan side as on the Jewish side.[28]

And what about their connections with the Aryan side?
They had connections, of course. And until 1941, they were very close connections. Only later, after the wall went up, they were harder to sustain. But no one, on either side, dreamed that those half-million people that lived in Warsaw would be murdered. It just didn't come into question, even though Hitler had talked about it in *Mein Kampf*.

Were the connections with the Aryan side mostly with communists?
What communists? What are you talking about? There were no communists. Our contacts were with the PPS.

And with military organizations?
They didn't trust the Jews. They were Sanation people.[29] All those gentlemen— "Bór" Komorowski and "Grot" Rowecki—said:[30] "We're not going to give the

---

27 p. 496 Glossary—First news of the extermination camps.
28 p. 492 Glossary—Aryan side.
29 Sanation (Pol. Sanacja, from Lat. *sanatio*—cleansing, purging)—the colloquial name given to the authorities that ruled Poland in the years 1926–1939 under Józef Piłsudski.
30 Tadeusz Komorowski (*noms de guerre* "Bór", "Lawina") (1895–1966)—general and politician. In 1943–1944 commander and later commander-in-chief of the AK. In 1944, he took

Jews weapons, because there's no way of knowing what they'll do with them, whether they'll even use them. Because Jews are no good at shooting."[31]

They believed that to be rooted in the Jewish culture?
I don't know what they believed, *relata refero*. Go ask them yourselves. It's pointless hypothesizing. Gomułka was of the same mind.[32] Throw yourselves at the walls with your bare hands, ten out of a hundred thousand will survive. But we aren't going to give you any weapons. Because we don't know if you'll use them, or they'll disappear, or you'll die. The truth is that they didn't have anything. It was a different mentality; those were different times.

Could you tell us anything else about the connections with the Aryan side at the point when the truth about the Holocaust became clear?
They were very difficult.

Do you see those difficulties only as their ill will?
They were weak, too. And anyway, they didn't trust us. They sent us instructions, of course, some garbage they cooked up. But it wasn't until after January 18 that they gave us the first weapons.[33] Notice that they themselves didn't fight. Not the AK,[34] not the AL.[35] None of them fought. The "Arsenał" job only came after the operation, the first corpses, in the ghetto.[36] I'm not getting above myself,

---

the decision to launch the Warsaw rising. In 1944–1945, a German POW; after the war he settled in Britain; Stefan Rowecki ("Grabica," "Grot") (1895–1944)—general and journalist. From 1911, a member of the clandestine scouting movement; in the period 1914–1917, in the Polish Legions, and from 1918, in the Polish Army. A commander in the Polish defense campaign in September 1939; from June 30, 1940, commander-in-chief of the ZWZ (Związek Walki Zbrojnej [Union of Armed Combat], later the AK); arrested on June 30, 1943, in Warsaw. Murdered by the Germans in August 1944 in Sachsenhausen concentration camp.

31 Edelman is in all certainty thinking here of Gen. Rowecki's dispatch to London of January 2, 1943, in which the then commander-in-chief of the AK reported: "There are Jews from all groups, including the communists, approaching us requesting arms, as if we had stockpiles. I gave out a few pistols as a trial. I am not certain that they will even use the weapons. I shall not issue any more weapons, because, as you know, we do not have [enough] ourselves. I am awaiting another transport [weapons drop]. Inform me what contacts our Jews have with London." Until fall 1942, the Warsaw ghetto received neither moral, material, nor military support of any kind from the authorities of the Polish Underground State. Very few groups (above all the Bund) maintained contacts with individual Polish underground organizations.
32 p. 497 Glossary—Gomułka, Władysław.
33 p. 500 Glossary—January operation.
34 p. 499 Glossary—Home Army.
35 p. 510 Glossary—People's Army.
36 p. 492 Glossary—Arsenał operation.

but I think, regardless of what anyone else says, that that was a caesura. When ten Germans were killed and nothing happened, then those boys mounted the "Arsenał" attack, because the AK Command didn't want to. It was the ghetto that gave them the push. I'm not talking about isolated assassinations, which did happen, but the first armed uprising was in Warsaw in 1943, on January 18, in the ghetto. The "Arsenał" came later, on March 26. Somebody in some book somewhere wrote that that's not true, because in Pińsk in 1943 someone sprang ten POWs from a prison and that was the first armed operation.[37] Well, it might have been.

Do you consider that the aid that came from the Aryan side was sufficient?
Well, first of all, they couldn't, and secondly, they didn't want to.

But you're still not answering the question.
What do you mean, I'm not answering?

Well, because if someone can't, there's nothing you can do about it, but if they don't want to, that's different.
It's hard to answer that; it's impossible to gauge. How much of it was ill will, or how many thefts there were—you couldn't tell that then, and you can't tell now. Times were different then. Every kid wanted a revolver. They might have sent five hundred, but only fifty reached us. They said they sent a hundred fifty grenades but only fifty turned up. Whether someone stole it, or something else happened, you'll never get to the bottom of it. Facts are facts.

How did the world outside the walls exist for the Jews in the ghetto? Did it give them hope?
It was the enemy. You don't understand. You see, it's not only your killer that's your enemy but also those who are indifferent. Today, Bujak has nowhere to live.[38] How many people will offer him a roof over his head? Ten out of a hundred? But if he's got a death sentence hanging over him, all one hundred of them will be his enemies. Don't you get that?

---

37 On January 18, 1943, a group of sixteen AK soldiers under Lt. Jan "Ponury" Piwnik took control of the prison in Pińsk (present-day southwestern Belarus) and sprang four of their comrades-in-arms.

38 Zbigniew Bujak was a Polish dissident who was in hiding from December 13, 1981, when Martial Law was declared in Poland, until May 1986, when he was arrested.

I get it.
And that's all there is to it. Enemies in the sense that if you went out onto the other side and said who you were, they would kill you.

Or not help you.
It's all the same. Not helping you and killing you are the same thing. I'm not talking about now, because right now you can still walk down the street. But back then, if one person didn't help you, someone on the next corner would kill you. They're incomparable situations. Bujak can walk down ten streets today and nobody will hassle him. They won't take him into their homes, but they'll smile at him.

Why did the uprising break out so late?
Don't say "late!" Why wasn't there an uprising in Auschwitz?! Were they beaten and harassed more there?! It's because there was no wherewithal. Why don't you have anything against Auschwitz or Mauthausen?! I believe that it was impossible to have staged an uprising any earlier. Notice that a few months before the outbreak of the uprising, we were told that there were waggonloads of weapons coming—and they never came... Don't be childish. Don't say things like that! In 1942, at some convention of Jews, the observant ones held that it was wrong to shoot, because this was the Lord God's will. All in its own time. Then the entire AK was afraid that if an uprising broke out in the ghetto, Warsaw would catch fire, and they would all be massacred, and that would have been too soon, because in one direction the front was five hundred kilometers away, and in the other two thousand.

In an interview with Hanna Krall about the suicide at 18 Miła,[39] you said that life shouldn't be sacrificed for symbols. You also said that you were convinced of that for the whole of those twenty days. I want to ask how you see it today?
The same way.

Is suicide really pointless if there is no other way out, if death by suicide is the only way?
Don't be ridiculous. We only have one life. I'm not a believer in suicide—what if there does prove to be a way out? The ones who didn't do it got out of there. You always have to hope for something.

---

39 See Hanna Krall, *Shielding the Flame: An Intimate Conversation with Dr. Marek Edelman, the Last Surviving Leader of the Warsaw Ghetto Uprising*, trans. Joanna Stasinska and Lawrence Weschler (New York: Henry Holt and Company, Inc., 1977); p. 517 Glossary—Suicide at 18 Miła Street.

So, you think that Mordechaj Anielewicz did wrong?[40]
You know, it's a beautiful thing to say: "A nation perished; its soldiers perished."

Yet you were incensed at Czerniaków for making his death a private decision.[41]
Yes, but Anielewicz didn't make his private or take a different decision. After all, by that stage, it was all over. There was no reason for him to kill himself. And over a dozen people got out because they didn't kill themselves. And six or seven of them are still alive today.

Are any of them still in Poland?
No.

Do you keep in touch with them at all?
No. I saw some of them a while back.

Tell us what you did after the uprising.
That's of no importance. All those details are of no importance.

We beg to differ; they are of importance to us.
Afterwards, I was on the Aryan side. It's all been written already in some book or other. You are precious.

Did you fight in the AL underground units after that?
After that, I was in the Warsaw rising. I was in the AL because the AK wanted to shoot me, because they said I had a counterfeit *Kennkarte* and I was a Jewish spy.[42] They locked me up in the kitty and there was supposed to be a court, or whatever they call it. I managed to throw a note out through the cellar and Kamiński got me out.[43] Well, I wasn't going to play with boys who wanted to kill me. The AK had me up against a wall several more times, because Jews are a bad idea, and the military police in the Old Town were all ONR, Falanga to the core. So, I was in the AL. Some guy from the AL said to me: "Marek, don't sleep here in this cellar. Come and sleep at Świętojerska instead." And he put his overcoat over me and slept with me so that they wouldn't shoot me. So, it isn't all as simple as you think.

---

40 p. 336 Rereading the List.
41 p. 494 Glossary—Czerniaków, Adam.
42 p. 506 Glossary.
43 p. 504 Glossary—Kamiński, Aleksander.

Men

We know that. That's why we're here.
Give me a break. You're kids. Don't listen to all that nastiness; it's not fit for any newssheet. Because the Polish nation, as you know very well, is tolerant. There was never any nastiness against ethnic minorities here, against religions, this is an extraordinary nation. Casimir the Great took the Jews in and put them on a pedestal and loves them to this day.[44] Finito. What's the point in talking about it? There's no need.

But perhaps we could talk about anti-Semitism? Because that's the very real memento of that tradition.
Son, what you need to remember is that Narutowicz wasn't killed because he was Narutowicz, but because he was elected with Jewish votes.[45] It wasn't the Jewish parliamentarians assumed to have voted for Narutowicz in the Sejm that were beaten up. It was the people who beat them up. It was no accident that Narutowicz was killed—after all, Niewiadomski was no idiot. He was an emanation of a particular segment of the people—a very large segment at that time. Jew-beating was a daily occurrence. Because the Church taught that it was the Jew that killed Christ.

But Fr. Zieja is a Catholic priest.[46]
But Fr. Zieja is one on his own. And apart from him there was Fr. Trzeciak and Hlond and all those who did that.[47]

But the idea that the Jews killed Christ isn't something that occurs to ordinary people in the street.
Well, what can I do about that? And yet all the anti-Jewish pogroms spilled out from churches. Now there are marches for Przemyk;[48] back then, they would go

---

44 Casimir III the Great (1310–1370)—king of Poland considered an outstanding ruler. He had Poland's Jewish communities brought under the jurisdiction of the royal courts.
45 Narutowicz, Gabriel (1865–1922). Engineer, constructor, and professor at the Zurich Polytechnic; first president of the Republic of Poland after its restitution in 1918 (December 9–16, 1922). Shot dead in Warsaw by the nationalist Eligiusz Niewiadomski.
46 Fr. Jan Zieja (1897–1991)—Polish Army chaplain, scoutmaster. In 1943–1944 chaplain of the Gray Ranks; wounded in the Warsaw uprising. From 1976, a member of KOR. An advocate for ecumenism and dialogue with Judaism.
47 Hlond, Cardinal August (1881–1948)—Salesian cleric, primate of Poland. In 1936, after the pogrom in Przytyk, he condemned racism and violence, but accused the adherents of Judaism of demoralization and called for the social isolation of the Jews. After the outbreak of World War II, he left Poland for Rome. From 1946, archbishop of Warsaw and Gniezno.
48 Grzegorz Przemyk (1964–1983)—philosophy student, son of the poet Barbara Sadowska, in 1983 tortured in custody at the Jezuicka Street Civic Militia precinct in Warsaw and died

out on the streets against the Jews. There really were priests who denounced Jews after what they heard in the confessional.

***

We are shocked, we won't hide that.
By what, though?

We're shocked at how starkly you put these things.
That's the way it is: all the weak ones are oh-so-humanitarian, but the strong ones will finish you off.

That's a pleasant vision of the world!
But it's obvious. Humans are derived from animals fighting for survival.

What I want to ask you is to what extent all that is a closed chapter for you?
No, it's all very much ongoing. Nothing has changed here. The Polish nation, which hates Jaruzelski, Brezhnev, Stalin, and Gorbachev, is weak. If it doesn't get up and fight, if it doesn't get stronger, it will lose in the same way. Strength is all that counts. Not only for the communists. In the West, too. Mitterrand respects strength. So does Reagan.

Back then in 1943, in the ghetto, did you think about all those connections with big politics?
But child, you can't reason like that! If someone is writing a poem, for instance, they think about making it a good poem, not about world politics. When you're sweeping the floor, you don't wonder whether the prime minister will be pleased with it. You want the floor clean. But it's all part of a bigger deal. Anyway, even in 1943 I knew it was hopeless in political terms. There might have been a chance of someone getting out alive, but that was all.

So, what was the point, in that case?
Don't be petty. It's better to do something than not to do anything.

And that's all?
…

***

---

in hospital. Przemyk's murder was one of the most highly publicized political crimes under Martial Law in the Polish People's Republic.

To go back to what we were talking about before, what happened to you after the Warsaw rising?
No, no, no. I don't have the patience for that. It's boring—and anyway, somebody somewhere already wrote all about it. It's not necessary. You don't need to know a person's whole biography; they have to be able to keep something to themselves.

But our readers are very interested.
It's not that easy. After the rising, I stayed in Żoliborz for another six weeks. Then a patrol came around that got me out as a typhus patient.[49] After that, I was in Grodzisk, and then, when the Russians came, "peace broke out" and I walked back to Warsaw, and so on.

Why didn't you leave Warsaw with the insurrectionists?[50]
For them to kill me? I'm not that naive. If I'd gone with the insurrectionists, there might well have been someone who'd have pointed their finger at me and said: "This guy's a Jew!" Before I'd have gotten to the place where they deposited their arms, the Germans would have shot me. There were all sorts of low-lifes in the rising, though Żoliborz was the best of the lot.

In what way the best? Do you mean that it was the least anti-Semitic?
Yes. There were the fewest ONR and Falanga people there, the fewest of the sort that thought the Jews should be finished off and that "Hitler did it for us." There was this one lieutenant, Tytus,[51] who said to me: "Marek, come with us . . . Or maybe not—how do I know who's in our unit? They could turn you over outside a camp." And that's why I stayed in Żoliborz in some cellar or other.

---

49 On November 15, 1944, five employees from the hospital in Boernerowo (now part of the Warsaw district of Bemowo) managed to smuggle seven members of the ŻOB out of the house at 43 Promyka Street, in the area occupied by the Germans: Celina Lubetkin, Marek Edelman, Antek Cukierman, Tuwia Borzykowski, Zygmunt Warman, Julek Fiszgrund, and Dr. Teodozja Goliborska. Cf.: Stanisław Śwital, "Siedmioro z ulicy Promyka," *Biuletyn ŻIH* 1968, no. 65–66, 207–210.
50 Many of those who had fought in the Warsaw rising and did not surrender to the Germans after its defeat, including some high-ranking military personnel, managed to mingle with the crowds of civilians leaving the city. Many of the Jewish survivors, however, even those who had fought side by side with the Poles in the insurrection, believed, not without reason, that it was not safe to join them, due to the considerable anti-Jewish sentiment in Polish society, including among the Warsaw insurrectionists, at that time.
51 Lt. Święcicki, an AK officer. A group of Jewish insurrectionists, among them Marek Edelman and Antek Cukierman, stayed in his apartment in the Warsaw district of Żoliborz (16 or 18 Krasińskiego Street) in October 1944.

You mean you were in hiding for six weeks? Were you alone?
No, no, there were quite a few people there. Ten or so. And then later the paramedic team came . . . But those details are less important. In any case, it all worked out. Oh, you can write that there was this Dr. Śwital from Boernerowo who organized it all. I'm not going to go into what happened after that.

But that's the most important!
Well, I can also tell you that one of the people in that paramedic team was Janusz Osęka. He was nineteen, brave, and good.

And what happened next?
After that, I lived in a house where the headquarters of the unit *Zur Bekämpfung der Banditen und Partisanen* was on the first floor,[52] and ten Jews living on the second floor—all those who made it out of the rising. And in the bathroom, there was a portrait of Hitler on the wall, and we all peed in the same bathroom. Then the Russians came . . . This Russian female light cavalry squadron with grey fur trimmings on their caps—gorgeous girls. And that's how the war ended.

And what happened to you after the war?
What do you mean, what happened to me? I had twenty-five lovers, a different one every two days—what do you want me to tell you?!

How did you come to be in Łódź?
There was a couch here, it was warm, and I lay down to sleep here. I'd had enough of keeping going—but that's also already been written down somewhere. In Warsaw, there was nowhere to lay your head, but here there was a couch, a pillow, and I lay down on the pillow and just stayed.

Where did you study?
In Łódź. And why? Ask Hania [Hanna Krall]; she wrote about that in that book of hers.

In which year did you come to live in Łódź?
It might have been 1945, or maybe 1946? I can't tell you.

---

52 *Zur Bekämpfung der Banditen und Partisanen* (Ger.)—For Combatting Partisans and Bandits.

Were you ever a member of the PZPR?[53]
Oh no, no, no! I had been wise to them for a long time. I knew what communism was all about even before the war.

In what way was 1968 important?[54] **What happened to you then?**
It wasn't important—what should have been important about it? The communists stop at nothing. They threw me out of my job, and that was all.

Where were you working at that time?
In the military hospital in Łódź. To be precise, I wasn't thrown out, I just wasn't allowed into work. The porter said I couldn't go in anymore. I wasn't thrown out because nobody spoke to me. It was just that the porter wouldn't let me in.

How long were you without a job?
I was never without a job. I went to some other hospital, where a friend took me on as his junior assistant. And then they threw me out of there as well—I think that was in 1970. And then, I was taken on at the hospital where I work now. My ward was created *ad personam*, because at that point there was a big uproar and an intervention. Back then, I still had acquaintances among the people in power. I knew Cyrankiewicz,[55] and Rakowski,[56] and they put in a word for me; they said such an important Jew, one who had stayed, couldn't be thrown out of work. So, they threw somebody else out, and gave me these twenty-five beds. And so, for more than ten years now I've been acting head of department. But that's not important. Those are minor details; even in the money there's only two hundred zlotys' difference.

But let's go back to 1968. Of course, I'm not going to ask you why you didn't leave the country, because that would be indelicate, but I will ask whether you ever thought about leaving.
I didn't. But I'm surprised you didn't ask me why my wife and kids did go.[57] Why don't you ask that?

---

53 p. 512 Glossary—Polish United Workers' Party.
54 p. 508 Glossary—March 1968.
55 Józef Cyrankiewicz (1911–1989)—Polish socialist activist, communist politician, and prime minister for several terms in the People's Republic of Poland.
56 Mieczysław Rakowski (1926–2008)—Polish communist politician who held various high offices in the 1980s.
57 p. 416 Rereading the List—Alina, Ala, Margolis [Margolis-Edelman].

Well, I'll ask: why did they go?
Firstly, my wife and children were harried more than me. Perhaps not more, but they worried more about being thrown out or not being allowed to sit tests. And secondly, when things are that bad, it's good to get those who are doing worse behind a wall, so that you have more room to manoeuver, so to speak. And that's it, that's all. No more to it.

I also want to ask you what you think about the current interest in the Jewish issue in Poland. Catholic papers devote a lot of space to Jewish culture.
Those Catholic papers are opposition papers—greater or lesser, but in any case, the opposition. *Tygodnik Powszechny, Znak, Więź, Przegląd Powszechny* are papers that are not all too popular with the Church administration. They represent the views of secular Catholicism, which believes in the few Christian ideals that are also at the heart of socialism. Jews are a very important subject in Poland. Not because of their presence, because there are no more Jews in Poland, but because of the past. Because the Church behaved despicably toward the Jews, in the two interwar decades, for instance. I'm not talking about the Church that is against the state today, the Church in which one hundred thousand people attend masses for Fr. Popiełuszko.[58] And the pope who beams down on the Gdansk Shipyards isn't a Church pope but a guarantor of freedom.[59]

But he has something in common with religiosity...
With religiosity? Garbage! With security! You have to understand! You are so naive. Do you remember when it was that most people went to church? From 1945 until 1948, to stick one up at the Reds; they started going during the war. And when was there any culture in the Church? In 1968, and now, when they're beating people up. The Church is the only place where the nation can take refuge. Don't be childish—it's all politics.

Well, maybe, but whose politics?
The nation's politics.

---

58 Jerzy Popiełuszko (1947–1984). Roman Catholic priest, chaplain of the Warsaw branch of the oppositional civil rights movement Solidarity, which he continued to support during Martial Law (1981–1983). He was kidnapped by Security Service officers, tortured, and drowned in a river.

59 Marek Edelman is referring here to Pope John Paul II (1920–2005), who, as a Pole himself, was to Polish society in the repressive 1980s at least as much a symbol of freedom as a religious figure.

But I want to repeat our question. How do you explain the interest in Jewish issues in the Polish Catholic press? Is it a need to make amends?
In a sense, yes. I suspect that those people are ashamed of the Church that held sway here between the wars.

But there's also some interest in society at large—
In Jews? Yuck. Jews are disgusting! I don't know, maybe there is some form of interest, but notice that this society no longer knows Jews; there are no Jews anymore.

But there is an interest in the past.
Well, yes, because it's exotic in a way. But essentially that doesn't prove anything. Look: in 1968 there were eighteen thousand Jews in Poland. And see how marvellously things worked out with people then. You even had the woman who worked in the Wedel chocolate factory shouting: "Moshe, go to Israel!" She wasn't bribed. Then again, this interest in the Jewish question might also be a question of opposition to communist policies. If the commies are against the Jews, I'll be for them.

But on the other hand, there's the notion of Judeo-communism.[60]
Of course. Look what the "real Poles" in the Solidarity movement did. They said: "KOR—Jews—commies."[61] That didn't catch on at its congress, but it did in the regions. They'd have knocked Bujak down on the street and called him a Jew. That was the work of the UB.

I'm not convinced it was the work of the UB.
Because you're just a kid.

---

60 Pol. *Żydokomuna*. The Polish name for the conspiracy theory which claims that communism is an order operated and perpetuated by Jews. In its Polish variant, it functioned as a mechanism by which to deflect the guilt for the communist takeover of Poland after the war from the Poles themselves by laying it at the door of the Jews. They, the "red traitors," the argument ran, were an instrumental force in the entrenchment of communism in Poland. Edelman's answers to this and the following questions reference the way that the security apparatus (here: UB; in the period in question properly *Służba Bezpieczeństwa*, SB—Security Service) in the People's Republic of Poland equated all forms of dissidence with Jews in order to discredit them.

61 KOR (Komitet Obrony Robotników, the Workers' Defense Committee) was an illegal, independent opposition organization in Poland which operated from June 1976 till September 1981. It took action on human rights issues, published underground literature, and laid the foundations for a civil society. KOR, later KSS KOR, was a significant contributor to the development of independent trade unions and the Solidarity movement.

So, you mean like with the Kielce incident?[62] It didn't matter whether it was the UB who did it or not; the main thing was that there was someone who could be provoked.

I don't think that's the same thing. I think that the authorities are constantly returning to the Jewish issue because they really think they can win something out of it. It worked back between the wars. And it worked in 1968. And now, look—only recently Kiszczak had the balls to say of Bielecki that all he has in common with this country is that he was born here...[63] In all honesty, it's unbelievable that there's such a problem with anti-Semitism in a country where there are practically no Jews anymore. But on the other hand, it's not about whether you really are a Jew. They decide who's a Jew.

Could you tell us where you stand on the book by Hanna Krall and your words in it? How do you judge—

I take the responsibility for what I say in it. Not for the author's comments on that.

Do you appreciate it?

I don't appreciate it because I don't know anything about literature. I mean, not in the sense that I don't appreciate it...

Do you like it?

I don't know because I haven't read it. Anyway, nobody talks to me about it much.

Could you say what it means to be a Jew today?

Where? Here in Poland?... It means siding with the weak, not siding with authority, because here the authorities have always beaten Jews, and today it's Solidarity that's being beaten. Bujak is beaten by the authorities. I think that always, regardless of who the one being beaten is, you have to stand by them. Give them a roof over their head, hide them in the cellar, not be afraid to do so, and, above all, be against those who are doing the beating. And that's the only

---

62 p. 506 Glossary—Kielce pogrom.
63 Czesław Kiszczak (1925–2015)—general and communist-era interior minister, co-author of many repressive anti-opposition measures in the Polish People's Republic, up to and including the introduction of Martial Law (December 13, 1981). The last communist prime minister of Poland; Czesław Bielecki (b. 1948)—architect, social and political activist, journalist, of Jewish descent, imprisoned by the authorities of the Polish People's Republic. Deputy to the Third Sejm of the Republic of Poland.

reason why you're a Jew today. Polish Jewry perished. All that vast Jewish culture perished, and it will never come back.

But it hasn't entirely perished. The memory of what used to be still remains.
No, don't talk nonsense. There is nothing left. Even though it is still there in memories, in Polish literature, there is no presence, and there never will be again. There is no presence when nothing is being created anymore.

In that case, could you say what it means to be a Jew not here, in Poland, but at all?
That is a very difficult thing to define. Jewry was a basin between the Vistula and the Dnieper. Everything that was in America, France, England, did not make Jewish culture. For what is a nation? A nation is people who create a common culture, and progress. A nation need not necessarily form a cultural or religious community. There are millions of Mohammedans in the world, but it is not one and the same culture. Those five million Jews between Odessa and Warsaw had the same culture. And even the same economic conditions. And that no longer exists.

Yes, that no longer exists, but on the other hand the state of Israel, which you say has no chance of survival, does exist.
The state of Israel has an entirely different culture. Even if it prevails, over time it will become an Arab state in cultural terms. And that is inevitable. It is not a Jewish state but a Mosaic state. Jews from Ethiopia, Egypt, China, transplanted to Israel, who have nothing more in common with each other than that they confess the Mosaic faith. And so, if they prevail, a new nation will emerge, a new culture, which will have nothing in common with Europe, Chagall, or Peretz;[64] with the Jewry that was here.

In your opinion, what should someone who says of themselves: "I am a Jew" identify with? Where should they seek their place?
If they consider themselves to be a Jew in Europe, they will always be opposed to authority. A Jew always has a sense of community with the weak.

---

64 Yitzhak Leib Peretz (1852–1925)—educated as a lawyer, the creator of modern Yiddish literature. Born in Zamość into a traditional Jewish family, he wrote poetry in Hebrew, Polish, and Yiddish, and was a master of Yiddish-language prose.

In that case, is there any difference between a Jew who stands with the weak, and weak non-Jews?
Is there a difference? No. None. Bujak, Kuroń, Michnik, Jaworski, Lis, Frasyniuk are Jews of this system.[65]

How would you like to end our conversation?
You are very nice to have come, you are very thorough. I'm very pleased to be able to speak to Poznań; I never thought that I would ever have anything to do with Poznań.

Thank you for talking with us.

Łódź, spring 1985

Marek Edelman died in Warsaw on October 2, 2009.

---

65 Zbigniew Bujak, Jacek Kuroń, Adam Michnik, Seweryn Jaworski, Bogdan Lis, and Bogdan Frasyniuk were all leading anti-communist opposition figures in the late 1970s and 1980s.

Back Then,
There Were Many Legends...

Szmuel Ron's Story

I used to be called Rozencwajg. I changed my name in 1951. Before the war, I lived in Katowice. That was where I was brought up, where I went to school— just before the war, to a Jewish high school in Będzin. When the war broke out, the Jews were hounded from Katowice. The wind blew us to Sosnowiec. It was then that I joined the organization Haszomer Hacair.[1] Over time, our educational, charitable, and, to some extent also, our political activities were replaced by military training; we became a combat group. But that didn't all come at once—Mordechaj Anielewicz was very influential there. When did Mordechaj come to us? I can give you the date almost precisely. It is connected with two events that I remember very well. In May 1942, my close friend Kalman Tencer died. That was one of the few instances when a man could die in his own bed and have a normal burial. We didn't always have that good fortune. And then in the June, I caught pleurisy. And that was a serious event, because back then it was not easy to treat. It was when I finally recovered, I remember, that Mordechaj came. That was the end of June or the beginning of July 1942.

He only came to us once, but he stayed for a long time. Until the moment when the letter came from Josef Kapłan informing us of Czerniaków's suicide.[2] And then Mordechaj went back to Warsaw. I think he was with us for two or even three months. He didn't leave right after that information came, and the letter itself didn't come at once. Mordechaj came to us with a mission, which he broke off—Czerniaków's suicide indicated that the stakes were higher than we thought. I'm not sure if he was with us for three months, but over two and a bit for sure.

Why did he come? Some very important people in our Haszomer Hacair group, such as Idzia Pejsachson or my friend Sewek Meryn, had become Trotskyites, to the great disillusionment of all the others. Such a great

---

1 p. 498 Glossary.
2 p. 505 Glossary—Kapłan, Josef.

misfortune! Mordechaj came partly in connection with that. He wanted to redress the line of their political thinking a little. I found out the other reason for his visit later, after he had left—it was a great secret. In those days, there was a legend, and there were many legends at that time, that Moniek Meryn, the chairman of the Judenrat in Sosnowiec,[3] was allegedly in such close relations with the Gestapo that he could bribe them. And Mordechaj wanted to go abroad to call on world leaders to protest. But during his visit he abandoned that idea.

Every day brought new tidings, worse than before. Every day buried what had happened yesterday, what had happened the week before, in archeological layers. The previous things ceased to exist. They didn't even exist in our thinking; you didn't feel the past, it wasn't there. Friends, family—gone; it was a different world, a different life. You couldn't even mourn what had passed. Mordechaj, when he arrived, described a reality to us that we both knew about and did not know about, both knew about and did not *want* to know about. I remember our first meeting with Mordechaj at a meeting, of which there were a few. With a map on his knee, he described the situation on the front in Africa to us. He was a great journalist, reporter, and political commentator. It was then that he started building our new way of thinking. I remember his words, which later became our slogan: "From Yugoslavia to Norway, from Slovakia to Ukraine, partisans are fighting. Shall our people be absent from among them?" At that point he didn't know that the partisan army in Lithuania was 90 percent made up of Jews. Yes. What we also didn't know at that point was that the Polish partisans would turn us away . . . That was also something that I had personal experience with. You see, ma'am, I've gotten old, dammit, and I haven't rid myself of those emotions. Those things are still alive to me.

I remember Mordechaj talking about the first experiences of the Holocaust. Places like Chełmno, Bełzec, Trawniki—not yet Treblinka—were familiar to me through him. And those stories about the vehicles with gases . . . He told us about it in detail, because one of our people had been there and managed to get away. I remember my physical reaction. I don't know how to portray it to you. Imagine—you're sitting here, I'm sitting here, and many other people of various ages, and somebody says: "I am condemned to death—there is no way out. And you are condemned to death—there is no way out; and this guy here is condemned to death—there is no way out. All of us, all of us: our

---

3   p. 504 Glossary.

neighbors, friends, family, children, old people, without exception . . ." Your mind can't take it in, your mind rebels against it. And I remember my physical reaction: my skull froze . . . I . . . I . . . I . . . lost my breath. We had no doubt that Mordechaj was trustworthy, that this was not flummery, fantasies, or fairy-tales. We believed that something of this sort not only could exist but already did exist. I remember telling my parents, and they accepted it. But I also talked about it to my friend Lipka's folks (he was our radio-tapping man). I told his father: "Listen up, sir: you, your wife, that grandfather of yours, and your sons, and I, and my parents, we are all condemned to death." That man slapped me round the face twice; he couldn't bear it. I had taken away the security of his life. I, a young whippersnapper—how old can I have been then?—was bandying around words whose meaning was incomprehensible. That was his reaction. I didn't feel he was being aggressive. It was he who thought that I was abnormal.

So Mordechaj told us this, and that was why we started talking about self-defense. At that point, the ghetto in Sosnowiec and Będzin was still open. The thought that we would have to defend ourselves by any means possible—with an ax, a metal bar, or our fists—was new to me. It took a while for me to accept that thought. Our group—the more mature ones, aged between eighteen and twenty, of whom there were a few dozen in Będzin and Sosnowiec—were all as taken aback as I was, I think. We were overcome with fear. Though I don't remember anyone doubting that we would follow him. It was clear to us that from then on, our lives would be taken up entirely with the thought of defending ourselves. Other groups, other organizations, did not accept that thought at once. But I don't want to talk about that. I'm not a historian to judge them. After the war, so many legends grew up, and I don't want to debronze them. Many issues hurt me a lot. That's one of the reasons why I don't want to publish my book.[4] Certain things have never ceased to burn me inside. In my book, I make some suggestions, and I leave that to my sons. Let them worry if it interests them. But I don't think it does interest them. In any case, those details are not important to history. In terms of self-defense, we from Haszomer Hacair treated a refusal as a weakness, as a betrayal. Betrayal not in the sense of disgrace; the thing was that we couldn't rely on such people. They were too weak to our mind.

I often spent time alone with Mordechaj. I had to be in hiding more than the others, and Mordechaj also had to be in hiding. Apart from that, I was a courier in Zawiercie, and it was I who took Mordechaj into Zawiercie. I was his minder,

---

4 Szmuel Ron, *Die Erinnerungen haben mich nie losgelassen*, trans. Esther Kinsky (Verlag Neue Kritik, Frankfurt am Main, 1998).

so to speak. I had a pair of fists, I knew the terrain well, and he was an outsider. I got him into the ghettos in Zawiercie, Będzin, and Sosnowiec.

I remember that I spent several nights with him in a cobbler's workshop. The workshop was outside the ghetto; the ghetto was still open. That was in Sosnowiec. We slept in the same bed there. And in Będzin our hideout was on a farm, among some beehives. Ah, and one interesting thing: I had taken a book by Władysław Spasowski with me from Katowice.[5] Do you know who Władysław Spasowski was? Ah, you young people in Poland today! Władysław Spasowski was a philosopher in prewar Poland. He wrote the book *Wyzwolenie człowieka*. That was like our bible. It was our vision of the future. Likewise, Kotarbiński was important to us.[6] Well, in any case, I gave Mordechaj that Spasowski, and he read it very eagerly.

We talked about a lot of things. But I remember that there was one area of Mordechaj's life that I knew nothing about: his private affairs. That was taboo. That was never spoken about. Nothing, absolutely nothing! Everyone asked him, but he let nothing slip. I didn't know—either then or after the war—and never met anyone who knew his personal affairs. Later on, I found out that he had a girlfriend. Mira [Fuchrer],[7] her name was. She wrote letters to him, and those letters were kept with us. I read them once. Not one word from one beloved to her beloved! Only the cause. He remained in my memory as a man who thought and acted without ceasing only in the cause. Day and night. You could speak of nothing else with him. Perhaps I'm exaggerating, perhaps that's one of those legends which we spoke about.

I remember that we used to meet frequently on an agrarian farm in Środula.[8] That was a safe haven to us. We used to sing and write poetry there, and make love, and work, and escape from all our various problems, and dream of the future, and talk politics—there was even a theater there! I remember that Mordechaj once conducted a youth choir singing Hanukkah songs there. I didn't know those songs back then, but I know that here, in Eretz Israel, they sing them in preschools. But those songs, at that time, were no kindergarten songs. They were fighting hymns.

---

5 Władysław Spasowski (1877–1941)—philosopher and pedagogue, left-wing teaching activist.
6 Tadeusz Kotarbiński (1886–1981)—philosopher, logician, and praxeologist, in the years 1919–1961 a professor at the University of Warsaw. Decorated with the Righteous Among the Nations medal.
7 p. 380 Rereading the List—Mira Fuchrer (Fuchter).
8 Środula—a working-class suburb of Sosnowiec. From November 1942 until August 1943, one of the city's two ghettos was in Środula.

Humiliation
September 1939

I said already that Mordechaj lived only for the cause. When he went to put his plan to Meryn—Meryn didn't accept it, of course—he didn't say that there was a resistance movement in the making. Mordechaj claimed that there was already a resistance movement in existence, and that he was at its head. We found that incredible. Everything we were doing was still at the fermentation stage, yet he was already able to speak calmly about the existence of a resistance movement. He threatened Meryn, saying to him: "You have to reckon with us." He had something more than charisma; it was an incredible strength. He had a huge influence on people. I don't know whether Mordechaj had any other contacts with the Judenrat. I only know about those with Meryn in connection with his trip abroad. Mordechaj abandoned his cooperation with Meryn when it transpired that his possibilities were one of those legends. He didn't particularly trust Meryn anyway. He reckoned with the possibility that if Meryn knew too much, he could betray.

As I already said, Mordechaj was not only an excellent political reporter and organizer, and a man of immense charisma; he was also a splendid journalist. He put together a newspaper with us at the drop of a hat. It was called *Przełom*. It was the Jewish revolutionary youth press organ. The Gestapo got hold of that paper, though I only found that out in prison. One moment. I was first arrested in Bielsko in January 1944, but I slipped them. Then they arrested me in the March, and that time I couldn't escape, because I was injured when they caught me. We were held in Katowice that time, and then in a prison in Mysłowice. That was a slaughterhouse, worse than Auschwitz. Every new inmate—Jew or non-Jew, political or criminal—who came into a cell was given a ceremonial "welcome" with a whip, a bullwhip, and so on. I was injured. They battered me and thrashed me, but I didn't let out a peep. I got a compliment from one guy for that, a criminal, I think: "We already had one hardnut Yid here, but they hanged him." What a nice reception! After that welcome, in the night, a gentleman came to see me. He went by the name of "Mr. Stach" in that prison, and he was respected. He was a communist, a Pole. I told him who I was and asked him if he'd heard of the "Przełom" group. Of course he had! He'd been interrogated by the Gestapo about it. Mr. Stach helped me out a bit, bigged me up with the politicals. The politicals kept together, and they had contacts on the outside, too. I asked them for just one thing—a dose of cyanide. I got it, too. It later turned out not to be cyanide; it was probably morphine. I didn't have to use it, luckily. I probably would have only gotten the shits. But as it was, not knowing what I had, I felt safer. I think it was that that kept me together in the first few hours at Auschwitz. But that's another story ... Let's go back to Mordechaj.

So, Mordechaj was well-known in Warsaw circles, but he wasn't known everywhere in Poland. At that time, people like Josek Kapłan, Tosia Altman,[9] and Arie Wilner were well-known.[10] Kapłan was already an "old man" by then—he was twenty-eight, I think. Mordechaj wasn't young, either; he was over twenty-three. Even I wasn't the youngest—I was twenty! Yes . . .

What we also knew about Mordechaj was that he had high-tailed it to Vilnius with Tosia and Arie Wilner when the war broke out. After a while, they decided to come back. They came to the conclusion that their place was with their nation, and that leaders of a youth movement couldn't afford to simply leave their organization. And they came back to Warsaw.

What else do I remember about Mordechaj? I don't recall him having a sense of humor. I also remember that he often talked about the Polish underground. Contacts were very poor, and it was hard to get arms from them. Neither the AK nor the AL supported the idea of self-defense in the ghettos. Arms were largely procured from two sources: either we bought scatterguns on the market, or from the Polish underground. I remember that Mordechaj tried to convince us that short arms, revolvers, were worthless, and that we needed to procure long-bores, rifles. That failed. But we had our own grenade manufactory. The gentleman who made them, Meir Szulman, is still alive here in Eretz Israel, in Holon. He was not a political man; he was a handyman. There was nothing he couldn't make—a broom out of nothing, false money, documents, grenades, an elegant dress . . .

Mordechaj also told us that in Warsaw conditions, if there was a round-up, he would order our people out onto the street, rather than to stay in hiding. For two reasons: to be able to put up resistance on the spot, but most importantly, to see. If you didn't see it all, you wouldn't believe that they were killing children, and you wouldn't be able to hate enough. And you wouldn't be able to fight enough if you couldn't hate. This wasn't about hatred of Germans, but about provoking in us the reaction of the need and skills to defend ourselves.

I remember this one scene, if you'll allow me: Cwi Duński and I had a portion of cyanide. We weren't sure if it was cyanide, so we wanted to try it out. We decided to give a little to a cat. But we couldn't! We were unable to kill a cat! And if you can't kill a cat, how can you speak of self-defense? There was this macabre "instruction" circulating among us, that we should practice by killing cats, to have that "cold blood." We couldn't do it. That was a problem. Aesthetes, we were, Boy Scouts, humanists, socialists, and who knows what else? We were better at philosophy than with a knife or an ax in our hands.

---

9   p. 334 Rereading the List.
10 p. 465 Rereading the List—Izrael Wilner, Arie, Jurek.

There were minor self-defense operations, but they were feeble. I was supposed to take part in one of them. I was dispatched on a mission that Mordechaj had planned in advance. I was sent to Hungary, but I never made it. Aside from me, members of three other groups also went: Haszomer Hadati,[11] Dror Frajhajt,[12] and Gordonia.[13] I was always very eloquent, you know; I could always talk and talk, but on that trip to Hungary I experienced some kind of dreadful block. How would I tell them over there in the free world about all these murders? How would I convince them that I was telling the truth? I talked to Karski[14] about it. He had the same thoughts and exactly the same experiences: he was not believed. I was very afraid that they wouldn't believe me. But we never reached Hungary. At the railroad station in the town of Oświęcim, our guide abandoned us, and simply fled. Then I and the guy from Gordonia hid in the sewers. What happened to the other two? I don't know. The next day, we headed for the ghetto. And our self-defense? I believe it was ineffective. There were both too few arms and too few fighters. There were groups in the ghetto which up to the last moment believed that not self-defense but saving themselves was the answer. Sure, there were armed fighters who attacked groups of Germans, but the Germans slaughtered them, knocked out all our boys. I think that was August 1943.

Now I will tell you about the letter from Mordechaj that came to us from the fighting ghetto. They had contacts with the Aryan side via the sewers, and that was how letters were sent. I remember one sentence from that letter: "I am happy; I have seen Germans killed." What became of that letter? What became of the archive? I don't know, I don't know. The fact that we kept an archive shows that we were thinking historically. I think we received more letters than one. It was also then that I read Mira's letters to Mordechaj, the letters of one beloved to her beloved—not a single warm word. Only the cause.

He never talked about anything. I remember I was curious about his life, and about that time a legend about Mordechaj attached itself to me. The legend went that his grandfather was a fisherman on the river Vistula, and that it was allegedly from him that Mordechaj had inherited his desire to battle storms. After the war, I met some people who had known him better than I had and refuted the story. Back then, there were all kinds of legends ... I had one very devout gentleman in my family. He used to tell the story that some Gestapo officer wanted to

---

11 p. 498 Glossary.
12 p. 496 Glossary—Frajhajt.
13 p. 497 Glossary.
14 p. 505 Glossary—Karski, Jan.

throw a *Sefer Torah* into the river,¹⁵ and at that moment, the Lord God paralyzed him. And that gentleman believed that, just like I believed, Mordechaj's grandfather was a fisherman. Another legend ran than the fighting ghetto hung out the slogan: "For our freedom and yours." Those words were bandied around among us; they were on everyone's lips. But that the slogan was painted on the walls of the ghetto in arms—that's untrue. It was just a legend that we wanted to believe in at that point.

He wasn't the fighter type who liked brawling, certainly not. But he certainly was a born commander and leader. The figure made by Rappaport is not entirely reminiscent of Mordechaj, his face wasn't like that.¹⁶ But the figure itself, the movement it embodies, is reminiscent of a commandant. I think Mordechaj was the antithesis of an aesthete, he was very realistic.

Tosia Altman was different. When she came to visit us, a few months before Mordechaj, though there were already considerable miseries all around, she went on about psychology and philosophy. Tosia Altman was the first person who encouraged us to go out onto the Aryan side—that was very important; it was a watershed in our thinking. How? With a nose like this, a mug like this, eyes like these? Do you know the concept of "With a nose like this," ma'am? A girl is different; she can dye her hair, for instance. But Tosia convinced me. At the beginning of 1942, I started going out of the ghetto. Over time, I gained confidence, and in the end, I came to the conclusion that it wasn't appearance but behavior that counted. Behavior was the most important thing. And on that count, I well-nigh reached perfection. I could travel in streetcars that were only for Germans, and if a Pole wanted to get in, I wouldn't let him. In fact, between you and me, it was Poles that scared me the most.

After my failed foray to Hungary, I lived in the apartment of a woman who—and I speak of her with great respect—had a very well-known profession, one of the oldest in the world. Aside from that, she also brewed moonshine. I went to see her once, for some moonshine, which we needed for bribes. I was about to leave, but the curfew was getting close, so she says to me: "Perhaps you want to stay?" Well, I didn't need asking twice. I stayed. She put me to bed on this narrow couch. In the night, her sixteen-year-old daughter comes into my bed. I started to fight her off, hands and feet, because back then I still had various principles. In any case, that wasn't what I was there for. Early the next morning, her mother said to me, straight out: "Listen, if you have any dealings with the police,

---

15 *Sefer Torah* (Heb.)—book of the Torah, a Torah scroll.
16 Ron is talking about the statue of Mordechaj Anielewicz in the Yad Mordecai kibbutz near Ashkelon, founded by Polish Jews in 1943.

you can stay with me." I told her I was a Jew, but that didn't make any difference to her. She was a very noble woman. Later on, her apartment became one of our most important hideouts. I lived there as her son. Zofia—that was her name—was also a janitor in an NSDAP house. And the full story was that she did a deal with Jesus: if she saved me, Jesus would save her son, who was on the German front. She was one of those Polish Germans,[17] like the Silesians, you know. She couldn't write in Polish, but she wrote in German; after the war I got letters from her. Zofia had this one gentleman, a son-of-a-bitch called Alojz. He wanted to rape one of our girls. I tussled with him, and he was as strong as an ox, like a maddened bull. And we couldn't make any noise while we fought, of course; we had to fight silently. He was her man; not the first and not the only one. She fought with him once, too—over me, because he wanted to blackmail me.

There was this one room and a little kitchen there. Policemen and various other types would come around, and it would all be conducted on the spot, no chit-chat. I'm a grandpa now, but I still blush whenever I remember it. But Zofia was a truly noble person. She had . . . of course! That's why I'm so sensitive to your eyes! She had your eyes! She didn't resemble a Pole at all; she was a typical Jewess. And she wasn't afraid to work for us as a courier. But she wouldn't take any money. In the end, I taught her to take it. She needed that money, because she had this dream of having a cow and a cottage after the war.

What else about Mordechaj? He succeeded in consolidating almost all the groups in Warsaw,[18] apart from Betar,[19] I think. You know, over the past few days since your telephone call, I've been in dialogue with Mordechaj the whole time. I don't know what else I can say about him. I know that in Eretz Israel there are very few people who have anything to say on the subject. Mordechaj was a typical introvert, and, as I said, lived and breathed only the cause, day and night. He was uncompromising. He was the type of ideologue and revolutionary who is interested only in the revolution. I remember he said: "We are the vanguard of the nation. The vanguard cannot exist without the nation. We have no right to stay alive." And we believed him. Nothing but preserving our dignity! To make peace with the thought that I had no right to live was amazing.

In 1962 or 1963, I was summoned to court as a witness in the case of a gentleman who had been a Jewish policeman in Będzin.[20] And I could say as many

---

17 p. 519 Glossary—Volksdeutsche.
18 p. 512 Glossary—Political relations in the Warsaw ghetto.
19 p. 493 Glossary.
20 p. 502 Glossary—Jewish Order Service.

things against him as in his defense. In the end, I asked to be relieved of the role of witness. During the trial, I talked to the man's lawyer. That was in his office.

I remember that the lawyer, a short guy like me, asked me why we opposed those who did not want to defend themselves. He stood in front of me, his feet planted wide apart, and started shouting out: "I am an officer in the Israeli army! I know what it means to send soldiers to the front, I've experienced orders like that! And it wasn't an easy thing for me. But you wanted grandmothers, aunties, cripples, the healthy, young, and old, all to defend themselves?! Where did you get the chutzpah? Where did you get the audacity?" He broke me because I sensed that he was right. Perhaps it was unjust that we back then criticized those who lacked the courage to defend themselves. Later on, I often thought that probably we didn't have the right to demand of them all that they defend themselves, that they put up resistance...

You asked when I left Poland. Via Auschwitz, and Mauthausen. One moment... I was arrested in March 1944. Katowice, Mysłowice—prison. Then Auschwitz and Mauthausen. And after that I never went there again. My feelings for Poland are like feelings for a once beloved old flame... whom I never want to see again. Please don't take that personally, ma'am. It has nothing to do with the people—at least not the people from your generation. I... No, I'm not going to talk about that!

Jerusalem, May 1989

Szmuel Ron died in Jerusalem in 2000.

Someone Must Have Pushed That Closet up Flush from Outside...

Conversation with Masza Glajtman-Putermilch

I was born in Warsaw in 1924 into a petty bourgeois family—my father was a merchant. We had a leather goods workshop. My mother belonged to the Bund from her youthful days.[1] My father was not a party man. I was given a socialist upbringing at home. I went to a Bund school, one of the CISzO schools.[2] The language of instruction was Jewish, of course. Each of the schools was named after a Bund leader. I went to the Grosser elementary school at 29 Karmelicka Street. We received a commune-style education—children should share with each other, see each other, and help each other. I was taught that from a young age.

And later, after elementary school?
After that, I started attending an ORT vocational school, also in Warsaw, on Długa Street.[3] I never finished that school, because in 1939 the years of education were interrupted for Jews. Children in the ghetto studied in secret and carried their books under their overcoats. And in late 1939, I moved from Warsaw to Miedzeszyn. In Miedzeszyn, I worked in the Medem Sanatorium.[4] I stayed there until the ghetto was sealed.

You mentioned before that you went to the same school as Marek Edelman, yes?
Yes, we went to elementary school together. The ORT was a girls' school.

---

1   p. 516 Glossary—Society for the Propagation of Labor among the Jews.
2   p. 514 Glossary—Schools.
3   p. 516 Glossary.
4   p. 508 Glossary.

And at the Medem sanatorium?
I was in the sewing workshop, I sewed. There were twelve of us girls from the Bund's youth organization, Cukunft Skif.[5] When I returned to Warsaw, they sealed the ghetto right afterwards.[6]

Why did you go back?
My parents were very insistent. They said that when the ghetto was sealed, we would be cut off from one another, and they didn't want that. My elder sister was in Russia at that point, and I was the only child at home, and they didn't want...

And your parents were already in the ghetto?
Yes, of course, they were in the ghetto. We lived at 47 Nalewki, and our apartment was inside the ghetto. So, we were "lucky," as it was called back then. We weren't expelled from our apartment. Whatever we had in the apartment we could sell for bread, whereas those who had to move left almost everything behind. Yes. But by selling our things,[7] we survived somehow until the deportation.[8] As I could sew a little, I would buy up old clothes left by the dead; my father unpicked them, we dyed the material, I sewed, and Mama sold them. Later on, I had to take care of it all myself, because my parents were very weak from hunger. I was really the last one who kept going, though I was swollen by then, too.

Please can you tell me about the deportation?
The deportation was... My mother was the first to be taken to that Umschlagplatz.[9]

When?
In July, that was at the beginning of the deportation. It was really thanks to Marek [Edelman] that I was able to save my mother. I remember I met him on the street with Michał Klepfisz,[10] and he sent me to the ŻTOS for a work pass.[11] When I went there and said that Marek had sent me, I was given two passes: for my mother and for me. At the Umschlagplatz they were supposed to let my mother go, but I couldn't find her. She was inside the building...

---

5   p. 494 Glossary—Cukunft.
6   p. 519 Glossary—Warsaw ghetto.
7   p. 515 Glossary—Smuggling.
8   p. 491 Glossary—*Aktion*.
9   p. 518 Glossary.
10 p. 404 Rereading the List.
11 p. 503 Glossary—Jewish Social Welfare Society.

Warsaw, intersection of Grzybowska and Żelazna

Which building?
It was a school, on Stawki Street, an elementary school. Usually, people were outside, on the square. Mama was inside the building. But I was lucky, I noticed her from outside. She was looking out of the window, and I saw her. I asked her to stay where she was, so that I could ... And that time, I freed my mother from the Umschlag, but a short time afterwards, they caught her again, with me. Unfortunately, it was a Jewish policeman who was taking her to the Umschlagplatz, and I raced after the waggon ... and asked him to take me too, because my father was also gone—or so I thought. Only later did it transpire that my father had escaped and gone into hiding. He came back, but at that moment, running behind that waggon, I thought my father was gone.

So, you wanted to go the Umschlag of your own free will?
Right then, I wanted to go voluntarily with my mother, but the policeman wouldn't agree to take me onto the waggon for anything. He kept saying: "You're young, you still have a chance, you could still save yourself; I just need five noddles."[12] And he said: "This is my fifth noddle." That was their slang.

And where did he catch your mom? Just on the street?
No. I had gone out of the house with my mom. We were standing in the entranceway. We wanted to go see what had happened to my father, because they'd taken him. And he—that Jewish policeman—was driving through our courtyard, through our Nalewki Street entranceway. He hauled my mother out right in the entranceway onto the street, and as I was running after the waggon, he kept whipping my hands to make me let go of the waggon. I think I fell onto the roadway. I was found by two Jewish policemen, and they ask me: "What's with you?" So, I say: "I'm going to the Umschlag." And they say: "You've no need to go there, because there's no one there anymore, and you aren't going with your mother." And then I went to my uncle's. I mean, my uncle wasn't there anymore, because he had died of starvation, but my cousin was still there, and she told me that my father had escaped on the way ...

---

12 In the initial phase of the liquidation of the ghetto (late July 1942), the rounding-up of Jews was carried out almost exclusively by the Jewish Order Service. Each officer had to supply five people—which they referred to in their slang as *lepki* (Pol.: noddles)—to the Umschlagplatz every day. Failure to supply the required number meant that the policeman himself would be put on the transport to Treblinka.

To the Umschlag?
Yes, on the way to the Umschlag, and he had gone home. I met my father at home.

And you never got to the Umschlag, and you didn't see your mom again?
I never went to the Umschlag again, I was only there that once. I never saw my mom again. I would like to say something about my mom now. My mom found out from Zygmunt Frydrych where the trains went,[13] but she had been talking politics in ghetto courtyards even before the *Akcja*, since the beginning of July 1942. She had been warning people that they should resist, because they were going to Treblinka, to their deaths. Nobody believed her. Until, one time, a guy from our house came back—I mean, he basically escaped from there. He was called Zycher. How had he gotten out? He jumped into a train carrying clothes that was leaving Treblinka. And then my mom started ordering everybody: "Don't let yourselves be taken alive! You all have axes at home: put them by the door, and when the Germans come, defend yourselves! Why go all the way to Treblinka to your deaths? Perhaps we can kill a German with an ax!" I would like to add that about my mom. She deserved that. Whenever I wonder why I was so fired for revenge, I think I got it from my mom.

You started working in the "'shop" with your father even before the end of the *große Aktion*.[14]
Yes. It was a saddlery 'shop on Szczęśliwa Street. We had to pay a lot of money for that workplace, of course. We were given the money by my uncle, my father's brother, who was still quite wealthy. In fact, I didn't actually work in the 'shop; it was only my father who worked there. There was an ordinance issued by the Germans that husbands covered wives, meaning that if the husband worked, that gave his wife the right to exist, the right to life.[15] So my father put me down as his wife. And it's a little comical, because the foreman of that shop was constantly trying to persuade me to leave my "husband"—how could such a young girl want to be with such an old guy? And if I really wanted an old man, then he was younger.

Did you live in the 'shop?
Yes. Each 'shop had its workers barracked. And then, on the day of the "kettle"—

---

13 p. 377 Rereading the List—Zygmunt Frydrych, Zalman.
14 p. 515 Glossary.
15 p. 510 Glossary—Number for life.

The kettle on Miła?[16]

Yes. That was in September. When they finished their segregation in the kettle, the Einsatzkommando raided our 'shop.[17] My father and I wanted to go outside to look for father's brother on Świętojerska, but the Germans took us by surprise. We ran and tried to hide. In the house where we were living, there was a hideout on the third floor. There was a closet that had been pushed up against the door of the room. It was a one-room apartment. The house had four stories, and all three upper floors had identical hideouts. And then I . . . But somebody had to push the closet back . . . So, I pushed my father into the room and pushed the closet back. I had nowhere to hide. There was a baby's cot in there, so I got under the cot. And the cot was covered with this plush cover, so I wrapped myself in the cover under the cot. And they came in . . . Ukrainians and Latvians—I could hear them talking, I couldn't see them. To get to the closet they had to move the cot a little to one side. And I heard the word: "szafa, szafa."[18] I realized that they knew it was a hideout. I don't know . . . That was all I could hear above the thumping of my heart. I felt one of them kick me. They got past, and I lay there, I don't know how long for—I couldn't define the time. They took them all out—there were more Jews in there. They evidently found a similar hideout downstairs. It had been agreed that that little room would be concealed on all three upper floors. When I came to my senses, I heard terrible cries, cries of pain. I came out. I heard gunshots. There were corpses everywhere on the stairwell.

The people they had found in the hideouts?
Yes, the people from the hideouts. I looked for my father, but I couldn't find him. They were lying in pools of blood. I turned over the corpses to see their faces.

They hauled everyone out of the hideout? No one was saved?
No one.

How many people could there have been in one of those rooms behind the closet?
Two, three, maybe five people. I lived with my father in the kitchen, and another family lived in the other room in our apartment, a couple—with my father there were five of us. But I don't know, perhaps there were more people in there,

---

16 p. 506 Glossary—Kettle on Miła Street.
17 Masza Glajtman-Putermilch is referring to the German police unit that until September 24, 1943, carried out blockades and roundups of people employed in the 'shops.
18 *Szafa* (Pol.)—closet.

because by the time we got there, the hideout was already closed. Somebody must have pushed the closet up flush from the outside . . .

You didn't find your father. Do you know what happened to him?
I know that they took him. That time, they took them all to Treblinka.

And anything else?
Nothing, absolutely nothing. There, by that closet, was my parting with my father.

What did you do with yourself?
I went to my street, to Nalewki. Above all, I went looking for my father's brother, who I didn't find at that point. I found him later, at Schultz's.[19] I mentioned my name somewhere, and somebody told me that there was a Glajtman working at the Schultz place. And I tracked him down. But that was later. And after the *Akcja* I went back to my own courtyard. That courtyard, I mean at 47 Nalewki, was where the barracks for the workers on detail[20] were. They worked at stations, shoveling coal, and they could bring bread in. And they smuggled clothing and bedlinen, all sorts of things—"rags," we called them—out of the ghetto. By the time they got back to the ghetto, it was almost the curfew hour, and you couldn't go out onto the street. So, they were very keen for someone to buy rags for them to sell the next day. So, I started to buy up rags. One person would always recommend another—you can buy this here, and you can get that there. The best things were ones that could be smuggled out easily and sold quickly. Pillowcases were very easy to smuggle: I sewed them into the linings of coats, under the padding. I got very good at that. And then they would unpick the pillowcase and take out the goods. That was the period when I ate best in the ghetto. The workers on detail would bring a bit of sausage and a few potatoes, and even a little coal so that you could cook the potatoes. And they would put eggs into flour, because when you're not hungry, your spirits are a little higher.

And where were you living then?
I was living in the same house on Nalewki, but not in our apartment. The janitor was a Jew. He had known me practically since I was born, and he gave me a room with a Jewish family. So, I had this little room with its own entrance. One time,

---

19 In the ghetto, there was one '"shop" called Toebbens-Schultz and another called K.G. Schultz. It is not clear which one Masza Glajtman-Putermilch is referring to here. Cf. p. 518 Glossary.
20 p. 521 Glossary.

I happened to meet a school friend on the street, and she said to me: "Masza, they're getting a fighting organization together, you know, would you like to?" And I agreed right away.

When was that? When did you meet your friend?
That was shortly before the January campaign.[21]

What was the friend's name?
Leja Szyfman.[22] We went to school together. Leja had a sister who was very active in the underground: Miriam Szyfman.[23] Through Miriam, Leja approached Marek Edelman. And in the end, I got a meeting with Marek. He asked me everything in detail: What do you do? Who with? And why? Marek had known my mother and my sister. His mother and mine were friends from the Bund. After that whole interrogation, he said to me: "Listen up: we're organizing a new cell on Zamenhofa right now, and I want you to be one of the organizers." He asked me if I could recommend anyone; I'd gained his trust. And so it was that I started work in the organization. We looked out apartments—that in itself was not a problem. There were enough empty apartments left by Jews who had been deported. But they can't be just any apartments, because when the uprising comes, we're going to need streetfront apartments, because we're going to have to shoot from the windows. We found an apartment for our group at 29 Zamenhofa.

"We" meaning who?
Lejwi Gruzalc[24]—later on, he was our commander; my Leja with her unofficial husband, Adek Jankielewicz[25] . . . There were ten of us: two girls and eight guys. We were barracked—we slept together, we lived together. Above all, we started learning to handle weapons. I was taught by Chaim Frymer.[26] He survived. He died here, in Eretz Israel. He was Pnina Grynszpan's husband. His group was on the other side of the street—the entrance was at 29 Miła, but the windows looked out over Zamenhofa. We organized ourselves in such a way that there were several groups close to one another, on the same part of the street, so that an attack would be more intense. And that's how it was. We attacked from both sides. On the other side of the street there were two groups, in fact: one a

---

21 p. 500 Glossary—January operation.
22 p. 457 Rereading the List—Lea Szyfman.
23 p. 457 Rereading the List.
24 p. 389 Rereading the List—Lejb Gruzalc.
25 p. 397 Rereading the List—Adek, Edek Jankielewicz.
26 p. 378 Rereading the List.

Selling

PPR group,[27] under Paweł [Bryskin],[28] and the other under Berl Brojde.[29] Our groups were in close contact. We had an agreed codeword to launch the attack. Someone from the other group threw a grenade, and then we started to attack.

And so, you started to learn to shoot...
Not so fast. Here I have to tell the truth: the instruction was theory-based, because we weren't allowed to shoot ammunition!

You joined the organization right after January 18, yes?
Yes, but there were already cells before that, known as "fives." My husband [Jakubek Putermilch] belonged to one of those fives,[30] he was in the Toebbens & Schultz yard.[31]

And do you remember January 18?
I remember very well.

Please tell me about it.
January 18... I'll tell you what I experienced myself. On January 18, I went into a hideout, I hid in an attic.

Where was it?
At 47 Nalewki; the entrance was via 49 Nalewki. They were connecting courtyards. And they belonged to the same houseowner. I want to talk about this so that others can get an idea of what it meant to spend time in a hideout. The hiding place was under the roof, in an abandoned apartment. The entrance to the room was through the kitchen stove: you opened the stove door and got into it, and then there was an opening into that concealed room. On that day, January 18, a woman with a baby wanted to go in there with us. There were several people standing there and on no account did they want to let her in, because the child might cry... I didn't react all that much, because I didn't really care much anymore; I was very lonely in that courtyard. I was all alone in the world, I had no one, and I had a feeling of complete indifference. Some of the people there were tearing at life, and that was quite normal. So, she, the mother of the child, swore that she would suffocate it if it cried. I remember that we could hear the

---

27 p. 512 Glossary—Polish Workers' Party.
28 p. 356 Rereading the List—Aron Bryskin, Paweł.
29 p. 355 Rereading the List—Berl Braude (Brojde).
30 p. 430 Rereading the List.
31 p. 518 Glossary—Toebbens-Schultz.

Germans—they were searching. As always, they were going around with their dogs trained to react to the scent of humans. And then all eyes... It was a large room, and we were lying on the floor, one beside the other. It was winter, and everyone had taken themselves bedclothes, or a duvet... And of course, she gave the child some Luminalets, so that it would sleep. But everyone was afraid anyway. Later, when I had children myself, I often found myself terrified at the thought that they might cry. This strange fear dogged me all the time my children were small. But that child didn't cry that time. The next day, we didn't want to go to that same hiding-place, because of that woman... Nobody wanted to go in there. On the corner of Miła and Nalewki there was a sewer. Some of us were young. We decided that we would go down into the sewer. We spent the whole day standing in the manhole, we didn't go down into the sewage. We moved down from the top a little, of course, because the manhole had these little holes in it which could be looked through. After that, the campaign ended.

Why did you go into hiding on January 18? How did you know about the campaign?
We knew quickly. When the detail workers went out to work, lots of them were taken to the Umschlag. I knew a few of the detail people, as I said; I bought wares for them. I remember that one guy—Izio Frenkiel, his name was—jumped off of the waggon going to the Umschlag and escaped. He told me who they had taken, and I knew almost all of them...

Let's go back to the period after the January campaign, to your lessons in the fighting groups.
So, we learned how to handle weapons, how to open grenades. Our weaponry was very meager. We had Polish grenades, and grenades of our own making; we had a few revolvers and Molotov bottles.

Do you remember any numbers? How many weapons there were for the group you were in?
Everyone except Leja had a revolver, so there were nine revolvers in our group. I had an FN 7, a Belgian revolver, and I had a grenade I had made myself.

Did you all have a grenade?
All of us.

Leja too?
Leja had a grenade—at least I think so. Because she was with Adek, they said that I should have the ninth revolver. At that point, not many people knew how

to handle weapons. There was this one, Abram Stolak[32]—he was in the brush-makers' 'shop,[33] on Marek's turf. He knew about weapons. And there was Koza;[34] I don't know his real name. He had a machine gun.

Where was that from?
I don't know. Maybe won from the Germans during the January campaign, or maybe bought from the Poles for big money?

Did you have any contact with the detail workers after the campaign? What were you living on?

The moment I joined the fighting organization, I had to stop everything else I had been doing up to that point. I lived with my group, but sometimes I would go over to the courtyard at 47 Nalewki, because I had a friend from the ORT school there. I found her again after the war in Canada.

What was that friend's name?
Ewa Alterman. She's alive in Montreal.

Was she in the uprising, too?
No. She survived Majdanek, and then Auschwitz, and was liberated on the *Toyte Marsh*.[35] They took her out of the bunker on May 3, but she survived. I found her through a friend from Warsaw. I met up with her a year and a half ago.

Please say a few more words about life in the organization.
Our organization was very clandestine. Naturally, there were even Jews we didn't trust. We couldn't leave our turf without permission. We would get passes. None of us had any money of our own, and we all ate the same—we lived very, very frugally. We saved up all our money for weapons. We were given bread for free by the bakers. Meat we never had. What kept us going was the desire for revenge. We wanted to live to see the moment when we could defend ourselves, when we could live to see *mitat kavod*.[36] Every one of us was waiting for that day. We knew that the liquidation of the Warsaw ghetto was coming. That was clear to all of

---

32 p. 445 Rereading the List.
33 p. 493 Glossary.
34 p. 445 Rereading the List—Icchok Suknik, Koza.
35 p. 495 Glossary—Death March.
36 *Mitat kavod* (Heb.)—death with honor.

us! We lived the whole time in expectation of the first day of the uprising. Each night, we set watchers, and observed the area from our windows, because the Germans always launched their campaigns in the early hours of the morning. They would surround the ghetto. We knew which direction they might come from—from Zamenhofa, from Gęsia. And that's how it was.

So, the first day of the uprising. April 19.
Yes. Well, we... I can see it all now... We went down to the floor below; we lived on the third floor. We took an empty apartment. I think there were five windows, two of us stood at each window...

How was the very beginning?
We saw the Germans entering the ghetto. I was on alert that night, I remember. I saw that something was happening: vehicles were on the move. The Jewish community building was on our street at that time, on the corner of Zamenhofa, and something was going on there, too. Interestingly, the Germans launched all their campaigns on Jewish holidays, but that was Easter Day. Using lamps, we communicated with the other group. I can't remember today how many times we had to flash our light. There are things that I'm only recalling now. I had forgotten about those lamps, and now it's so real again; it's all coming back... In the early morning, very early, they marched in, singing—sure of themselves. We started to attack them. Within a moment, the room was red with fire, and rubble was raining down on us. We would do this: throw a grenade, and then down under the window. Polish windows are quite high, and we hid behind the walls under the windows. And we had barricaded the entrance through the gateway into the courtyard. It was agreed that as we started to withdraw from our positions, we would set the barricades alight. We were to throw bottles full of incendiary material onto the wooden things. I dragged a table there, I remember. The gate was closed.

You were to set the barricade alight when you withdrew?
Yes. The barricade was built in the gateway, from the inside, and the gates were closed. One of us was designated—Mejlach Perelman.[37] He had that mission; he was to set the barricade alight. We withdrew into the attic, and all the attics had openings in the walls, so that you could pass from one house into the next. We had prepared that in advance. The boys had worked very hard to hack holes in the walls—Polish walls were a meter thick. Via the attics, we withdrew to Miła Street.

---

37 p. 426 Rereading the List—Majloch (Mejloch, Melach) Perelman.

After how many hours did you start to withdraw?
I don't remember.

More or less. An hour? A few hours? Toward the end of the day?
It was a short time, but I don't know how long. At moments like that, it's absolutely impossible to gauge time. We withdrew via the attics because we had no more ammunition—that I remember! When we had fired all the bullets from our pistols and thrown all our grenades, we withdrew. The attack on us was incredible. We were a handful of youngsters. I mean, we had virtually no weaponry at all, and they were hammering us with machine guns... There were thirty of us. Three groups, for that whole column of troops. In our group and the other one, no one was killed. The boy with the machine gun was killed. He was in a group near Muranowska. The boy with the machine gun was standing on a balcony, and they shot him dead; he was killed. We withdrew. The Germans couldn't get to us, because Mejlach had set the entrance on fire. They could have only gotten in through the windows, but they were too high up. We managed to withdraw.

Where to?
It was 29 Miła, 31 Miła, 33 Miła—I don't remember exactly. I remember we had one problem as we withdrew: the houses weren't all the same height. So, we had to jump from a fourth floor down to a third floor, for instance. In moments like those, we were on the outside of the building, and there were Germans all along Miła, who started firing on us as we jumped. I remember that when at last we reached the designated place, we found lots of Molotov bottles. They had been prepared there by another group. In the night, we returned to Zamenhofa. We wanted to reach Central Command, where Mordechaj Anielewicz was, at 29 Miła, but they had moved to 18 Muranowska.

To 18 Miła.
Yes, to 18 Miła. 18 Miła was a house that led through onto Muranowska; that's why I got confused. But the entrance to the building was off Miła. I went to the bunker, but Mordechaj wasn't there.

But when was that? The next day? A moment ago, you said that you returned to Zamenhofa in the night.
Yes. It was... On Zamenhofa everything was in ruins. We knew that on the opposite side of Zamenhofa, at 29 Miła, was the other group. I was chosen, and one other boy, and we went over there. I remember that we had only to cross the street, but it was almost impossible. The Germans were patrolling the street constantly.

Two soldiers marched back and forth, and we could see them. There were burned bits all over the street because they had set the house at 29 Miła alight right away.

It was the next day that you got across to Miła?
I don't remember if it was the next or the one after that.

Why were you sent there?
We wanted to receive further orders. I remember that we wrapped our shoes in rags so that we couldn't be heard. The streets were completely empty, silent, and then the echo of steps carries a long way. I stepped on a piece of metal, and how it rang! The shooting began. There were only two Germans, but they fired madly. And I flew! I knew where the entrance was, I remember. Melach didn't go across. He waited until things quietened down a little. Once I had gotten across, I waited for him on the other side. I didn't want to go in alone, and in any case, I was afraid that the Germans would catch me or see where I went in. A moment later, Melach also managed to run across the street. It was twenty meters or so—no! no way was it twenty! Eight meters at most—the width of the street. When we reached the bunker at 29 Miła, it turned out that Mordechaj wasn't there. We stayed there overnight.

So, was Mordechaj at 18 Miła at that point?
Yes, he'd already gone over.

And who was at 29 Miła?
All the fighters from both the groups that our group was working with. That was Paweł [Bryskin's] group, from the PPR, and Berl Brojde's group from Dror.[38] The next day, Mordechaj came over, and then we were given the order to shift to guerrilla fighting. That meant that we were to pool all our ammunition, and only twos were to go out.

What does that mean: "twos were to go out?"
We didn't have enough bullets. We thought that perhaps we just might get something more. But he—Mordechaj—explained to us that unfortunately there would be no more ammunition. Then I told him what we had left: two bullets and a few bottles. So Mordechaj said: "Now the Germans are systematically setting house after house alight, dousing them in kerosene and setting them on

---

38 p. 495 Glossary.

fire." They wanted to burn the ghetto down completely; they would go in at the first floor and send the whole house up in smoke.

"The twos will hide on the first floor, and when the Germans come in to burn it down, we will kill them." So, each day, two of us went out, and lay in wait, concealed, in one of those houses, for the Germans. And the Germans weren't prepared for that, so, out of the blue, through the element of surprise, we were successful. And then the fighters brought in a few more weapons.

Did you ever go out on one of those operations in a two?
I was sent once.

Where was that? Do you remember?
Yes, of course. 40 Miła? It was on the even-numbered side, I remember. 42? 44? Maybe 46.

Do you remember the operation?
Precisely, precisely. The Germans usually went into the stairwell and set the first floor alight. The doors were wooden, so it was very easy to set them on fire. The Germans doused all the entrance doors in kerosene. We lay on the first floor and listened.

Who were you with?
I was with that Majloch Perelman. We always wanted to be together. Later on, he went out once more on one of those operations and was killed. I wasn't with him then; he was with a boy from another group. Well, but that time, we chose a room on the first floor, and dragged some furniture in there to screen ourselves. We wanted to be able to see them as soon as they were in the stairwell, and not let them get any closer. And the room where we waited for them was perfectly opposite the entrance. We knew which house they would be going into because they went systematically. There were no surprises. They weren't armed, and they were carrying all the incendiary materials... But later, they caught on, so our twos could only operate that way at first. And so, we opened fire. But one bullet, the last one, we were to save for ourselves, for if they caught us... So as not to fall into their hands alive.

How many of them went into the house?
Two. We saw two. Sometimes, only one went in. But that time, there were two.

Were they both killed?
Yes. But we couldn't leave. We had to wait till nightfall, and we went back in the night.

Did you take any weapons from them?
Yes. Two Parabellums.

And what happened after that?
I never went on any more of those forays. But Mejlach went a second time, and they found him... He came back to us wounded, crawled back... On his stomach... We were at 18 Miła. When they discovered 29 Miła, we moved to 18 Miła, the place where Mordechaj later died. After that, Marek took us to his group, at 30 Franciszkańska.

When did you move to Franciszkańska from 18 Miła?
I don't know—it was in May, but which day? I know I left the sewer and went into the forest on May 10.

But before the tenth. The twos...
I'd like to tell you a little about that boy, about Majloch. When we moved to the bunker at 18 Miła, we found Majloch on the rubble. The house at 18 Miła had been burned down in 1939, and the bunker was underneath the burnt-out house, in the cellar. It was a Polish-style cellar, where coal was kept. He was lying there on Miła, underneath an eiderdown, hidden. He waited there until nightfall. He was wounded in the stomach. The other guy who had been with him had been killed. Majloch had his own revolver with him and had hidden the revolver of the guy who had been killed. He told us where, in which house, he had hidden it. He had opened the stove door and hidden it in there. He asked us to go and get the revolver. He knew how important a revolver was to us. We told Mordechaj that we wanted to carry him down into the bunker, but Mordechaj said that Majloch wouldn't make it. The entrances into the bunker were very narrow. You had to crawl; only young people could do it. Mordechaj said: "He'll get stuck in the passageway." I was standing over Majloch and pleading Mordechaj to let me, that I would pull him, and that the boys from my group would help and that I was begging him to take the boy into the bunker. But he said: "It will be better for him to die over there; over there he will have a better death." And Majloch asked us to leave him the revolver, because if he... And we also knew that now that house was next. That was 18 Miła. The rear wing gave onto Muranowska, and that wing was still standing, so we knew that if not that day, then the next, they would reach it, go in, and burn it down... So, we asked Mordechaj to let him, because otherwise he would burn alive... Majloch knew, too... He said: "Just leave me the revolver, I don't want to burn." I remember he had to be taken up onto the second floor. Two boys carried him. It looks so

easy today: carry him upstairs. But the stairs were knocked out there, and there was no way to get up, and that's why it was a good hiding-place, so to speak, because the Germans couldn't get up there. But we had the order to take the revolver off of him, because a revolver was of great importance. There were some other people in the same hiding-place up there. They stayed alive, and later they told us how incredible the screams had been. He burned alive; he was burned alive . . . I remember I took tea, a bandage, prepared water . . . But Majloch was no longer. So, there it was. Mordechaj gave that edict: "Don't take him into the bunker and take his revolver." I understand—he knew that a revolver with a few bullets could kill several more Germans. I would like to stress at this point: we had gone into battle, but none of us had any hope of staying alive. There was just one slogan that united all of us: revenge—to salvage the Jewish honor, the honor of the Jewish nation. And with that slogan we went into battle. We knew that death awaited us. We had risen up against a regular army that had made the whole world tremble. Death was perfectly clear to us.

What else do you remember from the time of the uprising? You were at 18 Miła.
18 Miła—that bunker was built by the Jewish rabble: thieves and porters; the *unterwelt*, it's called in Yiddish.

The demi-monde. Was the bunker built to commission for the organization?
No. They built it for themselves. But they knew about us, they had heard. And they themselves suggested that we go there. They gave a few of the compartments in the cellar over to us. They fed us. Their compartments were beautiful, with tiled floors. There was water in the bunker. They asked us—they didn't have any weapons, but they asked to join up with us and fight with us. They had a lot of respect for us, the citizens of that bunker.

So, they stayed in the bunker to the end?
I think so. I wasn't there by then, but a group of fighters from 18 Miła saved themselves. Later on, they came to the garbage men's bunker on Franciszkańska. One of them was a guy called Jehuda Wengrower.[39] Jehuda had been shot back before the uprising; they'd hit him in the lung, but he had managed to escape from them. They'd shot him while he was posting our flyers to the ghetto inhabitants on walls. We wrote that people shouldn't surrender, that they shouldn't go voluntarily to

---

39 p. 464 Rereading the List—Jehuda (Juda) Wengrower.

their deaths, that everyone should defend themselves with whatever they had—an axe, or anything iron. That was shortly before the uprising. When the uprising broke out, he was in the bunker at 18 Miła. And the Germans threw gas grenades in there. Do you know, I'm the only one who was in that bunker at 18 Miła. And Marek in Poland . . . I was there . . . I don't remember—for a few days, maybe two or three. Until Marek came and took our whole group, the people from the Bund.

Do you remember when that was?
I can't say precisely. A few days before 18 Miła was blown up. We all went. Only without Majloch Perelman . . . there were nine of us.

And why did you want to go with Marek?
We wanted to! Shall I tell you the truth? I can now. We had a grudge against Mordechaj because of Majloch. Angry that he ordered us to take Majloch's weapon and didn't let us take him into the bunker. He had good intentions—today I can understand that, but at the time . . . Majloch was wonderful. A good fighter, a wonderful friend, intelligent—he had every quality. And he always took the hardest tasks on himself. Afterwards, after the war, I met his classmates, and I had to tell them about every detail. Majloch wrote our group chronicle every day.

Has the chronicle survived?
No.

What happened to it?
To the chronicle? I sewed all the boys these little drawstring bags, and each of them put their personal things in them and wore them on a string around their necks. I kept the chronicle in my own bag, along with all the photographs that I still had from home. And I also had the photographs of another of the boys, who asked me to keep them, because if he was killed, the photographs would remain. When we were at 29 Miła, there was water, and we all washed. And there were even beds—and us with so many sleepless nights behind us . . . I even found pajamas there, I remember, and I put the pajamas on, and hung the bag on this stand next to me. I woke up when they started pounding at the bunker with hammers. And there was this one boy with us, Chaim Frymer, who knew his way around the bunker very well. He said: "Listen, there's a dugout underneath the wall, and we can get out that way!" But then our commander—of course, at this point I had completely forgotten about my little bag—gave the order: "Don't go into the dugout!" And then the Germans blew a hole right through, and we

could see the blue sky. The Germans started to throw grenades in. Those who were standing closest—the commander and a few other people—were killed by the first grenade. That was when Leja [Szyfman] was killed. We saw it. Chaim ordered us to retreat into the dugout.

And why did your commander, Lewi Gruzalc, not allow you to go out through the dugout?
Because he said we had to open fire on them.

Not flee, but fight?
Not flee . . . But we had no chance. We went—in Yiddish you say *kiddush ha-shem*[40]—to our extermination. And when we saw our comrades fall down dead, we started to retreat. The Germans had us all right there in front of them. They would have killed us one after the other. There was no point in that, so we retreated. Chaim went last, I remember. They shot a hole in his jacket. We sat in that dugout all day, and then we went to 18 Miła.

We already spoke a little about the bunker at 18 Miła. Perhaps you remember something else?
I remember that there were a few compartments inside, and that there were people living in all of them. In our compartment there was no flooring, just earth. There were folding beds and paillasses in there. Some people lay on the ground, others on the paillasses. I already spoke about the "room" belonging to the *unterwelt*; I remember it very well. They invited us in. It was beautiful in there. Their compartment was like a salon compared to ours. We used to go to them for water, and they shared their food with us. A big kitchen had been built in the corridor, and that's where the cooking was done, at night. Because night was day and day night.

Which of the fighters were in that bunker?
Almost all our group; seven of us. Majloch was still with us. It was from there that he set out on that sortie. Gruzalc was no longer there, and neither were Leja or Dawid Hochberg.[41] Those three were no longer with us. It was also there, at 29 Miła, that the fighters from Group B, the reserve group, were killed. There were also the other fighters from 29 Miła and the group from Zamenhofa.

---

40 *Kiddush ha-shem* (Heb.: in sanctification of the Name of God)—an expression indicating readiness to bear the ultimate sacrifice, to die in the name of one's faith.
41 p. 394 Rereading the List.

Humiliation

Was Mordechaj there, too?
Yes, and Jehuda Wengrower and Mordechaj Growas,[42] and his friend Margalit [Landau].[43]

Jehuda Wengrower didn't survive the war, did he?
No. I started to talk about him, but I'll finish his story when we talk about getting out via the sewers. I want to remember who else was at 18 Miła.

I presume Mordechaj was with his girlfriend?
I don't know anything about his girlfriend.

Tamar?[44]
No.

Marek Edelman came to the bunker at 18 Miła and took the Bundists to the bunker at 30 Franciszkańska.
Yes. It was incredibly hot in there because the bunker was in a burned-out house. Some of the fighters had already left it. When we arrived, we didn't find many of them there. They came back a day or two later. Marek was with us, of course, a few people from his group, and a few from Hanoch Gutman's[45] group. After a short while, Marek sent our group to another bunker, because the Germans were starting to close in on us. They hadn't found us yet, but Marek was of the opinion that he ought to split the fighters up; perhaps they would be able to save themselves in another bunker. At that point, when the uprising was over, we all said that if we managed to get out of the ghetto, we would go and join the partisans.

Why do you say, "at that point, when the uprising was over?"
Well, because we weren't fighting any longer! There were no weapons.

---

42 p. 389 Rereading the List—Mordechaj (Merdek) Growas.
43 p. 409 Rereading the List—Margalit Landau, Emilka.
44 Tamar's surname is unknown. Melekh Neustadt claims that Tamar survived the attack on the bunker at 18 Miła and was killed in the Wyszków forests (Melekh Neustadt, *Khurban uMered shel Yehudey Varsha* (Tel Aviv: Executive Committee of the General Federation of Jewish Labour in Palestine and the Jewish National Workers' Alliance in U.S.A., 1947), 164.
45 p. 390 Rereading the List—Henoch, Hanoch, Gutman.

So, Marek sent your group to a different bunker. Where to?
To 5 Gęsia, I think. Not far from Nalewki. We went to 30 Franciszkańska the next night, because, as I said, night was day and day was night. But by then there was no longer anyone there. The bunker had been discovered, and the people killed. Stasiek Brylensztajn [Brylantsztajn] was killed, and Berek Sznajdmil[46] . . . Only Janek Bilak[47] survived, and . . . Adolf? from Gutman's group? No. He was called Szlomo Alterman.[48] We went back to the bunker at 22 Franciszkańska. But that bunker had been razed entirely.

How did you find out what happened in the bunker at 18 Miła?
On May 9, I think, or maybe it was May 8, a group of surviving fighters came over to us from that bunker. Among them were Merdek Growas, Jehuda Wengrower, Tamar, Pnina Zalcman[49] . . . I can't remember anybody else. They told us. We found out from them. They's made it. They'd found a way out of that bunker. They had gotten out and gone to sit in some cesspit and saved themselves that way.

Do you remember what they told you?
They said that when the Germans started throwing in gas grenades, Mordechaj gave them the order to shoot themselves, to shoot each other. But whether that's how it was? I don't know. That's what Merdek Growas told us. Some were gassed, and some killed themselves, that's what he said . . .

Do you know how many people were killed there?
I can't say. Now I want to explain why we went to what they called the garbage men's bunker. To the place that Jehuda and the others from Miła came to. In that bunker there was a tunnel dug out that led to the sewers. And that's why we went there, because even then we had had the idea of trying to get out of the ghetto via the sewers. We sent Kazik Ratajzer.[50] Kazik was supposed to forge contacts with the sewerage workers.

So, Kazik went out onto the Aryan side?
Yes. He had a good appearance.

---

46 p. 449 Rereading the List.
47 p. 345 Rereading the List.
48 p. 334 Rereading the List.
49 Neustadt (ibid., 164) lists Pnina Zandman, a member of the Warsaw Haszomer Hacair, as having been killed on May 10, 1943.
50 p. 432 Rereading the List—Simcha Ratajzer, Kazik Simcha [Rotem].

Portraits

In the uprising, he was in a group with Szlamek Szuster.[51]
Yes, now I want to tell you about Szlamek. I first saw him in the Franciszkańska Street bunker. In comparison with us—and we were all seventeen, eighteen—Szlamek looked totally like a child.

How old was he?
Sixteen, but he looked a lot younger. There was one more little one, Lusiek Błones,[52] the little brother of one of the fighters; he was twelve. He had a special task: collecting bottles on the street, which we then filled with incendiary material. We called him our "youngest fighter." But Lusiek didn't have a gun, while Szlamek was an armed fighter, a member of the organization.

Which group was Szlamek in?
Hanoch Gutman's, in the brushmakers' yard, where Marek's group was. There was one more group there, the one that Pnina Grynszpan belonged to: Hersz Berliński's[53] group. Szlamek went with us from the ZZ bunker[54] to the garbage men's bunker.

Why do you call it the garbage men's bunker?
Because that was the house where the Jews who transported garbage out of the ghetto in peasants' waggons lived. And they built a bunker there for themselves.

Let's get back to Szlamek's story.
On May 10, before we went into the sewer, a group of a few people went to check out the route, because Kazik hadn't come back. When they went down into the sewage pipes, they met him, and came back for us. The manhole leading down into the sewer was on Franciszkańska, close to the Vistula. And the sewers were built in such a way that the closer to the Vistula they were, the higher they were. Because the sewage was more powerful. All the excrement from the whole of Warsaw flowed that way because it all flowed into the Vistula. When we went down into it, I remember we said that the sewer wasn't so terrible after all. I knew what the sewer was like, because in January I had sat under the manhole cover during the first campaign.

---

51 p. 454 Rereading the List.
52 p. 350 Rereading the List.
53 p. 342 Rereading the List.
54 The ZZ (Pol. *Zakład Zaopatrywania*, Provisioning Authority) bunker, run by Abraham Gepner, was at 30 Franciszkańska Street.

How big was the group that went down into the sewer with you on May 10?
Forty of us. Cywia Lubetkin[55] (Icchak Cukierman[56] didn't take part in the uprising at all), Marek was with us, Szlamek Szuster, Tuwia Borzykowski,[57] Pnina... Forty of us came out of the sewer, but more of us went in. Some stayed down there, and they were killed afterwards... Szlamek was among us. We stood in that sewer for forty-eight hours. But the people on the Aryan side had no way of... They were looking for someone with vehicles who could get us out. They explained that to us later, but at the time, we didn't know what was going on. We reached the manhole on Prosta and waited there. But that shaft was small, and we couldn't all stand there. I should point out that the manhole is the only place in the sewer where there's no water and it's dry. But as long as we were walking, we were in water the whole time. There were rats scurrying about all over us, feces floating around—and the stench... We had candles with us, but they wouldn't burn, because there was no oxygen.

How long did that hike through the sewers take?
A very long time. Because it's a long way from Franciszkańska to Prosta. It was impossible to stand upright in the filth. The sewer was very low, and you had to be bent over the whole time. Cywia and Marek decided to split us up and send us to other manholes. Jehuda Wengrower was with us. Do you remember? I talked about him. He had had his lung shot through before the uprising, and afterwards he was in the bunker on Miła when the Germans threw the gas in. He was very weak. He couldn't walk by himself. In the sewer, he walked behind me and held onto my hips. I had to drag myself and him. We were in the sewer for forty-eight hours. He drank the sewer water and kept fainting. I told him it was poison, but he couldn't stop himself. He thought the water would bring him round, and that he would be able to survive. In the sewer it was impossible to overtake the person in front, to get past them. But what could you do? You could spread your legs apart and pass between their legs. And I could see that he was fading. So, we decided that we had to try and save him: we spread our legs—it looked like a sporting challenge—and each of us passed him forward between our legs. He was completely covered in the shit. But he finally made it to the manhole. There, it was impossible to fall down, it was such a tight

---

55 p. 413 Rereading the List—Celina Lubetkin.
56 p. 361 Rereading the List—Icchak Cukierman, Antek.
57 p. 353 Rereading the List.

squeeze. Cywia Lubetkin said that we had to be spread out over several shafts. After forty-eight hours, Kazik opened the manhole cover and told us to come out. But that was forty-eight hours later, and in the meantime, some of the fighters had been sent off to different shafts. Someone had to be sent to bring them back. Szlamek and one other fighter, Adolf [Hochberg],[58] were standing next to Cywia, who said to them: "Listen, go and bring them back here!" They wavered for a second . . . We were in unbelievable conditions in that sewer. I can't possibly describe it to you. It was . . . I remember being close to suicide. I'm not even talking about the hunger, but all the rest of it! We were tired out and resigned. Szlojme Alterman, from Gutman's group, kept my spirits up. He said: "Just a little longer, you'll see, we'll get out, we'll be saved." And Jehuda had such a strong will to live! He tried to keep himself alive with that filthy water. So, when Cywia spoke to them, Szlamek thought about it, and Adolf also hesitated for a moment. Then Cywia said: "We're waiting for you; go!" We got out, but Szlamek wasn't back in time. By the time they returned, the Germans were already at the manhole on Prosta . . . We climbed out very fast. One after the other, one after the other. And threw ourselves down onto the floor of that truck. The Germans hadn't got there then. But we looked like corpses. Corpses emerged; corpses plastered with filth!

Did any Poles see you?
Yes, yes. A ring gathered at once.

What time was it?
It was daytime by then. A beautiful May morning.

Was there one truck, or more?
One. Cywia asked right away what they would do about Szlamek and Adolf. They said: "There's another truck." But there was no other truck, and they perished—Szlamek, who went back with Adolf, and the ones who had been sent to other manholes . . . I don't know exactly what happened. I heard only that the Germans shot them all. Nobody survived. And nobody knows any details; there were no witnesses. Perhaps Kazik knows more?

---

58 p. 394 Rereading the List.

How many people can there have been in that other group?
Not that many. But who knows whether they all got out? Perhaps some of them stayed in the sewers. Forty of us got out.

And forty of you boarded that truck.
One on top of the other.

And where did the truck go?
Outside of Warsaw, to Łomianki.

Why to Łomianki?
In Łomianki there was a coppice, and around it a German settlement. There, we met up with Aron [Karmi's] group. They had gotten out on April 29. In that coppice you could only sit down, because if we stood up, we were visible.

How long did you stay in that coppice?
I think about two weeks, or maybe a week and a half.

Were all those who came out through the sewers on May 10 in the woods?
No. Marek and Cywia didn't go into the woods. They went into hiding on the Aryan side.

And did you want to go to the woods?
Yes. We joined the partisans in the Wyszków forests after that. But after six months I got sick, and I went back to Warsaw. But when the Polish uprising broke out in 1944, I took part in that uprising.

Please can you tell me about that?
I was in the bunker at 64 Żelazna. Several of us, including Marek and some others, wanted to join the rising. On Żelazna Street, we met a Polish officer from the AK, and we wanted to fight as a Jewish group, but they wouldn't let us . . .

What did you decide?
We each went to fight alone.

Did you have a weapon?
Yes, but not from the AK. I had my own gun. My husband, Jakubek, was on the barricades, and my job was to tend the soup kitchen. We were on Żelazna, Twarda, Topiel, and Tamka Streets, and after that for a long time on Warecka.

"We," meaning?
My Jakubek, me, and two fighters who are now in Canada: Bronek [Szpigiel] and Halina [Chajka Bełchatowska]. And there was another mother and daughter with us. They both survived the war. The daughter now lives here, in Eretz Israel.

Did you leave Warsaw again after the rising?
No. After the rising, we went down into the cellars. At first, we were on Śliska, and later at 38 or 39 Sienna. And then we escaped into the sewers again because they started getting close to our bunker. We thought it was Germans, but it was some Jews who knew about us and wanted to tell us that Warsaw was free. But we were afraid that it was Germans, and in the night, we went down into the sewers. And later on, I roamed the rubble with another woman, Falkowa—she's still alive in Canada. We wanted to find out from Poles, we couldn't believe that Warsaw was liberated.

So, you were in the bunker from the end of the rising until January.
Until January 22, 1945.

But why didn't you leave Warsaw with the Varsovians after the rising?
Because we Jews were afraid to go with everyone else—both Germans and Poles were a danger to us.

How many people were there in the bunker on Śliska?
Thirty-two.

All Jews?
Yes. That bunker was discovered, and very few people stayed alive. They killed them on the rubble. In the next bunker there were ten of us. I was there with Jakubek, my husband; and Pnina Grynszpan.

In which year did you leave Poland?
In 1945, in March.

Where to?
To Romania. We left in a group: Pnina with Chaim [Frymer], Kazik with that journalist woman [Irena Gelblum],[59] and my husband and me.

---

59 p. 381 Rereading the List—Irka (Irena) Gelblum.

Did the journalist go back to Poland?
Yes, in 1947. She couldn't get used to life here. She desperately wanted to study.

When did you reach Israel?
From March until October we were in Bucharest, and then we travelled via Constanța to Israel. I arrived on October 26.

Did you marry here?
No. We are a married couple from the forest. We were together forty-one and a half years. We went through that whole Gehenna together. When my husband was writing his book,[60] I typed it up on the typewriter. I fought for every detail, because Jakubek was *dugry*, which means frank, truthful, and he wanted to write the whole truth, even if that truth was not so pleasant. He was of the opinion that he shouldn't alter anything, that history would judge everything. But Antek [Cukierman], for instance, was against that. He held that those who were no longer alive could not defend themselves, and that that was inadmissible.

And you fought with your husband to try and persuade him to omit certain facts, is that it?
As I was typing it up, I sometimes tried to smooth things over a little, but he was very precise, and read every sheet, and refused to agree to my changes.

Was the book published in the version as written?
Yes, absolutely!

When did your husband write it?
When we were on the Aryan side, Antek came to us, brought each one of us— there were four of us: Jakubek, Halina, Bronek, and I—a pen and said: "This is a present from me on the anniversary of our escape from the ghetto. Write everything down, start writing right away." Jakubek made notes, and when we came to Eretz Israel, he would write in the evenings, after working hard. It took him many years to write it, and then the book lay for a very long time in Lohamei Ha-Getaot.[61] They didn't want to publish it.

---

60 Jakub Putermilch, *BaEsh ubaSheleg* [In Fire and Snow: Memoirs of a Fighter] (West Galilee: Beit Lohamei Ha-Getaot & Ha-Kibbutz Ha-Meuchad, 1981).
61 p. 508 Glossary.

Why not?
I don't know; there must have been some reason. I can imagine why, but I don't know for certain.

Was it published after Icchak Cukierman's death?
No, after Cywia [Lubetkin]'s death.

Thank you.

Tel Aviv, May 1989 and October 1999.

Masza Glajtman-Putermilch died in Tel Aviv on November 6, 2007.

I'm Telling You so Superficially Because I Don't Remember

Conversation with Pnina Grynszpan-Frymer

Start your story from the beginning, if you would. Where you were born, where you lived... Do start.
I was born in 1923. There were eight of us children; I was the youngest in the house. They used to call me "the scrapings," because when I was born, my parents were already advanced in years. It was a sensation that my mother had become pregnant—she must have been forty-something. So, in our house I was treated like a doll. Everybody loved me, adored me, I was dreadfully spoilt.

What did your father do?
He had a kind of carrier's office. He had a large flat waggon, and horses, and he transported various goods to stores. He would transport whatever came along.

But your mother didn't work, of course?
Mama didn't work. She ran the house, and one of my sisters helped her.

Was your family religious?
Not particularly.

What does "not particularly" mean?
Mama kept the house kosher because my grandfather, who visited us frequently, was devout. He also lived in Nowy Dwór, with his daughter, my father's sister.

What did your grandfather do?
Well, in fact, it was his waggon that my father worked on. Grandfather had very much wanted my father to get an education because he was very gifted. Our family was a large one. It was always fun at our house. Lots of friends came round to my brothers and sisters; it was an open house. My mother was a typical *yidishe mame*.

When my brothers started work, mama would get up at five in the morning and dash to the bakery for fresh bread rolls and to prepare their breakfast. One of my brothers lived and worked in Warsaw, and he only came home for shabbat. He was an official in a large faïence and porcelain firm at 1 Przechodnia Street. I don't know if you know where that is. It's probably not there anymore. Everything's changed.

Where in Nowy Dwór did you live?
At 1 Mickiewicz Street. I went to Poland last year and saw my house.

Was that the first time you had been to Poland since you left?
The first time since 1945, when I emigrated with Masza and Kazik [Ratajzer].

You were born in 1923. That means you got to attend school before the outbreak of the war.
That's precisely the thing! I was still too small when I saw the other children going to school, and I was so jealous that I resolved to go with them. My cousin took me to the ceremony for the beginning of the new school year, and I liked it a lot. They started reading out the names, and I heard "Papier, Frajda." My maiden name is Papier; I am "Papier, Pinia." Papier Frajda didn't come forward, so I plucked up my courage and said "Present!" And so it was that I connived my way into school. I remember that all the children marched to the synagogue that same day, and Rabbi Neufeld spoke to us there. I was very happy, but at home they all laughed at me and wondered at how I had been so bold as to do such a thing. The next day, I took a notebook and a pencil, and I went to school. And I attended that school as Papier, Frajda. Perhaps Frajda was in a different class?

What kind of school was it?
An elementary school, a Jewish one, but we learned everything in Polish. And the school principal was a Pole.

Was the Jewish language taught there?
No. Once a week we had a Jewish religious studies class, also in Polish, and once a week one hour of Hebrew.

Did you speak Yiddish at home?
Yes. We all spoke Yiddish, but our parents could also speak Polish. Once, they noticed at school that I hadn't handed in my birth certificate. But I didn't even have a birth certificate. So, when a birth certificate had to be made out for me, they added a year on—they wrote that I was born in 1922. And to this day, I have

Ger—Góra Kalwaria, Iłża, Suchocin

that error in all my papers. If it was ten years' difference ... but it's only a year, so it's not worth changing. In 1936 or 1935 I finished elementary school. But at home I was always treated like a little girl; I was given a very short leash. I wasn't allowed to go out anywhere in the evenings.

Did you go to another school after elementary school?
No. That's precisely the thing. I wanted to learn more, but at home I was treated like a little child and forced to wait a year. In any case, further study would have incurred costs; I would have had to go to Warsaw, because there was no high school in Nowy Dwór. And then the war broke out. I felt that I was adult enough to become independent. I told them that I wanted to go and live with my brother, in Warsaw. In any case, the whole family had decided to move to Warsaw at that point.

Why?
Because things were closing in with the Germans, they were harassing the Jews badly. They would take young people away for labor in the night. We packed up the house—I mean we gave the furniture and certain of our valuables to a Pole for safekeeping. (We never met that Pole again.) And in October, or maybe November 1939, we went to Warsaw. We went to live with Dawid. But it was very cramped there, and one of my brothers rented an apartment for his wife and children. There were already grandchildren in our family! My sister also rented an apartment and moved there with her husband and little boy. A few months later things seemed to have settled down a little in Nowy Dwór. We thought we would be able to go back home, so two of my brothers went to Nowy Dwór to check things out. They rented an apartment and started to work. Then they had my father go back. In Warsaw it was getting worse and worse, with work and with life in general. Things were closing in from all sides. And then came the ghetto and we had to wear armbands.[1] Eventually, the ghetto was sealed. My father insisted that we return home. So, we said goodbye to my brother Dawid and went to Nowy Dwór, into that ghetto, which was in the area known as Piaski.[2]

---

1   p. 517 Glossary—Stigmatization of the Jews.
2   The ghetto in Piaski (the poorest part of the city) was established in early 1941. The area was enclosed by a wooden fence with barbed wire. In May 1941, there were four thousand Jews living in Nowy Dwór. Following a selection in the ghetto, the Germans left seven hundred fifty people as labor, and the rest were marched to the prison camp in Pomiechówek. In the second half of 1941, Nowy Dwór was designated a center for concentrating Jews prior to deportation to the extermination camps. Jews from Czerwińsk, Wyszogród, Zakroczym, and other nearby towns were moved into the Nowy Dwór ghetto. The liquidation of the ghetto began on November 20, 1942. All the transports were sent to Auschwitz. The last one left Nowy Dwór on December 12, 1942.

Otwock, Mińsk Mazowiecki, Żyrardów

Dawid's apartment in Warsaw, where you lived with your mother, was inside the ghetto, which by then was sealed. So how did you get out?

It was very difficult, that's true. But one day some Jews from Nowy Dwór came on a smuggling sortie. We had good—Aryan—looks. And they took us with them. My mother and I dressed to look like Polish peasant women, and we traveled with them by train to the Nowy Dwór ghetto. We succeeded.

So, you swapped the ghetto in Warsaw for the ghetto in Nowy Dwór. What kind of a switch was that?

I was very pleased to be back because I met friends from my school years. But I really didn't like the life there. It was such a small area, and very closed in. Every day, Jews were taken to work in Modlin. I also went to work, of course.[3] I volunteered, because I didn't want to sit around at home.

What sort of work was it?

We worked with wood. I don't remember exactly; we stacked some kind of beams. In the mornings we would leave the ghetto with our yellow patches. When we came back in the evening, we came back via the German *wacha*.[4] I only had a patch on my front, but I should have had one on my back, too. A Gestapo officer at the *wacha* came up to me once and gave me a hefty clip round the cheek for that patch. When I got back home, I didn't tell my parents, but I decided I wouldn't go back to work. When my parents found out about the whole incident from other people, they decided to hide me, and not send me to work.

When was that?

It might have been in 1940.

It couldn't have been in 1940 if you only arrived in Nowy Dwór from Warsaw in 1941.

Not in 1940. It was in 1942!

In 1942?

No, not in 1942. It might have been in early 1941.

---

3   Pnina probably started work in Modlin in the early spring of 1941, because it was shortly after her return from Warsaw, before the "disinfection" down by the river (May 1941), and before the Nowy Dwór Jews were sent to the camp in Pomiechówek. See Pnina Grynszpan-Frymer, *Yameynu hayu haLeylot* [Our Nights Were Days] (West Galilee: Beit Lohamei Ha-Getaot & Ha-Kibbutz Ha-Meuchad, 1984), 37.
4   *Wacha* (Ger. *Wache*, used in the Polonized version *wacha*)—guardpost.

So, you started work in Modlin right after you arrived in the Nowy Dwór ghetto?
No, not at once, but shortly afterwards. I don't remember exactly whether it was in 1941 or in 1942. I think it was spring 1942 that I was going to Modlin to work.[5] I'll tell you exactly. In the summer of 1942,[6] I told my parents that I didn't want to be in the Nowy Dwór ghetto any longer, and that I wanted to go back to Warsaw with the smugglers. And then, the Germans announced that all the Jews had to put all their furniture and clothes—all the things from their apartments—out onto the street and go down to the Vistula. And there they would undergo quarantine.[7] When I heard about this, I told my parents and brothers that we had to flee, because they were planning something awful. I told them that we should go over to Legionowo and wait it out there, but they wouldn't listen to me—they had always treated me like a little girl. They said that since I was so afraid, they would send me with the smugglers to Legionowo. "You can wait it out there, and then either come back to Nowy Dwór or go to Warsaw." And what happened? They took all the Jews down to the Vistula. Ordered them naked into the river. And then they hounded them to Pomiechówek, to the camp.[8] They finished the elderly off at once, the children and invalids, too . . . I found out

---

5   Pnina is off by at least a year here. Throughout the conversation there are similar errors regarding the time when particular events took place. The footnotes correct or supplement her memory wherever possible.
6   In fact, the summer of 1941.
7   In May 1941, the Germans announced in Nowy Dwór that all the inhabitants of the ghetto had to undergo disinfection. They were ordered to leave their homes and put all their possessions out onto the street. See Grynszpan-Frymer, *Yameynu hayu haLeylot*, 38.
8   Grynszpan-Frymer, *Yameynu hayu haLeylot*, 38: "When the ghetto residents had carried out the Germans' orders and put all their possessions out onto the streets, and left the houses empty, they were ordered to undress, and were driven naked, men and women together, to the place where the Narew flows into the Vistula, to wash in the river. They suffered dreadful cruelties there—some were tortured and killed, women were raped; many found their deaths in the waters of the river. Those who did return to Nowy Dwór after the disinfection found none of their belongings there; all their possessions that they had put outside their houses had been looted. The people were herded onto the town square, where a selection was carried out. Just a few hundred were qualified as fit to work; they were permitted to return to the ghetto. Among them was my brother Mates, and Mosze, the husband of Małka; they made the selection thanks to the director of the brewery, Pelcer. All the others, some 4,000 people, including my father, mother, and the other members of my family, were sent to Pomiechówek, which was essentially an extermination camp." The prison camp in Pomiechówek near Nowy Dwór Mazowiecki existed from March 1941. Jews from nearby towns began to be interned there in July 1941. On July 7, 1941, the Germans selected 3,250 Jews from Nowy Dwór and herded them into the camp. At that point there were some six thousand there. In early September 1941, the surviving Jews were released from the camp and marched to the border of the General Government under the escort of military police and SS officers. In all, an estimated fifty thousand prisoners passed through the Pomiechówek camp, of whom fifteen thousand

about all this in Legionowo from the smugglers and went straight to my eldest brother in Warsaw.[9]

And what happened to your family?
Yes. Of course. Some of my family were in Pomiechówek, and the two brothers who had made the selection were left by the Germans in the ghetto to work.

Can you say exactly who in your family ended up in the camp in Pomiechówek?
My parents, my grandfather—my father's father—and my sister Małka and her child.

And your sister's husband?
He was also left in the ghetto after the selection. My brother Zysiek [Zygmunt Papier][10] was also in the camp. Terrible things happened there: they killed elderly people, they killed children, they killed the sick. The Germans didn't let them work; they were just finishing those Jews off. My mother had typhus in the camp. She concealed that from the Germans, of course. And the Judenrat of the Nowy Dwór ghetto tried to smuggle a little food into Pomiechówek every day. My brother-in-law managed to take my father and my sister and her child out of there.

And your mother and grandfather?
They killed my grandfather. But my mother and my youngest brother, Zysiek, stayed in the camp. When they had finished off almost all of the Jews in Pomiechówek, they marched those who had stayed alive to Legionowo. On the way, the Germans built these huge campfires and had the Jews jump over the fire; those were the kinds of tortures they devised. Mama and Zysiek somehow managed to make it from Legionowo to Warsaw, back into the ghetto. You can imagine how overjoyed I was when I saw them.

Can you tell me when your mother and Zysiek returned to the Warsaw ghetto?
It might have been in late summer 1942.[11]

---

are thought to have been murdered. Cf. Michał Grynberg, *Żydzi w rejencji ciechanowskiej 1939–1942*, (Warszawa: Państwowe Wydawn. Nauk, 1984), 79–86.
9 Pnina reached Warsaw in June 1941 after about two months in the Nowy Dwór ghetto. See Grynszpan-Frymer, *Yameynu hayu haLeylot*, 39.
10 p. 424 Rereading the List—Zysie Papier, Zygmunt.
11 This was after the liquidation of the camp in Pomiechówek, so it was in September 1941.

Were you in Warsaw during the *große Aktion* in July and August 1942?
Yes, yes. I'll tell you. Mama and Zysiek came back to Warsaw shortly after me. We worked in Landau's 'shop[12] on Gęsia Street.[13] My brother Mendel had been working in the same 'shop as a carpenter for a long time; it was thanks to him that Zysiek and I got that work. I also worked the carpentry machines. Zysiek and I had security because of course we were working for the Germans—making closets for them. That company was called... Ostdeutsch...[14] something or other; I've forgotten what it was called...

Never mind. And what about living arrangements? Did you all live together?
I lived with Zysiek and my mother with Dawid at 40 Nowolipie Street.

And what did your mother do?
Mama was at home.

And Dawid?
Dawid sold porcelain and faïence to Poles who came into the ghetto, and they took the goods out onto the Aryan side. And my sister-in-law was at home, she didn't work.

Can you tell me when you started work for Landau?
From 1942.[15]

Can you remember more precisely?
Which month I got in there? I can't remember precisely.

Spring? Winter?
Spring. One moment: I think I've gotten confused. I'll put myself right now. My father was with my brothers in Nowy Dwór, and they started to organize themselves some work. I remember they set up a restaurant in the house where they lived. And it was even quite successful. And it was then that they took Mama back to Nowy Dwór; the smugglers took her back. That was after Pomiechówek.

---

12 p. 507 Glossary—Landau's 'shop.
13 Pnina started work in Landau's 'shop in the fall of 1941. She was the only woman among its eighty workers. This carpentry workshop, run by Aleksander Landau, its prewar proprietor, was at 30 Gęsia. See Grynszpan-Frymer, *Yameynu hayu haLeylot*, 46.
14 Ostdeutsche Bautischlerei-Werkstätte—a carpentry workshop at 75–79 Gęsia Street.
15 Pnina worked in Landau's 'shop from the fall of 1941. See Grynszpan-Frymer, *Yameynu hayu haLeylot*, 45.

My father wanted Zysiek and me to come back, too, but Dawid kept us in Warsaw. And it was then that we got the jobs with Landau, and Mother went back to Nowy Dwór.

So, your mother wasn't with you during the *große Aktion*?
Yes. That's precisely the thing. When the deportation started, the purge of the Schultz yard, that's what they called it—mother was no longer with us. The Germans sealed off the street and did a big round-up. I happened to be at home at the time, not at work. Zysiek and Mendel were in the 'shop. Dawid wasn't home either. Dawid's little girl was with her grandmother on Karmelicka Street, and I was with my sister-in-law. I don't know why I was at home. And suddenly we heard that the street was sealed, and that there was a deportation. They were telling us to leave the house and go out onto the street.

Do you remember the date?
I don't remember the exact date, but it was summer. Whether it was July or August, I don't remember exactly. So, I said to my sister-in-law that I would rather we didn't leave the house. We could hear the Germans' shouts. I said to her: "Let's lock ourselves in and hide somewhere." But she didn't want to: "No, because if they come, they'll kill us. We have to go out; everyone is going out." We could hear them running down the stairs. "We absolutely have to go down!" I let myself be persuaded, and I went out with my sister-in-law—Sara, her name was. We went downstairs. The whole street was full of people! We went into the file.

With some hand baggage?
With no baggage. We had nothing. While we were standing in the line, I saw my friend, Heniek Rotszajn. He was a policeman in the ghetto. He had come to Nowolipie because he was afraid that they would take me away. He found me in that line with my sister-in-law and told me that he would run to Landau's factory for a manager to take me out of the line. Because of course I was working and so I was covered, because I was working for the Germans! So, I said to my sister-in-law: "Sara, remember, when the manager comes, tell him that you're Zysiek's wife." Zysiek also worked at Landau's. Sara was afraid, she didn't want to. And Dawid, Sara's husband, had been at Karmelicka Street, at her mother's. When he heard that there was a deportation on Nowolipie, he ran over and watched us from a distance. After a while, Heniek, the policeman, came back, with someone from Landau. They went up to the Germans, and the manager said that he had to take me, because I was needed for work. When he came up to us, I told him

The Street.
Warsaw. Intersection of Chłodna and Żelazna in July 1941, Hipoteczna, ?

that this was Zysiek's wife, but he said that he could only take me out ... And I was saved; he took me out. When my brother Dawid saw that they were taking his wife away, he joined the file himself, voluntarily.

And they went to the Umschlagplatz together?
Yes. Dawid thought that if he went with Sara, then he could save her. He thought that they would jump out of the wagon together.

But they didn't?
They didn't. They weren't saved. Their child stayed with her grandmother.

Was the child saved?
No. The child went with her grandmother when they sealed off Karmelicka Street. But that was a little later, and they were sent to Auschwitz or Treblinka on a different transport.

But you went back to your work in the 'shop?
Yes. And I was barracked on Gęsia. We weren't allowed out of there. My sister Adela was living in the small ghetto[16] at the time, on Prosta, with my brother-in-law and my brother-in-law's mother; he worked as a cutter at Toebbens. When she found out about the selection on Nowolipie, she was very worried about me. She asked around people and found me on Gęsia. She somehow managed to get to me in the large ghetto. She brought me a little food, I remember. A few days later, there was a blockade on Nalewki, and that time, my brother Mendel, who also worked for Landau, was sent to the Umschlag with his wife and children. But I stayed with Zysiek at Landau's, at 30 Gęsia. By the time of that kettle, we Landau workers were living on Miła.

Do you remember the exact address?
It was 6 Miła, I think. I also wanted to say that my cousin [Josek Litman[17]] from Nowy Dwór also managed to get a job in that 'shop. He was also a Warsaw ghetto fighter later on. It was then, when we were living on Miła, that our "five," our group of five fighters-to-be, was organized. There was a Haszomer Hacair group working at Landau's. Landau's daughter [Margalit, Emilka, Landau] was also a member of that organization. She brought a whole group of her Haszomer Hacair comrades to work there, and so they were covered. Josef Kapłan and

---

16 p. 519 Glossary—Warsaw ghetto.
17 p. 413 Rereading the List.

Miriam Hajnsdorf,[18] his girlfriend, and Josek Farber[19] were all working in that factory then, too—later on, all of them were fighters. If you have heard of the first uprising in the ghetto, in January 1943, you must know that it was that group from Haszomer Hacair that led the fighting. In that shop, I could tell that there was something going on among the young people. One of them, Josek Farber, would often talk to me, and he often told me that he was tired, that he hadn't slept all night. So, I ask him: "What happened that you didn't sleep?" So, then he says to me: "I was in the sewers in the night." So, I ask him: "What were you doing in the sewers?" "Ah, I wanted to go from one street to another," he says, "so I went via the sewers." So, I say: "What? Have you gone crazy? Are you unconscious? What does it mean—you go into the sewers in your clothes?" So, he laughed. I knew there was something going on. For a few days, Josek told me all kinds of stories. So, in the end, I say to him: "You know what, Josek, I get the feeling that something is being organized in this factory. You're friends with Miriam [Hajnsdorf] and Josek Kapłan. I want to be with you, too." So, he laughed. And he didn't want to tell me exactly what was going on. And then there was another round-up in Landau's 'shop. I remember that I was running up to the attic to hide, and some Gestapo officer, or maybe it was a Latvian or a Ukrainian, grabbed me from behind and dragged me into the file. I remember that as I was standing on the street among those people, those workers, they started to sort us: some to the right, others to the left. They ordered me to go to the right, but I yelled that I wanted to go to the left. Some Ukrainian pulled me over to the right by force. Those who were on the left were sent to the camp. There was a rabbi there, as well, I remember—Blumenfeld, his name was.[20] He went up to a German and asked to be released, saying that he was very sick. And then the German pulled out his pistol and shot the rabbi dead on the spot. And that terrified me! I thought to myself: There are so many workers here, but they're all standing around so indifferently, and they're so afraid. There are so many Jews here—I mean, we could attack the Germans!

Was that the first time you had seen a situation like that?
Yes, yes. I mean, there was just a handful of those Germans—five, maybe. And even though we were unarmed, we could have throttled them, at least. I don't know, but not given in... That was when I started to rebel inside, somehow. Us so defenseless, putting up no resistance. After that, I talked with Josek Farber

---

18 p. 391 Rereading the List.
19 p. 370 Rereading the List.
20 Grynszpan-Frymer, *Yameynu hayu haLeylot*, 54: "Rabbi Blumental."

about it. He was already in the fighting organization, but I didn't know that. I asked him: "What will become of us? We're so defenseless; we're not putting up any resistance, yet we're going to our deaths anyway." One of the workers overheard that conversation. I don't know if you've come across the name: Hirsz Berliński from the organization Poalej Syjon Smol.[21] Berliński was in the *hanhallah*,[22] I don't know how to say that in Polish. And one day, Hirsz came up to me in the factory and started to talk with me. He asked about my family. I told him that out of all my family, only myself and my youngest brother Zysiek were left in the ghetto. And then there was my cousin, Litman, and his mother and his sister Chajale. Berliński said that he would like to meet with me one evening, in my apartment or his, and talk. When we met, a few days later, he told me that he had overheard my conversation with Josek Farber. "You should know that we are organizing small groups of five here. You are with your brother and cousin; if you can choose another two young people, then we'll make a new five. We'll be learning to handle weapons." And we organized a "five."[23]

Who else made up the five?

Two young workers who I recommended. One was called Włocławski, and the other Blumsztajn. They both worked at Landau's. I don't remember their names, but it's all written down in my book. I'm telling you so superficially because I don't remember. We had meetings once a week. We were taught various things—all theoretically, because back then we still had neither weapons nor grenades. In January 1943, when there was another liquidation campaign, I was too late to hide, I remember. Zysiek managed to hide, but Josek Litman and I had to go down and join the file. They marched us to the Umschlagplatz. And then, as we were walking to the Umschlag, that group from Haszomer Hacair: Josek Farber; Lilka, I mean Margalit, Landau's daughter, and the others, started shooting, and throwing grenades.[24] Josek Kapłan was no longer with us. The Gestapo had come to Landau's some time earlier, I remember, and taken him away. He underwent terrible tortures and didn't give anyone away. In the

---

21 p. 510 Glossary.
22 *hanhallah* (Heb.: management)—here: the ŻOB command.
23 Pnina's "five" was organized in December 1942. See Grynszpan-Frymer, *Yameynu hayu haLeylot*, 59.
24 Among the fighters who launched the self-defense operation in the column of people going to the Umschlagplatz on January 18, 1943, were Josek Farber, Tosia Altman, Miriam (Josek Kapłan's girlfriend), and Margalit Landau. Later on, Pnina found out that Mordechaj Anielewicz had also taken part in the operation. See Grynszpan-Frymer, *Yameynu hayu haLeylot*, 60.

end, the Germans killed him. And then, on the way to the Umschlag that day, Landau's daughter was shot dead in the fighting.

Do you remember what happened on the Umschlagplatz after that?
Yes, of course. We stood on the square and waited to board the train.

Was there a selection?
No. They shoved everyone into the wagons like cattle. Finally, the wagons were full, but we were left; there was no room for us. They told us that we would be going on the next transport. My cousin and I decided that we would try to escape. We managed to slip out of the file, and we ran to the cellar of a large house on Niska. It was dreadful in that cellar—corpses everywhere, and people close to the end, moaning and begging for water.

Were they people who had escaped from the Umschlagplatz?
Evidently. They had escaped and hidden there. They couldn't go out onto the street because the whole area was surrounded. When it got dark, we decided to get out of the cellar; we were afraid that we would expire there. On the street we met Josek Farber and the others from Haszomer Hacair. And Josek said: "Stay with me! We're a group. We have to get up to the top floor of this building, and then we'll think what to do next." It was a street-corner house. We took a door off and laid it on the window of the neighboring house. We wanted to use it like a ladder, to get across. The risk was huge; we could have been killed if we were noticed by the Germans, or simply have fallen. But we made it; we got across. We found ourselves inside an apartment which was full of beautiful furniture amassed by the Werterfassung.[25] We hid in the closets. It was so terribly cold, I remember, that we were afraid we would freeze to death. But we had to stick it out there until the morning. In the morning, we went out. On the street, a *werkszuc*,[26] a Jew, came up to us. We asked him to help us get out. We gave him money, I remember, and he took us out. Josek Litman and I managed to get back to Miła. How Farber got out I don't know. On Miła I met my brother Zysiek, who had also hidden out in a cellar for the two days of that January campaign. A short time later, I met up with Berliński again. By that time, Landau's factory was no longer there; it had been shut down. "Now we will be barracked as a fighting group," Hirsz Berliński told me. One night, we made our way via the rooftops

---

25 p. 517 Glossary—Werterfassungsstelle.
26 p. 521 Glossary.

and attics to the brushmakers' yard at 34 Świętojerska. Marek Edelman was the commander of that yard.

When did you move into the brushmakers' yard?
It must have been at the turn of January and February 1943. I was in a group with Zysiek and Josek Litman. The group commander was Berliński. We lived there like a family, but we weren't allowed to leave the premises.[27] Out of all our group the only one legally employed was Awram Diamant, who worked in the 'shop kitchen. Sometimes I would get a pass out. Once when I was out on such a pass, I met some people in the ghetto who had escaped from the Nowy Dwór ghetto in December.[28] From them, I learned that my whole family had been deported. My brother Mates could have saved himself. His line manager wanted to pull him off the transport, but Mates refused to leave his family: "If you can take my parents, and my sister, brother-in-law, and their child off too, then great. But if you can't save them, I'm going with them." And they all went.

Please tell me when you met Marek Edelman.
When I was barracked in the group at the brushmakers'.

How do you recall that meeting?
I remember that I was sent to Marek's group—Marek was the area commander, and the group commander was Jurek Błones[29]—to take him some incendiary bombs and grenades. I also remember that Marek would hold these night alerts to check our readiness. He would look, watch in hand, how long it took us to get ready to attack. I got to know Marek better. I often went over to see them;

---

27 Blumsztajn and Włocławski from Pnina's original "five" did not move to the brushmakers' yard; they "gave up the fight." Pnina's group, like other groups, numbered ten people. Its members were Alek Erlich, Jur Górny, Bronka Manulak from Łódź, Abram Stolak, Stefa, Szaanan Lent, Zysiek Papier, Josef Litman, and Pnina Papier. Pnina lived in one room with Zysiek, Bronka, and Josek; Berliński, Górny, and Erlich lived in a second; and all the others in a third. They ate bread with jam and drank tea and ersatz coffee. By that time, the boys had weapons: pistols, grenades, and homemade Molotov cocktails. At night, they would go out in pairs to put up ŻOB flyers and posters in places that Jews passed by on their way to the workshops. They would wear gumboots or wrap their feet in rags, so as to move about the ghetto as quietly as possible. They also learned to handle firearms. See Grynszpan-Frymer, *Yameynu hayu haLeylot*, 62–64.
28 The people whom Pnina met were probably members of the Nowy Dwór Judenrat, who were sent to the Warsaw ghetto instead of to Auschwitz because they had cooperated with the Germans. Theirs was the last transport out of the Nowy Dwór ghetto (December 12, 1942), and it comprised forty-two members of the Judenrat and their families.
29 p. 350 Rereading the List.

I was friendly with that group. Marek was very cold and very brave. He was a responsible man, so I felt safe with him. I remember that later, during the April uprising, after the liquidation of the brushmakers' yard, we went over into the central ghetto, to the bunker at 22 Franciszkańska. Marek was the organizer of that move. He led three groups over: mine—Hirsz Berliński's group, Henoch Gutman's Dror group, and his own, a Bund group. When we finally made it, I went up to him; I was very down. He said to me: "Pnina, just so you know, I will take care of you, you'll be under my protection, don't be afraid." That I remember. Marek has been to us in Eretz Israel a few times, and I always reminded him of that. I felt strong when I was near him. I was in Poland recently, and I spoke to him on the telephone. We didn't meet up, because I went looking for him in Łódź, but he was in Warsaw. I only went to Poland to tour all the camps and to see Nowy Dwór. I hadn't been there since the liberation. Back then, Chaim [Frymer], my husband, wouldn't let me go. He was afraid for me, because there was an incident that a guy from Nowy Dwór went back to his home, and some Poles killed him. I don't know whether, if I had been back to Nowy Dwór then, in 1945, I would have gone this time, in 1988. I didn't want to go to Poland, but the whole time it had been bothering me that I hadn't said farewell to the house I was born in.

Did you find your house in Nowy Dwór?
No. There's a new building there now. We lived on the main street of Nowy Dwór, near the church and the park—a beautiful area. I remember that as a child I used to love going to that church. I had friends who were Poles, and I used to go on church processions with them—I liked that a lot. I went to Nowy Dwór with Tadek [Rajszczak],[30] a Pole. He didn't want me to go alone. In a house near the place where I used to live, I noticed a woman in a second-floor window. I asked her who she was, and she told me she was called Andzia. Then I introduced myself. And she remembered me . . . I didn't recognize her, but who did she turn out to be?! She had worked in our house as a servant! But you know, I couldn't get over the fact that she didn't invite me into her home even for a minute, that she wouldn't come down to me, even for a second. But she spoke to me; she listed all the tenants who had lived in our house.

You spoke to her through the window like that?
Yes. I was standing at the bottom. I found that very hard.

---

30 p. 431 Rereading the List—Feliks Rajszczak.

Please could we go back to where we left off about your work in the "fives?" You said you had your own instructor. Who taught you to handle firearms?
That was Hirsz Berliński. And later, once we were in the brushmakers' yard, we had a boy in our group who had been a soldier in the Polish army.

What was his name?
Abram Stolak.[31]

Do you remember any other operations before the uprising?
We organized money for the group.[32]

How?
We had to go looking for rich Jews who were keeping hold of their money because they thought that they could save themselves that way. We asked them nicely, but sometimes that didn't work, and then we took money from them by force.

How did that work, taking it by force?
Well, it was very unpleasant. We searched them, sometimes we arrested them, sometimes we threatened to kill them. We explained that they were going to be finished off in any case, so why shouldn't they leave us their money? But they believed that we would get all the Jews killed.[33]

Did you have a weapon?
I didn't have a weapon. Only the boys had weapons; the girls were given grenades and Molotov bottles. I only got a pistol toward the end of the uprising, when my brother was injured—it was his pistol.

---

31 p. 445 Rereading the List.
32 p. 495 Glossary—Expropriation operations.
33 In one of these operations to "organize" money for the combat group (which were known as "exes"), the participants were Abram Stolak, Hirsh Berliński, Zysiek Papier, Pnina Papier, Josek Litman, and Erlich. In the night, they made their way, masked, through the attics, to a bunker indicated by Diamant. When they stormed it, they were astounded at the standard of comfort that they saw: the bunker had electricity, tiled walls, nice furniture, and a radio receiver. The fighters set about persuading the residents of the bunker to hand over their fortune to the organization, since the Germans would confiscate it all anyway. The negotiations were conducted by Berliński. In that time, Pnina searched the women (finding diamonds on one of them), and the boys the men (they found gold and money), and they combed the whole bunker too. When the residents of the bunker began to protest, Berliński threatened to use his gun. Afterwards, Bluma, wife of Hirsz Wasser, bought weapons on the Aryan side. See Grynszpan-Frymer, *Yameynu hayu haLeylot*, 68–70.

Could we talk about the uprising now? Do you remember the first day?
The uprising started in the central ghetto on April 18. They only entered our area on April 19. But we had the information that the Germans had entered the ghetto. I remember that we were in our apartments, standing at the windows, observing the terrain. I remember that the entranceway to the house that stood at the entrance to the brushmakers' yard was mined. The mine was the responsibility of Hanoch Gutman's group. And when the Germans entered the area, Kazik disarmed it, and it exploded.[34] A few of them were killed and quite a lot wounded. They hadn't been expecting anything like that at all! After that we had to fall back. But even though we knew that it was only a minor setback for the Germans, we were overjoyed. The next day, when they marched in, they were better organized—they had tanks. And then we started to fire on them from the windows and throw grenades and incendiary bottles at them.

How many bottles did you have?
One, and one grenade. The bottle in one hand and the grenade in the other. We had a few extra bottles and grenades . . . I think it was two days later that we had to leave the brushmakers' yard. We couldn't hold our positions there because everything was on fire. The Germans fired on us with artillery. We had to retreat to the central bunker, which had been prepared beforehand.

Where was that bunker?
Also on Świętojerska.[35]

Was anyone from your group killed in the first days of the fighting?
Not from mine. But as we were retreating via the attics to the bunker on Świętojerska, we found Michał Klepfisz dead. Then we retreated to the central ghetto.[36] It was very difficult, because the houses were all in flames. I remember that we choked dreadfully because of the smoke, and our hair caught fire.

---

34 This took place on April 20, 1943. The mined gateway was close to the guardpost at the corner of Wałowa and Świętojerska Streets. The attack by a detachment numbering three hundred soldiers under Jürgen Stroop was launched at approximately 3 p.m. Stroop commanded the assault in person. The insurrectionists allowed them to come up to the gateway before they detonated the mine. That operation killed twenty-two Germans. Cf. Bernard Mark, *Powstanie w getcie warszawskim* (Warsaw: Idisz Buch, 1963), 63–64.
35 The brushmakers' central bunker was at 34 Świętojerska Street. See Grynszpan-Frymer, *Yameynu hayu haLeylot,* 77.
36 The fighters spent two days in the Świętojerska Street bunker. After that, three groups were selected that were to move to the central ghetto. They comprised members of the Dror, Bund,

How big was the group which you retreated in?
Thirty people, perhaps.

Who led the group?
Each commander led his own people. My group was led by Hirsz [Berliński]. The various ten-person groups met up en route; each one came from a different point—I mean a different house. We had our feet wrapped in rags, so as to move quietly, so that the German guard wouldn't hear us. We went by night, of course. We had to climb over the wall to get into the central ghetto.

Was anyone killed while you were moving to the bunker at 30 Franciszkańska?
Yes, one of our fighters was killed.

Do you remember who it was?
I remember that he was called Cwi. He was from Praszker's[37] group.

So, you eventually reached the bunker at 30 Franciszkańska.
Yes. There, we waited for Cywia [Celina Lubetkin] to contact us. We wanted to know what we were to do next. That house was on fire, too, I remember. It was quite cramped in that cellar bunker. I remember that there was water, and we found a little food. We ate, and lay down to sleep; we were all completely done in. After a while, I woke up and felt that my head was spinning and that I was weak. I started vomiting: I was poisoned by the smoke from the burning house. I just managed to wake Josek Litman before I fainted. Panic broke out in the bunker because we were all half-poisoned. It was early in the morning, so it was starting to be dangerous in the ghetto. We had to go back over the wall. But I had no strength. Josek and Zysiek carried me, and then they threw me over onto the other side like a sack of potatoes.

Where was the bunker that you wanted to move to?
It was the honeymen's bunker.

What does that mean?
I don't know. Perhaps they traded in honey?

---

and Poalej Syjon Left groups, respectively. The Hanoar Hacyjoni group under Jakub Praszkier remained in the brushmakers' yard. See Grynszpan-Frymer, *Yameynu hayu haLeylot*, 78–79.
37 p. 429 Rereading the List—Jakub Praszkier (Praszker).

What street was that on?
I think it was at 6 Gęsia. We spent one night there, maybe two, and then we went back to 30 Franciszkańska.

Did you make contact with Cywia in the end?
Yes. While we were still at 30 Franciszkańska, somebody came from Cywia with the instruction that the groups should split up, because we couldn't all be together in the same bunker. And that was when I left with the group going to Gęsia. Two people went from each group. I was with Masza and Josek Litman, and Berek [Sznajdmil], and Szlojmele. When we reached Gęsia, they didn't want to let us in. They were afraid.

Were there any fighters there?
There weren't any fighters. But we told the people in that bunker that if they didn't let us in, we would break in by force. Then they let us in, and they were even nice to us. As I said, a night or two later we went back to Franciszkańska—we didn't want to be separated from the others. When we arrived at Franciszkańska, it turned out that the Germans had discovered the bunker, and open fighting had ensued; I mean, the fighters had come out onto the street.

Who was in the Franciszkańska bunker when the Germans attacked?
Marek [Edelman] was there with his group, my brother with Berliński's group, and my group. All those who hadn't gone to Gęsia.

Was anyone killed in that battle?
Henoch Gutman and my brother were seriously wounded. From the PPR Jurek Grinsztajn [Grynszpan][38] was wounded, I think. Stasiek [Brylantsztajn][39] from Marek's group was killed (I don't remember his surname), Berek [Sznajdmil], also a Bundist, was killed, and Josek [Abram Ejgier][40] from Gutman's group. Before they shot Josek, he made this speech to the Germans, yelled at them from the window, that we would avenge ourselves in any case.[41] The situation in that

---

38 p. 390 Rereading the List—Jurek Grynszpan.
39 p. 355 Rereading the List.
40 p. 368 Rereading the List—Abram (Abraham) Ejgier (Eiger).
41 The bunker at 30 Franciszkańska Street was betrayed to the Germans on May 1, 1943. The fighters decided to fight despite being promised that their lives would be spared if they surrendered. Berek Sznajdmil was the first to leave the bunker, and he was killed at once. The second fighter managed to launch a grenade before being shot dead. A few Germans were also killed in the battle. Josek [Abram Ejger] shot and threw grenades from the second floor before being

bunker was dire: the wounded were suffering, and then the Germans close by. They wanted to blow us up with dynamite. We decided to move to a different bunker via a tunnel. Above all, we wanted to get the wounded out. A few of the boys went with the wounded to protect them. One of them was Szaanan Lent from my group, a young, beautiful, very brave boy born here, in Eretz Israel. There was also a guy from the Bund; I don't remember his name. When we pushed the first of the wounded into the tunnel, we heard the Germans start to fire. All the wounded were killed.[42]

In the tunnel?
Yes, in that dugout. The Germans threw gas bombs in there, and our fighters suffocated.

And what happened to the rest of you?
We started to block up, stop up, the entrance to the tunnel with whatever we could, so as not to suffocate in the bunker. We sat there until the evening. The Germans tried to blow us up, but they failed. In the night, we moved to the garbage men's bunker. The remnants of us, those who had survived. Cywia came over from 18 Miła to see us there. She came with Chaim Frymer, my future husband—that's when I met him. I remember that I was on guard duty when Chaim came towards the bunker. I asked him for the password, but he wouldn't give it to me; he just laughed. And by that time, I had my brother's pistol, and I wanted to shoot him. I thought he was one of those Jews who wanted to denounce us to the Germans. In the end, I called someone, and then everyone laughed at me—they told me he was a fighter. So, when Cywia came, they held council, all the commanders: Marek, Berliński, and Cywia. They were pondering what we should do next. They decided that we should send a few people through the sewers onto the Aryan side and make contact with Icchak Cukierman.

So, who went out?
Josek Litman went out, Janek Bilak from the Bund, Jurek Błones, and somebody else. But they were back before long because the manholes were all covered by the Germans. In the early morning, Cywia wanted to go back to 18 Miła, but

---

wounded and falling from the window. The Germans ran his body through with bayonets. See Grynszpan-Frymer, *Yameynu hayu haLeylot*, 82.

42 Szaanan Lent started shooting at the advancing Germans. Pnina was standing in the entrance to the bunker, when she saw her wounded brother. She tried to pull him inside, but she couldn't. In the shootout, both Lent and Zysiek Papier, Pnina's brother, were killed. See Grynszpan-Frymer, *Yameynu hayu haLeylot*, 83.

Chaim said to her: "You're my commander, but this time I won't carry out your order!" Cywia agreed; it was too dangerous to walk about the ghetto in daylight, and they stayed with us in the bunker. It was that day that the bunker on Miła was discovered. You could say that Chaim saved Cywia's life—if they had gone back to Miła, they would have perished with Mordechaj and the others. Cywia always remembered that it was thanks to Chaim that she cheated death that time.

When did you learn about the attack on the bunker at 18 Miła?
I learned about it just as we were supposed to go down into the sewers.

Do you remember which of the survivors from Miła were with you in the sewer?
Tosia Altman and Juda Wengrower—they were wounded.

What did they say about what happened on Miła?
They said that the Germans had found the bunker. They knew they had no way out. And when they started to smell gas in the bunker, they took cyanide—those of them who had any. Tosia and Juda were wounded in the attack. I remember how she just sat with her head bowed, holding her forehead. Tosia was only with us in Łomianki, and after that she went to Warsaw; she didn't join the partisans. And Juda died in Łomianki and was buried there. That was probably because he drank the water in the sewer—he couldn't stop himself.

Let's go back to the ghetto. What happened after that?
The commanders decided that ten people had to be sent via the sewers out onto the Aryan side. They chose a few people from every group. From my group they chose Abram Stolak and me, from the Bund Marek sent Jurek Błones, his sister [Guta Błones],[43] her friend Fajgele [Władka Peltel],[44] and Jurek's younger brother Lusiek—oh, and Abrasza Blum.[45] This group was to find somewhere to get a foothold on the Aryan side and wait for the next groups. And then we were all going to go and join the partisans together. When I found out that I was to go down into the sewer and jump into that filthy water, I was really upset. A friend from my group, Bronka Manulak,[46] said: "Pnina, you ought to dress better, so you look decent when you get out." She went to Masza and said: "Masza, you

---

43 p. 349 Rereading the List—Guta Błones.
44 p. 426 Rereading the List—Fajgele Peltel, Władka [Międzyrzecka, Meed].
45 p. 347 Rereading the List.
46 p. 416 Rereading the List.

wear a nice skirt. Give it to Pnina, so she isn't so ragged." But Masza said: "She's going down into the water anyway; what does it matter to her what skirt she's in?!..." I was very scared. Finally, we went down into the sewer.

Who was the leader?
Jurek Błones. Jur knew the address we were supposed to go to. So, I said to him: "Tell me what the address is. I don't know, perhaps we'll have to flee on the Aryan side, and we'll get split up. Then where will I go?" But he wasn't allowed to tell me the address. I was very frightened. In the sewer, each of us held our own firearm. We waded through the water with candles in our hands. There were ten of us. We're walking and walking, and suddenly we hear noises. We were convinced that we'd come up against some Germans, because we knew that the manholes were covered. So, who could it have been? Only Germans! But a moment later, we heard talking in Polish, and our password: "Jan." It turned out to be Kazik [Ratajzer]'s group. Kazik had been in the ghetto before and had been looking for us in the bunkers. He'd been on Franciszkańska, but not found anyone there. By then, Kazik was so resigned that he had even thought of committing suicide.

Who was Kazik with in the sewer?
With some plumbers, Poles,[47] because he didn't know the way very well. Rysiek [Maselman][48] was also with him; I think that was his name. Was he a Jew or a Pole? I don't know. There were four of them altogether. Because Kazik couldn't find us, the plumbers wanted to leave him, they wanted to go. But then Kazik took them with his gun. He said he would kill them if they wouldn't go with him.

Didn't the plumbers have guns?
No. They were doing it for money. But in the end, we met up. You can imagine that meeting! Kazik told us that we had to tell all the groups in the ghetto to come down into the sewer, and that he would organize trucks to take us into the forest. So, two of our ten went back into the ghetto for the other fighters. One of them was Szlamek Szuster. We waited in the sewer for a signal from Kazik. He was supposed to organize those trucks, but it was very difficult. Krzaczek[49] helped him on the Aryan side. We waited a full forty-eight hours. Around fifty

---

47 Bernard Mark gives the names of the Polish sewerage workers: Wacław Śledziewski and Czesław Wojciechowski. See Mark, *Powstanie w getcie warszawskim* (n.p.: Nakład Związku Patriotów Polski w ZSRR, 1944), 128, 131.
48 p. 417 Rereading the List—Rysiek Maselman (Moselman).
49 p. 408 Rereading the List—Władysław Gaik (Krzaczek, Kostek).

people joined us from the ghetto, among them Josek Litman and the survivors from Miła. We didn't have contact with every group in the ghetto, so we weren't able to inform everybody. So, we sat in that sewer for forty-eight hours! We were absolutely drained, with no food, no water, no air, and the wounded... It was dreadful in the sewer. Some people wanted to commit suicide. Forty-eight hours' waiting! Marek and Cywia decided to divide people up into groups and have them wait under different manholes. Because if the Germans had discovered us, they would have finished us all off at once. So, we split up. Then we heard a hammering on the manhole cover. Kazik opened the manhole and said: "Come out!" And the trucks were standing on the street.

How many trucks were there?
Two. We started to drag ourselves out onto the street. How did we get out? It was a miracle. With our last vestiges of strength, we climbed up the ladder in the shaft. They hauled us out like rags. I was dotted with ulcers. We were all unrecognizable in that truck, we looked so dreadful. The Germans were close by. We had to close the manhole cover and flee fast. Many of them didn't manage to get out in time. More than thirty of us got out; the rest stayed inside. They tried the next day, but the Germans were guarding the manhole. They all gathered in that one shaft and decided to emerge at the risk. There was nothing for them to go back into the ghetto for. When they emerged, there was a shootout. They shot too! They were cut down, all of them. None of them were saved... But we were taken out to Łomianki.

Do you remember the street when you came out of the sewer?
It was on Niska.

Not on Prosta?
I think you're right—on Prosta, I'm very sorry.

Do you remember there being people on the street?
Yes. There were Poles standing there looking at us and marvelling.

Marvelling?
Well, not as fighters, because I don't think they knew that, but marvelling at the state we were coming out in.

Did you have your weapons with you?
Yes, but we didn't emerge with our weapons on view. Not until we were in the truck did Kazik say that anyone who had a gun should hold it ready. We were to

drive through the German checkpoint on the bridge over the Vistula. And we did it!

Was the truck covered with a tarpaulin?
No, it was open.

How did you get through the checkpoint?
One of the fighters was dressed in a German uniform if I'm not mistaken. He saluted them, and they let us past.

And so, you reached Łomianki without incident?
Yes...

Did anyone return to Warsaw to check what had happened to the fighters who were left in the sewer?
I don't remember, but it's possible. We were only in Łomianki for a short time, maybe ten days. After that, we left for the Wyszków woods, to join the partisans.

How long were you with the partisans?
Until July 1944.

And then you went back to Warsaw?
Yes, to join the Polish rising.

Can you describe your return?
A courier, Lodzia [Silverstein], came to the Wyszków woods with Stach, a Pole. They were supposed to take me and Chaim to Warsaw. But Dow Szniper, the commander of our group, insisted that he wanted to go. Chaim was to sub for him in the woods. And I didn't want to go. I didn't want to be kept in hiding on the Aryan side; I didn't trust them. I protested, but it did no good. In the end, Chaim backed down, and I went to Warsaw with Dow. There, we were taken to an apartment at 24 Rakowiecka, where there were already two fighters in hiding—Chana Fryszdorf[50] and Janek Bilak, Bundists. When the Polish rising broke out, the owner of the apartment came to us and told us we had to leave. We were four fighters; we had weapons. So where could we go? I didn't want to go out. Even if the Germans were to come, well, there was a dugout, and we could

---

50 p. 407 Rereading the List—Chana Kryształ-Fryszdorf.

hide. I thought we shouldn't go out onto the street—we were Jews, after all. But they decided that we were going out. On the street, we joined a large group of Poles who were going somewhere with bundles. It was Hanka [Fryszdorf], who was a Varsovian, that decided we would go with them. Before long, it transpired that the Germans were taking them to Szucha Avenue, to the Gestapo.

When you joined the group of those Poles, didn't you see that there were Germans leading them?
We saw, but we mingled with them specially, so as to hide. Not only were we Jews; we also had guns. Janek said that he was going to throw his gun away because he was afraid. He was a 100 percent Jew in appearance. So, I say to him: "If you want to throw your gun away, give it to me. I'm not throwing my Vis away!" Hanka didn't have a gun. She was eight months pregnant at that point, her husband had been killed in the woods. When we reached Szucha, we realized that we were in a trap. And then Dow fired, and they killed him at once. So, they're taking us to the Gestapo, and I'm carrying two pistols. I didn't know what to do. I decided that I would do the same as Dow—I didn't want to be tried and tortured, and ultimately betray who I was. They made us go into a courtyard. I wrapped both my pistols in a nightshirt and left the package outside the Gestapo building; the Germans ordered everybody to leave their bundles on the street. After a while, they drove us out onto the street again and told us to wait. They said they would be checking our *Kennkarten*,[51] but I didn't have a Kennkarte. But I did have a pot with peas in it, which I'd hidden photographs of my family in, and a watch on a gold chain that I'd been given by my mother. A Gestapo officer came up to me, and I said to him: "I don't have my *Kennkarte*; I was so disorientated when I ran out of the house that I just grabbed this pot with peas in it, so that I would have something to eat." At that, he laughed out loud, and walked off. Some other Gestapo officer came out of the building and said that he needed four women and two men to go onto the barricades with stretchers to recover the Germans who had been killed. And they chose me! They took me into the building and gave me a white apron and headscarf with a red cross on it. As that German was dressing me in it, he ordered me to tie up my hair under the headscarf. How I must have looked! The Germans warned us that if we tried to escape, we would be killed by the German soldiers who were in the trenches. So, I thought to myself: that's exactly what I'm waiting

---

51 p. 506 Glossary—*Kennkarte*.

for! Because to come back to the Gestapo? Well, I'd rather they shot me dead on the street! I threw away my flowerpot with my photographs and hid the gold watch in my bra. On the barricades, we didn't see any dead Germans. The Polish insurrectionists wanted to shoot us, but I shouted that we were Poles too, and that we wanted to come over to them, to join the rising. And they helped us! I remember how happy I was.

Was Hanka with you?
No. She stayed at the Gestapo headquarters. The Germans killed all the men, but let the women go, and they went to a shelter on the insurrectionists' side. And I was taken by the insurrectionists to their command center. They asked me who I was. So, I—after all, I was among Poles—said that I was a Jewess. I told them that I had come in from the forest a week before the rising; that I was a fighter from the ghetto uprising. They didn't believe me, and I had no papers. They charged me, that I was a spy, and that I was collaborating with the Gestapo. And they decided to finish me off. They took me to a prison, to some cellar—I never saw such dreadful lowlifes in my entire life as there were there. They interrogated me every day, and every day I had to start by telling them my life story. I told them that in the woods we had been in contact with the AK, but they didn't believe me at all. It was a mistake to tell them that I was a Jew—but I thought that since I had managed to elude the Gestapo, I was saved, safe.

And how did their investigation end?
At one of the interrogations, there was an officer who had served in Modlin. And I was telling them the story of my life again. I said that I was from Nowy Dwór, told them what my name was, and that my brother had been a telephonist in Modlin. And that officer knew my surname. It was a miracle! He saved me! Then the AK let me go, but they ordered me to go live with a Jewish family that they knew and said that they would be checking up on me every day. When I arrived there, the family was terrified of me. It transpired that one of the sons of the woman who owned the apartment had been arrested by the AK on charges of collaboration with the Germans. And so, the family thought that since I had been sent by the AK, I must be their spy.

Were you there long?
Almost until the end of the rising. While I was with those people, I met up with my commanding officer from the woods, Stach. Thanks to him, I got a uniform, and became a courier in an AL group.

And after the rising?
I didn't leave Warsaw after the rising. I had nowhere to go. With my looks! I was afraid. Masza, Jakubek [Putermilch] and I[52] holed up in a bunker and stayed there until January.[53]

When did you leave Poland?
In March 1945.

How?
Our group was sent by Icchak Cukierman. We left illegally. In Lublin, we procured documents stating that we were Yugoslavs returning from the concentration camps to our country. First, we went to Romania via Czechoslovakia and Hungary. We were there for half a year until we finally reached Eretz Israel.

Will you ever go to Poland?
No.

Thank you.

Tel Aviv, May 1989

Pnina Grynszpan-Frymer died in Tel Aviv on November 17, 2016.

---

52 Halina (Chajka) Bełchatowska and Bronek (Baruch) Szpigiel were also in the same shelter. See Grynszpan-Frymer, *Yameynu hayu haLeylot*, 131.
53 Until January 22, 1945. See Grynszpan-Frymer, *Yameynu hayu haLeylot*, 132.

We Were Just Rank-And-File Soldiers

Conversation with Aron Karmi

Could we start our conversation with your story of your home and your family?
I'm from a small town, from Opoczno, which until 1939 was in the Kielce province. Later, during the war, the town was annexed to the Łódź province. We lived in a house above the bakery, which belonged to our father. There were seven of us children, and our parents. Our name was Chmielnicki: Eliezer Chmielnicki—my father, Ester—my mother, four sons, and three daughters. My eldest brother came here, to Israel, in 1935: Zeev—Chmielnicki Wolf. He came as a sportsman, for the Makkabi games,[1] and stayed here.

Is Zeev still alive?
He's alive, he's alive. My second brother, Moszek, was with me in the Holocaust; we were together on the train to Treblinka, but he didn't stay alive. He taught me how to jump out of the train, but when he jumped out, he hit his head on a telegraph post. He lived for two weeks longer.

Did he jump out before you or after you?
After me, because I was younger.

Let's go back to the prewar days. Were your parents religious?
Yes, it was a religious family, but not a superstitious one. I mean, we were members of Gordonia,[2] for instance, and we attended gymnastics clubs.

And that didn't bother your father?
No, it didn't. But on Saturdays we went with him to synagogue. Once a week, not every day—religious people go every day.

---

1 p. 508 Glossary.
2 p. 497 Glossary.

Were your parents also from Opoczno?
No. They were born in Końskie, not far from Opoczno.

And do you remember your grandparents?
Not my grandfathers, but I remember one of my grandmothers, my mother's mother. She died in our house, back before the war. And I bear the name Aron after my grandfather on my father's side.

Did you speak Yiddish at home?
At home? We spoke Yiddish and Polish with our parents. We spoke Polish because we had a *chanut*[3] with baked goods. All our clientele were Polish. They came to town from the countryside for the market. With my brothers I spoke Hebrew.

How many Jews lived in Opoczno before the war?
Three thousand and something.

Was your father's bakery in the Jewish quarter?
On the edge. The Jewish quarter started from our house. Berka Joselewicza Street was the main Jewish street in Opoczno.

What kind of school did you go to?
I went to a few schools. First to cheder for two or three years, then to a Polish school, and then to a state school that only Jews went to. But all the subjects were in Polish. It was a small school; it was in the Esther House. From that school I moved to Tarbut[4] and I studied a few subjects in Hebrew. I had started vocational school when the war broke out.

And when did you join Gordonia?
I was a Boy Scout at the time; I was eight. My brothers drew me in. We had fun, played games, and had various kinds of meetings, like in the Scouts. And later on, we learned Hebrew and sang songs about Palestine.

---

3   *Chanut* (Heb.)—store.
4   p. 514 Glossary—Schools.

Otwock, ?, maybe Wiązowna

And meanwhile, war was looming.
In 1938, some fugitives from Germany came to us. One family came to live in our house, and they told us who the Germans were. So, when the Germans entered Opoczno, the fear was enormous. Attacks on Jews in the street began on the very first day. They would be rounded up for work in the city. There were days when people came back from that work beaten up dreadfully. Later, in early 1940, the armband started. There wasn't a ghetto at that point, but there was already a Judenrat and a Jewish district.

Were those the same streets where Jews had lived before the war?
Yes, but those who lived outside that area had to move. And after that, they surrounded us with barbed wires and hung up a sign: "Jewish district—no entry." And that was the ghetto. I think that was on May 8, 1940.[5] But the Judenrat was established a month after the Germans' entry. I remember that right away they took three hostages and said that we had to pay twenty thousand zlotys in war tribute, because it was the Jews' fault that there was a war.

Who were the three hostages?
My father—Eliezer Chmielnicki, Mosze Kacenelebogen, and the third was Icchak Chmielnicki, but he wasn't from our family.

Why did the Germans choose those particular people?
They chose some of the more important citizens in the town. Kacenelebogen traded with the countryside—he bought grain from the peasants and sold it to the mill, Icchak Chmielnicki had a "vulcan" (that's what people used to call a glassworks) and a limestone quarry.

What happened to the hostages?
This *makher* showed up, that's a guy who can cut any deal, and he went to the commanding officer of the German military police, and said: "Give me those three Jews, and I'll bring you the dough. They've had their fright now, and now they'll go to the residents and collect the money." That was how he talked them round. And the officer liked the makher's idea.

---

5 The ghetto in Opoczno was established in November 1940.

Do you know his name?
Mordechaj Rozental. He spoke German *perfekt*, because he had lived in Germany, and he was a trader in Opoczno. He and the three Jews collected the money in eight hours. And then the guy from the military police said to Rozental: "Give me a list of the twenty richest Jews, the most important Jews in Opoczno." And that was the Judenrat. The Germans couldn't choose people themselves because they didn't know them.

Was your father also a member of the Judenrat?
Yes. There was a doctor, and religious people, and political activists. The director was Fredlewski.

How did the Judenrat in Opoczno behave?
Well—not a hundred percent, perhaps, but in comparison with other cities, until 1942 they behaved well. After that it was different.

What do you mean by "different?"
When the Germans started the executions, the firing squads . . . That was a different thing entirely. Before that, you could buy yourself out; for money have someone else sent to work, but after that it was more difficult. The Judenrat started to collaborate with the Germans more—it had to.

Was your father in the Judenrat until the end?
No. Later on he fell sick, with his heart. He worked in the Judenrat until 1942.

Did you work in the ghetto?
Yes, in my father's bakery. Every Jew had a ration card and would get seventy grams of this black bread a day. And I baked the bread. Other Opoczno Jews went to work on the peat bogs. There were a few details where people worked for the Germans. The people in the peat bogs worked barefoot, and caught typhus, and so there was an epidemic. There was the ghetto by then. When they moved in the Jews from outside the district, each family took one family in. And then there were those who had escaped from Wielun, from Łódź, from Płock. At that time, there were around four and a half thousand Jews in the ghetto. But there was no food because they had shut us in. The state of the sanitation was dreadful, and then the typhus. And once, out there on the peat bogs, some Volksdeutsche beat up the Jews. There was this one who used to go about with a big dog, and he loved to hit; he broke lots of Jews' arms and legs. So, the Jewish workers didn't want to go to work. But by then, you couldn't buy your way out anymore, so they fled.

Do you remember when that was?
In June in 1942. Then the military police came in and ordered the Jewish police to arrest all those who had escaped. And the police went into the town and arrested them. About twenty people. They were taken to the synagogue. That's where the lock-up was. They were arrested around six or seven in the evening. In the city it was announced that those people were to be shot. So, their families went to the synagogue and told them. And then they broke out some of the planks and fled. The next day, the military police came to take them away, but there was no one there. They had all fled. The Opoczno military police called in the Gestapo from Tomaszów Mazowiecki, and they shot about two hundred people in the city.

They took people at random, did they?
Yes, off of the street, from their homes. Two hundred people!

Do you remember that day? Did you go into hiding then?
Yes. The whole family hid. The people from the SS came over from Tomaszów, and they took the makher, Mordechaj Rozental. They wanted Rozental to find those twenty people, but Rozental refused. He said: "I'm not going to do that, because I know what you want to do with them." And then they went and hunted down those two hundred people, and somehow, Rozental escaped from them. Three days later, he returned to the ghetto. And precisely on that day, Moritz, this criminal from the military police, happened to be in town. And Moritz met Rozental in the Community and ordered him to go with him. They were going down the stairs, and on the last step, Moritz shot Rozental in the heart. Yes... Before they deported us, they reduced the ghetto in size. There was less and less food and it was more and more dangerous. And we young people knew what was to happen to us. In the spring of 1942, we got underground newspapers from Warsaw.

What newspapers?
Słowo Młodych. That was the Gordonia paper, Eliezer Geller had done it.[6]

Your later commander in the uprising?
Yes. In that paper, Geller wrote about Ponary,[7] called for protests, and encouraged us to fight. A friend of mine, the son of the Hebrew teacher, hid the

---

6   p. 381 Rereading the List.
7   Ponary was an execution site some six miles from Vilnius, on the route to Grodno. During the Soviet occupation of Lithuania (1940–1941), trenches had been dug in the woods around

papers in a hiding-place in his house. And his mother made soap to sell, and she put the soap in the same place. They lived on Grobelna. But when the Germans reduced the ghetto in size, they had to move to another apartment very quickly, and they forgot about the hiding-place. The Germans raided the place, and they found—both the soap and the newspapers. They took the newspapers to Radom, to the Gestapo, and started to look for the criminals. The community organization wanted to give them money, bribe them, but the Gestapo demanded the person who had written the newssheet. And then the boy's father turned himself in to them. They arrested him. They examined his handwriting, and it turned out that it wasn't him. But we had taken the actual guy—Aba Lebendiger, his name was—out of town. We took him to Skała, to some Polish guy, and then to Częstochowa. Then his sister turned herself in to the Gestapo. And though it turned out that she hadn't written it either, the Germans took Aba's father, his sister, and his younger brother, and shot them. All three of them. Two or three weeks later, on April 27, 1942, they arrested thirty people in the night, most of them Zionist and communist activists well known in the town. The chief of the Polish police,[8] Zawadzki, went from house to house with a list, and arrested those people. They took them to the Community, took three of them—they selected every tenth one—to the lock-up in Tomaszów, and then to Auschwitz. But those twenty-seven people were shot, not far away, by the river. One of those twenty-seven, a member of Gordonia, was only wounded. He managed to crawl to the hospital; the hospital can only have been one hundred or two hundred meters from the river. Somehow, via some channel or other, Moritz found out about it. He went to the hospital and finished the injured guy off in his bed. And after that came the deportation. From those clandestine newspapers, we knew that

---

Ponary where fuel tanks were to have been installed. After the Germans invaded, mass executions of Jews from Vilnius and the surrounding area, Soviet POWs, and others were carried out there. The victims were marched to Ponary on foot, driven there in motor vehicles, or taken by rail. The perpetrators of the executions were SS and German police personnel, as well as massed platoons of Lithuanian collaborators. The massacres of Jews in Ponary began at the turn of June and July 1941 and continued until July 1944 (the last murder in Ponary was carried out by the Germans on July 20, 1944, when they shot three thousand Jews from Vilnius). The bodies of the victims were initially buried in situ. In September 1943, however, probably at least partly in connection with the release of the information about the Katyn massacres, a campaign to exhume and burn the bodies was launched. Some seventy thousand to one hundred thousand people are estimated to have been murdered in Ponary, most of them Jews.

8   p. 511 Glossary.

Einsatzgruppen[9] were going from town to town and carrying out a deportation. We knew they were getting closer to us. People started to make shelters; some people went to Poles in the countryside. They wanted to save themselves. We lived in a house on the boundary of the ghetto, as I said. The barbed wire passed through our courtyard. The next-door house was on the other side. That house was a cinema, before the war, the fire department had been there. I knew all the entrances and exits from the cinema, and we made a plan: if something were to happen, we would go into the cinema, and stay there as long as we needed to. And in the bakery, we had a bunker. And my entire family went in there. Only my father didn't hide, because he had this card stating that he was needed for work. So, my mother and my siblings went into the shelter in the bakery, and we, meaning I, my brother Moszek, and our cousin from Łódź, piled wood on top of the shelter in the bakery, and went into the cinema.

When was that operation?
We went into the cinema on September 22, 1942, because we knew that the next day the penal gang was coming. And it did. They surrounded the town in the early morning.

How exactly did people in the town know that the Einsatzgruppen would be coming on September 23?
Because the day before, they had been in Tomaszów, and apart from that, the Jewish police knew. And on September 23, they went through the ghetto shouting that everyone was to go out onto Kilińskiego. Kilińskiego Square was where they used to trade horses before the war. And everyone went out onto Kilińskiego Square, almost the entire town. "Anyone who hides will be killed!" they shouted. And we heard the shouts and the rifles. We had been sitting in the cinema since the previous evening, sitting under the *bama*, under the stage. And the night passed, and the day passed, and it was too frightening to go out and see what was happening there, in the ghetto. On the second night, we ran out of water, and we really needed a drink. You can go hungry, but it's hard without water. So that second night, I climbed quietly out of a window. I went home to the bakery. Everything was open wide, things strewn around. You could see that the Germans had been, that they had searched. The wood that had covered the bunker was strewn around; there was no one there . . . We decided to sit in

---

9   p. 495 Glossary—Einsatzgruppen.

the cinema for another day. The day before, the Germans had celebrated the end of the Opoczno Judenrein campaign. Od nekuda ahat Judenrein.[10] Their boss addressed the officers and soldiers, and the Ukrainians. And we, in the cinema, we could hear everything. No, it's impossible to describe it... We couldn't sit upright in the cinema; it was low, and there were rats scurrying about all over us. And we didn't know whether it was day or night—it was dark the whole time. We could only tell by the noise on the street.[11]

So, you were there for two nights and three days?
Yes. And all that remained in the ghetto was the Community and the Police—two blocks. Two hundred people—employees of the Judenrat and the *hiyunim*, those who were still necessary. We came out on the third day in the early morning. We went along Berka Joselewicza Street towards the Community. There was a Jewish policeman standing outside the Community, and he signaled to us with his hand that we shouldn't come any closer. We hid. We saw a military police patrol. They were still looking for people who had been in hiding, and whenever they found anyone, they killed them. Later on, we met my father, mother, and siblings in the Community. It was my father who had opened the bunker in the bakery on the second day, because in the Judenrat they had made a list of all those who were "necessary," and they could stay in the ghetto with their families. But neither I nor my brother was on that list. So, when I came to my father, my father burst into tears and said: "Oy leaba sheroe et ha-banim chozrim ve lo yahol laazor lakhem.[12] What shall I do now?" We had to flee at once. My father, brother, and cousin went into hiding inside the ghetto, but I went to a Polish man. He had worked for us at the bakery for twenty years. He spoke Jewish with us. He had often repeated: "If you're in need, come to me; I'll help you." And he wanted to help me, but he was so terrified when he saw me... The Germans killed Poles if they found Jews in their houses; there had been cases like that where we lived. But that Polish guy lived close to the cemetery, and there was this house there where the dead are washed. So, I went there. I sat up in the loft and waited. I don't know what I was waiting for, but I waited. I think I was waiting for a good day. Stasiek, that employee of my father's, brought me warm food and milk, but he was very frightened. And I sat there with those dead people in the night. The next day, Stasiek told me that they were shooting in the ghetto—I couldn't go

---

10 *Od nekuda*... (Heb.)—One more place free of Jews.
11 The Opoczno ghetto was liquidated on October 27, 1942.
12 *Oy leaba*... (Heb.)—Woe to the father who sees his sons returning and cannot help them.

Portraits

back there. And so, several days passed. One day, my father came to me, with a funeral. He brought a spade for me, and I went back into the ghetto with them. That very day, the military police made the announcement that those who had been in hiding could come out, and they would go on the list. And that was really what happened. It turned out that there had been lots of people in hiding, some people came back from the countryside. We were in the ghetto for four more months. Until January 5, until the next deportation. Two weeks before January 5, 1943, the military police came to the community offices and said: "Well, you survived the war. You made it. Anyone who has family in Palestine will be able to go. There will be an exchange: for every German, we will give ten Jews," that's what they said. There were even jokes that they would be turning Poles into Jews yet, because there were so few of us left. And that trick of theirs worked. A great many people who had been living in the countryside, on Aryan papers, put their names down for that exchange. After all those murders, after all those deportations? It would have been illogical—not to believe them. Because what does those two hundred people mean? What does such a number mean? Would they perform such miracles specially for two hundred people? Well, and you wanted to believe them... We all put our names down on the list. We had family here, in Palestine; we had my brother. There were some who added their names to other families'. On January 5, they told us that we could only take five kilograms with us, because there wasn't much space in the waggons. Well, what can you take in five kilograms?! And with that baggage, we went to the waggons.

Did the waggons leave from the ghetto?
Yes. The waggons took us to Ujazd. That's a village between Opoczno and Koluszki, near Tomaszów. There were just two SS men and Polish policemen with us, no Ukrainians or German soldiers. At that point we still believed... In Ujazd was the central point where Jews from other places were also brought; they were going to Palestine on the exchange, too!

How many people were there in Ujazd?
Two waggons from Opoczno—about four hundred fifty to five hundred people: two hundred families. I don't know how many there can have been altogether. We arrived in Ujazd toward evening. It was a large village. We went in through a gate, which they shut behind us. Then we saw huge numbers of Germans and Ukrainians. We started to suspect that it was a trap, that this was not Palestine. But we wanted to believe, we wanted to live. So, we waited. They told us that we would be spending the night there, and in the morning a train would come. A train would come, and we would travel west, to Germany, from Germany to

Switzerland, and the exchange would take place there—that's what they told us. We sat up through that night in Ujazd because there was nowhere to lie down.

What kind of rooms were you in?
They were abandoned Polish peasants' houses that had been specially "prepared" for the Jews. They packed us in, twenty to a house.

Could you have escaped from there? Did anyone try?
No, you couldn't. The entire site was surrounded by Ukrainians; they warmed themselves around campfires. One of us tried to escape, and they killed him. And in the morning, it was "Quickly! Quickly!", and riding crops, and whips, rifle butts, schnell, schnell, line up in fives. And the march began . . . A march to the railroad, a three-kilometer march in the snow. The snow was all dry. It squeaked as we walked. We had to keep together. The first victim was a rabbi from our town. We set off running in fives, and the Germans started to shoot. The rabbi couldn't keep up with his line, so a German went up to him and said: "You're making a mess here." He pushed him aside and put a full series through him with his Schmeiser. Then I saw blood in the snow . . . That red and white . . . And then that thought came into my head again—is this an exchange? Surely it's a trap! I heard shots behind me. Everyone thought that they were being shot at. And we shrank in on ourselves, we grew smaller, and we ran, like dogs, like cats, like terrified animals. How can I describe it? We ran like that for three kilometers. There were a number of victims along the way. At the railway station, they ordered us to form ranks. The train wasn't there yet. They ordered us to put our packages on the ground and step forward ten paces. Some among us had a little money, or some jewelry, or family photographs in those bundles. So, when they turned around to look at their bundles, the Germans killed them. That was another sign for us. It had really been clear to us since Ujazd that this was not Palestine, but we still couldn't understand why they were doing it. Why were they moving us? I mean, they could just have shot us! When they killed those few people at the station, I think everybody stopped believing, or almost everybody. Some said: "We have to get through this." They believed and gave the rest a little comfort. "We'll see which direction the train comes from. If it comes from the east, and we go west, we can have hope. But if it comes from the west, and we go eastward, then this will be our last journey." And so, we waited. And every moment was like an hour, and every hour like a day. It was cold, we had had nothing to eat, and we hadn't slept the previous night. And then the train came. I don't remember whether from the west or from the east. In the ghetto, when they had been putting us on the list, they had said that we would be going by passenger train. But this was

a freight train. Ukrainian guards jumped out of the train. Now everything was clear to us. But now it was too late, we couldn't do anything; we just had to wait. And the order: "Die ganze Scheisse heraus!"[13] The Ukrainians formed two lines, the doors to the train were open, and they're pushing us. The people who were already in hauled the rest up. And so, they pulled and pulled until the wagon was full. When the wagon was full, an SS man would come up with a Schmeiser and use it to make this circle—he didn't shoot, but everyone drew back, and then he would call to one of the Ukrainians: "Give us some more people here!" And so, there were one hundred twenty, one hundred thirty people in one wagon. They shut us in. And then there, inside, the real tragedy began—spasms, screams, crying, laments ... But I've already described that ...

Please go on.

Go on? ... The wagon stood for many hours. How many? It's impossible to say. It's not that nobody had a watch, only that time was abnormal. It's impossible to explain. We stood there for a very long time—or perhaps it wasn't long ... More wagons rolled in, already loaded up, until at last the whole train was ready to depart. When it set off, the questions started again. Where are we going? And we were going toward Koluszki, westward. And again, that small hope. Perhaps there would be an exchange after all? There was a tragedy in the wagon. A mother suffocating her child, a baby. The people standing next to her try to claw the child off of her. But she won't let them, saying: "Let it die here, not in the gas." We already know where we're going: to Treblinka. But we're going west. Perhaps it won't be Treblinka after all? There are people shouting: "Don't let her do it, don't let the child be suffocated!" People are shouting all kinds of things: "I have money with me, what will I do with the money? We're going to our deaths! What have I done my whole life? I made money, what can I do with money now?" Then the train stops and takes on coal, and then takes on water. Every time it stops, Ukrainians open the door, come in, and loot. They shout: "Give us money, give us money!" If not, they'll shoot us dead! And everyone gives them what they have ... So, we're going to Treblinka, now we know. "But in Koluszki," we say, "we'll find out for sure. If we go to Łódź, there's hope." In Koluszki, we stop. We can tell that they're doing some kind of maneuvers with us, uncoupling the locomotive and shunting it to the other end. The people standing by the windows say that the locomotive has to take on water. But it wasn't about the water—the locomotive was being coupled up to the other end. And then we set

---

13 *Die ganze* ... (Ger.)—All this shit out of here!

off from Koluszki toward Warsaw, Małkinia, to Treblinka. We're traveling east. And from then on, nobody is in any doubt. We all now know we can't expect anything else . . . We're going to Treblinka. Everybody is standing with their families. I was standing with my family, too.

Who from your family was in the wagon?
My father, my mother, my elder brother. One brother was in Russia, the second here in Palestine, and that was my third brother, Mosze. Mosze had already served in the army; he was a platoon commander. And my three sisters—one older than me and two younger.

How old was your youngest sister?
Nine. The other one thirteen. And Bracha, the eldest, was pregnant. Her husband was standing next to her. We were all standing together, the whole family. Moszek was pondering what to do. He said out loud: "Now there's no hiding it; we have to say it openly: we're going to Treblinka." And then my father says to us, to me and to Mosze: "I'm already fifty-one. Some people die at my age. And it's far easier for me to come to terms with that than for you. You young ones should give it a try. Try to jump out of the train. If you succeed in escaping, I will go to paradise. For whoever saves one soul from Israel saves the world entire."[14] He gave us a little heart. Mosze said: "This is the last chance because this evening we will reach Warsaw, and from Warsaw to Małkinia there are *wachy* posted. Here, we could still jump out." He taught us that because he was a soldier, and he knew. It was awful. I can't talk about it. I find it so hard with Polish, and it's not easy for me to name everything. What does it mean to escape? What does it mean to try? What does it mean? First you have to part with your family. How can I leave them? Where are they going? There were no answers to all those questions. And finally, we resolved. And we started to bid our parents farewell. As I was about to say my farewell to Bracha, my elder sister, then she burst into tears: "But this child that is not yet born, surely it has not sinned, why it?" And then I broke down completely and said: "I'm staying!" And all the time the train is traveling on, and there is less and less time, that time ahead of us. My father is adamant that we should jump out. Our cousin from Łódź was with us; there were three of us. My father says to us: "If you jump, then perhaps there will be some vengeance for our blood?!" The fact that I am alive is thanks only to my

---

14 For whoever saves one soul from Israel . . .—*Kol ha-mekayem nefesh ahad keilu kiyem olam male tu tez ha* (Heb.) [in:] *Mishnah Sanhedrin* 4:5. (Correct translation: Whoever saves one soul, it were as though he saved the world entire.)

father. We ourselves wouldn't have had any initiative of our own had it not been for our father... As my father was persuading and persuading us, my mother asked: "Where are you sending them? What about their little sisters?" That was a mother, you understand? "We'll all go together!" But then my father started again, and this time my mother understood, took money out of her hidey-places, and started to bid us farewell. She also took money from our little sisters. She gave it to all three of us. And she blessed us for our journey... And so, we were resolved to jump. But how to do it? Where the little windows were, there were iron bars. And by the windows stood those with the strongest elbows. The weak ones, who couldn't breathe, and were begging for a little air, couldn't get to the window. We announced that we were going to jump. We said that other people could jump with us. We said we had to hurry, that there was no time to lose. Now it was still possible. And then those people, who all that time hadn't let anyone else get close to the window, started to help us. Moszek said to us: "You come behind me." He supported himself on people's shoulders and climbed over their heads. He flowed as if on water. People held him up, helped him. And that's how we got to the window.

How many of you resolved to escape?
I can say for certain how many jumped out before me, but how many after me—that I don't know. I was second, and Mosze third. But before we jumped, we had to pull out the grille. Everyone wrestled with it. I'm sure that others had tried that grille before us. And we succeeded. We didn't have a lot of strength, but we did it. We put the grille on the ground. And that was like our little ladder, so it was easier to climb up to the window. And then Mosze instructed us once again: "Listen well, you have to jump out of the train with your legs. You have to catch hold of that iron bar above the window, twist your whole body around, and lie on the window on your stomach. And then slide down and push off from the wagon with all your strength, so that your legs don't fall under the train wheels." Everyone who jumped as Mosze taught us did it right. Those who didn't have such instruction didn't always make it. One woman from our town, Jofka Kacenelebogen, jumped, and the train severed both her legs. She died there, by the train, the next day. Some Poles found her. I was second to jump, and the one who went before me had to try twice, because he was in a kapote and his kapote got tangled up. And he only jumped on the second attempt, that Edelsztam. And one more thing Moszek taught us. We could hear shooting the whole time. One wagon in three had this hut with guards. And they would shoot along the windows. So Moszek said to us: "You hear that round? And another round? And another? And now there is a break. Because the guard has to reload

his magazine after three rounds. You have to jump after the three rounds." So, we waited, and then after every three rounds, one of us jumped. I threw my overcoat out first and then jumped. Beforehand, I agreed with Moszek that I would stay in the same place, and he would come to me. We also had a password: the tune "How good to climb mountains." Mosze could whistle it. By then, it was night. I jumped into a ditch—full of snow—like a cat. The snow revived me a little at once. And I stood there and waited, and waited... After a while, I thought that perhaps it wasn't such a good idea to stand and wait just like that, because it was a rather bright night. There was a little birch coppice, a young wood, there. And I waited for the melody there, in that wood. But Mosze didn't come. After the war, I found out that Mosze had hit a telegraph post and had gone back to Opoczno with a wound in his head. Every night he had walked a few miles, hiding in the woods by day, and in the end, he got there. In Opoczno he went to Bolek Kosowski, a school friend. But Bolek couldn't keep him in the house, so Mosze hid in the woods, and Bolek took him food every day. A family called Jakubek lived nearby, and they followed Bolek, tracking him. They saw that there in the woods there were three Jews: one was from Łódź, the second Mosze, and our cousin, Lutek Lerer. Franka Kacenelebogen is here, in Israel. She was in hiding in the barn at Adamek's farm, and from the barn she saw the military police come and kill the three of them. After the war, people said that it was Jakubek who had denounced them. I don't know whether he was jealous that Adamek was getting money, or whether it was about something else. You can't know that. But that's what the Poles said after the war.

So, your brother never came. What did you decide to do?
My brother never came. I had only one address in Warsaw.

Eliezer Geller's address?
Yes. I didn't know how to get to Warsaw. I went to the first peasant I found—I had to get something to eat and drink—and I said: "Give me something to eat; I'll pay you." He gave us some food.

"Us"—you mean you weren't alone?
I was with one other guy, Rozencwajg, from my wagon. And the peasant brought us sausage and bread, and vodka, and tea. We paid him and fell asleep. While we slept, then he took out all our money, took everything we had. So, when we woke up, we didn't know what to do. We said to the peasant: "You look here, we jumped a train going to Treblinka."—We couldn't say: "You robbed us." That wouldn't have helped.—"Give us some information as to where we can spend a

day or two or tell us how to get to Warsaw." Then he sent us to another peasant. That village was called Wilchelmów; it was not far from Podkowa Leśna.

How far was it to Warsaw from there?
Twenty kilometers? The other peasant was hiding Jews, he lived in Podkowa Leśna. We went to him in the night. He was a good peasant. He fed us, and then showed us how to get to the station. I got a scarf and a bit of cotton wool from him, as if I was going to the dentist. So that people wouldn't see my face. And the other guy looked like a Pole; he wasn't similar. And so, we took the train to Warsaw. In Warsaw . . . Shall I tell the whole story?

Today please just tell me how you managed to get into the ghetto.
In Warsaw it was difficult to get into the ghetto. The easiest way was with a work detail. But for that you had to have papers; and first you had to have them made out. So, I got some papers made out. But that's a whole long story that I'll pass over here. Anyway, one day I got locked up on Szucha.

The Gestapo caught you? How did that happen?
That was the first time in my life I'd ever been to Warsaw. I needed a safe place, and I was sent to 9 Długa Street. I got the address from the Pole who made out my papers. On Długa, there was this old woman, and she took people in for the night. She asked me how long I wanted to be there for. I said: "I don't know—maybe a day or two." So, she said that I had to register, and then I would get a food ration card. I said that I was tired, and that she should register me.

Did she know you were a Jew?
Yes, but we didn't talk about it. She registered me with the janitor herself. And every morning, I walked around the outside of the ghetto, I wanted to figure out how I could get in. On the third day, as I was walking out of the entranceway, this guy grabbed me by the scruff of the neck and said: "Stop right there, kitty! Where are you from?" I tried to wrest myself free of him, but I couldn't. The police were there right away. And it was the Polish police that arrested me. They took me down to the precinct. I had my counterfeit papers, which said that I was supposedly from Płock. I knew that they'd been bombing there, and that they wouldn't be able to check up on me in the town hall there.

What papers were they?
An *Arbeitskarte*. So, I spent the night at the police station, and in the morning, they took me to Szucha Avenue, to the Gestapo. I was there for six days, and

The Street

every day for six days they beat me. There was blood coming out of my ears, out of my nose, out of my wounds. After the interrogation I could barely drag myself back to the cell. I had to go down three floors, into the cellar; that was where the cell for Jews was. Whenever they caught a Yid with false papers on the Aryan side, they would dump him in that cell. And every Sunday they took the people from that cell into the ghetto, to 103 Żelazna, to be shot by firing squad. I didn't know what 103 Żelazna was, I didn't know anything, I was in Warsaw for the first time in my life. When they took me to that cell on the first day, I think there were about seven people there. Every day, two or three more came in. We were all interrogated every day. The people who carried out the interrogations had these planks and would thrash us over the head with them. "Tell us where you got these papers from!" And I would say: "I don't know." "Who are you?" So, I say I'm Cholawski because those were the papers I had. When they had beaten me up good and proper, I knew that there was nothing for it, I had to give in. So, I'll tell them I'm a *Mischling*—a mix, a half-Jew. That's what the people who were in with me advised me to do. When I told them that I was a half-breed, they stopped beating me. That was a start—they stopped beating me. They gave us food once a day. Ersatz coffee and potato peelings; the Poles were given the potatoes. And so on for six days. They shaved us, took our clothes, and gave us prison stripes. And eventually, Sunday came around. I remember that in the cell, we sang "That last Sunday." The next day, they took us all in an SS vehicle, this kind of open truck, to the ghetto. We sat in the middle of the vehicle, with Germans carrying rifles on either side. We were all weak; none of us had any thought of fleeing—we couldn't even move our arms.

How many people were there in the truck?
Twenty-three. Among us there were Poles who had stores in Warsaw. I heard their conversations. They were Poles; their grandfathers had been Jewish. They took people to the third generation. None of us admitted to each other that we were Jews, so I thought I was the only one, the only original Jew. We arrived at Żelazna. Schnell, schnell! They ordered us to stand by the wall, and at the foot of the wall there were a few corpses. They hadn't had time to clear them away. But they didn't order us to stand facing the wall; we stood facing them. One of them, an older man, held our papers. And there was also a group of armed policemen in front of us. And we're just standing there. But we can't stand, because it's cold, because we're hungry, because we're weak. We're all shivering. And again, every minute like an hour. I remember I closed my eyes. I had to stand, but I didn't want to look. I didn't want to see them loading their rifles. And the older guy is reading out the sentence, and I'm getting hot—this mass of heat's flooding down

from my head. And I hear him saying: "Obediently reporting, Mr. Brandt,[15] das ist dreiundzwanzig Mischlinge." And Brandt says: "Aaah, Mischlinge!" And then he comes up to the row and asks each one of us: "Name!" One says: "Pacholski," the second: "Krzyżanowski," the third says: "Krakowski," another one says: "Leszczyński . . ." And at that, Brandt says: "Alle sind 'ski'! You ain't been Jews yet; you still gotta see what it means to be a Jew!" And he saved us, that Brandt.

***

We ended our previous conversation with the story of how Brandt saved the lives of twenty-three Jews. Let's go back again to the time when you were in hiding in Warsaw before the Polish police took you to Szucha.
I traveled here and there, and I was also in Opoczno.

Ah, yes. Please tell me about that journey.
While we were still in the ghetto in Opoczno, my father called all his sons together and said: "See here: in the cellar, there is money buried." It was in glass jars in three places. "If any of you stays alive, you will be able to save yourselves." And you could only save yourself with money. So, I went. I don't know where I had the strength from, to go to Opoczno at that point! After all, there was nobody left there by then! Again, I traveled as if to the dentist's, in a headscarf. I arrived by train in the early evening. I went to see that Stasiek who had worked for us in the bakery. He lived near the Jewish cemetery; I spoke about him. I wanted him to help me. He told me that the ghetto was guarded by the police. At night, patrols were posted there, and in the daytime, laborers took out the things that had been left behind by the Jews. And if they found anyone, they would shoot. Stasiek's sister had a boyfriend, Romek. He was well-known in the town for his bravado. Romek and I went into the ghetto in the night. We dug in the frozen ground for five hours. We got one jar out. I left the rest; perhaps one of the others was still alive, or maybe I myself would be in need at a later date. I gave Romek some of the money and said: "This might not be enough for you, but I need this cash very badly; I can't get myself any papers made without it." I was afraid that he might shoot me there and then, so I showed him the place where the second jar was buried, and I told him that it was for him. And he agreed; he believed me.

---

15 Karl Brandt—an officer in the rank of Untersturmführer, the head of Section IV B (Jewish affairs) in the Gestapo in Warsaw; later, one of the commanders in the Sonderkommando der Sipo-Umsiedlung, co-perpetrator of the liquidation of the Warsaw ghetto in the summer of 1942.

Does that mean that Romek dug up his share later on?
I don't know, I think so. I never saw him after that.

Do you know what happened to the third share?
I don't know and I don't want to know. At any rate, when I said goodbye to Romek, I was very afraid that I wouldn't get out of the situation alive. I told him that I was going back to Warsaw that same night, but I didn't go. It's possible that he didn't want to do anything bad to me, but I preferred not to risk it. I spent that night and the next day at the home of a guy who lived in a cottage down by the river. Before the war he used to repair bicycles. He did a great deal for me. That day was very important to me.

And then you went back to Warsaw by train?
Yes. And then I came into contact with this woman, she was called Chłopikowa. I don't know whether that was her name or a nickname. She lived at no. 15 on the Market Square. She made documents at home. She had all the stamps. You just had to give her a photograph.

Ilana Cukierman[16] told me that in Warsaw you were in an apartment that the Gestapo entered.
That was at Chłopikowa's. It wasn't until later that I was at 9 Długa.

Can you tell me about that?
Yes, of course! That happened before I went to Opoczno. That Chłopikowa woman was making my papers for me. Her husband traded with the ghetto—in sausage and vodka. They would smuggle it in through a hole in the wall. And one day, exactly when I was there, the Germans caught him. Someone came and said that. And they had two apartments. They themselves lived on the second floor, and on the third they had an empty apartment that was padlocked. So, what was to be done with this Adam? Meaning with me.

Did she know that you were a Jew?
Of course! "Come with me!" she says to me. And she locked me in on the third floor. I knew that the Germans would come and raid the place. But there was nothing in that apartment, only a table and a few chairs; there was this army blanket lying on the table, and then there was a closet.

---

16 Ilana Cukierman (1930–2009)—Israeli artist and experimental radio art curator.

There was nowhere to hide?
Yes. But it was evening. Windows had to be covered, but they didn't live up there, and the windows were bare. Through the window I could see Chłopikowa's husband and the Germans. So where can I hide, what can I do? All that was left was that closet. I opened it. And inside—sausage, these headscarves . . . So, I thought that if they came to do a search, they would look in the closet first of all. I looked again at that green blanket. I thought—there's a blackout order. So, I climbed up onto the window and stretched out the blanket, held it up by the corners and stood on it to hold the bottom edges down. And I stood there like that on the windowsill. And then I hear them coming up to the apartment. He opens the padlock and they come in. They start talking to the Germans. And that Jeruminiak—oh! I remembered his name now!—starts saying to them: "I'll give you sausage and vodka . . ." And he laid some money on the table, he wanted to bribe them. And it worked.

How long were you standing there in the window?
How long? A month! I couldn't tell you how long it lasted; maybe fifteen, maybe twenty minutes. A moment later, the Poles came back into the apartment and started kissing me. "How did you think of that?! We were sure that was the end of us. If you survived that, you'll survive the war!" The next day, I went to Opoczno.

Yes. I know that story already. So, let's go back to that Sunday at 103 Żelazna.
Very well . . . Brandt had us taken to the Werterfassung. We were to work for the Germans there. They took us to Niska Street. It was a huge house, and inside, there was a large courtyard. Each of us was given a little metal token with a number on it. When we arrived there, I started talking with the Jews, and they tell me that I should be pleased to have gotten that token, because a token like that cost two thousand zlotys at that point.

Yes, because the number on that token meant that you were employed, "legal," not a "wildcat"[17] in the ghetto.
Yes. Employed, and employed well at that. Jews had a lot of work there. But of course, my plan wasn't to get a good work detail, I wanted to get to Eliezer Geller. I asked when we would be going to work. They said that in the morning.

---

17 The term "wildcat" had two meanings in the ghetto: before the uprising, a "wildcat" (Pol. *dziki*, lit. "wild one") was a person who had remained in the ghetto after the *große Aktion* without authorization in the form of a "number for life," while during the uprising it referred to individuals or groups fighting independently of the ŻOB or ŻZW, without political affiliation.

The Street

Where were you billeted?
In the same block. All the Werterfassung laborers lived there. We went straight to the kitchen; it was a kitchen for that block. In the kitchen, I thought to myself, there might be some people from the organization. So, I casually asked if anyone happened to know Eliezer. "Because he's my cousin," I said, "and I don't know where to find him." I hoped that in that way he would get wind of the information that I was looking for him. In the morning, I was supposed to go to work. But when I was in the bathroom, I saw that a plank had been broken out. I thought that someone must already have escaped that way. I broke off another piece of the plank and left the place. I found myself on Niska Street, outside the Werterfassung block. There were quite a lot of people on the street. They were going to work at dawn. Later on, during the day, the ghetto was empty. I saw a woman walking along with some bread. I went up to her and asked her where she had the bread from, where there was a bakery. She told me that the bakery was at 5 Niska. I went there, and said to the guy: "I've just been released from Szucha Avenue; you can see what kind of a state I'm in." My head was shaved, and I looked like a skeleton. "I want to stay with you for a day or two until I find my cousin," I said to him.

Why did you go to a bakery?
Because I was brought up a baker. And I say to him: "In return for you keeping me here for two days, I'll work for you." So, he started to laugh—I didn't look like a worker. While we were talking, the guy's father came in, the owner of the bakery; his name was Gefen.[18] He had this trumpet by his ear, because he couldn't hear well. So, his son, Paweł, shouted that I'd got out of Szucha and wanted to work for them. And the father started to laugh as well. And he says to Paweł: "Take him upstairs, give him some clothes, and give him something to eat." And when I'd washed and dressed, I was a different man.

Why did you escape from the Werterfassung? You could have tried to contact Eliezer from there, too.
I didn't trust the Germans. But in that bakery, I started to talk about my cousin again. Two days later, Paweł told me that if I wanted to return their kindness, I could help build a shelter under the bakery. They worked every night for several hours.

---

18 According to the telephone book dating from the turn of 1939/1940 and the memory of a relative of Lejb Gefen, his bakery was at 35 Niska Street.

What was the shelter like?
They had a cellar beneath the bakery. They had walled up the entrance to the cellar and made a masked entrance underneath the oven in the bakery. We had to carry earth out; it was a lot of work. I started to help them, but it didn't last long, because on the third day, two fighters from the ŻOB came asking for Chmielnicki Aron. The baker didn't know what was going on; he was afraid they might be narks. But they told him that I would be in good hands; that Chmielnicki's cousin had sent them for me. And to me they said: "We got an order from Eliezer Geller to take you to him." They even had with them a letter I had once written to Eliezer from Opoczno. I said goodbye to the baker's family and went with them.

And where did they take you?
They took me to the brushmakers' yard. Geller was the commander of the Gordonia group at 32 Świętojerska.

How many people were there in that group?
About ten or twelve. Not far away there was another group, an organized commune. That was a reserve group. They were waiting for weapons.

Did Geller's group already have weapons?
Of course! We each had a weapon. But to be able to get into a group like that, there had to be a weapon for you. When I went to Geller, he took me straight into the armed group. That was a big day for me!

That was in February 1943, right? Please tell me about your meeting with Geller.
Yes, it was February. And the meeting? On the first night, Eliezer took me into his bed. We talked all night. He wanted to know about my father, my mother, my sisters, the whole town... I was the first person who was able to tell him in detail about it all, in the greatest detail. In that way, he was able to experience the whole tragedy with his family. Whenever I wanted to cut my story short, he protested: "No, no, tell me, I want to know everything." And I told him everything. When I had finished, he said to me: "Listen, we haven't been organized here for long; up till now we had no weapons. Even now, we don't have enough for everyone. There are guys and girls who want to join us, but there is no space for them for now. Because everyone who joins the organization has to have a weapon. You are an exception." And he pulled out a Parabellum 38 and says: "You're getting a weapon on the day after you arrived, because I know you have lost your whole family; that you have no one. I feel the same as you. And this is the last moment

that we can take revenge; that we can die as we want to, and not as they want us to." I remember those words precisely.

How old was Geller?
Twenty-five? He was a soldier. He had been in the army for two years before the war, and there weren't many like him among the fighters—maybe four, maybe five? And Geller had soldiered in the September campaign; he had been at Kutno.

How long were you in the brushmakers' yard?
Two weeks, I think.

Now let's talk about life in the group of fighters: from the moment of your meeting with Geller until the outbreak of the uprising.
We lived in a commune. There were twelve of us. We lived in an attic and learned to use our firearms. We stockpiled food. Sometimes people would give us food of their own free will, but sometimes we had to take it by force.

How did you do that?
A group of three or four guys would go out, to a bakery, and say: "You have to supply twenty loaves of bread a day to the organization. And if you don't supply them, we'll come and take them ourselves. But if we come ourselves, we'll take more than twenty." That usually ended amicably, but there were some who didn't want to give us anything.

And what then?
Well, we had to take people like that to prison. I remember two prisons in our area, on our turf, I mean on the premises of the Toebbens & Schultz 'shop; I remember two prisons: 56 Leszno and 76 Leszno.

What were those prisons like?
ŻOB soldiers stood there on guard day and night, and locked up inside there was a Jew who, for instance, should have donated half a million zloty, because that was what the Command had ruled, but he didn't want to. We needed that money for arms, and that Jew had made it collaborating with the Germans. If he didn't want to hand over the money, he would be arrested and locked up until he did give it.

And if he remained adamant despite the prison?
That did happen once, I remember. One guy was in prison until the uprising broke out. And on April 19, on the first day of the uprising, we were given the order from the Command to release him.

What was that man's name, do you remember?
He was called Opolion.[19] I was on guard; I was watching him. In the other prison, there was a guy who had collaborated with the Gestapo: he would send the Germans to our addresses. We caught him with papers from the Gestapo, with passes in his name. He was inside until April 19, too, but we didn't free him.

What happened to him?
He was shot.

What was his name?
Misza Wald. He was imprisoned on Leszno, at no. 56. Lilit [Regina Fudem],[20] our *kasharit*,[21] brought the order to release the one and shoot the other. There was also another Jew in prison at no. 56 on Leszno. I remember that he was known as Pilotka. He had collaborated with the Germans, too, and he was also shot. But that was earlier, in March. I remember that execution. A group of fighters surrounded the prison, read him out the sentence, and shot him. It was Szymon Heller[22] of Haszomer Hacair who shot him, they lived at 67 Nowolipie. It was at night. Pilotka was shot in the cellar, and afterwards they stuck a piece of paper to him saying: "This is what will happen to anyone who collaborates with the Germans." And they threw him out onto the street and left him.

Was Pilotka a policeman?
No, he was a nark—he went looking for our hideouts.

Do you remember any other prisoners?
I remember this one devout Jew, who was called Fingerhod, I think. In prison, he wanted us to give him a tallit and tefillin[23] so that he could pray. We gave him all that, and I think he stayed there for two weeks and wouldn't give us any money. But in the end, he did! I mentioned the case of Opolion. Now I'll tell you how we carried out the Opolion operation. Guta [Błones], one of our girls, dressed up like a lady—she put on a fancy hat and went to see him. But before

---

19 In her book, Vladka Meed mentions an Appolion, a factory owner in the ghetto; this was probably the same person. (Vladka Meed, *On both sides of the wall* [Beit Lohamei Ha-Getaot, Ha-Kibbutz Ha-Meuchad, 1977], p. 191).
20 p. 380 Rereading the List—Regina Fudem, Lilit.
21 *kasharit* (Heb.)—courier.
22 p. 393 Rereading the List.
23 Tallit and tefillin—prayer shawl and phylacteries, the two little black boxes containing passages from the Pentateuch that male Jews put on to pray.

that, we had been following him to know his daily schedule. He was a Jewish line manager at the Toebbens 'shop. He collaborated with the Germans and made big money, because every Jew wanted to work, and to get a job in the 'shop, you had to pay a bribe.

So, Guta dressed up like a lady and went to see him . . .
Yes. We had found out that Opolion had family in Palestine, and Guta went to pass on their respects. His apartment was always guarded by some *werkszuc*. Guta had a photograph of Opolion, and her task was to recognize him on the street. After work, he was always escorted home by the *werkszuc* or an armed German. The arranged signal was that Guta, when she recognized him, would make a sign with her hat, and we would then know that that was Opolion. And that's what happened. When Guta started talking to him, our boys went up to him; one of them was Michałek [Klajnwajs].[24] He asked him: "Are you so-and-so?" And the other guy says: "No; my name is Opolion." So Michałek answers: "Oh yeah? Then it's you we want."

Was Opolion alone that day?
No, he was with the *werkszuc*. But we cut him off. We took Opolion into the entranceway, from the entranceway up into the attic, and via the attics took him to our prison at 76 Leszno. He stayed there until April 19 and was released, like I said.

But he gave no money?
No, he was stubborn.

Let's go back to our conversation about life in the commune before the uprising. How did you manage for heating, for instance?
As we went about through the attics, we would find various pieces of furniture that people had thrown out of their apartments. We took them for fuel because we had a tiled stove in our apartment. Before we took the furniture into the apartment, we took it apart. And then we would have a guessing game. We would ask: What's this? A table? A closet? A chair? Whoever guessed right, won.

Won what?
Nothing. Just won.

---

24 p. 403 Rereading the List—Henoch (Heniek) Klajnwajs, Michałek.

What else did you do on Świętojerska?
They told us that we had to dig a tunnel from Świętojerska all the way to the gate via which the Germans could come in again to take Jews out. We lived in the attics. We went down into the cellars and dug the tunnel there. We carried the sand in sacks on our backs two or three blocks further on, so no one would notice that we were digging. When we reached the gateway, our group planted a mine there. That was the only mine that exploded when the Germans entered! There were mines in other places too, but they didn't explode.

You also made passages through the attics.
Yes. We knocked holes in the walls. They made a plan for us of where to hack, and we hacked, because we were just rank-and-file soldiers. There was a passage via the attics through all the houses on that street. And from the cellar of the last house, we dug a tunnel under the street. So, you could get over to the oddnumbered side of the street via that tunnel. There was a plan to make passageways like that throughout the ghetto. Each group did it in their own area. We started on Świętojerska, and then when we reached Toebbens, we started to dig there. If we had had more time, the whole ghetto would have been done like that, so that we could have gotten around only via the attics and the tunnels.

A sort of attic-tunnel labyrinth?
Yes. What we managed to do helped us considerably afterwards, during the uprising. The Germans used the streets, and we the attics and tunnels, to get from one building to the next.

How much did you manage to do on the Toebbens' shop premises—because you didn't finish Świętojerska?
No. Świętojerska was finished by the people who came after us, and at Toebbens we managed to do the whole of Leszno.

Why did you move to the Toebbens premises after two weeks?
Two of our boys, Szymon Lewental[25] and Jehuda Koński,[26] went up to the wall, because they were due to receive a package with weapons from the Aryan side. But some nark saw them and turned them over to the Germans. When they were taken, our Command ordered a state of emergency. All the groups changed addresses, because humans are only humans, and if they're pressed too hard, they can spill.

---

25 p. 411 Rereading the List.
26 p. 405 Rereading the List—Juda (Jehuda) Koński.

What happened to those boys? Were they killed?
Yes, they were killed. At the Gestapo their fingers and toes were crushed in this press. They were completely blue with pain, but they didn't spill on anyone; they didn't spill anything!

Were those boys from your group, from Gordonia?
Yes. A Jewish policeman who was at the interrogations told us about them. Pinkiert's people[27] also told us what the boys looked like. But back then we didn't know that they hadn't spilt, so for a whole week, we were in a state of emergency. We moved places, and every group went to a different shelter.

Would you like to talk about any more operations before the uprising?
I remember that when we arrived at Toebbens, we didn't take up our positions right away. For a week, we stayed in the cellar and waited for the Command to call off the state of emergency. It was dreadful in that cellar. There were a lot of us, fighters from several groups. We had weapons, but we were holed up day and night. And the waiting...

Did you have enough to eat in the cellar?
Food wasn't a problem. It was brought to us. But there were forty people down there. Stuffy, hot, and that waiting ... for a week. When at last the information came that we could come out, we took up our positions; we went to 76 Leszno. That was the place for the Gordonia group. We also had a reserve place. If anything happened, we were to go to Dawid Nowodworski's[28] group at 67 Nowolipie, near Smocza. They were our neighbors—from Leszno we could reach them via the attics.

Were the 'shop employees' living quarters at 76 Leszno?
Yes. There were 'shops every few blocks. There was a 'shop at 74 Leszno and one at 80 Leszno. The 'shop laborers lived on the lower floors and we on the top floor. We walled up the entrance to our apartment, but we had a way out via the attic; we got into the apartment via a ladder.

How many people lived there?
Ten or twelve people—our group.

---

27 Employees of the funeral parlor owned by Mordechaj Pinkiert, which operated in the Warsaw ghetto.
28 p. 421 Rereading the List.

Could you list the names of the fighters in your group?
Certainly! Jacek Fajgenblat,[29] Jakubek Putermilch—Masza's husband, Michałek Klajnwajs, Kuba Wajs,[30] Genek Fingerhut,[31] Leja Korn,[32] Guta Kawenoki[33]—she was from Łódź, Adek Himelfarb,[34] Marek Blank,[35] and me—Aron Chmielnicki.

Did you know them well?
I got to know them well then—before and during the uprising. We were together the whole time. When we lay down to sleep, I remember, there was a round—

A round of what?
Aron finished, Michałek starts, Michałek finished, Kuba starts . . .

But what?
To tell your story: where you're from, how you came to join the group, what happened to your family . . . We wanted to get to know one other. In that way, we became as close as if we were one family. And we lived like one family. We took money from people—sometimes we took half a million—but we ourselves had no money. We lived on black ersatz coffee, and on bread and jam, I never saw meat in that period—for dinner there was soup, sometimes there was a small piece of sausage. Money was sacred; it was for arms.

Were there any pairs among you?
Leja Korn was with Jehuda Koński. But when he was killed, she was very miserable, and didn't want to get together with anybody.

Did Leja survive?
No; I'll tell you about her later. And Guta [Kawenoki] was single.

Who did you like most of all in your group?
I liked Michałek most, he was kind of original.

Did Michałek survive?
Nobody survived from my group except Jakubek and me.

---

29 p. 369 Rereading the List—Jakub Fajgenblat, Jacek.
30 p. 462 Rereading the List.
31 p. 372 Rereading the List.
32 p. 405 Rereading the List—Lea Korn (Korun).
33 p. 402 Rereading the List.
34 p. 393 Rereading the List.
35 p. 347 Rereading the List.

Can we talk about the uprising in the ghetto now?
I won't say anything about the first uprising, the January uprising—I wasn't in the ghetto at that point.

Yes, I know. I'm asking about the April uprising, the second uprising in the Warsaw ghetto.
In March, Eliezer Geller was designated by the Command the commander of eight groups. He was the commander of the Toebbens 'shop premises, the way Marek Edelman was the commander of the brushmakers' yard and had four groups.

Who was the commander of your group?
Jacek Fajgenblat. Jacek survived the uprising but perished later on in Warsaw. He was in a shelter with Guta and a few other people. But there was a spill, and they were killed. Before that, Jacek had been in the woods with us, but then he went back to Warsaw, to the Aryan side, and was killed.

...The April uprising.
On April 18, in the night, we sensed something. The next day was Erev Pesach.[36] But before that I have to tell you something, to show you who the Germans were. The whole time, they played around with us, sending some for extermination, and giving others numbers, tokens, and go play, little girls, go play, little boys... Another month longer, another week longer... In the ghetto it was always about how to be productive, how to carry out all their orders. But it was all one big sham, one big deception. A week before April 19, the Germans announced that it would be possible to bake matzah for Pesach. In previous years, that hadn't been the case. Well, if you could bake matzah for Pesach, that meant that Pesach was going to be peaceful. There was no white flour in the ghetto, only dark flour, so people went to the rabbi to ask whether they could make matzah from dark flour. The rabbi answered that in times like those, one could. And you would see people on the streets going about after work with these white duvet covers; they would be getting matzah for Pesach from the bakery. Everyone was preparing for the seder.[37] And then in the night of April 18, the Germans surrounded the ghetto. But I didn't see it, because it was dark; we just heard vehicles driving around, and engines running. Not until dawn did we see it all. Every morning, the 'shop laborers went to work—some to the 'shops inside the ghetto, and others to their work details on the Aryan side. That day, those who worked in

---

36 Erev Pesach (Heb.)—the eve of Passover.
37 Seder (Heb.)—the solemn, festive supper on the eve of Passover.

'shops inside the ghetto went to work as normal, but those who went on work details were stopped. They were told: "*Zurück, zurück!* Nobody is going out today." And that was a sign to us that something was going to happen. We had been preparing since the night. We received the information from the central ghetto and the brushmakers' yard that they were also being surrounded. They surrounded all three ghettos, but they only went into the *merkazi* ghetto, the central ghetto, and that was where they started. Our boys received them with grenades, and we at Toebbens heard the shooting from the morning, so we knew that the campaign had begun. We could tell from the shots whether it was ours or the Germans—ours were pistols and grenades, but the Germans had heavy rifles. At that point we didn't know how that first engagement ended. We were on alert the whole time; Eliezer ordered all groups to take up their positions. We went down to the third floor at no. 76. The windows of that house gave out onto the wall, because Leszno was divided; there were Poles living on the other side. We observed the wall and waited for the Germans. They always approached the ghetto along the wall on the Aryan side and entered by Karmelicka Street. But we didn't see anything. They only went into the central ghetto. I said, we heard shots. We didn't know what to do, we waited in suspense. That same day, we decided to build barricades in the stairwells. We went into the courtyards via entranceways, and every courtyard was a square—there were stairwells on all four sides. And we barricaded the stairwells up. We dragged down everything we could lay our hands on—furniture, straw mattresses, pots and pans—and threw it all onto the stairs so that they wouldn't be able to get up. And we were on the third floor. We spent the whole day barricading the stairwells. Over in the central ghetto there was shooting, and we're preparing for battle. Before evening, we received the order that part of our group should go over to Dawid Nowodworski, where the mine was that didn't detonate later on. We went to help them guard the house, because the Germans were supposed to be passing via the Befehlsstelle,[38] not far from Nowolipki. It was from there, from the Befehlsstelle, that they went out in the early morning into the central ghetto and that they were supposed to return. And we had put a mine down there, of course. Three of our guys went down into the cellars and tried to detonate it. But they were left with their tongues on their asses, as they say. I'm joking, but it was a tragedy. Those boys came back crying. When the Germans passed that way and the mine didn't detonate, we threw a few grenades after them, out of sheer frustration and fury, but we didn't hit any of them. But we threw them! To show them! Then we

---

38 p. 493 Glossary.

went back onto our turf. That was April 19. On April 20, Toebbens, the owner of the 'shop, called his Jewish line managers, and started shouting at them. He told them he didn't want that gang, meaning us, on his premises. "What goes on in the central ghetto is nothing to do with us. We have one duty—to work. And nothing will happen to anyone who works. And we have a second duty—we have to get all these machines out of here, because the factory is to be evacuated to Trawniki, and we are to carry on working there." That's what he said, that Toebbens. We knew what that meant: work for as long as you're needed, and then to the gas chamber.[39] But it was easier not to believe that, you understand? It wasn't that we didn't believe. We believed that it was true, but it was easier... Perhaps even so, perhaps even so? We all wanted to delude ourselves, do you understand that? Eliezer came to us and told us that we had to be ready for the morning of April 20. We were to attack the Germans as they were walking along under the walls toward the central ghetto. That lunge of ours was to be a sign of solidarity with the central ghetto. We weren't going to wait until the German came to us, until he had destroyed one ghetto and would come into the next. Eliezer said that he would throw the first two grenades, and then we would all shoot. And so, we're standing there under the windows and waiting. We can hear them—coming in song toward the central ghetto. They're singing that song *Wir horten die Juden*...[40] They marched into the ghetto with that song. We can see them; they're marching in rows of five. It's a mass of armed soldiers, with heavy rifles, with grenades, just as they go to the front. So, they're walking along under the wall, and we can see them from the third floor. And then Eliezer took out two grenades and threw them, one after the other. That was our sign that the battle was beginning. A few bodies fell, and the rest started to move along under the wall. Then their officer started shouting at them, so they moved out from the wall a little and started shooting at the windows. There were only twelve of us, but they were pounding as if it were a regiment. The noise was terrible. During that shootout, Toebbens—he was at no. 74—came to the window and yelled: "*Nicht schiessen*, I live here! I'm Toebbens!" He was wounded. We were all certain that after a shootout like that, the Germans would come into the ghetto, but they didn't come in. They went on to the central ghetto.

How many Germans can have been killed on that occasion?
They say forty, but I don't know. We didn't count them at the time. Ambulances came to take them away. There was a group at no. 74, too, a communist one,

---

39 p. 496 Glossary.
40 *Wir horten die Juden*... (Ger.)—We're gathering in the Jews...

commanded by Hesiek Kawa. After that, the Germans were attacked at no. 36 by Beniamin Wald's group. And that's how the Germans went to the central ghetto that day, attacked every bit of the way. That was April 20. We found out later that the Germans had wanted to give the Führer a present: Ghetto Warschau Judenrein. Because April 20 was Hitler's birthday.

Was anyone from your group killed in that first onslaught?
Two days later, the first girl was killed; she was called Korngold [Lea]. No one had been killed from our group at that point.

Please go on.
That was April 20. Toebbens called the line managers in again, and started yelling at them again, and threatening them. He said that the workers had one day to report to 80 Leszno,[41] there was a collection point there, and they would go from there to the Umschlagplatz. But there was no one who would go there of their own free will; no one believed that anymore. A few months previously they would have gone. But now everyone had a shelter, a cellar of some sort, or an attic, and everyone went away and hid.

Did really no one go to 80 Leszno?
Well... A few groups went. They believed that they were going to Trawniki. I think they maybe took about five thousand people from the whole place that time.

And how many people were there in that area at that time?
Twenty thousand? There were forty-five thousand in the whole ghetto. But I wanted to talk about something else. While the "deportation to Trawniki" was going on, we received the order to send Chańcia Płotnicka, our kasharit, to Będzin. She was to tell them there what had happened where we were. She received her instructions from Eliezer Geller. I was there when he gave her the various letters. Eliezer told her that the next day she would be taken out of the ghetto somehow. And it was that next day that the workers went to the Umschlag. Michałek [Klajnwajs], me, and two other people were to take Chańcia to 80 Leszno, where a *werkszuc* was to be waiting for her. He was in our organization, Meir Szwarc, his name was, he was a Bundist, and, like Lilit, a courier for Eliezer. As we were walking down the street with Chańcia, a German patrol appeared out of an entranceway, and stopped us. "There's no way through

---

41 The gathering point for those being transported from the Warsaw ghetto to the extermination camps was at 84 Leszno.

here," they say. Michałek—he was very smart—said to the German: "My family is here, in this next house, and I want them to go to 80 Leszno with us." The German agreed and said that he would take them there. So, the German takes Michałek and Chańcia, and we're standing on the other side of the entranceway; they were on the street. And the German goes into the entranceway with them, while Michałek picks up some packages from the ground (there were packages left in every entranceway) and says: "I have family in the next house too, and I want to take them as well." But Meir Szwarc was waiting in the next entranceway, Michałek knew that. And as soon as he went in through the entranceway, he gave a sign to Chańcia and Meir to escape. But he himself opened fire. He killed one on the spot and wounded the other. Some other Germans heard the pistols, ran into the entranceway, and started shooting at them. They hit Szwarc. he got a round in his shoulder but managed to escape. He came to us in our cellar at 76 Leszno. That was Stefan Grajek's[42] shelter. He lived in that house.

What does "Stefan Grajek's shelter" mean? Did he build it?
It was a party shelter, where some people from Poalej Syjon Smol were in hiding: Lejzer Lewin,[43] Jochanan Morgensztern,[44] Stefan's wife, and others. Entrance to the shelter was by a password. You had to say: "Jan." That was our contact point. If we lost each other, we gathered there, and went on to our next job from there. Meir went to the shelter, marking the entire route with his blood. But luckily, the Germans didn't follow him, and our people washed the blood away quickly. Chańcia didn't come back.

What happened to her?
They caught her and sent her to Treblinka...

Please go on.
Now the difficult thing began. We had to shoot, but we weren't getting any grenades or new bullets. Our supply of ammunition ran out very soon; on April 23, I think. And precisely on April 23, the Germans started to go into the entranceways.

---

42 Stefan Szalom Grajek (1916–2008)—activist for the underground party Poalej Syjon Right in the Warsaw ghetto, later chairman of the organization of Jewish veterans. After the war he lived in Tel Aviv.
43 Lejzer Lewin—activist for the underground party Poalej Syjon Right and the Jewish Social Welfare (Pol. Żydowska Samopomoc Społeczna, ŻSS) in the Warsaw ghetto. After the war, he lived in Israel.
44 p. 419 Rereading the List.

We're on watch upstairs and observing which entranceways they're going into. Szymon Heller was with us. He was the only one who had a rifle, we had pistols, grenades, and Molotov bottles. Whenever we saw any Germans, we would give him a sign, and then he would open fire with his rifle. After each of these attacks, we would move along to the next building, and so the Germans thought that there were many of us and that we had a lot of rifles. But there was a small group of us, moving along from attic to attic, from house to house. And though we shot at them, it was all so meager in comparison with their force. We wondered what would happen when our bullets ran out. We decided that each of us would save our last bullet for ourselves, so as not to fall into their hands alive. Because every death is easier and lighter than Treblinka—and we knew what Treblinka meant. When I think about it all today—at the time, I didn't ask, I didn't know anything—but today, when I think about it, I don't recall us ever talking about retreating from the ghetto. Nobody talked about that. We only said that we wouldn't let ourselves be killed easily. So, what would happen when our arms ran out? Each of us knew what we had to do with our last bullet. The Germans are starting to go into houses. They had a different tactic every day, sometimes changing it every few hours. And we didn't have a well-functioning command; even communication between groups was poor. Eliezer came to see us again, on the third or fourth day, and told us what had happened in the brushmakers' factory. He told us that our mine had exploded. Oh, how delighted we were: something had succeeded after all! Eliezer also told us about the central ghetto: our boys had burned out two tanks there, and not suffered particularly large losses. That also gave us heart. But we're hungry. After a few days without food, we're hungry. What to do?

Wasn't there a stockpile of food?
There wasn't. How?! We only ate what we happened to find in an apartment—a little rice, a few potatoes. The bakeries weren't baking bread. If there were any stockpiles anywhere, people had taken them into their shelters. In the first days in the shelters there had been food to eat. But later? So, we were hungry. But at no. 76 there was a bakery on the ground floor. We went there. I saw that there was flour, I saw that there was an oven—there was everything, only there wasn't any yeast. So, I made bread without yeast. In wartime, bread can be baked without yeast. I baked three hundred flatbreads. That was the seventh or eighth night. We divided up that bread among all the groups in our area. Each group got a few of those flatbreads. That was all very well, but when I baked the bread, smoke came out of the chimney—and the Befehlsstelle was next-door. They must have seen the smoke, but they didn't come into the ghetto. The Germans didn't go into the ghetto at night. They came in in the morning and blew the oven up!

You said that the Germans frequently changed tactics.
Yes. After a few days, they started to use the Jewish police to search for people. They ordered them to go into houses, into cellars and apartments, and shout out that everyone was to leave the building because they were going to set them alight. People were very afraid of that; they didn't know what to do. Some started to come out. They went to 80 Leszno; a few every day, every day *ktsat*.[45] Those who had a good shelter stayed. We also decided to change our tactic. We came down from the attics and were in the courtyards more. The Germans started to enter apartments quietly and carry out ambushes. They informed their artillery on the Aryan side which house, which attic, we were shooting from, and then their artillery started firing on us. When the artillery started firing on the attics, then we went lower down. When the Germans saw that even the artillery wasn't working, they started to set houses alight. They set house after house on fire, and in that way, a great conflagration grew up. We already knew that fire from the central ghetto. And then we saw another, similar fire from Świętojerska. The three fires got larger and larger, and we had nowhere to retreat to. All our passageways were very useful in the first few days, but not later, when the houses started to burn. The Germans surrounded the house from which Szymon Heller had shot at them. Our whole group was in that house. They burst into our apartment, and then Eliezer gave the order to jump out of the windows into the courtyard. We jumped from the third floor. Some made it, they got through to Dawid Nowodworski.

How is it possible to jump safely from the third floor?
There was this mountain of garbage there, and we jumped onto that garbage.

Did anything happen to anyone when they were jumping?
Eliezer let himself down from a window by a sheet, and then jumped, but twisted his arm—it hurt him badly. Szymon Heller was the last to jump, and they shot him dead. They shot at him from a window, and he died on that mountain of trash. After some time, we went back to him, but his rifle was no longer there.

What did you do with his body?
We took it away. But where did we take it? Into the stairwell. We couldn't do anything with it. He was dead. The shootout was still going on the whole time . . . Houses were burning, and we were going about via their attics. Wooden structural beams were burning and crashing down in front of us.

---

45 *Ktsat* (Heb.)—a little.

And then we couldn't pass any further. We had to leave one house like that via the stairs. There was nowhere to go. We could do nothing more. We had no means; there was no ammunition. That was the most terrifying.

Do you remember when Szymon Heller was shot?
We left the ghetto on April 28,[46] after ten days of fighting. I think Szymon was killed on the eighth day. On the ninth day we were completely exhausted. What do I mean by exhausted? We had been going from shelter to shelter, from hospital to hospital; we had a number of wounded. The hospitals were in the shelters. One was at no. 76. There was even a real doctor there. I don't know what his name is, but I know that he is alive in America. Stefan Grajek told me that that doctor's alive, only that doctor . . . We had six wounded in that hospital. On April 28, we received the news—all fighters were to report to 56 Leszno, to the shelter. We were going to try to get out of the ghetto.

Were all the fighters from the Toebbens yard to meet there?
Those who received the news. Someone was sent to each group with that information. And the Jewish police was going about the ghetto and shouting: "Tomorrow we are starting fires, tomorrow we are starting fires! Come out!" Those words—"Tomorrow we are starting fires"—flooded the ghetto like a deluge. We had nowhere else to go . . . I remember that that day, before we went to 56 Leszno, we were also given the order to set the factory on fire. We had no more weapons, but we could start fires! They were starting fires in houses, and we in factories. Gasoline, and start a fire! A bigger and bigger conflagration . . . That night at 56 Leszno we found out from Eliezer that there was a way of leaving the ghetto via the sewers. And from there they would take us into the woods, and we would be partisans, and go on waging war against the Germans.

Do you know who organized the exit via the sewers?
All I know is that the previous day, Eliezer had sent Stefan Grajek out onto the Aryan side via the sewers. He had a safe house on the other side, at 27 Ogrodowa. There was already a group there that had left the ghetto previously. The janitor of that house on Ogrodowa was a PPR man, and he cooperated with the fighters. The way through the sewers was known to some extent because we had been obtaining weapons and information via the sewers. There were specialists for the sewers, including those who ran weapons.

---

46 In the night of April 28/29, 1943.

Does that mean that you didn't undertake any more major operations in the ghetto?

No. Eliezer sent ten fighters one more time to set factories on fire. I was among them. We went to 76 Leszno. And when we had carried out our task, we went into the shelter; it was in the same building as the factory. There were eight, maybe nine people there, a few of them party members, but civilians, without weapons. Eliezer wanted them all taken out of the ghetto with us. We took them all with us.

Who were the people that you took?

From Poalej Syjon Lewin and Morgensztern, the leaders of that organization. With them we first went to the hospital. I said, we had wounded there. I remember that to get into the hospital, you climbed through a tiled stove ... That meeting with the wounded was very difficult. We already knew that we were going out into the woods, but we couldn't tell them anything. Because they couldn't go out with us. Can you imagine that? Eliezer went up to Meir Szwarc—he had a wounded shoulder, not his legs, and he could walk—and asks him: "Tell me, can you go all that way with us?" Meir answered that he could. "Then I'll take you!" Then Eliezer turned to Guta [Kawenoki]: "Guta, you're staying here. We can't leave the wounded alone without help."

Guta wasn't wounded?

No, she wasn't wounded. I often thought about that. At that point, Guta started to cry terribly. She said: "Because I'm a woman, I'm no good for the partisans?" And all this was going on in the room in front of the stove, with the wounded lying on the other side.

But they didn't hear it?

No, they couldn't hear. Guta begged Eliezer to allow her to go with us, that she wanted to fight. And then Leja Korn—I said I would say more about her—whispered to Eliezer: "Eliezer, I'll stay."[47] And she didn't wait for an answer. She went straight inside through the stove. I'll never forget that moment. Leja stayed there. And staying meant waiting for them to burn the house down. Szwarc went with us. That same night, we went down into the sewer for the first time. That was in the night of April 28. One of us smelled gas. We thought that it was the Germans, and we started to retreat.

---

47 Cf. Hela Rufeisen-Schüpper, *Pożegnanie Miłej 18: wspomnienia łączniczki Żydowskiej Organizacji Bojowej*, (Krakow: Beseder, 1996), 101: "Lea Korun volunteered to stay with the wounded."

But how we went down into the sewer is a whole story in itself as well. First, we enlarged the opening that the smugglers had used to traffic goods; we took out a few bricks. The first people to go down into the sewer had no experience and didn't really know how to do it. If they went down headfirst, they couldn't get any further, because the sewer was deep. So, they came out and went in again—this time feet first. And after that, one taught the next, and then it was easier.

How many people went down into the sewer on April 28?
I think that there were about thirty or so of us. So, when that first group drew back because of the gas, we decided to wait for Eliezer and the others. But Michałek [Klajnwajs] said: "If I had some planks, I could put them down inside the sewer and wait on them." Not far away, there was a bakery; I knew it. And of course, I know that in bakeries there are these boards which the bread is baked on. We took all the boards from the bakery. Each of us got one and was responsible for it. Later on, those boards were a great help to us, when we had to walk for such a long time, and on the way stop and wait, and then go on again. We went back into the sewer a second time that same night. We couldn't wait any longer. The fire was getting closer and closer. Before we set off, we waited for the people in the sewer. Perhaps someone else would come, perhaps someone else? There were about forty of us, from various groups, but all of us from the Toebbens & Schultz yard.

Who was the leader of that group?
Eliezer, our commander. But it was his first time in the sewer as well. Stefan Grajek, who knew the way, was already on the Aryan side. He was supposed to organize a truck and pick us up when we got out.

Did he organize it?
No, he didn't manage it. He got in touch with Icchak Cukierman, but he didn't manage it.

Was there anyone else in the sewer who knew the way?
No. None of us had ever been in the sewer before. The most important person was Geller. He gave the orders. And so, we started walking. We knew that we had to go in a diagonal line and get to 27 Ogrodowa. And that's how we went: in a diagonal line. Some of the sewers were so low that we had to walk bent over. There were also wide, deep, high sewers, but in those there was a lot of water. In the low ones there wasn't much water, but in the high ones it reached to our chests.

Dying

Not only water?
Yes, not only water. It stank terribly. We held our weapons above our heads so that they didn't get wet. We were tired, and hungry, and everything all together. We split up into groups. Some went through these sewers, some through others. In the low sewers we waited; we rested on the boards.

Did you have to wait, did you have to rest?
We had to wait because we didn't know how to go on.

So, one person went on in front, checked the route, and came back for the group, yes?
Yes. He checked this sewer and that sewer, and then we went on. We often had to go back and change our route. None of it was organized, of course, there was no plan.

How long did that "journey" last?
The "journey" went on until three at night. We thought that there would be a truck waiting for us ... At last, we reached the manhole. We thought—well, this should be the way out. But we couldn't all stand there because someone could have heard us. And only Eliezer and Nowodworski stood there and waited ...

For Grajek?
For Grajek. And there, up there, there were military police officers walking about. Finally, Grajek came, banged on the manhole cover, and shouted: "Jan!"—that was our password. So, we were to get out! Grajek had arranged with the janitor that we would go into 27 Ogrodowa, go up to the attic, and wait there until the next day. And the next day there would be a truck. There were Poles living at 27 Ogrodowa, it was not far from the manhole. But they lived on the lower floors; the other floors—up to the seventh—were empty. Quietly, like cats, we climbed out of the sewer.

Those forty people?
Those forty people! Each of us ran to the entranceway, then to the stairwell, and up the stairs right to the top, into the attic. We go into the attic, but we can't understand why they've taken us there. And then they tell us that the truck is coming the next morning.

Did everyone manage to get there safely?
Yes. Those forty people flitted across in complete silence. So, there we were in that attic. I can hardly speak of sleep because we were all wet. We wait until morning. But in the morning, there's no truck either. Stefan came with Eliezer. He brought us... bread rolls! This basket of fresh bread rolls. You're laughing?

Yes, because I can imagine these tormented people in stinking clothes, with bread rolls in their hands.
Precisely. Everybody got one bread roll, where they would have needed about two loaves of bread. Evidently Stefan couldn't procure any more.

That was the 29th?
Yes. At... it might have been nine thirty, Eliezer came again, without shoes, and without his leather jacket. What had happened? Some blackmailers had caught him. They had taken his money, his shoes—they had taken everything, and left him like that. Not Germans, Poles—*szmalcownicy*.[48] And he had had a gun! But he wanted to resolve it quietly, because he was afraid that they might discover us too. They caught him not far from Ogrodowa. We gave him something to put on. Eliezer told us that there was still no truck, and that we would have to wait until morning, because in the daytime we couldn't go anywhere anyway.

And how did you manage with your wet clothes?
Each of us had our own personal stove. The warmth of our body dried our clothes. First, we wrang our things out, and then they dried on us.

But there was no water?
None at all.

Only those rolls?
Well, not only them. After that there was also ersatz coffee.

Who brought the coffee?
Franka, a courier, but not from our beat. And then there was dinner—we got bread and sausage, and something to drink. The most important thing was for us to be quiet, so that nobody would hear us. That was very difficult. After all that we had been through, we couldn't sit so quietly for hours in the attic. At

---

48 p. 518 Glossary—*Szmalcownictwo*.

one point, from downstairs, from the courtyard, we heard shouts of: "Jew!" "Policeman!..." We were sure that they had discovered us. Do you understand? We ready our weapons and are on full alert. We say: "Well, this is the end, the end of the Warsaw ghetto. Each of us has a bullet for themselves." And so, we wait ... But it turns out that it was some kids playing "Jews and policemen." After that, Eliezer came back again. He brought the information that a truck would be coming in the early hours of the morning. We tried to sleep a little, to rest. At four in the morning, it came. Quietly, we went down from the attic and onto the truck! Only the old ones from Poalej Syjon stayed behind. I think there were eight of them. Stefan took them to the shelter in the house on Ogrodowa. They were in no state for the woods. Sitting in the truck was a Pole from the PPR, Krzaczek.

The same one who took the other group of fighters out on May 10?
Yes. And Tadek [Tuwia Szejngut][49] from Haszomer Hacair was also there. He was shot dead during that second exodus from the sewer. There were thirty or thirty-two of us on the truck. We lay down side by side, our weapons hidden. The agreement was that if there was any trouble, we would throw grenades, and Krzaczek would drive on. It was early in the morning. People are starting to go out on the streets—this one with milk, that one sweeping up outside a house. And those people see us—oh my God! And they flee into their entranceways. We're headed out of Warsaw. We know that there's a turnpike at the city boundary and that there's a guardpost there. Krzaczek reminds us about the grenades again. He drives up to the guardpost. The Germans are checking more or less one in five. When Krzaczek drove up to them, they were in the process of checking someone. So, he swerved around them ... and drove on. They didn't shoot. We drove past. It worked! But it might not have worked.

It might not have ... How long were you in Łomianki?
I think we spent three weeks sitting in that coppice.

Did anyone bring you food?
Nobody brought us anything. Not only was there no food, but there was also no water either. Stefan had stayed in Warsaw; so had Eliezer. With us was Dawid Nowodworski; he was commander. We waited there for the partisans to take us into the woods.

---

49 p. 447 Rereading the List—Tadek (Tuwia) Szajngut (Szejngut).

So how did you manage for food?
Dawid Nowodworski was under order not to let us out of the coppice—nobody was to see us. But we had no water. So, we broke the order, and in the night, we would creep over to a well. We didn't have anything to eat, either. We had to think of something. We decided to organize some food without Nowodworski's knowledge. That operation was carried out by me and Michałek. Early one morning, we left the wood—I look like a Jew, he's similar to a Pole. We're walking through the young coppice toward the road. We stand at the roadside and wait. I on one side; he on the other. We see a peasant coming along in a cart.[50] Michałek goes out onto the road, and I stand on the other side, behind the peasant's back. Michałek asks him whether he has anything to eat. And then the peasant looks around and sees me. He quickly realized what was going on, and asked: "And where are you from?" "I jumped a train to Treblinka," I say, right away. "I'm a Jew. Can you help me at all? I'll pay you." "How can I help?" "You can buy me a loaf of bread and bring a little water." "And how will I bring it to you? Where will you be?" "We'll be right here, in the same place." I can see that he's a decent peasant; you can tell things like that straight away. But you have to be on the safe side. So Michałek and I agreed that we would go on one more kilometer in the direction of the village and meet him there. If he came with the police, we would see them sooner. But he came alone and brought a loaf of bread. He didn't have water; he had milk for us. We paid him and asked him to come to the same place at the same time the next day and bring another loaf.

Did he come?
Yes. We divided up that first loaf among the hungriest. On the way to the coppice, we couldn't help ourselves and we drank a little of the milk. The next day we gave him money for bread again. We told him that we were with a family that had also jumped out of the train. Then the peasant told us that he was a party man, but not from the PPR; he was from some nationalist party. He was called Kajszczak. Later, he came to us with a whole cartload of bread. In Łomianki, Juda Wengrower from the central ghetto was with us. He had been at 18 Miła, and so in the coppice he was very sick—poisoned by gas. He had desperately wanted to drink in the sewer and had drunk that stinking water. He died a few days later in Łomianki. And then Kajszczak, with that cartload of bread... When he saw

---

50 This was Bronisław Kajszczak (codename "Sylwester"), a Pole, AK soldier, and resident of the village of Dąbrowa near Łomianki. Kajszczak and his son Józef supplied the Warsaw ghetto fighters with food in the Łomianki woods. He also gave shelter to Jews in hiding.

the dead Juda, he stood to attention, saluted, and said: "For the Warsaw ghetto fighters, I will do everything!"

When did you leave Łomianki to join the partisans?
We spent another few days with the other group, the one that came on May 10. Then, two trucks came and took us into the woods. There, each of our groups got two or three Russians who had escaped from prison, and they were our guides.

When did you leave Poland?
In May 1945.

But you didn't leave with the same group that Masza Putermilch left with?
No; we left shortly after them.

Via Romania?
Yes. In Bucharest we were given certificates, and on October 28 we arrived in Palestine.

Have you been to Poland since then?
No.

Will you go?
Perhaps. I want to. I'll come for the fiftieth anniversary of the uprising. I've sworn to.

I'm pleased. Thank you for our conversation.

Tel Aviv, May 1989 and October 1999.

Aron Karmi died in Tel Aviv on November 26, 2011.

Well, I'm Here, Aren't I?!

Conversation with Luba Gawisar

Tell me what year you were born in.
In 1924, in Warsaw, and more precisely still, in the Holy Ghost hospital.

What is your maiden name?
Zylberg. Listen, and I'll tell you.

Go on.
First, we lived on Wrzesińska, in Praga, and later in Saska Kępa. My father had a cigarette wholesale business, and Mama was at home. I had no siblings—I was this spoilt only child. Our family was assimilated, and my environment exclusively Polish.

Did your parents never speak Yiddish to each other?
Sometimes. But I disliked that very much.

Why?
I don't know, I didn't like that language. I remember that Cywia and Antek also used to speak Yiddish when they didn't want us to understand them.

So, you lived in a Polish world?
Yes, absolutely. I went to Polish schools; I had Polish friends. Only one of my girlfriends was a Jew. A very intelligent one . . . I met her later in the ghetto. She was in a very bad way—she looked terrible, and she was kind of strange. I don't think she had anything to eat, and she was ashamed to say so. I don't know what became of her . . . Anyway, before the war, I was a communist. When I was eleven, the nanny of the sister of that Jewish girlfriend of mine signed us up for Pionier,[1] a youth organization. The organization was illegal, of course. So, for me, an only child from a good home, it was all very exciting. I was a salon communist, you know.

---

1 p. 510 Glossary—Pionier.

And then came entirely non-salonesque times.
Yes. I remember the dreadful chaos in the soul of that spoilt only child. And of course, the thing with the Jews started right away. I simply couldn't understand what kind of a world I was in. And the armbands right away... Everything changed. My girlfriends, boyfriends, and on the other side me. And then we had to move into the ghetto. We went to live in a large room on Gęsia, close to Okopowa. In the same apartment there were some people who had come from outside Warsaw. We hadn't been able to take much with us into the ghetto, but I had all my books, and my journal.

Did you carry on writing in the ghetto?
Yes.

And what happened to your journal?
How should I know what happened to it?! The same as to everything! It went up in flames, most likely.

Tell me about your family's life in the ghetto at first.
I don't remember much. I don't think my father worked. He sold various things—Mama's furs, rings...

Do you remember the hunger in the ghetto?
Of course! People died of hunger.

But I'm asking about your family.
I didn't go hungry in the ghetto.

You worked, didn't you?
Yes. I worked at the post office.[2] I think it was on Grzybowska. That job was very important to me: I met some remarkable people there. Among us was a first violinist from the Warsaw Philharmonic, and Erna, the wife of a bank director. I loved Erna dearly! And then there was Leon Machtyngier,[3] the journalist. I liked him very much, too, he was very intellectual. Later on, when they liquidated the

---

2 The post office was on the corner of Zamenhofa and Gęsia Streets in what had formerly been a mansion belonging to Prince Stanislaus Augustus. The package office was on the corner of Grzybowska and Ciepła.
3 Leon Machtyngier—typographer for *Nasz Przegląd* (a Polish-language Jewish daily with Zionist leanings).

Arrests

small ghetto, the post office was moved to Gęsia, I think, and they ordered us to live there. I was with Irena [Gelblum], Jurek [Grasberg],[4] and some others. It was there that I tried to make the first soup of my life. It wasn't a success.

Did you see your parents?
Yes. Sometimes I went to see them, sometimes they came to see me. They didn't go hungry, only at that time there were constantly raids. I remember that we were constantly hiding. I survived one selection in the Community.

Did you get a "number?"
No, they took me to the left, and Erna, too—a great many people . . .

To the left, meaning for transport?
Yes. I remember that Gestapo officer, he was handsome. I was saved by an acquaintance of my father, who went up to the German and said something to him. Because I had some document in my pocket that was good at that point. But afterwards I went into hiding again. We had this hiding-place under the roof. I remember that we always got stomach aches and diarrhea during those operations.

Did your parents have any papers that protected them from deportation?
Mama worked at the Werterfassung. My father was at home, in hiding.

How did you get out onto the other side?
Well then, I shall have to tell you about Jurek Grasberg. We were married. Before we left the ghetto, some rabbi married us. Jurek was a scoutmaster, and had an older friend, Professor Kamiński.

The same Kamiński that pulled Marek Edelman out of the cellar?
I don't know anything about that. Do you think it was the same one? Such a small world! Kamiński played a very important role in my life on the Aryan side. He helped me a lot. Well, Jurek wanted to organize a group of scouts that would cooperate with the ŻOB. I know that Anielewicz didn't agree to that. He said that scouts could join the organization individually, but not as a group. One day, Jurek informed me that I was going out onto the Aryan side. I had the perfect looks, the Polish, too, without a trace of an accent: after all, I didn't know Yiddish. The plan

---

4 p. 388 Rereading the List—Jurek Grasberg.

was to rent an apartment that would be a point of contact with the ghetto. The ŻOB was also to make use of the apartment. And so, I went out . . .

When, do you remember?
Don't you ask me about dates—I never remember dates. It was between the first and the second Aktion. You know, I have no sense of time at all in terms of the past.

How did you get out?
Through a bribed *wacha*. Some Jewish policeman took me out. Jurek arranged it all. He gave me the address of some woman in Wola, I wrote the telephone number of Kamiński's courier down somewhere on my body, and I went out . . . On the other side of the wall, I took my armband off, and I was immediately set upon by some *szmalcownicy*, two young Poles. I told them to leave me be, that I was a Pole and I had been out looting. "You're a Yid, we're going to the police!" I don't remember whether or not I gave them money . . .

But they left you alone?
Well, I'm here, aren't I? But that was just the beginning.

Did you manage to say goodbye to your parents?
What a question! I saw them two or even three times more after that. I went in and out between the ghetto and the Aryan side . . . Listen, I don't know how it is that I can sit here so calmly and just tell you about it. Well, anyway. I went to that woman's place in Wola and called Kamiński's courier. I think I was there for a few days, waiting for papers. The only contact I had at that point was with my girlfriend, a Polish girl. Her father was a carpenter, and Alina was beautiful, only terribly dark-haired. I was always dreadfully scared when I walked along the street with her. One morning, very early, two Gestapo agents came into my room in that apartment in Wola. "Papers!" "I don't have any." "You don't have any because you're a Jew!" I don't know what that woman might have had to do with that.

So, what happened?
Nothing special. I'm here, aren't I? One of them was a Pole, a *Volksdeutsche*, and the other a German. He had a ratlike face that I'll never forget. "Get dressed!" he said to me. "Whether you are or you aren't, we're going to the Gestapo." "Very well." I got dressed. Then the *Volksdeutsche* took me into another room and said: "Listen, you know Jews on the Aryan side." "Of course I do," I said.

But you didn't say who you were?
No, but it was completely obvious. I had no papers, I had nothing, and I was still such a little girl. And here he was, telling me that I had the right looks, and that he would give me an apartment on Nowy Świat, and the right papers, and money. But I knew, even in the ghetto, that there were Jews who collaborated with the Germans. All I had to do was tell him where Jews lived, and after a while they would send me abroad—that's what he said. Incredible working conditions, no? And though I had never been in a situation like that, I think my survival instinct told me how I should react. You know, when I talk about it today, I think it's like a fairy story.

It's all unreal.
Unreal, a different incarnation, different, like it's not my life. Well, so they believed me. They let me stay there and arranged to meet me the following day near the philharmonic. They left, and within half an hour, I was out of there.

And where did you go?
To Alina's. But shortly after that, Kamiński came. And he helped me a great deal. By then, there were no Jews left in the small ghetto. And all those houses were now at the disposal of the city hall, and you could rent an apartment there. So, Kazimierz—that was Kamiński's codename—went there with me, as my uncle. (At that point he was already the editor of *Biuletyn Informacyjny*.[5]) He helped me to rent an apartment at 5 Pańska. There were two rooms and a kitchen in the attic. Alina's father installed a high bookshelf under the roof, and underneath it he made a drawer that could be pulled out. So, if there were Jews staying with me, there would be a hiding-place. Because of course Jurek was supposed to be coming, and my parents, and maybe someone from the ŻOB! And there would have to be somewhere to hide weapons.

Were you afraid of what was going to happen on Pańska?
I don't think so. But in fact, I can't recall what state I was in at that time.

In a sense, life on the Aryan side was more dangerous than in the ghetto.
No, absolutely not. I found it a lot better on the Aryan side. Anywhere but there, anywhere but in the ghetto! What would be, would be. It would all be over

---

5   *Biuletyn Informacyjny* was the leading press organ of the AK.

sometime, anyway. I was very busy and didn't spend too much time ruminating on it all. Only I missed my parents very much. And once, I went to see them. I went in with the Poles who went looting. And I was coming out with them, but right outside the wall, some Shaulists[6] caught us. And they just took us.

Where to?
They always took people to the Gestapo. But I didn't get that far—after all, I'm here now, aren't I? At one point I thought to myself: I have nothing to lose. And I escaped into an entranceway, and up some stairs into an attic. They chased around, yelling. But I'm here. And the second time I went into the ghetto, the January campaign was in progress.

What do you remember?
My mother and father were living on Stawki at that point. I remember we were standing on some square, and then we managed to hide. The next morning, I went out via the wacha. There were no Germans there, only a Polish and a Jewish policeman—I gave them money. My father walked me there. That was the last time I saw them. I slept with my mother in her bed that night in the ghetto. She gave me this ring.

You went back to Pańska.
Yes. And Alina's father even bought me furniture at the market. And then Irka came, and Jurek came. He hadn't been able to get my parents out, I don't know why. Mama had the worst sort of looks—blue eyes, but too dark hair. They were in the ghetto to the end.

Do you know any details?
No. They perished. Like everyone. They were very pleased that I was on the other side.

Tell me a little about life on Pańska.
Tadek [Tuwia Szejngut] would sometimes come over. Someone would bring weapons, or I would go somewhere and bring weapons home. And Tadek would take them into the ghetto.

---

6 "Shaulists" (Lit. Šauliai)—members of Lithuanian and Latvian nationalist riflemen's associations who volunteered in German police units and participated in the extermination of the Jews.

Were those pistols and grenades?
Just pistols.

Do you remember how much you paid for them?
No. Jurek paid. I didn't know anything about the financial issues. Before the uprising, Antek came. Instead of Jurek [Arie Wilner]. His role was to maintain ties with the Polish underground, and to procure arms for the ghetto, of course. And during the uprising, Kazik [Ratajzer] appeared.

But Antek wasn't yet living with you at that point?
No. We were together later. I don't remember what den he had at first. Well, and then the uprising broke out. We were sitting in the evening by the window, and Antek was with us. The window was open. But we were on the floor because someone could have seen us. My neighbor was a glazier. "Mrs. Kowalska, close your windows, or some Jew will come crawling inside," he called to me. And the ghetto was on fire. I went down there by the ghetto a few times. Where was the merry-go-round?[7]

On Krasińskich Square.
Yes, of course! I went down there several times. But it was dangerous; people could see what was playing out on my face. And then Kazik came to Pańska with that letter from Anielewicz.[8] Kazik doesn't remember that. But I remember him standing with Antek in the third room, and Antek was white and red, and Kazik had these three-quarter-length pants on. And they read the letter. Anielewicz wrote about how our dream had come true, you know, that there

---

7   Before Easter 1943, a merry-go-round was put up on Krasińskich Square in Warsaw which probably continued to operate in the initial days of the uprising. It belonged to a local funfair. Visible from inside the ghetto walls, and recalled by Polish and Jewish witnesses alike, it came to be seen as an unequivocal symbol of the attitudes of parts of Polish society toward the Jewish uprising, and more broadly to the extermination of the Polish Jews. The writer Czesław Miłosz, who described the merry-go-round in his poem *Campo di fiori* (1943), made it an enduring metaphor for the Poles' indifference toward the murder of the Jews.

8   The famous letter from Mordechaj Anielewicz to Icchak Cukierman, dated April 23, 1943, with the words:

"[. . .] my life's dream has come true. It has been my lot to see the Jewish defense in the ghetto—in all its greatness and glory . . .," was smuggled out of the ghetto by employees of the Pinkiert funeral parlor. The original, written in Hebrew, was lost along with the entire ŻOB archive at 18 Leszno during the Warsaw uprising. Cukierman's translation into Yiddish has survived, as has the translation into Polish made by Adolf Berman for the Polish underground. As Icchak Cukierman writes in his book *A Surplus of Memory*, the differences between the three texts are considerable.

was an uprising. It was very hard when Kazik came. You have to understand that I didn't really know what they were doing. I took care of the apartment. Later on, it proved very important—Cywia and Tuwia [Borzykowski] came there.

Who else came?
Marek, and a few months later Krysia [Sara Biederman].[9] They all came to Pańska when the apartment on Komitetowa was compromised. And later we organized them another apartment, on Leszno.[10] But I was on Pańska practically the whole time. Our courier, Edek, also a scout, was caught. He knew a huge number of addresses, so we moved out for a month, because we didn't know whether he wouldn't split. Many years later, in the kibbutz, Antek told me that Edek didn't betray anyone. I heard that he jumped out of a window at the Gestapo, but Kazik says they shot him in the street. At that time, Irena and I were living in Żoliborz, but Antek and Kazik spent the days roaming the streets. They got knocked about dreadfully. So even though we were very afraid, we went back to Pańska. I want to tell you about the evening on Pańska when we all finally returned there. One day, Antek said to me: "Give me the keys. I'm going back to Pańska, I don't have the energy to wander about like this anymore." "Alright," I said. "I won't give you the keys; come home this evening." I bought some food, lit the stove, and they gradually came back: Antek, Irka . . . I remember that evening as if it was yesterday. First there was a knock, our characteristic knock. Antek came in, his hat pulled down over his eyes . . . We sat by the stove until late at night, and Antek talked. He talked endlessly. He could tell stories like no one else—true ones and made-up ones. That was a magical night. At times, I forgot where we were. Shortly after that, they went to 18 Leszno, and I stayed with Jurek.

Did Jurek have counterfeit papers, too?
No; he looked like a hundred Jews. But I went about town, met up with the Jews whom we gave money to. I had people I looked after. But above all, I kept house and procured food. I had this huge bag, I remember . . . You know, I think that there were Jews in hiding in the apartment opposite ours.

Didn't the Poles suspect anything?
I don't think so. Everything was fine, except that they couldn't understand why Irena and I didn't go down into the shelter when there was an air barrage. I

---

9 p. 343 Rereading the List—Sara Biederman (Biderman), Krysia Serafin.
10 Cywia Lubetkin and Icchak Cukierman were in hiding before and during the Warsaw uprising in an apartment at 18 Leszno Street. The archives of the ŻOB and Dror were also kept there.

explained to them that we were terrified of the shelter. But in fact, we all sat up there and were delighted that they were bombing. And it never occurred to any of us that one of the bombs could fall into our place. You know, now I recall the feeling that was constantly with me at that time. It was like something's suffocating you all the time, but quietly. A constant tension, unease, that is unbearable. It's this silent depression that doesn't leave you, even for a moment, is with you all the time, like a shadow. Fortunately, there was always something going on. Antek was always sending me somewhere. I went to see Guzik[11] a few times. He was a representative of the Joint.[12] He gave me dollars for my wards.

And then came the Warsaw rising.
The day before the rising, Kazik came to Pańska and said: "Go to Grodzisk to see Krupnik and bring him back here."

Who was Krupnik?
Krupnik and Domb were two Jews. They had escaped from Pawiak prison a few months previously. They were in hiding in Grodzisk, living with some Poles. Antek had found out about them somehow and sent me there every month with money for them. So, Kazik came and said: "In a day or two there's set to be an uprising; go for Krupnik, he might come in handy." Krupnik was a sewerage engineer. The Germans had let them down into the sewers to repair something, and they had escaped from Pawiak via the sewers. Kazik said that there was a plan to rescue some Greek Jews from Pawiak, and that's why he needed Krupnik. It was very late, but Kazik said: "Go!" So, I went. I spent the night in Grodzisk, and in the morning, I took that guy Krupnik—he looked like a hundred Jews, but I bandaged him up here and there; his arm, part of his head—and we set off. In the same train, but separately. I wasn't allowed to sit next to him. I took him to the address that Kazik had given me. But what happened? While I was in Grodzisk, Domb and his wife started to cry: "Bring Irenka to us. Our only daughter, Irenka, is with a family in Saska Kępa. Bring Irenka to us." What could I do? And do you know who the family was?

---

11 Dawid Daniel Guzik (1890–1946)—financial director of the Joint (an American charitable organization) in Poland. He gathered and distributed funds for the ŻOB in the ghetto and on the Aryan side and supported Jews in hiding. After the war, he helped to organize illegal emigration to Palestine. Killed in an air crash in 1946.
12 p. 492 Glossary—American Jewish Distribution Committee.

Transport
Warsaw

Mrs. Strzelecka?
Yes, Jadwiga Strzelecka. Somehow, she found me here, in Israel, many years later.

But what happened then?
I went to Saska Kępa, the rising broke out, and that was it. I was stuck. No way back to Pańska—and Jurek alone there. Two or three days later, I went down to the river Vistula, by Poniatowskiego Bridge, and I thought: perhaps there'll be someone going to Warsaw. And then I see this boat, two young Germans. I started to tell them that my mother was on the other bank. And they told me that I wouldn't get through anywhere, that I wouldn't be able to get downtown. But they were very decent, because they told me that they could take me, and that they were coming back that afternoon, so if I wasn't able to get through, they would bring me back to Saska Kępa. And it did prove impossible for me to reach the city. I went back to Mrs. Strzelecka's.

How long were you stuck there for?
I was there until the end of the rising. Jadwiga tells me that after the rising, she went with me by train to Grodzisk, but I don't remember that. We took Irenka back to her parents. Three years ago, someone called me up and said, in Polish: "This is Irena." "Irena who?" I asked. "Irenka, I was called Domb." "That little girl??" I asked. And she said: "An old woman!" She's a psychologist, she lives in Argentina, and she has a granddaughter now. And that's the whole story.

While you were in Kępa, Jurek Grasberg was killed on Pańska, on the first day of the uprising, I believe. Do you know anything else about his death?
Kazimierz [Aleksander Kamiński] knew how it happened. While I was still living in the kibbutz, Kazimierz wrote me a letter in which he told me explicitly that he knew that it was people from the AK who killed Jurek. He wrote that Jurek had begged them to get in touch with Kamiński, that he would vouch for him... But I think they were in a hurry.

Do you know if they killed him in the apartment or in the courtyard?
Definitely not in the apartment. I know that he left the apartment with a gun, the idiot! He wanted to fight; he was going to join the rising.[13]

---

13 This is how Icchak Cukierman tells the story: "When the rising broke out, Luba was stuck in Praga and Jurek in the locked apartment. One day passed, and then another. Jurek heard shots. And he must have understood what was happening and gotten excited. When he had nothing left to eat, he started pounding on the door for someone to let him out. The neighbors

And after that?
After that, we were all in Grodzisk. I met Ala Margolis and Inka [Adina Blady-Szwajgier] on the street. And Lodzia [Silverstein] was with us too, and Cywia, Marek, Tuwia [Borzykowski] . . . Before that, they had been in Żoliborz, on Promyka Street. They stayed there after the rising, and we had to get them out of Warsaw somehow. So, I went to Kraków for Kazik—he was the expert on the sewers. But they got out somehow with a paramedic patrol. When we came back to Grodzisk, the people from Promyka were already in our apartment. The next day, we had a major delousing, I remember. We stayed in Grodzisk until the end of the war. I traveled a lot because there was nobody else who could. I went to Częstochowa, and I took money to Stefan Grajek in Kielce.

And what was he doing there?
Hiding out. He was always in hiding. And do you know that downstairs in that house in Grodzisk there was a military police precinct? It was a very good place. Somehow, we managed to survive there until the end. When we heard the army entering the city, we all went out onto the street. And when I saw the tanks, I don't know what happened to me. I got some kind of terrible hysteria, and I fled back into the house. I cried and cried and couldn't calm down. It was so empty and hopeless. It was then that I really felt how lonely I was. It was hard after the war altogether. In some respects, it was harder than during the war, when you were constantly on alert. But after the war there was nothing. There was nothing left . . .

You recently came to Poland for the first time since 1945, since you left.
Yes. I found it very hard. But I was moved by Warsaw, which was once my city.

Thank you, Luba.

Tel Aviv, May 1989 and October 1999.

Luba Gawisar died in Tel Aviv on November 8, 2011.

---

came, opened the door, and apprehended him. He tried to explain something to them, told them that he was a close friend of Hubert [Aleksander] Kamiński, one of the leaders of the AK, and hoped that they would believe him. But they turned him over to the Polish military police, which had formed hastily, and he was killed there." This version of Jurek Grasberg's death differs from that recounted by his wife, Luba Gawisar. There is no trace of the source of Cukierman's information.

Truth Be Told, I Left My House in 1942 and Never Went Back

Conversation with Adina Blady-Szwajgier

These are the photographs I took in the Lohamei Ha-Getaot kibbutz.
Yes. I saw Antek and Celina there. Her I'd met before, in Poland. Oh, these are photographs from our years together. This is how I remember them. Antek was in Poland, too. Before 1968. After that he looked terrible. I saw him in *Shoah*.[1]

And this is the grave of Tuwia Borzykowski.
Well, if you had told them then that they would die in Israel, normally, in bed, they would have considered it a miracle. You envied everybody who died. Few people could answer the question: "What's with your parents?" with: "Luckily, they're dead."

Did they say that with a sort of bitter irony?
No, entirely seriously. "Luckily, they're dead."

You saw the insurrectionists when they came out of the sewer.
Yes, yes. Only I was a long way from the manhole; I was around the corner.

Was that on May 10?
Yes. I don't remember much. Dirty, unshaven, bent over, and they're climbing onto a truck. There were some people there watching.

How long did it take?
Seven minutes, five minutes? To me, it took a year. Faster, faster, faster, and the fear—that's all I remember.

---

1   *Shoah*—nine-and-a-half-hour French documentary about the extermination of the Jews in Treblinka, Auschwitz, and Sobibór, made by Claude Lanzmann in 1985.

Did you go to see them in Łomianki?
No, I never went there. A few days later I met up with Marek on Śnieżna.[2] And I'll tell you a brief story about Marek. It was a beautiful July day. That was back before the ghetto was sealed. I had come to work at the hospital in a very pretty prewar two-piece crepe suit. The fact that it was crepe is important because that's a material that shouldn't get wet. I went to the window, and there, outside the building, Marek was watering the lawn. When he saw me in the window, he calmly turned the hose on me. I leaped out of the window—it was the first floor—and we started to fight on the grass.

That was a long time ago, wasn't it?
Yes, but you know, an old person, even though they are physically very tired, and can't do much, is still the same on the inside. Perhaps they just understand a little more than before. What's known as tolerance I think is a function of age. All the rest is the same—the dreams, the feelings, the desire for action: you're still the same. It's only the awareness of your own impotence that forces you to change the way you look at the world. And that's probably why you remember the past so well in your old age and return to it increasingly frequently.

When did you first go to Israel?
It was 1970. Precisely when it was all kicking off in Poland; it was December.[3] I was in Paris at the time, and I went there on a pilgrimage for Christmas. That was the cheapest way—and it was the only way I could get to Israel back then. I was in Israel for just three days. I went to see my father—I hadn't seen him for forty years.

Adina Blady-Szwajger or Szwajgier? Inka Świdowska. So many names.
Ah, I didn't learn the story behind the first part of my maiden name, "Blady," until I graduated from high school. Have you ever heard of the Cantonists? Under the tsars Nicholases, young boys were called up into the army. Jewish children were taken for forty years. They didn't take only sons. So, Jews would give their boy children up to Ukrainian peasants for adoption. And my great-grandfather on my father's side was one such child given up for adoption—hence the Ukrainian surname "Blady." But my great-grandfather's surname was Szwajgier. After the war, they lost the "i" in my surname. Inka is the same as Adina, and the surname Świdowska is from my second husband.

---

2   Marek Edelman claims that it was at 24 Śmiała Street (conversation with H.G., January 1, 2000).

3   This is a reference to the workers' strikes on the Baltic coast in December 1970.

So, you didn't take the surname of your first husband, Szpigielman?
We never had a civic wedding.

What about the wedding you mention in your book?[4]
That was a religious wedding. Before the war, you had to have a religious wedding to be able to have a civic wedding. We were married by Rabbi Posner, a military rabbi.

What was your occupation surname?
Meremińska. And that wasn't a random surname. The funniest thing is that it was a Jewish surname, it was the surname of friends of ours, who were already dead back then. It was important to have a surname that you wouldn't forget if anything happened. There were cases like that. But I couldn't forget that surname because they were my parents' closest friends.

I know that you were born on March 21, 1917, in Warsaw, in the same house that your mother was born in, at 30 Świętojerska. It was a long, corridor-like, three-room apartment, because that's what Warsaw apartments were like before the war, that's what you told me. You lived with your mother and grandmother; your father was not present. You only met him many years later, in Israel. Would you like to tell your father's story?
Well, my father was a Nansen passport holder,[5] a stateless citizen. I think he was a member of the SR; he didn't like the Bolsheviks. As a student he was sent into exile for *posyelenie*.[6] From there, he escaped to Poland during World War I. He studied biology. He was a Russian Jew from a very devout family. He had run away from home because he wanted to study. He came from Chernobyl—or Radomyśl; that's what it was called. But here in Poland, in 1920, I think, Nansen passport holders were held to be potential friends of the Bolsheviks. So, his right to remain was rescinded, and he had to leave. We used to meet up with him at Zionist congresses in Europe. After that, he came back to Poland once more, in 1926. But when he left again, in 1927, we didn't see each other until 1970. Mama didn't want to go to Palestine. Above all, she had never been a Zionist, didn't know the language, and apart from that, my grandmother was still alive then, and couldn't be left.

---

4 Adina Blady-Szwajgier, *Wspomnienia lekarki* (Zeszyty Niezależnej Myśli Lekarskiej, Warsaw: Niezależna Oficyna Wydawnicza, 1989).
5 Nansen passport—an identity document for refugees and stateless citizens introduced on the initiative of Fridtjöf Nansen in 1922.
6 *Posyelenie* (Rus.)—forced resettlement.

And what kind of a family was your mother from? A more assimilated one?
Absolutely. My grandmother's family had still been religious; her father was a *gabbe*, gabbai. That's something like a sacristan; it's not a *shammes*.[7] A gabbe is like an "under-rabbi."

That was your great-grandfather? Your grandmother's father on your mother's side?
Yes. But all his children were assimilated. My grandmother—I have no idea how this came about—was brought up in a Polish noble family in Izabelin, on the Niezabitowski family estate near the eastern border. But she did go to the synagogue once a year.

On Yom Kippur?[8]
Of course. And she prayed at home at the festivals. She had this beautiful prayerbook, bound in leather, with an ivory clasp. Naturally, there was no question of a kosher kitchen or anything like that in our home. But there was one amusing story connected with my grandmother. It was this: at Easter, she didn't eat bread. In that monstrously unkosher household, where bread and matzah both lay on the table, my grandmother would only eat matzah. Only... she ate that matzah with butter and ham!

And your mother's father?
I didn't know him. He died tragically; in 1914, I think. He was a merchant with a very small factory making uppers for boots, and he had some business with Russia. He went to Russia on business and never came back. He was killed by the carrier and robbed. I know that the carrier stole his entire portfolio of bills of exchange—a fortune. That meant that my mother had to break off her medical studies at the Sorbonne and went back to Warsaw to my grandmother and started work. Later on, she graduated in biology. But as for assimilation, well, those are all erroneous terms.

Let's talk about that for a moment.
Well, at present, the term "assimilation" is used to describe the departure of those people from Judaism. Well, no, that's not true. Here we can speak of external assimilation, assimilation in terms of clothing, and language—after all, they spoke Polish. But that didn't change the fact that they were Jews.

---

7 *Shammes*—rabbi's assistant who takes care of the synagogue.
8 Yom Kippur—the Day of Atonement; a fast, and the holiest day in the Jewish calendar, marking the end of the ten Days of Awe.

And they were aware that they were Jews.
But absolutely, absolutely! That whole vast stratum that was the Jewish intelligentsia never for one moment lost the sense that they were the Jewish intelligentsia. There were Zionists among them, there were some who, the language issue aside, agreed with the Bundists: here, where we are, we are citizens of this country with equal rights.

Could you define more precisely what this awareness of their Jewishness meant, aside from their awareness of distinctness?
It wasn't an awareness of distinctness! Do you consider that if someone considers themselves a Pole, that is an awareness of distinctness? No! That is my own culture existing alongside the Polish culture, which is also my own. I pray elsewhere, I do not agree with the interpretation that Christ was God. In the Jews' understanding, Christ was one more prophet. Had he been the Messiah, the world would have been saved. But it hasn't! Some people can be Protestants; some can be Greek Catholics.

So, it's above all a difference in faith?
Not only. It's a difference in traditions, in culture.

But tradition and culture—particularly in Judaism—have their roots in religion, in faith.
I don't know. I don't think so. I'm talking about people who emancipated themselves from religion entirely. And the Jews emancipated themselves from religion more than other nations. That happened out of necessity. Remaining within their religion was tantamount to remaining within a cultural ghetto. But that didn't mean that those people became unbelievers. It's amusing, but most of those who called themselves assimilated went to the synagogue once a year.

What school did you attend in Warsaw?
I went to a Jewish school; the language of instruction was Polish, but we learned Hebrew. Before the war, one didn't go to elementary school; there were eight or nine classes in high school. It was a rather Zionist-oriented, secular high school; there were no religious studies classes.

Was it Jehudija, the girls' high school where your mother was the principal?
Yes. Eight classes a week in Hebrew: four classes of literature and language, and four classes of history of the Jews, including the history of the religion. So, I was absolutely brought up in a Jewish cultural milieu.

Were there lots of Jewish schools in Warsaw?
Oh yes, lots, a great many. One moment—what do I remember? Kalecka, Posnerowa, Pryłucka, Jehudija, Hawaceles... And then the boys' schools—the Merchants' Congregation, Hinuch, Laor... I think there were about ten Jewish schools.

Were they state-supported?
In Warsaw two girls' schools and I think two boys' schools were supported by the state. The rest were private. At Jehudija, the income from fees went toward the upkeep of the school.

How long was your mother principal of that school?
For twenty-five years. At first it was a four-grade school on Dzielna Street, later it gained the status of a state high school.

After your high school finals in 1934, you went to Warsaw University to study medicine. What was studying in Warsaw like between 1934 and 1939?
Well, it was inevitably something of a shock. You have to understand—I mentioned it—we were, even in spite of our profound connections with Polish culture, with theater and literature, immersed in a Jewish environment—entirely. We didn't encounter antisemitism on a day-to-day basis—until university.

I suppose so. You can hardly have encountered it, given that you were living in a Jewish environment.
And if we did have contacts with Poles, it was with those who wanted those contacts with us.

Did your mother have any Polish friends who visited your home?
No. But very few people came to our home at all. My mother worked all the time—during the day at school, and in the evening at Jewish courses for the illiterate.

In that case, what notion of antisemitism did you have as a seventeen-year-old going to university?
The whole idea seemed blown out of all proportion to me. It was as distant as talking about pogroms in the Ukraine. You see, I lived on the edge of the Jewish quarter, on the corner of Świętojerska, near Krasińskich Square, and my closest friends were the children of the janitor—who was in fact the only Catholic in the tenement.

We talked about assimilation. What do you think about attitudes like Hirszfeld's?[9]

Ah, Hirszfeld is an entirely different story. Hirszfeld was from a very religious family, as was his wife, but also a very rich family. The Hirszfelds were Warsaw restauranteurs. One of their restaurants was the Piccadilly restaurant on Bielańska, in the Jewish quarter. It was known for its chulent,[10] which attracted the whole of the government every Saturday. The Hirszfeld family had a lot of restaurants, as well as a pasty shop on Nowy Świat. Hirszfeld himself committed apostasy purely and simply for the sake of his career. Purely. He was a world-famous scholar and wanted to be the director of the Hygiene Institute, but he was told outright that only a Roman Catholic could be director of the Hygiene Institute. So, he apostasized today, and received his nomination tomorrow. Before the war you couldn't be a Jew to be a director. And that's why the Hirszfelds weren't liked on the Jewish street, or later on in the ghetto. Jews don't like apostates at all, you see, but situations when people change their religion out of conviction can be open to some degree of understanding. It's hard to hold anything against Cardinal Lustiger[11]—who in any case never denied that he was a Jew. I'll tell you another story. In Poland there was a lady doctor called Dr Szymańska.[12] And that lady, and an immensely intelligent, brilliant woman she was, also changed her confession—during the war. In February 1945, I was working in the Central Committee of Jews in Poland.[13] One day, Dr. Szymańska showed up there, who had been a fairly close acquaintance

---

9   Ludwik Hirszfeld (1884–1954)—physician, microbiologist, immunologist and serologist, an outstanding scientist. During the war he spent time both in the Warsaw ghetto and on the Aryan side. From 1945, he was a professor at the University of Wrocław. Hirszfeld's name became a metonym for behaviors typical of apostasized and assimilated Jews who refuted identification with the Jews.
10 Chulent—a hot dish (meat on the bone, beans, onions, and potatoes, often served with kishke), kept in the oven from Friday and served for dinner on Shabbat.
11 Jean-Marie Lustiger (1926–2007)—until 1940 Aron Lustiger, a French Roman Catholic clergyman and theologian of Jewish descent. From 1981 archbishop of Paris, and from 1983 a cardinal.
12 Dr. Zofia Rozenblum-Szymańska (1888–1978)—physician, social activist, initiator and founder of the Friends of Children Society's Pedagogical Clinic. Prior to 1939 she conducted research in Dr. Korczak's orphanage. She was head physician in the Institute for Children with Special Needs in Otwock. When confined to the ghetto, and later in hiding on the "Aryan side," she helped others. After the war she lived and conducted her scientific work in Warsaw. In 1979 her memoirs were published under the title *Byłam tylko lekarzem* [I was only a doctor] (Warsaw: Instytut Wydawniczy PAX, 1979).
13 Central Committee of Polish Jews (Pol. Centralny Komitet Żydów Polskich, CKŻP), Poland-wide Jewish organization with its roots in the Jewish Committee founded in Lublin in July 1944 and liquidated in 1950. It brought together all the Jewish parties in Poland, except religious factions. Its main functions were to bring aid to survivors, repatriate Jews from the USSR, and organize Jewish emigration from Poland.

of my mother's. She had returned from some convent, where she had been in hiding. She looked dreadful—she was a very ugly woman in any case; there are some like that. Because I knew her, I took her home with me. At the time, I was living with my husband and my mother-in-law in Grochów. I was a little apprehensive because my mother-in-law was a small-minded kind of Catholic. But to my astonishment it transpired that the two ladies were as sweet as honey to each other. One day, Mrs. Rozenblum—Dr. Szymańska—and I were walking toward what is now Wiatraczna roundabout. Back then there was a statue of the Virgin Mary there. At one point, by the statue (I was to Mrs. Szymańska's right), I was almost smacked in the mug: she crossed herself with such flourish that I jumped backward. I tried to pretend that nothing had happened, but I failed. And at that point she told me a story. Before the war she had worked in a patients' fund. She had a patient there, a herring trader, I think, a Mrs. Chana Ogórek, who had six children. And back then, a home visit cost money. One day, Dr. Rozenblum came to work to her insurance fund, and found out that this Mrs. Ogórek had paid for tabs for a home visit for all six of her children. They had all fallen sick, and that on a Friday. The doctor was terrified because it could have been diphtheria. She hurried over. She comes into the room, and there—the table laid with a white cloth, on the table a challah loaf, and Mrs. Chana Ogórek in her holiday wig and holiday clothes.[14] "Mrs. Ogórek, what happened? Where are the children?" "My children are out on a walk." "So, what happened?" "Ma'am, if I had asked you to come to have fish with a poor Jewess, would you have come? No! But I bought six tabs for half an hour apiece, so you have three hours for us. Please sit down, ma'am, and you shall eat the Friday supper with us." And so during that walk, Dr. Szymańska said this to me: "You see, I have been through various potential philosophical systems, but when all that happened, in order to be able to go on living, I had to believe that my sister, my loved ones, and Mrs. Chana Ogórek with her six children are there somewhere, are alive somewhere, and that I would be able to meet them again. And I found that in Christianity. I didn't stop being a Jew, but I believe that I will meet them all again." Can one reproach her for changing her religion? There were not many such cases. As a rule, Jews changed their faith for the sake of their careers, to make their own or their children's lives easier. And that's why the Jews don't like apostates—you can be a non-believer, but to change your confession for the sake of your career is simply disgusting duplicity. And for that reason, the Hirszfelds were not liked in the ghetto. They were ostentatiously Catholic—and that was truly dreadful.

---

14 Orthodox Jewish women often shave their heads after marrying and wear a wig or turban instead.

Did you meet Hirszfeld again after the war?
Yes, in Wrocław.

Was he a pleasant man?
Well, I'm not objective. From the moment Hirszfeld had his book published,[15] we hated him.

Why?
Because his explanation that he left the ghetto because he wanted to salvage his dignity is inacceptable! The way to salvage your dignity was by staying in the ghetto. He simply got out because he had the opportunity. And everyone had the right to try and save their life. Apart from that, he ascribes to himself what above all Zweibaum did in the ghetto.[16] Zweibaum himself wrote a response to Hirszfeld in some article.[17]

And what about Makower?[18]
He was an entirely decent man, though not the wisest—after all, he wrote an exceptionally stupid book.[19] How can a physician write a book without writing about his hospital at all?! But he was truly decent. And the fact that he was a police physician[20] is not bad in itself. Aside from that, he was quite a doctor. And I have my own personal reasons to be grateful to him: when they took my mother to the Umschlag, he was the only person who had the courage to go there. He went at five in the morning. Except that it was too late. Those people had gone straight into the wagons.

---

15 Ludwik Hirszfeld, *Historia jednego życia* [The story of one life], Warsaw: Instytut Wydawniczy PAX, 1967.
16 Juliusz Zweibaum (1887–1959)—histologist, from 1945 a professor at the University of Warsaw and the Medical Academy in Warsaw. Author of a work on the epidemics in the Warsaw ghetto entitled: "Kurs przysposobienia sanitarnego z epidemiami w latach 1940–42" [A course in paramedic preparation with the epidemics in the years 1940–42] (*Archiwum Historii Medycyny* 1958, bk. 3/4).
17 Juliusz Zweibaum, "O książce L. Hirszfelda," [On L. Hirszfeld's book, in:] *Kuźnica* 1947, no. 13.
18 Henryk Makower (1904–1964)—before the war a doctor of internal medicine in Łódź; in the Warsaw ghetto head of the infectious diseases ward at the Berson and Bauman Hospital. He taught clandestine classes for medical students in the ghetto and was a physician in the Order Service. In January 1943, he and his wife fled the ghetto and went into hiding in Miłosna, outside Warsaw. After the war a professor of microbiology at the Medical Academy in Wrocław.
19 Henryk Makower, *Pamiętnik z getta warszawskiego, październik 1940 – styczeń 1943* [Memoirs from the Warsaw ghetto, October 1940—January 1943] (Wrocław: Ossolineum, 1987).
20 He was a physician employed in the Jewish police service in the ghetto.

The Street.
?, Różycki Bazaar in Warsaw, ?

Was that on July 30?
They took her on the 29th, and Makower went there on the 30th in the morning.

Did they take her from home?
From home, from home. I was at the hospital at the time.

And you never heard anything of your mother again?
No. All I know is that that transport went straight onto the wagons. I spent all night looking for someone who would go there, who would call, who would do something, who could...

You yourself couldn't...
What could I do?!

Didn't you find anyone earlier than that?
No. People were afraid... I asked one man, who was quite well known, but he was afraid. I dashed about all afternoon, all night... It wouldn't have done any good anyway—they went straight onto the wagons.

How did you find out...
Quite simply, I came home and there was no one there.

Had it been a street blockade?
Yes, the street, the street. And just a note left: "Honey paid for, coupons[21] cut out. Don't do anything stupid. Kisses to you." Honey paid for; coupons cut out... I still have that note.

Let's go back to your student years. To your real encounter with antisemitism.
Well, I studied at the time of the "bench ghetto,"[22] didn't I? Will that do?!

Let's talk about that. How many Jews were there in your year?
Well, the *numerus clausus* was in force. Ten percent could be accepted. So out of two hundred thirty or two hundred forty people, twenty were Jews. I remember the election of our year captain. Granted, they weren't all ND-ers,[23] but there

---

21 Coupons: colloquial name given to food ration cards in the Warsaw ghetto.
22 p. 513 Glossary—Prewar antisemitism in higher education.
23 p. 509 Glossary—National Democracy.

were enough of them for an ND-er to be elected year captain. That particular guy changed a lot later on. He was the son of Professor Loth, Felek Loth. But back then, he was a bludgeon-swinger, a knuckleduster. We essentially had no contact with the Poles at all.

Do you mean that it was the Polish side that was averse to any form of relations?
Absolutely, absolutely.

Did you personally experience any form of aggression?
The aggression came later. At that point there were just differences. In Professor Loth's labs, for instance, in the dissecting room, Jews would be given one specimen per three students, but non-Jews had one between two: because the Jews didn't supply enough corpses. I'm not even talking about the minor meannesses: "Oh, here comes Chajka," or the pushes and shoves. But the Jew-beating started in the spring of our first year. The troubles always flared up in the spring—God only knows why. I think some Polish student was killed in Lwów during some riots, and it all started on the anniversary of his death.

What was the beating like?
It even happened in the lecture theater. But usually, the gangs would gather in the university courtyard, and wait for a Jewish student to come along on their way to lectures.

Did the Jewish students defend themselves?
Oh yes. I never experienced a beating, but my closest friend took one on the noddle. And every year in the spring, they would close down the university. On the whole, we usually had no classes for half of the third semester. That's how we studied. Later on, I think I was in my third year, was when the "bench ghetto" began. One day, our grade record books were taken away, and when we got them back, there was a purple stamp in them: "Seat in odd-numbered benches." So, we didn't sit down again until the end of our degrees. There were only two lecture theaters where we sat down: in psychiatry, under Professor Mazurkiewicz, who refused to let his benches be numbered, and with Professor Michałowicz, who said: "I am a senator of the Republic of Poland, and no auditor is going to give me orders!" Of course, they smashed the windows in his clinic. And a few Jewish lecturers stood with us. There was this one Dr. Rychter. She came in for her lecture once and saw that half of the students were standing up, so she said: "Please sit down!" One of our fellow students

went up to her and showed her his grade record book, and she stood up, too. "This affects me, too," she said.

And were there no Polish students who came to your defense?
If there were thirty of them in my year, that was all. And do you know who they were? Above all communists. There was a group of students who had been relegated from Poznań, among them Helena Wolf. They stood firmly by us. There were also a few democrats, though not many.

Did you have any form of contact with Poles in private?
Not really, only at the university. They had their own medics' association and we had ours. They had Bratniak, and we had the Association of Jewish Medical Students. There was one joint organization, Życie,[24] and I belonged to that, and met up with left-wing Poles there.

And on the streets?
I never came into contact with anything like that. Probably because I wasn't recognizable; I didn't look like a Jew.

But what about the atmosphere on the street? How did the street take the ND right wing? What was the real extent of its influence?
I would say it was tolerated. They had extensive influence among young people for sure. I think it was a combination of the increasingly fascist atmosphere and the economic dissatisfaction—it was by no means as wonderful between the wars as they make out nowadays. And then there was a good deal of youthful stupidity in it as well. The saying went: "Whose fault is it? The Jews' and cyclists'!"

Is Polish antisemitism different to, say, French antisemitism?
No, it's the same phenomenon. Perhaps just on a different scale. Here antisemitism is more visible than elsewhere because the Polish street is very poorly educated. And antisemitism is nothing other than a form of ignorance. Moreover, the role of the clergy before the war cannot be over-estimated—it was dreadful. And this country has always been very Catholic and listened to the Church. Antisemitism is in all certainty a function of ignorance, just as every form of racism is a function of ignorance. And let us not forget that an educated person is not necessarily an enlightened one. Polish antisemitism is quite simply very

---

24 p. 508 Glossary—"Life" Socialist Youth Organization.

ordinary racism, you know—and that it is more pronounced than anti-Arabism, for instance? No wonder. One can dislike Arabs, or Czechs, and that's all it is. Things are entirely different when I don't like somebody whom I have to live with. And the other question is this: why do you think 1968 happened? It seems to me that it was precisely the intellectual Jewish youth that realized what they were facing, and initiated unrest. And the communists might have wanted to get rid of that element.

Is there any difference between prewar and contemporary Polish antisemitism?
You mustn't forget what role the Jews played in Poland after the war. In any settling of accounts of the crimes of Stalinism today... I can't say that there were no Jews involved. Don't think that there was no revenge in that. Jews are not angels.

People are not angels.
People aren't, but Jews aren't either.

Even so, I don't believe that that was the foundation of contemporary antisemitism.
It is certainly in part the foundation. You have to remember that the majority of the Jews who returned from Russia after the war went straight into the best positions, ones that they wouldn't have been able to hold before the war. It was easier for a Jew to obtain a position like that than for a Pole. That was a very clever policy of Stalin's.

Above all, it can be put down to...
...to Stalin's antisemitism, and to the fact that Jews were believed more than Poles. The Poles hadn't survived the Holocaust, you see, but the danger to them after the war was often greater than the danger of war had been. I think that after the war the Poles—many of them—lived through a monstrous nightmare. And that, unfortunately, is identified with the Jews.

That begs the stereotypical question about contemporary Polish antisemitism with no Jews in Poland.
People on the street don't believe that there are no Jews in Poland. Because they say, "just how many of us are there," but we are visible. Take a look: those few Jews are well-known intellectuals, sometimes artists. And everybody is constantly asking: "And this one? Is he a Jew?" Polish antisemitism rears its head

so much because it was here, in Poland, that it all happened. But people—often Jews—abroad, who didn't experience the war in Poland, don't realize what went on here. In Paris I was asked why the Poles didn't smash Auschwitz. What was I to answer to such stupidity? It's hard to discuss with something like that.

I have the impression that you're trying to justify Polish antisemitism somehow.
I'm not justifying Polish antisemitism. But neither do I think that it was as widespread as people elsewhere in the world think. I'm by no means defending people who denounced Jews, like *szmalcownicy*. But I have to say that the elite of Polish society, even the prewar ND people, behaved in an exemplary manner. But the rabble... The rabble, which was antisemitic...

In any case, it was often not out of antisemitism that people like that denounced Jews; often, they did it for money.
Oh yes. And they were more visible. I mentioned to you that the captain of our year was a guy who liked to wield a club. So, it was 1939, September, shortly after Poland's capitulation. We went to find out what was to become of us. The university had been partly bombarded. Our dean's office was in Collegium Anatomicum on Chałubiński Street, where it is today. The acting dean was a Professor Lauber, a half-German, half-Pole. And he said calmly to us: "Don't forget, to you they are the occupier, but to me it is my fatherland. We don't need Jews as doctors—or Poles either." We went out. On Jerozolimskie Avenue I went into a store where there were cigarettes at monopolist prices. At that time that was a rarity, because of course the cigarette factories weren't operating.

Did you smoke at the time?
Of course! Did you ever see a medical student that didn't smoke? Apart from anything else, people started to smoke in the dissecting room, because the smoke was said to mask the smell of the formaldehyde. It's not true. But we all started smoking in the dissecting room. So I went into this store, put five zloty down on this wooden shelf, and said: "A pack of Płaskie, please." And then I saw on the other side of the shelf Felek Loth, the ND guy, the captain of my year, whom I'd never spoken a word to. My first instinct was to back away, but ultimately—what was it to me? He was just the sales assistant. "Don't you recognize me, my friend?" "I don't recall us ever having been friends." At which he says: "You know, ma'am, these six weeks have been enough. You can absolutely shake hands with me. I am very ashamed." Later on, Felek Loth left a beautiful record. He sat through most of the war in Pawiak prison. But we knew perfectly well how he behaved.

Not all our people who were caught in roundups perished in the "Gęsiówka."[25] And that was thanks to Felek. The Germans held *Schwanzparaden*[26] for the Jews they apprehended, but Felek, who was a prisoner-physician, never found any to be a Jew. I met him later, during the Warsaw rising. His father, Professor Loth, was a bestial antisemite before the war, a racist—in one of his scientific papers, he claimed to have proven the inferiority of the black race on the basis of intestine length or something. And those people, Felek's parents, took Jews into hiding in their home. So, it varied. And when the rising was over, Felek said to me: "Don't go with the hospital, because there are all sorts of people here, who are saying that there are Jews with you." Felek is no longer alive. He just died. It's important not to forget that a large proportion of Polish society behaved very beautifully—the elite, of course, but that is always less visible than the rabble.

Why didn't you leave Poland—either after the war, in '56 or '57, or even in '68?[27]
In '57 it didn't even enter my head. And after the war, I didn't think of leaving even for a moment.

Yet most of your close friends were leaving.
No; most of my close friends left after '68. I absolutely didn't identify with those who left in '46 and '47!

Antek, Celina, Kazik, no?
No. They were Zionists; they had their cause. They would have emigrated sooner or later if there hadn't been a war. They were just going home. I was at home in

---

25 The colloquial name for the prison established inside the Warsaw ghetto in June 1941, in the former Polish military prison on Gęsia Street. The decision to establish a prison inside the ghetto was taken when it transpired that the number of Jewish prisoners being held outside the ghetto was increasing rapidly. At first, the plan was for a prison for one hundred to one hundred fifty people, but two months before the *große Aktion*, some one thousand three hundred Jews were being held there. From the prison's establishment, the majority of those held there were petty smugglers caught on the "Aryan side"; sentences were usually three months long. A large percentage of the prisoners were children (around 40 percent in May 1942); Adam Czerniaków petitioned for their release on several occasions. From the end of 1941, the prison yard was the site of executions of those convicted of leaving the ghetto; the first of them was carried out in November 1941 and the second a month later. The prison was run by the Jewish Order Service, but the death sentences were carried out by the Polish police.
26 *Schwanzparade* (Ger.—lit. "tail parade")—checking whether a man was circumcised, a method frequently used by the Germans to "establish" his racial identity.
27 1946, 1947, 1956, 1957, 1968—the years of the successive waves of Jewish emigration from Poland.

Poland, but they weren't. It is irrelevant now, which of us was right, and we will probably never resolve that. I was at home here. The fact that things were bad here was no proof that this wasn't my country. This homeland behaved badly not only toward the Jews, didn't it? And anyway, after the war it behaved least badly toward the Jews. Many people left because they believed they couldn't live in a cemetery. But I felt that this cemetery shouldn't be abandoned. And after 1956 there were fewer reasons to leave even than before. It's true that there were antisemitic moves, in the army, for instance, but most people were simply taking advantage of a chance to emigrate that they hadn't had for years. Things only turned bad for the Jews in 1968.

And the Kielce pogrom?
Above all, I didn't believe that that happened spontaneously. Somebody must have had their ax to grind. And in any case, I was already used to such behavior from the rabble.

So, you were able not to hold society as a whole responsible for that incident?
Yes, yes. I told you: this is my country.

And in '68?
Well, in '68 there were a number of issues. On the one hand it seemed to me important to oppose evil here, where we were. But there were also some very prosaic reasons. To be able to emigrate, you had to have either support or money—and I had neither the one nor the other.

Don't you think that you would have found support in Israel?
Possibly there. But Israel was the last place I would have thought of.

Why?
Too many Jews. "Yids, Yids, everywhere, I scream, I roar, I call..." But seriously, at that time I was decidedly underwhelmed by Israeli politics[28]—as I was by Polish politics. Indeed, I am still underwhelmed today, even though I have far warmer sentiments toward the country now than I used to. After all, Israel is a

---

28 The reference here is to the policies of the state of Irael in respect of Arab countries, above all the annexation of Jordanian and Egyptian territory following the Six-Day War in 1967.

theocratic country. That's not for me—I might as well go to Iran. At times I am very afraid that what we have here is also a nascent theocracy. But to return to your question: at the time, I had two children, it wasn't easy, I didn't have the energy to emigrate.

Were you separated by then?
More or less. My husband wouldn't have gone with me. In fact, in the end it was 1968 that finally divided us. In the end, he finally came to believe in a difference between anti-Zionism and antisemitism. Apart from anything else, I was loathe to emigrate, because I was always of the opinion that an émigré is half a person.

But is a Jew in the diaspora not a permanent émigré?
No, not at all. Poland is my country. I speak Polish, feel in Polish, think in Polish, regardless of the fact that I'm not an assimilated Jew but a Polish Jew. There is the concept of a "Polish Jew."

What do those two words mean to you?
It's hard to understand. It's not something that you can explain; you have to feel it. This combination of two nationalities, two cultures, forms one whole, and has one name: a Polish Jew.

Can you say of yourself that you sometimes feel Polish and sometimes Jewish?
I think so. When I'm in France, among the French, I represent Poland—I'm a Pole.

Are the expressions "a German Jew" and "a Polish Jew" equivalent expressions?
I think the German Jews felt more like Germans. They assumed from the Germans that conviction of German superiority. I remember the Jews who came to us via Zbąszyń. That was in 1938, when the Germans expelled the pseudo-Polish Jews. Some of them came to Warsaw, and one family lived in our house for a while. Jewish families took those expellees in. The homes of the intelligentsia in Poland were never luxurious, there's no doubt about that. Anyway, the family of a Berlin tailor came to live in my intellectual, that is, not wealthy, home. How afraid they were that it would be dirty! Because we were only Poles . . . They considered themselves better than the Polish Jews, just like the Polish Jews were better than the Litvaks.

Can we go back to 1968 for a moment?
Terrible things happened back then. Similar to what happened after the war with the "bespittled reactionary dwarf."[29] But did all those persecuted Poles emigrate then? No!

Only at that point those Poles couldn't really emigrate, but the Jews in '68 could.
That's true. But even so. It was the same evil.

Did you have any issues at work at that time?
Not in 1968. It was a little delayed. I lost my post in Szczecin in 1970. But nobody forced me to emigrate.

I think many Jews in Israel or America would be at a loss to understand how, after all that happened here, you can feel at home. And they would doubtless brandish the well-known stereotypes of the "antisemitic nation," "land of cemeteries," and "they never really wanted us here."
First of all, it's not true that we were never wanted here: it varied. And that it's a cemetery? I said already: some people find it hard to abandon their cemetery. And I want to lie in this cemetery! Not in any other. In some cemetery where half the graves are symbolic. And apart from anything else, why does it not surprise anyone that Hanna Krall never emigrated, for instance?

Perhaps the difference is that she was a child at the time?
But do you know how mature, how adult those children were?! Can you even imagine those children? Those children who said of us: "They're like children; they don't understand anything, because they've never yet been dying of hunger"—they used to say that of us! "Or perhaps they're afraid and want to be with us?" Imagine: we wanted to play with those children! But they were a hundred years older than us, believe me. In my book I wrote about this one six-year-old Jasia. She remembers everything perfectly. Today she's a fifty-year-old woman. When I was taking little Jasia to her new guardian, I asked her on the way: "Jasia, do you remember your surname?" "Yes. My name is Jasia Ostaszewska." Jasia's new guardian had a little store selling bread rolls on Leszno Street. She spoilt Jasia dreadfully. I used to go round there once or twice a week. Once, I was walking down Leszno with Jasia, and she said to me: "Yids used to

---

29 "Bespittled reactionary dwarf" (Pol. *zapluty karzeł reakcji*)—a derogatory expression used in the People's Republic of Poland period to refer to Home Army veterans.

live here." I was afraid to say anything in response; perhaps it's better that she should think like that ... But after the uprising, when her guardian decided to tell her that she wasn't her real aunt, the little girl asked, confounded: "So you knew that my real name is Jasia Jelenkiewicz?" Can you imagine that?! For two years, a six-year-old child said nothing at all, even to those closest to her! She had been pretending to us all that she knew nothing, remembered nothing! And you say they were children?! Children who had cowered behind closets and knew that they mustn't make a sound?! They were adults!

Did you ever come across children who were childlike in the ghetto?
At the beginning, in the hospital, before the deportation. After that, all of them were absolutely adult.

...So, you didn't emigrate?
I didn't emigrate because I was at home here. But now? Am I at home here? You might say, like Mr. Warszawski...[30]

... "a little less at home."[31]
I don't know? Sometimes I am "a little less at home." Sometimes...

You mentioned that you moved to Łódź shortly after the war because Marek Edelman and Ala Margolis were there. In which year did you leave Łódź?
In 1960.

Why?
Purely for professional reasons. In Poland there was a shortage of pediatric pulmonologists. There were several in Łódź; there was Łagiewniki, Professor Anna Margolis's school. But in Szczecin there was only one specialist for the whole province.

---

30 Dawid Warszawski, real name Konstanty Gebert (b. 1953)—journalist, translator, writer, anti-communist activist before 1989 and activist in the Jewish community in the course of its reconstruction after 1989; editor-in-chief (1997–2000) of the Jewish monthly *Midrasz*. He lives in Warsaw.
31 The title of an article by Dawid Warszawski, printed in the September 1989 issue of current affairs periodical *Polityka*, a polemic with a sermon delivered by Polish primate Józef Glemp on July 15, 1989.

Let's talk about the Warsaw rising for a moment. That's also a significant part of your life.
It all started at 24 Miodowa Street—that's where I was living with Ala and Zosia [Renia Frydman].[32] At five that morning, I was alone at home. When I heard the first shots, I ran out into the stairwell and saw a Polish officer in the uniform of the Carpathian Brigade!

In your book, you say that you burst into tears when you saw him.
Well, sure! What do you think? I ran downstairs. It transpired that they had a hospital in the basement of the house. So I went to the commander, and "revealed myself," so to speak. I stayed in the hospital straight away. The girls got back to Miodowa three days later, and we were in the hospital until the end—until August 29, I think. All of them there were killed—the commander, "Pobóg," was killed, and both surgeons, who were Jews as well. One of them, Koenigstein, the son of a well-known Warsaw ENT specialist, was shot dead by someone unknown—probably not by the Germans—in the hospital courtyard. Ala and I were left alone—and there were forty wounded there. All our group was with the AL on Świętojerska Street. They came to take us to Żoliborz as they were retreating after their entire command was killed on Freta Street. But we couldn't go because there were those forty wounded. Later on, we had problems trying to evacuate the hospital. The chief councilor for Warsaw North was my future husband. And he sent us downtown via the sewers, to the Śródmieście district, to try and organize somewhere for the wounded to go. We were supposed to go back the following day, but in the meantime the Old Town was evacuated, and they wouldn't let anyone back the other way—it's hard to pass both ways in a sewer. Some of the wounded made it through, those who couldn't walk were left behind. After the war, on January 23 or 24 we went back to Warsaw, I went to Miodowa Street and found charred corpses in the beds—the Germans had burned them. So, after that we worked in this bandaging station on Moniuszki Street, and from there we went to the hospital on Mokotowska, and we stayed there until the end of the rising. We didn't leave Warsaw until October 11.

But not with the hospital?
No. By some miracle I managed to procure a convoying pass for myself, one nurse, and twelve wounded. They asked me where I was taking them. To Milanówek, to the Red Cross hospital.

---

32 p. 376 Rereading the List—Renia Frydman, Zosia Skrzeszewska [Wysocka].

Who were you "convoying?"
Ala was the nurse, and the wounded were the two wives of the two Jewish doctors who had been killed, one of them with her child, and some insurgents.

And where did you go?
We really did go to Milanówek. We spent the night there, and then we all went our separate ways. Ala and I went to a village near Milanówek, to a peasant's barn, and there we had the pleasure of catching lice. We had managed to get through the whole rising without lice!

In one of our previous conversations, you mentioned that Felek Loth, a fellow student of yours, warned you not to leave Warsaw with the hospital because "there are people here who are saying that there are Jews around you."
Yes. Those Jews were Ala, and the two women, who also looked "very much not." But the hospital on Mokotowska was a mixed civilian and military hospital, so we had a choice: either to go with the civilians to Pruszków, or to go with the army as POWs. So, we went to Milanówek.

In our previous conversation, you compared dying, death in the ghetto, with death in the Warsaw rising.
Dying is always the same. Believe me, I'm a doctor . . . It's like Marek said in his interview with Hanna Krall: "It's people that have come to an agreement among themselves that it's a different way of dying, it's people that have decided that. But you die the same way . . ."[33]

Does that mean that there's no difference whether you die with a weapon in your hand or in a gas chamber?
It's probably easier with a weapon, but there's no difference. No death is less worthy or less heroic. The only thing is that if you die with a weapon in your hand, you often don't know that you're dying. It's beforehand that it's better, before you die, because you're not thinking about dying at all, you're only thinking about fighting. A soldier doesn't think about dying, a soldier thinks more about killing, about victory. People have simply come to an agreement that death with a weapon is better, more beautiful. It's the same death. It's only the "before" that counts. And apart from that, if you're armed, you have no fear.

---

33 See Hanna Krall, *Shielding the Flame*.

So, what about the injections for the children? Was that to spare the children the fear?
Can you imagine what the deaths of those who went to the gas were like? Can you possibly imagine that? And those children? In one of her books, [Zofia] Kossak-Szczucka writes that people who had profound faith had more chance of surviving. To me, that's garbage. But there is one sentence there . . . When she writes about how tiny children, who couldn't even walk yet, were taken to the gas, and one little child waved "bye-bye." Or another one, being taken to the gas, asking: "Mommy, why is it dark in here? I wasn't naughty!" Adults have fear, too . . . And your question about fear I will answer with a prewar joke. A bankrupt merchant is walking across the Poniatowski Bridge and meets an acquaintance. "What's wrong?" "It's all over for me; I'm off to drown myself." "Look out! There's a car coming!" "Oh no!!" Shall I tell you what fear of death is? If mothers can abandon their children?

Do you think that there was anybody who wasn't afraid of death at that time?
If people committed suicide—and they did, as you know—then one of the reasons why they did so was out of fear, out of fear of the road to death. If I have to die, then at least let death be momentary. Let me not have to go to my death.

So, was it fear of going on living, that kind of life, and waiting for death? Was it fear of that kind of death?
Of that kind of death. Of the gas chamber.

And the orthodox Jews, who went to their deaths reciting the "*Shema Israel*?"[34]
Now that's something else. There is the concept of *kiddush ha-shem*.[35] They were dying as a burnt offering. In any case, that doesn't mean that they weren't afraid. But God was with them. I don't know, maybe it's easier to die with God.

---

34 *Shema Israel* (Heb.: Hear, o Israel) are the first words of the prayer that devout Jews recite night and morning.
35 *Kiddush ha-shem* (Heb.)—sanctification of the Name. This is how religious Jews refer to a martyr's death.

Pits

And another stereotype. Of the elderly, bearded men who went to the transports and then to the gas chambers with the words *Shema Israel*, people say cruelly that they "went like sheep to the slaughter."
Everybody went like sheep, I can tell you. The people of Warsaw left the city after the rising like sheep. There were three military police officers and a hundred thousand people, but nobody threw themselves at the officers. Because the officers were armed, but the people were defenseless. And that sufficed for them to go like sheep. Couldn't they have thrown themselves at the officers and then scattered?! All of Warsaw went like that . . . But those who recited the *Shema Israel* were not going like sheep. They were commending themselves to God, who had decided to smite the chosen people once again.

We're talking about fear of death. Do you think it's impossible that a person who is powerless in the face of death can understand it and come to terms with it enough so as not to feel fear?
There is something that is called the instinct to live, and it is an immensely strong instinct. And that bankrupt merchant on the Poniatowski Bridge, resolved to die, instinctively jumps back out of the way of a car that might have killed him. People in the gas chambers clawed their way up . . . Over one other . . . It seemed to them to be worst at the bottom . . .

In your book, you write that fear is connected with defenselessness.
Yes, of course.

Aren't we always defenseless in the face of death?
No, no. None of us thinks about death with fear, even though we know we will die. Apart from that, I think people are more afraid of taking a long time to die than of death itself. They are afraid of torture: they were afraid of the road that led to death. But if you are armed, that means you will die at once. When I was taking Marek along the street, I asked him whether he had a gun. Because it was obvious that if they caught us, Marek would pull out his gun, kill someone, and they would kill us. And that would be it! And we wouldn't have to worry about Szucha, beating, tortures, and that long dying. Why do cancer patients beg to have the unnecessary torture of dying cut short?

You write that you only came to know the fear of death after some time. When the Gestapo officer put a pistol to your temple, you didn't feel any fear.
Yes, in such moments of finality there is no more fear. It was as though it had already happened. As if I was already on the other side. But I was very frightened

when I was carrying money under my shirt for our wards, and I passed a patrol. When I finally reached home, the money was soaked through.

But on that occasion, you were frightened of being arrested. That wasn't fear of death.
Well, that's very hard to tell apart. I would have preferred to have cyanide with me, so as not to have to reach Szucha. Today, here, over tea, we can analyze it all calmly. But that was simply fear; I was afraid. It was undoubtedly more fear of the way of dying, of everything that might happen beforehand, than of death itself. A person at risk of death doesn't think precisely what it is that they are afraid of—there are just two thoughts within them: fear, and the desire to save their life, which is often instinctive. Those who jumped the train going to Treblinka—they were simply saving their lives.

Do you think that faith can "insure" people against fear? Do you believe in God?
I can't give you an unequivocal answer to that question. Back then, God was not here. It's a very difficult question. Is he not here? I don't know. Back then he certainly covered his face, even if he was here ... He bottled it.

Can God bottle it?
In my memoirs there is a woman called Janina. She had three sons. At that time, one of them was in England, in the RAF;[36] the second was in Auschwitz; and the third, who was seventeen, was with her. He was in the underground, very actively involved—I think he was a nationalist, in the ONR. Anyway, he got caught in some round-up, and ended up at the Kripo. Our contacts managed to get him out. Shortly afterwards, he was killed—on the street, with a gun in his hand, in action. Mrs. Janina Plewczyńska was an incredibly religious woman; her house was full of sacred pictures. What she did for us—and she did a great deal—she did out of her sense of Christian ethics. Marysia [Bronisława Warman] and I went to see her when we found out about her son's death.[37] We saw her standing in front of a reproduction of the Black Madonna, and she was shouting insults at it: "It's all lies! You're no Mother! You wouldn't have allowed it if you had been a Mother!" But Janina didn't stop being a believer.

---

36 RAF—Royal Air Force.
37 p. 370 Rereading the List—Bronka Feinmesser (Fajnmesser), Marysia (Warman).

That kind of shouting is a very human way of talking with God.
I think there are a lot of Jews who have nothing to do with the rituals, but of whom one couldn't say that they weren't believers.

People often recall how human they are; they speak of being Human in inhuman conditions. We have spoken about faith, which can make a person dignified. Could we talk about the opposite of what we call a worthy life, being Human, about the limits of humanity? Can a person cease to be human in their behavior? Would you agree with the opinion that a human can cease to be Human; that they can start to be animalistic, or even turn into an animal?
When I think about the Muselmanns,[38] I think that a Muselmann didn't stop being human; they simply ceased to exist. But the Germans? They are a puzzle to me. With that most profoundly encoded notion of orders and discipline of theirs, they were capable of doing anything. Were they human? Perhaps their cruelty is also a human attribute? After all, our experience, our history, offer evidence that such behaviors exist in the human dimension. Evidently there is a sort of evil, a Satan, in the human. Even in the Old Testament we read of the cruelest cruelty.

Let me repeat my question: can a human cease to be Human?
I saw mothers who abandoned their children out of fear. Because they thought that without children, they would make it through. Can you imagine that? That is rock bottom, the absolute rock bottom of humanity. That was what fear could do.

So no?
So, no. But human cruelty is worse than animal cruelty. Animals don't kill for pleasure.

Do you, as a doctor, recognize the right to euthanasia?
Only in one case. When a person is suffering terribly and there is no hope for them.

Is a person, a doctor, in a position to decide that "there is no hope any longer?"
I am of the opinion that life that is no longer there should not be prolonged mechanically—the life of a person who is already practically dead.

---

38 Muselmann (from the German)—a word widely used in Auschwitz and other German concentration camp slang to denote a prisoner so emaciated and exhausted that they had lost the will to live and had become indifferent to everything, to the point of catatonia.

When they are "spiritually" dead, you mean? Are you talking about the situation when a person is only existing biologically?
Yes, and is also experiencing terrible suffering. But on the other hand, I think it is impossible to allow the right to euthanasia, because there could be abuses. People do have the right to decide about their own life, though.

Really?
If they know that there is no hope, and they are suffering inhumanly...

How can we know that there is no longer any hope?
Well, we refer to what medical knowledge tells us on the subject.

In that case, do humans have a right to suicide?
Of course! That is the right of every human.

But there's always a chance. I'm reminded of what Marek said about the suicide on Miła. After all, a few people from that bunker saved themselves.
There isn't always a chance. Sometimes there just isn't any more... And the matter of the bunker? They thought there was no way out.

Was Korczak a hero?
If he was, then it wasn't only him. Korczak was not the only one who acted like that. There was Stefa Wilczyńska;[39] there was Esterka Winogron[40]—my schoolfriend; there were children who went with their parents, and parents who went with their children. But if we're talking about Korczak himself, he had no other choice.

He could have gone out onto the Aryan side. He could have saved himself.
Not at that point, he couldn't leave the children. He received an offer at the Umschlag, but he couldn't have done that.

Did you know Korczak?
Of course. I used to go to his house with my mother as a child. And in the ghetto, I used to go to the orphanage. We had some of Korczak's children in

---

39 Stefania (Stefa) Wilczyńska (1886–1942)—studied natural and medical sciences in Belgium. From the moment Dr. Korczak opened his orphanage at 92 Krochmalna Street, she was his closest colleague; she died with the children in Treblinka on August 6, 1942.
40 Esterka Winogron—a carer in Dr Korczak's orphanage. She died with the children in Treblinka on August 6, 1942.

our hospital. And there were conflicts between him and our head doctor [Anna Braude-Hellerowa].[41]

Why?
Well, Korczak was a very difficult man, very difficult. He was incredibly mistrustful, hot-tempered, suspicious. As far as I remember, he accused the hospital of some kind of dishonesty, absolutely groundlessly. He was not an easy man; he was no angel. He was a terrible oddball—he even wrote that of himself.

You saw Korczak going to the transport with the children.
Yes, I saw that procession; they passed under our windows.

Were you standing at the window?
Yes, yes... We saw Korczak pass. And there was something momentous about it. They were accompanying the children.

Can you reconstruct that moment precisely?
We were standing at a window on the second floor. We were standing to one side, by the right-hand frame. We watched them walking down the middle of the street. We didn't move—the Germans would have started to shoot.

They were walking down the middle of the street parallel to the window?
Yes. We saw them approaching.

Who were you standing with at the window?
There were a lot of us standing there. I remember well that Zosia Skrzeszewska [Renia Frydman] was standing with me—she saw her parents and her sister...

How were the children walking?
By four—certainly: that's how the Germans lined people up. Or maybe by six? Korczak was walking at the front, among the children, I think. Then a few rows of four, and then came Stefa Wilczyńska. And then came the girls—Esterka Winogron and Natka.[42] The smallest children were walking at the front, then the

---

41 Anna Braude-Hellerowa (1888–1943)—pediatrician and community activist. She ran the Berson and Bauman Children's Hospital from 1930 until it was closed down in 1942. She was deputy director of the last hospital in the ghetto, at 6/8 Gęsia Street. Probably killed during the uprising in the ghetto.
42 Natka—a caregiver in Dr Korczak's orphanage. She died with the children in Treblinka on August 6, 1942.

older ones. I think Esterka was at the end. So, the children weren't left alone at the back.

That means that there were at least four carers.
Yes, at least. I remember the ones I knew: Esterka—my schoolfriend, Stefa, Natka...

Was Natka young?
Young? No, she was my age: twenty-something.

So, she was young!
No. At that time, a sixteen-year-old girl was young.

How many children were there with Korczak?
Forty? Fifty?

About a large classful?
A large class... I don't know, I don't know...

So, you only saw the moment when Korczak and the children passed by under the windows?
Yes. It was like this, you see: the hospital was on the corner of Leszno and Żelazna Streets. The window where we were standing gave out onto Żelazna. The children walked along Żelazna toward Nowolipki, so we only saw them on that short stretch. That's all. We couldn't even move by that window. And they just filed past below us. And after the children came other people... The children weren't abandoned, they weren't terrified, or lost, do you understand? That's important. Korczak did his duty to the end, to the very end. And if doing one's duty is heroism... You know, one thing upsets me in all of this. Why is it only Korczak who ever gets mentioned?

Probably because people need symbols.
But what about those young girls? That was even more than Korczak. He didn't really have a choice. That procession was the logical consequence of his life. But those young girls? They probably could have saved themselves.

Well, yes, but the stance was the same.
But that's precisely it! Their stance meant even more—they were twenty years old! Going into battle, risking your life—that's entirely different than taking the

decision to go to your death in cold blood. When you are twenty, you really want to live... Those girls' names are not on any monument. Why not? Because Korczak was famous, and they weren't? Yes, Korczak was a great writer, but their deaths remained nameless.

That's how the world's built, I think—we express our fortunes and misfortunes through those great figures.
Perhaps. I don't know. I don't like it... I'll tell you a funny story about Korczak. It was at the beginning of the war. Korczak boarded a streetcar. He was standing, and next to him some guy was sitting down. And the guy says to him: "Merchant, sit down!" Korczak remains standing. "I said sit down, merchant! What, is the merchant waiting for me to plant him down?!" "When this merchant was a colonel in the Polish army, he planted people like you in the kitty and not on a seat, you piece of shit!"

Tell me how you joined the ŻOB.
I've written about that in great detail.

In great detail? You wrote that Marek ordered you to go out onto the Aryan side.
And that was it!

And that was it? That was all?
Yes, they gave me an address, ordered me to go to this place and that place, and that was all! The ŻOB command met in our home, in the ghetto, on Gęsia Street. Marek was there, Welwł Rozowski[43] was there; Abrasza Blum would come over.

How long had you been living on Gęsia Street?
One moment... my mother disappeared on July 29; at that point I was still on Świętojerska. They threw us out of there two or three days later.

Was that because the ghetto was being reduced in size?
Not only. The brushmakers were moving in there.

The "'shops" were being installed there, is that it?
Yes. Then I slept in the hospital for a few nights. And we stored our things in a little room opposite the hospital, on Leszno.

---

43 p. 438 Rereading the List—Welwł (Wolf) Rozowski.

"We stored" meaning who?
My husband, who went to live with his parents, me, and a few other people. It all disappeared after that. I took a huge trunk with linen, porcelain, and vinyls there, I remember.

And after that you lived on Gęsia?
Then came the day when the children were taken to the hospital on the Umschlag.

When was that?
August 9, or maybe 11. I don't know! August 9, I think. Then came the apartment on Pawia. We were barracked.

The hospital personnel?
Yes. We lived together then—Marek, Stasia [Rywka Rozensztajn],[44] [Ala] Margolis, the Kielsons.[45] We were on Pawia until the kettle. And it all ended on September 4.

I don't understand. The kettle on Miła lasted from September 5 to 12.
Nonsense! It all ended on September 4! We were kettled for two or three days, and then taken out of the kettle to Gęsia. We never went back to Pawia. There was a hospital at 6 Gęsia Street, and one rear wing was taken over by hospital personnel. And there, Welwł lived with us, along with Alik Zarchi, the fifteen-year-old brother of my girlfriend, whose parents had been killed.

Were you brave in the ghetto back then?
I can tell you that back before anything happened, some of us were childishly brave. I took advantage of my appearance, for instance, to go out onto the Aryan side just for shit, pardon my language. For nothing. To buy a bit of sausage or better vodka. That wasn't bravery. That was more like stupidity, showing off. But then I was twenty, and we couldn't imagine that they would lock us in and that it would be like it was.

---

44 Stasia—Rywka Rozensztajn (1912–1999)—lived in Warsaw at Miła Street. She attended a CISzO Jewish school and studied at the Warsaw Academy of Fine Arts. She was a Bund activist in the Warsaw ghetto. After the Warsaw uprising, she was taken from Pruszków as labor to Germany, along with Marysia Sawicka. After the war, she lived in New York, where she remained until her death.

45 Dola Kielson, a nurse, shot dead in Otwock in 1943; her sister Dr. Hela Kielson, a doctor of internal diseases at the Berson and Bauman Children's Hospital, who lived in Sweden after the war; and Aleksander Kielson, their father.

When did you first hear of Treblinka?
Directly after the first campaign. Someone who had jumped a transport came back to the ghetto. I don't remember his name.

Was it then that everything changed, that a breakthrough in the understanding of the situation came?
Well, that was the final certainty ... That this wasn't resettlement. Because we had had our suspicions before that. I mean, with all that had been happening in the ghetto all that time ... Only, as Marek says, people truly couldn't believe that so much bread could be wasted.

How long were you in the hospital on Stawki?
A few days less than everyone else. I wasn't with them anymore when the personnel were moved to Pawia, and they started going into the hospital on Stawki to work. It was Marek who took me out of the hospital and left me in an apartment on Nowolipki. In fact, I only found out about all of that from *Shielding the Flame*.[46] I think it was on August 11 that they threw the hospitals out, and I joined them on August 14 or 15. And after that we were together until the end, until September 4. So, I was on Stawki from mid-August until the end, until the kettle on Miła. Three weeks. We entered the kettle on September 4, and we were in the kettle for two days.

On September 4 or 6?
The street blockades came first, and then the kettle. After that there were isolated roundups. Police officers grabbed five Jews at a time. And the campaign ended on September 8.

So, the kettle lasted ...
From September 4 to 8. Only Marek writes that from 6th because we probably arrived there on 6th. From 4th for sure!

Do you think that Bartoszewski[47] would have quoted Marek if he'd been wrong?

---

46 Krall, *Shielding the Flame*.
47 Władysław Bartoszewski, "Ludwik," "Teofil" (1922–2015)—historian, writer, journalist, social activist, politician, and diplomat; co-founder of the Żegota Council to Aid Jews, an organization run by the Government Delegation for Poland, part of the Polish Government-in-Exile. Fought in the Warsaw uprising; imprisoned by the occupying authorities and after the war by the authorities of the People's Republic of Poland. Scholar of the history of the AK, and of the extermination of Poles and Jews during the war. Chairperson of the International

Where could Bartoszewski have checked it? Who knows when it was? I know for sure that it was the day when all the sick were brought to our hospital. But whether that was the 4th or the 6th? I think it was the 4th.

You already had numbers when you entered the kettle on Miła. How were they given out?
In the hospital... We left the hospital with numbers. I wrote about that—when we were ordered to go into the kettle, we went to the hospital, and there it transpired that the hospital had been given a certain number of numbers, and the Chief just had to hand them out... By then, all the hospitals were on the Umschlag, all the patients had been taken there; the staff were with the patients ... And we left the hospital with numbers. Those who had numbers got out, but the rest went...

How many people went?
They ordered fifty doctors to be left. The others went straight into the kettle; I don't know how many...

Were those fifty doctors from all the hospitals, ones who didn't already have numbers?
Yes, to the Umschlag...

Did all the doctors and nurses who went into the kettle have numbers?
No. Most did, but there were some "wildcats" among us. And you either got out of the kettle or not, irrespective of the numbers. They just counted us out, and at one point said—that's it... And lots of people who had numbers went.

How were the numbers shared out?
That was dreadful... We told the Chief that she had to do it. She didn't want to. If she hadn't done it, all the numbers would have been taken by the other hospital, and no one from ours would have been saved... The heads of departments were given them automatically, but the rest, that just depended...

What did the numbers look like?
Look like? A bit of paper, a stamp on a slip of paper.

Council of the National Auschwitz Museum, twice minister of foreign affairs, and a senator in the fourth term of the parliament of the Third Polish Republic. In 1965, he became one of the first people to be decorated with the Righteous Among the Nations medal.

Numbers for life...
Yes, numbers for life.

Where did you go after the kettle?
To Gęsia. We didn't go back to Pawia.

Are you very tired?
No, no. We can go on talking.

Could you talk about those days in the kettle?
I'll tell you something funny. The whole thing is kind of blurred—those four days are as if it was one day. Nothing happens in order, do you understand? We're sitting somewhere...

Inside a building or on the street?
In a building, I think, we're sitting on the floor... It's very amusing, but somehow, when I was leaving the hospital, I managed to smuggle out half a liter of pure spirit. How did I do that? I know we drank that spirit. Did we have anything at all to eat? I can't remember at all; I don't think so. I know that when we finally made it out, we were dreadfully hungry, and searched the entire apartment on Gęsia for something to eat.

And is sitting on the floor and the spirit all you remember from the kettle?
We slept somewhere, also on the floor. I know that there were screams. And then they herded us out onto a street, and we stood there for a dreadfully long time. It was something like the camp rollcalls they describe, you know. It all happened in the summer, so it wasn't that awful. We stood there in fours. One moment. When we were leaving the building, we tried to stick together. I know that Hela Kielson had something wrong with her leg, so I held her hand the whole time. And I held Stasia's hand, too. And there we stood. There were Germans shouting. Somebody somewhere shooting, of course. There was always shouting and shooting. There was no gateway there, it was some kind of barrier. And there were Germans standing there. At one point we moved forward, and they started counting... those fours. And directly after us there came the shout: "Halt!" Marek was behind us—I think he was in the last or second-to-last four.

And did you have to show your numbers?
No.

But there were some "wildcats" among you.
Yes, for instance Stasia, Welwł's wife. I was holding her hand the whole time. And that's all. That's all I remember of that. Nothing really happened. We sat in some cellar and waited—hungry, dirty, a little cold because it was night-time. And that's all.

And fear?
No . . . I don't know. I think we were a little afraid as we passed the Germans, because of the "wildcats" among us. But they just counted. And suddenly we realized that some of those with numbers had been left behind.

Was anyone from the hospital with a number left behind?
Oh, yes. Lots of people were left behind. After that, all kinds of things happened, you know. Some people managed to get out somehow. Later on, we sent our numbers to the hospital by ambulance.

To which hospital?
To the Umschlag, because the hospital was only deported a few days later. We got out, and they deported the hospital later . . . A few more people managed to save themselves.

How many people were there working in the hospital on Stawki?
About two hundred.

Do you remember the Umschlagplatz clearly?
It's changed so much now that it's very difficult. After a while I can call up a picture of it in my mind: aha, so here's the door, here's the entrance to the hospital, here's the cellar, here are those windows. Like that. But everything outside that is completely different. The ramp isn't there . . .

Could you draw the place as it was?
With one exception. I know which way I left the hospital to go out onto the Umschlag. I know what the two parts of the building looked like. One wing was the hospital and out-patient clinic, and the other wing was the waiting room, so to speak—that's where they gathered the people awaiting transport. Then I somehow see myself after the wagons have left, gathering up the abandoned children . . . But somehow, I've lost the route that you took to get to the wagons. I can see two separate pictures: the wagons and the Umschlagplatz. The part "between" has gotten lost somewhere.

Why did you write your memoirs?
Because at one point I realized that it should all be preserved. Though I had huge reservations about writing.

Why?
It seemed to me that no one would understand any of it anyway, and in any case, people want to forget about it, they aren't interested in it. And there was no need to write it all down for those who had lived through it. But in any case, it shouldn't be lost. And one more thing. A stereotypical way of thinking about the ghetto had emerged, a dreadful stereotype. I don't know—Marek didn't succeed, and neither did I, in correcting the lie, in explaining that the people who were locked up in the ghetto were not a herd of cattle. When people talk about the ghetto, they only talk about death, and about how miserable dying there was. Nobody talks about life, or about the heroism of those ordinary people, about their struggle to remain human, to survive as humans.

Could that stereotype be illustrated with an image of "high society in the cafés and skeletons on the sidewalks?"
Precisely! Cafés for the rich! And it's not true. Ninety percent were hungry, most of them dying of starvation. Those who bathed in luxury were "How many? One!"—five percent, ten percent. And the concerts, the clandestine classes! Now that was saving our humanity! And the work on hunger disease?![48] In those conditions! Can you comprehend that? Doctors who were themselves dying of hunger, undertaking research of that caliber! And the improbable efforts of doctors to save human lives? In those conditions?! That was heroism—everyday life! But the stereotype is of a passive waiting for death. Nobody talks about the fact that it was one of the most heroic places in the whole war. And that's what I was trying to write about, but I don't think I succeeded.

---

48 Hunger disease is a pathological syndrome manifesting in metabolic disorders caused by chronic undernourishment. The study of hunger disease was launched in 1942 on the initiative of Dr. Izrael Milejkowski. The group of more than ten physicians from the Warsaw ghetto worked under the scientific leadership of Dr. Julian Fliederbaum. Their method involved monitoring the clinical progression and biochemical changes occurring in children in the six- to twelve-year-old age group and adults aged between twenty and forty. The object of study was cases of malnutrition, without other complications, in people recruited from shelters for expellees. The outcomes of the study, which was financed by the Judenrat but interrupted due to the deportation of the majority of both scholars and subjects to Treblinka extermination camp, were published after the war as *Choroba głodowa. Badania kliniczne nad głodem wykonane w getcie warszawskim w roku 1942* (Warszawa: American Joint Distribution Committee, 1946), and in English translation by Myron Winick, ed., *Hunger Disease: Studies by Jewish Physicians in the Warsaw Ghetto* (New York: John Wiley & Sons, 1979).

Resettlement ... Deportation

Isn't it that you didn't succeed because you couldn't have succeeded?
I don't know, I think it's all too hard to retell. Just as Marek failed to say that death in the ghetto was the same as death in the uprising. But that's precisely what he meant—that these two deaths were of equal status, and that it was only people who devised the idea that it was better to die with a gun in their hands. So, they decided to die that way, too. And I failed to say: Listen, it wasn't the Holocaust that was important, and that people were being killed; the heroic ethos was the way those people lived!

Why is that so hard to convey? Because it is beyond our powers of conception?
Yes, and perhaps a little because people say: "Moshe, go to war! Yoyne, go to war!" When Poles came into the ghetto, they really did see crowds of ragged people milling about on the streets—because if there were four hundred thousand people in those few streets, and an average of ten people to a room, there was nothing but misery to be seen!

If the ŻOB hadn't sent you out onto the other side, would you have wanted to go yourself?
No. I argued with Marek about that, and it was only Abrasza [Blum] who put an end to our dispute. I didn't want to go out simply because I didn't want to be alone, I wanted to be with them to the end. There was no heroism about it!

We already spoke about Korczak as one of the symbols of the ghetto. Let's talk about another stance: about Czerniaków.
At the time, in the ghetto, we asked ourselves whether someone like Czerniaków had the right to commit suicide. We were of the belief that death ought to serve a purpose. Meaning that instead of committing suicide he ought to have (which is basically garbage as I see it now that I'm old) thrown everything aside and taken charge of the resistance movement. That's what we young people thought back then. But today I know that Czerniaków was quite simply a decent man. He didn't believe what was going to happen, like ninety percent of the people... no, not ninety percent—a hundred percent!

Up to a point.
Yes, to a point. Czerniaków, like everyone else, believed that it was a matter of holding out. And he thought that carrying out the Germans' orders would help us to hold out... But when that delusion ended... No, no; he was a decent man.

And the attitude of you young people to the Judenrat?
I knew a few people in the Judenrat and I knew that they were decent people who worked hard and were doing what they could. Zygmunt Warman,[49] for instance—he was the most upright man I knew; we considered him the conscience of our entire group. Even though there were thieves and blackguards among them, I always remembered that not all of them were, just as anywhere else.

So, you probably don't agree with what Ringelblum[50] wrote about Czerniaków and the Judenrat.
Ringelblum writes a lot of garbage. Marek doesn't consider him the wisest either, to put it delicately. I knew him well, very well even. Ringelblum was my history teacher at Jehudija for four years. Not a bad historian, but a stupid man. He was the teacher with the crass jokes.

Somewhat poor?
Bad, silly, bawdy jokes were his specialty. When he made jokes about a girl, it was tasteless to say the least. He educated us in the spirit of historical materialism. To tell the truth, it impressed us a little. He was very left-wing, like all of the PPS Left, which was more communist than the communists. And God bless him for it! But there was another thing that I couldn't stand him for. You see, I was the principal's daughter. And he was the only teacher who made anything of that— he favored me in a completely idiotic way. Once, he corrected a paper of mine in which I had used far too many punctuation marks, and he wrote this comment:

---

49 Zygmunt Warman (1905–1965)—the son of the head of the Lublin Judenrat; a 1927 law graduate from the University of Warsaw. Secretary of the Judenrat in the Warsaw ghetto, from January 1943 on the "Aryan side" under a false name. In the Warsaw uprising, a soldier in the ŻOB group in a detachment of the AL; after 1945 a solicitor and attorney in Warsaw, from 1956 a Supreme Court judge.

50 Emanuel Ringelblum (1900–1943)—Jewish historian and social and political activist (Poalej Syjon Left). In the Warsaw ghetto, the initiator of a group called Oneg Shabbat, which archived and documented life in the ghetto. The documentation amassed by Oneg Shabbat, known as the Underground Archive of the Warsaw Ghetto, or the Ringelblum Archive, is one of the most important bodies of documents on the Holocaust. In February 1943, he left the ghetto with his wife and thirteen-year-old son and went into hiding with his family and thirty other Jews in a bunker codenamed "Krysia" at 81 or 84 Grójecka Street. On the eve of Passover in 1943, Ringelblum went back into the ghetto. In July 1943, he is known to have been in the labor camp in Trawniki and was rescued by Polish and Jewish underground activists (Tadeusz Pajewski and Róża Kossower). He then returned to the shelter on Grójecka. On March 7, 1944, the bunker was discovered, and its Jewish inhabitants and the Poles looking after them (the Wolski family) taken to Pawiak prison. A few days later, they were all executed by firing squad in the ruins of the ghetto.

"Typical Szwajgier punctuation marks." Afterwards, he probably realized that he'd overstepped the mark, and he crossed out "typical Szwajgier" in such a way that he almost tore my notebook. How could he?! I mean, it wasn't only my name, but my mother's—his principal's—as well! That doesn't show him in the best light, does it?

We started talking about Ringelblum in connection with his opinion on Czerniaków and the Judenrat.
Yes, well he writes about the Judenrat from his ultra-left-wing point of view: all bourgeois, thieves, and bandits. Not true! Garbage! There were thieves, but there were also quite a few decent people.

Do you remember your reaction to Czerniaków's suicide?
I think it was above all a case of our realization of what was really happening to us. I told you that some people thought he shouldn't have killed himself because of the resistance. Everybody understood that his death was a refusal, that he didn't want to have any part in the worst. Today I think that Czerniaków's death was the same kind of death as Zygielbojm's.[51]

Do you really think so?
You disagree because Zygielbojm was in London? But Czerniaków's death was a protest just like Zygielbojm's.

Only Zygielbojm could have lived.
Well, yes, but Czerniaków could also have counted on surviving. And what about Szeryński?[52] And all those other scoundrels? They all believed they would survive.

But Czerniaków wasn't a scoundrel!
No... Perhaps Czerniaków was weak? But he was a decent man, for sure!

How did you write your book? I know that you were in hospital at the time, in Łódź, on Marek Edelman's ward, and that it was 1986.
I wrote that book in six weeks. It was there that I realized that time was passing, we are not immortal, and I had one duty left to fulfil. Marek says it was "screaming from me."

---

51 p. 522 Glossary—Zygielbojm, Szmuel.
52 p. 517 Glossary—Szeryński, Col. Józef Andrzej.

Did you tell Marek that you were writing the book?
No. I just gave him the manuscript without telling him what it was—I was counting on his laziness. But I miscalculated—he read those papers. He came and said to me: "I've sent it to be typed up."

In your book, you wrote: "I couldn't live like the others, like those who went out into the big wide world and started over." After you left the ghetto, you felt as though you weren't from here: "I was always there, behind that wall."[53] How is it today? What world do you live in today?
Things were different then and now. Back then, through all those months of incarceration, one missed Warsaw awfully. The ghetto, with its milling crowds, wasn't Warsaw. One really missed a bit of green. The walls ran in such a way that we couldn't even see the Krasińskich Gardens. I remember that I was sick once, and someone who had been on the Aryan side brought me a flowering red bean plant...

And nowadays? Many people left and started over. What about you?
After the war, I couldn't find my niche in Warsaw, but that passed fairly quickly. And now? I don't think I'm able to be as happy as other people. Perhaps even more so now than before... You know, I have no reason to complain of poverty; I made a little money with that book.

Do you mean that ironically?
No, not at all. And I don't even need the money! It's only useful for making my children's lives a little easier. But me? I really have need of very little besides a book.

So where are you—more here or more there?
No, now I'm in this world. Perhaps partly because I don't allow myself such internal emigration anymore, because Polish issues are too important to me. Perhaps if I lived in France, it would be different. It's true that I don't have the skill of enjoying life—perhaps that's what's remained. But I'm here, in the midst of all these Polish issues.

When we talk about your being here, it's impossible to forget that that other world was in the same place. In your book, you write: "In this huge, modern city, there is no trace of what happened, but when I close my eyes..."[54]

---

53 Blady-Szwajgier, *Wspomnienia lekarki*.
54 Ibid.

But when I close my eyes, I'm back on that street with those people . . . If I say "Nalewki," that has nothing in common with what is now Nowotki. And I can see it when I close my eyes. There is the fire station, the park gate and fence, and the people, and on the corner is a cold meats store, only I can't make out the sign . . . I can see it, you understand, but it's too far away for me to read. I cross the street. In front of me there's an entrance gate, and beyond that, three courtyards, it's a kind of precinct or arcade—lots of stores, little shops, and a crowd of people. And here is the Doll Clinic, on the second floor, in that entranceway. It's all so clear . . . And there's a man standing outside the store with his hat pushed back on his head, and sitting beside him a woman selling bagels; a little further on is a cart with oranges . . .

And that street is real?
Very, very much so . . . Truth be told, in 1942, I left my house and never returned to it. And today? I live in the new Warsaw. And when I walk back from, say, the Ministry of Health, I walk through the Krasińskich Gardens. When I come out onto Nowotki, I wonder where I am. Of course, it's Nalewki. From the Krasińskich Gardens I always come out onto Nalewki, never onto Nowotki.

And when you pass close to the Umschlagplatz?
I go to the Umschlagplatz twice a year—on All Saints, and on April 19.

Do you avoid it?
Apart from anything else, I have no business there, because there is nothing anyone needs on Stawki.

And when you go there on those two occasions every year, the "film replays," yes?
Of course, of course.

And does the film sometimes replay here, in your apartment in Ochota?
. . .Well . . . yes, sometimes it does—when I read something, see something, when someone asks me something—then it replays . . .

Does it sometimes happen out of the blue?
No, no. Sometimes I have recurring dreams in the night . . . I dream about Śnieżna Street and the race with the German motorcycle. I'm walking along the street, I'm in a hurry, but I can't walk—that happens a lot in my dreams. But I have to get there before the Germans; I have to get Marek out of that apartment.

And when you're awake?
No, no. I think you repress things like that, both consciously and subconsciously. You couldn't function otherwise! But I'm constantly aware of the particular past that I am from.

So, for you, that world is a past that doesn't intrude on your present?
It's a past that changed everything . . . I told you—I left my house in July 1942 and never went back . . . And I shall never be at home anywhere again! Only sometimes do I dream of home . . . I think we're all homeless, really.

All of you who experienced that?
Yes. I think so. Where we are now, where we live—these are all just apartments . . . Apartments, do you understand! You know, it's amusing! You have the impression that everything everywhere around you is unreal, somehow.

That past is real.
Yes. But not what happened during the war. By "that past," I mean what there was before the war. That home, that life was real. That was true. You know, it's funny—when I was in a somewhat difficult situation financially for many years, that also seemed unreal to me!

The prewar years. And the war, the ghetto, the Umschlag? Was that reality? I'll put it differently. Is there a place for that world in today's world? Or are they two separate worlds separated by a clear line?
No, everything is a continuation of that. That world is part of this world. Because you see, if it were possible to go back . . . Then it could be a closed chapter! But a return is impossible. What happened is irreversible. We will never be able to go back to our point of departure. So, everything that happens now is a continuation of that. The here and now is somehow unreal, and it became unreal because of that. Everything, everything is different. And it's probably all a surrogate of what there should be. There's just no going back to real life.

I think that almost everyone has places or situations in which they feel comfortable, at home. Do you?
No, no. Sometimes, when the children were small, sometimes with my grandson, but those are fleeting moments. And you know, I don't mean to say that our lives ended there—no! They just changed entirely, and there is no returning to what was and what should be . . . And now we have to find our place in this alien world.

So, it's not true, what you wrote in your own book, that "it all receded into the gloom of history"—it's not like that? It all lives in the present, and not in history?
Perhaps. It's inside me.

You and a few other people. And since that's the case, then it's real; it is in this world. I started going to the Umschlagplatz many years later, when you were there, but to me it's not the place where the gas station stands. I see a different place entirely, and it is this recalled picture that is real.
It's a caesura. Nothing in Poland is the same anymore; everything has changed.

You're talking about the changes around us, but I think that the changes within us, in our thinking about the world, are far more important.
Both around us and within us. This used to be a rich, mixed forest. Then one day a lumberjack came and cut all the birch trees down. And it's no longer a mixed forest. Apart from anything else, a mixed forest has much greater chances of survival than a homogeneous forest. This is an entirely different Poland, believe me.

Did you read the discussion in the press sparked by Jan Błoński's article in *Tygodnik Powszechny*?[55]
I think I know most of those texts. I remember the shameful voice of Siła-Nowicki[56] well. His text surprised me—back then he was still considered a decent person.

The debate was not, as was frequently claimed, about Polish-Jewish relations, but about the Poles' responsibility for the Holocaust, and their guilt.
Responsibility, not guilt.

Well, if we talk about guilt, we are defining responsibility. An important voice in that debate is Zygmunt Bauman's text in *Aneks*.[57] Bauman says that reason was the most disastrous force, and obedience, and that the logic of

---

55 Jan Błoński's article "Biedni Polacy patrzą na getto" [The Poor Poles Look at the Ghetto], first published in the Catholic current affairs weekly *Tygodnik Powszechny* in 1987, later reprinted many times and translated into several languages, was the point of departure for the highly turbulent debate, conducted largely in the press, on the attitudes of Poles to the Holocaust, and the extent of their co-responsibility, guilt, and part in the murder.
56 Władysław Siła-Nowicki (1913–1994), lawyer, author of press articles, defender of right-wing, nationalistic views.
57 *Aneks*—political quarterly published, initially in Uppsala, later in London, by Jewish émigrés who left Poland after the events of March 1968.

reason necessitated consent to crime. Logic flew in the face of emotions and destroyed values. Thus, Bauman claims, immoral reason co-existed with illogical morality at that time.
And he's right.

He goes on to say that that inhumane world dehumanized its victims, forcing them to use logic, to switch into self-preservation mode.
He's right. But you know, the notion of the Poles' guilt as understood in the West is meaningless. Over there, people have no idea what it was really like. I suppose it would be fair to speak of one type of guilt—too few people were saved. In terms of the thing itself, the Holocaust—the Poles could not have done anything at all. Save rescue individuals.

Thank you.

Warsaw, winter 1990.

Adina Blady-Szwajgier, Inka, died in Warsaw on February 19, 1993.

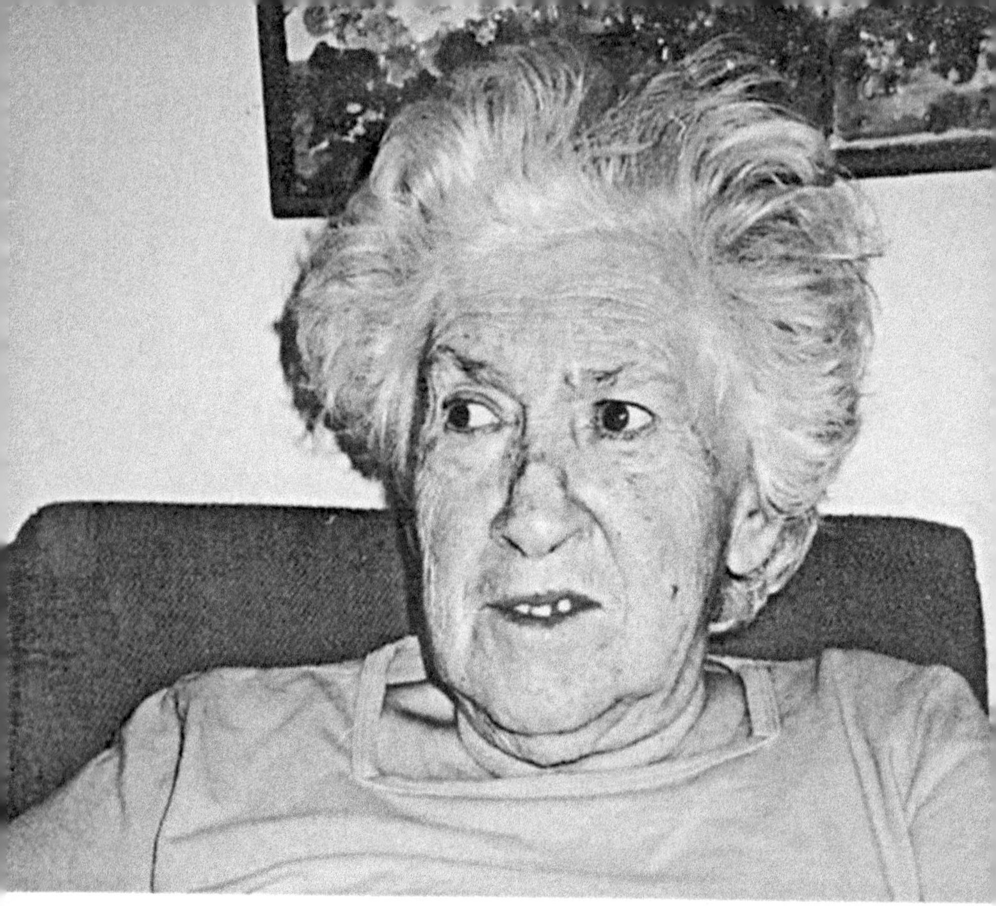

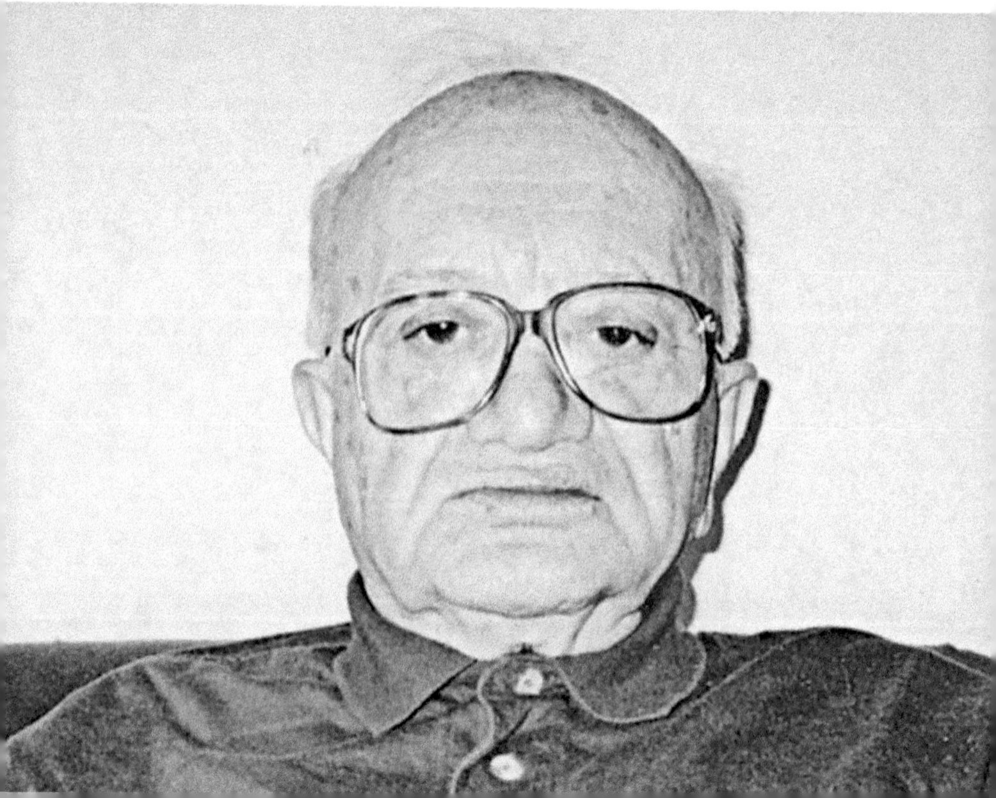

And That's All My Life Story

Conversation with Halina [Chajka] Bełchatowska and Bronek Szpigiel

Halina: My name is Halina Bełchatowska. I went to a public elementary school. My mother was a bookbinder. She was a member of the Bund. I didn't have a father; he disappeared or something, I don't know what happened to him. I lived with my grandmother and mother on Smocza Street, in the Jewish district. In the ghetto I lived on Smocza at first, and then every few months in a different place. I was a member of Cukunft. Before the war I used to go to the Medem Sanatorium, whenever I had time. We mended linen and clothes. I was born—I don't remember when, in 1919, I think. In the ghetto I worked in a soup kitchen on Nowolipie, it was a Bund soup kitchen. I cooked and washed dishes there. It was a soup kitchen for poor people. And that's all my life story.

***

Chajka, you once told Zbyszek Bujak how you jumped a train headed for Treblinka.
Bronek: He asked if we went belly first or ass first.

Belly or back to the car, you mean?
Halina: Belly.
Bronek: I think back.

***

Halina: I jumped that train to Treblinka. That was in August 1942. I was taken off of the street. I was living on Smocza, and they caught me on Smocza . . . on Nowolipie. And they took me to the Umschlagplatz. I jumped that train. I only spent a few days on the Umschlagplatz.
Bronek: They took you from the 'shop, Halina, with the whole group, not from home.

Halina: I don't remember.
Bronek: It was November 11, in 1942. They surrounded the entire ghetto. And Welwł Rozowski's group went into hiding together.

Which "'shop" was it? Roerich's?
Bronek: Yes. We mended tarpaulins for the army there, but there were people there who couldn't sew. I worked in the impregnation 'shop. That was somewhere else. It was a branch of Roerich's on Nowolipki and Smocza.

***

So how did you manage to jump the train?
Halina: Through the window.

How? Was the window open?
Halina: No, it was us opened the window.

How could you have opened it? The windows were barred.
Halina: There were seven of us. And we all tried to open the window.

Was it a Bundist group?
Halina: Yes.
Bronek: They all held hands.

Who was there?
Bronek: Lusiek, Guta, and Jurek Błones, Mojszele Kojfman, Brucha Einstein,[1] Welwł Rozowski, Lola Wiernik from Łódź, Bruch Zalcman, and Minia Wajsgruz. She was such a beautiful, innocent little girl; I think she was sixteen. It was Rozowski opened the window. And first to jump out of the train was Kojfman, because he said he had papers and he had a better chance on the Aryan side.

Were all of you in that group from the Bund?
Bronek: Apart from that one girl from Łódź. She was from Poalej Syjon Left.
Halina: Lola Wiernik.
Bronek: That's right. See, she remembers! Her father was a Bundist. And her brother-in-law was well known in the Bund. Pat, his name was. Am I right, Halina?

---

1 p. 368 Rereading the List—Cypora Einstein.

Halina: No. She was Wiernik.
Bronek: It's a well-known name, Wiernik. There was a carpenter who built Treblinka. He was Wiernik,[2] too.

***

Bronek: That Welwł Rozowski, he was extraordinary. And Kojfman had been on the Aryan side. But his money had run out and he returned to the ghetto and worked with us in the 'shop. And he jumped first, because he had papers from the Aryan side, and said: "I'll get by out there, I have more possibilities than you."

And how did they pull the bars out?
Bronek: That was Welwł Rozowski. He had a, what do you call it . . .
Halina: . . .saw.
Bronek: A saw. He was already a member of the organization. Everyone from the organization had a saw.
Halina: We hid them in our boots.

Did you have a saw, too, Chajka?
Halina: I don't remember.
Bronek: And that Lola—she was wealthy. And in the wagon, Rozowski said: "Who has dollars?" So, she pulled out some small change and gave some to everyone. How much did you get? Five dollars?
Halina: I don't remember. Maybe ten.
Bronek: Everyone got dollars. And Chajka had bread, so she shared her bread. Chajka always went about with a full breadbasket, because then if she was caught . . . And they jumped. But Guta Błones twisted her leg. They jumped out before the train got going; it was just shunting between tracks.

So, they jumped out right outside Warsaw?
Bronek: Yes, the train hadn't gotten going. It was just beyond the Umschlagplatz. Welwł pushed them all out through that little window. The Ukrainians were already sitting on the train.
Halina: And shooting.

---

2   Jakub Wiernik escaped from Treblinka in August 1943. At Celina Lubetkin's request, he wrote an account of it that was sent to the Polish government-in-exile in London.

So Welwł jumped last?
Bronek: Yes.

And what happened to the ones who jumped out?
Bronek: They called to each other with a codeword. And some Polish boys noticed that there were Jews there and that they could earn something on them. And ours said: "Take us to the ghetto and we'll pay you." Is that how it was?
Halina: I think so.
Bronek: So, the group waited until the detail workers came back from work and went into the ghetto with them.

And you, Bronek, were in the 'shop at that point?
Bronek: Yes, I was at Roerich's. they didn't catch me that time.

***

Where were you living at that time?
Bronek: On Nowolipie. What number was it?
Halina: Sixty-something.[3]
Bronek: Oh! Sixty-something!

Who were you living with?
Bronek: Mojsze Kojfman. Welwł Rozowski. He wasn't with us seven days a week, because he had a wife, Rywka Rozensztajn.

And did she live on Dzielna?
Bronek: Nooo. By that time, she was with the hospital. She lived on Dzielna at the very beginning.

***

Bronek, how did you come to join the ŻOB?
Bronek: I remember clearly. The fives were being organized. There were no weapons yet.

---

[3] According to Marek Edelman, that group was living at 67 Nowolipie Street (conversation with H.G., Jan. 1, 2000).

Selling

When did the fives come into being?

Bronek: It was in the October. In 1942. Hersz Lent[4] was our technical manager. He taught us because he had a revolver. And Welwł was our commander for *tsures*. Do you know what that means?

Yes: for problems. Did Hersz work at Roerich's too?

Bronek: He was something more than a janitor there. It was a kind of made-up position. Hersz was a streetcar driver before the war. Back then, that was an important, party post. If we managed to get those positions from the PPS, it was a miracle. And Hersz Lent was one streetcar driver; the other one was Abram Feiner.

Was Lent a Bundist?

Bronek: He was from Poalej Syjon Left. And so, when people write about all that, he's left out.

You mean they don't write about him?

Bronek: Because he wasn't from the Bund.

How did Hersz Lent die?

Bronek: That's a very tragic story. Two Polish streetcar drivers came looking for him into the ghetto. They wanted to take Hersz and his family into hiding. And Hersz went to Berliński because his son was in Berliński's group.

Hersz's son Szaanan?

Bronek: Yes. But his son didn't want to leave the ghetto. And so, his father didn't go either.

Szaanan was born in Palestine, wasn't he?

Bronek: Yes. He was a beautiful lad, beautiful.

And how did Szaanan die?

Bronek: In fighting, on Świętojerska, in the brushmakers' yard, in Berliński's group.

And his father?

Bronek: He was taken from Roerich's 'shop to the Umschlag.

---

4 p. 410 Rereading the List—Szaanan Lent.

***

Who was in Rozowski's group?
Bronek: Szlojme Szwarc,[5] Igła . . .

Zygmunt Igła?[6]
Bronek: Zygmunt, Gabryś Fryszdorf,[7] Hanka Fryszdorf, Chajka Bełchatowska. And one more. He was killed with Merdek Growas's group. I remember his face. And I was in that group, and Tobcia Dawidowicz.[8] Nine people.

Thank you, Chajka. Thank you, Bronek.

Montreal, December 1999.

Halina Bełchatowska (Chajka) died in Montreal in March 2002.
Bronek Szpigiel died in Montreal on March 9, 2013.

---

5   p. 456 Rereading the List—Szlomo Szwarc.
6   p. 396 Rereading the List.
7   p. 378 Rereading the List—Gabriel (Gabryś) Fryszdorf.
8   p. 363 Rereading the List.

I Know What I Know, and I Remember What I Remember

Conversation with Kazik Ratajzer

You know, a few years ago, I was in Warsaw with a group of our young people.[1] We were walking the route to the Umschlagplatz, and their guide said: "This is the Heroes' Route." "What heroes?!" I yelled. "What heroism? What are you talking about? What? We were victorious? Was I able to defend my parents in the ghetto? Was I able to defend anyone at all? One more heroism like that and there'll not be a single Jew left alive!"

But you did rescue people—you more than anybody else. Literally: you took dozens of people out of the ghetto.
But you know what? If we had put our minds to that and not to the uprising, perhaps I could have taken hundreds out? Perhaps that was possible?! For honor, for history... For honor and for history you have to have a homeland, tanks, and maybe even the atom bomb!

So, there were no heroes in the ghetto?
Listen, I wouldn't call all of that "heroism" so glibly. I think you can speak of humanitarian attitudes and behaviors, of a sense of duty to those close to you. You can call them comrades-in-arms if you wish; I don't like that expression. If I could do anything for them, I was prepared to do anything, anything at all. I didn't know that I would make it out onto the other side, that I would be able to get back into the ghetto. It was one huge madness, going out and going back in of your own free will.

And that's not heroic behavior?
Call it that if you want. I was aware that there were people waiting for me, that they trusted me, and were counting on me. How could I have let them down?

---

1   Every year, groups of Israeli high school students go on "delegation" to the extermination camps in Poland and visit sites of remembrance connected with the murdered Jews.

So, what would you call your stance? Friendship? Loyalty? A sense of responsibility?
All of that together. And only at the end would I call it heroism. But I don't actually think there are that many people so keen to call us heroes. Here, at least. To this day, the State of Israel has never decorated a single fighter from the ghetto uprising or the partisan army.

What does that mean?
It means that they don't see us as heroes.

But that's a different story.
Yes, that's a different story.

***

In a conversation I recorded years ago, Marek Edelman told the story of how the AK got hold of him during the uprising and locked him in a cellar. Marek threw a note out of the cellar window, Kamiński happened to be walking along the street, and somehow managed to get him out of there. Years later, it transpires that the story is true, but the protagonists were different. It was Julek Fiszgrund in the cellar in the Old Town. And Kazik who found the note.
Listen, that all sounds very pretty, but I never found any note. Fiszgrund really was arrested by the AK, but there was no miracle coincidence afterwards. As far as I remember, someone came to us and told us. It could have been Zosia [Renia Frydman], Fiszgrund's girl. Naturally, Julek was in grave danger, so I didn't stop to think, I didn't ask anyone. I just went right over to the AK guys. After all, I considered myself a first-class member of the AK after the battle to defend the Courts.[2] "What do you want from him? I know him well—he's an upstanding Pole!" and so on…

You resolutely played the Polish AK member card?
Yes. You know, I was cocky, and I didn't stammer in Polish like I do nowadays—so I got him out. And that was that.

---

2   The insurrectionists took the courthouse at Leszno Street on the first day of fighting, August 1, 1944, and were essentially left unassailed by the Germans for several days. On August 6, the German assault on the northern part of the downtown Śródmieście district began. The courthouse was defended by the battalion "Chrobry I," whose soldiers were recruited from the National Armed Forces (NSZ), and the battalion under Cpt. Sosna. On August 7, the AK fighters retreated to the Old Town.

How long were you in the group at the Courts?
A few days—I don't remember precisely. I would guess it was five days, or maybe six? There was a hospital for the insurrectionists in the basement of the Courts, and I was there until the order was given to evacuate the hospital.

But how did you come to join them? Did you just go up to the group and say you wanted to fight with them?
Listen, the situation came at me by surprise. I was walking down the street, and suddenly I walk into this insurrection. I happened to have a revolver with me, and I thought I might come in useful.

When did you meet up with Antek and the rest?
I think it was the next day. I went from the Courts to Leszno.[3] I was worried about them, and I knew they would be worrying about me. But they were all there: Antek, Marek, Celina . . . And I said to them: "Listen, we have to join. Either here or there. I'm in the AK, because I ran into their insurrection on the street, and there happened to be an AK unit nearby, at the Courts."

But you decided to join the AL because it would be safer?
Yes. We already knew that the AK had a bad attitude toward Jews.

You already knew about Jurek Grasberg's murder?
Yes. I went back one more time to my unit at the Courts. I'll tell you something funny. The guys in that unit were a group that had known each other before; they even had some sort of military ranks. I was the only rank-and-file outsider. When I joined them, I was given a police uniform, and they called me "the Cop."

Why did you get a police uniform?
Because they didn't have any other.

And it was important to be in some kind of uniform to look more military?
Yes. Things like that gave you self-confidence. And listen. One night, those boys from the AK were sitting around and talking. I was asleep, but at one point I woke up and I heard that they want out, because the insurrection has no chance, and they have to get out of there. I sat down with them and I'm listening to them saying that they gotta get out of Warsaw in the early hours of the morning, because everyone's gonna be slaughtered, and so on and so on. So then, get this, I say to them: "You should be ashamed of yourselves! We ought to take the Jews in the ghetto as our example!" They were shocked. And listen, they decided to stay!

---

3   The ŻOB fighters were living at 18 Leszno at the time.

So, when you gave the ghetto as an example, did you admit to being a Jew yourself?
No way! Are you kidding? Absolutely not, never! Not because I was particularly wise. It was intuition. Good intuition. Well, how was Jurek worse than me?![4]

So how did you come to join the AL? How did you get into the AL?
Well, Antek had direct contact with the AL the whole time. And there was this guy, Witold,[5] I think his name was. Antek and I went to the staff company, sorted everything, and that was it. We decided that we would join as a group from the ŻOB.

Who was in the group?
I can count easily enough: Antek, Marek, me, Cywia, Grajek, Marysia Sawicka,[6] Marysia Warman and Zygmunt Warman, Stasia [Rywka Rozensztajn], and [Józef] Sak,[7] too. We weren't all together. After all, we didn't know when the uprising would break out, and each of us had our own affairs in the city. Inka wasn't with us then, for instance. The group wasn't complete.

Was Marysia Sawicka with you in the ŻOB group?
Yes, of course. She was with me afterwards on Leszno, too, right to the end.

But Marysia wasn't a member of the ŻOB.
No, but she was one of us.

What do you remember of those days with the AL in the Old Town?
One of my tasks was to find a way to Żoliborz via the sewers.

Who gave you that task?
The AL staff company. Antek had obviously told them that I had experience. They assigned me a group of a few people. Each one of those guys had some form of military experience, and I, a greenhorn, had no idea how to give commands. So, I went up to one of them and said: "Listen, I'll talk to you, and you organize them and do what you want. I'll lead you through the sewers, and that's all." The guy was happy, he was suddenly a commander, and I was happy too.

---

4   Kazik is referring to the murder of his Jewish friend Jurek Grasberg, who had believed that the AK would welcome him to fight.
5   Franciszek Jóźwiak (Witold) (1895–1966)—member of the PPS, the Polish Legions, and the Polish Communist Party; co-organizer of the PPR in 1942, commander of the People's Guard [Gwardia Ludowa] staff company, and later also the AL staff company. After the war commander-in-chief of the Citizens' Militia (the communist police force), member of the Polish United Workers' Party Central Committee's Politburo.
6   p. 441 Rereading the List—Marysia Sawicka.
7   Józef Sak (1899–1965)—a literature teacher in Częstochowa before the war; organizer of the Dror underground high school in the Warsaw ghetto. After the war, he emigrated to Israel.

And you went?
Yes, we reached Żoliborz, assured ourselves that we were in the right place, and returned to the Old Town. And a few days later, Antek (and I think Marek and Cywia were also involved in the decision) ordered me to push back through to Leszno, to our base. I absolutely didn't want to go, I thought it was madness. Go into territory that was shortly to be German? I mean, everything was on fire there. But Antek was firm—I was to go and that was it. So, we went. Nastek [Lt. Anastazy Matywiecki] took us part-way. He guided us through the AL positions, and further, almost to our destination. On the way, as he saw what was happening—it really was madness, everything burning, and crowds of people streaming toward the Old Town, and us heading stubbornly in the opposite direction—Nastek wanted to convince me to turn back. But I had set my course. I remember the words I said to him: "A goat would go back. I didn't want to go before, but now I'm going, and that's that." And I said to my people: "Anyone who wants to go back should go, I'm going on." No one went back, we all went together. The next morning, the Germans came and set the house alight. Somehow, we made it. Afterwards, we sat in those cellars on Leszno for weeks.

Did you find what Antek sent you for? You went for the ŻOB archives, right?
Listen, I wasn't looking for anything. That whole archive interested me about as much as last year's snow. I don't understand what I went there for now, and I didn't understand then!

Well, yes, but what did Antek say when he gave you the order to go to 18 Leszno?
That we had to go because there had to be . . . a base there!

In your book[8] you say that you went for the archives.
It may be that that's what he told me, and then explained that there had to be a base there. Look, Antek in his book[9] basically wrote: We sent Kazik because we knew that we could rely on him.[10] But because Antek is no longer with us, I can't ask.

---

8   Kazik (Simha Rotem), *Memoirs of a Warsaw Ghetto Fighter*, trans. and ed. by Barbara Harshav, (New Haven: Yale University Press, 1994).
9   Zuckerman, *A Surplus of Memory*.
10 In his book, Cukierman writes: "The decision was taken to establish an AL rebel base at Leszno 18. We sent a group of our comrades there [...]. The idea was to move people who weren't vital to the war to hold the base at Leszno, which we would use for retreat if necessary, and, meanwhile, for preserving the archive and the armory. [...] I must note that Kazik was a fighter and was very vital to us, but he knew the bunker and the way to it, and we relied on him to lead the group and organize it on the spot." Zuckerman, *A Surplus of Memory*, 469.

But you never asked him after the war what he sent you to Leszno for?
No, I didn't.

Why not?
Listen, I didn't want to go back to those subjects at all. I didn't go anywhere near that whole period. Either with Cywia or with Antek.

You never ever talked about it together?!
No. Sometimes we would reminisce over something, but I never dug, and they never explained. When Antek was so keen for me to write our story down, he would always say: "Listen, there are things that only you and I know. You have to write it down." I had no need of either writing or talking. For me it was all over. I wanted them all to just leave me in peace. And once, I said: "OK, fair enough, I agree. But tell me, what about you? Are you writing, aren't you writing? You should write, too." But he didn't say as much as half a word to me. It wasn't until after his death that I found out that his story had already been told at the time of our conversation.

Do you have a grudge against him for that?
I don't have a grudge against anybody. I just want to understand why people did what they did and not otherwise.

And that's a situation you don't understand?
No, I don't understand it. How can I understand that Antek didn't tell me he'd already written his story?!

Did you think you were close friends?
Listen, I think so. You know what, perhaps you'd have to define what friendship is. And apart from that, I think that telling the truth, total truthfulness, those are difficult things. Look: being in a friendship with someone means being prepared to help. And I'm sure that Antek would never have refused me help. Sometimes I think that all the differences and misunderstandings between us came about because I was never, never ever, a party man. That way of thinking, that the party is more important that anything else, is alien to me. That's how it was with Antek, and it's the same with Marek. In that respect they were no different to each other. Look: Marek wrote that little book about the ghetto.[11] But he only wrote about the Bund.

---

11 See anonymous English translation, Marek Edelman, "The Ghetto Fights" in *The Warsaw Ghetto Uprising*, Literature of the Holocaust, accessed October 2, 2022.,

Well, yes, but that was his intention. That text was a report for the Bund cells in America.
Precisely! That's what I'm talking about: about the Bund for the Bund! I talked to Marek about that many years ago; I said to him: "Listen up, man, I think it was a bit different, wasn't it? And what about me? Did I come back to the ghetto to get you Bundists out, or not to get you Bundists out?! I don't understand what you're saying to me. It's some language I don't know. You can write whatever you like about the Bund. But that doesn't mean you can pass over everything else in silence!"

Do you know anything about Jurek Grasberg apart from that he was killed on Pańska?
No; I don't know anything else at all. Perhaps I feel a little guilty. Although: no, I don't. Truth be told, I don't feel guilty about anything. And that incident was like this. That same day, or a day earlier, I sent Luba [Gawisar] to somewhere in Saska Kępa to bring this little girl back from there. And Luba went. And because the rising broke out, then she couldn't get back. And I wasn't there, at Pańska, by then. (I had been living with them—Luba, Irena [Gelblum], and Jurek—for a while before that. But after that big spill, Antek and I moved out to Polska Street.) I found out about it all a day or two later.

Does that mean that there isn't anyone who might know any details?
No.

And it was Aleksander Kamiński who knew that it was AK people who murdered Jurek?
Yes. And I don't know how he knew.

***

---

https://writing.upenn.edu/~afilreis/Holocaust/warsaw-uprising.html. Original Polish version, see: Marek Edelman, *Getto walczy* (Łódź: Nakł. C.K. "Bundu," 1945).

Hala Mirowska in Warsaw, Piaseczno, Wiązowna

Marek likes to spice up his stories with an anecdote about how you served as an altar boy for mass in a hospital after the Warsaw rising. Was that in Boernerowo?
Yes, and it's true. One day Luba came to see me in Kraków. (I was with Irena at the time.) And she said: "Listen, Antek: Marek and the others are in Żoliborz, and we have to get them out." I didn't stop to think. Though I was livid . . .

Because of the incident with the foray to Leszno?
Yes, because of that. But I said: "OK." We arrived in Warsaw in the early hours of the morning, and it turned out that they had already been gotten out, and they were in hospital. And since the priest needed an assistant, and I was suitable . . .

***

Let's go back to that lost thread of your friendship with Antek.
Listen, I often went to see Antek. When Cywia was still alive and later, after her death. I always had the issue of whether or not to take him a bottle, but I thought, he'll find one either way, so I used to take one. After Cywia's death, Antek was always reminiscing about her. He talked about her a lot. And I listened and didn't ask questions. Perhaps analyzing what happened back then came to me too late. It's possible. But it couldn't have been any other way. I just didn't want to talk about it, and I didn't, for many years.

Why didn't you want to talk about it?
The way of life here was certainly a major factor. When I came to Palestine in 1946, there was no space for pondering those things. In 1947, I was called up, and before long I was fighting in the war for independence. Apart from that, people were kind of suspicious of us immigrants from Europe. Perhaps I was over-sensitive. I had the impression that they looked at us and thought that since we had managed to save ourselves, there must have been something wrong with us. Because the decent ones had been killed, they were no longer. Within a very short time, I had changed my identity. If I was asked where I was from, I would say: "Petakh Tikva."[12] Why Petakh Tikva? Because people who lived in Petakh Tikva couldn't speak Hebrew very well. They spoke Yiddish and other languages, but Hebrew least of all. So, if I said "Petakh Tikva," no one asked me anything else, and I didn't have to answer any of the whys and wherefores.

---

12 Petakh Tikva—a city around ten miles northeast of Tel Aviv.

And only those closest to you knew the truth?
Yes. There were a few of them: Antek, Celina, and Jakubek and Masza, Luba [Gawisar], Pnina [Grynszpan], and Aron [Karmi]. There was just one local person who knew everything. That was this woman who took me in right after I arrived. Cipora Czyżyk. She gave me the key to her apartment, hardly asked me about anything, and let me sleep.

***

How did you reach Eretz Israel?
Illegally.

Who were you with?
I was alone.

Nobody you knew?
I don't remember, but I don't think so.

You arrived by ship.
From Marseilles. They intercepted us just outside Haifa, interned all several hundred of us, and we were stuck in Atlit[13] for about six weeks. And when they released us, buses came... You asked who was in that group. Well, then. Most of the group were people I had spent the previous more than one and a half years with, doing those various operations in Germany.[14]

You're referring to the operation known as "Revenge," right?
Yes. So, the buses took us to Aba Kowner's[15] kibbutz. You must have heard of it. And they all decided to stay there. But I got up the next morning and said: "I'm

---

13 Atlit—a small town between Hedera and Haifa where illegal immigrants to Palestine were interned. After World War II, the British administrators of Palestine (British Mandate Palestine: 1917—1948) permitted the entry of one thousand five hundred Jews every month. Illegal immigrants were sent to internment camps, usually in Cyprus. Between 1946 and the first half of 1948, seventeen thousand legal and thirty-nine thousand illegal immigrants arrived in Palestine.

14 Nakam (Heb.: "revenge"), a group of Holocaust survivors under Aba Kowner that in 1945 attempted a mass operation to kill six million Germans, by poisoning the mains water supply of Nuremberg, and, when that failed, German SS prisoners held in Allied POW camps, by poisoning their bread. After a few months, Kowner was arrested. The operation was in no respect a success.

15 Aba Kowner (1918–1988)—Haszomer Hacair activist in Vilnius, leader of the Vilnius partisans; Hebrew poet. During the final deportation campaign in the Vilnius ghetto in September 1943, he masterminded the escape of Jewish soldiers to forest partisan units; he was also the

going to Tel Aviv." They all asked me: "Kazik, have you gone mad?" And actually, it wouldn't have taken much to push me over the edge. "What? Why? You have everything here: a home, a job, green lawns!" "Precisely," I said, "that's just it: I didn't work for any of this."

How large was the Nakam group that came with you from Germany?
Maybe thirty to forty people. In the end, almost all of them left the kibbutz apart from Aba and Witka.[16]

Did your girlfriend, Irka, also come to Eretz Israel at that time?
Yes.

But then she returned to Poland?
Yes. I don't remember whether we came together or whether she wasn't already here before me? I remember that when we high-tailed it from Germany, I was with one other guy, and we escaped to France. But Irka was somewhere else.

But you didn't go to Tel Aviv together?
No.

You weren't a couple by then?
Yes and no. She was in Haifa, you know, and I was in Tel Aviv.

***

Why don't you want to talk about the Nakam group?
Because I think that, fifty years on, I can't explain to anyone what that crazy idea was all about.

That's a convincing argument.
If we could have talked about it in 1946, 1947 . . . But today?! No logic would be capable of understanding it. What sort of crazy people thought up something so dreadful? Such revenge? Who could understand it?! The world today no longer

---

leader of Nakam (see note 335 above), which comprised soldiers from the Jewish Brigade and other Jewish survivors. In Israel from 1945; from 1946 in Kibbutz Ein Horesh.
16 Witka Kempner Kowner (1920–2012)—Jewish underground activist in Vilnius: in May 1942, she and two others blew up a train carrying German soldiers. She also took part in many other operations, including the rescue of sixty Jews in October 1943. After the war, she and her husband, Aba Kowner, were active in Nakam. In 1946, she went to live in Kibbutz Ein Horesh in Israel.

needs our story; it's full enough of terror and violence as it is. Why should I give anyone any more cruel ideas?! I don't see any reason.

Other former group members don't seem to share your reticence. I recently saw a documentary on Nakam.[17] Your former comrades talk in considerable detail, as far as their memory permits, about those operations in Germany. Could you see yourself telling the same story sometime?
I don't know, perhaps. I don't have a problem with that.

In what sense?
In terms of the race for popularity in history, I have no trouble dropping out.

What have you retained from that experience?
Listen, it was just an episode. We didn't succeed in doing what we set out to do. There are things I truly regret. But the fact that our main operation didn't work is something that I can only be pleased about, because I don't know how it would be possible to live with it if it had worked. It really was madness. Fifty years ago, I saw it all differently. I changed my mind not today, but several decades ago.

***

When did the ŻOB come into being? What date do you use?
What does "come into being" mean? On paper? Are you asking about when it actually began operating? I don't know how to count it. I can only recall facts. One fact is that the first uprising in the ghetto was in the January.

Those street battles on January 18, 1943, you refer to as an "uprising?"
I can refer to them differently. Do you have a better word?

Some call it the "January campaign," or "operation."
Campaign? No—it was the Germans who mounted the campaign.

Now you're meaning the deportation campaign?
Yes. But we could use "resistance," or "organized battles," if you want. I was already in a fighting group by then. I had no weapon. I was holed up in an attic with Celina and some others. There were probably several dozen of us. You

---

17 *Revenge*—American documentary film from the 1990s.

know, I don't even remember if I had a metal bar or anything, or only a wooden club. So, in terms of when the ŻOB was called into being, you'd have to refer to documents, which may or may not have survived.

I suspect that there are no surviving documents. But there are at least two dates in circulation. Celina writes that the ŻOB was founded on July 28, 1942, and Marek says that it was founded on October 15, 1942, when the halutzim[18] came from Czerniaków.[19]

Listen, I can't add anything to that. I think that Cywia is right. And I'll explain why Marek considers himself right. And the two arguments aren't contradictory. The ŻOB was called into being by Zionist, Halutz, organizations—call them what you will—during the biggest deportation. They had about two revolvers, so I heard. I don't know whether someone spilled, but in any case, the Germans destroyed their "huge" stockpile, and people were killed. And that was it, no more ŻOB. But Marek is referring to the time when the ŻOB was recreated, as it were, and the Bund joined it. For him, that's the date that counts, that's the point where the ŻOB starts.

So, if someone asks you: "When was the ŻOB founded?", what do you say?
I say: "That's not my field; I'm not a historian." And I really don't know. I know what I know, and I remember what I remember. Either I was an eyewitness, and then I can be sure, unless I've forgotten a little and I'm wrong. But if I wasn't an eyewitness, what can I say?! The truth is that everything we did happened between January 18 and April 19, 1943.

Do you remember how you joined the ŻOB?
Yes, that I do remember. When I was in Czerniaków on the farm, Rebeka Pasamonik[20] approached me and asked me to take some letters into the ghetto for Lutek [Rotblat].[21] I knew Rebeka from before the war, she was a few years older than me.

Was Rebeka a member of Akiba?[22]
No, she belonged to Hanoar Hacyjoni.[23] Before the war she lived on Czerniakowska and I lived on Nowosielecka, so we knew each other.

---

18 p. 497 Glossary—Halutz movement.
19 Czerniaków—a suburb of Warsaw, where a kibbutz-style farm operated until late 1942.
20 p. 424 Rereading the List—Rywke (Rywka, Rebeka) Pasamonik.
21 p. 434 Rereading the List—Lejb (Lutek) Rotblat.
22 p. 491 Glossary.
23 p. 498 Glossary.

Does that mean that that sortie was your consent to working in the ŻOB?
That's how I read it. I didn't get any official letter, but I don't think anyone did.

Do you remember when that was?
In November or December 1942. In December, the place in Czerniaków was shut down, and we all went back into the ghetto.

How did you get into the ghetto?
With a work detail. Easy, you might think. But what it took to convince them that I was a Jew?! You have no idea! They wanted to take me to a German. They were obviously afraid that I had ill intentions. They saw that I had nothing on me—no potatoes, no bread, nothing! But once they were satisfied that I was one of them, they gave me some stuff to take through the wacha.

And where did you have the package? Sewn into your coat lining?
Yes.

And then you went back to Czerniaków?
Yes.

***

In Czerniaków there was a farm where a group of Halutzim worked. How did they come to be there?
Listen to how that worked. A Volksdeutsche would get permission from the German authorities to employ, say, a hundred Jews. And he could take whoever he wanted. And that's how it was in Czerniaków. And the fact that most of the people who worked on the farm were members of Zionist organizations is another matter.

Your parents and your sisters were among them. Do you know how they got that work?
No.

You had two sisters, right?
Yes, and a brother. My brother was killed in 1939.

How was he killed?
During the bombardment of Warsaw. My brother, my mother's parents, and my mother's sister and brother-in-law were all killed then. But I was only wounded.

***

Workers on detail

Did you ever hear that there was a Scout troop that wanted to join the ŻOB as a group before the uprising, and Mordechaj Anielewicz didn't let them?
Listen, I didn't hear about it at the time. But it's no wonder that I didn't because I didn't conduct negotiations of that sort.

Did you hear about it later?
Yes.

From Luba? Or from someone else?
From Luba, I think. Or maybe from Kamiński himself? I don't remember.

There's a similar story, you know, not entirely verified, that Anielewicz wouldn't let an entire unit of the ŻZW[24] join the ŻOB. Why?

Because he didn't want to agree to a "foreign body" within the ŻOB. Apparently, he was prepared to scatter the ŻZW members across various different ŻOB units.
Perhaps. But I don't know anything about that. One thing I can tell you: apart from Akiba, which I belonged to, all the others were in groups according to their organizations or parties. But we were scattered in among the others.[25]

Why was Akiba scattered?
Perhaps for the same reason that you mention. But that only occurs to me now. There weren't many of us, that's true, but there would have been enough for one group.

* * *

---

24 p. 501 Glossary—Jewish Military Union.
25 "In the central ghetto, there was a small Akiba division under the command of Lutek Rotblat. In the brushmakers' yard, there was a small Akiba division under the command of Jakub Praszker" (Marek Edelman, conversation with H.G., November 1999). According to Israel Gutman, this was a division of the organization Hanoar Hacyjoni. Edelman and Ratajzer remembered this group as belonging to Akiba.

Selling

Before the uprising you were in Beniamin Wald's[26] group, billeted on Leszno.

When the Germans took us there from Czerniaków, they put us up somewhere on Miła. By then, there was no longer any problem with apartments in the ghetto; there were huge numbers of empty houses left behind by the Jews who they had deported in the July campaign. But after the battles in January, organized groups were formed, and I was assigned to Wald's group in the Toebbens factory.

What did you do in the period before the uprising?

Listen, we did a great deal, but I'm terse, so I'll tell you in brief. Above all we sourced weapons and ammunition. In theory, there were two or three possible routes. In practice, things were worse. The only possibility was the Polish underground, which had a small quantity of weapons, but was rather unwilling to give them to us.

By "the underground," do you mean the AK, the AL, or both?

Listen. In fact, from the AL we only got a few firearms when the fighters went out into the forests. Before that, in the ghetto, there was only the AK. But I think there is a vast difference between the aid that the AK talks about, and what we actually received. I suspect much of it disappeared en route. We certainly received a few dozen revolvers, and that was all.

Do you remember any of the details of how they were transported?

On the Aryan side we had Jurek Wilner, Arie. And it was him who organized that aid. And the actual smuggling of the firearms into the ghetto? I think that was Jewish work. That revolvers would be brought in two by two in sacks of carrots or potatoes smuggled in by work details. People would pass through the guardpost trembling, but somehow it worked. I never ran guns into the ghetto, but I remember that I did go out onto the Aryan side once on a mission to get some. Someone told us that there were guns for us buried in a certain place. We went there, and dug and dug, but we didn't find shit! That was that. The second method was to buy firearms on the other side of the wall. Those were usually German guns, but not only. The war was over,[27] you know, and people had all kinds of things stashed away in their cellars. That was very risky. And the third possibility was attacking Germans and taking their weapons. Those were the methods available to us. So, from the Germans we had what we had gotten in

---

26 p. 463 Rereading the List.
27 Kazik is referring here to the failed September 1939 military campaign to defend Poland.

January—not much. Then the few dozen revolvers from the AK. And whatever else we could buy. We bought ammunition, and in the ghetto, we made Molotov cocktails, and hand grenades that we had to light ourselves. That production line was supervised by Michał Klepfisz; he had military experience. (You could count those who had served in the army before the war on the fingers of one hand. All the rest were young kids who were fourteen or fifteen when the war broke out.)

***

Did you ever meet Jurek Wilner on the other side?
No, I never saw him on the Aryan side. But I couldn't have seen him, because he was caught in January 1943, I think.[28]

Do you know any of the details of how Jurek was rescued from the camp?
What I know is that some Pole—I don't remember his name . . .

Grabowski?[29]
Grabowski! Heniek Grabowski got him out. I was very friendly with that Grabowski later on. He helped us a lot. I often used his kiosk.

What do you mean?
Grabowski had a stall selling food. And it was a superb contact point that I used to go to. Grabowski was a friend of Jurek's and, like you say, by some miracle managed to get him out of the camp and took him into hiding in his own home. But Jurek wanted to go back to the ghetto. After the war, Grabowski was decorated with the Righteous Among the Nations medal.[30]

Did he offer aid in return for money?
No, no, no money. Absolutely not.

---

28 Arie Wilner (Jurek) was arrested in an apartment on the Aryan side on March 6, 1943.
29 p. 387 Rereading the List—Henryk Grabowski, Heniek, "Słoniniarz."
30 The Righteous Among the Nations medal was first awarded in 1963 by Yad Vashem in Jerusalem, pursuant to a resolution passed by the Israeli parliament. On the basis of documentation and eye-witness accounts collected by Yad Vashem, a committee chaired by an Israeli Supreme Court judge awards Righteous Among the Nations medals and titles. Trees used to be planted in the Garden of the Righteous in the grounds of Yad Vashem to commemorate the Righteous; today, commemorative plaques are put up. Of the 27,921 citizens of 51 states honored to date, 7,184 are Poles (data from the end of 2021).

Is Grabowski still alive?
You know, I think he died recently. I remained in touch with him the whole time. I told you that I want to go to Poland and visit everybody. But there aren't many left now.

Who do you want to visit?
Tadek [Rajszczak] is gone. I would like to meet his wife. Hela Balicka is there.[31] Heniek Grabowski's wife is, too. And in Łódź there's Alina, the sister of Stefan Siewierski,[32] who was killed. And that's all.

When you go to Poland, do you meet up with Irka?
No. Not really. She is often in Italy. Sometimes she writes to me or calls, but you know, our youth ended almost fifty years ago.

***

Let's go back to our conversation about life in the fighting group before the uprising.
Basically, we did one thing: we learned to handle the weapons we had. And we attempted to get funds to buy more at all costs. This we called "exing." And since people were unwilling to give us money, well, sometimes we had to use force. We didn't like doing that, but we believed that everything would be lost anyway, so we didn't have any particular scruples.

Do you remember any particular situation, any particular "ex?"
I couldn't not remember! My first name—what used to be my pseudonym—is connected with one of those stories. It was in Henoch Gutman's group, not Beniamin Wald's; they transferred me after a little while. Or perhaps I wanted them to transfer me to Gutman, whose group was in the brushmakers' yard. I don't remember. Anyway, so one day, we went out on one of those missions. It was just the two of us, Gutman and I—or maybe there was someone else with

---

31 Helena Balicka-Kozłowska (1920–2004)—before the war a member of the PPS; during the war of the underground Union of Youth Struggle (Związek Walki Młodych, ZWM). In the Warsaw uprising, a soldier in the AL. After the war, she remained in the ZWM; decorated with the Righteous Among the Nations medal. Author of the memoirs *Mur ma dwie strony* [The wall has two sides], (Warsaw: Bellona, 1958). She lived in Warsaw.
32 p. 443 Rereading the List.

us. We went to this wealthy household, but the guy didn't really want to give us any money. And then suddenly, Gutman shouts: "Kazik! Put this gentleman right, would you?" I immediately understood what he meant, and I played the part.

The part of a boy from the Polish underground?
Yes: the idea was that I'd come over from the Aryan side to help the Jewish fighters, and so on. And after that, it got about in the ghetto that the AK was sending its own people into the ghetto, that they were being so helpful to us.

And from then on, you often played the valiant AK guy.
There was another situation related to that one. The Jewish police arrested a large group of people and locked them up in some shed. We decided to get them out. I remember that before the operation, I went on a recce to check the place out and plan our options. And then a few of us went back. All we had to do was order the policemen to let the prisoners out.

The Jewish police were unarmed. Was the group guarded just by the Jewish police?
Yes. The Germans relied on them—after all, they carried out orders to the letter. But we showed up with guns. We ordered the policemen to lie down on the ground; they lay down one of top of the other. Our boys had their faces covered, but I didn't. I spoke Polish to our people, and I think I told the policemen that I was from the AK, too, that this was a joint job. We freed all the people. They didn't need telling twice—a few minutes, and the shed was empty. The whole story got around the ghetto like wildfire. People made God knows what out of it. And the pseudonym Kazik stuck to me, so I live with it.

Even your wife calls you Kazik.
Even my Israeli grandchildren call me Kazik.

Aren't you sad that you aren't Simcha?
No, absolutely not. I don't like the name Simcha, but I wasn't asked; they named me it after some grandfather. And another "ex." This was a rich guy, some merchant—I don't remember either his name or the place. I know that he had a very pretty daughter. When we showed up there, he wasn't home, so we took the girl with us to force him to give us money. We had places we could keep the people we sort of arrested.

Aron Karmi told me a lot about the "exes," and he calls those places prisons.
OK, so be it—prisons. So, the girl wrote her father a letter, and we waited. In the end, he came, but he didn't want to give us any money, so we locked him up, too. But he was stubborn—we tried everything. I even threated to kill him, but he wouldn't budge. At one point, he gave us some money, and said to me: "Listen, I have a daughter. I'd like you to take my daughter with you back onto the Aryan side." I'd have loved to do that. But what could I tell him? That I wasn't really a Pole? I didn't want to do that. So, I just said: "OK, I'll think about it, and if the opportunity arises, I'll let you know." The guy gave us that bit of money only because he wanted to save his daughter, not because he was scared of us. He knew we weren't going to kill him.

Did you ever kill anybody that didn't want to give you money?
No, no way. We killed two people, but they were collaborators. One was called Pilotka, and the other was the chief of police. Maybe there was someone else, but I don't remember.

***

Do you remember your first group, Beniamin Wald's group?
I don't remember the others, only Wald himself. I know he was short, shorter than me, but that's all.

Wald was killed at Toebbens', right?
I think so.

Who do you remember from Henoch Gutman's group?
There was Cypora Lerer[33] and Szlamek Szuster, and Adolf Hochberg, and Dwora Baran.[34] There was Abram Ejger, and Gutman's girlfriend, whose name I don't remember. If Marek can forget, so can I, right? It's not only a commander's privilege.

In your book you write that there were four girls.
There may have been; evidently the fourth one didn't make much of an impression on me.

Were there ten people in the group?
At least—maybe even twelve.

---

33 p. 410 Rereading the List.
34 p. 339 Rereading the List.

***

When did you meet Marek?
I can't remember precisely, but it was there, at the brushmakers'. There was probably some sort of cooperation between our groups, because on the second day of the uprising, Henoch [Gutman] and Marek appointed me commander of the patrols that went out to recce in the central ghetto.

There must have been cooperation. After all, Henoch was a group commander and Marek commander of the whole area.
You know, in fact it was a little different from the way people think now. I know that Marek is God in everybody's eyes, especially in Poland—a sort of Jewish king. But I don't need to pay homage to anybody!

You only ever recognized Antek as your commander, didn't you?
No, no, no, it's not like that. You know, Marek was a commander inside the ghetto. But on the Aryan side he, like Cywia, was holed up inside all day long. It was Antek who took care of everything—and I worked with him the whole time. It was Antek who was Anielewicz's successor. Today we can call it this or that: area commander, commander of the uprising, but at the time, during the uprising, each group was more or less independent. Of course, we maintained contact with each other whenever possible, but it wasn't always possible. So that independence was rather forced. It wasn't like it is in the army, where you have a commander behind you, giving orders to each soldier, and above all there's a hierarchy, and communication. We didn't have any way of remaining in contact when the Germans were inside the ghetto. At times when a commander was most needed, we were all reliant on our groups.

I take it that you met up mostly at night, when the Germans had left the ghetto.
Of course. We looked for each other in the ruins and told each other about our experiences during the day. I tell you, all the notions that function nowadays just don't fit that situation. And when I'm asked how many rifles we had, I answer that it was irrelevant whether we had two or a hundred. Well? Even if we'd had a hundred, so what? Would we have won the war?! But we had nothing!

***

Would you like to talk about Dwora Baran?
What can I tell you? When I went out of the ghetto on May 1, she was still alive. They were all still alive. When I went back, I found no one. The only person I met in the sewers was Szlamek [Szuster]. I only saw him for a moment.

And Szlamek told you what had happened?
Yes.

Tell me.
Well, what can I tell you? That the Germans attacked, and Abram Eiger was killed, and Dwora Baran was killed. And Henoch was wounded. The remnants joined Marek's group.

Did it all happen at 6 Wałowa Street, in your base?
No. We had had to leave 6 Wałowa that day, because the Germans had set fire to the house. We went downstairs in the night and went to look for a place. Because of course we had no alternative prepared.

And was it then that you found Franciszkańska, the Provisioning Authority's bunker?
No, before that we were in some other place.

At 34 Świętojerska?
Perhaps. I went out scouting for a bunker that would accommodate several dozen people. It was then that I frightened those people in that bunker, because I was going down the stairs, and at first, all they could see was my legs in these high black leather SS-man boots. Luckily, I don't think any of them had a gun. But there was no room for us in that bunker.

And it was after that, at Franciszkańska, that most of your group was killed?
I can't be sure of that, because I wasn't there, but from what I know, yes. I asked Marek for the details recently, but he says he doesn't remember.

***

Do you remember any situations in which you shot and hit, and maybe killed someone?
I don't remember shooting my revolver and killing anyone. I think I killed a lot of people, but not with my revolver, with grenades. We would throw them from the second floor when they were on the other side of the street. It was very close. It would have been hard not to hit them. One got hit on his helmet and was set alight, and then the others next to him . . . I saw situations like that. And then the ones killed by the mine . . .

...that exploded in the entranceway on Wałowa? One of the two that had been prepared, and the only one that exploded.
Yes, those were the first people killed on our turf. How many of them there were? I don't know. But listen, it wasn't me who did that, either! Though I was supposed to. My commander, Henoch Gutman, came up, and snatched the detonator out of my hand, and it was him who pulled it. I was waiting with the mine until more of them had gotten through the gateway. And that's what happened—half of them were inside and half outside, and then Henoch ran up to me. A moment later, everything was up in the air.

Do you remember your reaction?
What a question! We were all dancing for joy. There's a difference between shooting someone directly and throwing a grenade, you know. I also had a situation where I shot at someone at close range, and I missed. I don't regret that, either. It was when we were being blackmailed on Komitetowa. A woman came to the apartment saying that she knew we were all Jews, and demanding money from us. I decided we would do the talking out on the street. We went out; I was walking along with her and Nastek. And suddenly Nastek shot at her—I don't know, once or twice. And ran off. But the woman was still walking, so I pulled out my revolver, and shot, too. I shouted that it was a round-up, and then I ran off. When I got back to Pańska, it turned out my bullet had stuck in the barrel.

You used to walk about the ghetto in an SS-man's uniform, is that right?
Yes, but I didn't use it for long, only during the uprising.

Wasn't that dangerous? In fact, why were you even walking about in that uniform?
It seemed like a good idea. You know, a German sees you from a distance and you're a little safer.

But a ŻOB member could have shot you from a distance!
But our people knew about my disguise. Everybody in the brushmakers' yard knew me. And in the central ghetto? Above all, I never walked about alone. The only time I was scared was on those steps going down into the bunker that I told you about. I could tell they were dying with terror, and that anything could have happened.

Do you remember where you had the uniform from? Did you take it off of a corpse?
I guess so. Where else could I have had it from?!

***

On April 20, the Germans entered the brushmakers' yard. First the mine explodes, detonated by you and Henoch. Then you launch grenades. You throw yours first, and shout: "Zapal!" That's what you write in your book. Did you really shout "Fire!" in Polish?
Yes, for sure. We usually spoke Polish. Though not all of us. Dwora was from eastern Poland, and she spoke Hebrew and Yiddish better. But with me they spoke Polish. I spoke Polish with Szlamek, too.

Do you remember whether you spoke Yiddish with anyone?
Truthfully? I don't.

What about with Antek?
With Antek? Outside the wall? Whenever I went out, I think I reported to him in Polish.

Would you say that your first language is Polish?
In a sense, yes.

Do you speak Polish better than Yiddish?
Yes. Though today neither my Polish nor my Yiddish are good. My Polish used to be good. But from 1946 until I think 1990, I didn't speak Polish at all. To Gina[35] never, not once.

And presumably you never spoke Yiddish in Israel, either?
No, no. Only Hebrew.

Do you remember who found Michał Klepfisz's dead body, and when?
I remember that someone found his body in an upstairs room. You know that we knocked holes in walls and had passageways through the attics?

Yes, I know. Aron Karmi talks about that, too. Do you remember where Michał Klepfisz was found? On Świętojerska or on Wałowa?
I don't remember.

Did you see his body?
Yes, for sure, it was lying in an attic. They brought it down into the courtyard and dug a grave somewhere there. That's all.

---

35 Gina Rotem (1930–2017)—painter and ceramics artist, wife of Kazik Ratajzer, born in Chorzów; she left Poland in 1942. She lived in Jerusalem.

Are you sure you buried Michał?
Yes.

Marek says you didn't bury him, that he was left where he lay, and then the house was destroyed by a bomb.
Let me tell you: he was our first man killed. If it had been a few days later, I agree with Marek, nobody would have thought about it. But he was the first, and the only one that day. I remember that we buried him at night, and so we were able to do it calmly, without fear.

Do you remember when Klepfisz was awarded the Virtuti Militari?[36]
No. I never heard anything about that.

Marek says that he heard the news in the ghetto, and that it was the most joyous news of the uprising.
Well, I'm hearing it for the first time from you, now. But think, how could it have come about that somebody, somewhere, so far away, could have come to hear about Klepfisz so soon?

Perhaps the information got out onto the other side somehow?
Somehow? How?! By fax? By telegram? By telephone to London? Garbage! It really is improbable.

***

A quotation from your book. "When only a handful of people were left in the Ghetto, everyone finally understood—unfortunately too late—that the fighters weren't the 'enemies of the people.'"[37]
Most people in the ghetto believed that any resistance would bring about its total liquidation. For a long time, they didn't believe that the Germans had resolved

---

36 The document confirming the award of the Silver Cross of the Order of Virtuti Militari to Warsaw ghetto insurgent Michał Klepfisz, Eng., is dated Feb. 18, 1944, and is signed by the Supreme Commander, Lt. Gen. Kazimierz Sosnkowski. Edelman (conversation with H.G., Nov. 1999): "One phone call was all it took for Sikorski to take the decision. I'm certain that we heard the information on the radio on the third or fourth day of the uprising."
37 Kazik, *Memoirs...*, 39.

to murder Poland's Jewry—even Europe's. And that's why they believed that underground activity would bring down disaster upon us. The change took time. You know, today, I ask myself a very difficult question, to which I find no clear answer. Back then I didn't even think about it. Recently, I tried to talk to Marek about it. The question is this: Who gave us the right to decide the fates of other people? It is possible that someone might have saved themselves had it not been for the uprising in the ghetto.

Does that mean that today you have no unequivocal answer to the question of what stance was the more justified at the time?
No, I don't have an answer. I know that for us, then, only that stance counted. But I'm asking: did we have the moral right to take that decision for others? You know, it's different when you have a Sejm or a Knesset, and representatives of society decide on behalf of others that they have to go to war. But here? We were vigilantes who for a long time were acting against the will of the majority. Well, what do you think?

Somehow my line of thought is simpler, and I don't think I would pose the question of moral right here. But I understand when you formulate it. My answer is unequivocal: Yes. I think that the decision to mount resistance was a declaration of responsibility for yourselves and others.
To me it's not that clear-cut. I'd like us to be able to think about it. And apart from that, I'll tell you that I didn't think in those categories. I thought about myself, and about how I was going to die. I didn't want to suffocate in a gas chamber. It's easier to die fighting; it's just quicker. All that talk about the uprising being for history, for the nation, for the Jewish honor, and so on, I find unconvincing. All those fancy words are good for ceremonies. Who thought about that at the time? Later on, here in Israel, you know, people used to say: "It was great fortune that you did that uprising, because otherwise? What a disgrace it would have been for the Jewish nation!" Well, I tell you: if I'd known then that they would talk like that, I wouldn't have done it!! I believe that human life is most important, not honor or anything like that. But let me make myself properly understood: I don't mean human life at all cost. No. I'm not thinking about situations when people debase themselves to live. I'm just asking this one question: What right did we have to decide for others? But nobody wants to think about that. It seems so obvious to everybody. There was this one religious Jew in the ghetto, Zysie...

...Friedman.³⁸ One of the leaders of Agudat Israel.
Yes, Friedman, I think. And he gave us his blessing, but he didn't go with us. There are various stances; I don't know which is more right.

***

I'd like to talk with you about the Jewish Military Union. This is an aspect of the ghetto uprising that's rarely addressed. Can you say anything about the ŻZW?
I know for sure that there were talks where our positions for the uprising were agreed, to ensure that we didn't shoot at each other. That happened right before the uprising; I think the ghetto was already under siege. I know that I took part in talks of that nature, but I don't remember any details.

Do you remember the name Chaim Łopata? Israel Gutman writes³⁹ that a ŻZW unit under Chaim Łopata fought in the brushmakers' yard.
I never heard of them. And as for Gutman, don't even start me on him. I can't be objective about him, so I'd rather you didn't ask me.

You got out of the ghetto via a tunnel built by the ŻZW.
Yes. That tunnel was right by their base on Muranowska. It may have been their headquarters; it may have been their only base. I know about everyone in the brushmakers' yard; after all, it wasn't such a vast premises. Where did Gutman get that from?

Since Gutman didn't give the source of that information, I asked him about it a few weeks ago. He cited the memoirs of Leon Najberg.⁴⁰ Did you see evidence of fighting⁴¹ when you got out onto the other side?
Absolutely. There was a lot of evidence. It indicated that the fighting had been fairly fierce. And then we heard what someone who lived in that house had to say about it—I think he was a streetcar driver, or maybe a power-station worker. We got to Muranowska in the night.

---

38 Zysie Friedman—before the war general secretary of Agudat Israel in Poland; journalist and editor of religious periodicals, and Hebrew lecturer; in the Warsaw ghetto a representative of Agudat Israel in the Joint community council. Killed in 1943 in one of the camps in Lublin.
39 Israel Gutman, *Żydzi warszawscy 1939–1943* [The Warsaw Jews 1938–1943] (Warsaw: Rytm, 1982).
40 Leon Najberg, *Ostatni powstańcy getta* [The last ghetto insurgents] (Warsaw: Żydowski Instytut Historyczny, 1993).
41 This is a reference to the battle that the ŻZW soldiers fought on their exit from the ghetto via the house on Muranowska.

What date was it when you left the ghetto?
I couldn't forget that. It was May 1. Marek sometimes says April 30, sometimes 29. You know, that surprises me, because I'm alive, and he could check; all he has to do is call me. And I also remember exactly when I went back into the ghetto. When I met that group in the sewer, when I was on my way back from the ghetto, they said to me: "This morning, Anielewicz's bunker was discovered," so it must have been May 8.

And how can you be certain that you left on May 1?
Because I went with a Bundist [Zygmunt Frydrych]. I didn't set any store by May 1, but he did. Why doesn't Marek mention that Zygmunt didn't want to go back into the ghetto with me?!

Why didn't Zygmunt want to go back into the ghetto?
Listen, he had a child. And apart from that, you had to be mad to go back. Does anyone go into hell voluntarily? And I don't hold it against him because that's human. But that's precisely why it shouldn't be covered up.

I understand that you left the ghetto to organize something for the others on the outside.
Of course. We didn't go for our own amusement. We weren't sent to save ourselves.

Was it Marek who sent you?
Marek was one of the people who decided that we should go. They came to me and asked me if I would go. I said OK. What? Should I have refused? The situation in the ghetto was such that I had nothing to lose. And you know what? Within a few minutes, we were on our way.

Did you like Frydrych?
I didn't know him before that. I met him a minute before we left.

Why do you think you and Frydrych were chosen?
I can't answer you that question.

You were resourceful, reliable, and had the right looks. Is that it?
Yes, I think so. But I wasn't the first to go out with the task of organizing assistance, you know. One of the people who had tried before me was Tuwia Borzykowski. But he came back.

Did he go out via the sewers as well?
Yes. There was no other way. That really was the only one.

But you found the tunnel dug out onto Muranowska?
Yes, but nobody found that tunnel before us, and afterwards it was unusable; the house was guarded by Germans. When we went out, we had more luck than sense that we didn't fall into their hands.

So, the tunnel went from a house on Muranowska?
Yes. The street was divided by a wall. You went in on Muranowska and came out in a house on the other side of the wall. But then you also had to get out of that house! We left the ghetto at night. So, we stayed there until the end of the curfew, until morning. We sat at the top of the house, on the stairwell. When it started to get light, we looked out through the window, and on the roof of the neighboring house, we could see that everything was smashed up and scattered around in pieces . . . The corpses had gone, but there was still a lot of blood. And suddenly a door opened, a guy came out, and shrank back, terrified. I can imagine what the two of us looked like. So, I said to him: "Listen, we just got out of the ghetto. We got stuck there during the uprising, and we only just managed to get out." He congratulated us, and so on, and it was he who told us that the house was guarded, but he showed us a hole by which we were able to slip out.

How did you find the tunnel?
It wasn't me who found it. I think it was Adolf [Hochberg] who came to me and told me he'd found it.

Where were you supposed to go once you were on the other side?
Zygmunt had Anna Wąchalska's[42] address.

Was it a private contact?
No. I must be fair! It was a Bund contact. I hadn't the faintest idea what we were going out to. You know what? It was all so "superbly" organized that when I think about it now, I can hardly believe it. I don't understand the leaders and commanders. How could only he have had the address?! How could

---

42 p. 463 Rereading the List.

they have been certain that we would make it through together? What if I'd survived and him not? Didn't I deserve the address too? Listen, those were cardinal errors!

Shouldn't those errors be put down to the extreme situation? It wasn't ill will, surely?
No, not ill will, but basic errors! They really could have thought a little more. You need leaders, people who take responsibility for you and others in difficult situations, not when everything is hunky-dory. In situations of mortal threat, everything has to be thought through in advance.

But weren't you in the ghetto in a situation of such extreme danger that it was hard to think everything through in advance?
Listen, I had no preparation, no training. But when I found them in the sewers, I told them clearly that under no circumstances were they to move from the manhole! As if I'd predicted what happened . . . I told them not to dare move! My best friend, Szlamek [Szuster] was there. I recently read your conversations with Masza and Pnina, and they tell you that. It's not that I want to defend myself now; I have no such intention. Cywia said to me: "Stop the truck!" But I refused. And I'm not going to defend myself; I see no reason. I told Marek that in my opinion, the ŻOB, its leaders and commanders—nobody thought that we might have to retreat, that we might not be able to go on fighting. Marek claims they thought about it.

From what happened in the bunker on Miła, from Anielewicz's attitude, you might think that the ŻOB commanders had not considered the option of retreat.
That's precisely what I'm saying! And everybody says the same—except Marek. We knew that we had no chance against the Germans, yet a few of us did survive. Nobody thought that we could stage an uprising and survive! And what then? What next? Nobody thought about that. They were all sure we would be killed, end of story.

But Marek said many times that the suicide on Miła was a mistake, that they should have looked for a way out, because there was always a chance.
A chance?! On what basis? Other than a miracle—and he never believed in miracles! Though I can tell you that I understand the idea of counting on a miracle. When they sent us to Leszno in '44, we were in an absolutely critical situation.

The Germans were approaching the house, and Józef Sak took out his cyanide and said that he was going to commit suicide. But I shouted: "No! You're not going to do that! Wait! There'll always be time for that." I didn't know what our chances were, but there might have been one. But the Germans were very close; we could hear them shouting. Marysia [Sawicka] and Irena [Gelblum] were with us. So, I say: "Call out to them that there are women here and go out. If I don't hear any shots, I'll throw down my revolver and come out, too." And that's what we did. Marysia, Stasia [Rywka Rozensztajn] and Irena went out first, and then the rest. I think they were a little spooked, too—I mean suddenly, out of the house next-door to the German command (we could hear them the whole time), there are these people coming out. After so many weeks. And as the Ukrainians were taking us down the street, an SS man drove past on a motorcycle and shouted out, pointing at us: "Jude! Jude!" So, my comrades started again: They're not going anywhere, let them shoot us on the spot. But I said: "Dammit, if they wanted to shoot us, they'd have shot us! Let's not make it easier for them." I almost had to drag them along. And you see, we all made it out; we all survived until the end of the war. We were taken to some church in Wola,[43] which was a marshalling point, and from there they sent people on to Pruszków.[44] So I say to them: "When we get there, we don't know each other, and we all go into different corners." We got to the church, and suddenly this SS man bursts in, yelling: "Where's that group from Leszno?" Let him look! If he knew, he wouldn't be asking, and since he's asking, it means he doesn't know. His problem. He's going from person to person, but there were dozens of people there. In the end, he gets to Stasia and asks her: "What's your name?" So, she told him. And he asks: "Since when?" He gets to Sak, same thing. "Since when is that your name?" It was clear that he recognized them. But he went out. Ten, fifteen minutes went by, and suddenly the order came for us all to get on the train. That's just what I'd been waiting for. They'd forgotten about Stasia and Sak. Shortly afterwards, we were in Pruszków.

***

---

43 At 16 Leszno, there was a Protestant church where the Germans were stationed. Kazik may also be referring to the Church of Our Lady at 34 Leszno.
44 On August 7, 1944, the Germans established a transit camp (Ger. *Durchgangslager*) on the site of the defunct Railway Repair Works in Pruszków for the civilian population that was gradually expelled from the capital during and after the Warsaw rising. Around five hundred thousand people passed through the camp.

Enclosure

Kazik, tell me in detail about that early morning expedition beyond the wall on May 1. How did you get to Anna Wąchalska's apartment from Muranowska?
Listen, it was all as normal. First up, there's this gang of *szmalcownicy*. I don't remember how many of them there were—fifteen, or maybe eight? But it was a gang, a proper gang. And suddenly, this truck drives up—I don't know if I said to Zygmunt or he said to me, or neither of us said anything—but we were on that truck. Somehow, we jumped on. Luckily. Then around the bend we jumped off again and carried on walking.

And nobody bothered you after that? I mean, you must have turned heads with your appearance after your "stroll" through the sewers!
Listen, it was early in the morning. At that time of day, in those times, there were quite a lot of ragged types roaming the streets. And we didn't look like Jews. That gang latched onto us because we ran into them right by the wall. They didn't have to think too hard to work out who we were.

Where did Anna live?
In Wola, on Krzyżanowskiego Street.

Tell me about that meeting.
Now that was not normal.

Was there only Anna in the apartment?
No, Marysia was also there, and their niece, Alina.

So, tell me about the not normal.
Listen, none of it was normal! The apartment looked like a palace to me. You can imagine. They let us have a wash. To this day I remember that bathtub, and that water, and the soap, and the towel. And the reception afterwards! The table was groaning—bread, sausage, vodka, don't even ask! It was as if there was a difference of centuries, or like the difference between hell and heaven—I don't know how to describe to you how it was to exchange death in the burning ghetto or a stinking sewer for a magnificent feast in the best company, within a few hours.

How did the Bund have the contact with Marysia and Anna?
Marysia was in the Iskra sports club,[45] or something. And she had Jewish girlfriends. I guess it went something like that.

---

45 Kazik is referring here to the Warsaw PPS sports club Skra.

When did you meet up with Antek?
That same afternoon. We had his number, and he came round to Anna's apartment.

Where was Antek living at that time?
I never went there, but I know he lived on Marszałkowska. So Antek got a full account from us. But I was naïve and stupid enough to believe that once I got out onto the Aryan side, everything would be sorted. All I had to do was get out and find Antek...

Did you smoke cigarettes at the time?
What? Cigarettes? Back then I smoked three packs a day. So, then it transpired that... that we would have to start everything over, because otherwise nothing would come of it.

How did Antek react to your story? Did he think that it was possible to get all the others out of the ghetto?
I don't know what he thought. It's certainly easier to say: "Do this or that," than just to do it. So, what transpired? It transpired that we couldn't count on any assistance; that we were on our own.

"We" meaning who?
The ŻOB people on the other side.

Can you name them?
Rysiek [Maselman] and Wacek.

Wacek who?
I don't know; I don't know his surname. The one who was killed with Rysiek the same day that we got that whole group out of the sewers. And then there was Frania,[46] a courier.

Frania Beatus who committed suicide?
Yes. She came with Antek to Anna's that day. She heard our story, and the next day she committed suicide.

---

46 p. 340 Rereading the List—Frania Beatus.

Do you remember how she did it?
Nobody knows. She just disappeared.

So how can you be sure that it was suicide? Perhaps she fell into the hands of some Germans or *szmalcownicy*?
I think she left a letter to Antek. I remember that it was clear to us at the time.

You said you were on your own.
Yes. We started to look. Four or five days later, when we still hadn't found any sewerage engineers who would lead the group through the sewers, I had a hard talk with Antek. He came and said to me that if we didn't go for the rest of them that day, he would go. That didn't make much of an impression on me. I said to him: "Listen, if you want to commit suicide, then go. I'm only going if and when I'm satisfied that there's at least a ghost of a chance not only of my getting there, but also of getting back out." I obviously convinced him because he didn't go.

Did you want to get a particular number of people out?
We wanted to get them all out.

All the ŻOB people?
All of them. Listen, when I went back into the ghetto that night to look for people, I was walking around in an empty ghetto. At one point, I met three people. I told them to wait for me, and I would take them out onto the other side. I went back the same way, but they weren't there anymore.

Do you think they were afraid of you, that they didn't believe you?
I think so, because how else could you explain it? I was prepared to take anyone, but I met no one.

So, the idea was that you would get as many people as possible out of the ghetto, organize transport for them, and take them into the woods, right?
Yes.

And the woods, the place in Łomianki, was thought up beforehand, was it?
Yes. That was the only thing thought up. But those woods weren't real woods; it was just a low-growing coppice. It was all really anything but normal.

Who thought up Łomianki?
I don't know; not me. But the Toebbens group had already been there for a few days.[47] And why had they been held there so long? I don't know. I think it was a miracle that they had survived.

Don't you think that there was quite simply nowhere else to take them; that it wasn't a question of poor organization but rather a lack of options?
I don't know. Perhaps. But there were people who were responsible for those decisions. There was Antek, there were the others that I mentioned. I don't know. That previous group had been sitting in those trees since April 29. The next one arrived on May 10, and then they sat there together for another two weeks or so. Couldn't they have got the first group out to the Wyszków woods before that, rather than keeping them there so long?! I don't know.

Marek recalls his conversation with Celek Celemeński[48] on the morning when the soldiers that you brought out reached Łomianki. He was convinced that the place wasn't safe enough for such a large group of around seventy soldiers.
Marek was right, of course! Every hour spent there was one too long. It was madness, you know. Or a miracle. Or all of that together.

Was the idea of going to join the forest partisan units born because people wanted it, or was it just easier to keep them hidden in the woods than in the city?
Listen, who could have known what was easier or where was better? It's true that there were very limited possibilities for hiding in the city. Ultimately, it wasn't a question of choice at all. The city was very difficult. Even if you did find a place, which wasn't at all easy, you were putting not only yourself in danger, but also the family that took you in. The risk was huge. Twenty-four hours a day. In my opinion, the underground army offered more opportunities, and a chance at life.

And you? You didn't go to the forest?
Because other people wanted me to be in the city. It wasn't my decision.

---

47 Marek Edelman (conversation with H.G., Nov. 1999): "The other group had been there no more than 2–3 days."
48 p. 358 Rereading the List—Jakub Celemeński, Celek.

***

Kazik, in the night of April 30 to May 1, you and Zygmunt Frydrych leave the ghetto via the sewers out onto the other side. You reach Anna Wąchalska and Marysia Sawicka on Krzyżanowskiego Street. That afternoon, Antek comes to see you. You report to him on events in the ghetto. You decide that you're going to organize assistance for the surviving insurrectionists, relying above all on yourselves. You're going to get them out of the ghetto to the safest possible place. What are your next few days like? What do you do? Where do you look for help?

Listen: that situation was the shock of my life. You can imagine—I come out of the ghetto, a world which has nothing in common with the world I find myself in literally a few hours later. But I remember, you know, that the people who are still there have only our help to count on. Their lives depend on what you're gonna do, what help you can organize. It was absolutely clear to me that every moment—literally every moment—was crucial. And it was also clear to me that I could only count on myself. I already told you: even in that first conversation with Antek, I realized that there was no one waiting for us, no one prepared to help us, yet we ourselves were impotent. What did I do? I ran around from morning to night like a poisoned mouse. I tried to remember anyone I knew, tried to look them up, meet them, while taking into account the lurking dangers to some extent. And I did crazy things. Like when I called in the assistance of the Polish policeman.

The one with the beak face?
Yes!

Do you remember his name? Mądry or Adamczyk?
Mądry! Now I know for sure. Listen: I met him on the street. I went up to him and struck up a conversation. Afterwards, when I told Antek about it, he shouted at me: "What?! Are you crazy? What are you doing?" But you know, if I hadn't taken that risk, those people wouldn't have been rescued.

What did you tell the policeman when you approached him?
He got the measure of the situation very quickly. After all, he remembered me from before the war, he knew my parents, lived in our neighborhood—he was already a policeman back then, and he looked like a decent guy. And you see, I wasn't wrong! Later on, he ran us guns to Częstochowa. He did it without money, he didn't take a penny from us, ever. And if he'd wanted to arrest me, he'd have done it right away, right? What did I say to him? I said: "Hello." I walked a way down the street with him, and he invited me home with him. Antek thought I shouldn't go, but I went.

We sat there over coffee, or tea, and I told him a little about the ghetto, about the uprising, I hinted that I had contacts in the AK. I controlled what I said, you know. There was one rule I always stuck to—I never noted anything down, and I never said even half a word that the other person didn't need to know.

You never found him after the war?
No. I emigrated straight away, and never went looking for anyone. A shame, but that's how it was.

But at the time, after you left the ghetto, you ran about like a poisoned mouse?
Yes. But the most important thing was to find sewerage engineers who would help us to get the others out.

How did you look for them?
Like I said: I hunted down friends, acquaintances, closer ones, more distant ones. Antek was probably doing the same, and the other guys, too: Tadek Szejngut and Rysiek [Maselman], and Wacek. Finally, we found our sewerage engineers through the king of the *szmalcownicy* on Prosta Street.[49]

Did you meet him?
Yes, but it was Krzaczek [Władysław Gaik] who made contact with him.

And where did Krzaczek come into it?
Antek knew Krzaczek. It was Krzaczek, of course, who had taken the Toebbens fighters to Łomianki. So, the first group with the sewerage engineers went into the ghetto on May 7, in the night, but they turned back.

Who was in the first group?
The two sewerage engineers and someone else. I think it was Rysiek.

Why did they turn back?
They said that the Germans had shot at them. That's highly possible. The Germans cut off our routes through the sewers. They would stand by the manhole covers and wait. And then there were gas canisters left lying in the sewers, which you would kick in the darkness, and they would explode. Sometimes they threw

---

49 Marek Edelman (conversation with H.G., Nov. 1999): "The sewerage engineers were a contact given us by the PPR, by Jóźwiak."

grenades down the manholes or started shooting if they heard footsteps down below. So, it's possible. The next day, I decided I would go. I took Rysiek. First of all, we went to the king of the *szmalcownicy*. One shot of vodka, two, three. That was where we took the sewerage engineers from. And suddenly, the king got the idea that I was a Jew. So, we said that we were from the AK, and we were going in to rescue this group of Poles that had been helping the Jews and had gotten stuck inside the ghetto during the uprising, and so on. In any case, I wriggled out of it somehow, and promised to prove my "Aryanness" when I returned. Off we went. And it was then that the impossible expedition began. The sewerage engineers came to their senses very rapidly. They realized what a risk they were taking with their lives, and in the end, they said that they wanted out, and were going back.

Once you were already in the sewers?
Yes.

Did you promise them a lot of money?
They had gotten their payment up front. And in addition, I had told them that they were going down in Polish history, that they were doing a heroic deed, and so on. I was appealing to their patriotic conscience as Poles. But when they said: "No," I had to take off the kid gloves. Up to then, I had used sweetness, with vodka, without. But this time I spoke to them sharply: "Listen, you have a choice. Either you go with me, or I leave you here, as corpses, not alive!" They believed that I wasn't joking and went on. On the way, they tried again, but I was resolute. "Listen, we're going to the end. When you're sure that we're in the ghetto, I'll go up, and you wait for me in the sewer." I told Rysiek that he was staying with them and the guns. And that's what happened. At one point, they said that we were in the ghetto. The rest you know.

How long were you walking through the sewers?
About two or three hours, I think. It was very hard going, because the water in the main sewer, which was over two meters high, was very deep. The other sewers were so narrow that we had to crawl on our bellies. It wasn't an easy walk.

Where did you come out?
A few dozen meters from the gate on Gęsia. I opened the cover, and saw a strong searchlight, which illuminated the whole area from Zamenhofa. It was as light as day. I had a second to think when I opened the cover. But since I didn't hear any shots, I slid out on my stomach, a few movements forward, and I was in the dark, in the rubble, and I was gone.

> You found nobody in the ghetto whom you could take out onto the other side. You met the three people who didn't wait for you, and the woman with the broken leg whom you couldn't find in the ruins, but no insurrectionists. You decided to go back. You went back down into the same sewer beneath the bright searchlight. The sewerage engineers and Rysiek were waiting for you.

Above all, I didn't want to go back.

You didn't want to go back onto the other side?
I didn't want to go back into the sewer. What for? I hadn't found anybody; there was no point in going back. I thought—I'll wait till morning, and the Germans will come and shoot me, the last Jew, here, on this rubble. I don't know how I pulled myself together and where I found the strength to pull the manhole cover aside and go down inside. "I didn't find anybody!" I called to them in this inhuman voice. We started to walk, but I was constantly calling out our codeword: "Jan! Jan!" And suddenly—but you know the rest, Pnina and Masza told you—they saw the light from my torch, and I heard noises. We all frightened each other—they me, and I them. Luckily, no one fired.

Was it close to the manhole?
Not very close, but not that far, either. We found them pretty quickly. Then I heard a brief version of what had happened on Miła. But above all, I thought that we had to get everyone down into the sewer.

How many of them did you meet?
Ten. Pnina Grynszpan, Abrasza Blum, Szlamek Szuster, Adolf Hochberg, Janek Bilak, Jurek, Guta and Lusiek Błones, Bronka Manulak, and Abram Stolak. I think that's all the names. I said to Szlamek: "Take someone with you and go into the ghetto for the rest. Bring everyone you find. We'll leave people along the way so that you don't get lost, and we'll chalk arrows on the walls. Have everybody wait under the manhole cover. And don't split up. Under any circumstances!" I remember I said that several times before we parted. And I went up and out to organize transport.

So, the whole situation wasn't exactly planned. The transport was still to be organized.
Yes, but the transport was relatively easy. There were transport offices, you called up, said that you wanted to move some furniture, and that was it. And that's what Krzaczek did. The best thing was that he drove the truck himself.

And before that, before the truck came?
When Rysiek and I climbed out of the sewer, there were already people on the streets. I went back to the king of the *szmalcownicy* to change my clothes...

And nobody bothered you anymore?
Listen, the fact is that neither the sewerage engineers nor the king of the *szmalcownicy* split on us. But our people were sitting in the sewers till the next day. They only came out early in the morning of May 10, because we couldn't organize it any sooner.

So, you changed, and...?
And I set off to look for Krzaczek, Tadek Szejngut. I had no contact with Antek. I don't even know if he knew that I had gone back to the ghetto. In the end it turned out that we couldn't get a truck for that day. And I was waiting for news from them that they were all waiting under the manhole cover.

How were you supposed to receive the news?
I told them that in the afternoon I would come back to the manhole cover and wait for it. And that's what I did. Between four and five, I went and stood by the manhole cover, and as I tied up my shoelaces, I slipped them a piece of paper into the hole. A moment later, I had the answer that they were all there.

Did it say on the paper how many people there were in the sewer?
No. But I could imagine, because the people I had met in the night had told me where the groups were, and more or less how many people had survived. I knew that there should be between eighty and a hundred people, and that's why there was originally mention of two trucks and not one. In fact, that meant, I remember now, that there was no chance of taking them from there that same day, because first I was supposed to find out whether they were all under the manhole cover. I was sure that we wouldn't be able to repeat the operation. It would be fantastic if it succeeded once. So, I received the answer that they were there and were waiting. Waiting for us to get them out of there as soon as possible. In the night, we went to the king of the *szmalcownicy* and got some soup together, and someone took it to them.

Was it possible to make soup for a hundred people?
Probably not. I don't know how we managed it; I haven't the faintest idea. But it was easier to make soup than to organize bread. Go get fifty bread loaves. Where will you get them from? But soup you can make at home; nobody will see how

much, and you're good. It was harder with lemons than with the soup. When they were in Łomianki, they asked for lemons. Do you know how hard that was—to get enough lemons together for each of them to get two slices?!

Why lemons?
I don't know. They'd survived a gas attack, they felt sick, and they asked for lemons.

So, that night there was soup, the lemons came later, and now it's early in the morning of May 10.
I showed up there at first light. I also asked Tadek, Krzaczek, Wacek, and Rysiek to come, and of course they did.

Did you know that Inka was standing just around the corner and observing everything?
I had no idea. If she saw it, why didn't she come up to me?

Would she have been able to help you with anything? Would she have been any use?
She could have helped me with a good word. You know, as they were coming out, Izrael Kanał,[50] the commander of the central ghetto, shouted at me: "Kazik, you got cover?" "What am I going to say to him?" I thought. "See all these people all around us? They're our cover!"

Were there a lot of gawkers?
Yes! More and more with every minute! I heard them saying: "The cats are coming out."[51] But it's good that they were there. They shielded us entirely—and the wacha for the small ghetto was very close by. It was all quite extraordinary. You can imagine: broad daylight, and these goings-on! I was outside the circle of people, the truck was standing a little way off, and next to the manhole were two of our people, because everyone climbing out needed a hand up. When people ask me how long it lasted, I say I don't know, but at least half an hour—there

---

50 p. 400 Rereading the List—Izrael Kanał, Mietek.
51 "Cats"—an expression used by Poles in Warsaw to refer to Jews in hiding. In his deposition, Mordka Purman (AYV, 0.3/260) said: "People used to call the Jews 'cats' at that time, because the Polish for 'used to have' sounds like 'miaow,' and all the Jews 'used to have' a house, 'used to have' a factory, etc., etc." Traders at the popular Kercelak market would say: "I buy gold, I take in cats."

were about forty of them. Each one had to climb up the ladder in the shaft, and then they had to be pulled out, because they weren't strong enough themselves, so I'd say about a minute per person.

As the insurrectionists were emerging from the sewer, a Polish policeman appeared, heading in the direction of the German guardpost.
Yes. I quickly realized I needed to stop him, so I went up to him, and said in a firm voice: "This is a Polish underground operation, being carried out by the AK, and I have to ask you not to pass this way." He turned back, of course.

So around half an hour had passed . . .
And then I see that there's no one else coming out. I slip inside the circle. I ask the guys what's going on. They say there's no one else. I go over to the shaft, bend down, shout down a few times, no one answers me. So, I say: "Close it!" And we're off. In the September we got a group of Jews out of the ghetto.

How did you find out about them?
I think that by some miracle, someone got out, and made it through to us somehow. I seem to remember that we were very surprised, because we hadn't thought that there was anyone left alive in the ghetto. There hadn't been any firing for a long time; everything had fallen silent. We were even afraid that it might be a trap. In the end, I took care of the matter. First, an apartment had to be found for them. I found something at 1 Mokotowska, with the janitor.

And this janitor agreed to take in a large group of Jews?
Yes, he agreed.

For money?
Yes, for money.

So how did you decide to get them out?
I decided to ask the policeman, Mądry, for help, the one we already talked about. I came to the conclusion that that was the safest solution for both them and me. Mądry was to wait by the manhole, they would come out, and if anyone said anything, Mądry would arrest them and take them to the police station.

But before that, someone had to lead them out of the ghetto via the sewers?
Of course. And somebody did that.

You don't remember who?
No. But it all worked out somehow, because they came out in the night, Mądry intercepted them at the manhole, took them to Mokotowska . . .

How many people can there have been in that group?
Twenty, or maybe more. On Mokotowska we had food prepared for them. We had no experience. They fell on the food, and it made them sick. It was dreadful. A few of them died, I think. We realized too late that we had made a mistake with the food. After all, they hadn't eaten for months. They told us that they would soak an eighth of a potato in a little water for several hours so as to have something to chew on later . . . I had Felek Rajszczak brought in to build a hideout there, but suddenly, a few days later, the Gestapo came and arrested them all.

How did the Gestapo know about them?
It turned out that the janitor's son was a nark. It was probably all planned out by them in advance.

You think that the janitor was working with his son?
Yes, probably. They arrested Felek as well, and he had a whole group from Poalej Syjon in hiding in his house. After a short time, we received a message from Felek; he sent it via some policeman. Felek didn't give anyone away, though they tortured him mercilessly. You can't imagine what he looked like. We did everything we could to get him out—the AK, the AL—we did whatever we could. But Felek helped himself, too. He just kept saying to them: "I don't know, I just don't know." And when the Gestapo started shouting at him: "What do you mean, you don't know that Antek and Kazik are Jews?!," Felek didn't miss a beat, and answered: "Now that I know they're Jews, I would tell you where they're hiding, if only I knew." He was a bricklayer, but a wise, prewar bricklayer. One day, they let him go.

And what happened to the group of Jews that had gotten out of the ghetto?
None of them survived. There were other blunders around that time, too.

How were they killed; don't you know?
No, I don't know anything about that.

Do you remember any names?
No. I was there, but I don't remember any details.

Were there any children among them?
No, there were no children, but I do remember that they were all very young.

Do you think that there might have been any more wildcat groups living in the ghetto at that point?
I don't think so. It would have been impossible. The Germans were in the ghetto the whole time. And the Jews had nothing at all to eat.

***

In your book, you wrote that Jurek Grasberg, Marek, and Cywia depended on people like you who could move relatively freely about the city. You said that all those who because of their appearance were forced to stay indoors learned everything through your filter. What effect did that have on your relationships? Do you think they found that hard to take?
Listen, I asked Marek that same question recently. He says that he didn't experience that negatively. He says that he was well aware of the situation in the city outside, and that he did go out. That's not true—Marek didn't go out! Perhaps once or twice he went with Inka or Marysia [Warman] to a meeting of the Bund leaders. But that was a huge and complicated operation. Listen, none of them went out.

None of them meaning who?
None of them. None of the people who were in hiding went out. They didn't leave their places! Listen, even if they had wanted to go out, they would have been putting everyone at risk.

What did they do, holed up inside for so many months? It was more than a year!
They talked; they probably drank vodka. We all drank vodka back then. Cywia even made eggnog. Maybe they made love? I don't know. And when we came back in the evenings, we would tell them everything, in detail, about the whole day.

***

Do you understand the attitude of those who decided to stay in Poland: Inka and Marek? Some people call Marek the guardian of the cemetery.
I don't know whether it's a question of understanding. That approach doesn't convince me. I don't believe that the dead need a guardian, they're done with

managing—for better or for worse. It sounds good: guardian. And I have no doubt that it's spoken absolutely genuinely. But it doesn't convince me. I respect it, but it can't only be that. Inka, who stayed like Marek, writes that she simply felt Polish!

I don't think it's quite like that, you know. Inka didn't feel Polish; I think she considered herself a Polish Jewess.
OK. She felt at home in Poland. Everywhere else she felt alien; she missed Polish books, the language, and so on.

Didn't you ever feel like that in Poland? Or, to put it differently: didn't you ever miss Poland like that?
No. Though I can't say that I was indifferent to Poland. More: I have a certain fondness both for the country and for the people, but I never missed it like Inka or Marek did. When the war ended, I left at once. I sensed that it was a different place by then. There wasn't anything left of everything that I had been used to. There was no Jewish life left in Poland, nothing of my world. So, there was nothing for me there. There was nothing binding me to it. "What am I doing here?" I thought.

Do you remember talking to Marek or any of the others about what to do next and where to go?
We had talked about that back in '44. They were already sure that if we had the misfortune to survive, they would go to Palestine. I'm not saying it was that clear for me, but I knew that I would leave Poland. But I don't think I ever even saw Marek after the war. The last time I saw them all was in Boernerowo, in the hospital. After that, of course, I had my "very important" mission to carry out: Antek sent me and Irena across the front, to Lublin.

Why?
Because we had to help the AL! Another absurd idea. In any case, I was given a codeword to some important colonel, and I was supposed to pass something on to him. And I did; a few hours later I was in Lublin being received by Gomułka.[52] I did what I had been sent to do. But whether Gomułka took any action on our information I don't know. Above all, they spent a very long time checking us out. Once I'd finished that special mission, I went looking for my parents. And fortunately, I found them.

---

52 p. 497 Glossary—Gomułka, Władysław.

We need to speak again about what happened in the sewer. When you lifted the manhole cover on May 10 and told them that transport was waiting, your friend Szlamek Szuster and, I think, Adolf Hochberg were sent into the side sewers for the insurrectionists who had spread out. Celina Lubetkin claimed that it was she who sent Szlamek, and Marek says that it was he who gave the order. Szlamek and the others didn't make it back in time. The truck drove off.

And that's all. I don't know any more. The ones who got out said that some people had gone into the side sewers because it was very uncomfortable to stand in the main sewer, and Cywia promised them that she wouldn't go without them. I didn't hear that, of course, so I don't know. Marek said—I asked him about it again recently—that he had promised to wait for everyone. In any case, I was the last to climb into the truck, and Cywia said to me: "There are still people down there, don't drive off!" But I categorically refused. I considered it too dangerous. I even said to her: "Here I'm not going to follow your order. When we've taken this group, we'll come back for the rest." And that's what we did. Except that they'd climbed out of the sewer beforehand, on their own. And they were all killed.

How do you know that the other group, the one led by Szlamek, got out and that they were all killed? Are there, or were there, any eyewitnesses?
None of us saw it. And those who probably did see it are dead. You know that when we reached Łomianki, Rysiek and Wacek didn't want to stay there, but someone had to take the group into the coppice. So, I stayed, and Rysiek and Wacek went back to Warsaw. I was supposed to wait for them in Łomianki.

And one more question, about the trucks. There were supposed to be two. There was one...
Everyone gives their own version, but nobody knows the truth better than I do, because it was to do with me. I know what I did. Marek, in his last book,[53] writes that I said that another truck was going to come but it didn't. But I didn't say that. I said that when we had taken them where they were going, we would come back for the others. There was no other truck.

And there wasn't supposed to have been one?
I don't know whether there was supposed to have been one. I know there wasn't one.

---

53 Rudi Assuntino, Wlodek Goldkorn, *Strażnik. Marek Edelman opowiada* [Guardian: Marek Edelman recounts] (Cracow: Znak, 1999).

So Rysiek and Wacek went back to Warsaw with Krzaczek?
Yes. They went straight back. And I waited. An hour passed, then two. I thought: This is impossible. They should have been here twice over by now. I sensed that something was wrong. I decided to go. When I reached Bankowy Square, I saw a crowd. I jumped out of the streetcar, went closer, and heard people talking about the whole story: "Some cats came out this morning, and these two got killed."

Were Rysiek and Wacek's bodies still lying there?
Yes!

And you saw them?
Yes! of course! I saw both of them. Pnina said that Tadek Szejngut was killed climbing out of the sewers. That's not true. Tadek was killed several months later, on Waszyngtona Street.

And what happened to Krzaczek? After all, they were together.
Listen, what happened to Krzaczek, I don't know. He definitely stayed alive that time. You heard the suspicions that Krzaczek was a Kripo agent. That on the one side he was doing stuff for us, but on the other he was collaborating. I don't know, I can't tell you. I know that he helped us: he drove the truck, and then took the whole group with us to the woods. And he did that twice. Had it not been for Krzaczek, the driver would have fled at once, but Krzaczek sat next to him with a revolver and ordered him to drive. That's a fact. Allegedly, there are other facts, too. We informed the AL of our suspicions that Krzaczek was an agent. I think they checked him out. And it's a fact that they sentenced him to death. Sometime later, we heard that Krzaczek was in Warsaw and wanted to meet me. Everyone was against my going to that meeting, but I believed that I should. After all, Krzaczek did do a lot for us.

That sounds a little like you don't really believe in his guilt.
No! How could I not believe in it? He killed those guys of ours.

And there's no doubt about that?
No! It's one hundred percent fact. Jasiek from Częstochowa is here; the sister of Lalo,[54] one of the guys killed, is here. I'm no historian, you know, and I haven't researched it all like it should be researched. But those people are convinced of

---

54 Icchak Windman (Lalo)—member of the ŻOB in Częstochowa. Kazik suspects that Lalo was killed in Warsaw, betrayed to the Germans by *szmalcownicy* (Kazik, *Memoirs*..., 68–69).

his guilt. Nonetheless, I believed I ought to meet with him, and I went to that meeting. He was in a dreadful state: unshaven, and in rags. The whole conversation between us faltered, somehow. He didn't say anything in particular; he just asked me for a few cigarettes.

And you didn't ask him about anything specific?
No. Listen, my thinking was this: I ask him if he killed them, he says no, and where does that get us? What arguments or evidence do I have? I decided I wouldn't ask about anything. I waited to see what he would say, but he didn't say anything. We stood about a bit on the street, but I didn't feel comfortable with him; he was so down-at-heel that people were looking at him, so we parted fairly quickly.

And no one knows what happened to him, how he died?
Not exactly. I heard that there were these two guys—one was called Zygmunt [Igła], I think, and was from the Bund—in hiding downtown somewhere. They were arrested by the Gestapo, and apparently Krzaczek went to the Gestapo to get them released. Word was that he was killed there, too. You know, it would have been idiotic of us to try to find out what really happened to him. It was all too risky, to push your nose in where you didn't need to. It happened, he disappeared somewhere—too bad. In any case, then, on Bankowy Square, there they were: Wacek killed, Rysiek killed. I was certain that one of the bystanders had informed the Germans that there were "cats" from the ghetto climbing out of the sewers. I decided not to go to the manhole cover on Prosta.

But you say that Rysiek and Wacek were killed on Bankowy Square, not by the manhole on Prosta.
Yes, because they had fled. But I don't know the details of the situation. Some people said they had gone by droshky. I don't know; nobody knows. I know that I saw them killed.

How many people can there have been in the second group, the one that didn't manage to get out of the sewer?
I suspect there might have been about fifteen people.[55]

That means that they hadn't managed to find everyone in the ghetto?
No, certainly not.

---

55 Marek Edelman (conversation with H.G., Nov. 1999): "There were about 8–10 people there."

Are the names of those killed by the manhole shaft apart from Szlamek Szuster and Adolf Hochberg known?
Listen, I don't know. Truth be told, I never tried to find out.

How can you know that there were about fifteen of them there?
The people who got out said so. Marek, Cywia . . . I think they knew how many people they sent away from the main shaft.

Don't you think that someone else could have joined them from the ghetto?
I don't think so.

Kazik, do you judge that situation at all? Do you consider anyone to have been guilty of anything?
Listen, I can't hold anyone guilty. I can only ask the question: since you promised, why didn't you keep your promise? Cywia was angry with me for not wanting to wait once they were all lying in the truck. If Cywia and Marek hadn't climbed out of the sewer and had waited for the others, I definitely wouldn't have driven off. Since that group took at least half an hour to get out, and the others hadn't made it back, God knows where they were! And the fact that both Cywia and Marek claim responsibility for the decision to send Szlamek for the others probably means that they both feel uncomfortable with it. You could wake me in the middle of the night and I'll tell you what I'm telling you now: I am sure that I took the right decision in not waiting for the others with that truck . . . We'd all have been long gone by now. And it certainly wouldn't have helped those fifteen either. But if someone wants to judge me because I shouldn't have driven off, that's their affair. I'll tell you just one thing. I told you everything as I saw it. And the rest—judgments—I'll leave to others: readers, historians, and so on . . .

Jerusalem, October 1999

Kazik Ratajzer died in Jerusalem on December 22, 2018.

None of It Is of Any Significance

Conversation with Marek Edelman

You know, I'm not in favor of you doing a second part of that thing. Because the other one was good. That was a shot on goal, but now?

But I want to try and supplement it, maybe add something to it. As far as possible. Marek, can we start by talking about the ŻZW?
The ŻZW? What do you care about that? You want anything to do with fascists?

Marek, seriously. There are quite a lot of memoirs about the uprising in the Warsaw ghetto, written by Zionists and non-Zionists. And nobody says anything about the ŻZW.
Because there's nothing to talk about.

In Poland you have talked many times about . . .
. . .about the ŻZW?

No, that's precisely it—you've talked about the uprising, but you've always been silent on the ŻZW. Perhaps it's worth talking about the facts.
About what facts? There were no facts!

For instance: Israel Gutman says that on the brushmakers' premises there was a detachment of the ŻZW commanded by Chaim Łopata. Was there a ŻZW detachment at the brushmakers'?
Oh, come on! What are you talking about? Do you imagine that anyone from outside could have existed there?! Impossible. Yes, yes. You're forgetting who you're dealing with. I'm no angel. When the communists attempted an "ex" of their own, I nearly killed them, too. Nowadays, anyone can talk. Eh, let them talk, what's it to me?

So, you never heard the name Chaim Łopata?
I think I heard the name after the war. So, what did they do on the brushmakers' premises?

I don't know.
Because they didn't do anything. They can't have been there. Listen, it's impossible that anyone was there.

…And that you didn't know about it?
No one could have given orders there without me. You're forgetting that we had the say-so there.

Marek, do you mean to say that no part of the ghetto was controlled by the ŻZW?
Apart from that house on Muranowska, no.

Did you know Dawid Wdowiński?
No. Who's he?

Doctor Wdowiński. He was a physician in the ghetto. And the chairman of the ŻZW's Political Council. He survived, and after the war had a book about the ŻZW published in America.[1]
Never heard of him. They had a Political Council? Oh, for goodness' sake, people can write anything. And don't exaggerate—they were vile.

Why vile?
They thought they were the most important because they got hold of a few weapons—from some nationalists or someone, I think.

Do you know who from?
Word was they were from some people from "The Sword and the Plow."[2]

---

1 Dawid Wdowiński, *And we are not saved* (London: Philosophical Library, 1964).
2 The Sword and the Plow (Pol. Miecz i Pług)—a clandestine political and military movement founded in Warsaw in 1939 by nationalist Christian activists (and as such fundamentally anti-Jewish).

In 1991 I spoke to a man who was called Józef Grynblatt[3] in the ghetto—Bednarczyk after the war—and he talked in quite a lot of detail about the ŻZW. He claimed to have taken part in their Military Council himself.
I never heard that they had any Military Council.

Ringelblum writes about a visit to their command at 7 Muranowska Street.
And what of it? They were a band of porters, smugglers, and thieves. They holed up in that house, fired a few shots, and fled the same day. There's nothing to talk about. It's possible that it was they who hoisted that standard.

Apparently, there were two.
Maybe.

When was the ŻZW formed? Some people say it was in July 1942.
Oh, come on! It was much later.

January 1943?
I think it was later. Whatever, I don't know. I'm old and I don't remember.

You met with them, didn't you? You, Antek, and Anielewicz?
Yes, their commander, Frenkiel,[4] came to us, and two other guys.

Leon Rodal?
I don't know.

And they came to the meeting with pistols.
And so did we.

They waved their weapons around and demanded to assume command from you?
We waved our weapons around, too.

What else do you remember about that meeting?
Nothing, nothing important. They wanted to take command, they said that they didn't want to talk, that they were going to kill us. So, we said that we could do bang-bang too, but nothing significant happened.

---

3   Conversation with Józef Grynblatt conducted by H.G. in July 1991 in Warsaw, recorded on audio cassette.
4   Paweł Frenkiel (1920–1943), officer in the Polish Army, one of the leaders of the ŻZW.

Where was the meeting? At their place on Muranowska?
No, somewhere on Nalewki. In our secret joint.

Was that after the January campaign?
Of course. Just before the uprising. A week, maybe two . . . I couldn't tell you. And they come demanding that we cede command to them because they're a military organization! And they had contacts. Which they did. And quite a lot of weapons. Compared to us they had a lot more. I mean, percentagewise they had more.

Were there other meetings besides that one? Do you think that Anielewicz met with them?
Nooo.

Why didn't the ŻOB integrate the ŻZW detachment into its own ranks?
Because they didn't want that!

Various sources claim that they weren't wanted as the ŻZW. The ŻOB command agree only to split up their members among its own units.
Not true, that's not how it was. We could certainly have taken those three groups of ten who wouldn't have split. We wouldn't have taken the whole trash–too dangerous.

But that "trash" wanted to fight, too.
And how do you know that? What they wanted above all was to get out of the ghetto. There were a few of them who fired a few shots; apparently, they hoisted a flag. I know nothing about that, but it's possible. And then they left. At once. And they got killed because they associated with God knows who. How many of them were killed on that roof? Fifty? Listen, what they wanted most of all was to get out of the ghetto. We didn't dig a single tunnel out onto the other side. But they had tunnels. One led out onto Muranowska. They also had some shady dealings with the bakers. They were just on the lookout to get out!

But they did have quite a lot of weapons. Were they stockpiling them just to get out?
I don't know. I mean, no one had any contact with them. Don't tell me what they were stockpiling, or what they were thinking, because you don't know.

Did they have bunkers of their own?
I don't know. I don't think so. They were just in that house on Muranowska. And that's all.

How many of them were there? Some sources say a hundred fifty.
No way!

Józef Grynblatt claimed that Anielewicz wanted to do a deal with the ŻZW, but Antek Cukierman was against it.
Not true. They had one thought in their heads: how to get out of there! They fired three salvos and got out the same day. That was probably their idea all along. And the idiots got themselves shot. But in the ghetto, they didn't exist. Neither in ŻTOS, nor in Centos[5]—they're not there.

Apparently, they had people in the Jewish police.
What do you mean, "they had people?" That they had been in Betar before the war? Maybe. And that's the end of it.

***

One of the unit commanders on your turf was Jakub Praszker. You never talk about him.
Because there's nothing to talk about. Those people had no personality, you understand? Apart from Antek, apart from Anielewicz, apart from Jurek [Arie Wilner]—they had no personality.

But they were just random people, in a random situation. They weren't trained soldiers.
It's not about soldiers! Soldiers weren't needed there. The more you were a soldier, the worse it was.

Because?
Because a soldier is something completely different. Notice that in wartime, civilians are best.

---

5   p. 494 Glossary.

So, in what sense weren't they good? What conditions didn't they fulfil?
They were small, browbeaten people.

Isn't that obvious?
I'm not saying there's anything wrong with that, I'm just telling you. Perhaps they were too old? Berek [Sznajdmil], for instance, who was a military man, couldn't cope with the tension. You understand what I mean—civilians! Civilians were capable of putting up resistance. Somewhere or other, I said: soldiers had learned how to fight in an open field, in trenches, this or that. But civilians didn't know how to fight. They just fought! If they had the will from within. And those were the best sort. Who were the boys from Kedyw?[6] Boy Scouts. Civilians. Teachers. Who was Rybicki? A teacher. The commander of Kedyw. Perhaps he had graduated from some cadet school twenty years before. But that was of no significance. And who were the military men? One was that dinner-hunter "Monter" [Antoni Chruściel]. But the ones on the barricades were just regular guys.

Can what you're talking about be extrapolated to the attitude of the ŻOB to the ŻZW? Civilians versus military men?
But where were they "military men?!"

Well, that's the image that has been created for them. Soldiers of the Polish Army, a predilection for uniform, an arsenal of good weapons . . .
Oh, get away with you! That was the *underwelt*. Military men?! What Jews were ever military men at the age of twenty? You know what? All that is fabrication. Today anyone can talk because there are no witnesses. In any case, I don't care. The more you write, the better, even if it's God knows what.

Is that really what you think?
Well, yes, because then historians read this stuff and say: "Ooh! He said . . ." But they can't verify who says what. And then one will write a Ph.D., another a postdoc, and so on and so on. I don't know why you're so intent on truth. None of it can be established any more. And quite apart from that, it makes me real sad when I read all these various things, these so-called testimonies. It makes me sad. For the people who were there and somehow managed to live. And now they're being screwed over.

---

6   *Kedyw* (Pol., partial acronym of *Kierownictwo Dywersji* ("Directorate of Diversion") was a Polish Home Army unit that conducted active and passive sabotage, propaganda, and armed operations against Nazi German forces and collaborators.

Why "screwed over?" If these stories are colorized, overstated, that only adds appreciation to the whole thing.
No, no! You can't bump your self-esteem with lies. Everyone has their five minutes. And that's fine. But you can't create myths.

***

Did you have some sort of conflict with the PPR unit?
Yes, I did. Because they would go out on "exes" and send out money to Gomułka on the other side.

Before the uprising?
Yes.

Unbelievable! And so?
Well, when we got wind, we caught them as they were heading out on their next job. And they never did that again.

Such were your powers of persuasion?
They wouldn't have dared.

Because?
They were afraid, simple.

***

Why did you write *The Ghetto Fights* in the third person?
Because it's a report. It was written with the people in America in mind.

For whom?
The only organization that was active there and helped the ghetto during the war, was the Workers' Committee.[7]

---

7 The Jewish Workers' Committee (Yid. Yidishe Arbeter Komitet)—founded in the USA in 1943 by Jewish trade union activists, mostly from the tailors' union. Its leaders were Dawid Dubiński, Jakub Pat, Adolf Held, and Beniamin Tabaczyński, all of whom had emigrated from Russia to the USA at the beginning of the century.

Was that a Bundist organization?
Ninety percent Bundists: [Dawid] Dubiński, [Jakub] Pat, [Adolf] Held, [Beniamin] Tabaczyński. I can't remember what all of them were called any more. It was them who went to Roosevelt, them who worked up the contact with London, and them who sent money. And the real reason was that so that the Zionists would get a leathering for what they did here: claiming that the Bund was opposed to fighting.

Celina wrote that [Maurycy] Orzech[8] put off joining the ŻOB.
He was the only one who had the wherewithal for a larger transport of arms into the ghetto. But when he went outside the wall, they shot him dead. That's such a nice story, but it's of no significance.

That was during those first July meetings?
Yes. It was around July 25, 26, or maybe 27.

Is anything known about the circumstances of his death?
No, nothing. He disappeared. Nobody knows anything. He just disappeared.

In *Doyres Bundistn* there's a note[9] on Maurycy Orzech which indicates that he was still alive for another year. At one point he tried to get over the border, was arrested in Kolomyia, taken back to Warsaw, and imprisoned at the Gestapo. And then: there were failed attempts to spring him. Orzech was murdered in August 1943 at the Gestapo, according to the author of that note.
Listen, he left the ghetto, it was July 26 or 27. He was supposed to call the next day, he didn't, and that was the last of him.

Perhaps he didn't get in touch with you, but someone somewhere saw him or met him?
This book you're talking about, it was written in America, right?

---

8   Orzech, Maurycy (1891–1943). Activist in Jewish and Polish trade unions, contributor to the PPS paper *Dziennik Ludowy* and correspondent for the American Jewish paper *Forward*. In 1940, deported from police custody in Lithuania (Kaunas or Vilnius) to the Warsaw ghetto. In the ghetto, he became a member of the Bund central committee. Left the ghetto in July 1942. In 1943, he allegedly attempted to escape abroad, was arrested in Kolomyia [now Ivano-Frankivsk, Ukraine], taken to the Gestapo headquarters in Warsaw, and murdered in August 1943.
9   The entry on Maurycy Orzech in *Doyres Bundistn* ([Generations of Bundists], vol. 2, New York: Farlag Unzer Tsayt, 1956) was written by Victor Shulman.

Yes.
Well, what can they know? And anyway, let them write whatever they want. He definitely died. There's no question of that if you ask me. I mean, we looked for him. We would have found him if he had been alive.

***

Did you have some kind of dispute with Antek about their post-war interpretation of the uprising, that it was only the Zionists . . . ?
He never said any such thing to me.

But he did say it publicly?
Well, yes. But you know, I have to say that in all of the ŻOB, apart from Masza [Glajtman-Putermilch], who hates Anielewicz to this day, there were no such differences along party lines.[10]

But they emerged strongly after the war, right?
Yes, because they wanted to prove to Israel that they were the best, that we weren't even there.

And you weren't mad about that?
No, it made me laugh. I said to Antek: "What? You guys did everything?! And without the Bund you would have been in contact with the AK?! Without me you would have had contact with the AK?! Who would have talked to you?!" "And Jurek [Arie Wilner]!" Antek yelled. "What about Jurek? Jurek couldn't get in with them."

But you could?
I knew them. Not because it was me, but because I had the name.

A Bundist name?
Yes. About [Adolf] Berman,[11] for instance, they knew that he was dancing at two weddings. And so, they didn't trust him. And those conversations with Antek weren't any kind of hugely important political talks. He laughed, I laughed, and that was all.

---

10 p. 512 Glossary—Political relations in the Warsaw ghetto.
11 Adolf Abraham Berman (1906–1978), communist, Polish and Israeli politician. During the war, secretary of Żegota.

You cut your first visit to Israel in the 1950s short by a few days. Why?
Because Antek was bugging me. He took me on a three-day tour of Israel. We went everywhere: The Dead Sea, the desert, and so on. I liked it a lot. And when we got back to the kibbutz, he says to me: "Well, then?" "Beautiful," I said. "But what did you like the most?" So, I said: "The landscape, the nature." "But didn't you see all the factories?" "There are bigger ones in Poland." "But these ones were built by Jews!" "So what?" And so on and so on, from one thing to the next, and then he says: "It's your duty to stay here!" "Kiss my ass!" I said and slammed the door. The next day, Antek came to the airport and wanted to give me some chocolate, but I don't like chocolate. "Leave me alone," I said.

I heard that when everyone wanted to eat you for Anielewicz's red-painted gills,[12] Antek defended you fiercely.
Well, he had to defend me on that, because it was him who told me about it.

***

Listen to this quote of Ben Gurion's: "They wouldn't listen to us. They sabotaged the Zionist idea with their death." And he goes on: "The tragedy that European Jewry is experiencing is not my immediate problem."[13] What do you say to that, Marek?
You know what? Ben Gurion was a small-town snollygoster. He had no vision. I have no doubt that the whole thing played into Ben Gurion's hands. Back then, their opinion was: the worse it was here for us, the better for them over there. I mean, they never came over here to Poland, wouldn't send us any money. They didn't want to help us out.

No financial aid ever came from Palestine?
Never. The AK and the London government helped us a little. But Schwarzbart?[14] That great Zionist! He wouldn't lift a finger. Antek even wrote him a letter:

---

12 In an interview with Hanna Krall (*Shielding the Flame*), Edelman said of Anielewicz: "Before the war, he lived on Solec. His mother sold fish, and if she had any over, she had him buy red paint and paint their gills so that they would look fresh." He came under immense criticism in Israel for those words.
13 Words spoken by David Ben Gurion, later the first prime minister of Israel, at a meeting of activists from the socialist party Mapai on December 8, 1942.
14 Ignacy Schwarzbart (1888–1961)—one of the leaders of the General Zionists, from 1938 a deputy to the Polish parliament. One of two representatives of the Jews in the National Council of the Polish government in London, along with Szmuel Zygielbojm of the Bund.

"We will curse you and your children to the third generation." Like it says in the Bible. And nothing! As far as I remember, that letter was written in August or September 1943 at 4 Komitetowa Street. I'm sure it reached him. I'm not sure that Karski didn't take it. And then, when Antek and Celina went over there... How many years was it that Israel had not a single good word to say about what happened here? The word was: we are the Jewish nation because we are fighting the Arabs. And they let themselves get slaughtered. And in fact, even today, those new Jews only rate themselves. They cut themselves off from the Jewish nation in Europe and are pretending that they can build a culture of their own. They just wrote off whole magnificent centuries.

Are you still resentful about that?
Listen, I think that some of it was for saving, but they didn't want to. And now they write in a language with no traditions, and don't even remember what they once had. The Jews were Europeans, but Israel will be a state with an Arab culture. I have nothing against that, but it doesn't have much to do with Jewry. Because Jewry was in Europe!

I wonder what you have to say about Celina's book.[15]
I can imagine what she might have written.

Celina says, for example, that it would have been hard to survive in the ghetto without the thought of the comrades in Palestine.
Oh, that's garbage! Who in the ghetto took any thought for the comrades in Palestine?! But I know she was saying that even at the trade unions congress in 1946 or 1947. She had to say it!

Celina's book is full of pathos.
Well, yes, because she was writing it for others. But Celina had a head on her shoulders.

Were Celina, Antek, and the others so very Zionist before all of that? Or was it all a kind of ideology after the fact?
During the war Zionism didn't play any role. In 1939 Palestine was an escape route. But you had to court Mussolini, like the Rebbe of Ger did, to be able to get

---

15 Cywia Lubetkin, *Zagłada i powstanie* (Warsaw: Książka i Wiedza, 1999).

there.[16] If truth be told, all the Zionists hated Schwarzbart and those Palestine Zionists. And afterwards, when those *shlikhim*[17] came, they jumped on the bandwagon. And Antek was in charge of that because he had the contacts. He helped organize that *aliyah*.[18] He had some buddies in the Foreign Ministry: Zarzycki, Jóźwiak. I don't remember how many dollars they were taking to let a Jew across the border back then.

Did their post-war Zionist engagement surprise you?
Nooo, we laughed about it together. Antek didn't emigrate that quickly, anyway, not for three years. Celina did. But she came back even faster. She slept on that bed right there for three months. She was pregnant at that point.

I sensed from various comments of yours that you felt somewhat abandoned, lonely, when they eventually left.
I never said that anywhere.

No, that's my interpretation. But you did write that you didn't really know what to do with yourself.
And you think they knew?! And then, in Israel, they were all in the shadows— Antek, Celina, and Kazik [Ratajzer] too.

But Antek and Celina were surely less lonely in their kibbutz than Kazik in Jerusalem?
I don't know. I don't think things went especially well for them. And that was no coincidence. It was a continuation of the same politics that Israel had shown during the war: we are the only army, only we here are worth anything.

***

Did Antek have an unfulfilled insurrectionist complex?
Some people said so, but that's not true.

And did the "Aryan" side bring him fulfilment?
He was a brand in himself over there.

---

16 The Rebbe of Ger (Góra Kalwaria) and his court left Poland at the beginning of September 1939.
17 *Shlikhim* (Heb.)—envoys.
18 *Aliyah* (Heb.)—immigration to Israel.

And he didn't have to be afraid of "looking similar?"
Not at all?! Antek looked like a hundred goys. Totally the Polish gentleman. *Schnapps getrunken* and the Germans were eating out of his hands. He totally looked the part. And he had the self-confidence.

And he could go about his business openly?
Completely openly.

And you?
I couldn't. Because I'm a Jew boy.

Did it bother you, having to sit about a lot?
No, no. I'm lazy.

That's now, but I'm sure you weren't lazy back then.
I was always lazy. I mean, when they blew that bunker up, I was asleep.

So, you say.
It's true. I would say if it was otherwise.

But at some point, you woke up?
When they were done.

So, what did you do between the two uprisings if you couldn't get out much?
I mostly drank vodka.

And you had a girlfriend back then.
Yes, a wonderful girl.

Was it very hard for you to be cooped up like that?
Not really. I'm fairly "adaptable." I went out in the evenings sometimes. And apart from that, there was essentially something going on the whole time, people would come by. I'll pass over Kamiński, who used to come by to see Jurek [Grasberg]. He was a 200 percent Jew boy, that one!

Who? Kamiński or Jurek?
Jurek. Kamiński wasn't completely *rein arishes gesheft*,[19] either.

---

19 *Rein arishes gesheft* (Yid.)—the proper Aryan stuff.

Did you have a weapon with you in those various hideouts?
Yes, always. We all did. Well, maybe not all of us, but I always did.

Did the women have weapons, too?
No-oo. What? The women?! Zielona Marysia [Luba Gawisar] with a gun? Or Irka [Gelblum], that crazy girl?!

***

When we talked fifteen years ago, you said some very acerbic anti-Israeli words: that as a nation it had no chance in a sea of a hundred million Arabs.
Because it has no chance, given Israel's hostile policy!

But there has been a fundamental change—increasing numbers of Israelis, not only among the elite, believe that compromise is necessary in order to be able to co-exist in the world over there.
Fifty years of those small-town politicians has not been good for them. But there is another thing that I said back then: that there is no chance of a European Jewish state; that they would Arabize.

That state is already largely an Arab state today.
Well, there you are, then. That's what I was talking about. But will they be able to make that Arab-Jewish state succeed? I don't know. That depends on international relations, on American politics, on Islamic fundamentalism; there's the matter of Jerusalem, and so on. And at the same time, it's a nation state, a religious state, where Christians are second-class and Muslims third-class citizens. That's asking for trouble. After three million people were murdered over here, they want to dominate, and not to have to reckon with non-Jews?! The secular ones succumb to the pressure of the religious ones, and a state like that is good for no one.

***

Do you know Antek's book?[20]
No, only excerpts someone translated for me.[21] But that's not a book about the ghetto. It's a book about the Zionist movement. What's that big-shot historian of theirs called?

---

20 Zuckerman, *A Surplus of Memory*.
21 The first Polish translation of Icchak Cukierman's book was published after this conversation with Marek Edelman.

Israel Gutman?
Yes, yes. He wrote a history of the youth wing of the leftist Zionist movement in wartime Warsaw. They're blinded. They don't see anything beyond halutzim and Zionism. They don't see the ghetto. They don't understand anything!

***

Marek, what date should be taken as the foundation of the ŻOB?
October 15, 1942.

Celina gives a different date—in July. "And the Bund joined the ŻOB in October," Celina writes.
Not true. The ŻOB was founded and started to operate when they came in from that farm in Czerniaków and the halutzers had a few people. And that was in the fall. I remember that it was terribly cold.

Luba says that Grasberg and the other Boy Scouts wanted to join the ŻOB as a whole troop, but Anielewicz didn't want to let them.
That's the first I heard of that. Perhaps, but I don't know anything about it. We had one Boy Scout; he sang beautifully. I forgot his name. He was killed at the streetcar terminus on Grójecka. That was after the uprising. Jurek, his first name was.

***

Is there a full list of the ŻOB members anywhere?
Neustadt has one.[22]

Who was counted as belonging to the ŻOB?
Anyone who was in one of the groups, one of the detachments.

And Inka?
She wasn't in the ŻOB.

And the fact that she was a courier outside the wall isn't enough?
Well, yes. But the two hundred twenty in the ŻOB were the ones who fought. And in addition to them there were the couriers: Władka [Fajgele Peltel], Zielona

---

22 Neustadt, *Khurban uMered shel Yehudei Varsha*.

Marysia, Irka, Marysia, Inka, and the others. You know, I knew those two hundred people in the ŻOB. It's not hard to get to know two hundred people in half a year. I don't mean I knew them all personally, but I knew their names and faces. I just can't remember where Henoch Gutman was killed; he was a loyal subordinate.

Ask Kazik, who was in his group.
I don't think Kazik can know that, either, because Gutman was killed later, after Kazik left the ghetto.[23]

On Franciszkańska?
First three, and then five people were killed on Franciszkańska, but he wasn't one of them.

Neustadt says that Gutman was wounded on May 2 in the battle for the bunker at 30 Franciszkańska. And that he stayed in the ghetto with his girlfriend and didn't leave via the sewers.
He certainly didn't leave. But in that battle at 30 Franciszkańska it wasn't him but Berek Sznajdmil that was wounded, in the head, and he died a few hours later. And it wasn't May 2, it was May 1. I don't remember Gutman being in the Franciszkańska bunker at all. But perhaps he was there. I don't remember having any contact with him after we left the brushmakers' yard.

And the only one killed at the brushmakers' was Michal Klepfisz?
Michał and the five people from Akiba. They were a bit useless.

Was there an Akiba unit? Kazik says they were scattered.
Yes, there was a small Akiba unit, five or six people.

Under Jakub Praszker?
I think so.

Do you remember Mejloch Perelman?
Of course.

---

23 In his book (*A Surplus of Memory*, 469), Antek Cukierman writes: "The decision was made to establish an AL rebel base at Leszno 18. We sent a group of our comrades there [...]. The idea was to move people who weren't vital to the war to hold the base at Leszno, which we would use for retreat if necessary, and, meanwhile, for preserving the archive and the armory [...]. I must note that Kazik was a fighter and was very vital to us, but he knew the bunker and the way to it, and we relied on him to lead the group and organize it on the spot."

The wounded Mejloch asked to be left his gun so that he could save himself from being burned alive. And Anielewicz ordered them to take his pistol, so that it didn't go to waste. That's what Masza says.
Well, Masza hated the Zionists. And she hated Anielewicz above all. But what she says is true.

Is it true that they could have gotten him out of there?
If he had been a Shomer,[24] they would have gotten him out, like Masza says. Though I buried both Shomers and Bundists... But in that situation, I can't tell you precisely. Strange things went on at 18 Miła altogether.

Who knows what went on there?
I know. The dozen or so people that got out of there knew.

It was under the stairs that you found them?
Outside the door. In any case, it's all the same, what difference does it make?!

Do you want to say anything about what went on at 18 Miła?
No, I'm not going to say anything.

Will you ever say anything?
No! That's not for telling.

They're not things that could be learned from?
No. You know, that was a situation... No, it doesn't do to speak ill of people who are no longer here. It's unnecessary.

Can't it all be justified in terms of the reality they were living in?
No, it can't.

But it was you who told me once that there was a different morality there.
But that's different!

What categories do you judge that situation by?
The categories from back then. According to today's categories, everything is fine and dandy. Because they say: a nation perished, its soldiers perished.

---

24 Shomer—member of a Zionist youth organization.

Yes. Without that suicide on Miła, the whole Zionist interpretation of the uprising...
...would not exist.

Precisely.
And that's their failure, between you and me. But it's not worth talking about. And apart from anything else, it's not true that the Zionists constituted any kind of formation back then. They truly did not exist as a political group. They were soldiers, Boy Scouts, people, friends, and so on. There weren't all those differences between us. That happened later. But that's a different matter. Things are different once you have freedom.

You got a few survivors out of 18 Miła. Who?
Yes. I think there were twelve people.

Juda Wengrower, Tosia Altman...
Jurek, the Boy Scout.

The one who was killed at the streetcar terminus afterwards?
Yes. Twelve people. They had lain down on the floorboards. The whores had made beds up for them. And they had gone to sleep.

The whores who you didn't let into the sewers? Or other whores?
There were no more. Those two were enough.

Why did you not let them in?
Leave it, will you?!

After all, they were decent whores. They looked after you all.
Yes. I had it especially good with them. Back when the ghetto still existed, they used to give me food every day.

They had maternal feelings for you?
Yes. They would come up to me on the street and put a bread roll in my pocket.

Always in the same place?
Yes. I think it was on Walicόw they had their spot.

And the two that you didn't let into the sewers?
When we came to no. 30, they hitched their skirts up and started scrubbing the floor.

To no. 30 on Franciszkańska?
Yes. It's all the same. They behaved very decently. They fed Lusiek.

The young Błones boy?
Yes, his lip was shot through.

And the ten people you sent out of the ghetto on May 8 through the sewers to the other side?
Janek Bilak led that group, those ten people.

Did they know where they were going? Did they have an address?
They knew more or less. Not exactly, but they knew something.

Did they know the layout of the sewers?
No, they didn't. But it wasn't that difficult. In any case, it's all the same. If they hadn't gotten out in one place, they would have gotten out in another. Either they would have gotten out, or they would have been killed. Like the ones after us. They got out. And they were killed. And that's all.

***

Was it possible that someone from the group that didn't manage to reach the main manhole via the sewer could have retreated to the ghetto?
No, no way.

But how do you know that, since nothing is known of what happened to them? After all, there are no witnesses.
Oh, stop it! I'm telling you—nobody went back because everyone wanted out. They emerged on Grzybowski Square, and they got killed there. They were tired, careless—whatever. They got killed.

Kazik suspects that someone must have denounced them and the area around the manhole was guarded.
Kazik shouldn't tell stories. He knows nothing. Now he has all kinds of ideas. But I'm telling you, it's of no importance. What is it you want? You're nagging. That's what happened, and that's all there is to it. It happened! And finito!

Do you think there were fifteen of them?
There were eight of them.

Kazik says fifteen.
Kazik doesn't know. I know.

Do you know who was there? Apart from Szlamek Szuster and Adolf Hochberg?
I do. That young Rozowski boy[25] was there.

The younger brother of Welwł?
Yes.

What was his first name?
I don't remember. Lejbl, I think. Anyhow, it's all the same.

Think for a minute more about who else was there.
What's it to you?!

It's important to me.
I don't know. Six or eight people.

Who sent them into the smaller sewers, you or Celina?
I did. I am responsible for everything.

So why did Celina say that it was her?
She can say what she likes, as much as she likes. It's not true that she could have a say. Nobody did. You're forgetting who you're dealing with. You ask and want to find out, but you won't find out. It was all me. Me and finito!

And those who were left behind...
That was chance. They all went back, all forty of them went back, but then it started to get uncomfortable there, and they started to return. Thirty of them returned. If it hadn't been so bad back there, none of them would have returned to the main shaft. And those few found a good hole and stayed there.

---

25 p. 437 Rereading the List—Lejb (Lejbl) Rozowski.

***

Was Masza a pair with Mejloch?
No. She was in a group with him. She was only sixteen or seventeen!

I always thought that in the ghetto that wasn't too young to be together.
No, that's a post-war fashion.

And back then?
No, they weren't even in any state to be together. Things like that, then, in that tension, didn't work.

***

Say something good about Anielewicz. So as to redress the balance at least a little from that image of the red-painted gills.
But there was nothing wrong with that!

Come on, you know well that many people were upset with you for that. Only a few treated it as a very human story devoid of pathos.
Precisely. Their family went hungry, and their mother wanted to buy bread, so she painted those gills.

But nonetheless, you hurt all sorts of patriotic, national, and various other feelings.
But why? Is painting gills banned?

Well, now say something else about Anielewicz. Did you know him well?
I knew him for half a year. From November till May. I was with him every day.

Did you like him?
…I don't remember…I don't remember! We worked differently. He was unpredictable. I was with Antek on the one side. And Anielewicz with that other guy … what was his name?

Hirsz Berliński?
…with Berliński on the other side.

In what way were they unpredictable?
Well, what did Anielewicz do? He went out on the street, shot a *werkszuc*, and then they killed two hundred fifty or three hundred people. He killed that *werkszuc* in the morning, took his revolver, and then at four or three in the afternoon, the Germans came in and murdered the whole street, everyone. He was irresponsible. Because he never saw the deportation. He came to Warsaw from Będzin, and he thought he could do God knows what. After the incident with the *werkszuc*, the Coordinating Committee[26] had him pulled from his post.

When did the incident with the *werkszuc* happen?
In March or April. But Anielewicz was very militant, intelligent. He just misjudged situations.

Anielewicz threw himself on Germans with his bare hands.
Exactly. I said he was crazy.

And he slipped the Umschlagplatz round-up?
Yes, that was on January 19.

***

And Jurek Wilner?
Jurek came back to the ghetto before the uprising. It was Grabowski who sprung him from the camp in Grochów. But he returned unrecognizable. His heels were black—he couldn't walk. He was totally beaten up, could hardly move and he was virtually gone. I used to have a notebook with Jurek's poems, he was a bit of a poet, you see. But I gave all that stuff to the museum in the Lohamei Ha-Getaot kibbutz.

Couldn't Jurek have been hidden away somewhere on the Aryan side so that he didn't have to go back to the ghetto?
Maybe he could have, but he needed a bit of warmth, a little care from people close to him. He came back in a dreadful state.

Did he have a girlfriend in the ghetto?
I don't know. I don't think so. But he was among his own. I'm not surprised that he didn't stay on the other side.

---

26 p. 502 Glossary—Jewish National Committee.

***

Why didn't Zygmunt Frydrych go back into the ghetto with Kazik?
I don't know, I couldn't tell you. Kazik believes that Frydrych let him down. Or it could have been Antek's policy. But Frydrych himself was rather skeptical, as I remember. He said: "Well, OK, but if we go back into the ghetto at night and don't have any addresses, we won't find anybody." And he was right: Kazik didn't find anybody in the ghetto. Listen, I don't know. I mean, Antek didn't know that Kazik went into the ghetto, either.

Exactly. Kazik told me that recently.
Well, yes, because I told him that not so long ago. Kazik got a lead to Krzaczek, did a quick bit of maneuvering, and went.

***

Zygmunt Frydrych moved in with some Polish woman after he got out.
Yes. That woman didn't want anything to do with us.

Why not?
You know, I can't understand that. She said: "All that happened is my business, leave me alone." She was besotted. Anyway, afterwards, she fled, moved away, leaving no trace. "That's mine!" she said. That child of hers must be about sixty by now. But she was remarkable.

Did you see her right after?
I saw her once. In 1945. I went to see her because I felt I ought to. She said to me: "Sorry, please don't come here." She adored Zygmunt the whole time. He had been going in and out of the ghetto. I can't even tell you what she was called. I knew her address, but I didn't know her name.

***

Neustadt wrote that Michał Klepfisz is buried at 32 Świętojerska. Do you remember who buried him and when?
Nobody ever buried him. It was a five-story house and it collapsed. And that's where he's lying. And then they built the Chinese embassy there.

Who lived at 18 Leszno after the ghetto uprising? Kazik wrote that Grajek and Tuwia Borzykowski lived there with you.
Not true. Celina, Antek, Stasia, and I lived there. Nobody else.

Stasia who?
Rywka Rozensztajn.

Welwł Rozowski's girl?
My girl. They lived together for a while at the beginning of the war. Stasia was very important to us; she was moral support for all of us.

Did Stasia have braids? Was it that Stasia?
She did. It was that Stasia.

Blond braids?
No, black ones! No, no, she was brown-haired. Or maybe she did have black hair? I don't remember that anymore.

Was she pretty?
Of course.

Does Stasia live in America?
Yes. She doesn't want to talk about what was.

Did she leave straight after?
Yes, in 1945 or maybe 1946.

Did you know that she was leaving?
Yes. I organized her departure myself. And before that I got her out onto the Aryan side. I was responsible for her.

When did Stasia leave the ghetto?
In late January or early February 1943. I can't remember now.

At the same time as Inka?
I think it was a few days later.

***

Was Inka very much in love with you?
Inka? No. No, never.

Marek, but when she talked about you, the way she talked about you, the way she wrote about you, how she behaved around you?
Listen. That's different. Her whole life depended on me. But I had lots of people dependent on me, only they didn't survive.

Inka never talked about anyone with such tenderness. She became an awkward young girl when she started talking about you, even though she was seventy-something by then. When I talked to her that time, in 1990, and asked about you, the first story she told me was about her crepe suit and about how you got her suit wet while you were watering the grass outside the hospital.
I'll tell you why. It's because I had her life in my hands from a very early age.

From the point when you sent her out onto the other side?
Even before that. I don't remember when it began. The thing is, from 1941 her life was in my hands. And not only her life. Tosia Goliborska and many others, the same. Even though I was a kid.

What do you mean: "in your hands?"
Just that, in my hands.

Because they were uncertain, and you knew what to do?
I don't know, I couldn't tell you.

Well, it wasn't because you had solutions that they didn't have. You were as defenseless as they were.
Well, no, but I was self-assured. And I had this vision that everything had to fit in the mold that I had in my head.

And did it fit?
It did. And if it didn't, then I made it fit. I was no angel.

Inka was a remarkable woman. Delicate, somehow, in a different way.
She's an artist. A fantasist. An intelligent fantasist. She knew how to create great myths.

But her book isn't mythologized, is it?
Nooo! When she was in hospital, in my hospital, in 1986, I said to her: "Write!" Every other day she would give me papers. Inka can write beautifully. Not everything has to be spelled out in detail.

"Because of what significance is it?" as Marek Edelman says.
Exactly. Of none.

So, you say you were no angel.
Stasia once told someone: "He was brutal, sharp, but he needed to be." I mean, she was older than me, but boy, did she listen to me! Though I learned everything I knew about life from Stasia. I knew her before, before all of that. She was a big shot in the organization, and I was just a kid.

In Skif?
Yes. Stasia had studied at the academy of fine arts in Warsaw. Maybe she had dropped out due to poverty, I don't know. But after that, during the war, she painted umbrella handles. And altered clothes that I unstitched.

How many years later did you meet Stasia again?
It was 1963 when I met her. And whenever I go to America, I always visit her.

***

Who did you like most back then? Who were you closest to?
I don't know, I couldn't say. They put me in a situation where I had to take charge, and then everything loses its significance.

Perhaps except for the need for closeness with another person?
Well, then, Stasia was important, the most important.

And of the boys?
Probably Jurek.

Which Jurek? Wilner?
No! Błones.

Jurek, Lusiek, and Guta Błones, wasn't it?
Yes. But that was slightly different. Because to me, he was a friend, but to him, I was the boss.

And you didn't have any friends for whom you were also a friend?
No. Or maybe Antek was a bit like a friend to me? I don't know.

Was Dawid Hochberg a nice guy?
I don't know. I remember he carried out orders well.

***

Where in the ghetto did you live?
At 36 Dzielna.

At 34 Dzielna there was a Dror kibbutz, and Chawka Folman lived there.
Yes, that's right, and I lived at 36 Dzielna, next door. But I had a few places. I also lived at Leszno.

And did you live alone on Dzielna?
No, with Stasia, with Rozowski. His parents lived there.

Till when did you live there?
Until the July campaign. I was on Muranowska for a while, too, at no. 44, I think, with Stasia's mother.

Did her mother go to the Umschlagplatz?
Yes. Her mother, her sister, and her brother. They rounded them all up together. On one day.

And Stasia was left alone?
Yes . . . Well, but she's not here now, so there is nothing to say.

Yes, she is.
No, she's not here anymore.[27]

When did you last speak to her?
Not long ago, a couple of weeks ago.

You said that Stasia was at some party three days ago.
Yes. It was sudden.

---

27 Stasia Rozensztajn died two days later on December 2, 1999.

Do you know what happened?
No, they don't know. People die.

Was Stasia a joyful person?
No, she wasn't joyful. But she did sing beautifully. She had a beautiful voice.

Do you remember what she sang?
She had these romantic, sentimental songs. "O, flow...," something along those lines. Now you ask, I can't remember. "O, go down to the gondola, my lover girl," she sang. And she painted nicely, and drew, and everything was lovely. Yes, now you've left your America trip too late.

A few days too late.
But in any case, if you'd met her, she wouldn't have told you anything. Various people went to visit her, but she didn't say anything. The only thing she told Paula [Sawicka] was that I was ruthless, but that I had to be.

When I first went to the Lohamei Ha-Getaot kibbutz, in 1988, and read my conversation with you to them, they attacked me viciously. And I had no idea why. And it was only when this one elderly, gray-haired lady stood up and asked with disbelieving outrage: "What does that Marek want? Does he want to be the Christ of all the Poles?" that I understood the reason for their anger. Are you pleased with the role that history in Poland has assigned you?
Listen, I share a similar way of thinking about life with many people in this country. Among us there is no place for nationalisms. In my way of thinking there is no place for a chosen nation, for a chosen land. The cause is respect for every life. And that's it. But there's no need to make a myth out of it.

But a myth has grown up. Whether you like it or not, there is a myth. Marek, do you realize how important Hanna Krall's book *Shielding the Flame* was here in Poland? In our conversations you don't usually appreciate it. That book made many people aware of you. And more: in a sense, that book created an image of you.
I think it created an image of Hania to a greater extent.

In a different sense.
Hania is a genius, you know. She can note every word like no one else. I didn't always want to agree to her conclusions, but, well... It's of no matter. I didn't say anything new there. I said it all already in *The Ghetto Fights*.

I'm talking about something else. The exceptional character of that book has nothing to do with the discovery of new historical facts. On the contrary: that book shows the reader that facts themselves, no matter how precisely conveyed, are of little value. But what I want to say is that the exceptional character of that book lies in its creation of an image of you that became extremely important to a certain generational community in Poland: that of heroic anti-hero, honest cynic, sensitive iconoclast... We all hear everything you say through the filter of that book.

How do you know that it was Hania who created that image? She did no creating! She merely reproduced what she heard.

So, it was you who were the great creator? That's who you were before Hania told the world about you, and that's who you are?
Yes, indeed.

In that case, it truly is a superb book.
Well, yes, Hania could always make her voice heard.

Inka in her book tells a story that is a combination of dream and reality. It's a story connected with Welwł Rozowski and his murder. Some *szmalcownicy* came to your apartment. Welwł went out to drum up money for them. And someone refused to shelter him over night. And Welwł was killed. You were left sitting in the apartment all alone. And Inka raced to reach you before the SS did. And then you walked down the street like a pair of lovers. And you had a revolver, and Inka felt safe.
Those are to some extent Inka's fantasies. Welwł did go to Senatorska Street, to see Salo Fiszgrund,[28] and his Polish landlady refused to let Welwł stay over. And nobody knows what happened to him.

And the apartment that the *szmalcownicy* came to was on Śmiała, not on Śnieżna, as Inka remembered it?
Yes, at no. 24 I think, but I'm not sure.

---

28 Salo Fiszgrund (1893–1971)—Bund activist in Krakow; a member of the Jewish National Committee in the Warsaw ghetto and on the Aryan side; after the war a member of the PZPR and the TSKŻ. Emigrated to Israel.

Was it really the landlady, or was it Salo Fiszgrund who wouldn't let Rozowski stay?
Basically, the landlady. I don't think Fiszgrund would have thrown him out. I think it was the landlady. I stayed over there once, and he was terrified that she would see. He was a typical Krakus.[29] And nobody liked him because nobody likes a Krakus.

How long were you hunkered down in that apartment on Śmiała?
24 hours.

And Inka came for you?
No, it was a guy who came. Władek Świętochowski. From Bronek Szpigiel. Bronek lived with him later on. And that Władek took me to a Mrs. Hornung on Noakowskiego Street. I was there for about ten days. She was a great woman, she brought good food. I think she was a Volksdeutsche.

***

Inka tried to commit suicide. She swallowed a whole lot of luminal. And you carried her out of the Żelazna Street hospital in a pink nightshirt.
A mercerized cotton nightshirt.

Where did you take her?
I took her out of the hospital onto the other side of Żelazna Street. Look: I have a scar here. Where is it?

On your right cheek. What mark is it?
A Ukrainian laid into me with a truncheon. And I was so mad at Inka that I left her on a second-floor window ledge. But what does that matter?!

Did you talk with Inka about those things after the war?
Only seldom, very seldom.

Inka once wrote that she very much hoped that by writing and talking she would manage to change the stereotype about the ghetto. And she added skeptically: "Marek didn't succeed, so I probably won't either." What didn't

---

29 *Krakus*—Pol. slang term for a person from Cracow. Edelman's comment references the age-old rivalry and antipathy that traditionally exist between Cracovians and Varsovians, as well as the stereotype of the Cracovian as tight-fisted; a pennypincher.

succeed was talking enough about life, love, work, and the ethos of day-to-day life.
Because people associate the ghetto only with death, not life.

That was what Inka always rebelled against.

***

Were people on the ghetto streets aware of the political and organizational differences between you?
No, not at all! The ŻOB was known in the ghetto as "the Party." "The party carried out that operation," is what people used to say. "The Party" meant the guys with the guns. And "the Party" was the law in the ghetto. It controlled everything from November 1942 to April 1943. Sixty thousand people answered to "the Party."

***

What language did you speak in the ghetto?
In the hospital Polish.

Never Yiddish?
Sometimes, perhaps. Everyone could speak Polish, but many people didn't understand Yiddish—Tosia [Goliborska], or Hela [Kielson], for example.

And you and Antek, what did you speak together?
Me and Antek? Do you know, I'm not sure. Antek usually told jokes in Yiddish, and he told a lot of jokes. But I guess we spoke both.

And what about Celina?
Celina spoke Yiddish too, and she could speak Polish better than Antek. Because Antek was trying to be Słowacki,[30] but it didn't work.

***

Marek, you went out onto the other side every day, with blood from the hospital for testing.
Yes, I did that for about a year.

---

30 Juliusz Słowacki (1809–1849): Polish Romantic poet and dramaturg.

Did you take patient files, too?
Yes, to the chief municipal physician.

Did you like to get out? Or were you a little afraid?
But I was legal! They could beat me up, but they couldn't do anything else to me. I was carrying blood—and I had my own affairs, of course.

What affairs?
Well, I had the blood, sure, but I also had newssheets. I took them from Kozia Street, from Rafał Praga's wife. And from other places, too, but I'm darned if I can remember where from now.

What else did you do?
Listen, I don't remember now. I forged contacts. Here I was supposed to have a meeting with Pużak,[31] there I had a message to deliver; all kinds of things went on. Nothing special. You'd have a house number, street, apartment number, and you had to leave a note, or pick one up, or tell someone something. But it all took an incredibly long time because I had to go everywhere on foot. I didn't drive.

Where were your newssheets printed? Do you remember?
Of course, I printed them myself. One of the printing shops was at 67 Miła Street and the other was at 36 or 38 Nowolipie; those were the main two.

Who else did the printing?
Stasia [Rozensztajn]. There was also this guy—Zyferman, his name was—and two other girls. One was called Blumka, I think.[32] Stasia did the mastheads.

***

I read about something recently that came as a great surprise to me. There is a testimony, used in the book by Basia Engelking,[33] which claims that the

---

31 Kazimierz Pużak (Bazyli) (1883–1950)—PPS activist, interned many times; in the years 1919–1935 a deputy to the Polish parliament. Sentenced to eighteen months' imprisonment in the Trial of the Sixteen in Moscow (1936); in the trial of the leaders of the PPS-WRN in 1948 sentenced to five years. Died in prison in Rawicz.
32 Her name was Blima Klog.
33 Barbara Engelking, *Zagłada i pamięć* (Warsaw: Wydawnictwo Instytutu Filozofii i Socjologii PAN, 1994, 189 [J.S., interview 35]: "One day, the Germans hounded us doctors out

following incident took place in the ghetto. A few days after the *große Aktion* was launched in July 1942, members of the Judenrat went into one of the ghetto hospitals and took a dozen or so medical students and doctors, purportedly to help out at the Judenrat. And then it transpired, that under police supervision, those students and physicians had to go along designated streets and force residents from their homes. Did you ever hear about an operation of that sort? That particular one or a similar one elsewhere?

No. That can't be true. That is invented.

***

Marek, will you tell me about Elżunia?
Everything.

Elżunia, Zygmunt Frydrych's daughter, had been in a convent in Przemyśl in the south of Poland.
And I think Inka brought her up from down there. Elżunia stayed on Krochmalna, at no. 5. The person who was looking after her was killed later, in the Warsaw rising. He had his leg in a cast, and they couldn't take him into the sewers. So, the Germans shot him and burned his body. After that, Elżunia went to stay in Pruszków. There, there was a field, where all sorts of people came by and chose themselves a child. Elżunia was taken by a miller to herd his geese. But then it turned cold, and the miller treated her very badly. So, a lady from Żyrardów came, saw that the child was shivering, and took her. The woman's husband repaired bicycles.

How old was Elżunia at that point?
I don't remember, exactly. Maybe six, seven, or eight?

Were you in touch with her at that time?
No, of course not! No contact from the August insurrection. And Elżunia would read the lady stories to help the lady to fall asleep. Elżunia was her best little daughter, and everything was marvelous. Then the war ended, and of course, Zygmunt told me to find his daughter. So, I started to try and track her down.

---

of the hospital at gunpoint, during a round-up of Jews. Each of us had to bring five to the Umschlag[platz]. We had to do it; there was no way out."

And when I showed up in this huge car with an American flag, some kids started yelling: "Elżunia, run; the Yids have come for you!" Then I went back a second time, and the lady told me that she couldn't part with her. In the end, she gave her up for some figure in dollars. I brought Elżunia to Warsaw. And that's what happened.

But that isn't the end of Elżunia's story?
When the Kielce pogrom happened, Estera[34] said to me: "You have no right to take responsibility for her," and she took Elżunia to Sweden. And there she was adopted by a lady from America. And in America, Elżunia had a bicycle, a pony, and a boat, graduated from college, and then got married and committed suicide. She poisoned herself.[35]

Did you think it was a good solution to send her away from Poland?
Mrs. Iwińska said that I couldn't take responsibility for other people's children.

Ala Margolis-Edelman says[36] that the woman from Żyrardów gave Elżunia up because you went to Cyrankiewicz,[37] who had her son released from prison. Is that how it was?
I did go, but not to Cyrankiewicz, only to the public prosecutor in Praga. Ala has no idea and is making things up. She never had a good memory. Cyrankiewicz wasn't even prime minister then.

Could you call it a barter: Elżunia the daughter for the release of that woman's son from prison?
No, no. And all that happened much later, two or three months later. When I took Elżunia from that lady, that boy—he was just a kid—was still at home. It was only later that he was arrested for the AK, because he'd been in the woods. And the Praga prosecutor did release him. But the lady from Żyrardów gave Elżunia up for money. At first, for a long time, she didn't want to, but when

---

34 Estera Iwińska (1886–1963)—barrister and Bund activist; the sister of Wiktor Alter, the leader of the Bund. In September 1939, she was held hostage with Stefan Starzyński, the mayor of Warsaw, but escaped and managed to flee to the USA.
35 Elżunia Frydrych, a chemistry freshman, poisoned herself in a California hotel on October 16, 1962.
36 Alina Margolis-Edelman, interview with Anna Bikont [in:] *Gazeta Wyborcza*, "Wysokie Obcasy" supplement, December 18, 1999.
37 Józef Cyrankiewicz (1911–1989)—Polish socialist activist, communist politician, and prime minister for several terms in the People's Republic of Poland.

she started counting and it turned out that there was quite a lot of money, she brought her to us herself.

Did you have any contact with that woman from Żyrardów later?
No, never. Why would I?

Did you know that Marysia Warman was in touch with the cigarette sellers?
Yes, of course. Józek [Ziemian] helped out the guys on Three Crosses Square, and Marysia used to go to the guys in the Royal Castle. They had this black-haired girl who they never let out because she was so dark. So, they kept watch over her, and because it was dark in there, they used to burn a candle-end. And the little girl was safe. Those guys sold cigarettes, too. Marysia used to take them money, but they were doing just fine themselves anyway.

How were weapons smuggled into the ghetto between January and April 1943? I read somewhere that Pinkiert's men used to transport weapons in hearses.
Hmmm, maybe.

But they were usually taken in via the guardpost, under potatoes or in a pillowcase, right?
Yes. And then there was that one huge consignment from the AK. We got fifty pistols and fifty grenades. That one came in over the wall on Parysowski Square. Michał Klepfisz organized it.

***

You always talk about your prewar life in such shorthand: Mom died young, Frania, tuberculosis, several schools, the end. Can you tell me something about Frania, for instance? Or: where did you live before the war? Who did you live with? Say more.
Frania always wore these thick fustian pants, and her skirt hung on a hook. Frania only wore her skirt on Sundays, to church. And those fustian pants had this reeeaaally big button-up flap at the back. It was big because Frania was a very big woman. Where I lived? 14 Franciszkańska. There were also some subtenants living there.

And they took care of you when your mom died?
I couldn't tell you. I supported myself.

How did you earn money?
I gave lessons. That girl Mania Kac wanted to learn Polish, and since she was dyslexic, I had my work cut out. And I earned my money. She never learned to read, but she was an amazing dancer and vocalist in the ghetto. Every week she acted in two children's plays. They were written in the Medem Sanatorium. One was called *Dolls*, and the other was about China. These two teachers, Giliński and Trupianski, wrote them, and Wanda Wasilewska translated them into Polish. They were *revolutsyonniye*[38] plays. The dolls rebel against being locked in the toybox. And Mania Kac was a dancer, the leading doll. And it was staged at our place . . . And then she had nothing to eat and died of starvation.

"Staged at our place"—what does that mean?
Skif organized this theater set-up on Krochmalna. Pola Lifszyc was the chief director, and Mania the lead dancer. She was still a kid.

Did you have any legal guardians after your mom's death?
I don't know. My mother's friend went to my school to get them to reduce my fees.

You mean you were completely alone?
Well? Can't you understand that? I was earning. I didn't have money for the streetcar, but I had enough to eat, and that was that.

***

In extreme situations, there are basically two opposing stances: the one we could term "Czerniaków's stance," and the other which we could call the ŻOB stance. The first is the stance of compromise crowned with tragic resignation. And the second is essentially the stance of a madman. From time to time, we wonder why history proves the madmen right, not the defenders of reason.

Czerniaków knew, just like we did, that all was lost. And in a situation where all is lost, you have to show character. You have to show that you can be opposed to that extreme situation. And although Czerniaków refused to play Rumkowski's[39] game, he was unable to hold out to the end. But assessments vary. Today, [Arnold]

---

38 *Revolutsionniye* (Rus.)—revolutionary.
39 Chaim Mordechaj Rumkowski (1877–1944)—head of the Judenrat in the Łódź ghetto; deported to Auschwitz in the final liquidation of the ghetto in late August 1944, where he was killed.

Mostowicz[40] claims that Rumkowski acted decently because he kept however many Jews—those who didn't perish in the Death March—alive. To be prepared to take responsibility for killing people because ten people in a hundred might survive is unfathomable... If that is morality, well, that's bad luck. To history, it's irrelevant whether those ten people survive. One person is entirely different. When they're lying there on a white sheet, and so on and so on. But in that mass...

Also individual people.
You know what happened in the Piotrków ghetto: when they ordered them to start selecting people for death, they shut up shop entirely, and came to Warsaw. "You kill them yourselves; we don't need to do any killing," they said. But Rumkowski killed.

So the Czerniaków stance is not the same as the Rumkowski stance. Because Czerniaków didn't want to send people to their deaths.
He had a different mentality. He was a middle-class senator, a gentleman engineer. He wasn't capable of fighting.

And neither was he capable of taking any other stance. Szmuel Zygielbojm didn't fight, either.
No, and those two deaths are different, too. One was weakness, the other was protest.

Why does history tend to approve the madmen? Why does Anielewicz get monuments and not Czerniaków?
Because Czerniaków handed out chocolate bars to dying children, and you don't get monuments for that!

And you're not angry at the world that it's constructed that way, that this is the way it divides up awards and oblivion?
No. Because that principle guarantees us a certain freedom.

It guarantees the chance to overturn the barrel that the other person wants you over?
Yes. More or less. But Czerniaków let himself be gotten over that barrel.

You say that without a shadow of a doubt?
Of course.

---

40 Arnold Mostowicz (1914–2002)—physician in the Łódź ghetto, prisoner in Auschwitz. After the war, a journalist and author.

He committed suicide. But perhaps that gesture can be read as an act of opposition, an act of bravery, in a sense?
No, I don't believe so. He wasted his chance. I've spoken about this a hundred times. He had colossal authority, and he could have said: "Gentlemen, don't give in, stand to fight!" We were nameless people. And he could at least have reinforced the passive resistance. But he did nothing. He didn't like the underground, the newssheets they brought him. He was afraid of all of that.

***

Marek, you have two splendid lives in one: the life in the ghetto, and the life on the other side. First the valiant soldier, and then the fantastic physician.
Because I always had good ideas.

So twice you had great ideas. Twice you had better ideas than others. But those two realities are fastened together by a staple: a decent man. Has the Lord God been more gracious to you than to others?
I don't know whether it's the Lord God's doing, but you know what? It's all the same thing. The second arises out of the first, and the third out of the second. You have to have a little bravery to do something oppositional. And in both cases, here and there, I did the same, always in opposition. You had to convince people to follow you. And I did. But I also made mistakes.

What kind of mistakes?
I underestimated what people are capable of. I overdid things.

Back then, in the uprising?
Oh, leave it! You don't understand anything about the uprising.

Can any of us, anyone who wasn't there, understand?
Sometimes people who don't ask questions and just listen can understand. But you want to know more. But you can't know more. Because it's not simply the case that you want to know something, so I have to tell you. I don't want to say anything at all anymore. I can't and don't want to talk about everything.

But my question is about those things that you do agree to talk about, while I, and others, circle around the crux of the matter and are still just as far away.
You know, if you were my lover and in bed would lie and listen to what I say, maybe it would be different. Because to know anything you have to be very close to a person. But you're a journalist who wants to pull something out of an abhorrent old Jew.

You talk to dozens of journalists...
Yes, and none of them ever found out anything.

Why do you talk to us all? Why are you still answering the same questions?
What harm does it do me?! Some guy or some girl comes around, yadda, yadda, yadda. But me? I don't deceive them. Did I deceive you?

I wonder why you really do it?
Look how accessible I am. I talk in such a way that everyone thinks they understand.

But you tell us half-truths?
No, the whole truth, only not the whole story. You can't know everything. Neither you, nor them. And I don't hold that against anybody. It's impossible to tell all that to a stranger.

I don't think it's only a question of being a stranger or being close. It's also a matter of time. I belong to a world fifty years later...
It's both.

Tell me, Marek, in the years after the ghetto, did you meet anyone who hadn't been there and...
...yes, yes, yes...

...and didn't live through what you did...
...yes, yes, yes...

...and yet you felt the connection was total...
...yes, yes, yes...

...and there were no barriers...
Yes, I did! A gorgeous girl. And passionate in everything, driven by passion. She pushed me because I couldn't be bothered. That was investment. She was invested with her whole life. But you're not. You want to write a book. You get what I'm saying?

A little, but not entirely.
Precisely. You have to be able to put your entire faith in the other person, and then amazing things happen.

Untitled

You're talking about love.
No, not about love. Yes, about love. I'm talking about various things. Not only about the ghetto. About everything. You have to be able to jump up on that roof one more time. Always. If it hadn't been for her, and two other girls, I would never have done all that. They pushed me: onward, onward! They were capable of thinking like me about the life of the other person. You have a guy here who's dying. They want to save him. But you have to be invested. And getting involved is a risk, a risk that twenty-five-year-old girls like them can't take. They would have needed pistols. I was never afraid to get involved, and they picked up on that. And a year later, half a year, they were the same. And we stayed together. Because all that is all the same. That one man today is those four hundred thousand then. And you just can't get into all of that, get into me. Because you don't want to.

You're right, I'm not . . . Are you very tired now?
No. I can die . . .

***

Marek, in all your statements, you never lose your confidence in your own judgments, and you often say of others that they're making things up or telling a pack of lies. Have you ever corrected yourself?
No, I don't correct myself. Sometimes I agree when other people insist. Those standards, for instance.[41] I didn't see them, but people say that they were there. So, maybe they were. I don't know.

But I'm asking about what you know and what you remember. About whether you have ever realized that for years you have been repeating an image to which you have become accustomed, but then suddenly a fact emerges that forces you to revise that image?
Huh?

Look, in *The Ghetto Fights*, you say that two trucks came to Prosta Street.
No, not true, impossible.

Marek, it's true.
You read it wrong. There were supposed to be two, but the second one never came. And in any case, that was all written with grand designs. Back then, that was necessary. And whether there were two vehicles, or one is of no significance.

---

41 Edelman is talking here about two flags, the Polish and the Jewish flag, that soldiers of the ŻZW planted on Muranowski Square at the beginning of the uprising.

Well, what was of significance?
Not details, but the whole. That first there was the ghetto and then the "Arsenał." And all that will remain of it all is Anielewicz, because in history it's never the case that all ten who snuffed it remain. Only the one. All that will remain of the ghetto is Anielewicz. And he is its symbol. And it's irrelevant whether he did or he didn't. In a few years, nobody will remember all those names. And that's right because that's how it is—the details cannot be of significance.

***

What makes the Holocaust so exceptional?
Ask Simone Weil, she'll tell you. Or the queen of Holland.

But what would you say?
Nothing. It's all garbage. I mean, think: what do you know about the Kościuszko insurrection? What do you know about the Napoleonic wars?

Well, nothing. But I never shared a challah with Kościuszko; with you, I did.
Aah, that's irrelevant. You know what? It was this major event that you can't describe. Finito. But people don't get that, and they ask about stupid things like what was on the left and what was on the right. But all that is of no significance.

For a moment longer I am going to insist that those details are of a certain significance. They are what enables us to imagine it all, at least to a small degree, they bring that world closer to us. Your red sweater, for instance. And the straps crossed over your chest . . . "Just think what I looked like back then," you said to Hania Krall.[42]
Well, I liked it.

We like it, too. Thank you, Marek. For everything.

Łódź, summer–fall–winter 1999–2000.

Marek Edelman died in Warsaw on October 2, 2009.

---

42 See Hanna Krall, *Shielding the Flame*.

Part Two

REREADING THE LIST: STORIES ABOUT THE SOLDIERS OF THE JEWISH FIGHTING ORGANIZATION

Irena Adamowicz was born in Warsaw in 1910. Brought up in a Catholic family, before the war she was active in the Polish Scouting Union (ZHP). She was a member of the girl scouting executive and also worked closely with young Jews in Haszomer Hacair. She was very friendly with Josek Kapłan. She studied pedagogy at the University of Warsaw.

During the occupation she was a courier for the Jewish underground. She first traveled to the Vilnius ghetto from Warsaw in June 1942, to tell Aba Kowner and Różka Korczak, the leaders of the underground organization there, about the ghetto in Warsaw. Thereafter, she also traveled to the ghettos in Kaunas, Siauliai, and Białystok. She liaised between the Home Army (AK) and the Jewish Fighting Organization (ŻOB), and often went into the Warsaw ghetto. She also visited the Halutzim who lived and worked on the farm in Czerniaków, Hela Szuster remembered. Irena was greatly helped by two older ladies, Janina Pławczyńska and Rena Laterner. (They carried letters and newspapers back and forth between the Jewish fighters and the Polish underground. After the April uprising, Pławczyńska and Laterner constructed a hiding-place for ten insurrectionists; they were killed along with them, apparently as the result of a tip-off.)

After the war, Irena Adamowicz lived on Dolna Street in Warsaw and worked in the Polish National Library. She took care of her elderly mother and lived for her wartime friendships—she wrote warm letters to Israel. (In 1958 she spent a few months in Israel visiting her Israeli friends; she returned very happy.) Irena was afraid of dying alone and sick. Toward the end of her life, she began to avoid social contacts, even with those closest to her. She died suddenly on an August day in 1973, on the sidewalk on the downtown Warsaw boulevard Krakowskie Przedmieście. (She was decorated with the Righteous Among the Nations medal in 1985.)

Chaim Akerman (Ankerman) was a PPR activist in the ghetto. He wrote? printed? distributed? the paper *Morgen Frei*, which was published in Yiddish by the communist and radical left-wing organization Młot i Sierp.[1] In the April uprising he fought in the ŻOB group under Paweł Bryskin, which made it through to the insurgents' command center at 18 Miła in early May. (This command center was a huge, well-equipped bunker belonging to the unterwelt.

---

1 The Hammer and Sickle Revolutionary Councils of Workers and Peasants (Pol. Rewolucyjne Rady Robotniczo-Chłopskie „Młot i Sierp")—a clandestine radical left-wing organization that operated in occupied Poland between 1939 and 1942. It was smashed by the Gestapo.

It was managed by Szmul Iser, who consented to let all the ŻOB fighters in.) Chaim was probably killed on May 8, 1943, when the Germans released gas into the bunker. Almost all those inside—one hundred, maybe one hundred fifty people—were killed.

Aleksander survived in the notes and memories of the ŻOB leaders. He was a left-wing activist and later insurrectionist. At the time, nobody recorded his surname. Marek Edelman remembers that he was thirty-something, a stout, broad-shouldered brunet, and wore dark glasses. A sharp-witted humanist, he spoke Yiddish and Polish well, and knew a lot about both literature and the military. A historian wrote: this was probably Fondamiński. And history has repeated that. Edelman says that Aleksander was nothing to do with Fondamiński, that Fondamiński had been killed much earlier, before October 1942. Anna Lanota, who knew Fondamiński, says that Aleksander was not Fondamiński, and that Fondamiński was probably killed in the *große Aktion*. Aleksander was (most probably) killed in the uprising, on May 8, in the bunker on Miła.

Jakub Chaim Meir (Majer) Aleksandrowicz was born on July 6, 1925, in Ostrowiec Kielecki [until the 1920s known as Ostrowiec nad Kamienną, and after 1937 as Ostrowiec Świętokrzyski] into a timber merchant's family. His father was called Szmul Josek; his mother was Malka. They lived in Ostrowiec at 15 Denkowska Street. Jakub studied in a yeshiva, but when war broke out, he cut off his sidelocks and joined the Jewish scouts from Haszomer Hacair; he was the secretary of the local cell. In October 1942, the Germans murdered eleven thousand Ostrowiec Jews. Jakub's parents and sister were killed in that campaign.

In December 1942 and in early 1943, a few young Jews from Ostrowiec went to the ghetto in Warsaw. Eiger Awram, Gertner Abek, Morgenlender Icchak, Horowicz Awram, Silman Basia and Silman Suja, Katz Nechemia, Aleksandrowicz Jakow—those names, in that way, were recorded by Dawid Sztajn. Jakub was one of the youngest ŻOBists. His friends called him Klostermajer, because he was as sharp a shooter as a well-known SS-man in the ghetto.[2] He fought in Dawid Nowodworski's group on the premises of the

---

2 Klaustermeyer, Karl Heinrich, SS-Oberscharführer, sentenced to life imprisonment by a court in Bielefeld in 1965.

Toebbens-Schultz 'shops. On April 23, a dum-dum bullet ripped his arm off. The insurrectionists did not take the seriously wounded boy down into the sewers. Jakub remained in the ghetto. He was eighteen.

Estera Altenberg was born in Międzyrzec Podlaski. She was active in Frajhajt, the youth arm of Poalej Syjon Right. She dreamed of emigrating to Palestine, so she joined the Borochow kibbutz in Łódź. (The Łódź and the Kielce *hakhsharas* were two of the biggest centers preparing young people for emigration.) She became the kibbutz seamstress.

After the outbreak of war, she moved to an agrarian farm in Sterdyń near Sokołów. When the Germans began to seal the ghettos, the Halutzim had to wind up the *hakhsharas*. Estera managed to get into the Warsaw ghetto. She was accepted into the ŻOB, to the Dror group under Beniamin Wald. Estera was friendly with Rebeka Glanc, who was killed in a ŻOB battle in Częstochowa in August 1943. Estera Altenberg had been killed in Warsaw a few months previously, in the April. She was twenty-seven.

Aron Alter, Antoś fought in the PPR group under Heniek Kawe. (On April 27, the fatally wounded Hesiek Kawe gave Antoś his pistol and watch.) Antoś is known to have gotten out of the ghetto via the sewers on April 29 and reached the Wyszków woods. The circumstances of his death are not known.

Małke Alterman, Mania was born in Żelechów in 1915. Mania's mother was a dressmaker, and her father delivered various wares to local stallholders. Her parents, devout and very poor, moved to Warsaw in the hope of a somewhat easier life. They lived at 4 Miła Street, in the heart of the Jewish district. Małke was a studious pupil at the Jewish-Polish elementary school on Bonifraterska Street. She had to help her parents out, so she started work and took courses at the ORT vocational school in the evenings. Somewhat against their will, and strongly under the influence of her sister Bina, who had been living in Palestine for several years, Małke became involved in the work of the Zionist movement. She and Pola Elster founded a youth group, Frajer Szomer, affiliated with Poalej Syjon Left. Małke herself grew up in the organization, and later taught and educated others.

In the ghetto, she worked in the public soup kitchen at 14 Elektoralna Street, helping those who were poorer still. She also became involved in underground work—distributing newspapers and acting as a liaison with Polish conspiratorial groups. She was probably killed during the April uprising.

Szlomo Alterman was also born in Żelechów. A lively, cheerful guy, he was interested in the secular life, and didn't want to attend cheder. Like his older sister Małke, he dreamed of the distant Land, and so joined Frajhajt. Szlomo had a job as a boy of all work in a soap manufactory on Nalewki Street. He studied on courses run by Tarbut, and he trained as a cyclist in the Hapoel sports club, activities he tried to keep hidden from his father. In the summer he would go on coeducational camps for young Zionists; this he kept strictly hidden from his father.

In the ghetto he was an electrician, and looked after fugitives from other, smaller towns. He worked briefly at the post office. In the April uprising, he fought in the Dror unit under Henoch Gutman on the brushmakers' premises, and later on Franciszkańska Street. On May 10, he went out of the ghetto onto the Polish side via the sewers. Masza Glajtman-Putermilch remembered that Szlomo sang well and was as beautiful as a dream. It was Szlomo who dragged her on through the sewers and gave her strength. He fought in a partisan unit on the eastern bank of the river Bug. He was killed in the summer of 1943 in the Łomża region, probably with his good friend and fellow ghetto insurgent Kuba Gutrajman.

Tosia Altman was born on August 24, 1918, in Lipno, near Włocławek. Her family was wealthy and progressive. Tosia was eleven when she joined the Haszomer Hacair youth movement. She attended a Hebrew grammar school and threw herself into working for her organization with the passion of an energetic, idealistic young girl. She was adored as an instructor by the younger girls on the Shomer summer camps. In 1938, following an internship in the city of Częstochowa, she began to work with the central executive of Haszomer Hacair in Warsaw. She continued to work with young people and was also the editor of the Hebrew paper *Ha-Navadim*.

At the beginning of the war, Tosia went to Vilnius with a group of other Shomerim. En route back to Warsaw shortly afterwards, she was taken into German custody on the border. She reached Warsaw in late 1939. She worked at the Halutz headquarters, traveling extensively around Poland as she had always done, visiting Shomer groups all over the General Government. In 1940, she organized a movement in Galicia, and in 1941 she visited Haszomer Hacair cells in Białystok, Baranowicze, and Vilnius. She traveled alone or with others. One of her close friends was Lońka Koziebrodzka. (Lońka fell into German hands en route from Białystok to Warsaw in November 1942. She had four revolvers and a newspaper on her person. She died of typhus in Auschwitz in March 1943.)

Tosia and Lońka, as Haszomer Hacair couriers, carried news and messages from ghetto to ghetto. In many places, they were the first to tell young people in enclosed ghettos that there was a need for them to rebel, for an uprising. Many years later, Szmuel Ron recalled Tosia Altman's brave, fiery speeches in the Będzin ghetto; it was they that "ignited his heart to fight." Familiar with the world outside the wall, she also lived there for some time before the April uprising. She procured arms for the ŻOB. At that time, in 1943, Tosia wrote letters to those who were far removed from the seat of the Holocaust: "With all my strength I resist pouring out all the bitterness that is building up within me onto you and your friends for your total obliviousness to us. [...] Israel is dying before my eyes, and I stand with arms folded and cannot help her. Did you ever try to break down a wall with your head...? I have but one wish: for the world to learn that Israel is so sick. For she is my closest friend..."[3]

Tosia went into the ghetto very shortly before the uprising. Perhaps because Jurek Wilner, her boyfriend, had returned, very sick, to the ghetto. In the first days of May, she was in the ŻOB command bunker at 18 Miła Street. There, around eighty other ŻOB members and over a hundred civilians were sheltering. On May 8, the Germans surrounded the five entrances to the bunker and released gas into it. A dozen or so ŻOB fighters survived because they found a sixth exit. Marek Edelman took them to 22 Franciszkańska Street. Tosia was one of that group. From there, on May 10, some forty insurrectionists made their way out onto the other side of the ghetto wall via the sewers.

A truck was waiting by the manhole cover on Prosta Street. The insurrectionists were taken to a coppice in Łomianki outside Warsaw. Tosia, with head

---

3   Letter sent by Tosia Altman to her friend Adam Rand, who lived in the Evron kibbutz in Galilee.

and leg wounds, was in no condition to fight with the partisans as she had so longed to do. A few days later she returned to Warsaw. She was taken into hiding, along with several other ŻOB members, in the attic of a factory producing celluloid materials at no. 10 on 11 Listopada Street in the district of Praga. The entrance to the vast, empty attic space was via a ladder that then had to be hidden. Over a dozen people sat on sacks of celluloid. It is not known how fire came to break out there on May 24. Hela Rufeisen-Schüpper, who had been in there just shortly beforehand, said afterwards that Tosia had been heating up ichthyol ointment to dress wounds. Or maybe someone had lit a cigarette? Within a quarter of an hour, the entire building had burned to the ground. Several people were killed in the fire. Zosia, whose surname is not known, Mojsze Szarfsztajn, Zygi Kirszenbojm, Marek Majerowicz, Icek Morgenlender, and Mania Grajek. Eliezer Geller and Meir Szwarc managed to escape. Tosia, and Szyfra Sokółka, who was known as Stenia, ran out into the street, badly burned. Some Polish police officers apprehended the injured girls, and handed them over to the Germans, because they were Jews. Both of them died in hospital because the Germans refused to allow them to be treated. Tosia was twenty-five.

Mordechaj Anielewicz, "Marian," "Malachi," was born in 1919 in Wyszków, but brought up in the Powiśle district of Warsaw, among the children of the Polish poor. Mordek's mother was a fish trader on the local marketplace, and he delivered fresh bread rolls at dawn. At his high school, Laor, he briefly sympathized with the revisionist organization Betar. Ultimately, however, he joined Haszomer Hacair, and became a well-known activist within that circle. His cell had its headquarters at 12 Rymarska Street, not far from the Saski Garden, in the Polish part of the capital. His friends from this period recall how "Marian" led them bravely in battles against Polish gangs with sticks. He was a very talented pupil, and was old enough to have passed his high school finals . . .

In the first weeks of the war, he traveled to the little border town of Kuty, just south of Kolomyia, to check out its potential as a marshalling point for smuggling Zionist activists into Romania. He returned to Warsaw after Poland's capitulation. In late 1939, he went to visit the Shomer activists in Vilnius for a few weeks. He was briefly arrested by the Soviet authorities. In 1940, back in the Warsaw underground, he co-edited the Shomer newspaper *Neged Ha-Zerem*, and ran classes for young people in the kibbutz at 23/25

Nalewki Street. In 1942 he visited the ghettos in Będzin and Sosnowiec. He was actively seeking a way to cross the Polish-Hungarian border.

He returned to the Warsaw ghetto on September 13, 1942. Marek Edelman said that he was uncompromisingly brave and filled with an inhuman desire for revenge. And that his unthinking bravery could be attributed to the fact that Anielewicz had never seen a deportation.

Even though a deportation campaign had been expected in the ghetto for many weeks, the operation launched on January 18 took the ŻOB by surprise. That day, Anielewicz's group—Elek Różański, Emilka Landau, Merdek Growas and others—were asleep in their apartment on Miła Street when the Germans surrounded the house in the early morning. The Shomers had a few minutes. They hid their weapons under their clothes and ran down into the street. They were led in a large group to the Umschlagplatz. On the corner of Zamenhofa and Miła, Anielewicz gave the signal, and they attacked with grenades. The Germans started to flee. Many of the Shomers were killed. Three, apparently, managed to take cover in a house on Niska Street. Anielewicz fought one of the Germans and managed to grab his rifle. He waited out the rest of the operation from a hideout. Then on March 13, Anielewicz ordered a German *werkszuc* on Miła Street to be shot, in order to take his pistol. In revenge, the Germans dragged around four hundred people out of the bunkers on Miła and Muranowska.

On April 19, Anielewicz was in the ŻOB bunker at 29 Miła, and then at 18 Miła. In the night of May 6/7, he went to Franciszkańska 30 with Mira Fuchrer and Celina Lubetkin. Marek Edelman urged them to stay. Mordechaj and Mira went back to Miła. On May 8, 1943, Mordechaj Anielewicz, the commander of the April uprising, was in the bunker at 18 Miła, with more than eighty ŻOB soldiers. When the Germans attacked, many of them committed suicide. "He was the only one of us who spoke of the nation's honor," Dr. Edelman remembered.

Chaim Arbuz was born in Warsaw. His father was a successful timber merchant. They lived in the Jewish district, at 41 Nowolipie. Chaim was tall, with red hair, blue eyes, and lots of freckles. He was well liked by his fellow Haszomer Hacair members. Chaim set up a Shomer library. Before the war broke out, he attended the Chinuch society's philological high school for boys at 27 Ogrodowa Street.

In the ghetto he worked in the library and took care of the house at Nowolipie. He lived with his parents at 72 Nowolipki. They must have been a wealthy family given that they could afford a housekeeper in the ghetto, recalls Leokadia Silverstein, formerly Hamersztajn, who cleaned the windows in their apartment ahead of the first Pesach festival in 1941.

Chaim's father worked in Hallman's carpentry 'shop; before the war he had been the co-proprietor of the factory. With his assistance, Szlomo Winogron's group set fire to the 'shop warehouses in February 1943. Chaim himself also took part in that operation. Ahead of April, Chaim bought guns and smuggled them into the ghetto.

In the uprising, he was a soldier in one of the Shomer groups. On April 29, he managed to get out onto the other side via the sewers. From Łomianki, he was moved, along with Merdek Growas's group, to the Wyszków woods. Before long, all contact was lost with that group of Jewish partisans. They are thought to have been killed by a unit of the NSZ. Chaim Arbuz was twenty-two.

Zachariasz Artsztajn was born in Pruszków in 1923. His parents were declared Zionists. His five siblings emigrated to Palestine in the early 1930s. (Zachariasz, the youngest, stayed with his parents, who didn't want to start their lives over.) One man who had a great influence on the boy was Abraham Koziebrodzki, a teacher and educator of Jewish youth in Pruszków. Zachariasz studied in Warsaw at Poznański's Jewish teacher training seminary, was an activist with Frajhajt, and was waiting for an opportunity to emigrate to Eretz Israel.

He was one of the better-known youth leaders in the Warsaw ghetto. In 1941 he participated in the clandestine Dror seminary at 34 Dzielna Street. (Among the teachers of the twenty young attendees were Icchak Kacenelson, Janusz Korczak, and Józef Sak. Stefa Wilczyńska gave talks about Palestine.) After that, he worked for a while in a steelworks in the town of Ostrowiec, and in 1942 on the farm in Czerniaków. (There were around one hundred Halutzim working there, along with fifty or so non-organization people, and a few Poles, though they—the Poles—worked separately, Hela Szuster-Kron remembered.)

On January 18, 1943, the Germans stormed the house at 58 Zamenhofa Street. Zachariasz was sitting in the room and reading Shalom Aleichem. The Germans entered the apartment, and he carried on reading, sitting facing the door. When they passed him, he turned around and shot one of them in the back. Henoch Gutman shot again, right after him. Someone else threw a grenade after the fleeing Germans. Meir Finkelsztajn was badly wounded. Zachariasz carried his friend to a safer apartment. His group, around forty boys, moved to 44 Muranowska Street via the roofs. After that, they defended themselves at 34 Miła Street. In February 1943, Zachariasz Artsztajn participated in the elimination of the Gestapo agent Alfred Nossig.

On April 19, he was in command of a large group of armed boys. His unit took up a position at the corner of Nalewki and Gęsia and was the first to shoot at the Germans as they entered the ghetto. Zachariasz did not leave the ghetto. His comrades did not find his group in the ruins. Someone recorded that Zachariasz Artsztajn stayed with Icchak Blausztajn, Josek Farber, and others. They defended themselves in the bunkers at 34, 37, and 38 Nalewki Street. When Nalewki ceased to exist, Artsztajn moved to Bonifraterska, apparently. He was looking for a way out onto the other side in the Mylna Street area.

Dr. Ryszard Walewski remembered that in the second half of May 1943, the ŻOBists, the PPR people, the ŻZW soldiers, and some "wildcat" insurrectionists joined forces. The ŻOB fighters were commanded by a Zachariasz. (This was almost certainly Zachariasz Artsztajn.) They were at 22 Franciszkańska Street, and fought at 11/13 Bonifraterska Street, where, Walewski remembered, they killed six Germans. Zachariasz's group also swept the sewers of mines. Chawka Folman said that Zachariasz was very masculine because he was tall and broad-shouldered. And that he had a round face. And Antek Cukierman that he spoke a Yiddish full of pathos and exclamation marks, but that it was a real language.

Eliezer Asz fought in the Hanoar Hacyjoni youth group in the brushmakers' yard. When Marek Edelman marshalled the insurrectionists from the brushmakers' premises to the central ghetto in the night of April 20, Eliezer and his group stayed on Wałowa Street.

Szlomo Baczyński was one of the youngest members of Haszomer Hacair in the ghetto. In the April uprising, he was a soldier in the group commanded by Szlomo Winogron on the premises of the Toebbens-Schultz 'shops. On April 29, he left the ghetto via the sewers. When the group of forty reached the manhole on Ogrodowa Street, Szlomo and Regina Fudem decided to go back for the other insurgents who had stayed behind in the ghetto. It is not known whether they died in the sewers or in the ghetto.

Dwora Baran was born in 1920, or maybe 1922, in Kowel, into the family of a petty goods trader who was both devout and a Zionist. She attended a Hebrew elementary school run by the Tarbut society, and then an ORT vocational school. In 1938 she went away to the Borochow kibbutz in Łódź. When the war broke out, Dwora remained in Łódź to guard the kibbutz's assets. After a few weeks, she went to Warsaw and joined the Halutz youth on the Czerniaków farm. There, she made friends with Hela Szuster. Together, they carried heavy baskets of cabbages. Hela says that Dwora was a romantic young girl.

When the October ŻOB was formed, she joined the organization in a Dror unit. In the initial days of the April uprising, she fought in Henoch Gutman's group on the brushmakers' premises, at Świętojerska and Wałowa Streets. (Kazik Ratajzer met Dwora in Czerniaków, before the uprising. He remembers that when the ghetto was burning and the acrid stench of burning bodies was everywhere, Dwora longed for the scent of the Volhynia forests.)

On May 1, the Germans surrounded the bunker at 30 Franciszkańska Street, where there was a large group of insurgents, among them Henoch Gutman's soldiers. Dwora bravely went out of the bunker and threw a grenade into the midst of the surprised Germans. On that day, Abram Ejgier, Abram Diamant, Staszek Brylantsztajn and two other insurgents were killed. The ŻOB members had no other shelter, so they remained on Franciszkańska. The Germans returned on May 3. That time, those who perished were Berek Sznajdmil, Szaanan Lent, Zysie Papier, Cypora Lerer, Jurek Grynszpan, Izrael Mittelman, Stefa Rozen, Majorek Szerman, Dwora Baran, and many others not remembered by name. (Kazik Ratajzer was no longer in the ghetto when his close friend Dwora was killed on May 3.)

Nate Bartmesser was born in Mogielnica in 1923, into a poor, devout family. Nate attended a Polish public elementary school. He started work at an early age. He learnt the tailor trade from his brother, at 42 Muranowska Street. He was a member of Frajhajt, and later of Poalej Syjon Right. In the ghetto, he was accepted into the Dror group. Nate is known to have been killed in the April uprising.

Heniek Bartowicz is one of the names of the April insurgents written down on the list of murdered ŻOB soldiers by its commanders. They gave him as having belonged to the PPR. I found no information about Heniek Bartowicz.

Frania Beatus was born in Konin. The Konin Jews were incarcerated in the ghetto in Ostrowiec Kielecki. On October 11, 1942, on the eve of the liquidation of the ghetto there, Frania escaped to Warsaw. She returned to Ostrowiec several times to get members of Dror and Haszomer Hacair into the Warsaw ghetto, among them Berl Brojde, the sisters Basia and Suja Sylman, Aba Gertner, and Icchak

Morgenlender. A short, chubby, ruddy country girl with a thick, flaxen braid, she looked very young, no older than fourteen. She spoke Polish well. And she was brave: great material for a courier, Hela Schüpper said.

Frania was sent out onto the other side in January 1943. She rented an apartment with a family somewhere in the downtown Śródmieście district. On April 13, she waited for Antek Cukierman by the ghetto wall. She had high heels on and carried a handbag, so as not to look so much like a kid. She took Antek by the arm and led him to 118 Marszałkowska Street. She was his first courier on the Polish side of the wall. From April 19, Frania began to cry constantly and talk about suicide. Reprimanded by Antek, she returned to her duties. She would take night-time telephone calls from Tosia Altman inside the ghetto, and in the morning run to Cukierman to pass on the information. She also organized hideouts for insurgents fleeing the ghetto.

On May 1, when Kazik Ratajzer and Zygmunt Frydrych reached Anna Wąchalska's apartment via the sewers, Frania was there. She was waiting desperately for her boyfriend, who never made it out. He was called Dawid Szulman, apparently. On May 10, Frania called Sara Biederman, who was in hiding in the apartment of a couple called the Balickis. She spoke of suicide again and asked someone to come and take the things she had, and thirty thousand zlotys. She left a detailed breakdown of the money she had spent, and a letter to Cukierman. Her body was never found. It is not known exactly how Frania Beatus died. She was seventeen.

Chajka Bełchatowska [Szpigiel],[4] **Halina,** was born in Warsaw in 1919. Her mother was a bookbinder who belonged to the YAF, the Bund women's organization. The two of them lived at 14 Smocza Street. In the ghetto, Chajka worked in the Bund soup kitchen on Nowolipie Street, and distributed Bund newspapers. After the *große Aktion*, she was employed in the Roerich 'shop. In November 1942, the Germans took several hundred people from the 'shops to the Umschlagplatz. Chajka was with a group of Bundists. They had saws in their boots, so they sawed through the window grilles in the railway wagons. First to jump was Mosze Kojfman, because he had good papers, and believed he could make it. Then the three Błones siblings, Lola Wiernik,

---

4 Names in square brackets are names used after the war.

Baruch Zalcman, Minia Wajsgruz, and Chajka Bełchatowska. Last of all was the group's leader, later a commander in the uprising, Welwł Rozowski.

In April 1943 they fought together on Smocza Street, on the premises of the Toebbens-Schultz 'shops. Also in the group was Bronek Szpigiel, Chajka's boyfriend. They left the ghetto via the sewers on April 30 and were transported by truck to Łomianki. And after that, on May 15, to the Wyszków woods, to the partisan units. Chajka and Bronek were in the woods until August 22, 1943. During the Warsaw rising, they went into hiding with Masza Glajtman-Putermilch and her husband Jakubek on 64 Żelazna Street, in the apartment belonging to Władek Świętochowski. Chajka and Bronek also lived briefly at 38 Sienna Street. They left Poland for Canada in 1946; they lived in Montreal. Chajka was sick for a long time. She died on March 27, 2002.

Hersz (Hirsz) Berliński, Jeleński, "Jeleń," was born in 1908 into an impoverished weaver's family in the Bałuty district of Łódź. He attended a cheder, and later the co-educational secular Borochow Jewish school. (The headmaster was Abraham Kagan, the father of Kazia Bergman and a member of Poalej Syjon Left. Kazia remembers her school friendship with Hersz.) In 1923 he joined Cukunft, but a year later, he and some friends switched to the youth movement of Poalej Syjon Left. He was the leader of a group of young weavers whom he whipped up to action against the ideology of the Bund and the PPS and encouraged to dream of Eretz Israel. His father grew very rich after the Great War. Hersz left home, and on occasion organized strikes in his father's manufactory. In September 1939 he left Łódź. He reached Warsaw after a series of forced halts: in a camp in Rawa Mazowiecka, in Częstochowa, and in Łódź.

In the ghetto, he found a job in Landau's 'shop. Many young people who sympathized with Poalej Syjon Left rallied to Berliński. He became their commander in the April uprising. His group fought under Marek Edelman's command on the brushmakers' premises, and later in the central ghetto. Berliński left the ghetto via the sewers on May 10 and, like the others, reached the Wyszków woods via Łomianki. A few weeks later, he returned to Warsaw.

He went into hiding in the district of Żoliborz on (the non-extant) Suwalska Street with Elek Erlich, a Poalej Syjon activist; Pola Elster, a courier for the Jewish National Committee (ŻKN); Hersz Wasser; and Bluma Wasser. It was probably then, at the request of Basia Bermanowa of the ŻKN, that he recorded his reminiscences from the ghetto. Erlich, Elster, and Berliński were killed on

September 27, 1944. Nobody knows the circumstances of their deaths. Their bodies were interred on April 29, 1945, in the Jewish cemetery on Okopowa Street.

Franka Berman was a member of Paweł—Aron Bryskin's—PPR group. She fought in the April uprising in the central ghetto. She was killed on May 8, 1943, in the bunker at 18 Miła Street. She was twenty-two.

Tosia Berman was probably Franka's sister, and probably a member of the same PPR group. She is known to have been at 18 Miła Street on May 8. She perished either in the bunker or in a Treblinka gas chamber along with the sixty others taken from 18 Miła Street.

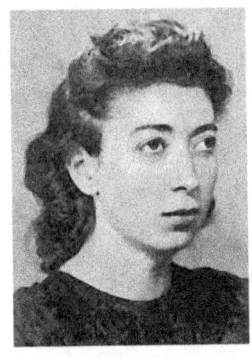

Sara Biederman (Biderman), Krysia Serafin, was born in 1922 in Warsaw. The family lived at 3 Dzika Street. Although they were poor, and her father wore a *khalat*, Sara graduated from high school, and in 1939 took the entrance examinations for the Architecture Faculty at Warsaw Polytechnic. She lived on Pawia Street. And then in the ghetto. During the *große Aktion*, Sara went into hiding with her parents in the cellar at 44 Muranowska Street. The Germans set the house alight and marched all those who had been inside to the Umschlagplatz. Sara's mother pushed her out of the train.

Sara was a member of Dror and worked on the Czerniaków farm with other Halutzim. They didn't try to escape from there because they had nowhere to go. They returned to the ghetto in November 1942. In January 1943 she was accepted into the ŻOB. She went to live with her fighting group, under Beniamin Wald, on the premises of the Toebbens-Schultz 'shops. On April 29, she left the ghetto via the sewers with the group of insurrectionists. She and Rywka Moszkowicz hid in the fields in Czerniaków, but they got split up, or lost each other? It is known that Kazik Ratajzer found the homeless Sara and took her to Hela Schüpper, who at the time had a hiding-place in the suburb of Rembertów. Another girl lived with them, too: Szoszana Langer from Akiba, whom Kazik had also found wandering the streets.

All three girls wanted to join the partisans and were waiting to be taken out into the woods. A Pole denounced Sara to a German on the street in Rembertów. She probably tried to run away and took two bullets to the abdomen. The German must have thought she was dead because he left her there. From Rembertów to Zielonka and then onward by two trams—Sara dragged herself back to Warsaw, to the apartment of Hela Balicka's parents. They put her in the hospital on Płocka Street. Marek Edelman remembers differently: some peasant found Sara on the street and took her on his cart to the Hospital of the Transfiguration on Zygmuntowska Street. Then Irka Gelblum took her to 5 Pańska Street, where Zielona Marysia and Jurek Grasberg lived.

In the Warsaw rising, Sara was with the ŻOB fighters. They join a unit of the AL: Cywia Lubetkin, Icchak Cukierman, Marek Edelman, Kazik Ratajzer, Irka Gelblum, and others. Cukierman sends Kazik's group to 18 Leszno Street for the ŻOB archives. They do not find the papers. A few weeks later, they are caught by the Germans. Sara is deported to a labor camp. After the war, Sara lived briefly at 38 Poznańska Street.

In 1946 she emigrated to Palestine. She wanted to live on a kibbutz; first she went to Yagur in Galilee, and later she was in Lohamei Ha-Getaot. She spent a lot of time with Chawka Folman, because she was constantly lonely and sick in spirit. She fled the kibbutz for the big city, but she never shook her sense of loneliness, and never recovered. She was wise, but had a sad life, a sad fate, Chawka says. Sara Biederman died in Israel in 1972.

Menachem Bigielman (Biegelman, Bejgelman) was born in Warsaw in 1919 into a very poor furniture trader's family. He lived in the Jewish district, at 19 Bonifraterska Street. Menachem didn't finish school. He was thirteen when he started work in a carpentry workshop. When he was seventeen, he joined the trade unions and the Halutz movement. He was the treasurer of the Warsaw Hehaluc Hacair. Later on, in the ghetto, he was the janitor of the house at 34 Dzielna Street. (The Halutzim had their kibbutz there.) Menachem was friendly with Jaffa Lewender, who was also in the Halutzim.

During the April uprising, he fought in Berl Braude's group in the central ghetto. On May 8, 1943, he was in the bunker at 18 Miła Street. That day, the Germans attacked it. Badly wounded and gassed, he managed to escape via the sixth exit that the Germans hadn't noticed. On May 10, around forty insurrectionists were led out of the ghetto via the sewers. Thirty more could not be taken out. Kazik Ratajzer remembered that among those who perished in the sewers were Sewek Duński, Lejbl Rozowski, Bronka Manulak, Jechiel Górny, Adolf Hochberg, Pnina Zandman, Menachem Bigielman...

Janek Bilak was born in 1920, probably in Warsaw. He attended the CISzO school, and was a member of the children's organization Skif, and later of the youth group Cukunft. He had finished learning a trade before the war broke out: he was a dental technician. In September 1939 he headed for the East, but from Białystok he was deported to Russia. Two months later he managed to return to Warsaw with his friends Lejb Gruzalc and Naftali Leruch. In the Warsaw ghetto, he and two other Bundists shared ownership of a rickshaw. That enabled him to support his family. He also proved of great assistance to the ghetto underground: after the *große Aktion*, he was able to move freely between the sealed areas. He lived on the brushmakers' premises, and he and Jurek Błones set up the Bund groups. In the Jewish uprising he fought on his own turf.

He left the ghetto via the sewers on May 10. Early in the morning, a truck drove up to the manhole cover on Prosta Street. Half-dead, they dragged themselves up onto the trailer. The truck drove them all to a coppice in Łomianki. The group waited to be accepted into Polish partisan units. Some of them returned to Warsaw to go into hiding in the city. Many were killed because they were denounced by local peasants. Others fell in engagements or were killed by Polish partisans. Janek was in a forest unit with Chana Kryształ and Gabryś Fryszdorf.

He returned to Warsaw in July 1944 and went into hiding on Rakowiecka Street with Chana Kryształ, Dow Szniper, and Pnina Grynszpan. In the early days of the Polish rising, the owner of their apartment threw them out. They were caught on the street and taken with a group of Poles to Szucha Avenue. The Germans let the women go but killed all the men.

Adina Blady-Szwajgier (Szwajger), Inka [Świdowska], was born on March 21, 1917, in Warsaw. Adina's mother, Stefania Szwajgier, was the headmistress of the Jehudija Jewish girls' grammar school on Długa Street. Her father, Icchak Szwajgier, emigrated to Palestine in 1927, where he wrote well-liked children's books. Adina—Inka—Szwajgier graduated in medicine from the University of Warsaw on the very eve of the war. She also got married shortly before the war, to Stefan Szpigielman, a third-year law student at the university.

In the Warsaw ghetto she lived with her mother at 34 Świętojerska Street. She worked in the Berson and Bauman Hospital, first on Sienna Street and later on Leszno, because the ghetto was shrinking. Before the *große Aktion*, the hospital was moved to Stawki Street, to the Umschlagplatz. Dr. Szwajgier saved children from a death in Treblinka: she gave them morphine, and the children died in their hospital beds. (One day, in late July, Inka came home from the hospital and found her mother gone. Only a note, written in haste: Coupons cut out, honey paid for.) By January 1943, the hospital was all but gone. Those who were still there, eleven people, were living at 6 Gęsia Street at the time. Marek Edelman "ordered" Inka, so she said, to go out onto the other side of the wall. She didn't want to go, because she didn't want to be alone, but she understood that it was vital to have trusted people on the other side. She went out on January 25, 1943. Maria Zarębianka sewed Inka a fur collar onto her overcoat so that she looked still less like a Jewess.

She lived with other people in several places, but the safest of them was 24 Miodowa Street, a large, bright room painted a lemon yellow. Inka, a ŻOB courier, took care of those who couldn't go out and about in the city. She ran guns, and distributed money, information, clandestine newspapers, tins of food, and candles. When there were lots of them on the Polish side after the April uprising, Inka was out running errands until the curfew. The hardest task was to find safe shelters. And they had to be moved frequently, from apartment to apartment, because the hideouts were constantly being shopped. She also traveled further afield, all over Poland, because she had safe looks: to Krakow, Częstochowa, and the camps in Poniatowa and Trawniki.

Stefan, her first love and first husband, was in hiding in a vegetable trader's apartment in the district of Mokotów. But he couldn't, didn't want to any longer. Inka took Stefan to the Hotel Polski on July 11, 1943. Two days later, all the guests in the Hotel Polski were deported to Auschwitz.

On August 1, 1944, Inka Szwajgier reported to the commander of one of the insurgent units. Two Jewish doctors also came out of cover, Dr. Ludwik Koenigstein and Dr. Bolesław Krzywonos. They worked together in the insurrectionist hospital on Miodowa Street. Ala Margolis and Zosia Frydman were nurses there. But the Jewish boys from the ghetto uprising weren't accepted into the AK unit in the Warsaw rising. (So, they went and joined the AL.) On October 11, Inka left Warsaw for Milanówek with a sanitary convoy.

After the war she was one of the first pediatric pulmonologists in Poland. She worked in Warsaw and in Łagiewniki, with Dr. Anna Margolis. In Szczecin, she founded a sanatorium for children with tuberculosis, and the children there never wanted to go home. She married a Polish insurrectionist, but their lives parted company in 1968, because there was too much that came between a Polish Jewess and a Polish Pole.

In 1986, Adina—Inka—wrote her reminiscences while a patient on Dr. Edelman's cardiology ward. Inka Szwajgier died on February 19, 1993, on the same ward in Łódź.

Marek Blank was born in Warsaw. In Gordonia he ran groups for younger children. In spite of his poor health, Marek joined Eliezer Geller's fighting group on the brushmakers' premises. Shortly before the April uprising, Geller's group was redeployed to the Toebbens-Schultz 'shop yard. Marek was supposed to get out onto the Aryan side to orchestrate help. He knew the way from the brushmakers' yard, but he didn't make it out of the ghetto. He joined the battle group on Świętojerska Street. He was probably killed at 30 Franciszkańska in the first days of May. He was twenty-one.

Icchak Blaustein (Blausztajn, Blojsztajn) was born in 1923 in Żyrardów, into a very poor family. He was still a child when he started work. He did not finish elementary school. He was a member of Frajhajt in Żyrardów. In the Warsaw ghetto he studied at the Halutz seminary at 34 Dzielna Street. He, Zachariasz Artsztajn, and several other boys helped to organize the armed underground movement. In the uprising he was the commander of one of the Dror fighting groups. He was killed in unknown circumstances.

Abrasza Blum was born on September 11, 1905, in Vilnius. He was brought up in a religious Zionist family. After studying engineering at Ghent Polytechnic, he came to Warsaw in 1929. He was unable to find work in his field, so he taught French and astronomy at the Popular University on Krochmalna Street. He was in the Bund's young leader corps. A few years before the war, he had married Luba Bielicka, a girl he had known from his high school in Vilnius. (Luba Blum-Bielicka became the head of the Nursing School. Later on, in the ghetto, the school was based at 1 Mariańska Street.) They had two children, Wiktoria and Aleksander, and they lived on Mylna Street. Later, in the ghetto, Luba lived with the children on Mariańska Street, and Abrasza in various places, so that his clandestine activity would not expose his family to danger.

Abrasza Blum was a member of the underground leadership of both the Bund and Cukunft for four wartime years. From late November 1942, he represented the Bund at inter-party councils in the ghetto and was elected to the presidium of the Coordinating Committee established by the Jewish National Committee (ŻKN) and the Bund as the underground representation of Warsaw's Jewish community in relations with the Polish underground. He did not want to leave the ghetto, even though his family was on the other side. (The children had gotten out in February 1943, and Luba shortly afterwards.) Physically weak, a warrior without weapons, he spurred people on to fight in word and deed. His voice was highly respected, because Abrasza was modest and wise.

During the uprising, he was with the Bund's ŻOB soldiers under the command of Marek Edelman, whose ideological education had been in Blum's hands. On May 5, Edelman's group was in a basement somewhere. The temperature was close to fifty degrees, because the ghetto was alight. The Germans were boring holes in the walls for dynamite. The insurrectionists, stripped almost naked, were lying under the beds, because that was where it was coolest. None of them were responsive anymore. Abrasza went over to Marek and said: "I think we'll get out of here." And then Marek got them up and took them to a different place. Such was the power of Abrasza's word, Marek Edelman said.

On May 9, Abrasza Blum went down into the sewers with Edelman and Celina Lubetkin, from the bunker at 22 Franciszkańska Street. (Thirty insurrectionists, maybe a few more, emerged the next morning on the other side of the wall.) A safe house was being sought out, and in the meantime, Abrasza was taken, briefly, to Władka Peltel, at 2 Barokowa Street.

He wasn't there for long. He was visited by Inka, the courier. She recorded that Abrasza was joyful, happy. And that he asked her for . . . a real cake from a cake store. The next day, around two in the afternoon, Inka ran over to Barokowa with a cardboard box tied up with colored string. But it was all over, Abrasza was no longer there.

Early that morning, the janitor, a Pole, had locked the door and gone to the Gestapo. Abrasza had tried to flee, sliding down sheets from the third floor. He fell and was taken away by the Germans in his battered state. It might have been possible to buy him out, as Władka Peltel was bought out, but he was taken from the Daniłowiczowska Street precinct to Szucha Avenue too fast. He was most likely killed on May 20.

Tola Blumenfeld belonged to the PPR. She was a ŻOB courier. She sold flowers by the ghetto wall, and once she smuggled a grenade into the ghetto in some flowers. It is also known that she was a rabbi's daughter, that she was very young, and that she had short, light hair. After the April uprising she apparently went into hiding with other survivors from the ghetto in a cellar on 14 or 24 Miodowa Street. That hideout, too, was reported by Polish neighbors. Tola was eighteen.

Guta Błones was born in 1917 or 1921 in Warsaw. She was the eldest sister of Jurek and Lusiek. She attended a CISzO elementary school and an ORT vocational school. She was active in the children's organization Skif, and then in Cukunft. Their mother died young, so Guta took care of her brothers and kept house. They lived on Smocza Street.

In the ghetto, the siblings stayed together. Guta worked in soup kitchens, and they kept a copier hidden in their apartment at 67 Nowolipie Street. Jurek Błones and Marek Edelman used to print the Bund newspapers there, and the girls distributed them throughout the ghetto. After the *große Aktion*, the Błones siblings had employment in the Roerich 'shop on Smocza. In November 1942, Guta, Jurek, and the youngest, Lusiek, were taken from the 'shop to the Umschlagplatz. In the train to Treblinka, they were in the group of Bundists with Chajka Bełchatowska and the others. They decided to jump. Ten of them, apparently. They all made it back to the ghetto.

In the April uprising they were together on the brushmakers' premises. Guta kept house for the insurrectionists and threw grenades along with her brothers. On May 10, they left Franciszkańska. Via the sewers, after over twelve hours, they reached Prosta Street. Kazik Ratajzer and Krzaczek drove them to Łomianki in the truck. After that, they were supposed to join the partisans in the Wyszków woods, but Jurek fell seriously ill. Guta was sick, too. The decision was taken to place them in hiding in the village of Płudy. Zygmunt Frydrych took them all to an agreed host. They were turned over to the Germans by the Pole who had promised them shelter. They were all shot on the spot. It was probably May 13, 1943.

Icchak Błones was born in Warsaw. His family lived at 28 Świętojerska Street. Icchak was in Jakub Praszkier's Hanoar Hacyjoni group. During the uprising, they fought on the brushmakers' premises. Praszkier did not take his group out to the central ghetto. His insurgents were killed along with some civilians when the Germans blew up the bunker at 8 Wałowa Street. Icchak Błones was not yet twenty-two.

Jurek Błones was born in Warsaw in 1920, 1922, or 1924. He attended the Michalewicz CISzO school on Miła Street. He was ten when he joined Skif; afterwards, he was a member of Cukunft. Jurek became an automobile mechanic.

In the ghetto he was active in the Bund underground. At first, he printed and distributed newspapers, and later he organized the purchase and transport of arms. He often went out of the ghetto. Thin, quite tall, and light-haired, he had safe looks. He could jump over the wall. Jurek was passionate; it was he who convinced Michal Klepfisz to make Molotov cocktails and take them into the ghetto.

In the April uprising, he was appointed commander of a fighting group on the brushmakers' premises. Later, when the "brushes" began to burn, Błones', Gutman's, Berliński's, and Grynszpan's groups, under Marek Edelman's command, made their way through to the central ghetto, to 30 Franciszkańska Street.

On May 10, 1943, Guta, Jurek, and Lusiek went out onto the other side of the wall via the sewers. Together with the others, they were taken to Łomianki, and a few days later to the Wyszków woods. There, Jurek fell seriously ill. He had a high fever and he had to be taken out of the woods right away. It was decided that Zygmunt Frydrych would find a place for him in the village of Płudy, where Rózka Klog-Wasserman was already in hiding. Celek Celemeński and probably Antek Cukierman went to the woods for Jurek. When they got there, they decided that they would also take Cimeret Wachenhojzer, who was sick; the 18-year-old Fajgele Goldsztajn, who took great care of Jurek (she didn't fight in the uprising; she and Jurek met at 30 Franciszkańska, and from then on, they were in a pair); and Guta and Lusiek Błones.

Zygmunt Frydrych took over the vehicle and its passengers on Wilson Square. Płudy was not far away, just across the Vistula, in what is now the district of Praga. The Pole who was supposed to be taking them in called the police. (Władka Peltel wrote that the Germans handcuffed them and paraded them through Płudy with signs around their necks reading: "jewish bandits, to be shot; this is how we will deal with Jews and those who help them.") They were all shot dead against a wooden fence opposite the Pole's house. That was on July 13, 1943. In 1946 they were buried—five Bundists and a Shomer girl—in the Jewish cemetery in Warsaw.

Lusiek Błones, Eliezer, born in Warsaw in 1930, was the youngest of the insurgents. He was thirteen when he fought bravely in April 1943. Lusiek Błones was a courier between the fighting groups in the ghetto. During the defense of 30 Franciszkańska, the Germans shot his lip through. (After that, Lusiek was fed patiently by two prostitutes, Marek Edelman recounted.)

He left the ghetto via the sewers on May 10. He was in Łomianki, and then briefly in the Wyszków woods. He was taken, with his sick brother and sister, to a safer place. The insurrectionists were handed over to the Germans by the Pole who had promised to shelter them. They were all shot dead on the spot, in Płudy. And the peasant afterwards complained in the village that he got too small a reward for the Jews.

Melach Błones was born in Warsaw. He was the younger brother of Icchak. Before the war he was a member of Akiba. His group, under Berl Braude, was billeted at 29 Miła, and fought in the central ghetto. Melach was killed on May 8, 1943, in the bunker at 18 Miła Street. He was about nineteen

Mosze Izrael Bojm (Baum) was born in 1919 in Jeżów, near Łódź. He was tall, imposing, and always wore a scout uniform. That was probably why he was known as "the Jeżów general." He was from a religious home. He had a Hasidic-like ardor for matters entirely unreligious. And like a Hasid, he was always singing.

He came to Warsaw after a few months of the occupation. In the ghetto, he lived in a commune and performed with the Hebrew dramatics group. In the April uprising, he was in Jakub Praszkier's Hanoar Hacyjoni fighting group. Like the others in Praszkier's group, never left the brushmakers' premises. He went into hiding in Herman's shelter on the brushmakers' premises, with Baruch Goldman, an architect, and others. In his account, from 1944, Goldman recorded that fighter Bojm was caught by a German patrol one night in late June 1943. He was shot on the spot, somewhere on Świętojerska Street.

Chawa Bonder (Brander) fought in Heniek Kawe's PPR group. She was killed on April 27 in the bunker at 74 Leszno Street.

Bernard Borg (Bork) was born on January 15, 1906, in Warsaw. His mother's name was Edla, and his father was called Jakób Lewenberg; he was a civil servant. (Somewhere it was recorded that in 1939 Bernard was living at 29 Gęsia Street.) He started working for his keep at an early age and began to communize equally early. He was a member of the Union of Communist Youth from 1926, and of the Communist Party of Poland from 1931. He was arrested for his political activity several times.

In the Warsaw ghetto he allied himself with the PPR underground. In the April uprising he fought on the Toebbens-Schultz premises. In his account, Borg mentions Mietek Goldsztajn, Różka [Rozenfeld?], Riva [Szmutke?], and a Comrade Ryba. From 74 Leszno they withdrew to 76 Leszno, and afterwards to 63 Nowolipie, where they joined forces with the group under Heniek Kawe. On May 1, the PPR people met in the bunker at 74 Leszno. They had a radio there. With red badges in their lapels, they all listened to the May 1 order issued by the great Stalin. There were seventeen of them: twelve men and five women. Comrade Szachne gave a speech.

On May 7, when the bunker was discovered, at Leszno 74 (from there, a sewer led to the courtyard at 71 Leszno, outside the wall) there were around one hundred fifty civilians and a few insurrectionists. (It was then that Itka Hejman shot herself.) The Germans blew up the entrance and marched them all to the Umschlagplatz. Bernard Borg was deported to Treblinka; he was also in the camps at Majdanek and Auschwitz.

After the war, he lived in the district of Praga, at 35 Targowa Street, in the house where he had lived before the war. He became the chairman of the Warsaw Jewish committee. He worked in the cooperative movement, was a civil servant and a culture activist, and represented the Warsaw ghetto insurgents at formal and official events. He died on May 17, 1968, in Warsaw.

Roman Born-Bornstein was born on January 14, 1898. He fought in the September 1939 defense of Poland. He was a physician.

In the ghetto, he was a lecturer in the clandestine medical faculty. In his account of how he left the ghetto, he wrote that he made his third attempt to get over onto the Polish side in the night of May 8/9. That time, he was in a group with Szlamek Szuster, Adolf Hochberg, Merdek Growas, and Abrasza Blum. In the sewers, they met Kazik Ratajzer. The group, of over a dozen, split into two. One group went back into the ghetto for the insurrectionists at 22 Franciszkańska Street and the groups under Artsztajn, Blaustein, and Farber, which were in hiding at 37 Nalewki. The other group, including Bornstein, waited under the manhole cover on Prosta. Only the group from Franciszkańska Street was taken out of the ghetto; Artsztajn's group from Nalewki Street could not be found. (Pnina Papier also left via the sewers in the night of May 8/9. She was in the group that met Kazik Ratajzer. Pnina remembered that night differently.)

In fact, it is not known whether Born-Bornstein was an insurrectionist. (Marek Edelman says that only insurrectionists left via the sewers that night.) After leaving the ghetto, he became physician-in-chief to the Polish People's Army (AL), in the rank of captain. And in the Polish Warsaw rising he fought in the unit "Chrobry II" and headed the sanitation service in Śródmieście. After the war, he lived in Sweden.

Tuwia Borzykowski, Tadek, was born in 1911 in Łódź. Before the war, his family lived in Radomsko. His mother was called Chaja and his father Szlama. Tuwia was a *yeshiva bokher*,[5] a trained tailor, and an activist in Zionist organizations. Autodidact, aficionado of Jewish literature, and proponent of the ideas of Borochow. He ran a library in Radomsko. When the Germans invaded, he hid several thousand volumes in an attic.

In mid-1940, he arrived in Warsaw. He joined up with the Dror kibbutz at 34 Dzielna Street, gave clandestine lectures on proletariat literature, and edited underground news bulletins. In 1942 he lived and worked with Halutz youth on the farm in Czerniaków. He tried a bit to be a courier but didn't really manage it: he looked too Jewish and was constantly being blackmailed.

On January 18, 1943, the Germans surprised the boys from Dror and Gordonia in their apartment at 58 Zamenhofa Street. The ŻOBists had three pistols and three grenades, metal bars, sticks, and bottles. The Germans burst into the room, first to shoot was Zachariasz Artsztajn. The group withdrew across the snow-covered rooftops to 44 Muranowska Street. Tuwia had to go into hiding because he had no gun. He hid in the shelter run by Naftali Nusenblat, an Akiba activist, at 44 Muranowska. (Later, during the uprising, around sixty people hid there. The ŻOBists Tosia Altman, Lutek Rotblat, and Rywka Pasamonik sometimes went there.)

On April 19, Artsztajn's group, which Borzykowski was assigned to, moved into position at 33 Nalewki Street. Tuwia stood on the balcony looking down on the corner of Gęsia and Nalewki Streets. The Germans surrounded the ghetto at 6 in the morning. When the German units moved in on the triangle enclosed by Gęsia, Nalewki, and Franciszkańska Streets, Artsztajn's group attacked first. The boys fired with their revolvers and launched a few grenades and homemade

---

5   *Yeshiva bokher* (Yid.)—yeshiva student, yeshiva boy.

bombs. For a moment, the serried ranks scattered into little groups glued to the wall.

Early in the morning of April 24, Tuwia, Halina, Jeremiasz from Haszomer Hacair, and Dorka Goldkorn of the PPR went down into the sewers for the first time in search of a way out. After an odyssey of several hours, they reached the next shaft. They hoped they were outside the ghetto. When they lifted the manhole cover, they saw the wall in front of them. Halina and Dorka were arrested by dark-blue policemen. Jeremiasz tried to escape and was shot dead on the spot. The bullet fired at Tuwia, who was just emerging from the sewer, hit the man just behind him. Tuwia slipped back down into the sewer, and with the wounded man on his back, set off on the long trek back. He heard the explosion of a grenade by the shaft.

On May 7, the next group attempted to find a way out beyond the wall through the sewers. At the corner of Zamenhofa and Wołyńska Streets, they were attacked by some Germans. Four ŻOBists were wounded, but three—Borzykowski, Growas, and Kanał—were able to take cover in the ruins. They made their way back to 18 Miła Street, but by then there was no one there.

Tuwia went down into the sewers again on May 9. He was in a group with Adolf Hochberg, Szlamek Szuster, Merdek Growas, Abrasza Blum, Jurek Błones, and Pnina Grynszpan (Pnina remembers there being ten of them). After wandering, lost, under the ground for several hours, they miraculously met Kazik Ratajzer, who was searching for the last insurgents in the ghetto.

In the woods, Tuwia contracted typhus. He had a forty-degree fever, and neither Dr. Skórnik nor Dr. Kirjasefer could do anything to help. He had to be taken back to Warsaw. He was the first to go back from the woods. On May 17, Antek and Kazik, who were taking him along Krzyżanowski Street to Anna Wąchalska, pretended they were drunk, because Tuwia was staggering so much. After that, they fought in the Polish Warsaw rising with the ŻOB group on the barricade at Mostowa Street.

On August 27, they managed to reach the district of Żoliborz via the sewers. After the fall of the insurrection, the ŻOB fighters did not leave the city. They took cover in a cellar at 43 Promyka Street, where they survived until mid-November. Taken out by a paramedic patrol, they reached a hospital in Boernerowo. They waited the war out in various small satellite towns around the capital. Tuwia Borzykowski found protection in the village of Blizne, in a house where Felek Rajszczak had built a shelter. A close friend, Lodzia Hamersztein, took him to an apartment in Brwinowo.

After the war, Tuwia Borzykowski worked in the editorial offices of *Unzer Vort* in Łódź. In 1949, he published his memoirs in Yiddish, but the censor had the book destroyed. That same year, Tuwia emigrated to Israel with his close friend Lodzia Hamersztein. They and other survivors from Warsaw built the Lohamei Ha-Getaot kibbutz. Lodzia left Israel later, in 1968, and settled in America. Tuwia stayed in the kibbutz and laid tiles. He was a loner, had no family, and was close friends with Celina and Antek. He died in 1959. His was the first grave in the kibbutz cemetery.

Berl Braude (Brojde) was born in Słonim around 1920. His family was religious, so Berl attended a cheder. Before long, he became an activist in Frajhajt, and started to prepare for the life of a pioneer in Eretz Israel on courses in the Borochow kibbutz in Łódź. A few months after the outbreak of the war, he went to Warsaw and lived in the Halutz commune at 34 Dzielna Street. In June and July 1940, he was the secretary of the kibbutz in Ceranów, near Małkinia. (Chawka Folman was with Berl on that farm.) During the day, the Halutzim worked the Polish landowner's farm, and in the evenings, they sang Hebrew songs and listened to Berl's talks.

In the fall of 1941, Berl's organization sent him to the town of Ostrowiec Świętokrzyski to prepare a group of Dror members to mount a defense. Some of them returned with him to the Warsaw ghetto. One time, Chawka Folman had to take Berl somewhere by droshky. His head was bandaged to hide his Jewish eyes and raven-black hair; his looks were too unsafe. Antek Cukierman said of him that he was an intellectual and had a Jewish charm.

On November 29, 1942, it was likely Berl Braude who shot dead the Gestapo agent Izrael First. (The execution was carried out on Gęsia Street, as First was returning to his home on Muranowska.) On January 17, 1943, the Germans apprehended Braude and the Dror group he was with and marched them to the Umschlagplatz. Berl jumped the train somewhere just outside Treblinka. He returned to Warsaw. In February 1943, he was appointed commander of the Dror fighting group in the central ghetto.

In the initial days of the uprising, they were billeted at 29 Miła, close to 44 Muranowska. They fought on Miła and Zamenhofa. On May 8, 1943, Berl Braude was in the bunker at 18 Miła. Wounded, he was unable to shoot himself, and asked one of his comrades for help.

Staszek, Stasiek, Brylantsztajn was born in Warsaw in 1922, to wealthy parents. Melekh Neustadt recorded that Staszek grew up on Nowolipie, a Jewish street; Masza Glajtman-Putermilch remembered that he had a deaf and dumb brother and lived in a Polish district. He also had a sister, Gienia, a nurse. He attended the CISzO elementary school at 29 Karmelicka Street, and was a member of Skif, and later Cukunft.

He joined the Bund underground and the ŻOB late, apparently, just before the uprising. He fought in Jurek Błones' group. Before he was killed at 30 Franciszkańska, he asked Marek Edelman for an address on the other side. "Still too soon," Marek answered—because he had no address. Masza Glajtman-Putermilch remembered how once, they were lying on the ground in a cellar, where it was dreadfully hot because the houses were burning. Staszek said to her then: "I would like to die by a bullet going in here and coming out here." Masza saw him dead—his head had been shot through. Staszek Brylantsztajn was killed on May 2 at 30 Franciszkańska Street. He was buried there along with four other ŻOB fighters.

Aron Bryskin, Paweł, was born in 1912 in Warsaw. (On the reverse of this photograph is the date 1931; Aron was 19). His parents came from Belarus. His grandfather Aron was a teacher, and probably his Jewish namesake. His father, Bernard, was a commercial agent. (In Lithuania, he had passed his examinations for the rabbinate in a well-known yeshiva, but he decided to "return to the question," meaning that he abandoned his faith. He married Miriam, the most beautiful girl in the area, and set off with her to Warsaw. In the 1930s, he went blind. He believed this to be a punishment, and so he "returned to the answer.")

They lived at 33 Gęsia Street. Aron was their fourth child. Róża was the eldest, and very beautiful; Josef and Szajne younger; and Natek the youngest. In 1914, Róża was sent to Belarus, to family. She never arrived; nothing is known of what happened to her. Josef was killed in 1920 in the war against the Russians; he had graduated in linguistics. Natek fell into a ditch on his motorcycle and lost his life that way. Szajne studied geography at the university in Minsk. She saw the war out in Russia.

Aron attended the school of crafts at 36 Stawki Street and worked in Klajnman's metal factory on Okopowa Street. He adopted the name Paweł himself, because he couldn't pronounce the "r" sound, and he was a conspirator. He was arrested several times for his communist activities. Shortly after the outbreak of war, he was released from jail and moved to Białystok, and from there deep into Russia.

He worked on a Jewish farm somewhere in the Crimea. When the Germans invaded Russia in 1941, Aron made his way back to Warsaw, because he wanted to be with his parents in the ghetto, Eryk Kamieniecki (Szajne/Sonia's son, Paweł's nephew), wrote to me.

In the ghetto, Paweł allied himself with the PPR underground. He worked in the Brauer 'shop at 28–38 Nalewki Street. In the April uprising, he took command of the PPR group in the central ghetto. On April 24, in broad daylight, he, Lutek Rotblat, and some other insurrectionists marshalled several hundred civilians from the bunker of the burning house at 29 Miła to the bunker at 9 Miła. There, hundreds of fugitives were camped out in three huge courtyards and in the cellars. When the flames from Meisels Street reached 9 Miła, the insurgents knocked a way through to 18 Miła.

On May 7, Anielewicz sent Paweł with a group of ŻOBists to look for a way out of the ghetto. (The group included Hela Schüpper, Szymon, Icchok Suknik, Lilka Zimak, and a few German Jews who had come to the ghetto from the Czerniaków farm.) They had Cukierman's address on Marszałkowska Street. Their plan was to climb out of the sewers on Bielańska Street, but they walked for a long time, from midnight until five in the morning, and lost their way underground.

They emerged on Tłomackie Street, in the vicinity of Krasińskich Park. They were noticed at once by some Polish police officers and a German patrol. They tried to scatter, shooting as they went. Hela Schüpper ran with Paweł. Some police officers caught up with her, but she managed to shake them off and hide in some ruins. She lost sight of Paweł.

On May 27, the Polish janitor of the house at 14 or 24 Miodowa denounced the Jews in hiding there. That was Paweł Bryskin's group: Zygfryda Simson, his girlfriend; Icchok Suknik, known as Koza; Wanda Ochron; and Lilka Zimak. (The janitor was allegedly executed sometime later by the GL.[6])

Zocha Brzezińska was a member of the PPR in the ghetto. She was a passionate girl, of extraordinary physical strength. She was in the fighting group under Michał Biały, which was formed in the latter days of July 1942. In the April uprising she fought in Heniek Kawe's unit in the 'shops. She was killed on April 27, when the bunker at 74 Leszno where some insurrectionists were hiding was flooded.

---

6   p. 510 Glossary—People's Guard.

Tosia Cebularz was a member of the left-wing underground in the Warsaw ghetto. She was killed in the April uprising, probably on the premises of the Toebbens-Schultz 'shops. She was twenty years old.

Jakub Celemeński, Celek, was born on March 14, 1904, in Warsaw. His family came from Jewish Gąbin. Though his father was a Hasid, his nine children were members of Bundist organizations. The whole family perished in Treblinka in the summer of 1942.

Celek's Polish was very poor, but he looked like a hundred Poles. And he was brave. So, he became a courier for the Jewish underground. He traveled around occupied Poland—to Krakow, Lublin, Piotrków—and across the border of the General Government, to Będzin and Sosnowiec. He carried information, news bulletins, money, and weapons. (Celek, like Michał Klepfisz and Władka Peltel, was a courier for Leon Feiner, the Bund's representative on the Polish side.) He slept somewhere on Poznańska Street in a doss house, and often visited Inka Szwajgier and Marysia Feinmesser at 24 Miodowa Street. Before Christmas 1943, he took them a Christmas tree. The girls were not at home. For years afterwards, jokes about his clumsy Polish did the rounds: "So, I standing with this kiss-me tree outside the durr but you not there."

In the last months before the April uprising, Celek bought up arms and ammunition and smuggled the goods into the ghetto. He recorded that with the help of the Polish socialists, the Bundists were able to buy two thousand liters of gasoline and considerable quantities of explosives. In May and June 1943, he went back and forth to the Jewish insurrectionists hidden in the Wyszków woods. After the failure of the Polish rising in 1944, he was deported to the camp in Mauthausen as an Aryan.

He survived. And left Poland. Celek Celemeński was a dressmaker in New York because that was his trade. Sometimes, he visited his ŻOBist friends in Israel. He never went to Poland. He died in New York on January 25, 1986.

Icchak Chadasz was brought up in a wealthy Warsaw family. He was a pupil at the Askola boys' grammar school at 11 Tłomackie Street and as a member of Haszomer Hacair. In the April uprising, he fought in one of his organization's four groups. He was twenty years old when he was killed.

Aron Chmielnicki [**Karmi**] was born in Opoczno in 1921. His father Eliezer was a baker. The family was religious, but not superstitious, in Aron's words—all the children, four sons and three daughters, were members of Gordonia and attended gymnastics clubs. Aron attended a cheder, the public Jewish elementary school in the Esterka House in Opoczno, and the Hebrew Tarbut high school. They spoke Yiddish with their parents, Hebrew among themselves, and often Polish in the bakery, because that was their clientele.

In September 1942 the Opoczno ghetto was liquidated. Aron's large family was deported to Treblinka. Aron and his brother jumped the train. His brother Mosze, injured on the tracks, was killed shortly afterward.

Aron made his way to Warsaw alone. He had only one address, inside the ghetto: that of his instructor from Gordonia, Eliezer Geller. Aron hid in several places and looked for ways into the sealed Jewish town. A szmalcownik denounced him to a Polish "dark-blue" police officer, who then turned him over to the Germans. Tortured at Szucha Avenue, he said he was a *Mischling*, a half-blood. He and twenty-three other prisoners, "half-bloods" like him, were taken into the ghetto. That happened in late January 1943.

Inside the ghetto, Aron Chmielicki, the son of a baker from Opoczno, went to the Gefen bakery at 5 Niska Street. First, he baked bread, because every Jew received a ration of seventy grams black bread a day, and helped to build a shelter beneath the bakery, because the ghetto was gearing up to defend itself. Then he found Geller, was given a revolver by him, and joined the fighting group at 32 Świętojerska Street. Gordonia was barracked on the brushmakers' premises, but shortly before the uprising, the group moved onto the premises of the 'shops. Aron took part in "exes," learned to shoot, and guarded the ŻOB jail on Leszno.

In the uprising, he fought in the group under Jakub Fajgenblat. On the first day, they were at 76 Leszno Street, alongside the group under Dawid Nowodworski. In the cellar at 56 Leszno, they found a shaft into the sewers. To reach it, they dug a tunnel more than a meter long. Then they set fire to the 'shop storerooms at no. 72. They left the ghetto in the night of 28/29 April. There were around forty of them.

They emerged early in the morning on the corner of Ogrodowa and Żelazna Streets and took shelter in the attic at 27 Ogrodowa. In that house lived a Pole called Ryszard Tryfon, who helped the insurrectionists. On April 30, they were all taken to Łomianki by Tadek Szejngut and Krzaczek. Three weeks later, the group was moved to near Wyszków. Their commander in the woods was Dawid Nowodworski.

In October 1945 Aron Chmielnicki reached Palestine, via Romania. For many years, he was a baker in Tel Aviv. He was called Aron Karmi. He lived a family life, and the life of his country. He died on November 26, 2011.

Nachum Chmielnicki was born in Otwock in 1919, the son of Dawid and Dwora Berger. Nachum grew up in Warsaw, in the Jewish district, and attended the CISzO school at 29 Karmelicka Street. Majus Nowogrodzki was in the same class as him, and remembers that Nachum was a math genius, of a quiet, even phlegmatic temperament, an immensely kind boy. After elementary school, he studied at the Wawelberg high school at 4/6 Mokotowska. He was a member of the Bundist Ring student union. He was expelled from the Wawelberg high school for taking part in the student campaigns against the "bench ghetto."

In the ghetto he was active in the Bundist underground. (His brothers were with him: the younger Aharon and the elder Icchak Szulim. Aharon was killed in the ghetto. Szulim, who had been a soldier in the September 1939 campaign, survived the war and emigrated to Israel in 1957.) In late 1942 Nachum was appointed commander of a Bund group in the Toebbens-Schultz 'shop yards. Marek Edelman remembered that Nachum was a tall, well-built man. He was killed in the first battles in the ghetto in January 1943. He was twenty-four.

Icchak Chrzanowicz was born in Ciechocinek. His father was a cobbler and a synagogue shammes. Icchak was a member of the local Frajhajt cell. He went to Łódź, to the Borochow kibbutz, to prepare for emigration to Palestine; he worked on an agrarian farm in the village of Sterdyń, near Sokołów.

In the April uprising he fought in the Dror group under Beniamin Wald in a 'shop yard. He perished in the sewers, probably with the insurrectionists from his group, on April 30 or May 1. He was twenty years old.

Nacha (Naszke) Cukier was born in 1922 in Ciechocinek or Ciechanów. Her parents were fairly well-off; they had a leather goods store. Nacha attended a Polish school and was an active member of Frajhajt. In 1938 she took a six-week self-defense course in the Warsaw suburb of Zielonka. In 1939 she spent time somewhere in the Białystok or Kielce region preparing for life in the new country (she was on the list of Halutzim who were shortly to have emigrated to Eretz Israel).

The war broke out, and Naszke moved to Warsaw. She worked with young people in the ghetto. She fought in Berl Braude's unit in the central ghetto and was killed on May 8 in the bunker at 18 Miła Street.

Icchak Cukierman, Antek, was born in 1914 in Vilnius. The home he grew up in was a Zionist one. Antek attended the Ezra elementary school, where the language of instruction was Yiddish, and a Hebrew high school. He had a fondness for Jewish literature in both languages. He was active in the Halutz movement in Lithuania, and later, from 1936, in Warsaw. He lived on the kibbutz in the Grochów district of Warsaw (an agrarian farm that had been in existence since 1920) and on the kibbutz at 34 Dzielna. He worked in the Landau brothers' carpentry workshop. Shortly before the war, he was accepted to study at the Hebrew University in Jerusalem.

In September 1939 he set off for Kovel with a large group of Halutzim. In April 1940, he crossed the border illegally, and reached Warsaw, Dzielna Street again. At that point several Dror members were living there, among them Celina Lubetkin. The young members of the Dror, like those of the Bund, the Shomer movement, the Left, and Betar, conducted underground activity in the ghetto. News bulletins were published and distributed, courses and seminars organized, and work with the poorest children undertaken.

After the *große Aktion* began in July 1942, the young Jews began to think about forms of self-defense, and of potential ways to take armed action in the ghetto. In December 1942 Antek managed to reach Krakow, where together with local ŻOB fighters he assassinated several German officers in the Cyganeria café. (Over a dozen Germans were killed.)

By January 1943, two ŻOB groups, those under Cukierman and Anielewicz, were battle-ready. The weapons were allocated. (There were not enough for the Bundists, Marek Edelman recalled bitterly.) The decision was taken to attack the Germans marching Jews to the Umschlagplatz. Antek fought on Zamenhofa, Miła, and Stawki with a group of his Halutz comrades.

The ŻOB representative outside the wall at that point was Jurek Wilner. When he was arrested, somebody else had to be sent as representative in negotiations with the Polish underground. Antek had the right looks, and no one in Warsaw knew him. Light curls, bushy moustache, and a proud bearing. Though his Polish was poor, his strong Vilnius accent was a fairly credible explanation. A typical Polish landed gentleman, until his singsong Jewish accent came through—he could quote both *Anhelli*[7] and Kacenelson, Edelman recalled.

---

7   *Anhelli*—a classic Polish prose poem by the Romantic poet Juliusz Słowacki.

On April 13, Irena Adamowicz called: talks with the AK were on the cards, and someone from the ghetto had to go immediately. Antek got a smart suit from Meir Szwarc, only the pants legs were too short—three-quarter length. With shirts slung over his shoulder like a Polish smuggler, he passed through the bribed guardpost. He found his first safe house at 118 Marszałkowska Street. Shortly afterwards, the uprising broke out in the ghetto. Antek was given two letters from Anielewicz. When Kazik Ratajzer and Zygmunt Frydrych left the ghetto on May 1, together they started to think about how to get the insurrectionists out. Ultimately, two groups of ŻOBists, some eighty people in all, were taken to Łomianki.

Antek didn't go into the woods; he stayed in Warsaw. Now, the salient task of the Jewish underground was to rescue the survivors: find hiding-places, share out the available money among their wards—the day-to-day issues of thousands of people living illegally. On August 6, 1944, at the beginning of the Polish Warsaw rising, Antek and other ŻOB fighters were admitted to a unit of the AL; the AK didn't want them. They fought in the Old Town, and later in Żoliborz.

In January 1945, the Halutzim moved to 38 Poznańska Street. They called their new home "the kibbutz on Poznańska." Lodzia Silverstein (formerly Hamersztein) wrote that Cywia and Antek were the life and soul of the kibbutz. It was a staging-post for both Poles and Jews gathering the necessary skills to emigrate. And Lodzia in the kibbutz was in charge of changing over dollars into Polish currency. Everything went as if by clockwork, and we lived like lords at that time, she wrote. Antek took charge of organizing *brikha*, illegal Jewish emigration to Palestine. He left himself, with Celina Lubetkin, in 1947. They founded the Ghetto Fighters' Kibbutz in Galilee and lived there for the rest of their days. Antek Cukierman died of a heart attack on June 17, 1981.

Mosze Cygler was born in 1918 in Żyrardów. His father was a laborer on the roads. Mosze became a cobbler. He was active in the Żyrardów Frajhajt group. During the war, he moved to Warsaw. Together with a group of Halutzim, he ended up on the Czerniaków farm. In the April uprising he was a soldier in the ŻOB and fought in the Dror unit under Zachariasz Artsztajn's command. Borzykowski remembered that a Moniek from his group was killed while on guard outside the bunker at 5 Miła Street. That was on April 24. It may have been Mosze Cygler that was killed at 5 Miła.

Czarny Mietek was embroiled in a dispute with Różka Rozenfeld because he wanted to defend the ghetto, but she wanted to go out into the woods. (He had probably also been in Spartakus before the war, like Różka Rozenfeld.)

On January 18, 1943, he was killed in the central ghetto. Probably nobody ever recorded Czarny Mietek's full name, but someone remembered his nickname.

Lejb Czerniakower fought in Heniek Kawe's group in the central ghetto. He was killed on April 27, when the Germans flooded his group's bunker at 74 Leszno Street.

Tobcia Dawidowicz was born on May 21, 1924, in Warsaw. Her father, Szymon Dawidowicz, was a leader in the Bund youth movement Cukunft, and the editor of the Bund paper *Jugnt Weker* (Yugnt Vecker). Tobcia attended the CISzO school at 29 Karmelicka Street and Mrs. Kalecka's high school at 25 Nowolipki. She was active in Skif, and then in Cukunft, and played sport in the Jewish club Jutrznia. In the first weeks of the war, Szymon Dawidowicz managed to reach Vilnius, and from there, America. (Tobcia's letters to her father have been preserved.)

In the ghetto, she took care of her mother, her brother, and several other children. (Her mother and brother were killed in the ghetto.) She delivered news bulletins and sang in the Cukunft youth choir run by Jakub Gladsztajn. (The choir performed in enclosed courtyards, and in apartments, but they could be heard out on the street, Marek Edelman remembered.) In the Jewish underground, Tobcia was in Welwł Rozowski's group.

When the houses on Leszno, Nowolipie, and Smocza were on fire, the insurrectionists went into the sewers. Tobcia had a twisted ankle and didn't want to be a burden. She stayed with the wounded: Chana Grauman and Szlomo Sufit. From Leszno, they moved to the ruins on Nowolipki. They had weapons and poison.

Dorka Dembińska was in one of the four groups of Jewish left-wingers in the April uprising. She got out of the ghetto via the sewers and joined the insurrectionists-turned-partisans in the Wyszków woods. In late June 1943 she left the woods with Dawid Nowodworski and a few others. On the way to Warsaw, the group was intercepted by a German patrol. Aron Chmielnicki wrote that they were all murdered in Łomianki. Dorka Dembińska was twenty years old.

Icchak Dembiński was in one of the PPR fighting groups during the Warsaw ghetto uprising. He may have been Dorka's brother. It is not known where, when, or how he died.

Abraham Diamant (Diament) was born in Sieradz in 1900. His father worked in a mill and was a devout Jew. Abram attended a Polish school and became an ardent Zionist in a youth movement. He worked as a laborer in a charcuterie. He joined the Polish army and served to the rank of corporal. In 1926 he married Etke Rozonowicz; a year later, their daughter Jochewet was born. At the beginning of the war, they moved to Warsaw.

The Germans resettled Abram's family into the Warsaw ghetto. On July 22, 1942, Jewish police officers marched his wife and daughter to the Umschlagplatz. From January 1943, Abram was barracked under Hirsz Berliński on the brushmakers' premises on Świętojerska Street. He alone of his group had legal employment—he worked in the kitchen in the brushmakers' 'shop.

In the uprising, he received a distinction, for his commander gave him, as an experienced soldier, a rifle. On April 20, he fired from a second-floor window at 32 Świętojerska Street. He allowed his targets to come close, as close as possible, and then he shot accurately. He killed seven Germans. On May 1, he was fighting at 30 Franciszkańska Street, defending a civilian hideout with some other insurrectionists. He took a bullet straight to the heart. He did not have time to pass on the precious rifle and fell with it into the ruins of the burning cellar. His body was not recovered.

Abraham Drejer (Drajer) was born in 1922 in Grójec near Warsaw. His family was very poor, so Abram was apprenticed to a tailor at an early age. He enrolled in Gordonia, but later chose Frajhajt. After the outbreak of war, he fled to Warsaw. He worked on the Grochów farm. In the ghetto, he was the janitor of the house at 34 Dzielna Street.

On April 17, when the Germans did a night round-up of social activists, he did not let them into the Dzielna Street kibbutz; everyone managed to escape before the Germans could get into the building. Abram Drejer, Fajwel Szwarcsztajn, and Zachariasz Artsztajn carried out sentences passed on Jewish Gestapo agents, including Alfred Nossig and Anna Michalewicz. In the April uprising, Abram fought in Zachariasz Artsztajn's group. He remained in the ghetto with the others.

Abraham (Abram) Herszek Drezner was born on May 25, 1921, in Ciepielów, fifty kilometers from Radom. His devoutly religious father, Szlama Dawid Drezner, was a poor glover. His mother, Hena Perla, also came from Ciepielów. They raised eight children. Abram studied in a yeshiva and attended a Polish elementary school. In 1935 Abram, his parents, and his siblings moved to Warsaw in search of a better life. Abram started work for a bookbinder, went to night school, and was active in Frajhajt.

In 1942 he worked on the Czerniaków farm with his sister and his brother Ezekiel. (His brother was the only one to survive the Holocaust.) After that, Abram lived in the kibbutz at 34 Miła and worked in a machine warehouse at 15 Leszno Street. In the April uprising, he probably fought in the Dror group. He was killed in unknown circumstances.

Sewek Duński was the son of Mojżesz Duński, a Bundist from the tsarist era and a cobbler at 3 Miła Street. Sewek attended a Jewish elementary school and was a member of Cukunft-Szturm, the Bundist self-defense group.

In the April uprising he fought under Jurek Błones. When on April 20 the Germans surrounded their group and there seemed to be no escape, Sewek and his bosom friend Julek Junghajzer crawled around to the rear of the German positions and bombarded them with grenades. The Germans briefly had to retreat. Sewek Duński left the ghetto on May 10. Masza Putermilch remembers that Sewek was still small, and very light-haired. He was killed either in the sewers or at the manhole on Prosta Street. He was eighteen.

Marek Edelman was born on January 1, 1919, in Gomel. Only shortly afterwards, his parents were living in Warsaw. Marek did not remember his father. His mother was a great socialist, and secretaried for the Jidisze Arbeter Froj (JAF). "She believed that all are equal and that everything would be fine here." Marek used to go on Skif summer camps and was brought up in a Bundist environment. His mother died before he did his school-leaving exams in the spring of 1939.

He printed the first clandestine Bundist news bulletins with Rywka Rozensztajn, Welwł Rozowski, and Blumka Klog as early as October 1939. He remembered the apartments to which they moved the copier: 29 Karmelicka, 26 Długa, 62 Pawia, 12 Nowolipie, and 30 or 32 Nowolipie. There, they kept the machine behind the oven, in a hole in the wall. Marek remembered Ziferman, who packed the bulletins. (He was shot dead later, during the *große Aktion*, in a house on Nowolipie Street.) Ziferman was always hungry. When it was a printing night, he would be given money and buy smelt, bread, and a kind of mett sausage at the market. In the mornings, when the edition was ready, Zosia Goldblat would come for the papers.

Zosia was seventeen and a beauty. (Three times Marek pulled Zosia from the Umschlagplatz.)

Marek Edelman was an errand boy in a hospital. He had a pass to leave the ghetto, because he took blood to the laboratory on Nowogrodzka Street. Then he would drop in at 24 Żurawia Street to see Mrs. Wąsowska, who was hiding Ignacy Samsonowicz, a Bundist from Piotrków. The most important person in the ghetto for the Bundists, and for Marek, was Abrasza Blum. Because he was unsullied, and the young people could believe him. Marek had a straight back and it never left him, he was always that way, Ala Margolis said. Perhaps from all that looking up to Blum?

In late December 1942, the AK gave ten pistols, so the ŻOB planned an operation. On January 22, they were to have attacked a Jewish police station on Muranów Square. They used the weapons before that, on January 18.

In January 1943, Edelman was in the hospital at Gęsia Street. He said that they could have taken shots at the Germans as they were deporting the hospital, but the boys didn't have confidence in their weapons at that point. After the January operation, he moved to live with the Bundists on the brushmakers' premises at 34 Świętojerska Street. (He was never employed there; he had a "number for life" from the hospital.) The poet Władysław Szlengel lived on the floor above, but the ŻOB fighters had no contact with him—that was a different world, Marek Edelman said.

In the April uprising, Marek Edelman was the commander of five groups on the brushmakers' premises. The "brushes" soon started to burn. In the night of April 20/21, Commander Edelman got four of the groups out into the central ghetto. (They managed to get through a hole in the wall, because Romanowicz took out a searchlight with a shot on target.) They went to 30 Franciszkańska Street and holed up in the cellars of a five-story building, around forty ŻOBists.

On May 1, the Germans attacked them for the first time. Five people were killed. Marek remembered, he told me, that on Franciszkańska he had hallucinations: he kept seeing Germans sitting around a campfire. When the military police attacked at 11 a.m. on May 3, all those in the bunker were asleep, unconscious. There wasn't even a lookout posted, so worn out were they. The commander poked his head out through an opening. He had to jerk it away hard to free himself from strangers' hands. The ŻOB soldiers found another hole and thought they could get out. (But it was then that a grenade blew Berek Sznajdmil's head apart.) Only Marek managed to jump out somehow. He escaped into another cellar, but his red sweater was easy to spot. Before anyone did see him, however, he managed to stop up the hole. He ran, shooting, climbed up a burnt-out flight of stairs, leapt along the scaffolding of hanging balconies, grabbed onto a dangling metal rail, and slid down it. He hid in the rubble, ready to spring, for several hours. (The Germans left the ghetto in the evenings.) Marek went back to 30 Franciszkańska Street. He dug out the entrance to the bunker. And took many of the insurrectionists out. (He was unable to take them all out.)

Celina Lubetkin wrote that he was a boy full of bravado and scorned all safety measures. Stasia Rozensztajn said that he was brutal, ruthless, and acerbic, but that he had to be. On May 8, the insurrectionists burned down the stretch of Gęsia Street where the hospital was. They wanted it to collapse altogether. Or the gas bottle to explode. (The bottle didn't explode, because they didn't know that oxygen doesn't burn, Marek said.) Probably on May 7 they moved to 22 Franciszkańska Street because they knew—so Masza Glajtman said—that there was a way into the sewers in the cellar there.

On May 9, they left there to go out onto the other side. Marek led them in the sewers. He was the commander down there, so afterwards he said that it was he who ordered Szlamek Szuster to go off into a side sewer, and he who left them down there—not Celina; only he bore the responsibility for that decision.

They were together until the end of the war, Marek, Antek, and Celina. In the same apartments—in hiding. And in the Polish Warsaw rising—in the Old Town and in Żoliborz. Marek Edelman had a good revolver and would go out to man a position on Mostowa Street. (He was in the 2nd Platoon of the Third Battalion. His commander, Witek the tramcar driver, was shot by the Russians afterwards.)

Marek Edelman often saved others, and then they were dependent on him. Pnina Grynszpan said that at Marek's side she felt safe during the uprising. Inka Szwajgier left the ghetto because Marek ordered her to. And toward the end of her life, she was on Dr. Edelman's ward in a hospital in Łódź, because she trusted him. As many others had. Marek Edelman did not emigrate from Poland. Throughout the post-war years, he stood up for good, for life, against evil, against death. He died in Warsaw on October 2, 2009.

Cwi Edelsztajn was born in 1922 in Warsaw. The family lived on Leszno. Cwi attended a Tarbut school. When his parents and one of his sisters emigrated to Palestine, Cwi enrolled in an agrarian school in Anusin, near Włodzimierz Wołyński, because he, too, wanted to prepare for life in the new country. (In his letters to his sister in Palestine, he wrote a lot about animals; he especially loved horses.) He was a member of Akiba, and later of Frajhajt. When the war broke out, he moved to Warsaw.

Cwi and his girlfriend Cypora Lerer were in Henoch Gutman's group, which fought on the brushmakers' premises. On the eve of the uprising, Cwi went into the 'shops to visit his sister. He didn't make it back to his group. He fought in Beniamin Wald's group. On May 6, he managed to get out onto the other side, together with Gedalia Rutman and a few other insurrectionists. They were all spotted by the Germans on Ogrodowa. They were probably killed at the police precinct in the ghetto at 103 Żelazna.

Cypora Einstein was born in 1914 or 1915 in Warsaw. She and her elder sister Brucha were brought up in a poor, religious family. They spent a lot of time at the Cukunft club at 26 Zamenhofa Street. Cypora went to school at 36 Krochmalna. Lively and energetic, she was also a paramedic in a Cukunft-Szturm unit.

In the ghetto, she worked in a hairdressing cooperative set up by Miriam Szyfman; their barber shop was an important rendezvous for the Bundist underground. Cypora, like Tobcia Dawidowicz, sang in Gladsztajn's Cukunft choir. In 1942 she persuaded Welwł Rozowski with tears to accept her into his fighting group. Cypora's sister, Brucha, was deported to Treblinka by the Germans during the *große Aktion*. (She was in the same transport as Bronek Szpigiel. She didn't jump from the train.) In April, Cypora probably fought in one of the 'shops. It is not known where or when she was killed.

Abram (Abraham) Ejgier (Eiger) was born on May 24, 1923, in Ostrowiec Kielecki. His father, Szyja Simcha Ejgier, came from Kraśnik. Abram's mother was called Łaja Hejne. They lived at 32 Iłżecka Street.

Abram arrived in the Warsaw ghetto in the fall of 1942 with Berl Braude's group of Drorists from Ostrowiec. (Abraham was a descendant of the famous rabbi Akiba Ejger of Poznań. And a cousin of Basia Sylman.) He was remembered as a quiet, unassuming boy, who fought bravely in the uprising under Henoch Gutman.

On May 1, during the fighting at 30 Franciszkańska Street, Abram was fatally wounded in the stomach as he was firing from a second-floor balcony. He started addressing the Germans bravely and portentously; they looked on, stunned. Shortly afterwards, Abram fell from the balcony, and the Germans finished him off with bayonets.

Eliahu (Elek) Erlich, was born in Warsaw, into a very poor family. They lived on Wołyńska Street in the Jewish quarter. Elek attended the Borochow public elementary school at 6 Zamenhofa Street. He was a member of the Zionist youth organizations Jungbor and Jugnt, and the sports club Sztern. He was a pursemaker by trade.

At the beginning of the war, he was in Brest, but he returned to Warsaw, to his family. Afterwards, he was active in the Jewish underground in the ghetto. During the April uprising, he almost certainly fought in the Poalej Syjon Left group. After leaving the ghetto, he managed to reach the Wyszków woods with the others. Shortly afterwards, he returned to Warsaw. He was killed during the Polish Warsaw rising in unclear circumstances, probably on September 27, somewhere in Żoliborz, with Hirsz Berliński and Pola Elster. In April 1945 they were reburied in the Jewish cemetery in Warsaw.

Jakub Fajgenblat, Jacek, was born in 1919 into a poor household in Warsaw. Directly after leaving elementary school, he began work as a laborer. He spent his free time in Gordonia clubs in Warsaw or Falenica. His gleaming black eyes expressed his strong inner rebelliousness and desire for something higher, one Jewish historian wrote of him.

In the ghetto, he was close to the young people from his organization. He spent several months preparing for their defense. At first the Gordonians were barracked on the brushmakers' premises, but shortly before the uprising, they moved to the Toebbens-Schultz 'shop. Jacek was a group commander.

On April 29, he left the ghetto via the sewers. With the other insurrectionists, he was taken to the coppice in Łomianki, and a couple of weeks later to the Wyszków woods. (His sister Sara Fajgenblat was also in the woods.) In early 1944, he returned to Warsaw with Guta Kawenoki, who was sick, and Zygmunt Igła. They found shelter in the cellars of a house that had entrances at both 14 Próżna Street and 6 Grzybowski Square. Sometime later, the Germans surrounded the house. The three ŻOB fighters had guns. They wounded a few of them and were killed in the fighting.

Awram (Abram) Fajner was born in 1915 in Warsaw. His father was a Hebrew teacher in a private school at 17 Zamenhofa Street. Awram lived with his family at 15 Gęsia. He learned the furrier's trade. He was an active member of the Bund. He took part in the September 1939 campaign to defend Poland and was taken prisoner. The Germans freed him from the POW camp along with the other Jews.

In the ghetto, Awram and his girlfriend, Miriam Szyfman, ran a hairdressing salon that served as an undercover Bund rendezvous. After the July deportation campaign in 1942, Awram worked in the Toebbens-Schultz 'shops on Nowolipie Street. He had links to the Bund paper *Di Jung Sztime* (Di Yung Shtime). He was killed on January 19, 1943, in the first fighting to defend the ghetto, on the premises of the Schultz 'shop.

Josek (Józef) Farber was born in 1921 in Warsaw. His father, a declared Zionist, Berl Farber, had a large ironmonger's store on Grzybowski Square. (In the 1920s he had had an ironmonger's store in Tel Aviv.) Józef never graduated from high school and devoted himself with passion to activism for Haszomer Hacair.

In the ghetto, after the *große Aktion*, he worked in Landau's 'shop, which was something of a Shomer hotbed. He was a courier for Mordechaj Anielewicz. In the April uprising, he commanded a Haszomer Hacair group in the central ghetto. When the insurrectionists left the ruins on May 9, they could not find Josek Farber's group. He most likely stayed in the ghetto with two other commanders, Artsztajn and Blaustein, and their last soldiers.

Józef Fass was the name of one of the April insurrectionists whom the commanders wrote on the list of murdered soldiers of the Jewish Fighting Organization. They gave him as having belonged to the PPR. I found no information about Józef Fass.

Bronka Feinmesser (Fajnmesser), Marysia [Warman], was born on January 22, 1919, in Warsaw, into an assimilated family. Mindla, née Fersztendig, Józef Feinmesser, and their three children Halina, Jakub, and Bronka lived at 62 Marszałkowska Street. (Halina studied Polish language and literature, and Jakub was an engineer, a graduate of Warsaw Polytechnic.) At the same address there was a stationery store run by Bronka's mother, while her grandfather had a store on downtown Nowy Świat. Bronka attended Perla Zaksowa's Jewish high school at 10 Krasińskich Square and passed her school-leaving exams in 1938.

In the ghetto she was a switchboard operator at the Berson and Bauman children's hospital, and attended medical courses run by Prof. Hirszfeld. She lived in the hospital and helped out as a probationary nurse. In the first days of September 1942, the Germans marched her mother and sister to the Umschlagplatz. Bronka ran over there from the hospital with two white aprons—she found her sister but could not find her mother.

She left the ghetto in October 1942. She had links to the Bund, and acted as a courier for the party, and later as a courier for the ŻOB. (Her sister, Halina, also got out of the ghetto. She was arrested in April 1943 and was most likely killed in Pawiak prison.) Bronka, now Marysia, lived at 24 Miodowa Street with Inka Szwajgier, and later in Marysia Sawicka's apartment at 18 Leszno Street. Like other girls from the Jewish underground outside the ghetto, she procured documents, looked for new hideouts, and carried money to her wards. Marysia with the "blue eyes" looked after the cigarette-sellers, Jewish boys on Three Crosses Square. (In the Jewish underground there was another Marysia, "Zielona Marysia"—that was Luba Zylberg.)

In the Polish Warsaw rising, she was a courier for the GL. And afterwards, she went into hiding with other survivors at 43 Promyka Street. All of them—seven at the time—were taken out of Żoliborz on November 15, 1943. Ala Margolis wrote that it was Bronka and Zosia (Renia Frydman) who brought the paramedic patrol from the hospital in Boernerowo. Dr. Śwital helped.

After the war, Bronka Feinmesser–Marysia Warman stayed in Poland with her husband. (Her brother Jakub also survived the war; he left Russia with Anders' Army and reached England.) They lived in Łódź, and later in Warsaw. Zygmunt Warman was a Supreme Court judge from 1956. Marysia Warman worked for newspapers and publishing houses. Until 1968. Then she was expelled from the state publishing house PWN, along with many other Jews. In 1969 she and her son emigrated to the USA; her husband had died in 1965. Marysia Warman lived in New York and worked for law firms. She died there on April 2, 2004, and is buried in the communal cemetery in Warsaw.

Pola Fidelzajt was a member of the Warsaw Poalej Syjon Right. In the April uprising, she fought in her party's group in the Toebbens-Schultz 'shop yards. She was caught in a bunker somewhere and taken to Majdanek and then to Auschwitz. She was twenty-four when she was killed.

Simcha Fidelzajt was Pola's husband. A Varsovian. He was a member of Frajhajt, and then of Poalej Syjon. He spent some time in a kibbutz in Królewska Huta near Będzin. In the April uprising they fought together in the group commanded by Marek Majerowicz. Simcha Fidelzajt was killed in unknown circumstances. He was twenty-five.

Gienek Fingerhut came from Łódź. In the Jewish uprising he fought in the Gordonia group on the premises of the 'shops. He left the ghetto via the sewers on April 29 and managed to reach the partisans in the Wyszków woods. There, he was killed. The circumstances are unknown; the date is unknown.

Cyla Finkelsztajn had connections with the Warsaw organization Frajhajt. In the April uprising she fought in the unit commanded by her boyfriend, Zachariasz Artsztajn. It is not known when and how she died.

Majorek (Meir) Finkelsztajn was born in 1921 in Warsaw. He was brought up in a poor family on Nowolipie. He was a member of the Dror underground.

On January 18, 1943, he took part in the defense operation with the group under Zachariasz Artsztajn. He was fatally wounded in the Dror apartment at 56 Zamenhofa Street. He was moved to a safe place, to 34 Miła Street. There was no way of getting a doctor to him, however, because at that time, everyone in the ghetto was in hiding. During a raid on the house on Miła, the Germans found Majorek Finkelsztajn and shot him dead there. Elsewhere, it was recorded that Artsztajn took his comrade to 36 Pawia Street, and that Majorek died there.

Motek Finkelsztajn was born in Warsaw in 1923. He lived at 39 Gęsia Street. His family was very poor, so Motek went out to work young. He spent his free time at Beit Borochow, the Warsaw seat of Frajhajt. He had a beautiful voice, so he was in the organization's children's choir.

For a few months in 1942, Motek worked on the Halutz farm in Czerniaków. On his return to the ghetto, he went to live in the Dror kibbutz at 34 Miła. He was employed in the Werterfassung warehouses on Niska Street. It may have been Motek Finkelsztajn—so Borzykowski wrote—and not Zachariasz Artsztajn, who with Abram Drejer and Fajwel Szwarcsztajn carried out the death sentence issued by the ŻOB on the 79-year-old Gestapo agent and writer Alfred Nossig.

In the uprising, Motek fought in Zachariasz Artsztajn's group in the central ghetto. After May 10, he stayed behind in the ruins with Artsztajn, Farber, Blaustein, and many others. It is not known when and how he died.

Luba (Ala) Fondamińska, Zylbersztejn, was born in 1914. Before the war, she was a psychology student at the University of Warsaw, and a communist activist, probably a member of the student organization Życie. Anna Lanota rented a room in the Zylbersztejns' apartment at 14 Waliców Street. She remembered that Luba's father was a petty trader, that Luba had a deaf-mute brother, whom she helped a lot, and that the whole family could use sign language. And also—that Luba was a friendly, diminutive blonde and didn't look like a Jewess at all.

In the spring of 1942, Luba was living with her husband, Efraim Fondamiński, on Franciszkańska Street, probably at no. 24, and she lent books to a little girl called Iza Szymel. One historian wrote that during the April uprising she and her husband were on the premises of the Transavia 'shop on Stawki and that she was killed on May 2, when the Germans attacked that area of the ghetto.

Efraim Fondamiński, Edward, came from a relatively wealthy family, Anna Lanota remembered, and had a brother; they lived somewhere on Pawia Street. Before the war, he was an activist with the Communist Party of Poland and graduated from the Warsaw Polytechnic in 1938 or 1939. He was not yet thirty at that point, Anna Lanota, his wife's friend, recalled. He was a tall, slender brunet with a pale, cleanshaven face and slicked-down hair, in appearance very much like a Jew. When he was arrested for communism, his mother sent him an eiderdown to the Pawiak prison—everybody repeated that to each other.

When he visited the Legiec family on Szczygla Street, he wore an armband, because he believed that gave him protection from the *szmalcownicy*. History has repeated that Fondamiński, from September 1942 secretary of the PPR ghetto committee, and his party's representative on the Jewish National Committee, was in the bunker at 18 Miła Street on May 8. Marek Edelman never met him. He said that Fondamiński was already dead in October 1942. (Edelman believed him to have been killed during the *große Aktion*.) One historian recorded that Fondamiński was killed in the bunker at 18 Miła Street. He was probably 33.

Towa Frenkel was born in Warsaw in 1920. A quiet, unassuming girl, she was a member of the Haszomer Hacair cell from the age of fourteen. When she had grown up a little, she was a dressmaker.

In the ghetto, she lived with her father on Chłodna, and later on Zamenhofa. (Her father died of typhus.) She worked in a small tailor's workshop with her friends Mira Fuchrer and Rachela Zylberberg. She was a member of a Haszomer Hacair fighting group. She was killed in the April uprising.

Sławek Friedman (Frydman), Bronisław Mirski, was born in Warsaw in 1918. He lived with his parents and his brother Mietek at 14 Walicόw Street, on the first floor. (In the rear wing, in the second courtyard, lived Władysław and Maksio Szlengel with their parents. The proprietor of the tenement was Ernestyna Golde.) His father, Ludwik Friedman, was a member of the PPS in 1905, and later belonged to the Bund. A trained pharmacist, he had worked for a drug wholesaler, but lost his job in 1931. He was active in the Commercial and Officer Workers' Trade Union, which had its seat at 25 Zielna Street. His mother, Ewa, came from Płock, kept house, and was interested in literature. The poet Władysław Broniewski used to visit them; he had known Friedman's mother back in Płock. The family was supported by Mietek, who was a lawyer and had qualified as both a judge and an attorney. Although his home was a Bundist one, Sławek's first language was Polish. He briefly attended the public elementary school at 10 Wolność Street, and later went to the high school run by the Merchants' Congregation at 14 Prosta Street, and Boys' High School No. 3 at Emilia Plater Street. In the 1935/1936 academic year, he started a degree in veterinary studies at the University of Warsaw, where he completed three years; he finished his course in Soviet Lvov in 1941.

He was keen to return to his family, all of whom were still living on Walicόw Street. In the fall of 1941, he returned to Warsaw, to his city, by train—with his heart in his mouth, he said. He entered the ghetto through the Courts on Leszno Street. Sławek Friedman was adopted by a friend of his father's, the Polish Legionnaire and engineer Roman Mirski. "That was in the ghetto. It was my parents' request to their friend; they wanted to secure me in some way, and he officially adopted me, in the Courts on Leszno Street." His parents perished in Treblinka shortly afterwards.

Sławek Mirski worked in the textile 'shop run by Anna Melita Feliks at 80 Nowolipie. Later, after the *große Aktion*, in a 'shop on Świętojerska Street:

Metalwerk Nr. 2, Heeres-Unterkunft-Verwaltung Warschau, in the offices of the chemical department, making products including Meide cosmetics. The manager of that department was Roman Mirski, Sławek's guardian. Mietek, Sławek's brother, had employment in the Judenrat. (He was in the ghetto with his wife, a pianist. They were both deported in January 1943.)

After the January operation, Mirski and two of his friends, Aron Korensztajn and Jerzy Lewita, had contacts with the underground via Sara Żagiel. (Bronisław Mirski remembers that Sara's surname was Żagiel, not Żogel, and that she brought news bulletins to the 'shop.) "I was never in the PPR. I wasn't in any party, but my group had contacts in the GL. I got my gun from the GL; it was a Walther. You could say that we were left-wingers." Their base was at 30 Świętojerska Street, and they learned to handle their weapons in the workshops at 4 Wałowa and in the cellars of 14 Nalewki Street.

During the uprising, Mirski was in charge of the shelter at 2, 2a, or 4 Wałowa Street, which gave protection to several dozen people—thirty, or perhaps even fifty. "Adaś Folman and I started to prepare that shelter after the January operation. There were two rooms, electric light, and a few straw mattresses. We dug a tunnel out onto Nalewki Street ourselves; I think we knocked through onto 14 Nalewki. Because that was where our aid from the Poles in the GL was supposed to come. We wanted to get out into the woods. I was the only one in the bunker with a gun. I remember that Henoch Gutman and his friends came into the bunker to see if the board-lined tunnel was suitable for an escape. It was never used. The boarding collapsed when the house went up in flames. The entrance to the bunker was concealed behind an earth-filled box. It might have been May 2 or 3 when the Germans discovered the bunker. I don't know how it happened. There was fire on the Nalewki side, and Wałowa was also burning. There was only one thing we could do: give ourselves up to the SS. And that's what happened," Sławek Mirski told me in Warsaw in 2014. "We all went out. They lined us up; I dropped my pistol into my pants leg and stood on it. We were hounded to the Umschlagplatz, but—I don't know whether it's appropriate to say it—there were no acts of violence on the part of the Germans. As if they were affording us a modicum of respect. And after that I was in the camps: Lublin, Budzyń, Gross-Rosen, Wieliczka, Płaszów, and Brünnlitz in Moravia. In Budzyń we were building a camp for future French POWs, whom the Germans planned to bring over after the war was won."

In the new reality, in the Polish People's Republic, Bronisław Mirski worked on the construction of a pharmaceutical factory in Jelenia Góra, and thereafter in the editorial offices of various publishing houses. In 1968 he was fired from the publishers PWN, because he wasn't enough of a Pole. For years, he lived with his wife in a backwater world. They lived in the Warsaw district of Grochów.

By the time I started visiting him for conversations, he was alone. Once, I asked for a pen. He gave me several, from different drawers, but none of them would write. "It's not worth buying any more now," he said. Bronisław Mirski, or Sławek Friedman, passed away on July 27, 2015.

Emus Frojnd was the son of the teacher and well-known Poalej Syjon Left activist Abraham Frojnd. In the Warsaw ghetto he and his family lived on Nowolipie Street, and his home was a rendezvous for underground Zionist activists. Emus distributed illegal press bulletins. In the April uprising he was in Hirsz Berliński's group. He was nineteen when he was killed.

Renia Frydman, Zosia Skrzeszewska [Wysocka] was born in Warsaw in 1923. Her father had married into a family of Warsaw antiquarians, the Kleinsingers. Renia's parents themselves ran an antique bookstore at 19 Świętokrzyska Street, and lived close by, at 15 Świętokrzyska. Renia attended Paprocka's high school at 27 Zielna Street for two years, and then Jehudija, where the headmistress was Stefania Szwajgier, Inka's mother.

Later on, in the ghetto, Renia studied for her school-leaving exams in Mrs. Szwajgier's home. (History was taught by Prof. Marian Małowist, French by Prof. Magitson, Latin by Braude, and Polish by Mrs. Weinberger.) Renia worked in the Berson and Bauman hospital as a nursing assistant. In July 1942, from a hospital window, she saw her parents and younger sister Broneczka on the Umschlagplatz but was unable to help them. (Renia's parents and three sisters were killed in the Holocaust.)

She left the ghetto with a work detail on April 1, 1943. Bronka Feinmesser and Inka Szwajgier had documents made for her and found her work as a governess. She and Ala Margolis lived with a family at 69 Różana Street, as Poles. They found the National Democratic views of their hosts distressing, however, so they fled. Zosia had good looks and decent papers and helped others in hiding in the Polish city.

After the war she graduated from the State School of the Performing Arts, and until 1957 was an actress in the Polish Theater. (The photograph is from that period of her life as an actress.) Later, she worked in the Jewish Theater under Ida Kamińska, at 2 Królewska Street. (Zosia learned her Yiddish lines using Polish letters.) She emigrated in 1969 with her husband and son. Zosia Skrzeszewska-Wysocka lived in Frankfurt am Main. "Warsaw is my city," she told me in a telephone conversation in 2014. Zosia Wysocka died on January 21, 2020.

Zygmunt Frydrych, Zalman, was born in Warsaw in 1911. He was brought up in a poor Hasidic family at 60 Nowolipki Street. His father had a small paper-bag factory. Zygmunt was an active member of Cukunft and attended a CISzO school. Afterwards, he worked in various Bund institutions, and contributed to the *Folkscajtung* (Folkstsaytung). After the outbreak of war, he was called up into the Polish army and shortly thereafter was taken prisoner in Królewiec. He was tall, with blue eyes and light hair. Strong, brave, and proud, he was perfect material for a courier. He was thus constantly shuttling between two worlds, the Jewish and the Polish.

At the beginning of the *große Aktion* in July 1942, the Bundists sent Zygmunt to find out where the trains going "to the East" were actually destined, and what was happening to people. He reached Sokołów, near Małkinia, and there he met Azriel Wałłach, the first fugitive from Treblinka. Frydrych returned to the ghetto with all the information he needed.

It was also Zygmunt, apparently, who organized the first arms convoy into the ghetto, in late December 1942. The AK gave them ten pistols. Around the same time, the Germans arrested Cila, Zygmunt's wife. She was caught in the house at 11 Świętojerska Street, on the Polish side. (That house was connected via its cellars with a house inside the ghetto.) Cila was killed in Majdanek. After that, Zygmunt got his 6-year-old daughter Elżunia out of the ghetto and placed her in hiding in a convent outside Krakow.

Marek Edelman remembers that it was Frydrych, not Antek Cukierman, who was to have replaced Wilner on the other side, but Zygmunt had not managed to establish contact with Henryk Woliński of the AK, and so Antek went. (Antek was also unable to forge that contact.) Zygmunt often went to see Joanna Prażyna on Koźla Street. From her apartment they would let milk down into the ghetto through the drainpipe, and after the milk, news bulletins.

On April 18, Zygmunt Frydrych went briefly back into the ghetto. During the fighting, he was with the Bundists on the brushmakers' premises. On April 30, the commanders of the uprising sent Zygmunt and Kazik Ratajzer to seek help outside the walls. They used the tunnel at 6 Muranowska Street. (A few days later, Kazik went back into the ghetto and took some 40 insurrectionists out.)

In mid-May, Zygmunt Frydrych transferred the sick Jurek Błones from Łomianki to Płudy. There were four other insurrectionists from the woods in the vehicle with them: Guta and Lusiek Błones, Fajgele Goldsztajn, and Chedwa Wachenhojzer. They reached their destination. They were let into the house, but early the next morning they were surrounded by Germans and shot dead in the courtyard. (The Polish houseowner had denounced them.) In 1946, the six insurrectionists were buried in the Jewish cemetery on Okopowa Street.

Chaim Frymer was born in 1920 in Gniewoszów in the Lublin region, into a religious family. Before the war, he lived in Warsaw, at 14 Muranowska Street. In the Warsaw ghetto he was a member of Akiba. When they split into fighting groups, he taught the ŻOB fighters how to use their weapons. Shortly before the uprising, some Polish police officers guarding the Jewish bank at 37 Nalewki Street arrested him, because they found a gun and a considerable sum of money on his person. Some other armed ŻOB fighters, most likely his bodyguards, sprang to his aid. Taken aback and terrified, the policemen let him go and even gave him back his gun and his money.

In the April, Chaim fought in Berl Braude's group on Zamenhofa Street and in the defense of the bunker at 29 Miła Street. After that, he and Rywka Pasamonik managed to reach the ŻOB bunker at 18 Miła.

Chaim left the ghetto via the sewers on May 10 and reached the Wyszków woods via Łomianki. He joined a group of Soviet partisans who had fled from German POW camps. After the war, he was briefly registered at 70 Płowiecka Street in Wawer. In 1945, he and his wife Pnina Grynszpan emigrated to Palestine. Later on, in Israel, he had a small shoe manufactory, as his father had done in Poland before the war. He died in Tel Aviv in 1972.

Gabriel (Gabryś) Fryszdorf was born in Warsaw in 1918 or 1921. His father was the gabbai in a prayer house. Gabriel attended a cheder and the CISzO schools at 22 Twarda and 36 Krochmalna Streets. He was a schoolfriend of Hanka Krysztal, Fajgele Peltel, and Celek Celemeński. He grew up with them in Skif, and later in Cukunft. He learned the trade of sales assistant. He was a boy with an attractive face and sad, pensive eyes, quiet and decisive, full of dignity in his behavior. *Tsurikgehalten*, withdrawn, as Marek Edelman put it.

In the ghetto, he worked in the soup kitchens on Krochmalna Street and then at 32 Świętojerska. (The manageress there was Miriam Klepfisz, the mother of Michał. The soup kitchens were also ghetto underground hubs.) After the *große Aktion*, he found employment in the Roerich 'shop at 80 Nowolipie Street.

In December 1942, a *werkszuc* caught three ŻOB members and locked them in Hallman's 'shop. They were to have been taken to the Umschlagplatz the next morning. That same night, Gabryś Fryszdorf and his colleagues from the Roerich 'shop disarmed the German guard and freed all three. Shortly after that operation, Fryszdorf and Rozowski went to live at 56 Nowolipie Street with a group that was shortly to become a fighting group. It included the brothers Szlomo and Meir Szwarc, the Juszkiewicz brothers, Zygmunt Igła, Bronek Szpigiel, Chajka Bełchatowska, and Tobcia Dawidowicz. The Bundists stopped going to work, acquired two pistols, obtained Molotov cocktails from Michał Klepfisz, and started to prepare their defense. In February 1943, on the eve of the scheduled relocation of Hallman's factory, Fryszdorf and a group of ŻOB fighters set fire to its warehouses, raw materials, and plant that was standing packed and ready for the move.

In the April uprising, Fryszdorf was Welwł Rozowski's second-in-command on the 'shop premises. They fought on Nowolipki and Smocza. When the Germans surrounded Winogron and Rozowski's group in the attic at 43 Nowolipki, Fryszdorf fired bravely from under the roof, allowing the insurrectionists to get away. On April 29, as the group was relocating to Leszno via an attic route, Gabryś again gave them cover. That same night, they managed to get out via the sewers to 27 Ogrodowa Street. They were taken to Łomianki, and not until May 19 did two trucks take them to the Wyszków woods.

The ghetto Bundists were unwilling to fight in the same unit as Russians and formed a separate group. Gabryś was their courier. He told Celek Celemeński how on April 19, 1944, they celebrated the first anniversary of the outbreak of the ghetto uprising. At midnight on April 18/19, they went into a village, armed. They took axes, picks, and shovels from a peasant, and destroyed the telegraph poles and cables on the road.

On June 15, Gabryś and a comrade accompanied a group of people returning to Warsaw. They were on their way back to the woods when some Germans appeared out of nowhere. Fryszdorf's companion managed to escape, but Gabryś was killed in the shootout. (Some twenty Jews were killed in the woods in two weeks in May.)

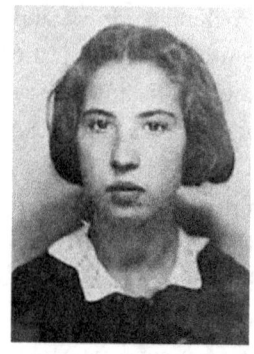

Mira Fuchrer (Fuchter) was light-haired, pretty, and warm, Marek Edelman remembered. She was born in Warsaw in 1920. In the ghetto she worked in a tailors' cooperative with Towa Frenkel and Rachela Zylberberg, who was known as "Sarenka." Mira used to attend Shomer meetings in high boots, a huge sheepskin coat, and a blue beret. She had slanting eyes and was strong and mysterious. Her friends from the organization knew that she was Mordechaj Anielewicz's girl and viewed her like a revolutionary from the Russian tsarist-era organization Narodnaya Vola.

In 1942, Mira traveled to other ghettos as a courier. She returned in a blue hat with a veil that obscured half of her face, her hair in a fashionable permanent wave, her eyebrows and lashes dyed black, a brightly colored dress—the picture of a young Polish lady. She was killed on May 8 in the bunker at 18 Miła Street, with her boyfriend Mordechaj Anielewicz and many others.

Regina Fudem, Lilit, was born in Warsaw in 1922. (In many sources, Regina's surname is erroneously given as Fuden. It was corrected here by Regina's brother, Leon Fudem.) Her father was a tailor, and poor, and her mother raised six children: Bela, Moszek, Herszek, Szymek, Regina (Renia), and Leon, as well as helping their father. They lived at 43 Nalewki Street. Lilit was awarded a study grant and attended four grades of the public elementary school at 20 Stawki Street. She was fifteen when she joined Haszomer Hacair. She started work young. In the ghetto, she acted in a Hebrew amateur dramatics club. She had the best looks of all of us, and was brave, her brother Leon said.

In the April uprising, she was a courier between the groups on the Toebbens-Schultz premises. On April 29, Lilit took a group of forty insurrectionists from Leszno Street out of the ghetto via the sewers. When they reached Ogrodowa Street, many hours later, Lilit decided to go back into the ghetto for two more groups. Szlomo Baczyński went with her. It is not known where or how they died.

Irka (Irena) Gelblum was born in Warsaw, probably on October 31, 1925 (she gave various dates of birth). Her family was wealthy; they lived at 49 Żelazna Street. (Her brother and parents perished in the Holocaust.) Irka had the right looks, and was spectacularly brave, so she became a courier. She left the ghetto after the January operation and travelled around some of the most dangerous and distant places in occupied Poland. On the "Aryan side," she lived with Luba Zylberg at 5 Pańska Street; prior to that in the ghetto they had worked together at the post office.

Before the uprising, they acted as a holding bay for weapons. Afterwards, the apartment at Pańska was used as a bolt hole for ŻOB fighters from the ghetto. Now the girls took care of Jews in hiding all over the city. They supplied them with money and medication, found new hideouts for them, and sometimes accompanied them out and about. Irka continued to travel around the occupied Polish territories. She worked a lot with Kazik Ratajzer; they were in a pair.

Irka Gelblum survived the Holocaust. She lived briefly in Israel. Then she lived in Poland, where she studied medicine for a while, and was a journalist. After that she lived in Italy and wrote poetry. She concealed her Jewishness under various names, in successive relationships. She never wanted to be Irka Gelblum again. She once told me that she had nothing in common with that person. She died near Warsaw in October 2009.

Eliezer Geller was born in Opoczno in 1918. His father, who owned an ironmonger's store, was a Zionist, and widely respected in the town. Eliezer, a Gordonia activist, attended a commercial school in Łódź, and then returned to Opoczno. He focused on setting up Gordonia cells in the Łódź district and in Greater Poland. Drafted into the Polish army in 1939, he was taken prisoner in the battle at Kutno.

In the second half of 1940, the Germans liberated him from the POW camp (along with all the other Jewish soldiers in the Polish army) and Eliezer was sent into the Warsaw ghetto, where he resumed his work for Gordonia: publishing the news bulletins

Głos Młodych and *Davar Ha-tzeirim*. He maintained contact with Natan Szwalbe at the Histadrut office in Geneva. He traveled extensively throughout occupied Poland and founded a Gordonia kibbutz in Częstochowa.

In the January operation he was a group commander. There were clashes with the Germans on Zamenhofa, Muranowska, and Miła Streets. In March 1943 he was appointed commandant of the Toebbens-Schultz 'shop premises. In the April uprising, his group defended itself in the house at 76 Leszno Street. On April 29, Geller and his soldiers left the ghetto via the sewers, emerging at 27 Ogrodowa Street. Eliezer did not go into the woods but remained in Warsaw in hiding. He lived close to Teatralny Square.

On May 24 he went to an abandoned celluloid factory with over a dozen other ŻOB fighters. It was a good place—spacious, empty, and with a Polish guard who ensured their safety. That day, he was to have met Antek Cukierman there. It may have been a match or an unextinguished cigarette that caused the fire. Eight people perished in the flames. Eliezer, badly burned, managed to escape to an apartment on Albert Street. (His host took care of him.)

In the summer of 1943, Geller reported to the Hotel Polski on Długa Street. Cukierman wrote that both Geller and Kanał, who went with him, were broken, and allowed themselves to believe in a chance of survival. On October 21, 1943, Geller was deported, in a group of one thousand eight hundred Jews, to Bergen-Belsen. It was from there that he sent his last letter. The Jews from Bergen-Belsen are known to have been murdered in Auschwitz.

Aba Gertner was born in Ostrowiec Kielecki, into a wealthy sugar wholesaler's family. His father's name was Izrael Dawid, and his mother's Rywka. Aba also had a younger sister, Bajla, who was shy, and wrote poems. (Bajla survived the war, but she did not survive the first days of July 1946. She was seventeen when she was killed in the Kielce pogrom.)

Aba attended the Jawne religious elementary school, and a Polish state high school. Sometime in 1939, he joined Haszomer Hacair. He ran the library of the cell in his town. In February 1943, he managed to get to Warsaw. In the April uprising, he fought on the Toebbens-Schultz premises. He was nineteen when he was killed.

Izrael Gertner was a member of the Bundist organization Cukunft-Szturm. He is known to have worked as a store assistant before the war. He was killed in the ghetto in the January 1943 defense operation.

 **Masza Glajtman (Gleitman)** [Glajtman-Putermilch] was born in Warsaw in 1924. Her father had a leather goods manufactory and was politically non-aligned. But her mother, Fania, née Stolper, was very progressive: she read books, went to lectures, and was a member of the women's socialist organization JAF. Masza attended seven grades of the Grosser CISzO school at 29 Karmelicka Street, and then the ORT at 29 Długa. In her own words, her family home gave her a socialist upbringing, and Yiddish as her mother tongue. (Her sister Chana went to the Bund school at 36 Krochmalna with Marek Edelman.) Masza and Chana were both members of Skif. (Stasia Rozensztajn was their *madrikha*, or instructor.) In the summer of 1939, the two girls went on a Cukunft summer camp to Włocławek.

From September 1939, Masza worked in the sewing room in the Medem Sanatorium in Miedzeszyn. She returned to Warsaw in October 1940, as the ghetto was being sealed. In the Jewish city, she lived at 47 Nalewki Street. She sewed, washed, dyed, and sold old clothes. After the *große Aktion*, she worked briefly with her father in the saddlery shop on Szczęśliwa Street; prior to that, she sewed leather goods at Brauer's. She was initiated into the ŻOB by her Cukunft comrade, Lea Szyfman. It was then that Masza met the Betar group living on Muranowska, probably at no. 17. She remembered Majorek, because he was fond of her, and she could procure arms through him.

After the January operation, Masza went to live with Lejb Gruzalc's group at 29 Zamenhofa Street. The purpose of barracking people in this way was to keep them together and get them used to a military-style rigor. Twice, she went out on "exes"; once they were collecting money, and on the other occasion they locked up "that Jew," in her words, in the jail on Miła Street, which was probably at no. 2.

In the April uprising, she had a Belgian FN pistol, and one homemade grenade, like the others in her group. They fired all their bullets, threw all their grenades, and started to retreat. From Zamenhofa Street to 29 Miła, and then to 18 Miła. She went there with Tasenkrojt and Jankielewicz. Masza was in the bunker at 18 Miła for a few days. She remembered that she could wash, and sleep in pajamas there.

When Marek Edelman went to see them there, the Bundists decided to stay together, so they went back with him from Miła to 30 Franciszkańska. There was a tunnel into another bunker there, Masza told me, and the Germans discovered it and threw gas grenades down it. And when she smelled the gas, Marek and the others stuffed the entrance with pillows. The next day, Marek opened the tunnel and got several of the insurrectionists out.

Masza heard from someone that when the Germans started to hack up the asphalt to get to the bunker at 18 Miła Street on May 8, Wafel Gruchal (that was the name Masza remembered) gave the order to open the window and fire at them. They killed him first.

Masza Glajtman left the ghetto on May 10. In the sewers, Juda Wengrower held onto her hips, and they made their way along like that together. He fainted repeatedly, and every time he came round, he drank the wastewater. From Łomianki she managed to make it to the Wyszków woods—she wanted to be with the partisans! She lived in the woods for half a year, somewhere by the river Bug, near the town of Kamieńczyk. They were filthy and lice-infested, so they would throw their clothes into anthills and the ants would eat all the lice from their clothes. (Her commander was Hirsz Berliński, but Masza spoke badly of him, because, she said, he would steal food and eat others' rations!) She once told me that it was there in the woods that she met Jakubek, who started making advances to her, though neither of them had any hope of surviving.

In the Polish Warsaw rising, the AK would not accept the Jewish group that they were in, so they joined the AL. Masza manned a soup kitchen in downtown Śródmieście, and her husband from the woods, Jakubek Putermilch, was on a barricade. After the rising, they did not leave Warsaw with the others, because they were afraid of being recognized by Poles and handed over to the Germans. They remained in hiding in the ruins of the city, on and around Śliska and Sienna Streets, until January 23, 1945.

In the March, Masza, Jakubek, Pnina Grynszpan, and Chaim Frymer were issued with papers from the Red Cross in Lublin, that they were Yugoslavs who had been liberated from the concentration camps. On the way to Czechoslovakia, Jakubek told Masza that they were going to Palestine. Masza Glajtman-Putermilch lived with Jakubek and their daughters in Tel Aviv. She died on November 6, 2007.

Wolf Gold was the name of one of the April insurrectionists whom the commanders wrote on the list of murdered soldiers of the Jewish Fighting Organization. They gave him as having belonged to the PPR. I found no information about Wolf Gold.

Dorka Goldkorn, Helena Brzozowska, was born in 1922 in Warsaw. She lived at 17 Pańska Street and was active in the Spartakus Union of Socialist Youth. Her father's name was Szymon, and her mother was called Sura Frajdenrajch.

In the ghetto, the young people from Spartakus had their meeting-place on Muranowska Street. In Dorka's group, there were five girls. Ludka Arbajtsman from Wronia Street was the youngest. (Later on, Ludka joined the GL, and was killed in the woods.) Renia Niemiecka came from a religious household. Esia Twerska had just arrived from Vilnius. Różka Rozenfeld was the leader of the group, and the instructor was Comrade Lena. From late 1940, they were in contact with Haszomer Hacair, and exchanged bulletins with them. In early 1941, the young socialists issued a Polish-language paper, *Strzały*, and the Yiddish-language *Baginen*. They set up a reading-room at 53 Nowolipie. In 1942 Spartakus joined the PPR. Dorka wrote that they pursued a fierce ideological war with the Bund, "which even in the ghetto conditions was absolutely negatively disposed toward the Soviet Union." In the latter days of July 1942, the Jewish communists in the ghetto formed a number of fighting groups under the command of Janek Biały [Szwarcfus]. Dorka's group lived at 49 Nowolipki, on the Hoffman factory premises. In the attic space at 51 Nowolipki, they filled burnt-out light bulbs with a mixture of sulfur and dynamite to make bombs of a sort.

On January 18, 1943, Dorka was on the 'shop premises. They had six revolvers and two grenades. Comrade Stach and a Shomer, Izrael, lobbed the grenades. Comrade Stach, a light-haired youth, was killed shortly after the January operation: he was arrested and threw himself at a German. Before the uprising, the young PPR members hacked out a route between the attics along Nowolipie, Nowolipki, and Smocza. (Geller's soldiers did the same on Leszno.) In the April uprising, Dorka Goldkorn was a courier for the groups fighting at 74 Leszno, 61 Nowolipie, and 51 Nowolipki. In that area, the communists and Zionists fought together.

Tuwia Borzykowski recalled the attempt to leave the ghetto via the sewers in the early morning of April 24. With him were Halina, Jeremiasz from Haszomer Hacair, and Dorka Goldkorn. After walking for several hours, they reached the next manhole. They hoped they were outside the ghetto. When they opened the manhole cover, they saw the wall in front of them. Halina and Dorka were arrested by the dark-blue police. Jeremiasz tried to escape and was shot dead. Tuwia managed to slip back down into the sewer and return to his group.

Dorka was taken to the Umschlagplatz, and three days later put on a train. The people in the wagon didn't want to escape, but they helped Dorka—they ripped up one of the planks in the floor, and Dorka slid down between the wheels of the thundering train. Some peasants in a hut at the trackside let her wash and gave her a colorful headscarf. They were afraid to let her stay for the night. Dorka picked a bunch of flowers, and went to Warsaw, to Szczygla Street, to the Legiec family. And after that, she returned to the ghetto, because she had nowhere to go.

On May 7, she was in the bunker at 18 Miła Street. She left there in a small group, via the sewers, and was taken to the woods in Radzymin. She was a courier between partisan groups. Probably in July 1943, the Germans staged a round-up, and caught Dorka and some others. She was interned in the camps in Ravensbrück, Auschwitz, and Bergen-Belsen.

After the war she probably studied medicine and was definitely active in the Łódź branch of the PPR. On January 17 or 19, 1947, she was traveling in a car with a W. Marczyński. Somewhere near Pabianice, they were dragged out of the car and shot. (Someone heard that the military personnel with her were released, and only Dorka was executed, because she was a communist and a Jew.) A month later, the Łódź paper *Walka Młodych* wrote that the driver had failed to stop when ordered by a patrol, taking it for an underground hit squad disguised as militia officers, and that was why the patrol had opened fire.

Icchok Goldsztajn was in a Bund group in the ŻOB. In January 1943, they had not been issued with weapons. They were caught and taken to the Umschlagplatz. A young Bundist, Boruch Pelc, briefly addressed all the Jews assembled there. They all refused to board the train, so they were all shot dead on the square. Icchok Goldsztajn was among them.

Izaak Goldsztejn was born in 1916 in Sokółka, near Białystok. He was a member of the religious Zionist youth movement Hanoar Hacyjoni. At the beginning of the war, he lived in Łódź, and later he moved to Warsaw. He cooperated with Jakub Praszkier, who in the April uprising was the commandant of their group on the brushmakers' premises. Izaak Goldsztejn was probably killed in the bunker at 8 Wałowa Street.

Jechiel Górny, Jur, Chil was born in 1908. He was one of the "old ones" in the ŻOB, because in 1943 he was 35. He belonged to Poalej Syjon Left. In the ghetto, he lived at 69 Miła Street. He contributed to the Ringelblum Archive Oneg

Shabat, keeping registers and making copies of documents. He was employed in the OBW—Landau's 'shop at 30 Gęsia Street. In the April uprising he fought in Hersz Berliński's group on the brushmakers' premises. He was killed on May 10, 1943, as he emerged from the sewer on Prosta Street.

Henryk Grabowski, Heniek "Słoniniarz" was born in 1913. From 1918, he was a Polish Scout. Before the war, he was in Irena Adamowicz's troop. (It was she who initiated him into the underground AK.)

In September 1941 Heniek cycled to Vilnius, Grodno, and Białystok as a courier for the Polish-Jewish underground. It was probably he who first brought back the news of the extermination of the Jews in Troki and Ponary. He was a close friend of Jurek Wilner, who frequently stayed with him and his wife Irena at 2a Podchorążych Street. (The apartment was also used as a hideout for Jews and an arms cache.) When Wilner, the ŻOB representative on the Polish side, was arrested, Heniek managed to spring him from the labor camp in Kawęczyn near Rembertów. Grabowski had a market stall with various wares (including bacon)[8] at the Kercelak market. After the annihilation of the ghetto, the stall was a prime rendezvous for ŻOB fighters in hiding across the Polish city.

After the war, Henryk Grabowski had an automobile workshop, and was later a taxi driver. He studied part-time at the polytechnic. (He was decorated with the Righteous Among the Nations medal in 1983. His wife Irena also received a medal.) He died in Warsaw in 1997.

Sara Granatsztajn was born in 1922 or 1924 in Warsaw. She attended the Jehudija Jewish girls' high school at 55 Długa Street. During her high school years, she became a member of Frajhajt. In 1940, she took part in the Dror seminar program at 34 Dzielna Street. On November 29, 1942, together with Dawid Szulman and Berl Brojde, she took part in the operation to execute Izrael First, a Gestapo agent.

In the January operation, Sara was rounded up on Muranowska Street with Tema Sznajderman and Lea Perlsztejn. They were probably killed in Treblinka. Chawka Folman remembered Sara from school and later from the ghetto.

---

8 Hence his pseudonym "Słoniniarz," which is derived from the Polish word for bacon, *słonina*.

She said that she was very wise, often blushed, and was in love with her elder brother Marek Folman.

Jurek Grasberg studied agronomy at the University of Warsaw before the war. His mother was a milliner and had a shop with smart hats. Jurek was a scoutmaster in the Polish scouting movement. Before he left the ghetto in March 1943, he worked at the post office with his wife Luba Zylberg, and Irka Gelblum.

After leaving, he went to live at 5 Pańska Street, in the ŻOB base on the Polish side of the wall. He cooperated closely with Aleksander Kamiński, the editor of the AK's *Biuletyn Informacyjny*. Jurek bought guns for the ghetto through his scouting and AK contacts. He wanted to organize a Scout group within the ŻOB, but Anielewicz would not allow it. Jurek had bad looks, so he did not leave his hiding-place for months on end. (Luba was already living with him.)

On August 1, 1944, when the Polish Warsaw rising broke out, Jurek was home alone. (Luba had gotten stuck in Saska Kępa.) When he heard shots, he boldly went out onto the street with a gun. He wanted to join the rising. A unit of the AK apparently apprehended him just outside the house on Pańska. They refused to cross-check his story that he was from the Jewish underground or his contacts with Kamiński from the Polish underground. They shot him, because he was a stranger, had a gun, and they thought he was a spy. Luba never had a photograph of Jurek.

Chana Grauman was brought up in a poor home on Pawia Street in Warsaw. There was a sewing room in their house, where Chana worked. She helped to support her elderly mother and sick sister. She was a member of a Shomer cell. After the *große Aktion* in the ghetto, she had employment in the Hallman workshop, and later at Toebbens' at 67 Nowolipki.

In April 1943, she fought on those premises in a Shomer group. Wounded, probably on April 22, she was unable to flee via the attics. Some boys from Gordonia: Chmielnicki, Fingerhut, and Fajgenblat, accompanied Chana and the wounded Szlomo Sufit to 76 Leszno Street, to the bunker which was known as the insurrectionist hospital. Chana did not manage to leave the ghetto via the sewers, and stayed with the wounded, with Tobcia Dawidowicz and Szlomo Sufit. Chana was twenty-one.

Mordechaj (Merdek) Growas was born in Warsaw in 1921. He was an instructor in a Warsaw Haszomer Hacair cell. On October 29, 1942, Merdek Growas, Elek Różański, and Margalit Landau, Shomer ŻOBists, carried out the execution of Jakub Lejkin, the deputy head of the Order Service, the Jewish police force in the ghetto. In the April uprising, Growas was the commander of a group in the central ghetto, in the region of Nalewki, Zamenhofa, and Miła. On May 10, he went out onto the other side of the wall.

Via Łomianki, he reached the Wyszków woods. He commanded a unit of ŻOB fighters that cooperated with the AK; those of its members whose names are known at least in part were Chagit Putermilch, Zandman Awraham, Joel, Izrael Krótki, Tamar, Berl Tasenkrojt or Taselkrojt, Julek Junghajzer, Izio Lewski, and Chaim Arbuz. When contact with the group was lost, and the Germans had not mentioned having discovered a unit of Jewish partisans, Antek Cukierman started to suspect that the Jews had been murdered by forest partisans from either the AK or the NSZ. He wrote a letter to Gen. Bór-Komorowski, the commander-in-chief of the AK. Apparently, he received some sort of answer. It may have been Growas's group, the group that was killed in Sadowne Węgrowskie.

Lejb Gruzalc was born in 1919. He lived in Warsaw. He was brought up in a Hasidic family. His grandfather prayed in the prayer house of Rabbi Twerski of Turzysk. Lejb was a member of the Cukunft's young printers' section.

In the April uprising, he was the commander of a Bund unit in the central ghetto. At first, they were barracked at 29 Zamenhofa. One of the ŻOB bases in the central ghetto was the bunker at 29 Miła. This was the billet used by the groups under Gruzalc, Rotblat, and Bryskin. On April 24, the house at 29 Miła was set on fire. The insurrectionists managed to evacuate, however. Three days later, Gruzalc and over a dozen other soldiers went back to 29 Miła. The Germans apparently found out about the insurgents' hideout from another Jew they had caught. They attacked the bunker with grenades. Lejb was the first to jump out, through a hole in the wall. He was hit by a bullet in the head and killed outright. He was twenty-four.

Icchak Grynbojm was born in Żyrardów in 1920. He was a member of Frajhajt. In the April uprising, he fought in the Dror group under Zachariasz Artsztajn. He did not make it out of the ghetto.

Jurek Grynszpan came from an intellectual home in Warsaw. He was a slender blond. And his breath whistled, Sławek Mirski remembered in 1951. Until January 18, 1943, he worked in Herman Brauer's workshop at 28–38 Nalewki. He was the commander of one of the four PPR groups in the ŻOB. His group carried out "exes" in the ghetto, but they had to abandon that mission, because other ŻOB members caught them sending money to Comrade Gomułka, Marek Edelman told me.

The day before the uprising, Grynszpan and a group of seven people reported to Marek Edelman and fought bravely on the brushmakers' premises. (Apparently, on April 19, his group was at 38 Świętojerska Street.) After that, in the central ghetto, Grynszpan's group staged a hunger strike, because they thought they had too few weapons—also something that Edelman remembered. On May 2, Jurek was badly wounded in the battle at the Provisioning Authority bunker at 30 Franciszkańska Street. A bullet pierced his lung. His comrades carried him into a courtyard somewhere between Nalewki and Zamenhofa Streets. Jurek Grynszpan died two days later. He was twenty-four or twenty-five.

Jakub Guterman was born in Warsaw. He was a member of Frajhajt. In 1942 he worked on the Czerniaków farm, and when that was liquidated at the end of the year, he returned to the ghetto. He lived in the Halutz commune at 34 Miła Street. In the April uprising, he fought in Zachariasz Artsztajn's group. He had a pistol of his own, and he fired from a balcony. He did not make it out of the ghetto. He was twenty-eight.

Henoch, Hanoch, Gutman was born in 1919, in the impoverished Łódź district of Bałuty. He was a teenager when he joined Frajhajt. He went to Warsaw with friends from the Borochow kibbutz in Łódź in the first weeks of the war. Later on in the ghetto, he worked in a detail: every morning, he went out with a group of Jews to work in the Okęcie district. He joined the Halutz commune at 34 Dzielna Street. Chawka Folman, who also lived on Dzielna, remembers that he was short, but good-looking, and loved to read.

In the summer of 1942, a group of several dozen Dror members was sent to Werbkowice, near Hrubieszów, to an agrarian farm. From there, the Halutzim were to have joined the partisans. Henoch Gutman was one of the organizers of that venture, and one of the few who returned from Werbkowice—the majority, arrested en route, or on arrival, in the sawmill there, were killed. In August 1942, he carried out a failed assassination attempt on Mieczysław Szmerling, the commandant of the Umschlagplatz.

Gutman fought in the first battles in the ghetto, in January 1943. Shortly before the April uprising, he and his group moved from the 'shops to the brushmakers' premises, swapping with Eliezer Geller. Seriously wounded at 30 Franciszkańska Street, he was unable to escape via the sewers. The Drorists moved him to Artsztajn's bunker, where he was left with a close girlfriend, Fejcze Rabow. It is not known how they died.

Kuba Gutrajman was a soldier in a left-wing group within the ŻOB. He was killed in the summer of 1943 fighting in a partisan unit near Łomża, with Szlomo Alterman and others.

Cypora Gutsztat was born in Warsaw, in a poor home. She was twelve when she joined Frajhajt. She went to school and prepared for emigration to Palestine. Together with others from the organization, she was accepted into one of the Dror fighting groups. In the April uprising, she fought in Henoch Gutman's group on the brushmakers' premises. She left the ghetto via the sewers on May 10. She was killed in the Wyszków woods while crossing the river Bug.

Miriam Hajnsdorf (Einsdorf) was born in 1913 in Warsaw, but until her late teens lived in Lublin. She attended a Polish school there. Her family moved to Warsaw in 1939. It was then that Miriam joined Haszomer Hacair. She studied in Słonim. In September 1939, she had plans to emigrate to Eretz Israel—her cases were already packed.

In the Warsaw ghetto, she was in a pair with Josef Kapłan, and lived with him at 46 Nowolipki Street. She was a Haszomer Hacair activist, along with Anielewicz, Kapłan, Tosia Altman, Szmuel Bresław, Juda Wengrower, and Arie Wilner. It was they who spearheaded the organization when it went underground. Miriam often traveled to other ghettos as a Shomer courier. She corresponded by letter with representatives of Jewish organizations across Europe. She was a representative for Haszomer Hacair in the ŻKN. In the April uprising, she fought in Szlomo Winogron's group on the Schilling 'shop premises. It is known that she did not manage to escape the ghetto.

Halina belonged to Haszomer Hacair. She took part in the April uprising. On April 24, she attempted to leave the ghetto via the sewers with Tuwia Borzykowski. (He was the only person who recorded her forename; nobody recorded her surname.) Halina was arrested by police at the manhole cover. It is not known where or when she was killed.

Aron Halzband was born in Żyrardów in 1916. His father was a tailor. All the children—five sons and a daughter—worked with their father in his workshop. Before the war, Aron was a member of Frajhajt, and in the ghetto, he joined the Dror fighters. In the April uprising, he fought in Berl Braude's group in the central ghetto. He was killed on May 8 in the bunker at 18 Miła Street.

Itkie Hejman fought in the April uprising in one of the PPR groups. She may have been under the command of Heniek Kawe. She was standing on guard outside the bunker at 74 Leszno Street when the Germans discovered the shelter and started to pump gas underground. That was on May 7. Bernard Borg recorded that Itkie Hejman shot herself at that point.

Rut Hejman was born in 1923 in Warsaw. She lived in the Jewish district, at 15 Nowolipki. She was a member of Haszomer Hacair. She was slender, not very tall, and had a delicate, pretty face. In the April uprising, she was part of Merdek Growas's fighting group, and was a courier for the ŻOB commandant, Mordechaj Anielewicz. She was most likely killed in the bunker on Miła Street.

Szymon Heller was born in 1920 in Kraków and was brought up in a wealthy intellectual family. He grew up in an assimilated household in nearby Wolbrom, and the family later moved to Warsaw. Szymon attended the Ascola boys' high school and was a cultural activist in Haszomer Hacair. The black-haired, handsome youth was popular with his peers.

In the ghetto, he worked in the education department of the ŻTOS, the Jewish social welfare office, and after the *große Aktion* in the 'shop run by Aleksander Landau, who was well disposed toward the Shomerim.

Shortly before the uprising, a death sentence was carried out on Pilotka, whom Antek Cukierman suspected of passing on information to the Germans. Aron Karmi remembered that it was Heller who carried out the execution, in the prison at 56 Leszno Street. (Others remembered that Pilotka was shot by Beniamin Wald.)

Szymon Heller was a good shot, so he was the only person in his group to have a semi-automatic rifle. On April 22, or maybe it was April 26, the Germans set fire to the house at 76 Leszno. The area commander, Eliezer Geller, ordered a retreat to 67 Nowolipie. The boys tied several sheets together and slid down them from the third floor. Beneath the window there was a garbage heap. Szymon was still firing on target. He apparently kept his promise to himself that he would not die until he had shot five Germans dead. He was the last to jump. He died on the garbage heap. He was twenty-three.

Adek Himelfarb was born in Falenica near Warsaw. His father, Herszel Himelfarb, was a Bund activist. (He survived the war and died in New York in 1964.) Adek had a sister (one that we know of). Hendusia, Adek's sister, had light braids and Bundist ideals. She took a job in the Medem sanatorium in 1940. In August 1942 the Germans deported the children from the sanatorium—there were maybe one hundred fifty of them—to the gas chambers in Treblinka. Hendusia didn't want to leave the children; she went with them so that they would be less afraid. (Marek Edelman told me about Hendusia.)

Adek Himelfarb stayed in the ghetto. In January 1943 he joined Jakub Fajgenblat's Gordonia group. Shot in the leg two weeks before the uprising, he left via the sewers and emerged on Ogrodowa on April 29. He is known to have been in hiding in his aunt's apartment for some time. The circumstances of his death are not known.

Adolf Hochberg was born in 1922 and came from Leipzig. He was not very tall, had light-colored eyes, was not good-looking, and spoke Yiddish with a German accent, Masza Glajtman-Putermilch remembered. He had come with a group of German youth to the kibbutz in Grochów back before the war broke out. In the ghetto, he joined forces with the Drorists.

During the uprising, he fought in Henoch Gutman's group on the brushmakers' premises. On May 9, he went into the sewers on Franciszkańska Street with a group of around eighty insurrectionists. In the main shaft beneath Prosta Street, it was cramped and airless. A dozen or more ŻOBists moved into smaller sewers. When the manhole cover opened and it was time to climb out, Adolf Hochberg and Szlamek Szuster were given the order to bring those people back. Adolf, Szlamek, and the rest did not return in time. They were killed an hour, maybe two, later, as they were climbing out of the sewer. Adolf Hochberg was twenty-one.

Dawid Hochberg was born in Siedlce on July 19, 1925. His father, Szlomo, was a bookbinder. Though religious, he was actively involved in the work of Poalej Syjon Left. Shortly after his son's birth, he emigrated to Palestine, and in 1941 he was in America. Dawid's mother, Dina Friedman, was a daughter of one of the Gerer Hasidim. In Siedlce, and later, from 1930, in Warsaw, she was a teacher in Bundist CISzO schools, and also ran a TOZ (Healthcare Society) children's home.

She and her son lived at 20 Nowolipki Street. Dawid attended the Laor boys' high school at 2a Nalewki Street and won a scholarship for talented pupils. He was a member of Skif and conducted ideological disputes with young Zionists at his school.

In the ghetto, Dawid lived with his mother at 43 Nowolipki Street. At 36 Krochmalna, there was a school and soup kitchen for Bundist children. Marek Edelman remembers that the young people from Skif put on plays for them twice a week. Mania Kac directed, Pola Lipszyc sang, and Dawid Hochberg acted. And that the boy was still almost a child, and his mother didn't want to let him join the ŻOB, wanting to protect him.

Hochberg's group was formed at the last moment, two, maybe three days before the uprising. Dawid was appointed its commander in the central ghetto. He fought in the area of Dzika and Miła. Masza Glajtman-Putermilch remembered differently than Marek Edelman. That the young Dawid was a soldier in her group, under Lejb Gruzalc. But both Marek and Masza remember that he was brave. In broad daylight, he and Berl Braude led several hundred people from the shelter buried under the rubble at 37 Miła to 7 Miła.

After that, they were at 29 Miła. There were five fighting groups in that bunker. (It was a large one. The insurrectionists had a radio there, and stored gunpowder.) On April 24, the Germans set the house on fire. The civilians were taken elsewhere, but the ŻOB returned a few days later. The Germans came again on April 27. (Apparently, it was another Jew who denounced the insurgents.) The Germans threw grenades into the bunker, but the ŻOB fighters fired back at them. Lejb Gruzalc was the first to be killed.

Wounded, Dawid gave his gun to his friend, Berl Tasenkrojt, and barricaded the entrance to the bunker with his own body. This bought time for both the insurgents and the civilians to escape, because it is hard to pull a dead man out of a narrow opening. Dawid Hochberg was eighteen. (It is not known how Dawid's mother, Dina Friedman, was killed.)

Zalman Holand was born in Warsaw in 1921. Like his father, he was a mechanic. He was a member of Akiba. He joined the ŻOB after the *große Aktion* when his mother and brother were killed. He worked in the Steyr und Daimler munitions factory outside the ghetto, where he mounted a sabotage operation, damaging hundreds of rifle bores. (The factory's director, a German, was apparently executed by firing squad for that reason.)

In the April uprising, Zalman fought in Dawid Nowodworski's group on the Toebbens-Schultz premises. He was killed there.

Abram (Awraham) Horowic (Horowicz) was born in Ostrowiec Kielecki on June 12, 1924. His father, Szmul Mendel, and mother, Chana Cukierman, lived with their children at 42 Rynek Square. Abram attended the Mizrachi school, and in 1936 graduated from elementary school no. 5.

Abram went to the Warsaw ghetto to fight. In the April uprising he was in a Haszomer Hacair group. On April 29, he left via the sewers, from the 'shops. Dawid Sztajn remembered that when he was in the attic on Ogrodowa Street, Awraham came up to him to say goodbye. He said he had to go back into the ghetto. He probably went (with Regina Fudem and Szlomo Baczyński) for the others. It is not known how or where he died. Abram was nineteen.

Icuś was an insurrectionist whose comrades knew him only by his forename. He was a member of Akiba in Warsaw. In the April uprising, he fought in Beniamin Wald's group in the area of the Toebbens-Schultz workshops. He was wounded by a splinter of a grenade.

On April 29, 1943, the insurrectionists were making their way to 56 Leszno Street. From there, they were to leave the ghetto via the sewers. The group Icuś was in didn't make it on time. He was most probably among those whom Regina

Fudem and Szlomo Baczyński went back for. It is not known where or when Icuś was killed. He was nineteen or twenty.

Zygmunt Igła—nobody remembered his surname. He was known as "Igła" [Needle] because he was the son of a tailor. Before the war, he worked in a store, and was an activist for the merchants' trade union. He was a member of Cukunft-Szturm, the Bundist defense groups. His entire large family was killed during the *große Aktion* in August 1942.

In the April uprising, Zygmunt fought in the group under Welwł Rozowski on the premises of the 'shops. On April 29, he left the ghetto via the sewers in a group of forty insurrectionists. The majority of them joined partisan units in the Wyszków woods. Tall, broad-shouldered, and well-built, he looked like a strapping Pole, and could thus risk traveling to Warsaw more than others.

In the fall of 1943, he was arrested. He was locked up in Pawiak prison, but they managed to buy him out. He lived for a while at Śliska Street, though he often returned to the woods. In January 1944, he went to Warsaw with Jakub Fajgenblat and Guta Kawenoki. All three briefly found shelter with Jabłoński, the janitor of the house that had entrances at both 6 Grzybowski Square and 14 Próżna Street. The courier Bronka Feinmesser maintained contact with them. Jabłoński, the janitor, was working with the AK. One day, the Gestapo knocked at his door. It appears that it was by chance, in the course of the raid, that they discovered the ŻOBists' hideout. Zygmunt Igła was shot dead in the chest where he was hiding, Marek Edelman said. They were all killed: Guta Kawenoki, Jakub Fajgenblat, Zygmunt Igła, and the janitor Antoni Jabłoński.

Mira Izbicka was born in Włocławek in 1921. She was eleven when she joined Haszomer Hacair. Her elder sister had emigrated to Eretz Israel, and Mira was preparing to go. After the outbreak of war, she, her younger sister, and her mother fled to Warsaw. In the April uprising she fought in a group with her organization. She died in unknown circumstances.

Szoszana Jakubowicz came from Nowy Dwór Mazowiecki. She belonged to Frajhajt. She worked on the farm in Czerniaków, and later, in the ghetto, lived with the Drorists at 34 Miła. In the April uprising she fought in Zachariasz Artsztajn's group. She never made it out of the ghetto.

Adek, Edek Jankielewicz. In the April uprising he fought in the Bund group under Lejb Gruzalc in the central ghetto. On May 10, he left the ghetto via the sewers and joined the partisans on the river Bug. Somebody remembered that Adek was killed in an engagement with the Germans some 4 miles from the town of Brok. Elsewhere, it is recorded that he fought in Janek Szwarcfus's group, and after an operation on the railroad tracks in Urle, the partisans hid out on the property of a forester called Bobrowski, who turned them over to the Germans. Almost all of them were killed, Adek Jankielewicz among them.

Masza Glajtman-Putermilch remembered differently again. Adek was wounded and in hiding in a large underground dugout (supported from within by wood and concealed from the outside with moss). Also in hiding with the wounded Adek was Rywa from the PPR, and someone else. It was late fall. The Germans discovered the dugout and killed them all. Someone probably denounced them, Masza said. How did she know that it was Adek Jankielewicz there? Because Adek had the most amazing woolen socks, very warm. And when the boys went there afterwards, they found them. But he wasn't identifiable by his face because it had been pecked clean by birds. And also—he had two photographs in his wallet, and that's how he was identified. Afterwards, Masza carried those photographs in her bra, and took them with her to Palestine. Adek Jankielewicz is buried in section 31 of the Jewish cemetery in Warsaw. His name is carved into the matzevah alongside those of the other members of Szwarcfus's group.

Józiek Jarost was a PPR courier between the ghetto and the city outside its walls. He was around twenty when he came to the Legiec family's apartment at 3 Szczygla Street before the uprising. He usually joined groups of workers on detail, or if he had to go about the city alone, he often bandaged up his face. His bad looks—very dark eyes and hair—were balanced out by his superb Polish and bravado.

He is known to have left the ghetto via the sewers on April 29 and to have fought in a partisan unit somewhere near Wyszków. He was wounded in the neck during a skirmish with the Germans somewhere on a forest track near Wyszków. His comrades patched him up and left him in a makeshift shelter. When they returned, two days later, Józiek lay dead, with his head cut off.

Lejb Jaszyński (Jasiński) was born in Warsaw. He was a member of Frajhajt. He worked on the Czerniaków farm. In the April uprising, he fought in Henoch Gutman's Dror group on the brushmakers' premises. On May 3, he defended 30 Franciszkańska Street. He was killed on May 10 as he attempted to climb out of the sewer on Prosta Street. He was twenty-two.

Michał Jaworski, Bronisław, Borys Najkrug, was born on July 12, 1911, in Baranowicze. He had seven siblings. His father, Max Najkrug, worked in a sawmill, and also enjoyed a certain standing in his synagogue. In the mid-1920s, the family moved to Warsaw. Borys went to France to study at a polytechnic. In 1935, he graduated from the officer cadet school in Zambrów; in April 1939 he married Celina Tandetnik of Radom, and they moved to 30 Prusa Street.

Borys took part in the defense of the Polish capital in September 1939, was taken prisoner, and escaped. In October he and his wife managed to reach the Russian-occupied East. They moved around between Białystok, Słonim, Baranowicze, and Lwów, eventually reaching the Radom ghetto. (And there Borys's wife and their baby son Robert stayed.)

Borys managed to reach the Warsaw ghetto in June 1942, where he lived with his parents on Dzielna Street. He was an instructor for the PPR fighting groups of five in the Toebbens-Schultz 'shop yards, and produced explosives, because he was a chemist by profession. His group was barracked on Franciszkańska Street. They wrote flyers on how to jump trains and made small bombs: lightbulbs filled with sulfuric acid.

On the first day of the uprising, Borys Najkrug happened to be in the bunker of the Jewish Military Union (ŻZW) at 7 Muranowska Street. In vain he pleaded with them to admit him into the ranks of their fighters. In his testimony, he wrote that by April 21, there were no longer any ŻZW soldiers at 7 Muranowska.

Najkrug and a group of other young people began to search for a way out of the ghetto. After a few days, they found the blocked-up entrance to the tunnel in the cellar of that house. They worked extremely hard to reopen it. Around twenty of them managed to get out onto the other side, into the building at 6 Muranowska Street. On the fifth floor they found a large group of Jews in hiding in an apartment with several rooms. They had a considerable quantity of arms. These were almost certainly the ŻZW soldiers who had left via the same tunnel a few days previously.

The next day, April 30, the house was surrounded by Germans. Some of them defended themselves. Many of them were killed on the spot; many of the others were deported to Treblinka. Bronisław Najkrug and a few others were taken to the Befehlsstelle, to the ghetto. A few days later, the Germans sent a second transport from the Umschlagplatz. Borys jumped the train just outside Michalin and returned to Warsaw. (His parents left the ghetto with the assistance of Włodzimierz Poleszuk, who then denounced them; they were killed in 1943.)

Borys Najkrug (from 1953 Michał Jaworski) survived the war. From 1944 he was an officer in the Polish People's Army (LWP) but was fired in 1968. He died on May 10, 2000, in Warsaw.

Jechiel fought in a Haszomer Hacair group in the April uprising. He may have been a member of the group under Merdek Growas. It has been recorded that it was he who fired from the automatic rifle, that he attacked the Germans as they entered the ghetto. He was the first insurrectionist killed on April 19 in the central ghetto. (Aron Karmi and Chaim Frymer wrote that Merdek Growas administered the coup de grâce to the badly wounded Jechiel.) Nobody recorded, nobody remembered Jechiel's surname.

Jeremiasz was a member of Haszomer Hacair. On April 24, he, Tadek Borzykowski, and other insurrectionists were searching for a way out of the ghetto. They made it to the other side via the sewers. Jeremiasz was shot dead by the manhole cover by a Polish police officer.

Joel of Haszomer Hacair was killed in the Wyszków woods with Merdek Growas's group. (It is not actually known whether he was in a ŻOB group during the April uprising.)

Julek Junghajzer was born in Warsaw in 1923. He was ten years old, when in a Hasidic cap and filthy, greasy kapote he first went to the Skif club at 29 Karmelicka Street. The other children didn't want to let the little Hasid in. Sometime later, the shy, grubby little boy went back to Karmelicka. He grew and studied in the organization. He started work at a young age, and after work he would go to the club and give classes for the youngest children.

In the Warsaw ghetto he distributed Bundist news bulletins and worked on a detail outside the ghetto. After the January operation, he went to live with a Bund fighting group at 32 Świętojerska Street. They were all preparing the defense. He worked in Michał Klepfisz's "factory" making incendiary bottles.

During the uprising, he fought bravely in Jurek Błones' group on the brushmakers' premises.

On May 10, he left the ghetto through the sewers. He reached the Wyszków woods via Łomianki. There, he was in Merdek Growas's unit. Julek found out that there were Bundists in the partisan detachment on the other side of the Bug. He found Chana Krysztal and Gabryś Fryszdorf, but they did not want to leave their group and join Merdek's. It has been recorded that Julek returned to Growas's detachment, and all trace of them was lost. Perhaps Julek was killed with Merdek Growas's group, or perhaps in the operation in Urle with Szwarcfus's group. His name is carved into the matzevah in the Jewish cemetery in Warsaw.

Efraim Juszkiewicz was a tailor and an activist in the youth section of the Igła Workers' Union. He was a member of the Bundist group Cukunft-Szturm. In the April uprising, he was in Welwł Rozowski's unit on the premises of the 'shops. On April 29 he made his way out, via the sewers, onto the other side of the wall. He fought in a partisan group near Wyszków. He was killed a few miles outside Mińsk Mazowiecki during an operation organized by the partisans.

Samuel Juszkiewicz was Efraim's brother. In the April uprising he probably fought in the same Bundist group in the 'shop yards. According to records, he was killed in Urle with Janek Szwarcfus's group. His name is carved into the matzevah in the Jewish cemetery in Warsaw.

Salke Kamień fought in Aron Bryskin's PPR group in the central ghetto. She was killed on May 8 in the bunker at 18 Miła. She was twenty years old.

Izrael Kanał, Mietek, was brought up in a wealthy, religious family in Bydgoszcz. He attended high school there and was active in the Akiba movement. In 1941, the Germans resettled them to Warsaw. Both his parents died very shortly after arriving in the ghetto. Izrael and his younger brother Salo lived in the Akiba kibbutz at 10 Nalewki. Izrael became a Jewish policeman.

When the *große Aktion* was launched on July 22, 1942, Izrael Kanał returned his truncheon and cap. At the founding meeting of the July ŻOB, Izrael decided to use his police cap only for Jewish underground operations. (He managed to get many people off the Umschlagplatz in the summer of 1942.)

The ŻOB passed its first death sentence in late summer 1942: on Józef Szeryński, the commandant of the Jewish Order Service. On August 21, Izrael Kanał rang Szeryński's doorbell. On the first shot, his pistol jammed. His second shot grazed Szeryński's cheek. Kanał had to flee. He rode off on his bike toward Nalewki Street. (People in the ghetto said that the assassin was a Pole, most likely from the PPS.) Izrael taught future insurrectionists how to handle their guns.

On January 20, 1943, the Germans launched an operation to liquidate the 'shops. Izrael Kanał and a few other armed youths fired the first shots on Nowolipie. The next time that Izrael used his policeman's cap was on the eve of the April uprising, in a raid on the Judenrat kitty at Zamenhofa Street. (The kitty was empty, so they arrested the son of the head of the Judenrat, Lichtenbaum. They got a considerable sum of money from the boy's terrified father: in the region of two hundred fifty thousand zlotys.)

The ŻOB commanders decided that Izrael Kanał, rather than Anielewicz, would be the commander in the central ghetto. This would free Anielewicz up, they thought, to move about the ghetto at will.

Izrael Kanał left the ghetto on May 10. In August, he returned to Warsaw from the woods, because he was sick. He had bad looks and no apartment, his friend Hela Schüpper remembered. He went nowhere without his pistol and did not want to leave the city. He was very depressed, and wanted to go back to the partisans, but that was not possible. Resigned, he reported to the Hotel Polski. By the time a hiding-place in Warsaw was found for him, he was no longer on Długa Street. In August 1943, the Germans dispatched a further transport of Jews from the Hotel Polski to Bergen-Belsen. Izrael Kanał was twenty-two when he was murdered in Auschwitz.

Ari Karliner. In the April uprising he was a soldier in the Shomer group under Szlomo Winogron in the Toebbens-Schultz workshops. It is not known where or when he was killed.

Herszl Kawe (Heniek, Hesiek, Kawa) was born in 1913 in Warsaw. His father was a barber on Nowolipie Street. Heniek attended a commercial school and worked in a drugstore. His political sympathies lay with the left. He became involved with the retailers' trade union at 5 Zamenhofa Street. Ahead of the uprising in the ghetto, he led a group of future fighters on "exes."

After that, he was a PPR group commander in the 'shop yards. He was badly wounded on April 27, when his base, the bunker at 74 Leszno, was flooded by the Germans. Hesiek gave his watch and his pistol to his friend, Aron Alter.

His comrades carried him to Nowolipie Street. Many of the insurrectionists from Hesiek's group were killed that day: Zocha Brzezińska, Chawa Bonder, Tosia Cebularz, Sara Klajman, Halinka Rochman, Aron Alter, Lejb Czerniakower, Adek Rozenfeld, Comrade Ryba, Lew Rudnicki—and their commander, Herszl Kawe.

Guta Kawenoki was born into a wealthy family that had moved from Białystok to Łódź. Guta's father was a textile factory owner and traded in cottage labor output, and her mother was a pharmacist. Guta was close friends with Anna Lanota (then Hania Rottenberg), and they attended the Zionist high school on Piramowicza Street together. Guta was older than Hania; she may have been born in 1913. She was short, and very joyful, Anna Lanota remembered. Guta worked for a dental technician and was active in the local Gordonia cell.

In 1940, she went to Warsaw. She joined the ŻOB along with friends from her prewar organization. Her group, under Jakub Fajgenblat, was barracked on the brushmakers' premises before the uprising. Later on, they fought in the area of the Toebbens-Schultz workshops. On the first day, they fired from the fourth floor at 76 Leszno Street. When the insurrectionists from the area of the 'shops left the ghetto via the sewers on April 29, Eliezer Geller ordered Guta to stay with the wounded. She cried bitterly and begged him to let her go. Lea Korn stayed with the wounded instead because she wanted to stay.

Around forty insurrectionists, Guta among them, reached the Wyszków woods. For a while, her group was in the region of Czerwony Bór on the river Narew. In late 1943, Guta fell ill, and had to return to Warsaw. She went into hiding in a shelter offered by Jabłoński, the janitor at 14 Próżna Street, with her commander from the ghetto, Jakub Fajgenblat, and the Bundist Zygmunt Igła. The Gestapo apparently found the address while investigating activity by the underground AK, with which Jabłoński had links. The three ghetto insurgents tried to defend themselves. But all three were killed outright. Guta may have been thirty.

Rachela Kirszenbojm came from Warsaw. In the ghetto, she lived in the Halutz commune at 34 Dzielna, and on the farm in Czerniaków outside Warsaw as long as the farm existed, until November 1942.

In the April uprising, she was in a Dror unit. Later, she fought in the Wyszków woods. She was probably killed in Czerwony Bór on the river Narew. She was twenty-two. A matzevah bearing Rachela's name was erected in the Jewish cemetery in Warsaw in 1945.

Sigi Kirszner, Zygi Kirszenbojm, fled Germany for Poland in 1938. In the Warsaw ghetto, he lived in the Halutz commune at 34 Dzielna, and then, for a few months, he lived and worked on the farm in Czerniaków. In the April uprising he was in the Dror group in the Toebbens-Schultz 'shop yards. He left the ghetto via the sewers on April 29 and went into hiding with several others in the bunker at 29 Ogrodowa Street. On May 6, the bunker was discovered; he was the only one who managed to escape. His next hiding place was in the Praga district, in an abandoned celluloid factory. He was killed on May 24, when fire broke out in the factory. He was twenty-eight.

Sara Klajman (Klajnman) was a member of a left-wing Jewish fighting group. She fought on the premises of the Toebbens-Schultz workshops in Heniek Kawe's group. It has been recorded that she was killed in flooded the bunker at 74 Leszno Street along with the other insurrectionists there. Elsewhere, she is reported to have gotten out via the tunnel from 74 Leszno into the cellar of the house at 71 Leszno, but to have been caught by the Germans shortly afterwards and deported to Treblinka. (The tunnel under Leszno Street was dug by the PPR before the uprising. The entrance was via concealed trapdoors in the cellar. There were several rooms in the tunnel, equipped with water, gas, and even electricity.) It is not known where and how Sara was killed. She was twenty years old.

Ziuta Klajnman (Kleinman) was brought up in the wealthy family of a Warsaw button-factory owner on Okopowa Street. She was a student at the University of Warsaw. She associated with young people with communist leanings who defended Jewish students' rights. She was killed in the April uprising fighting in one of the four PPR groups in the ŻOB. She was twenty-six.

Henoch (Heniek) Klajnwajs, Michałek, was born in 1917 into a wealthy, assimilated Warsaw family. He joined Gordonia quite by chance and became fanatical about Eretz Israel. Heniek dreamed of living by the sea, so he went to do his *hakhshara* in Gdynia.

And then he was in the ghetto. He sold lemonade—colored water with a little saccharine—and belonged to a Gordonia group in the ŻOB. On April 20, he and Meir Szwarc were escorting the courier Chańcia Płotnicka out of the ghetto. They were stopped by some Germans. Michałek did not lose his head and offered to take the Germans to a bunker where they would find Jews in hiding. When they entered the narrow entranceway at 74 Leszno, Michałek shot at one of the Germans, and all three insurrectionists managed to escape. (Michałek was strong, brave, and had good ideas, Aron Karmi said.)

Heniek Klajnwajs left the 'shops on April 29. He was in the Wyszków woods several weeks. He wanted to go back to Warsaw to get to Hungary, and then to Palestine. It is known that he was killed with Dawid Nowodworski's group. It is not known in what circumstances.

Icchak Klepfisz was the name of one of the April insurrectionists whom the commanders wrote on the list of murdered soldiers of the Jewish Fighting Organization. They gave him as having belonged to Dror. I found no information about Icchak Klepfisz.

Michał Klepfisz was born on April 17, 1913, in Warsaw. His father had been a Hasid in his youth, but later turned away from religion and joined the Bund. His mother was a teacher of Polish language and literature in public schools. Michał was brought up in a Bundist home, at 30 Świętojerska Street. As a student at the Warsaw Polytechnic, he ran the athletics section of the Bund's sporting union, Morgensztern.

After the outbreak of the war, he got out to Lwów, and on to Donetsk. When he returned to Warsaw he lived on the Polish side of the wall. There he called himself Tadeusz Mecner. He often went into the ghetto. As a polytechnic graduate, he knew how to make explosives, and he had "factories" producing incendiary bottles in the Dubiel family's apartment on Franciszkańska, at 3 Górnośląska, and at 48 Pańska. Some of the materials that he devised were also produced inside the ghetto. One time, he was arrested near 48 Pańska. He ended up on a transport to Treblinka. He managed to jump the train, however, and return to Warsaw.

Midday, February. Flour smugglers are at work by the wall on Parys Square. Someone whistles, a few boys run up to the wall, the flour people vanish into thin air. For a moment there is no one to be seen. Michał climbs astride the wall and begins to throw huge packages down into the ghetto. Within ten minutes, the boys took receipt of two thousand liters of gasoline and kerosene, and tens of kilograms of potassium chloride. The next day, three fighting groups were making incendiary bottles.

On the day of his thirtieth birthday, April 17, 1943, Michał bought a revolver. He got into the ghetto with his gun. And then, when the uprising broke out, he didn't want to go back out. He was in Jurek Błones' Bund group on the brushmakers' premises. On April 20, his group was surrounded in the attic of a house on Świętojerska. "We'll all be killed if we don't hack ourselves a way out!" Michał said, and without waiting, he took the machine-gun fire raining down on them from behind a chimney flue on himself. Jurek's group made it through to the neighboring attic. Michał's body was found by his comrades that evening, riddled with bullets.

Michał Klepfisz was the first insurrectionist killed in that area. They buried him in the courtyard. They buried him because he was the first, Kazik Ratajzer said. In YIVO in New York there is a copy of the certificate of the Order of Virtuti Militari, Silver Cross, awarded to Klepfisz. Majus Nowogrodzki wrote that this should be stressed.

Juda (Jehuda) Koński was born on January 1, 1922, in Siedlce. His father was a devout tailor. Juda attended a Tarbut high school. In the ghetto he was in the Gordonia fighting unit that was barracked on the corner of Dzika and Stawki. Juda was in a pair with Lea Korn. Shortly before the April uprising, Juda Koński and Szymon Lewental organized a shipment of guns into the ghetto. They were caught by the wall mid-operation and were tortured viciously for several days at the Befehlsstelle. They both died from their wounds. They did not give their comrades away.

Aron Korensztajn was a librarian before the war. He was initiated into the ŻOB after January 1943 by Sara Żogel. He, Mirski, Folman, and some others dug the tunnel from Wałowa Street out onto Nalewki, because Polish aid was expected to come from Nalewki.

In the April uprising, he and Mirski were responsible for the shelter at 2a Wałowa Street. He fought in Jurek Grynszpan's PPR group on the brushmakers' premises. Sławek Mirski remembered that the Germans caught Aron and deported him to a camp. Aron Korensztajn was a little over thirty in 1943.

Lea Korn (Korun) was born in Łódź in 1918. She was still a teenager when she left to live in Tomaszów to do her *hakhshara* with Gordonia. She studied Hebrew diligently, because she very much wanted to live in Palestine.

In the Warsaw ghetto she took care of children. Before the uprising, she went to live in the Gordonia commune at the intersection of Dzika and Stawki. After that, during the uprising, she fought with her group on the Toebbens-Schultz premises.

On April 29, the insurrectionists left that area via the sewers. Lea decided to stay with the wounded—Chana Grauman, Szlomo Sufit, and Tobcia Dawidowicz—in the bunker at 76 Leszno Street. She herself volunteered to her commander, Eliezer Geller. (Her boyfriend, Juda Koński, had been murdered a few weeks before the uprising.) Aron Chmielnicki remembered how bravely Lea climbed through the stove into that hiding place.

Alma Kornblum (Kerenbrum), Elma, Karolina, was brought up in a rich family on Nalewki Street, in the heart of Warsaw's Jewish district. In 1937 she joined Haszomer Hacair, and it was there that she took the name Alma. She sang and drew beautifully. She and Lodzia Hamersztajn belonged to the Tel Amal kibbutz at 23 Nalewki. Lodzia said of her that she was popular, respected, and had naturally pink-flushed cheeks.

In the ghetto, she looked after children in courtyard kindergartens. In the April uprising she fought in the Shomer group under Dawid Nowodworski on the premises of the 'shops. On April 23, Alma's friends found her in the attic of the house at 76 Leszno. She was twenty-two.

Lea Korngold was killed on April 22 in the Toebbens-Schultz 'shop yards. Only Aron Chmielnicki remembered her name.

Hela Kożuch (Farbman) was born in Pruszków in 1922. Her father was a fairly rich merchant. The family lived on Prusa Street, and Hela attended a Polish public elementary school, Hela Szuster remembered.

In February 1941, after the liquidation of the Pruszków ghetto, the family moved to the ghetto in Warsaw. Hela worked with the Halutzim on the farm in Czerniaków. She was a member of a Dror fighting group. Hela's surname has been forgotten, because she was always known as "Kożuch [sheepskin]," because of the coat in which she arrived from Pruszków. It is not known where or how she was killed. She was probably left behind in the ghetto with Artsztajn and other Dror fighters.

Izrael Krótki was a member of Haszomer Hacair. In the April uprising, he fought in the central ghetto. He was killed in the Wyszków woods with Merdek Growas's group.

Chana Krysztal-Fryszdorf was born on March 22, 1920, in Warsaw. Her grandfather was a devout man who traded in animal hides, which he imported from deepest Russia to his store. Her father abandoned his religion and became a  teacher. He was friendly with Jewish writers including Peretz, Nimberg, and Brenner. He married his cousin Etta Lothe and established a manufactory producing summer shoes known as *"bosaki"* [barefoot shoes]. They had two daughters and two sons. The whole family lived at 33 Gęsia Street. Chana and her siblings attended CISzO schools, and belonged to Skif and then to Cukunft, because they were a Bundist family. Chana learned dressmaking on courses at the ORT.

In the ghetto she got together with Gabryś Fryszdorf, a friend from her prewar Skif days. She worked with other Bundists in the Roerich 'shop on Smocza. Their leader was Welwł Rozowski. Shortly before the uprising, Rozowski's group took over a two-room apartment on the top floor at 56 Nowolipie. Chana recorded that they made incendiary bottles and sang a lot there.

On April 19, Chana was on guard. When the Germans entered the ghetto via Smocza Street, the Bundists and the Halutzim took up positions in the attics and at the windows on the top floors on Smocza. They attacked with their bottles. They held out in the ghetto until May 10. They left via the sewers and were in the Wyszków woods together.

In July 1944, shortly after Gabryś's death, Chana went back to Warsaw from the woods. Until the Polish Warsaw rising in August, she remained in hiding with several others at 24 Rakowiecka Street. When the rising broke out, the landlady threw the Jews out onto the street. Chana was arrested by the Gestapo. As a prisoner on Szucha Avenue, she cleared away the bodies of the dead—and in the confusion on the street, she managed to escape. Miraculously, she found some other ŻOBists.

In September, in a cellar occupied by the insurrectionists, and with a little care from Bernard Goldsztajn, she gave birth to a son, whom she named Gabryś. After the rising, she left Warsaw with the Poles. She was taken in by a peasant as the widow of a Polish soldier and saw the war out in his house.

She spent a few months in Łódź. In 1946, she emigrated to America via Sweden. And there she met up with her sister Szyfra Mendelsund, her husband, Henoch Mendelsund, and their children. In 1952 they were joined by their brother Salomon Kryształ. And together they formed a family (in the words of Szyfra, Chana's sister.) For thirty years, Chana was a secretary at the YIVO Institute for Jewish Research, in New York. She died in 1989.

Krzaczek, Kostek (Władysław Gaik), was born in 1912. It is not known what school he went to or what kind of a family he was from. Apparently, his father was a Pole who had been exiled to Siberia. Apparently, Krzaczek was a policeman before the war.

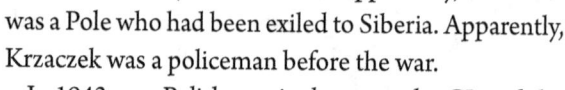

In 1943, as a Polish courier between the GL and the ŻOB, he helped to get the insurrectionists out of the ghetto. He accompanied both groups—the group from April 29 and that from May 10—on their journey to Łomianki. He helped to rescue some eighty people.

In June 1943, he was appointed a captain of the GL. He was dubbed Krzaczek [bush] because he was short and stocky. He had a short moustache and eyes that invited trust. The ŻOB knew of his good contacts with the underworld, the police, and the underground. Krzaczek was fast, brave, and a loner; he had no family. That was how Antek Cukierman remembered him. Jovial, hot-tempered, and a great risk-taker, he was unstinting in sacrifice. That was the description of him given by Comrade Legiec, who had known him for years.

Krzaczek was suspected of collaborating with the Germans. He allegedly denounced Icchak Windman ("Lala"), a ŻOB fighter from Częstochowa who was killed on his way to Skarżysko to pick up some guns in July 1943. He was suspected by both the Jews in the ŻOB and the Poles from the AL. The AL sentenced him to death. Then, Krzaczek disappeared. In late 1943, Kazik Ratajzer met him on the street. Krzaczek was destitute and terrified, gave no explanations, and merely asked Kazik for cigarettes.

It has been recorded that he was third on the lists of hostages shot in October 1943. The information has also survived that he was shot at the Kripo precinct on Zielna because he went to pull out some Jews who had been arrested. (He allegedly had NSDAP papers.) In fact, it is not known whether Krzaczek was working for the Germans. And it is not known how he died. It is known that without Krzaczek, it would have been impossible to get eighty people out of the ghetto.

Margalit Landau, Emilka, was born in Warsaw in 1926. Her father, Aleksander Lejb Landau, had been the coproprietor of a furniture factory before the war. In the ghetto, its German owner appointed him manager of the factory. The OBW carpentry 'shop was at 30 Gęsia Street. Thanks to Margalit's father, who employed many Shomerim, the 'shop became a hub for the ghetto underground.

Margalit was herself a member of Haszomer Hacair. She was a brave girl. She assisted Elek Różański in preparing for and carrying out the death sentence on the attorney Jakub Lejkin, the deputy head of the Order Service. In January 1943 she took part in the first battles on Zamenhofa and Niska. She was one of those rounded up in that operation. She was probably murdered on the Umschlagplatz. She was seventeen.

(Aleksander Lejb Landau, his wife, and their son went to Vittel from the Hotel Polski. They were murdered in Auschwitz in 1944.)

Stanisława Legiec was born in 1916, **Władysław Legiec** in 1902. They were Polish left-wing activists. (They were called Legiec, not Legec, their daughter Ewa pointed out.) In 1943, their basement apartment in the Polish part of Warsaw, at 3/5 Szczygla Street, was a point of contact for the left-wing ghetto underground. (They lived there with the four-year-old Ewa.)

They cooperated with Władek Gaik (Krzaczek), a Pole who was active for the ŻOB, whom Władysław had known before the war. One of the Jewish couriers who regularly visited the Szczygla Street apartment was Jurek Zołotow. Other frequent visitors were Tadek Szejngut, Józiek Jarost, Rysiek Maselman, and Benek, who was killed in the ghetto uprising. Dorka Goldkorn spent three weeks in hiding with them. People came from Białystok, Lublin, and Małkinia. The Legieces mediated in the production of counterfeit documents, and in organizing safe houses for people leaving the ghetto both before the April uprising and after it. In 1944, before the Polish Warsaw rising, the janitor of the house on Szczygla warned them that the Gestapo were on their trail. They fled the city.

Stanisława and Władysław Legiec lived in Warsaw after the war. Stanisława worked in the Women's League, and Władysław in the civil service. Władysław died in 1968, and Stanisława in 1975. (They were awarded the Righteous Among the Nations medal in 1994.)

Beniamin Lejbgot, Michał Czarny, was born in Warsaw in 1910. Before the war, he was a Polish Communist Party activist and worked in an Orbis travel office. In the Warsaw ghetto he was one of the leaders of the GL. In January 1943, his group defended positions at 78 Leszno, on the premises of the 'shops. Lejbgot was killed along with Pola, Estera, and Awram Fajner on January 19 or 20, 1943.

Szaanan Lent was born in 1926 in Neveh Sha'anan, a suburb of Tel Aviv. He was a few years old when he and his parents moved to Warsaw. His father, Hirsz, was a streetcar driver and was active in Poalej Syjon.

In the ghetto, his parents asked their son to stay with them. His answer is said to have been: "I won't stay in a shelter like a mouse. I will fight for the honor of the Jewish nation." Szaanan took part in the April uprising in the group under Berliński. From the brushmakers' premises, he moved with Commander Edelman to the central ghetto. It has been recorded that he killed three SS men in the battle for the bunker at 30 Franciszkańska Street. He was badly wounded and asked a comrade to accelerate his death. Szaanan Lent died on May 3.

Cypora Lerer was born in 1920 in Poczajów in Volhynia. Her father was a bookkeeper. Cypora attended a Polish public school, and later dressmaking courses at the Krzemieniec ORT. In 1938 she went on *hakhshara* to Łódź, to the Borochow kibbutz. In the Warsaw ghetto, she apparently worked in Janusz Korczak's children's home. She was the girlfriend of Cwi Edelsztajn, a ŻOBist.

A few months before the April uprising, she joined one of the Dror fighting groups. She fought on the brushmakers' premises under Henoch Gutman. She was killed on May 3 at 30 Franciszkańska along with many others.

Jaffa Lewender (Lawender) came from Piaseczno outside Warsaw. Before the war, she was a member of Frajhajt. Driven out of Piaseczno in February 1941 with all the other Jews, in the Warsaw ghetto she went to live in the Halutz commune at 34 Dzielna Street. She was a member of one of the Dror fighting groups.

In January 1943, Jaffa was sick with typhus. She is known to have survived the January operation. In the Jewish uprising, she may have been in Berl Braude's group with her close friend Menachem Bigielman. It is not known where or when she was killed.

Szymon Lewental was born and brought up in an assimilated Warsaw family. He joined Gordonia with a Christian friend. Like several other Gordonians, he dreamed of attending the marine school in Gdynia. After the war broke out, he stayed in Warsaw. He became involved in the ghetto underground. His good Polish skills and good, Polish looks enabled him to move about outside the ghetto on business for the Party (this was the ghetto name for the Jewish underground).

Szymon took part in the first battles in January 1943. Shortly before the uprising, he and his close friend Juda Koński were caught in the act of smuggling guns into the ghetto. The ŻOB boys were interrogated for several days at the Befehlsstelle but betrayed no one. Their bodies, returned to their families, were barely recognizable. Szymon Lewental was twenty-six.

Jerzy Lewita came from Łódź. From January 1943 he was a PPR member of the ŻOB. He, Korensztajn, and Mirski dug the tunnel from Wałowa out onto Nalewki. (Nobody ever used that tunnel.) He fought in Jurek Grynszpan's group on the brushmakers' premises. It is possible that, like others from that group, he was killed at 30 Franciszkańska.

Izio Lewski came to Warsaw from Russia in the summer of 1941. In the ghetto, he was a member of Paweł Bryskin's PPR group. On April 19, Izio was in the Toebbens-Schultz 'shop yards and did not manage to get back to the central ghetto. He probably fought in the Gordonia unit under Jakub Fajgenblat. He left the 'shops on April 29. In the Wyszków woods, he fought in the unit under Merdek Growas. He was killed with his comrades, probably murdered by Polish partisans.

Chaim Libert was born in Warsaw in 1911. He was the brother of Lejb Jaszyński. In 1936, he went to the kibbutz in Żyrardów on *hakhshara*. He married a local girl and was active in the Poalej Syjon Left cell there. In the Warsaw ghetto he joined a Dror fighting group. He was killed in the January 1943 operation.

Mosze Liliensztajn (Liliensztejn), Moniek Oczyść, was born in 1914. His mother was called Tauba, and his father Lajzer. Mosze came from Warsaw.

He was a barber by trade, and that was probably why he became known as Moniek Oczyść ("*oczyść*" means "shave off" in Polish). Before the war, he belonged to Cukunft-Szturm. In the ghetto he worked in a barbers' cooperative on Nowolipie Street, and later helped out in a hospital.

When the Bundists were barracked on the brushmakers' premises in January 1943, Moniek didn't join his comrades; he stayed with the last hospital, at 6/8 Gęsia Street. (It was in an empty former boys' orphanage building; the Germans had taken the children to Treblinka.)

After that, Moniek Liliensztajn belonged to Lejb Gruzalc's Bund group in the central ghetto. Before the uprising, he went out on "exes" to raise money for the Party. During the April uprising, he was on Gęsia Street, in the hospital.

On April 20, the Germans liquidated the hospital. Some of the personnel, and a dozen or so patients, took cover in the cellar bunkers. Marek Edelman probably saw Moniek on May 7 or 8. (Dr. Polisiuk wrote that on May 13, thirteen people dug in in a cellar at 6 Gęsia Street, and that the hospital director, Dr. Braude-Hellerowa, was among them. Moniek Oczyść was probably also in that cellar.) It is not known how many days later Liliensztajn was taken to Auschwitz. After the war, he was briefly in Łódź; he registered with the Central Committee of Jews in Poland and gave the address 31/10 Piotrkowska Street. Then he lived in Givat Olga, near Tel Aviv, and worked in a tire factory. He did not want to tell his story. Masza Glajtman remembered him. He died alone in the 1970s, a Bundist in Israel.

Józef (Josef) Litewski was born on May 21, 1912, in Łódź. His father, Chaim Hersz, was a devoted Zionist. The large family—for Józef had five siblings: the eldest was Chaja, the youngest Sura, and the others were Szewa, Mordka, and Szulim—lived in Łódź, at 32 Zgierska Street. After Hebrew elementary school, Józef attended an evening high school and was apprenticed to a locksmith. He did military service and wanted to study at the polytechnic in Haifa.

The war started, and Józef was called up. He was taken prisoner at Kutno. On being released, he had to move into the ghetto. He escaped from the Łódź ghetto to the Warsaw ghetto. He became a Poalej Syjon Right activist and attended vocational courses, after which he was taken on at Toebbens. In the April uprising, he fought on the 'shop premises, probably in the group under Marek Majerowicz. It is not known how or when he was killed. (Neither is it known who from his large family survived.)

Josef (Josek) Litman was born in Nowy Dwór Mazowiecki in 1919. His father was a trader. Josek moved to Warsaw after elementary school. He was a locksmith by trade. In the ghetto, he worked in Landau's 'shop. In the April uprising, he fought in one of the Poalej Syjon Left groups.

He left the ghetto via the sewers on May 10 and went to the Wyszków woods. Once, in June 1943, he was leading Dawid Nowodworski's unit across the river Bug. In a village outside Ostrów Mazowiecka, Josek and a comrade were attacked by the dark-blue police. Wounded, he hid his gun in a haystack and crawled back into the woods. He died before his comrades (among them Hirsz Berliński) could come to his aid. It was recorded that this happened on June 28, 1943.

Lolek was nineteen in April 1943. In the ghetto, he joined Haszomer Hacair. His forename was remembered by Kazik Ratajzer. (Nobody recorded his surname.) In the evening of April 29, Lolek and Adolf Hochberg took Kazik and Zygmunt Frydrych down into the sewer.

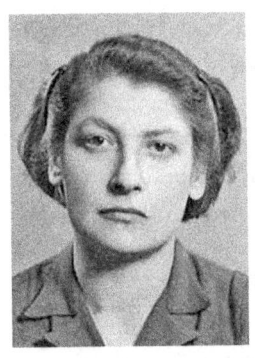

Celina Lubetkin, Cywia, was born on November 9, 1914, in Byteń, Polessia, a shtetl where one street was illuminated by gas lamps. Her religious father had a grocery store in the shtetl. Celina, her four sisters, and her brother attended the Polish elementary school, and they had a teacher called Berl who taught them the sacred language of the Bible and the Jews. Their father belonged to the religious party Mizrachi, their brother to the Revisionists, and Celina to the Halutz youth group Frajhajt. She went on *hakhshara* camps and took her political involvement very seriously. In 1938 she moved to Warsaw and became a coordinator for emigration preparation courses. In August 1939, she went to Geneva for the Zionist Congress. Celina was always serious and responsible. And that, Marek Edelman said, was probably why people obeyed her like a commander.

In September 1939, she made it through to Kovel on foot. Four months later, her party comrades sent her back to Warsaw to organize activist work in German-occupied territories. Celina went to live with the Halutzim at 34 Dzielna. Living together, studying together, the underground news bulletins, working outside the ghetto—all this was intended to give them at least a minimum sense of security.

In January 1943, Celina was with the Dror at 56–58 Zamenhofa Street: forty boys and girls under Antek Cukierman's command. They had four hand grenades and four revolvers, bars, sticks, and bottles filled with acid. They did not let themselves be marched to the Umschlag. They attacked the Germans on Zamenhofa. Then they battled their way through to 44 Muranowska and fought there, too. From Muranowska to 34 Miła, to the base used by the Dror youth from the Czerniaków farm. They were defending themselves the whole time, attacking the whole time. This was the first time that Jews in the ghetto had killed German soldiers, and they managed to get hold of a few rifles and grenades. For the first time, they believed in their power, Celina wrote.

In the April uprising, she fought without a weapon in the central ghetto. She was an emissary of hope, moral support, the young soldiers' unofficial commander. On the third day of the uprising, with Tuwia Borzykowski, she joined the group at 29 Miła. On the evening of May 7, Celina, Mordechaj Anielewicz, and Mira Fuchrer were in Marek Edelman's bunker at 22 Franciszkańska. Marek tried to persuade them to stay over. Mordechaj and Mira did not want to, so Celina and Marek walked them back to 18 Miła. For some unknown reason, Celina went back to Franciszkańska with Marek.

On May 10, they left the ghetto—those who had been at Franciszkańska with Marek Edelman, and the dozen or so who had survived Miła. They waited for a long time in the sewers before Kazik Ratajzer opened the manhole cover. Once they were in the truck, Celina told Kazik that they had to stop the vehicle. Because there, in the sewers, there were still people. With no hesitation, Kazik ordered the driver to drive off. (They couldn't have waited, he said with certainty; it would have been too dangerous for all of them. Among those left down in the sewers was Szlamek Szuster, Kazik's best friend.)

After that, between May 1943 and August 1944, Antek, Celina, Marek, and Stasia lived in various places in Warsaw: on Komitetowa, on Pańska, on Leszno... (Celina, like Marek Edelman, never went out, because she had the wrong looks.) Celina and Antek lived in great poverty; for a long time, they had no money from the organization. Not until July 1944 did the Zionists send them a half-kilo of gold and forty thousand dollars in a backpack. (Celina and Antek hid it all at 18 Leszno, and it all went up in smoke.)

In the Polish Warsaw rising, Celina wore an AL armband, like other ŻOB fighters. When Żoliborz capitulated, she was on guard duty. And nobody told her it was over, nobody came to relieve her, so she went on standing there with her rifle. By some fluke, Marek saw her there in tears, and took her to Tosia

Goliborska's apartment on Promyka Street. The seven ŻOB fighters in the cellar on Promyka Street were taken out by a paramedic patrol. They found an apartment in Grodzisk, outside Warsaw. And they stayed there together until the end of the war. After that, from Lublin, Antek and Celina started to organize illegal emigration to Palestine. That consumed them immensely.

In 1946, Celina attended another world Zionist congress, in Basle. After that, she and Antek emigrated to Palestine. They founded a kibbutz in Galilee and named it after the ghetto fighters. In the mid-1970s, Celina fell seriously ill. Ala Margolis went to visit them on the kibbutz once and found Celina lying in bed and Antek completely unable to cope. Ala promised Celina that she would come back and help her die once there was no other way. (Ala said that nobody called her when Celina was dying.) Marek Edelman also promised that he would come and ease Celina in her suffering. (He was only informed after she passed away; he couldn't even make it to her funeral.) Celina or Cywia Lubetkin died on November 7, 1978, and Antek a few years later.

Marek Majerowicz (Meir Meirowicz) was born in 1911 in Garwolin and brought up in a religious home. His father owned a tobacco factory in Warsaw. Marek became involved in social activism as a high school student. After that, he studied law at the University of Warsaw, was the head of the students' union, an active member of the Szul-Kult association board and was passionate about music. He wrote a little for the Polish press.

In September 1939, he managed to get to Lwów. He returned to Warsaw in mid-1941. In the ghetto he was the editor of *Nowe Tory*, the paper of Poalej Syjon Right. In the April uprising Majerowicz was the commander of his party's group. From their base at 31 Nowolipie, he forged a passage over the rooftops to 36 Leszno. It is not known when and in how large a group he went out via the sewers onto the other side. All that has been recorded is that at the manhole cover on the Polish side, the ŻOBists were noticed by the military police. Marek and his friend managed to escape. On May 24, Marek was with a group of insurgents in the celluloid factory at 11 Listopada Street. He was killed in the fire there that day.

Manfred came to Poland with a German youth group before the war. Perhaps he was one of the thousands of Polish Jews exiled from Germany in 1938. Nobody recalled his surname.

Manfred went to live on the Halutz kibbutz in the Warsaw district of Grochów. In July or August 1942, he escaped a transport to Treblinka. He returned to the ghetto. In the ŻOB Dror group he prepared for armed resistance. In the April uprising he was in Artsztajn's group in the central ghetto. He did not leave the ghetto walls. It is not known when and how he died. He was twenty-one.

Bronka Manulak was born in Łódź. She grew up in a family of ardent supporters of the Zionist movement. (Bronka's parents and her grandfather, Abram Manulak, a Łódź weaver, all belonged to Poalej Syjon.) Her father, Azriel, was a vendor, her mother a dressmaker. Bronka attended the Borochow school and was a member of Jugnt, the youth arm of Poalej Syjon Left. Like most of her peers from Zionist organizations, she was preparing to emigrate to Eretz Israel.

In 1939, she fled from Łódź to Warsaw. When the ghetto was sealed, she worked in the brushmakers' 'shop. In the April uprising she fought in Hirsz Berliński's group. She was killed on May 10 on the trek from the ghetto via the sewers with Sewek, Lejb, Menachem, Szlamek, Jechiel, Pnina, Adolf, and others. She was twenty years old.

Alina, Ala, Margolis [Margolis-Edelman] was born on April 18, 1922, in Łódź. Both her parents were doctors—her mother, Anna, a superb pediatrician and radiologist; her father, Aleksander, an internist and hospital director, and a respected Bundist social activist. In December 1939, Dr. Anna Margolis sent Ala and her brother Janek to stay with an aunt in Warsaw. She herself waited for her husband, who had been arrested. (The Germans had taken Ala's father hostage and murdered him at Radegast station in December 1939.)

In early 1941 Dr. Margolis was living with her children in the Warsaw ghetto. (She worked in the Berson and Bauman hospital: first on Śliska Street, and thereafter on Leszno, Stawki, and Gęsia.) Alina started to study at the Nursing School on Mariańska Street. That was an exterritorial place, she recalled. Pink, candy-striped dresses, starched collars, three white buttons, short sleeves with stiff cuffs. And the apron with the crossed straps fastened with buttons. And dark blue capes. The girls were safe until the *große Aktion*. Luba Blum-Bielicka, the director of the school, saved our lives and protected our souls, Ala said.

She left the ghetto after the January operation. Outside its walls, she met Renia Frydman, now Zosia Skrzeszewska, whom she knew from the hospital in the ghetto. They moved in together on Różana Street in the Mokotów district. Then they were both couriers for the ŻOB insurgents. Their wards were in hiding in the Okęcie district. (Ala didn't know whether they survived.) In April, she often went to stand by the ghetto walls—not for too long, because it wasn't safe. Ala carried money to people in hiding in Warsaw, and aid to the camp in Piotrków.

In the Polish Warsaw rising in 1944, she and Inka Szwajgier helped out in the hospital on Miodowa Street. In November 1944 she went with a paramedic patrol to Żoliborz. She managed to get several ŻOBists out of the cellar on Promyka Street. (There were seven of them: Antek Cukierman, Celina Lubetkin, Marek Edelman, Tuwia Borzykowski, Julek Fiszgrund, Zygmunt Warman, and Tosia Goliborska.)

After the war, Ala studied medicine in Łódź, in the same year group as Marek. Dr. Alina Margolis-Edelman was a pediatrician and social activist. She established foundations and supported existing ones (Médecins du Monde in France and Dzieci Niczyje in Poland, to name but a few). She treated and helped children in dozens of places across the globe.

From 1972 she lived in Paris, and later for a short while in Warsaw again. She said that her life was the way it was not because her parents had been doctors and social activists, and not because she had seen so many "filthy, withered wax dolls" in the ghetto. She said she had always done it for herself, that this was her way of saving herself. Alina Margolis-Edelman died on March 23, 2008, in Paris.

Rysiek Maselman (Moselman) was born in Warsaw and attended the Borochow public school. His mother was a Poalej Syjon Left activist. Rysiek became involved with a group of young left-wingers. In the ghetto he was a courier between the ŻOB and the Polish side. Rysiek looked like a rough laborer; he wore a heavy leather jacket and high work boots. He was muscular and light-haired. He found a way out onto the Polish side through the Jewish cemetery, squeezing between dead bodies. It was he who informed the Legiec family of the ghetto uprising.

On May 8, he went back into the ghetto with Kazik Ratajzer and the sewerage engineers to save the surviving insurrectionists. By chance they met some ŻOBists in the sewers. They agreed to guide them out. The insurgents went back to the ghetto for their comrades, and Kazik and Rysiek went to organize the exit.

On May 10, Rysiek stood guard by the manhole cover on Prosta Street. It is known that the first group of insurrectionists drove off in the truck to Łomianki.

The second, which had become lost in the side sewers, did not make it to the vehicle. When they emerged from the sewer later, the manhole cover was surrounded. A shootout ensued. The insurgents defended themselves briefly. They were all killed.

Rysiek Maselman and Jurek Zołotow, who had organized the operation, were shot by the Germans a short distance away. (The Legieces remembered that Rysiek and Jurek met in a cafe on Bankowy Square. The Germans surprised them there. Jurek managed to throw a grenade before he was killed. Rysiek was shot dead by the wall of the Saski Garden on Żabia Street.) Kazik and Antek Cukierman recorded that the boys' bodies lay on the street somewhere near Bankowy Square. They had allegedly been attempting to get away by droshky and someone had denounced them to the military police. Rysiek Maselman was eighteen when he was killed.

Szoszana Mastbojm was brought up in a wealthy Łódź home. She was a member of the Hanoar Hacyjoni movement from the age of fourteen. She spent a lot of time in a kibbutz run by the organization, and there she met her closest friend, Jakub Praszkier. They had planned to emigrate to Palestine together. In the April uprising Szoszana fought in Jakub's group on the brushmakers' premises. She was most likely killed with him and others in the ruins of a house on Wałowa.

Izrael (Srulek) Mittelman was born in Lublin in 1919. His father was a fruit trader. In the early 1930s, the Mittelman family moved to Warsaw. Srulek was apprenticed as a lathe-turner in a locksmith's workshop, and in addition dashed to classes at Skif.

Later, in the ghetto, he fought in the April uprising in the Bundist group under Lejb Gruzalc on Zamenhofa and Miła. He gave Masza Glajtman a few photographs for safekeeping because she had a drawstring bag and was already looking after other photographs and Mejloch Perelman's diary. (Masza said that it was a striped bag that she had sewn out of a mattress cover. The bag was left behind in the bunker at 29 Miła.)

The Germans threw a grenade into the dugout at 30 Franciszkańska, where there were maybe 5 or 6 soldiers, Masza Glajtman-Putermilch recalled. They blocked up the opening with pillows to keep the gas out. It was then that Izrael Mittelman was killed.

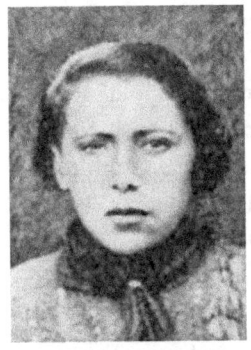
Basia (Batia) Mordkowicz was born in 1922 in Sulejów. Her father was a religious Zionist and a member of the Mizrachi party. Basia and her siblings belonged to Frajhajt. In 1938, she went on *hakhshara* to the Kielce region. In the April uprising she fought on the premises of the 'shops in the Dror group under Icchak Blausztajn. They were probably in a pair. She never left the ghetto.

Icchak (Izak, Icek) Morgenlender was born in Łódź on May 27, 1923. The family then moved to Ostrowiec Kielecki, because Izak's father, Josef Juda, came from Ostrowiec. The school registers record that Izak Morgenlender achieved an overall good grade in the 1933/1934 school year and was promoted into class 5. Before the war he belonged to Bnei Akiva, the youth arm of the Mizrachi party. Somebody remembered that Icek sang beautifully, that he had a moving voice. In the Ostrowiec ghetto he was active in Haszomer Hacair.

In February 1943 he managed to get into the Warsaw ghetto, because he had heard that the ŻOB wanted to put up a defense there. In the April uprising he fought on the premises of the 'shops. He left the ghetto for the Polish side via the sewers. His final place of shelter was the celluloid factory in the Praga district. He perished with others in the fire on May 24, 1943.

Jochanan Morgensztern was born in Zamość in 1905. His father was a religious man who traded in cottage wares and was interested in the Jewish national cause. Jochanan attended a cheder and a Polish elementary school. He edited the newspaper *Zamoszczer Sztyme* (Zamoshcher Shtime). In the 1920s, he became an activist for Poalej Syjon Right and the League for Aid to Workers in Israel. By this time, he was living in Warsaw, but travelled on party business to Galicia and the Dąbrowa Basin, and to Vilnius. He reported on those visits in his columns for the party daily *Dos Wort* (Dos Vort) and its weekly *Bafrajung Arbeter Sztyme* (Bafrayung Arbeter Shtime). Shortly before the war, he visited Palestine. Like many others, he wanted to emigrate. Morgensztern was

the Poalej Syjon Right delegate to the 21st World Congress of Jews in Geneva, and the secretary of the League for Aid to Workers in Israel.

In the Warsaw ghetto, Jochanan Morgensztern was one of the "old" activists in the Jewish underground. He represented his party on the Jewish National Committee and the Coordinating Committee. Afterwards, he was in the staff company of the ŻOB, responsible for the organization's finances. He had employment in the Schultz 'shop. During the April 1943 uprising he was on the Toebbens-Schultz premises. He went out onto the other side via the sewers on April 29. Morgensztern did not go with the insurrectionists to the woods in Łomianki. He went into hiding in the bunker at 29 Ogrodowa Street. There were around thirty people there, most of them from the same party. The Germans discovered the party bunker on May 6. They took all those inside to Szucha. The women were sent to the camp in Majdanek, and the men were shot on the spot.

Rywka Moszkowicz, Zosia, came from Będzin, and was brought up in a poor working-class family. She worked as an assistant in a material store and dreamed of Eretz Israel. When she was seventeen, she moved to the Frajhajt kibbutz in Kielce. There, she worked in a factory. After that, the organization sent her on a self-defense course. The kibbutz with which she was connected numbered around two hundred fifty members before the war. Now, in the conditions of incarceration, the young people began to organize themselves again. She was in the Będzin ghetto until the summer of 1943.

At Celina Lubetkin's request, she found a way to get to Warsaw. She was a courier for Antek Cukierman. She also traveled to the camp in Częstochowa. On August 1, 1944, she was walking along Twarda Street. She was carrying money for people in hiding in the city. A German was driving past and took a shot at her that hit its target. Zosia managed to reach the home of her Polish friend Stasiek Dutkiewicz. Stasiek took her to the hospital on Śliska Street. Rywka Moszkowicz died on the operating table.

Natek was a Jewish Boy Scout and a ŻOB courier. Before the war, he had been a high school student and lived on Niska Street, Masza Glajtman-Putermilch remembered. Natek worked with Aleksander Kamiński. He was recruited into the ŻOB by Jurek Grasberg in mid-1943, after the April uprising was over. Natek took care of people in hiding. He also worked with Kazik Ratajzer and a little with Antek Cukierman. He was a frequent visitor to 5 Pańska, where the ŻOB commanders lived in hiding.

One day, Natek was arrested. Apparently, a list of around twenty addresses of Jews in hiding was found on him. The finding of Igła, Fajgenblat, and Guta Kawenoki was linked to Natek's arrest. Marek Edelman said that the incident on Próżna Street had nothing to do with Natek. (Jabłoński, the janitor who was hiding the insurgents, was a contact point for the AK, and the German raid on Próżna was in connection with an "ex" carried out by the AK.) Kazik Ratajzer said that Felek Rajszczak was confronted with Natek at the Gestapo headquarters, and that Natek was dreadfully beaten up. And when he was taken out of the building, he made a run for it, so they shot him. Someone else remembered that the Germans took Natek to Próżna Street, to Jabłoński. Marek Edelman said that the Germans took Natek to the intersection of Senatorska and Miodowa, to one of the apartments on his list, and that despite being handcuffed, he managed to slip them. He surfaced again in Brwinów or Milanówek in December 1944. He joined Żegota, where he worked with Stasia Merenholc. Both Ratajzer and Edelman said that Natek did not denounce anyone.

Natek or **Jurek** was an insurgent. Only Marek Edelman remembered him. He was tall, handsome, didn't look like a Jew, and had a song about scalliwags that he sang beautifully. In the April uprising he was probably in Merdek Growas's group. He probably left the ghetto on May 10. He had nowhere to sleep, so he rode the tramcars. Once, he fell asleep at a terminus, and a German shot him dead.

Renia Niemiecka was born in Warsaw in 1919. She came from a wealthy Hasidic family. (Her father was a Hasid of the Sochaczewer rebbe.) Renia grew up in the Jewish district, on Franciszkańska Street. She attended a public elementary school, and then high school. Before the war, she became involved with the left-wing youth. She apparently belonged to Spartakus. Her friend from that organization, Dorka Goldkorn, noted that Renia suffered considerably due to her father's religious zealotry. In the ghetto she was a member of Jurek Grynszpan's PPR fighting group. She was killed on April 20 on the brushmakers' premises.

Dawid Nowodworski was born in 1916. He came from a Warsaw working-class family. His mother was a midwife. Dawid helped out in a small store on Gęsia and was an active member of his Haszomer Hacair cell. In the ghetto, he lived with his partner, Rywka Szafirsztajn, at 23 Nalewki Street, and later at 6 Leszno. They administered the ghetto Haszomer Hacair cell's finances. They also listened to the radio in secret and noted down news to publish in the underground news bulletins.

On August 17, 1942, Dawid was rounded up on a ghetto street and deported to Treblinka. He managed to escape from the camp, however, and return to the ghetto. (A notebook in a yellow cover filled with writing in green copy pencil has been preserved in the Ringelblum Archive. The ten sides of text, begun in Yiddish and continued in Polish, are almost illegible. This is Dawid Nowodworski's manuscript about Treblinka and his escape from it, dated August 28, 1942, the first written account by an escapee.) Later, in the September, Dawid won employment in the 'shop owned by Landau, who supported the Shomers. In the April uprising, Nowodworski commanded the Haszomer Hacair group on the Toebbens-Schultz premises. Their base on the first day of the uprising was at 67 Nowolipie.

Nowodworski left the ghetto on April 29. He reached the Wyszków woods via Łomianki. He sometimes went back into Warsaw. He was looking for contacts who could help him and a group of others to get to Hungary, and from there to Palestine. Once, as he was on his way from the woods to Warsaw, he and some other insurgents were stopped. They were allegedly denounced by a Volksdeutsche who asked them the way. They allegedly attempted to defend themselves. Among the others who died with Dawid Nowodworski were Rywka Szafirsztajn, Heniek Klajnwajs, Dorka Dembińska, Szymon Szejntal, and Izrael Romanowicz. This was in late June or early July 1943.

Sewek Nulman lived in Warsaw. His father, a war invalid, had a newsstand on the corner of Gęsia and Lubecki Streets. Sewek attended the CISzO elementary school on Karmelicka Street. In the ghetto, he was the janitor of the house at 60 Leszno, where left-wing youth would meet. (Both his father and his brother sympathized with the movement.)

In July 1942, Sewek became involved with the PPR group of five under Michał Biały. He wrote poems and tried to print them on a copier and distribute them among friends. In the April uprising he fought in Heniek Zylberberg's group in the central ghetto. He was killed on May 8 in the bunker at 18 Miła Street. One historian recorded that he was 28. He was definitely younger than that, Masza Glajtman-Putermilch said.

Józef Obersztyn (Obersztajn) was born in Łódź. His father was the bookkeeper in a factory owned by his friends, the Mazur brothers. After the outbreak of war, the family moved to Warsaw. Józek's father died of starvation in the ghetto. The Germans deported his mother and sister to Treblinka. In the April uprising Józek was in Henoch Gutman's Dror group. On May 10, he left the ghetto via the sewers. He was killed in the Wyszków woods. He was twenty years old.

Wanda Ochron was a member of a group of Jewish left-wingers. In the April uprising she fought in the central ghetto in the unit under Paweł Bryskin. On May 7, 1943, she was sent out onto the other side of the wall via the sewers with a group of insurgents to find help for those inside the ghetto. They were noticed at the manhole cover. Those who managed to escape went into hiding somewhere on Miodowa Street. The Germans came for them at the end of May. It was then that Wanda was killed. She was twenty-two.

Abraham Orwacz was born in Warsaw in 1922. His family lived on Okopowa Street. When the war broke out, Abram and his friend Elek Różański set off for the East. They returned to Warsaw shortly afterwards. In the ghetto they both belonged to Haszomer Hacair. Abraham Orwacz was killed in the April uprising.

Michał Oszerowski fought in a Haszomer Hacair group in the April uprising. He is known to have been wounded in the ghetto and to have died in the Wyszków woods. He was in his twenties.

Chawa Pachoł was born in Kielce in 1918. She belonged to one of the Dror groups. She was killed in the first days of fighting in the ghetto in January 1943.

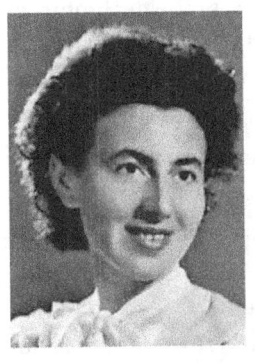

Pinia, Pnina, Papier [Grynszpan-Frymer] was born in Nowy Dwór Mazowiecki in 1923. Her grandfather had horses and a flatbed waggon, so her father delivered wares to local stallholders. Pinia attended a Jewish elementary school and was keen to continue her education. But the war started, the ghetto started. Pinia worked in a detail, in a sawmill in Modlin. She escaped to Warsaw in mid-1941, when the Nowy Dwór ghetto began to get increasingly cramped. After the *große Aktion*, she got a job in Landau's 'shop, with her brother Zysiek and her cousin Josek Litman. In the factory, Pnina noticed that her colleagues were secretive, had important matters to attend to, and were constantly conspiring. She was desperate to be one of them. She was initiated into the ŻOB by Hersz Berliński sometime before January 1943.

After the January operation, Pnina's group was posted to the brushmakers' premises at 34 Świętojerska. Their commander was Berliński, and the group members were Josek Farber, Abraham, Abram Stolak, Josek Litman, Zysie Papier, Bronka Manulak, and others whom Pnina did not remember. In the April uprising, Pnina had one bottle and one grenade. On April 20, she went into the central ghetto with Commander Edelman, to 30 Franciszkańska Street.

On May 8, Pnina went down into the sewers with Jurek Błones, Abram Stolak, and others. Their task was to seek an exit route for the insurrectionists. They wandered for a long time in the water, with guttering candles in their hands. When they heard noises, they were certain that it was Germans. The noises fell silent, and both sides waited. At last, someone said: "Jan." That was their codeword. Miraculously, Kazik Ratajzer had come upon Pnina's group. Only a moment before, he had been convinced that there was nobody left in the ghetto.

Pnina was in Łomianki and the Wyszków woods. In late summer 1943, she returned to Warsaw. She lived in hiding at 24 Rakowiecka Street with the Bundists Chana Kryształ and Janek Bilak. In the Polish insurrection she was a courier and was given a uniform with an AL armband. After the Warsaw rising, she did not want to leave the city, because she was afraid that Poles might denounce her to the Germans. She went into hiding with Masza Glajtman and Jakubek Putermilch in the ruins of the city until January 22 or 23, 1945.

In July 1946, she registered with the Central Committee of Jews in Poland, giving her address as 38 Sienna Street. After that, she emigrated to Palestine via Romania. She married Chaim Frymer, a ghetto insurgent and forest partisan. They lived in Tel Aviv. Pnina Grynszpan-Frymer died on November 17, 2016.

Zysie Papier, Zygmunt, was born on May 3, 1917, in Nowy Dwór, near Warsaw. He was the elder brother of Pinia. After elementary school, he worked in a porcelain factory, and trained in the Makkabi sports club. At the beginning of the war, Pinia and Zysie escaped to the Warsaw ghetto. (Those who stayed in Nowy Dwór were killed in Pomiechówek.)

After the *große Aktion*, Zysie found employment in Landau's 'shop. He and his sister joined Berliński's group in the ŻOB. Zysie Papier was killed on May 3, when the group of insurgents was attacked in the bunker at 30 Franciszkańska.

Rywke (Rywka, Rebeka) Pasamonik was born in 1921 in the Warsaw district of Czerniaków, into a religious, relatively wealthy family. Her father, Szyja Pasamonik, owned an old tenement at 92 Czerniakowska Street, near Nowosielecka Street. They lived on the second floor, in the corner apartment, in three rooms, a one-time Polish neighbor remembered. (There were both Poles and Jews living in the house, and on the third floor there was a small prayer house, a Hasidic *shtibl*.) Szyja Pasamonik kept cows and horses in the courtyard and sold meat in the abattoir (in the same tenement, on the Nowosielecka side). Rywka had an elder brother, Mejloch, who was already married; a younger sister; and a younger brother still, Menaszke. Rywka was modest but elegant—she was no ragamuffin. Black, curly hair, tall and rather thin, the neighbor remembered in 2013. She was idealistic and brave, a friend from Akiba remembered. Against her parents' wishes, Rywke joined Haszomer Hacair, and in 1938, without telling them, she went to live on a Shomer kibbutz.

In 1940, the whole family went into the ghetto, the neighbor said. Someone remembered that Szyja Pasamonik took the cows from his Czerniaków farm with him. One day, the neighbor recalled, Szyjowa came back to Czerniakowska Street for Rywka's trousseau, which she'd left with one of the Catholic women for safekeeping, but the woman denied all knowledge, and Siejowa went back to the ghetto empty-handed (Szyjowa, Siejowa, because she was Szyja's wife).

Rywka ran the Akiba kibbutz at 10 Nalewki Street. For a few months in 1942, she worked on the Halutz farm back in Czerniaków. In the April uprising she fought in Berl Braude's group. During the escape from the bunker at 29 Miła Street, Rywka was wounded. On May 8, she was at 18 Miła. Like many others, she did not want to fall into the Germans' hands alive; first, she shot a girlfriend, and then she shot herself. None of Rywka Pasamonik's family returned to the Czerniakowska Street tenement.

Rebeka Pekier. In the April uprising she was a ŻOB courier on Leszno. I found no information about Rebeka Pekier.

Boruch Pelc was born in Warsaw. He was the son of a Bundist printer from 14 or 16 Rymarska Street. It was at Boruch's father's place that the Bundists printed their first flyers, in 1939 and 1940, on his "pedal-op." In the ghetto, Boruch was in a Bundist group in the ŻOB. His group was waiting for weapons. (They never obtained any because the Zionists did not give the Bundists any weapons in January.)

They were rounded up on January 18, 1943. They went to the Umschlagplatz as a large group. They were unarmed, so could not shoot. Boruch briefly addressed the sixty Jews gathered there. None of those who had been rounded up boarded the train. They were all shot on the spot by van Eupen, the commandant of Treblinka I. Boruch Pelc was seventeen, maybe eighteen.

**Fajgele Peltel, Władka [Międzyrzecka, Meed]**, was born on December 29, 1921, in Warsaw, and lived at 64 Leszno. She was brought up in a Bundist environment. She had a good appearance and spoke Polish without a Jewish accent—she was able to be a courier for the Jewish underground in the Polish part of the city. Michał Klepfisz organized her exit from the ghetto. She left via a guardpost with a work detail on December 5, 1942.

She went to live in a cellar at 3 Górnośląska Street, with Stefan Machaj, a worker whom Klepfisz had known before the war. (Machaj was very helpful to them, smuggling arms into the ghetto and providing shelter to many people. After a while, his intermediation began to be linked to compromises of security. Machaj was shot dead by the Germans, and his ambiguous role was never fully clarified.)

Władka worked as a dressmaker and was a courier for Leon Feiner, the Bund's representative outside the ghetto. She often took news into the ghetto, and smuggled arms. Her main contact was her schoolfriend, Jurek Błones. Later on, during the uprising, Fajgele often went to stand by the wall.

After May 10, Abrasza Blum took shelter in her apartment at 2 Barokowa Street, waiting for another place. The janitor denounced them. (That janitor was later sentenced by the AK.) Four Poles and a German came to the apartment. Abrasza attempted to slide down a rope made of sheets, but they were on the fourth floor, and the sheets gave way. There must have been a dark-blue police officer close by. Fajgele and Abrasza were taken to the police precinct on Daniłowiczowska Street. Fajgele was released for ten thousand zlotys, which Anna Wąchalska brought to the policeman. (Abrasza Blum had been taken to Szucha Street the previous night.)

In the summer of 1943, Władka travelled a lot around occupied Poland. Leon Feiner sent her to Zielisławice, Koniecpol, and Częstochowa on behalf of the ŻOB's Coordinating Committee. She carried information, money, medicines, and clothing for Jews working in the camps. She also visited the Jewish partisans in the Wyszków woods. This went on until the Polish rising in 1944. At that time, she was living at 36 Twarda Street. After the Warsaw rising, she left the city with Beniamin. They made a brief halt at 40 Targowa Street in the Praga district.

After the war, Władka Peltel and Beniamin Międzyrzecki (they were now called Meed) lived in New York. Władka Peltel died in 2012.

Majloch (Mejloch, Melach) Perelman was born in Warsaw in 1917 or 1921. He attended a CISzO school, and was a member of Skif, and later of

Cukunft. He was brought up by his stepmother because his mother died young. Majloch was gentle, and probably for that reason well-liked. (Masza Glajtman-Putermilch remembered that he sang opera arias beautifully.)

In the April uprising, he fought in Lejb Gruzalc's Bund group in the central ghetto. The insurgents would go out on "twos": when the Germans went into a house to set it alight, two fighters would hide on the first floor and attack the arsonists. This operation only worked a few times, however, because the Germans soon caught onto the new tactic.

Majloch twice went out on "twos." And the second time—that was probably at 80 Gęsia Street—he was badly wounded in his lungs and belly. His partner was killed. So Majloch hid his friend's pistol in an oven and managed to crawl to the bunker at 18 Miła. The dying man could not be carried into the bunker, because the entrance was too narrow. He was moved into the attic at 37 Muranowska. He asked them to shoot him, or at least leave him a pistol. Commander Anielewicz ordered the gun to be taken because every bullet could kill one German. The house at 37 Muranowska was set alight the next day. People heard how slowly and horribly Majloch burned alive. (Masza Glajtman-Putermilch heard Majloch's screams for decades of her nights.) All the Bundists left 18 Miła and went to Franciszkańska, to Commander Edelman. They blamed Anielewicz for that death to the end.

Lea Perelsztajn (Perlsztejn) was born in Sokółka, near Białystok. She was from an educated, wealthy merchant family. She graduated from the teacher training college in Grodno, and taught Hebrew in the surrounding towns. From 1935, she helped to build the Halutz movement in Poland: she was active in Vilnius, Łódź, and Warsaw.

From the summer of 1940, she worked with a group of several dozen young Jews on the farm in Czerniaków; they grew rhubarb, tomatoes, cabbages, celeriac, and cucumbers. They slept in the stables on straw mattresses, and even received a minimal wage for their labor. And the gate was always open. Thanks to the owner of the estate, Zatwarnicki, who was now its manager, life on the farm was relatively safe. The farm protected people even during the *große Aktion*. It was also a rendezvous for the Jewish underground—from there, newspapers and weapons were smuggled into the ghetto, and there, contacts with the Polish underground were made. Hela Szuster (after the war Kron) wrote that although they worked hard, Czerniaków was paradise! Lea Perelsztajn was the leader of the Halutzim there.

When in November 1942 the farm was closed down, they all moved back into the ghetto. Lea was a member of one of the Dror fighting groups. On January 18, 1943, she was rounded up on the street along with Sara Granatsztajn and Tema Sznajderman. She was thirty when she was killed.

Chana (Chańcia) Płotnicka was born on April 3, 1918, in Płotnica near Pińsk, into a Hasidic home. Chańcia and her sister Fruma[9] never went to school. The eldest, Zlatkie, taught them Polish and Hebrew. When Chańcia was fourteen, her brother Eliahu initiated her into Frajhajt, most probably against the wishes of their religious father. Chańcia wanted to emigrate to Palestine, but she first had to prepare for work in the new country. In 1936, she went on *hakhshara* to Baranowicze, and attended Halutz seminars.

Early on in the occupation, Chańcia and her sister Fruma were Halutz couriers. (Fruma was killed in Będzin in 1943.) For a while, Chańcia was on the farm in Grochów. Later on, she worked for the ŻOB in the Warsaw ghetto. She usually traveled to the ghettos in Białystok and Będzin to encourage young people to put up resistance.

When the April uprising broke out, she was just setting off on another mission to Będzin. Heniek Klajnwajs and Meir Szwarc were escorting her out of the ghetto. On a boundary street, at 5 Karmelicka, they were caught by some Germans. As they were being taken to 80 Leszno, where people who had been rounded up waited for extermination transport, the insurrectionists made a bid to defend themselves. The boys managed to escape. Chańcia Płotnicka was killed on the street. She was twenty-five.

Stefan Pokropek was a Pole who greatly aided the ŻOB underground in Warsaw. He was born in Milanówek in 1906. He was a stonemason by trade, and a PPS man in his ideals. He lived at 80 Washington Street. He hid a 17-year-old boy called Rysiek there, and also gave shelter to the ghetto courier Tadek

---

9   **Frumka Płotnicka** was born in 1914 in Płotnica near Pinsk. Like her sister Chana, she was a member of Frajhajt. As a Halutz activist, she visited kibbutzim in Białystok and Łódź. After 1939, she was one of the most active of them all. She traveled all over the country on counterfeit papers, working with Tosia Altman, Arie Wilner, and Leon Perlstein. She wrote some of the first reports on the extermination of the Jews in eastern Poland and maintained contacts with Halutz representatives abroad. In later 1942, she organized the resistance movement in the Będzin ghetto, and it was there she died, on August 3, 1943, during a defense operation.

Szejngut, and others whenever necessary. He intermediated in contacts with the AL underground and bought up and stockpiled weapons for the ghetto.

His apartment was denounced by a Jewish Gestapo agent called Czarny. (Antek Cukierman remembers that Czarny survived the war, was never brought to justice, and after 1968 emigrated to Sweden.) On July 7, 80 Waszyngtona Street was surrounded by Germans. Stefan Pokropek was wounded with a gunshot through the door. He finished himself off before the Germans could get into the apartment. His daughter Basia and Kazik Ratajzer managed to jump out through a window. In that raid, Rysiek, the boy in hiding there, Tadek Szejngut, and Stefan Pokropek were killed. The Germans took Pokropek's body, and it is not known where they had it buried. (In the year 2000, Stefan and Eleonora Pokropek were awarded the Righteous Among the Nations medal.)

Jakub Praszkier (Praszker) was born into the family of a poor Łódź Hasid in 1913. He was brought up by relatives because his mother died young. He was a sickly child, but keen to learn. He started work at an early age and was active in the Halutz organization. He ran the *hakhshara* office in Łódź and was the favorite instructor of the young people there. On the kibbutz, Jakub became friends with Szoszana Mastbojm, with whom he was planning to emigrate to Palestine.

He stayed with Szoszana in the Warsaw ghetto. Until March 1943, they wrote letters abroad and maintained contacts with young people from their organization scattered across other ghettos. Somewhere on Leszno they founded a Hanoar Hacyjoni kibbutz. Jakub Praszkier was a group commander on the brushmakers' premises. They did not attempt to move into the central ghetto. They stayed at 8 Wałowa Street, in the bunker, in the ruins, with a group of civilians. It is not known when or how they died.

Ignacy Puterman was accepted into Lejb Gruzalc's Bund unit even as the uprising was underway. He was not a Bundist himself; he had more communist leanings. (His father was a Bundist who had been exiled to Siberia.) Ignacy was killed in action at 30 Franciszkańska Street, on May 3, 1943. He was nineteen.

Chagit Putermilch was born in Warsaw in 1922 into a Hasidic family. She had a brother, Jakubek. The family lived at 62 Nowolipki. Chagit attended a Tarbut elementary school and a high school for commerce. She was a member of Haszomer Hacair even before the war.

In the April uprising, she was on the premises of the 'shops, in the same group as her close friend Awram Zandman and his sister Pnina. It was a Shomer group, probably the one under Szlomo Winogron, or perhaps Dawid Nowodworski. On April 29, Hagit and Awram left the ghetto via the sewers. They were in the Wyszków woods in Merdek Growas's group—Bundists and Shomers together. And then one day, all contact with them was lost. When inquiries were made about them in the surrounding villages, the peasants said that those Yids had been killed by some AK men.

Jakubek Putermilch, the brother of Chagit, was born in 1924. They were brought up in a devout home at 62 Nowolipki Street. Before the war, their parents ran a store, where Jakubek often used to help out. Their mother, Hadasa, was very wise, and had the talents of an attorney, a friend of Jakubek's remembered.

In the April uprising he was in Fajgenblat's Gordonia group. He left the ghetto on April 29. He was in a partisan unit near Wyszków. He returned to Warsaw prior to winter 1943. He and Masza Glajtman—they were a married couple since the woods—went into hiding at 6 Twarda Street and 64 Żelazna, with Władek Świętochowski. They were in hiding-places until the end of the war, and even a little beyond. Masza remembered that they first went out onto the streets of the nominally free city on January 22, 1945. They lived briefly in Wawer, at 81/9 Płowiecka Street. And then they emigrated.

They lived in Tel Aviv. Jakubek worked in a construction company and recorded his Warsaw memory in fountain pen: the beginning in Polish, and then in Yiddish. Masza typed the text up and was not allowed to alter so much as a comma. Jakubek Putermilch died on September 9, 1984.

Fejcze Rabow, Cypora, was born in 1921 into a large, poor family in Suchowola near Białystok. She was a good student at her Polish school and took care of her siblings. When she was fifteen, she joined the Halutz movement. In 1939 she went on *hakhshara* to a kibbutz in Łódź.

In the first months of the war, she fled to Warsaw. She worked on the farm in Czerniaków. A short girl, with a worried face and dreamy eyes—that was how someone remembered her. From fall 1942, she was imprisoned in the Warsaw ghetto. It was probably in January 1943 that she joined one of the Dror fighting groups.

During the April uprising, Fejcze fought on the brushmakers' premises. She stayed in the ghetto to take care of her wounded friend, Henoch Gutman. She is known still to have been in hiding with other soldiers somewhere in the central ghetto on May 9. It is not known where or how she died.

Feliks Rajszczak was born in Warsaw in 1902. He was a communist and a master bricklayer. He built his first hiding-place for Jews on Twarda Street; it was accessed via a tiled stove. The Rajszczak family lived in the apartment on Twarda, and behind their tiled stove lived survivors from the ghetto: Lejzer Lewin, Tuwia Borzykowski, and Stefan Grajek.

Feliks Rajszczak was arrested on January 11, 1944, because he was denounced by a Pole who had also previously denounced a group of fugitives from the ghetto in hiding on Mokotowska. (Rajszczak had been planning to build them a hideout there.) Feliks was cruelly tortured but gave no names away and confessed to nothing. He was released from Szucha for a large bribe. He was not deterred and continued to aid Jews. The ŻOB bought a cottage in the village of Blizne, and Feliks built another hideout there. This one was never used, however, because the Polish Warsaw rising broke out.

Rajszczak had two children: Tadeusz (1929–1996) and Mirka (1926–1944), known as Sziksa. Both of them aided ŻOB members on the Polish side of Warsaw, as their couriers. (In the Warsaw rising, Tadeusz was a rifleman in the AK battalion "Miotła.") After the war, Feliks was quartermaster in a Civil Militia precinct in Warsaw. He was reluctant to cultivate his contacts from previous years. He died in 1977. (The entire Rajszczak family—Weronika, Feliks, Tadeusz, and Mirka—was decorated with the Righteous Among the Nations medal in 1978.)

Aron Rajzband was remembered by Celina Lubetkin. She recorded that he came from a small Warsaw satellite city and was resettled into the Warsaw ghetto. He worked on the Czerniaków farm. Before the uprising he joined the Dror group under Berl Braude. He was the oldest, and very caring toward the younger soldiers. Celina saw Aron in the Dror bunker on Miła Street on the third day of the uprising. It is not known where or how he died.

Lejb Rapaport was born in Bielsko into a wealthy manufacturing family. During the war, he was in Ostrowiec Świętokrzyski, and he joined the Halutz movement there. He went to Warsaw with a group of young people because he wanted to fight. Lejb's family went into hiding on the other side of the wall and tried in vain to persuade him to leave the ghetto.

In the April uprising, Lejb Rapaport fought under the command of Beniamin Wald in the Toebbens-Schultz 'shop yards. He was killed in the early days. He was twenty-one.

Symcha Ratajzer, Kazik Simcha [Rotem], was born in 1924 and brought up in the Warsaw district of Czerniaków. His father, Cwi Ratajzer, was a Hasid of the Rebbe of Piaseczno, and prayed in a prayer house on Czerniakowska Street (perhaps the same one in which Rywka Pasamonik's father prayed, at 92 Czerniakowska). His parents had a soap manufactory at 24 Podchorążych Street. Symcha was the eldest of their four children. He briefly attended a cheder, and then a public elementary school where Polish was the language of instruction and there was one Hebrew lesson a week. He learned his trade in the school at 26 Grzybowska and was a member of the religious Zionist organization Hanoar Hacyjoni.

In the summer of 1942, he lived with distant family in the country near the village of Odrzywół, south of Warsaw. Toward the end of the summer, after the *große Aktion*, he returned to Warsaw. He found his parents on the Czerniaków farm and stayed there with them until the farm was liquidated in November 1942. After that, in the ghetto, they lived at 34 Świętojerska. (In the same house, dozens of ŻOB fighters found shelter during the uprising—until the house went up in flames.)

Symcha joined the ŻOB sometime before January 1943. He was in Beniamin Wald's group at 60 or 62 Leszno, on the premises of the Toebbens 'shop. Like others, he was preparing to defend the ghetto residents. Shortly before the April uprising, he was reassigned to Henoch Gutman's group on the brushmakers' premises (at Świętojerska, Bonifraterska, and Wałowa).

April 20, around three in the afternoon. Kazik is standing at the lookout point at 6 Wałowa Street. The Germans are approaching from Franciszkańska, along Wałowa. As they come up to the entrance, Kazik gets ready to detonate the mine they have prepared. His commander is less patient and pulls the cord ahead of him. German soldiers are killed. On April 21, the brushmakers' premises go up in flames. The groups under Gutman, Berliński, Błones, and Grynszpan, under Marek Edelman's command, manage to find a way through to the central ghetto.

They go into hiding at 30 Franciszkańska Street, in the Provisioning Authority bunker.

In the night of April 30–May 1, Kazik and the Bundist Zygmunt Frydrych are sent to seek help for the insurgents. They're walked to the tunnel leading out under Muranowska Street onto the other side of the wall by their comrades Adolf Hochberg and Lolek. On May 8, Kazik goes back into the ghetto, but finds nobody in the ruins. On his way back, in the sewers, he hears a group of insurrectionists who have lost their way.

On May 10, around forty ŻOB fighters emerge from a manhole cover onto Prosta Street. They climb into a waiting truck and drive off in the direction of the Żoliborz district. Kazik has done his job, and now he leaves that group in the woods and goes back to Warsaw for those who did not manage to get out in time. But he is too late—he hears from gawkers that there was a shootout at the manhole cover, and they were all killed. One more time, in September 1943, with the help of a Polish policeman called Mądry, Kazik got another twenty or so people out of the ruins of the ghetto. He found a place for them at 1 Mokotowska Street. (They were starving and weak. Many of them died. The others were denounced by a Pole.)

Kazik had the perfect looks, like a backstreet boy from Czerniaków. He was Antek Cukierman's courier. He lived variously at 4 Komitetowa Street, 5 Pańska, 6 Wolska, and 18 Leszno. He smuggled people, bought guns, and traveled around the General Government: to Krakow, Koniecpol, Częstochowa, and Skarżysko-Kamienna.

On August 1, 1944, he joined an AK unit that was attacking the Courts. He stayed with them for a few days as a Pole. (He didn't want to stay longer because the AK boys didn't like Jews.) After that, he fought in the downtown Śródmieście district in an AL unit. Sometime during the Polish August rising, he was given the order to locate the ŻOB archive, which had been hidden at 18 Leszno. He and a group of ŻOB fighters went back there, into what was by then German-occupied territory. They lived there as fighters in the ruins for several weeks. They never found the archive. Then they were deported to the camp in Pruszków. For years after the war, Kazik remained furious that the lives of so many people had been put at risk for some papers.

In February 1945, he left Warsaw. He wanted to take revenge on the Germans and was for several months a member of the conspiracy under Aba Kowner. He reached Palestine in mid-1946. He was an officer in the Israeli army and fought in the 1948 and 1967 wars. Kazik Ratajzer, in Israel Simcha Rotem, lived in Jerusalem with his wife and two sons. He often went back to Poland, because he was from there, a little, and felt at home there, a little. He died on December 22, 2018, in Jerusalem.

Halinka Rochman was one of the youngest members of the ŻOB's left-wing youth. In the ghetto, she joined forces with the Spartakus faction. Her father found her a hiding-place outside the ghetto, but Halinka did not want to go. From July 1942, she drilled self-defense in the group under Janek Biały. In her apartment at 42 Leszno, the young communists learned to handle weapons. At 51 Nowolipie, they produced grenades and Molotov cocktails. Halinka Rochman was killed in the uprising on April 27, shielding Różka Rozenfeld with her own body.

Izrael Romanowicz lived in the Warsaw district of Ochota before the war. He learned the locksmith's trade in a vocational school at 26 Grzybowska and was a Cukunft activist. In the ghetto he worked as a fireman at the Berson and Bauman children's hospital on Śliska Street. After the *große Aktion*, in the summer of 1942, he was given a job in the Schultz 'shop.

In the April uprising, he fought in the Bund group under Jurek Błones. When the Germans set fire to the brushmakers' premises, five groups attempted to break through a gap in the wall into the central ghetto. In shoes wrapped in rags, they walked along in single file. Suddenly, the Germans illuminated the street. Izrael Romanowicz took the spotlight out with a single, well-aimed shot, and they were all able to pass safely on.

On May 10, Izrael was evacuated to the Wyszków woods with the group of insurgents. He, Dawid Nowodworski, and a few others wanted to return to Warsaw. Not far from Łomianki, they were all apprehended and murdered, probably as a result of a denunciation.

Lejb Rotblat, Lutek, was born on October 14, 1918, in Warsaw. He came from an assimilated family and lived on Twarda Street. He attended a Polish high school. His mother, Miriam, was the director of an orphanage on Grzybowska Street, and then at 27 Twarda. As a teenager, orphaned young after his father died, Lejb considered emigrating to Palestine. In 1937, he passed his school-leaving examinations and became a youth leader in Hanoar Hacyjoni. Tall, handsome, and talented, Lutek was very popular with his peers. During the occupation, he joined Akiba and became one of its leaders.

In the ghetto he ran a refugee reception point at 32 Zamenhofa Street, worked in the Jewish community store, and was active in Akiba. He also helped his mother out at the Youth Center at 18 Mylna Street, and, after the *große Aktion*, in the boarding school on Wołyńska Street (the last boarding school in the ghetto). Lutek lived with his mother at 44/35 Muranowska. (When Jurek Wilner escaped from the camp in Kawęczyn, he went into hiding in Lutek's apartment.)

Lutek was one of the first to call for armed resistance. On the eve of the April uprising, he was appointed commander of the newly created Akiba group, which before long joined forces with Icchak Blaustein's group. Shortly before May 8, he took all those closest to him to the bunker at 18 Miła: his mother, a relation of hers called Dolcia, and Hela Schüpper.

When on May 8 the Germans surrounded the ŻOBists' last base and started to pump gas inside, the insurrectionists did not surrender. Many of them decided to commit suicide. Hela Schüpper heard from Tosia Altman that Lutek gave his mother poison and shot her. And finally killed himself. Dolcia managed to escape from Miła but died in the sewer.

Jechiel (Chil) Rotblit was a Shomer in the unit under Szlomo Winogron. In the April uprising, he fought in the Toebbens-Schultz 'shop yards. It is not known how Chil died.

Cwi Rotman was a member of Dawid Nowodworski's Haszomer Hacair group. In the uprising, he fought in the Toebbens-Schultz 'shop yards. On April 29, he managed to escape the ghetto with the group of insurgents. He joined a partisan unit in the Wyszków woods and was killed in 1944 during an operation on the river Bug near the town of Brok. He was twenty-three.

Stefa Rozen came from Warsaw. In the ghetto, she had employment in Dreier's locksmiths' 'shop on Smocza. She was accepted into a Poalej Syjon Left group. In the April uprising she fought on the brushmakers' premises. She was killed on May 3 with Szaanan Lent, Zysie Papier, and many others in the bunker at 30 Franciszkańska Street. She was twenty-two.

Jardena Rozenberg was born in Warsaw in 1923. Brought up in a wealthy religious family on Nalewki Street, Jardena was a pupil at Jehudija, the Jewish girls' high school at 55 Długa Street. Against her parents' wishes, she joined Haszomer Hacair and became an instructor. She was preparing for emigration to Palestine on the kibbutz of her organization at 23 Nalewki. She was short, quiet, and unassuming. In the ghetto, she taught children in clandestine classes. She was killed in the April uprising in a situation not remembered by anyone.

Rachela Rozencwajg was born in Sulejów near Piotrków, into a family with Zionist traditions. Her father, a Jewish community official, sympathized with the League for Aid to Workers in Israel. Rachela joined the Halutz organization Frajhajt. On a kibbutz in Kielce, she prepared to emigrate to Palestine.

During the war, she was in the Warsaw ghetto. She joined a Dror fighting group, and in the uprising fought under Zachariasz Artsztajn's command in the central ghetto. She was killed in the ruins along with her closest friend, Abraham Drejer. She was twenty-four.

Adek Rozenfeld was the brother of Rózka Rozenfeld. In the April uprising Adek fought in Heniek Kawe's group in the Toebbens-Schultz 'shop yards. It is not known where or when he was killed.

Michał Rozenfeld, Michał Biały, was brought up in an intellectual family. He studied psychology at the University of Warsaw, was a member of the communist party, and was active in the Życie students' union. At the beginning of the war, he was in Lwów, but in 1941 he managed to reach Warsaw. He worked as a youth instructor in the CENTOS boarding school on Wolność or Leszno.

Michał Biały [Rozenfeld] and Janek Biały [Szwarcfus] began organizing fighting groups of five in the ghetto as early as July 1942. Anna Lanota remembered that sometime in early August, Michał turned up at the brushmakers' 'shop (where she and her brothers were), gave her two hundred zlotys, and said: "Tomorrow morning at five, a detachment of Jews is leaving the ghetto to go to work. Join them and give the money to the German at the wacha. He'll either let you through or shoot you."

Before the April uprising, Michał Rozenfeld joined the ŻOB staff company as the PPR representative. Kazia Bergman remembered that it was Michał who gave her the order to leave the ghetto and work for the party outside its walls. And that before that, she had accompanied him on meetings with "Stary", meaning Lewartowski.[10]

Michał Rozenfeld fought in the central ghetto. On May 8 he was sheltering in the bunker at 18 Miła Street. He was one of the dozen or so who survived the attack on the bunker. He left the ghetto on May 10 via the sewers.

---

10 Józef Lewartowski—a communist, and in the ghetto a member of the anti-fascist bloc. Killed in the *große Aktion*. His pseudonym, Stary, means "old" or "old man" in Polish.

In the Wyszków woods, he was in a group with Janek Szwarcfus. He also took part in the derailment of the train in Urle. After that operation, the whole group hid in the village of Krawcowizna. They were surprised by a detachment of Germans. Though they defended themselves, they were all killed on the spot. Michał Rozenfeld was 27. After the war, the partisans from Szwarcfus's unit were buried in the Jewish cemetery in Warsaw.

Różka Rozenfeld was born in 1921 in Częstochowa or Warsaw. Her family lived in the Jewish district, at 14 Muranowska. Her father traded in shoes. Różka graduated from Mrs. Zysfeld's commercial high school at 2a Nalewki Street. Before the war, she belonged to the communist students' union, and during the occupation she established a Spartakus youth group. A short, dark-haired girl with a strong character, she was always full of verve.

Różka trained a left-wing fighting group from the Herman Brauer factory. She taught them to shoot in an empty apartment on Muranowska. Różka wanted to leave the ghetto and go into the woods. During the April uprising she fought in Hersz Kawc's group on the premises of the Toebbens-Schultz workshops. (She was apparently in the same group as her brother Adek.)

She got out of the burning ghetto via the tunnel leading from the bunker at 74 Leszno to the building on the opposite side of the street, at 71 Leszno. Różka was caught on May 7, 1943. As she was being taken back into the ghetto, she made a run for it on Nowolipie. She was shot dead on the spot, somewhere near no. 42. There is also another story about Różka. This may have happened earlier. In late April or early May, Michał Jaworski jumped a train near Michalin station. While he was looking for his cap among the debris scattered along the trackside, he found an ID card from the Schilling workshop, made out in the name of Różka Rozenfeld, with her photograph on it.

Lejb (Lejbl) Rozowski was the younger brother of Welwł. Before the war, he had belonged to Skif and Cukunft. He was a quiet, unassuming boy. Someone remembered that before the uprising, he made wicks for incendiary bottles, and that he was swollen from hunger.

In April he fought in the Bund unit under Jurek Błones. On May 10, he did not make it out of the sewer when the truck was waiting at the manhole cover. Like Adolf Hochberg, Szlamek Szuster, and over a dozen others. They were too late. Lejb was killed in the sewer, or perhaps on Prosta Street, when the Germans surrounded the manhole cover. He was twenty-three.

Welwł (Welwel, Welwl, Wolf) Rozowski was born in 1916 in Warsaw and brought up in a family with Bundist traditions. He attended a Jewish elementary school and high school and had started a university degree program. In 1926, he joined Skif. In time, he became a member of the Cukunft leadership, and a Bundist youth instructor.

Welwł Rozowski, Marek Edelman, and Stasia Rozensztajn printed Bundist news bulletins on a duplicator (the same duplicator that they had taken from the school on Karmelicka Street in September 1939). They were assisted by Blumka Klog. In November 1942, the Germans caught a group of Bundists in the Roerich 'shop, and took them, along with many others, to the Umschlagplatz. In the train to Treblinka, the Bundists held hands. Somehow, they sawed through the window bars and jumped out one after the other. Welwł was the last to jump.

They all made it back to the ghetto. Ahead of the April uprising, Welwł Rozowski was appointed commander of a Bundist group on the Toebbens-Schultz premises. He fought in the area of the Roerich 'shop. The insurgents managed to retain control of the houses at 8–10 Smocza until April 29; that day, the Germans set fire to Smocza Street. That same night, via the rooftops, they moved to Leszno Street, to join Geller's group. That same night, they left the ghetto via the sewers.

Welwł did not go into the woods. He and Marek Edelman went into hiding on Śmiała Street in Żoliborz, probably at no. 24. In late May, they received a visit from some *szmalcownicy*, who took everything, and demanded more. Welwł went to try and find money. Him, because he looked slightly better than Marek. It is known that he went to Salo Fiszgrund on Senatorska Street. Władka the courier (Fajgele Peltel) recorded that the curfew was already in force when Welwł was apprehended by a German railwayman on Elektoralna Street and taken to a dark-blue police precinct. Marek did not know what happened to Welwł after he left Senatorska. It is not known where or when Welwł was murdered.

Eliahu Różański, Elek, was born in Warsaw in 1923. He lived on Nalewki Street, attended a Jewish high school, and from 1937 was a member of a Warsaw Haszomer Hacair cell. A round-faced, smiling high schooler. And always weighed down with books. After the outbreak of war, like many others he obeyed Col. Umiastowski's call and went east beyond Poland's border.

In 1940 he went into the Warsaw ghetto. In July 1942, when the first ŻOB groups were being formed, he became an instructor for one of the "fighting fives." During the *große Aktion*, he jumped a train to Treblinka and went back into the ghetto. Elek was in a pair with Margalit Landau. When the underground commanders resolved to punish the Jewish Gestapo agents, Elek reported to carry out the execution. He shot Jakub Lejkin, deputy commander of the Order Service, on October 22, 1942. (He was assisted in his preparations for the operation by Margalit Landau and Merdek Growas.)

On January 18, 1943, he was with Margalit in Anielewicz's group, which attacked the Germans. Fatally wounded, he lay all night in a fever. Elek died in the early hours of the morning in an apartment at 61 Miła Street. (The Germans had probably murdered Margalit the previous day on the Umschlagplatz.)

Mosze Rubin was born in 1919 in Berlin. He was one of the many Jews expelled from Germany in 1938. Mosze was quick to learn Polish and find his feet in his new environment. He was the leader of a refugee youth group. He joined Frajhajt, and later Jungbor Poalej Syjon, a youth activist organization.

During the war, he remained in Warsaw. By trade a printer and graphic designer, he was a specialist document counterfeiter. Until November 1942, he worked on the farm in Czerniaków. In the April uprising he fought in the central ghetto, in the group under Artsztajn. Somebody remembered that Mosze had a mouth organ, and often played Beethoven. He was killed in the ghetto ruins sometime after May 10, 1943.

Lew Rudnicki came from a relatively well-off Warsaw family. Before the war, he worked in a store selling accessories on Nalewki. A short, always serious boy, he was a member of a left-wing youth movement. In the ghetto he had employment in Hallman's 'shop on Nowolipki.

During the April uprising he fought in the Toebbens-Schultz 'shop yards. When the insurgents ran out of ammunition, Lew Rudnicki committed suicide. According to another record, Lew was killed along with Heniek Kawe's group in the bunker at 74 Leszno when the Germans flooded their bunker.

Gedalia Rutman (Rotman) was born in Warsaw in 1923. His father had a small store on Twarda Street. Gedalia grew up in the Jewish district. He attended the community school on Śliska, and then a Jewish high school. In 1937 he joined Hanoar Hacyjoni. He conducted its choir.

In the April uprising, he fought under Beniamin Wald's command in the Toebbens-Schultz 'shop yards. On May 6, he and a group of other insurgents managed to get out of the ghetto. They were all apprehended by the Germans on Ogrodowa Street. They were taken to the ghetto precinct at 103 Żelazna. Gedalia was shot on the spot because he had a grenade in his pocket.

Com. Ryba was one of the April insurrectionists in Heniek Kawe's PPR group in the Toebbens-Schultz 'shop yards. He and the others died on April 27, when their base at 74 Leszno Street was flooded.

Rysia [Gryngruz?] was born in Łódź or Konin. She attended a Polish high school. At the beginning of the war, she was in Radomsko for a time, and then in Ostrowiec. She arrived in the Warsaw ghetto in late 1942. She had good looks, and was brave, so she also traveled to the ghettos in Krakow and Częstochowa. She became a ŻOB courier.

In late December 1942, she went back to Krakow and brought three Krakow ŻOB members to the ghetto in Warsaw: Izrael Zilberman, Naftali Zimak, and Lejb Troks. She was killed on January 18, 1943, during the first battles in the ghetto, or caught at that time and killed in Treblinka. She was twenty-five. (This may have been the Rysia whose surname was Gryngruz, because one historian mentioned a Rysia Gryngruz who was a courier.)

Salka was in Zachariasz Artsztajn's group. She may have joined the Drorists during the uprising, or perhaps she moved to their group from a different one. The only person who remembered Salka was Tadek Borzykowski. On April 25 or 26, they were billeted at 7 Miła Street. They had no more bullets, the burning houses were crashing down, and the smoke, dust, and fire were hindering breathing and visibility. Salka began trying to talk the insurgents into committing suicide. Apparently, her words fell on fertile ground. Tadek Borzykowski wrote that he had difficulty taking her gun away from her. That night, the group managed to make it through to 18 Miła. Salka was probably killed there on May 8.

Jerzyk Sarnak was brought up in an intellectual family. He was musical. In the Warsaw ghetto, he worked with his father in the Brauer metalworks. During the *große Aktion*, Jerzyk's parents and sister were in hiding in a bunker on Nalewki. They were caught and taken to the Umschlagplatz. They resisted boarding the train, so the Germans murdered them in the yard, along with around forty others. It was then that Jerzyk joined a Jewish left-wing fighting group. In the April uprising, he fought in the central ghetto in the group under Paweł Bryskin. He was around twenty when he was killed.

Marysia Sawicka was a friend of Gina Klepfisz, Michał's sister, before the war. They would meet up at the Skra sports field and run (The races were each 800 meters long . . .) races together, Marysia in the PPS strip, and Gina in the Bund's Jutrznia squad. During the war, Marysia and her sister Anna Wąchalska hid Gina in their apartment at 23 Dworska Street. After that, they hid Lodzia and Irenka Klepfisz, the wife and daughter of Michał. They also gave shelter to Genia, the sister of Kazik Ratajzer, and to little Zimra Rawicka, who was taken there by Zygmunt Frydrych.

After the April uprising, Marysia gave immense help to Kazik Ratajzer and other ŻOB fighters in Warsaw. She hid them in her apartment at 18 Leszno; for a while there were as many as nine people living there. She rented out apartments in her name, and carried information, money, and weapons. She took part in the Polish Warsaw rising. Marysia Sawicka was a ŻOB courier, Marek Edelman said, without hesitation, in the year 2000.

After the war, she worked in an office and in a preschool, and sewed summer dresses. She lived alone and longed for signs from her friends from Israel. She died on August 17, 1996, in Łódź. She was 91. (She was awarded the Righteous Among the Nations medal in 1964.)

Hela Schüpper (Rufeisen-Schüpper) was born in 1921 into a religious family in Krakow. Her grandfather was a *soyfer*, a scribe, at the court of the Bobover tzaddik, and her father a cantor in a synagogue. Hela, who attended a Polish girls' school, grew up in two worlds: the Polish and the Jewish. She graduated from a commercial high school and worked as an official in a laundry company. She had links with the religious youth movement Akiba.

In late 1940 she went to Warsaw on *hakhshara*, because she wanted to prepare to emigrate to Eretz Israel. She became a courier for the Halutz movement, traveling between Krakow, Warsaw, Sanok, Rzeszów, and Lwów with counterfeit documents for people from the underground, she ran guns and distributed news bulletins, and also took boys from the Krakow ghetto to partisan units. She was in the Warsaw ghetto from the end of January 1943, living with Lutek Rotblat and his mother at 44 Muranowska Street.

When the April uprising broke out, she was supposed to have been going to Bochnia, near Krakow, with money and information, and to smuggle a pistol there. By the wall, she was shot in the leg, and she stayed in the ghetto. On Muranowska Street, she took care of Jurek Wilner, who was sick, just rescued from the German camp in Kawęczyn. In the night of May 7, Hela left the bunker at 18 Miła Street. She remembered that her group had been sent out by Anielewicz.

Ten or eleven of them had gone, to bring help. They had Antek Cukierman's address. They went down into the sewer via the cellars at 22 Franciszkańska Street. Someone from Marek Edelman's group led them—Hela couldn't remember the name. They were supposed to emerge on Bielańska Street, but their guide lost his way. They opened the manhole cover on Długa Street, right in front of some Polish police officers, who demanded money from them. A German military police officer appeared. The insurgents defended themselves by firing a few shots and fled. Hela saw Paweł Bryskin for a moment, but then she was alone. She still does not know what happened to Paweł, Zygfryda Simson, Wanda Ochron, Koza, Lilka Zimak, the boys from Germany who had come to the ghetto from Czerniaków, Szymon, who had been walking in front of her through the sewers, or any of the others, whose names she does not remember. She somehow got away.

She went to hide in the celluloid factory in Praga before the fire broke out there. After that she was in Rembertów. She was blackmailed, so in July 1943, her good Polish landlady took her and Szoszana Langer to the Hotel Polski. From there, she was taken to Bergen-Belsen with one thousand five hundred other people. She spent twenty-two months in the camp. She never returned to Poland. From 1945, Hela Rufeisen-Schüpper lived in Israel, in the Bustan Ha-Galil moshav. She died on April 23, 2017.

Mieczysław Siekierski, Motek Teller, was born in Warsaw in 1908. His mother was called Chaja and his father Mordche. Motek Teller had graduated from university before 1939 and was an engineer. He ran a tannery at 58 Żelazna Street.

He survived the war, and in 1947, in his application for decoration, he wrote his ŻOB biography. "On August 14, 1942, I was captured and packed into a cattle car going to Treblinka. Outside Wołomin I miraculously managed to escape from the train. After the operations in the ghetto died down, I went back there and lived in the 'Nowolipie' labor camp. I found contact with the ŻOB and put myself under the orders of the organization. My immediate superior was Abram Celnik, a master locksmith from the locksmiths' 'shop at Nowolipie no. 44."

He said that from November 1942, he was a member of the PPR group in the ŻOB. At the end of January 1943, he took part in the elimination of Gestapo agent Pinie. In February he threw sulfuric acid at Mops, the commandant of what he called the "Jewish militia" on Nowolipie Street. In the March, he took part in the elimination of Blumsztein, the manager of the joinery 'shop, in his apartment at 39 Nowolipie. Between December 1942 and April 1943, he made hundreds of hand grenades filled with cheddite for the ŻOB. In the April uprising, he was shot in the leg somewhere around Smocza and Nowolipie.

After the war, engineer Mieczysław Siekierski became the director of a fur factory on Puławska Street in Warsaw. In 1946 he and his wife Irena were living at 22/3 Nowy Świat.

Stefan Siewierski was the nephew of Anna Wąchalska and Marysia Sawicka. He was born in Łowicz in 1921. He graduated from the Konarski high school before the war, and belonged to OMTUR, the PPS youth wing. Through his aunts, who raised him, and his younger sister Halina, he became involved with the Jewish insurgents. He smuggled arms and food into the ghetto.

When on May 10 the insurrectionists emerged from the sewers on Prosta Street, Stefan was nearby, shielding the group. After that, he traveled to the woods in Łomianki several times with arms. In Warsaw, he shuttled between many people in hiding, helping to take care of them. A number of stories about his death have been recorded. Stefan was given a revolver by the ŻOB. His excitement was so great that he couldn't sit still at home, and ran to a cake store, where a German noticed the pistol in his pocket and shot him on the spot. Or: when Abrasza Blum and Fajgele Peltel were denounced by the janitor of the house at 2 Barokowa Street, Stefan decided to take revenge on him. The revenge failed, and instead, the janitor managed to inform on Stefan to the Gestapo. There is a third story, told years later by his sister, Halina. It was May 21 or 23, 1943. Stefan put on a German uniform and pretended he was marching several rounded-up Jews somewhere. In this way he managed to take them from Łomianki to join the partisans. When he returned to Warsaw, he looked in at a restaurant on Dworska. The military police noticed the pistol in his pocket. They took him to his aunts' house on Krzyżanowskiego Street, looking for arms and Jews. The only person at home was Zosia (Zimra), but nothing happened to her because she didn't have "those looks." They took Stefan to Szucha. They beat him badly, so he told them that he would show them a place in the woods where there were Jews. Out on the road, he made a run for it, and they shot him on the spot.

And a fourth, told by Kazik Ratajzer. It was in late May, and Antek, Kazik, and Stefan were taking the last group of Jews from Łomianki to the Wyszków woods. They were pleased that it had worked! On Krakowskie Przedmieście a photographer took a snapshot of them. That evening, Kazik found out from Anna Wąchalska that after the operation, Stefan had gone to a bar, laid his pistol on the table—foolhardy bravura?—the clientele all held their breath, and the police nark did not hesitate, and shot Stefan in the head. (Stefan Siewierski was awarded the Righteous Among the Nations medal in 1965.)

Zygfryda Simson. In the April uprising she fought in the central ghetto in the PPR fighting group. Her commander was her close friend Paweł Bryskin. On May 7, 1943, Zygfryda, Paweł, Wanda Ochron, Lilka Zimak, Icchok Suknik, Hela Schüpper, and a number of others managed to escape the ghetto. Paweł, Zygfryda, Wanda, Lilka, and Icchok went into hiding on Miodowa. On May 27, they were denounced by the janitor. They were all killed.

Chana Skulska was born in Krzemieniec in Volhynia. She joined Frajhajt at a very early age. She was warehouse manager in the Borochow kibbutz in Łódź. After the outbreak of the war, she went to Warsaw. In early 1940, she worked on the kibbutz in Grochów, and when the Germans closed that down, she went to live in the Halutz commune at 34 Dzielna. She also spent some time on the farm in Czerniaków.

In the April uprising she fought on the Toebbens-Schultz 'shop premises in Beniamin Wald's Dror unit. She was twenty-four when she was killed.

Szmuel Sobol was brought up in a poor family in the Warsaw district of Praga. He didn't finish elementary school because he had to start work young; he was a locksmith. In 1935 he joined Frajhajt. He was a sportsman in Hapoel, and an activist in the self-defense groups of Frajhajt Szuc. He worked with groups of Halutzim, in the ghetto and on the Czerniaków farm. In April 1943 he fought in Berl Braude's group in the central ghetto. He was killed on May 8 in the bunker at 18 Miła Street. He was twenty-three.

Stach was a light-haired youth—that was how Dorka Goldkorn remembered him. He joined the Jewish police in order to be a little safer and have somewhat more freedom of maneuver. On January 18, 1943, Comrade Stach launched the first grenade on the Toebbens-Schultz premises. The second was thrown by a Shomer, Izrael. After that, but before the uprising, Stach organized an attack on the police precinct at the intersection of Nowolipki and Smocza. Someone noted down the number on his cap, however, and before long, he was found. As he was being arrested, Stach attacked a German, who shot him dead on the spot. He was twenty-five.

Abram Stolak worked in the Brauer factory on Nalewki Street after the *große Aktion*. In the April uprising he was a soldier with the Poalej Syjon Left group. A Polish Army reservist in the rank of corporal, he was one of their best riflemen. On May 10, he managed to leave the ghetto via the sewers, and went with the others to join the partisans in the Wyszków woods. Masza Glajtman-Putermilch remembered that he drowned in the river Bug because the boat he was in sprang a leak. (His companion, Chaim, saved himself because he could swim.) Abram was twenty-six.

Szlomo Sufit was born in Warsaw in 1921. He attended the Hinuch boys' high school for humanities at 8 Krasińskich Square (in 1936, the school moved to 27 Ogrodowa Street) and was a member of Hanoar Hacyjoni. During the war, he joined Akiba. In the Warsaw ghetto, he was an instructor on the organization's kibbutz at 10 Nalewki. A very genuine boy, well brought-up, and very handsome, dark-haired, with big blue eyes, Hela Schüpper remembers.

In the uprising he fought on the premises of the Toebbens-Schultz 'shop, the adjutant of his group's leader, Dawid Nowodworski. On April 28, badly wounded in the leg, he was moved to the insurgents' hospital in the bunker at 76 Leszno Street. He was not in any condition to manage the walk through the sewers. With other wounded fighters, and his close friend, Chana Grauman, he remained in the ghetto under the care of Lea Korn. It is not known when or how the Germans discovered the bunker at 76 Leszno. It is not known when or how Szlomo Sufit was killed.

Icchok Suknik, Koza, was born in Warsaw in 1920. His father, Majer Suknik, and his mother, Cesia Lament, came from Chmielnik, but had married in Warsaw in 1917. His father was a pursemaker. He sewed and mended sacks, canvases, and jute covers in his workshop at 14 Twarda Street. The family lived at 44 Pańska. Icchok had two brothers. In 1929, his father went to Belgium and worked with his brother in a fur factory. (In that period, many breadwinners of poor families sought any work they could find, any work at all outside Poland.)

Icchok attended the craft school on Stawki. He was full of the joy of life, a confident, though sometimes belligerent boy. He was a member of Haszomer Hacair. He learned to shoot well on military training courses and had the rank of sergeant. His mother and youngest brother were killed during a bombardment in 1939. His father ran a bakery on Grzybowska Street in the ghetto until he died of typhus in November 1941.

At the beginning of the war, Icchok worked on the Halutz farm in Pniewy near Warsaw. In September 1941, he and a group of friends managed to get to Częstochowa and join the Shomer kibbutz. He worked on an agrarian farm in Zawiercie. A group of about twenty of them were issued work permits for a farm in Żarki. (A photograph of the Żarki Shomers has been preserved, showing Icchok, Amnon Klukowski, Chagit Elster, Awram Zylbersztajn, and Lodzia Hamersztajn.) In the spring of 1942, they were visited by Arie Wilner, who urged them to prepare for defense. Shortly after that, the kibbutz was disbanded, because the Shomers did not have enough food. Most of them went into the Częstochowa ghetto.

Icchok managed to get to Warsaw. When the resistance began to form, Koza established two workshops where the young people made hand grenades. In Lutek Rotblat's apartment he taught them how to handle weapons.

In the January 1943 operation he was in Anielewicz's group. He gave cover to a fugitive by throwing a grenade on target. In the April uprising he fought in the central ghetto in the unit under Merdek Growas. Koza had an automatic rifle and twenty bullets. On May 7, his commanders sent him and Paweł Bryskin out of the ghetto to organize help for the insurgents still inside amid the burning buildings. He was killed on Miodowa Street along with Paweł and the others, because the Germans were tipped off about their hideout by the Polish janitor.

Basia Dwojra Sylman was born on January 7, 1924, in Ostrowiec Kielecki. Her father, Chaim Fiszel, a merchant, came from Zawichost. Her mother, Marjem Kajle Eiger, was related to Rabbi Ejger. They lived at 23 Kunowska Street.

Basia, her younger sister Sara, and a group of Dror members from Ostrowiec came to the Warsaw ghetto in late 1942. The girls' mother also reached Warsaw. She was in hiding in relatively good conditions and tried in vain to persuade her daughters to leave the ghetto. Basia fought in April and May 1943 under Henoch Gutman on the brushmakers' premises. The circumstances of her death are unknown. She was nineteen years old.

Sara (Suja) Sylman, sister of Basia, was born on May 15, 1926, in Ostrowiec Kielecki. And, like her sister, she belonged to Dror. She was killed sometime between January 18 and 21, 1943, in the first armed clashes in the Warsaw ghetto. She was seventeen.

Icchak Symplak was brought up in a poor family in the Warsaw Jewish district. He was recorded as having been a slight, short boy with a broad back and a mature face. In September 1939, he had wanted to emigrate to Palestine via Vilnius. In the Warsaw ghetto, he aligned himself with Dror. Sometimes he would leave the ghetto and travel to Krakow as a Halutz courier. He was killed in the January operation. He was twenty-two.

Rywka Szafirsztajn, Julia, was born in 1919 in Warsaw, into a poor, religious family. She lived at 14 Nowiniarska Street and worked in a weaving manufactory. As for many others in the Jewish district, her youth organization was both school and entertainment to her. Rywka was a member of Haszomer Hacair. She and Dawid Nowodworski managed the finances of several cells.

In the April uprising she fought with a Shomer group in the Toebbens-Schultz workshops. On April 29 she left the ghetto through the sewers. Via Łomianki she reached the Wyszków woods. She, Dawid Nowodworski, and a group of other insurgents were killed as they were on their way back to Warsaw from the woods. It was probably late June, or perhaps early July 1943.

Tadek (Tuwia) Szajngut (Szejngut) was brought up on Jewish Nowolipie. He learned metalworking at the Grzybowska Street Community school and was a member of Haszomer Hacair. He was stocky, muscular, of medium height, and had large, workworn hands. He moved slowly, like an elephant, and spoke little; he had a slight stammer. Tadek never let anyone down. He wore a kapote and a dark blue cloth cap—he looked like one of the porters from Żelazna Brama. (That was how others remembered him.)

He traveled to Częstochowa and Krakow and went back and forth between the ghetto and the Polish side of the city. He lived for a while with Michał Klepfisz and Władka Peltel at 3 Górnośląska Street, and often went to visit the Legiec family on Szczygla Street. He was close friends with Gaik. He smuggled arms and clandestine newspapers into the ghetto, and never parted from his pistol. In early April 1943, somewhere near Okólnik, Tadek killed a young man, a Jewish Gestapo agent.

After the ghetto uprising, he grew close to Kazik Ratajzer and Antek Cukierman. On July 7, he went to the apartment at 80 Waszyngtona Street to see Stefan

Pokropek. That day, a guy called Czarny was supposed to deliver some guns. The Gestapo surrounded the house, because Czarny was their agent. Kazik and Pokropek's daughter managed to escape through a window. Rysiek, Stefan Pokropek, and Tadek Szajngut were killed. Tadek was twenty-three or twenty-five.

Moszek Szarfsztajn came from Warsaw. He was a member of Haszomer Hacair, and later of Dror. In 1942 he worked on the Czerniaków farm. In the April uprising, he fought in the group under Berl Braude in the central ghetto. On May 6 or 7, he managed to leave the ghetto. He went into hiding in Praga, in the abandoned celluloid factory at 11 Listopada Street. He was killed in the fire on May 24 with other ŻOBists.

Szymek Szejntal. In the April uprising he probably fought in a Haszomer Hacair unit. After that, he managed to reach Łomianki with others. He was light-haired, like an Aryan, wore a German uniform, and "disoriented the Germans," Masza Glajtman-Putermilch recalled. He was in the group under Dawid Nowodworski that set out to return to Warsaw. Szymek, Dawid, and the others were killed in unknown circumstances.

Majorek Szerman came from Warsaw. He was a boxer in the Bund club Jutrznia, but did not belong to Cukunft, Masza Glajtman remembered. In the April uprising he fought bravely in the group under Lejb Gruzalc. He was killed on May 3 in the battle at 30 Franciszkańska Street. He was twenty-two.

Szlomo is only known by his forename. He was "older," Tadek Borzykowski recorded. He was probably over thirty. He was stocky, with a tanned face and repertoire of choice language—a true Warsaw porter. He only joined Artsztajn's group at 29 Miła when the uprising was already underway. He was given an old hunting rifle and handled it boldly. It is not known whether Szlomo survived the uprising, whether he survived the war.

Sara Szlubowska (Szelubowska) joined a Halutz organization before the war. Chawka Folman roomed with her at Dzielna Street, and remembered that Sara was tiny, and braided her hair.

Her name was on the list of murdered ŻOB soldiers. She was recorded as having been a member of Dror. But in fact, Sara survived the war. After the liberation of Auschwitz, she reached Palestine. She lived on the Shfa'im kibbutz.

Rywa Szmutke fought in the PPR group on Leszno and Smocza in the first days of the uprising. Someone somewhere recorded that she threw grenades with

Eliezer Geller. She was probably in Heniek Kawe's group at 74 Leszno, next door to Geller at 76 Leszno.

Rywa spoke very poor Polish. When she emerged from the sewers into the city after the uprising, she went to Szczygla Street, to the Legiec family, for help, because there were others still waiting in the sewers. She looked dreadful: dirty, ripped clothes, and excessive agitation. She talked incessantly about her comrades who were still in the sewers, and that they had to be gotten out. The Legieces went to check out the manhole cover: there was nobody left to rescue, and there were Germans milling about in the area. Rywka refused to believe it. Toward evening, she ran from Szczygla, presumably to try and rescue her comrades. Nobody ever saw her again.

Tema Sznajderman, Wanda Majewska, was born in 1917 in Warsaw, into an assimilated family. Someone remembered that she was very thin, delicate, and unusually brave. She had links to the Halutz movement. At the start of the war, she went to Kovel, and then to Vilnius, with Antek Cukierman. When she traveled to Poland's eastern regions, she used the name Wanda Majewska. Someone counted that she went to the Białystok ghetto twenty times, smuggling people, arms, and money.

In January 1943, she returned to Warsaw with eighty thousand roubles from the chairman of the Białystok Judenrat, engineer Efraim Barasz. (Someone wrote of Barasz that he was an obedient executor of German orders, and the money for the ŻOB was intended as a way of seeing him through to a time without Germans.)

Shortly before the January operation, Tema smuggled in instructions on how to fill lightbulbs with sulfuric acid to make incendiary bombs. She was caught on January 18, 1943, with Lea Perelsztajn and Sara Granatsztajn. It is not known whether the girls were killed at the Umschlagplatz or in Treblinka.

Berek Sznajdmil, Abram, Adam, was born in Łódź in 1904. His father was a poor Hasid from Lithuania. Berek attended a cheder, and later he was able to go to a good Łódź high school because with a teacher's help he was exempted from tuition fees. According to the historian Melekh Neustadt, Berek wanted to become an attorney, to defend workers and socialists.

Berek embarked on a law degree at the University of Warsaw. He gave private tuition and worked as a bookkeeper in a company on Długa Street. For several years he was also active in Bundist organizations. He was an instructor in Cukunft-Szturm. Majus Nowogrodzki remembered him clearly, because for five years, Berek rented a room in Majus' parents' apartment at 7 Nowolipie Street, where the editorial offices of the *Folkscajtung* and the Central Committee of the Bund were also based. Sznajdmil's real forename was Adam, but he was known to everyone as Berek, because he was an ensign in the Polish Army, and was as strong and brave a Jewish soldier as Berek Joselewicz. Majus remembered (differently to what Neustadt recorded) that Berek came from a small town on the Polish-German border, somewhere near Koszalin, and that in the last summer before the war, he and Berek had climbed Mięguszowiecka Edge in the Tatra Mountains.

Berek passed out of officer cadet school shortly before the war started. He fought in the defense of Modlin, and then managed to get to Lithuania. A few months later, he returned to Warsaw, to the ghetto, because he wanted to be with Ruta. (Ruta Perenson and her young son were killed during the uprising, at 8 Wałowa Street.)

When Szmuel Zygielbojm left Poland in December 1939, Sznajdmil joined the Bund leadership, and was the party representative on the Coordinating Committee. It was he who put the entire Bund underground structure in place. Together with Abrasza Blum and Bernard Goldsztajn, he edited the paper *Za Naszą i Waszą Wolność*. He sometimes left the ghetto. He returned shortly before Pesach and the April uprising. He was with the Bundist group on the brushmakers' premises. He was killed on May 3 at 30 Franciszkańska Street. (A grenade blew his head apart.)

Dow Szniper came from Staszów. Before the war he was a shoemaker. In the April uprising he fought in a Haszomer Hacair unit. He left the ghetto via the sewers on April 29 or perhaps May 10. Like Gabryś Fryszdorf, in the Wyszków woods, he was the commandant of a group of ŻOB insurgents.

Masza Glajtman remembered him from their time in the woods. Dow was older than all the others; he could have been thirty. He was short, and very black-haired; nice, but couldn't get lucky, and perhaps that was why he came on to all the girls, she said.

In July 1944, he went back to Warsaw. He went into hiding at 24 Rakowiecka with Pnina Papier, Chana Kryształ, and Janek Bilak. When the Polish August rising broke out, the owner of their apartment ordered them out onto the street. They tagged onto a group of Poles carrying bundles. Before long, it transpired that the Germans were marching them to Szucha. Just before they reached the

Gestapo precinct building, Dow took out his gun and fired. He was killed on the spot. According to records, this took place on August 5, 1944.

Szyja Szpancer was a tailor before the war and was active in Jewish trade unions. In the April uprising, he fought in the PPR group. He was killed on May 8, 1943, in the ŻOB staff bunker at 18 Miła Street.

Bronek (Boruch) Szpigiel was born in 1919 in Wyszogród, his father's native town. (His grandfather's house still stands, at 3/5 Rynek, the main town square.) His parents moved to Warsaw when Bronek was just over a year old. They lived at 30 Pawia Street. His father made felt spats and dabbled in politics. There were both Bundists and communists in the family. When the war broke out, Bronek and his brother moved to Białystok. He returned to Warsaw shortly afterwards.

In the ghetto, he became involved with the Bundist underground. On January 17, 1943, he and his comrades resolved not to let themselves be rounded up and taken to the Umschlagplatz, so the next day, they hid in an attic. After that, they began to prepare to defend themselves. Hersz Lent of Poalej Syjon Left taught his group of five to handle weapons. Bronek worked in the Roerich 'shop. He lived on the 'shop premises with a group that later, in the April uprising, operated under the command of Welwł Rozowski.

On January 17, 1943, a ŻOB member, Awram Zandman, was placed under arrest in the Hallman 'shop because a bottle of some kind of acid had been found on his person. The *werkszuc* wanted to hand him over to the Germans, but Anielewicz, Fryszdorf, and Szpigiel went into the 'shop brandishing their guns and freed him.

In the April uprising, Bronek fought on his home turf: Smocza, Nowolipki, and Leszno. He left the ghetto on April 29. From May 15 until October 18, 1943, he fought with the partisans in the Wyszków woods, according to a testimony signed by Cpt. Marek Edelman. ("We didn't know how to go about in the woods, and then there weren't enough guns," Bronek commented.) Later, he and Chajka Bełchatowska went into hiding in Warsaw. During the Polish Warsaw rising, they lived with Jakubek Putermilch and Masza Glajtman at 64 Żelazna Street, in the apartment of Władek Świętochowski.

After the Polish rising, they didn't leave the city with the Varsovians, because they were afraid of the Poles. They hid among the ruins on Sienna Street, with Pnina Grynszpan, nine of them altogether. They had no food, no water. Bronek spent days digging a well in one of the bunkers with a tin plate. The earth was soft, and he dug through to water at a depth of just a meter. They only left the bunker on January 23 or 24, because they didn't know that the war had ended.

Bronek Szpigiel and his wife Chajka Bełchatowska left Poland in 1946. From 1948 they lived together in Montreal. In Canada, Bronek made bags, because no one wore felt spats anymore. From March 2002, Bronek lived in Montreal without Chajka. He died on May 20, 2013.

Szlama, Dawid Sztajn, Sztejn [Stein], was born on September 1, 1924, in Ostrowiec Kielecki. His father, Berek Lejzor, was a bookkeeper and worked in a bank. Dawid had three brothers, all of whom finished high school before the war. The maiden name of his mother, Alta Cypa, was Honigsberg. She was a very good woman, Dawid Stein wrote from Haifa, and kept a warm-hearted house. The family lived at 16 Zatylna Street in Ostrowiec. Dawid attended a Polish elementary school, studied Hebrew in the afternoons, and was a member of Haszomer Hacair.

Later on, there was a ghetto in Ostrowiec. Dawid's father was killed during the deportation in October 1942. His mother was taken to Treblinka, and his brothers were killed later: Motek in a partisan operation, and the other two shot by the Germans for escaping from a camp.

The light-haired Jadzia, a courier sent by Anielewicz, made seven trips to the ghetto in Ostrowiec, and managed to smuggle seven people to Warsaw, before the Germans caught her at the wacha and she was killed. (No one remembered Jadzia's surname.)

Dawid Sztein was to have been the eighth, so in March 1943, he decided to make his own way to Warsaw. He had just one address in the ghetto: 56 Leszno. Through the gate in the ghetto wall by Leszno, he recognized Szapsel Rotholc, previously a well-known boxer, now a policeman in the ghetto. "Are you crazy, man?!" Szapsel hollered. "Everyone else is trying to get outta here, and you wanna come in?" It was April 1943. Dawid hid in an empty apartment on the Polish side of Leszno, and waited for a work detail, to sneak into the ghetto with them. Szapsel took all his money for that advice, four hundred zlotys.

The people who lived at 56 Leszno were called the Fogelnests. And in the cellars of the house, money for the underground was extorted from rich Jews. It was this cellar that Aron Chmielnicki referred to as the ŻOB prison. Dawid was posted on guard outside the cellar prison at the time when a rich man known as Opolion was being held there. Opolion was guarded by four people in rotation: Dawid, Kuba Fogelnest, Danek Fogelnest, and a girl. They all lived in one room, which was also a bread store, where bakers brought sacks full of bread for the Party.

Friends of Dawid's from Ostrowiec, Izak Morgenlender and Abram Horowicz, put him in touch with Nowodworski, who accepted Dawid into his group. "I didn't fight, because I didn't have a weapon; I was a reserve," he wrote from Haifa in 2003. A few days later, Morgenlender took Dawid into a bunker where there were several dozen people, including ŻOBists. Smugglers would get out of the ghetto through the house at Leszno, but they were unwilling to reveal where the entrance to their tunnel was. Eventually, though, the people in the bunker managed to spot them.

The ŻOB fighters managed to leave the ghetto via the tunnel on their second attempt. They were led by Regina Fudem. In the night of April 29, they reached 27 Ogrodowa Street. The next day, Tadek Szejngut, Krzaczek, and Józek [Jarost?] took the insurgents to the woods near Łomianki. Six days later, Krzaczek went back to them with some food. After that, someone took them twenty rifles. A little further away, in more dense woodland, two Russians were waiting for them. Dawid Stein was one of the partisans. He spent 18 months in the woods. The Germans carried out periodic roundups, and by the end, there were only a handful of them left: Aron Chmielnicki, Bolek, Staszek, Janek, and Dawid. When the liberation came, they were in the woods near the village of Dobre. Dawid Stein and his wife Basia emigrated to Romania, and on October 28, 1945, by ship from Constanța to Palestine. In Israel he worked on building sites and was a major in the Israeli army. He lived in Haifa.

Moniek Sztengiel came from Warsaw. In 1942 he and his group moved to the Dror base in Werbkowice. He was one of the few who managed to escape when the Germans surrounded the Halutzim. Wounded, he returned to Warsaw. In the April uprising he fought in the group under Icchak Blaustein in the central ghetto. Moniek Sztengiel was killed in the ŻOB bunker on Miła Street. He was seventeen.

Mietek Sztern aligned himself with the left-wing youth in the Warsaw ghetto. On one occasion, he stole a typewriter from the management of one of the 'shops and wrote proclamations on it in his apartment at 53 Nowolipie Street. In late February 1943, he was involved in the arson attack on the Hallman workshops. (The ŻOB wanted to prevent the machines being taken out of the ghetto and warned that the camps in Poniatowa and Trawniki meant death.) Shortly afterwards, Mietek Sztern went out on a second arson operation. Somewhere on the Schultz premises, he fell from a roof and was killed. He was seventeen.

Dawid Szulman was born in Warsaw. He attended a Tarbut school, and before the war went to live on the Halutz kibbutz in Ostrowiec. He returned to the Warsaw ghetto with a group of friends, and in the April uprising they fought in a Dror unit. It was apparently Dawid who carried out the death sentence on the Gestapo agent Izrael First. That was a Dror operation, masterminded by Berl Braude and Antek Cukierman. (The sentence on Lejkin was carried out by members of Haszomer.) Dawid Szulman was a foreign citizen, but he burned his papers and stayed in the ghetto. He was apparently the boy whom Frania Beatus, Cukierman's courier on the Polish side, was waiting for. Dawid was killed in the uprising; he was eighteen. Frania committed suicide; she was seventeen.

Genia (Gienia) Szulman was born in Warsaw and brought up in a wealthy family. (Her father was a construction entrepreneur.) They lived in the Jewish district, at 36 Pawia Street. But Genia's first language was Polish; she only learned Yiddish later. Both she and her sister Maryla were active members of Frajhajt. It has been recorded that Gienia was subtle and genuine. And that one time, she helped a homeless boy—she organized a collection for him and found him shelter. In the ghetto, she aligned herself with Dror, and in the April uprising she fought in one of its groups. Nothing is known of when, where, or how Genia Szulman died.

Szlamek Szuster was born on April 18, 1926, in Pruszków, into a bootmaker's family. His father had a store selling hides, and some purse-making machines at 7 Komorowska Street. The family lived at the same address, in a single room with a kitchen. Szlamek's father was known as Mosze the Bootmaker, Hela Szuster-Kron, Szlamek's elder sister, wrote me from Tel Aviv. Their mother, Bela Szuster-Aronowicz, helped their father out. Szlamek attended first a Polish elementary school on Piłsudski Street, and later a Jewish one in Warsaw, at 11 Poznańska Street. In the evenings, he studied religion and Hebrew with his grandfather. Both he and Hela were active members of the Halutz movement Frajhajt.

In February 1941, the Pruszków ghetto, which had been in existence barely three months, was liquidated, and the Pruszków Jews were moved into the Warsaw ghetto. At first, the Germans held them in an empty school building, but later, Szlamek's family moved to live with his maternal aunt, Fajge Sztajn, at 31 Nowolipie. Szlamek was enterprising and supported his family from smuggling: he would go to Pruszków, bring various bits and pieces back with him, and then sell them with his mother on the street in the ghetto.

(Hela, his sister, was initially in the Halutz kibbutz at 34 Dzielna, and later, from March 1941 until early December 1942, worked on the Czerniaków farm. Szlamek joined her in early 1942 and stayed there till the end. Hela Szuster-Kron remembered the names of the Pruszków Jews who were on the farm: Zachariasz Artsztajn, Hela Farbman, Pola Zylberberg, Guta Tamboryn, Cyla Kiwkowicz, and Balbina Synalewicz.)

In the April uprising, Szlamek was in Henoch Gutman's Dror group on the brushmakers' premises. He fought valiantly. He assumed command when Gutman was wounded on Franciszkańska.

On May 10, he and several dozen other ghetto soldiers went out of the ghetto. They waited a long time in the cramped, airless sewers. They spread out from the main shaft in small groups, because there was less water and more air in the smaller sewers. When at last the manhole cover on Prosta Street was opened and they could climb out, Szlamek and Mosze Rubin were sent back for the others—that was what Hela Szuster heard from Cywia Lubetkin after the war. They didn't get back in time. The truck carrying the insurrectionists had to drive away. Szlamek Szuster and over a dozen other ŻOB fighters were killed an hour or two later at the manhole on Prosta.

Szulamit Szuszkowska came from Warsaw. In the April uprising, she fought in Merdek Growas's Shomer group. She was killed on May 8, 1943, in the ŻOB command bunker on Miła. She was twenty-one.

Meir Szwarc was born in Warsaw in 1916. He was a member of the younger generation of Bundists. In the ghetto he was a rickshaw driver, and later a *werkszuc* in the German workshops. In the April uprising he was in Rozowski's group in the Toebbens-Schultz 'shop yards. He was shot in the shoulder as he and Heniek Klajnwajs were escorting Chańcia Płotnicka out of the ghetto.

Meir left via the sewers with others on April 29. He didn't go to Łomianki, but stayed in a bunker on the Polish side, at 29 Ogrodowa Street. He managed to get out before May 6, when the Germans discovered the bunker. He went into hiding in a factory in Praga, the same factory where the fire broke out on May 24. He managed to escape that time, too. A Polish woman opened her door and hid him in her closet. But when the Germans had finished searching her apartment and left, she opened the closet to find Meir dead. He probably died of a heart attack.

Szlomo Szwarc was born in 1911. He was Meir's elder brother, a tailor by trade, and, like Meir, a member of the Bund. In the ghetto he lived at 58 Nowolipie, and thereafter on Prosta. After the *große Aktion*, he worked in the Toebbens-Schultz 'shops on Nowolipie.

In the April uprising he fought in the group under Welwł Rozowski. He probably left the ghetto on April 29. He was in the Wyszków woods for a time but wanted to go back to Warsaw. Somewhere en route, someone denounced him, or caught him. All that is known is that he never reached Warsaw. It is not known how he died.

Janek Szwarcfus, Janek Biały, was born in Warsaw in 1914. Before the war, he was an active member of an illegal communist movement and was imprisoned in Mokotów twice. He fought in the September 1939 campaign to defend Poland.

In the ghetto he had employment in the Toebbens and later Roerich 'shops. There, he formed a group of young communists, whom he taught to handle weapons. Together they made grenades and carried out "exes."

In the April uprising he fought in the central ghetto. He was tall and light-haired, and that was probably why he was known as Janek Biały [Janek White]. (And he had an unusual delicateness about him, remembered Anna Lanota, who met Janek in the woods.)

He left the ghetto and managed to reach Łomianki, and then the Wyszków woods, to join the partisans. (The Jewish insurgents organized themselves into four units of between fifteen and twenty people. Two of them were east and two west of the river Bug. They were stationed fifteen kilometers apart. The commander of two, and maybe even three of the groups, which also comprised Russian fugitives from various camps, was a Red Army solider called Siemionov.)

Janek talked about neither his family nor the uprising. (Nobody talked about the uprising, Anna Lanota said.) Janek Biały did bold things in the woods, Marek Edelman remembered. In late August, he was tasked with blowing up a German military train traveling to Małkinia.

In the night of August 31/September 1, Janek's group positioned their explosives at the station in Urle, and then hid in a forester's house near the village of Krawcowizna, in woodland belonging to Duke Radziwiłł. The forester, Jan Bobrowski, notified a German unit stationing in Tłuszcz. The partisans barricaded themselves into a barn and managed to defend themselves for a relatively long time; two of them succeeded in escaping. Janek Szwarcfus, Michał Rozenfeld,

Tola Rabinowicz, Samuel Juszkiewicz, Guta Tajchler, Józef Papier, Rachela, Zosia (recorded in one place as Ida), Rutka, Chaim Cyrenajka, Emil, Edek, someone known as "the Rabbi," Stefan, a fifteen-year-old boy called Wacek, an official from the Order Service in the ghetto, and two others whose names nobody remembered, were all killed. Adek Jankielewicz may also have been among them. The names of many of them are recorded in the Jewish cemetery in Warsaw. (The attempt to blow up the train caused a two-hour interruption in rail traffic on the Małkinia route. After the war, the forester was sentenced to death.)

Fajwel Szwarcsztajn was born in Żyrardów in 1916 into the family of a poor tailor. Fajwel joined Frajhajt and played sport in the Hapoel team. From 1940 he was in Warsaw. In 1942, he worked on the Halutz farm in Czerniaków.

After that, in the ghetto, he lived in the Halutz commune on Miła. He was one of those who carried out the death sentence on Alfred Nossig. In the April uprising, he fought in the unit under Zachariasz Artsztajn in the central ghetto. He was twenty-two when he died.

Lea Szyfman was probably born in 1922 in Warsaw. She was brought up in the family of a poor trader on Ostrowska Street and in Bundist organizations. It was she who brought Masza Glajtman into Lejb Gruzalc's group, which was billeted at 29 Zamenhofa Street. Later, in the April uprising, they were also together. Lea was not given a revolver, only a grenade, because she was in a pair with Adek Jankielewicz, and he had a gun. She was killed on April 27 in the bunker at 29 Miła along with Lejb Gruzalc, Dawidek Hochberg, and others.

Miriam Szyfman, Lea's sister, was probably born in 1915. She attended the Michalewicz CISzO School at 51 Miła. Afterwards she did dressmaking courses. She was active in Bundist organizations as a youth instructor. In the ghetto she established a hairdressing cooperative on Nowolipki, probably at no. 21. Quiet and unassuming, she lived with Awram Fajner in a small second-floor room on Gęsia Street. Miriam organized the distribution of Bundist news bulletins. Someone wrote that she was a poor conspirator because everyone could tell from her gleaming eyes that a news bulletin had just come out.

After September 1942, it was dangerous to try and move between the different residential parts of the ghetto—the Germans punished this with death. At that time, Miriam was working in the Roerich 'shop, and as a courier. Her most frequent destinations were the central ghetto and the brushmakers' premises, and she usually slipped between them with work details. She would steal German uniforms in pieces from the tailors' workshop. Then she and other girls would sew the pieces together in the night, because the uniforms were to be necessary in the uprising. She learned to shoot at 34 Świętojerska Street.

Shortly before April, someone brought in a new Browning. Miriam loaded it, but it was damaged, and one of the bullets shattered the bone in her leg. During the uprising, she was in the hospital bunker at 6 Gęsia Street. Marek Edelman saw her on May 6 or 7. Her leg was in a cast, and she couldn't move. She was said to have committed suicide when the Germans attacked the bunker on May 10. It is not known when Miriam Szyfman, distributor of Bundist news bulletins, died.

Władek Świętochowski was born in Warsaw in 1918. Before the war, he attended a school of commerce. During the occupation, he was an employee of the Warsaw Electrical Power Plant's fire service. From April 23, 1943, until mid-June that year, he was sent into the ghetto about every other day to secure substations and monitor the conflagration. Świętochowski, a socialist, assisted the Jews he met. The insurrectionists came to him at the substation during the night, and Władek showed them where there was water, and gave them food, alcohol for their wounds, cigarettes, matches, and the daily newspaper, which they devoured hungrily, because they were keen to know what the people of Warsaw thought about their struggle. (Władek Świętochowski recorded his experiences in the ghetto shortly after the war.)

He built a hideout in his apartment at 64/11 Żelazna. He took in the two Grossbard sisters, and a mother and daughter. After the Jewish uprising, he brought Chajka Bełchatowska and Bronek Szpigiel, and Masza Glajtman and Jakubek Putermilch out of the woods, and they lived with him, too. He built another hideout for members of the ŻOB in an apartment at 18 Leszno, leased under Marysia Sawicka's name. When Rozowski was denounced, Władek took Marek Edelman from Śmiała to Noakowskiego Street, to the home of Mrs. Hornung. He regularly went into the woods with Władka Peltel and Lodzia Hamersztajn. He took people back to Warsaw: Pnina Grynszpan, Dow Szniper, and others. After that, he took part in the Polish Warsaw rising. He was deported to Germany.

After the war, he returned to Poland and lived in Kłodzko, where he ran a store. Thereafter, he returned to Warsaw, and became an important company director, but he refused to join the communist party, and he was fired. He fell very low, reduced to piecework such as assembling ballpoint pens, or soldering pots for a locksmith, but he remained cheerful, and cultivated his friendships with his occupation-era wards. It was around 1968 that his serious problems began. Perhaps it was because he received packages containing oranges, and beautiful dresses for his daughter. He was interrogated, and tailed, until he began to fear going out onto the street. He died in a peculiar state of isolation in 1997. (Władysław and Władysława Świętochowski were awarded the Righteous Among the Nations medal in 1968.)

Guta Tajchler worked in a stocking manufactory and was a member of the communist youth organization Spartakus. In the April uprising she fought on the premises of the Toebbens-Schultz workshops, probably in the same group as Janek Szwarcfus, her closest friend. They left the ghetto on April 29. Via Łomianki, they reached the partisans in the Wyszków woods. Guta was killed in the operation at Urle railroad station on August 31, 1943. Janek Szwarcfus and his whole group were murdered in the village of Krawcowizna after that operation, denounced by a forester. Their bodies were buried after the war in the Jewish cemetery in Warsaw. Guta's name is not listed on any of the more than a dozen matzevot.

Niuta Tajtelbaum, Rywa, Wanda Witwicka, was born on October 31, 1917, in Łódź. Her father, Majer Tajtelbaum, came from Łęczyca. He was a religious man and a wealthy factory-owner, and in 1914 emigrated to America. (He returned after a few years.) Niuta attended a Beit Jaakow religious school for girls and the Aba high school in Łódź. As an advocate of left-wing ideas, she caused her family a lot of problems. She was a member of the Union of Socialist Youth, the Communist Union of Polish Youth, and Spartakus, and was an instructor in the illegal children's organization Pionier, so she was repeatedly expelled from school. She nonetheless passed her high school finals in 1936 and started a history degree at the University of Warsaw. She joined a committee for the defense of Jewish academics, a group established after the introduction of the "bench ghetto."

After the outbreak of war, she fled to Lwów, where she worked as a cleaner in a German barracks and studied at the Teaching Institute. In September 1941, she went to Warsaw, into the ghetto. She moved in with her sister, Ina Warszawska, on Dzielna Street. She and her friend from Łódź, Kazimiera (Kazia) Bergman, were among the first to join the PPR in the Warsaw ghetto. From around January or February 1942, Kazia remembered, they were active in a group of five (Bela Krakowska from Łódź; Henia Mączkowska, later Anita Duraczowa; Różka, whose brother was in the organization known as Trzynastka;[11] and the two of them) and would meet up on Leszno. Niuta was their instructor. Kazia Bergman didn't remember their having a gun.

She left the ghetto on the Party's orders during the *große Aktion*, but returned frequently in her capacity as a courier for the PPR and the GL. She ran guns, delivered news bulletins, passed on information, and trained the PPR "fives." The last time Kazia Bergman saw Niuta was on October 16, 1942. (She remembered the date precisely because it was her birthday.) Niuta was assisting some Soviet POWs escaping from incarceration. She was also preparing to go into the woods. Apparently, her closest collaborator was Franciszek Bartoszek; she was a member of his GL special group. She took part in many operations in the city. (Somewhere it was noted down that it was she who covered Bartoszek on January 17, 1943, when he planted a bomb in the Mitropa restaurant.)

There was a story about Niuta Tajtelbaum. A small young girl with bright, innocent eyes, a colorful country scarf on her head, and long, straw-colored braids down her back walks into a German government office holding a basket. She stops timidly in the doorway and explains that she is there on a personal matter. A tall, stocky German with SS badges rises from behind a desk. He stares at the girl, confounded, and then shouts: "Gibt es bei euch auch eine Lorelei?!"[12] The girl is transformed from a humble peasant into a fearless Judith, whips out her revolver, shoots, and vanishes.

The background to this story is probably an incident from early 1943: Wanda Witwicka shot three Gestapo agents living on Chmielna Street. One of them survived and was taken wounded to hospital. So, Wanda dressed up as a doctor, marched into the hospital, and shot both the policeman guarding his room, and the surviving agent himself.

---

11 The "Trzynastka" ("Thirteen"), properly the Office for Combatting Usury and Speculation, got its colloquial name from its address: 13 Leszno Street. It was a Jewish institution in the ghetto, subordinate to the Gestapo. It existed in 1940 and 1941, and in fact controlled the Judenrat and infiltrated underground organizations. Members of the "Thirteen" were eliminated as collaborators by Jewish underground formations. In 1941 it was subsumed into the Jewish Order Service.

12 *Gibt es* ... (Ger.)—Do you people have a Lorelei, too?

On April 20, the ghetto uprising had already begun. Late that afternoon, Bartoszek's GL group attacked a machine gun positioned on the corner of Nowiniarska and Franciszkańska that was firing on the brushmakers' premises from outside the wall. They shot two Germans dead and retreated to safety through Traugutta Park. One of the GL group members was Niuta Tajtelbaum. She is known to have been wanted by the Germans for a long time, and arrested on July 19, 1943, in the entranceway of the house where she lived, at 21 Poznańska Street. It is also known that no subsequent arrests were made, so she cannot have given anyone away. It is not known whether she was murdered in the Pawiak prison or on Szucha Avenue.

Tamar was a member of Haszomer Hacair. She was Merdek Growas's girl, Masza Glajtman-Putermilch remembered. Tamar was murdered along with Merdek's group in the woods.

Tamara was killed on the first day of the uprising together with Heniek Zylberberg, on the corner of Nalewki and Gęsia. Tamara, like Heniek, belonged to the PPR. They had thrown the first grenades and incendiary bottles from 33 Nalewki. The battle lasted no longer than two hours; the insurrectionists killed two Germans.

Berl Tasenkrojt (Tasenkraut, Taselkrojt) was born in 1921 in Warsaw. He was a member of the Bund, and in the April uprising he fought in the group under Lejb Gruzalc at 29 Miła, and on Zamenhofa and Dzika Streets. He was a large, strong guy, the closest friend of Dawid Hochberg. Berl's father was a butcher. Masza Putermilch remembers that for Pesach she made kishke that Berl had brought from his father shortly before the uprising, but that they never ate it.

Berl left the ghetto on May 10. On May 19, he reached Wyszków with a group of other insurgents. Berl and Julek Junghajzer fought in Merdek Growas's forest unit. It is unclear how Growas's group died. They were probably all murdered by Polish partisans.

Szlamek Tenenbojm was a member of one of the PPR fighting groups. In the April uprising, he fought on the Toebbens-Schultz premises. I found no further information on Szlamek Tenenbojm.

Lejb Troks was born in 1920 in Mogielnica, near Warsaw, and brought up in a tanner's family. He attended the Jawne school for children of the religious, and a Polish elementary school. He helped his father with the hides and spent his free time at activities run by Frajhajt, with his sisters Chana and Perla.

He spent the summer of 1942 working in the fields in Ceranów with a group of Halutzim from Ostrowiec. He also travelled to the Kraków ŻOB. Chawka Folman remembered him. Lejb and his friends from the Ostrowiec Dror cell stole into the Warsaw ghetto illegally, because they wanted to fight. Lejb Troks was killed in the first clashes in the ghetto on January 18, 1943.

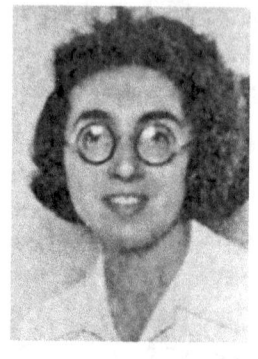

Cimeret Wachenhojzer, Chedwa, was born in 1916 into a poor Warsaw family. She joined Haszomer Hacair at a very young age. Shortly before the war, she started a degree course at the university, and she was active in her organization. She was responsible for educating young Shomers.

In the ghetto, she lived with her elderly mother at 49 Miła. She gave lessons for a pittance. She was tiny, with black hair and glasses. Her face was ashen gray, and she was thin and diminutive. One of her Shomer pupils remembered her as always having been weak and sickly. Nothing is known of where or in which group Cimeret fought in the uprising.

She left the ghetto via the sewers and reached Łomianki. The plan was to find somewhere she could be in hiding because she was not suited to life in the woods. Several notes mention that Cimeret was tasked with writing an account of the events of the final weeks in the ghetto. (Perhaps it was expected of her because people knew that she had written a diary, which she had given to Irena Adamowicz for safekeeping.)

When Zygmunt Frydrych arrived in the woods to take the Błones siblings to a hideout, the weakly Cimeret went with them. They are known to have reached Pludy, where they were killed. On January 11, 1946, the Bundists' bodies were moved to the Jewish cemetery in Warsaw and laid to rest in a common grave. Cimeret Wachenhojzer, a Shomer, was buried shortly afterwards in the same cemetery on Okopowa Street by her comrades from Haszomer Hacair.

Kuba Wajs was remembered by Aron Chmielnicki only by name. An Ostrowiec Dror member also remembered a Kuba from the Toebbens-Schultz 'shops; this was probably the same boy. If so, he is known to have guarded Opolion, the rich Jew imprisoned on Leszno for refusing to give the organization any money. The same Kuba is also known to have been killed on the third day of the uprising.

Mojsze Waksfeld is one of the names of the April insurgents written down on the list of murdered ŻOB soldiers by its commanders. They gave him as having belonged to the PPR. I found no information about Mojsze Waksfeld.

Beniamin Wald was born in 1920 into a religious family in the Czerniaków district of Warsaw. He attended a cheder and a yeshiva. He joined Frajhajt, probably against his father's will, and agitated for emigration to Palestine among the poor. Though he was as young as any of the others, he was known as Tatele [Yid. daddy], perhaps because he was warm and caring.

At the start of the war, he worked on the farm in Grochów. After that, he went into the ghetto. In the January 1943 operation, he fought on Zamenhofa and Miła Streets. In April, he was appointed commander of the Dror group at 36 Leszno. Shortly before the uprising, Wald carried out the death sentence on Pilotka, because Antek Cukierman was afraid that Pilotka would reveal their hideout to the Germans. (They held him in the cellar at 56 Leszno, but despite their beatings, Pilotka refused to admit to anything. Perhaps Pilotka was actually sniffing around them so much because he wanted to join the group, Marek Edelman wondered.) On April 30 or May 1, Beniamin Wald led his group down into the sewers, but the Germans had the manhole at the other end, on Ogrodowa Street, covered. The whole group was killed.

Wanda was a Pole and helped Jews in hiding in the Polish part of the city. Only Marek Edelman remembered her. He said she was a dressmaker and lived on Marszałkowska, not far from Nowogrodzka. It was apparently Anna Wąchalska that initiated Wanda into the Jewish underground. Marek Edelman was sure that Wanda survived the war.

Olek Wartowicz is one of the names of the April insurgents written down on the list of murdered ŻOB soldiers by its commanders. They gave him as having belonged to the PPR. I found no information about Olek Wartowicz.

Anna Wąchalska was the elder sister of Marysia Sawicka and the aunt of Stefan Siewierski. Anna was born in 1895 in Warsaw. The widow of a railwayman and PPS activist who had been exiled to Siberia, she made her home, at 23 Dworska Street and later 44 Krzyżanowskiego Street in Wola, a safe haven

for many Jews. It is hard to establish exactly how many people passed through her apartment, how many she took care of during the occupation years, how many survived the war thanks to her dedication. Anna and Marysia's home was also a rendezvous for couriers from the Jewish underground.

When Kazik Ratajzer and Zygmunt Frydrych left the uprising to seek help for those still in the ghetto, the first place they turned to was Anna Wąchalska's home in Wola. When the courier Władka Peltel was in trouble, Anna gave her the papers of her deceased daughter Stanisława. And when Władka was arrested, Anna went to Daniłowiczowska Street to rescue her child. (And she got her out.)

After the Polish Warsaw rising, Anna, Zimra Rawicka (whom Anna had been sheltering), and Halina Siewierska, Stefan's younger sister, were taken to Germany as forced labor. Anna had both girls registered as her daughters. All three returned to Poland from Berlin in April 1945. Anna, weak and sick, lived in Łódź, and died there in 1966. (She was awarded the Righteous Among the Nations medal in 1964.)

Eugenia Wąsowska-Leszczyńska was born in 1906. During the occupation, she worked for the Red Cross. She also collaborated with the Żegota Council for Aid to Jews and the ŻOB. Her tasks included finding apartments for her Jewish wards, supplying counterfeit papers, distributing underground news bulletins, and delivering reports, briefs, and correspondence. Her apartment at 24/4 Żurawia was home to the Żegota office. Eugenia gave shelter to both Polish and Jewish underground activists (the Bundist Ignacy Samsonowicz lived on Żurawia Street from January 1943), and kept the Bund archives, as well as guns for the ŻOB.

Eugenia took part in the Polish Warsaw rising. After the war, she lived in Warsaw with her husband, Ignacy Samsonowicz, by then called Tadeusz Leszczyński. She was a copy editor and publisher. (In 1985 she was honored with the Righteous Among the Nations medal.) Eugenia Wąsowska-Leszczyńska died on May 8, 1987, in Warsaw.

Jehuda (Juda) Wengrower was born in Warsaw in 1920. He attended the Tarbut elementary school on Nowolipki, where his mother was also secretary. After that, he went to a school on Gęsia Street. Juda was a member of Haszomer

Hacair, an instructor and ideologue for the movement. In 1942, he was entrusted with the Shomers' war archives. He kept them somewhere on the Polish side.

Juda left the ghetto frequently. He returned shortly before the uprising and joined one of the Hashomer fighting groups in the central ghetto. He took a bullet from the Germans even before the uprising broke out, as he was distributing flyers. He was one of the dozen or so who managed to escape from the bunker at 18 Miła Street. Masza Glajtman remembered that those people hid in a latrine pit, and then went to Franciszkańska, where she met them. Everybody remembered that Juda was poisoned by the gas. As they walked through the sewers, he was very weak due to his wounded lung and the severe poisoning. He fainted repeatedly, and every time he came round, he would drink the filthy water. He died in the coppice in Łomianki on May 10 or 11.

Icchak Wichter is one of the names of the April insurgents written down on the list of murdered ŻOB soldiers by its commanders. They gave him as having belonged to Poalej Syjon Left. I found no information about Icchak Wichter.

Izrael Wilner, Arie, Jurek, was born on November 14, 1917, in Warsaw. His father owned a leather goods factory. They were a wealthy family and lived at 6 Przechodnia Street. Izrael attended a private high school. He was very shy by nature, and oscillated between despair and hope, someone wrote. From 1936 he was one of the leading instructors in the Warsaw Haszomer Hacair cell. In the spring of 1939, he went on *hakhshara* to the kibbutz in Słonim. He wanted to leave for Eretz Israel as soon as possible, but his organization ruled that he had to stay in Warsaw. In 1938, he wrote in his diary: "The question is not about the potential to change the situation. There is only one possibility now: to influence others and change their awareness. To act like a revolutionary, like a rebel."

When the war broke out, Israel went east. After that, he spent time in Łódź, Warsaw, Lwów, and Vilnius. He spent a few months in hiding in the Carmelite convent in Vilnius as the pet of the mother superior. He only returned to Warsaw in early 1942. (His parents and sister Guta lived on the "Aryan side.") In the summer of 1942, he called on the Jewish youth in Częstochowa to take up arms in self-defense.

Jurek was not in the Warsaw ghetto during the *große Aktion*. When he came back from Silesia, he went outside the ghetto as a ŻOB representative on the Polish side. He lived with his sister on Marszałkowska Street. (There was an SS men's club in the same house.) He nonetheless went into the ghetto frequently. He was there on January 18, 1943. He apparently fought in the first battles.

A few weeks later, in March, he was arrested in an apartment on the corner of Wspólna and Poznańska following a tip-off. The Gestapo found guns, and his notes (Jurek also wrote poetry). He was tortured cruelly for several days at Szucha, but he didn't reveal anything about the ŻOB; he insisted repeatedly that he was avenging his parents' deaths. After that, he was taken to Pawiak prison, and was by mistake added to the list of prisoners to be sent to the labor camp in the old brickworks in Kawęczyn near Rembertów. News of what had happened to him reached his friends. Marysia Jiruska and Heniek Grabowski managed to get him out of Kawęczyn. He was very sick and did not want to stay in Polish Warsaw.

He returned to the ghetto, to his friends. (When he was being operated on by a doctor in Lutek Rotblat's apartment, Hela Schüpper held the sieve with the general anesthetic.) On May 8 he was with Anielewicz and the others at 18 Miła Street. It has been recorded in many places that it was Jurek Wilner who called on the insurgents to commit suicide. Because "there are events that shake you, send your thoughts along new routes never previously walked by human feet."[13]

Jehoszua Szlomo Winogron was born on May 1, 1923, in Warsaw, into a wealthy family. His mother's name was Adela. His father, Abraham, had a metalworking factory on Bonifraterska Street: he made elevators, balconies, and beautiful ornamental elements. His father did his best to give his children a good education. The elder children studied abroad, and Szlomo was a model student at the Chinuch high school, and a Haszomer Hacair activist.

In the Warsaw ghetto he ran one of the Shomer cells and was the co-editor of the paper *Neged Ha-Zerem*. He was a *werkszuc* in the Hallman 'shop on Nowolipki. (His sister Esterka, born in 1915, was probably one of the carers in Dr. Korczak's orphanage. As late as July 18, 1942, she put on a performance of Tagore's *The Post Office* with the children.)

In February 1943, Szlomo Winogron and a group of over a dozen other ŻOB members set fire to the Hallman workshops and confiscated furniture storage. In the April uprising he was the commander of a Haszomer Hacair group, and

---

13 Quote from Jurek Wilner's diary, after Melekh Neustadt.

deputy commandant on the Toebbens-Schultz premises. He was wounded in the arm covering the retreat from Nowolipki to Leszno. He was the last to jump from the second-floor window. It is not known whether he was killed at that point or shortly thereafter.

Zeew Wortman was the name of one of the April insurrectionists whom the commanders wrote on the list of murdered soldiers of the Jewish Fighting Organization. They gave him as having belonged to Haszomer Hacair. I found no information about Zeew Wortman.

Hirsz Wroński was born in August 1924 in Warsaw and brought up in a family with Zionist traditions. He attended the Bundist Michalewicz school at 36 Krochmalna Street, but when he was twelve, he joined Jungbor, the youth arm of Poalej Syjon Left.

In the ghetto, he worked with his party. In his small room on Nowolipie Street he hosted meetings of Jugnt Poalej Syjon Left instructors. He fought in the April uprising, probably in Berliński's group. It is not known how Hirsz Wroński died.

Herman Zając was expelled from Germany in 1938 and went to live in Łódź. He was a Halutz and went to live and work in the local *hakhshara* community. After the outbreak of war, he fled to the East. In the April uprising he fought in the Dror group under Zachariasz Artsztajn. It is unclear how Herman Zając died. He was twenty-five.

Mosze Zajfman, Aron, was born in 1909 in Brańsk, near Białystok. His father traded in hides. Mosze attended a yeshiva. When he was seventeen, he was married to a girl from Góra Kalwaria, probably a daughter of a Gerer Hasid. Mosze made a living giving Hebrew lessons, and later got a job as a bookkeeper in a local sawmill.

In the years 1930–1931 he served in the Polish army. He was active in Poalej Syjon Right. In 1941, the Germans closed the sawmill down, and sent all the local Jews to the Warsaw ghetto. There, Mosze mended shoes. He was probably in his party's group in one of the 'shops. He was killed in the April uprising.

Abraham (Awram) Zandman was born in Warsaw in a very poor family. He was a member of Haszomer Hacair. Someone recorded that in January 1943, Zandman threw sulfuric acid at a *werkszuc* in the Hallman 'shop. He was caught by some factory security guards, who found the acid on his person, and freed at gunpoint by Anielewicz, Fryszdorf, and Szpigiel in masks. In the ghetto, Awram was in a pair with Chagit Putermilch. It is not known which group he fought in during the April uprising. It is known that he was killed in the woods by the river Bug with Merdek Growas's group. He was twenty-one.

Pnina Zandman was the younger sister of Awram. She was also a member of one of the two Haszomer Hacair groups operating in the 'shops. Masza Glajtman met Pnina at 22 Franciszkańska and remembered that Pnina did not leave the ghetto with them on May 10. Masza also remembered that Pnina went back to 18 Miła Street. She was probably killed there on May 8.

Izrael Zilberman (Zylberman) came from Ostrowiec Kielecki; he was born on July 1, 1923. His father, Eljasz, from the borough of Lipsko, had a small food store in Ostrowiec, perhaps in the house where they lived, at 17 Tylna Street. Izrael's mother, Chana Pesla Hermolin, probably also sold wares in the shop. Izrael attended a vocational school and was a member of Frajhajt. He was sickly and had poor eyesight.

It is known that he took part in the Krakow ŻOB operation codenamed Cyganeria on December 22, 1942 (when Jews bombarded the Krakow café of that name with grenades, killing a few German officers). After that, Izrael managed to get to Warsaw. It is known that he was killed on January 18, 1943.

Lilka Zimak was born in 1920 in the Warsaw district of Praga. Her father was a trader. Lilka attended elementary school. She was a member of Frajhajt, wrote articles, and displayed her poems on the wall in the organization's base. She collected subscriptions for the purchase of land in Palestine and was awaiting her chance to emigrate to work that land.

In the Warsaw ghetto, she lived on Gęsia Street with Berl Braude's Halutz group. In the April uprising she fought with her group in the central ghetto. She was also a courier for Izrael Kanał. She left the ghetto on May 7 in the group under Paweł Bryskin. Their task was to seek an exit route for those left inside the ghetto. Lilka was killed on May 27 on Miodowa Street with Paweł and several other insurgents.

Naftali Zimak was born in 1922. He was the brother of Lilka, and also belonged to Frajhajt. During the war, he spent some time in the Częstochowa ghetto, after which he returned to Warsaw and worked on the farm in Czerniaków. He also took part in the Krakow ŻOB operation codenamed Cyganeria in December 1942. Celina Lubetkin recorded that he also carried out a death sentence on a Jewish traitor in the Krakow ghetto.

He was wounded in battle in the Warsaw ghetto in January 1943. In the uprising, he fought in the Dror group under Berl Braude. Naftali Zimak was killed in April 1943.

Sara Żogel (Żagel, Żagiel) was born in Warsaw. She was active in the Zionist youth organization Hercelija and graduated from a Polish high school. Sławek Mirski remembered that she came from an intellectual family. In the ghetto, she lived on Kupiecka Street and worked in the von Schoene 'shop. She was a member of the PPR.

In the April uprising she was a courier for Jurek Grynszpan's PPR group on the brushmakers' premises at 38 Świętojerska Street. (Sławek Mirski was in that group.) She was 29 when she was killed.

Jurek Zołotow was the son of the well-known (and repeatedly incarcerated) communist Hirsz Zołotow and a teacher from the Jehudija high school. (Jurek's mother was also a communist. She was killed in the *große Aktion* in the ghetto.) Jurek played the violin and read lots of books. He took his final school-leaving examinations in the ghetto. (He may have attended clandestine classes held in the apartment of Stefania Szwajgier, the prewar principal of Jehudija.)

Prior to the April uprising, he often left the ghetto and returned with a gun, newspapers, or instructions from his comrades in the PPR. Władysław Legiec remembered that Jurek was tall and slim and wore a tattered school blazer with blue darts. He had good papers, and lived on Wąski Dunaj Street, in a single room with the family of a painter and decorator. His hosts treated him like a son, but Jurek didn't stay there long: he had to flee from some *szmalcownicy*.

It was Jurek Zołotow and Rysiek Maselman who rescued the insurgents who left the ghetto on May 10. They drove the fighters to Łomianki and returned for those who had not made it out of the sewers. They were both killed not far from Bankowy Square. Władysław Legiec remembered that Jurek managed to lob a grenade before he fell. He was not even twenty.

Heniek Zylberberg was the commander of one of the PPR groups, which operated in the central ghetto. He was probably killed on April 19 on the corner of Nalewki and Gęsia. He was twenty-one.

Rachelka Zylberberg, Sarenka, was born on January 5, 1920, in Warsaw, in a religious family. She convinced her parents that she should be allowed to study, so she attended Jehudija and, somewhat less officially, belonged to Haszomer Hacair. Her two brothers were members of Betar. Early on in the war, Rachelka, her sister Rut, and her close friend Mosze Kopyto went to Vilnius. (Mosze had previously belonged to Betar and was a close comrade of Anielewicz's in the organization.)

In Vilnius, all three of them joined the Shomer kibbutz. (Rut emigrated to Palestine in 1940.) In 1941, Rachelka gave birth to a daughter, Maja. Shortly afterwards, Mosze was murdered. Sarenka found a safe place for her daughter and returned to Warsaw. (Maja, Sarenka's daughter, was known to have been called Jadwiga Sugak in her Lithuanian family. Despite many attempts, she was never found, Reuven Aloni, the widower of Rut, Rachelka's sister, wrote from Israel.)

Sarenka worked with her mother in a little store in the ghetto, at 34 Nowolipki, and contributed to the preparations for the defense of the ghetto. She was killed on May 8 in the bunker on Miła.

Luba Zylberg, Zielona Marysia, [Gawisar] was born on May 8, 1924, into an assimilated family in Warsaw. Her father owned a cigarette wholesale business. Luba lived with her parents in the Saska Kępa district. She described herself as a spoilt only child who dabbled in salon communism. In the ghetto, she was with her parents on Gęsia Street. They survived by selling off increasingly worthless possessions. After that, Luba worked in the post office.

She left the ghetto after the *große Aktion* at the urging of her husband, Jurek Grasberg. With the assistance of Aleksander Kamiński, she rented an apartment in the attic of 5 Pańska Street, which shortly afterwards became one of the ŻOB's bases outside the ghetto. There was a large bookshelf there, and underneath it a drawer which led into a hiding-place. Several ŻOB fighters spent time in hiding on Pańska Street in Jurek and Luba's apartment: Marek Edelman, Celina Lubetkin, Antek Cukierman, Tadek Borzykowski, Kazik Ratajzer, Irka Gelblum, and Tadek Szejngut. Luba was known as "Zielona Marysia," to distinguish her from the other Marysia, Feinmesser, who was known as Marysia with the blue eyes, or "Niebieska Marysia." (Luba had an earthy complexion, while Bronka had blue eyes.) Zielona Marysia took care of Jews living in the city, taking them money, or sometimes some good news.

On the eve of the Polish Warsaw rising, she was on the other side of the river Vistula, in Saska Kępa, at the home of Jadwiga Strzelecka, and was unable to get back. She was not at Pańska Street on August 1 when some Poles killed Jurek Grasberg, who had left the apartment because he wanted to join the Polish rising. (He had a gun, and looked like a Jew, so they killed him because they thought he was a spy.) Zielona Marysia carried on her work as a courier.

From 1946, Luba Gawisar lived in Israel: at first in the Lohamei Ha-Getaot kibbutz, and later in Tel Aviv with Menaszke, her children, and her grandchildren. She was close friends with Kazik and his wife Gina. She missed Polishness but was unwilling to go to Poland. She died on November 8, 2011.

Moszek Zylbersztajn was the name of one of the April insurrectionists whom the commanders wrote on the list of murdered soldiers of the Jewish Fighting Organization. They gave him as having belonged to the PPR. I found no information about Moszek Zylbersztajn.

LISTA POLEGŁYCH W OBRONIE GHETTA WARSZAWSKIEGO.

/Przynależność organizacyjna oznaczona jest następującymi inicjałami: "SZ"-Hoszomer-Hoszair, "D"-Dror,"A"- Akiba,"G"-Gordonja, "B"-Bund, "FF" -Poalej-Syjon-Prawica,"PL"-Poalej-Syjon -Lewica,"HN"-Hanoar-Hacyjoni,"L"-Lewica.

1. Anielewicz Mordchaj /Sz/
2. Altman Tosia /Sz/
3. Aleksandrowicz Jakób /Sz/
4. Asz Aliezer /HN/
5. Aresztajn Zachariasz /D/
6. Altenberg Astera /D/
7. Alterman Szlomo /D/
8. Arbuz Chaim /Sz/
9. Bresler Izmul /Sz/
10. Blones Mejłech /A/
11. Berman Franka /L/
12. Baum Moses /HN/
13. Blones Iechak /HN/
14. Brojdo Berl /D/
15. Biegelman Menachem /D/
16. Blausztajn Iechak /D/
17. Bartmesser Kute /D/
18. Baran Dwora /D/
19. Blones Jurek /B/
20. Blones Guta /B/
21. Blones Lusiek /B/
22. Brylantsztajn Stasiek /B/
23. Brzezińska Zacha /L/
24. Blank Marek /G/
25. Baczyński Szlema /Sz/
26. Chadasza Iechak /Sz/
27. Umielnicki Nachum /B/
28. Dukier Yesia /D/
29. Cywier Mosze /D/
30. Chrzanowicz Iechak /D/
31. Cebulare Tosia /L/
32. Dolek Libeskind /A/
33. Drenger Symek /A/
34. Drajer Abram /D/
35. Dresner Abram /D/
36. Dobuchno Szaul /D/
37. Dawidowicz Tauba /B/
38. Dunski Cewek /B/
39. Dembiński Iechak /L/
40. Dembińska Dorka /L/
41. Diament Abram /FF/
42. Alek /Sz/
43. Edelsztajn Cwi /D/
44. Krlichman Sujka /G/
45. Einsdorf Miriam /Sz/
46. Eiger Abram /B/
47. Fajner Abram /D/
48. Finkelsztejn Majorek /D/
49. Fass Józef /L/
50. Frenkiel Toba /Sz/
51. Farber Józef /Sz/
52. Finkelsztejn Motek /D/
53. Furmanowicz Yesia /D/
54. Folman Marc /D/
55. Puterman Izaac /B/
56. Finkielsztajn Cyla /D/
57. Fryirych Zalman /B/
58. Fajgenblat Jakob
59. Blum Abram /Abrasza/ /B/
60. Finkelsztajn Abram /D/

61. Fidelzajd Symcha /FF/
62. Fidelzajd Pola /FF/
63. Goldsztejn Izaak /B/
64. Granatsztajn Sara /D/
65. Gutrajman Kuba /L/
66. Gold Wulf /L/
67. Grauman Chana /Sz/
68. Guterman /D/
69. Grynbaum Iechak /D/
70. Gutsztat Cypora /D/
71. Gutman Henach /D/
72. Geresuni Cedalia /D/
73. Granzalc Lejb /L/
74. Grynszpan Jurek /L/
75. Gertner Israel /B/
76. Górny Jechiel /PL/
77. Gertner Aba /Sz/
78. Grzęca Sloszana /D/
79. Holand Zalman /A/
80. Hajman Ruth /Sz/
81. Heller Szymen /Sz/
82. Haleband Aron /D/
83. Hochberg Adolf /D/
84. Hochberg Dawid /D/
85. Kajman Itka /D/
86. Kimelfarb Adek /G/
87. Icek
88. Liblika Mira /Sz/
89. Jaskinski Lejb /D/
90. Jandzielewich Adek /B/
91. Joszilewicz Afruim /A/
92. Igla Zygmunt /D/
93. Jakubowicz Szoszana /D/
94. Kaplan Józef /Sz/
95. Karliner Arje /Sz/
96. Kerenbrum Alma /Sz/
97. Kmiel Salka /L/
98. Kirszner Sigi /D/
99. Klepfisz Iechak /D/
100. Kirszenbaum Rachel /D/
101. Kac Jankeil /D/
102. Kozlubrodzka Lonka /D/
103. Klepfisz Michal /B/
104. Klejnman Ziuta /L/
105. Kawa Meniek /L/
106. Klajnman Sara /L/
107. Konski Jehuda /G/
108. Korn Leja /G/
109. Klejnasja Moniek /G/
110. Katowicz Szoszana /D/
111. Kacenelson Cwi /D/
112. Kozuch Hela /D/
113. Landau Margalith /Sz/
114. Lejtowicz Lejb /Loban/ /D/
115. Litenki /FF/
116. Laver Cypora /D/
117. Levental Szymon /G/
118. Litman Josef FL/
119. Levin Gina /D/
120. Lilienstejn Moniek /B/

121. Lewski Izio /L/
122. Lent Szaman /TL/
123. Libert Chaim /D/
124. Lewender Jafa /D/
125. Mordkowicz Basia /D/
126. Manfred
127. Mittelman Israel /B/
128. Moselman Rysiek /L/
129. Manelak Bronka /PL/
130. Morgenlender Icek /Sz/
131. Morgensztern Jochanan /TP/
132. Majofes /L/
133. Wajcrowicz Marek /TP/
134. Kulman Sewek /L/
144. Nowodworski Dawid /Sz/
145. Nozyce Iechak /D/
146. Niemiecka Kenia /L/
147. Cohron Wanda /L/
148. Oszerowski Michał /Sz/
149. Obersztyn Jozef /D/
150. Orwacz Abraham /Sz/
151. Pelc Baruch /B/
152. Perlsztejn Leja /D/
153. Pachoł Chawa /D/
154. Pasmanik Rebeka /A/
155. Praszkier /MH/
156. Perelman Mejlech /B/
157. Putermilch Jakób /B/
158. Papier Zygmunt /TL/
159. Płotnicka Chajcia /D/
160. Rozowski Israel -Wolf /B/
161. Rozental Chaim /D/
162. Romanowicz Israel /B/
163. Rozowski Israel /B/
163. Rozowski Lejb /B/
164. Rudnicki Lew /L/
165. Rozenfeld Ruska /L/
166. Rozen Stefan /TL/
167. Rotman Cwi /Sz/
168. Rysia /D/
169. Rutman Gedalia /A/
170. Rotblat Lutek /A/
171. Rotblit Chil /Sz/
172. Rozenberg Jardena /Sz/
173. Rubin Mosze /D/
174. Rozencweig Rachel /L/
175. Rapoport Lejb /D/
176. Rabow Fejcia /D/
177. Rajngewirc Moniek /D/
178. Rubeńczyk Mosze /D/
179. Rrlutowska Sara /D/
180. Szwarc Salome /B/
181. Sznajdmil Abram /Berek/ /D/
182. Szyfman Miriam /B/
183. Szwarc Meir /B/
184. Szuszkowska Szulamith /Sz/
185. Szwarcsztejn Feek /D/
186. Sztengel Moniek /D/
187. Sznajderman Tema /Wanda/ /D/
188. Sylman Suja /D/
189. Szulman Dawid /D/
190. Szmplak Icchak /D/
191. Sufit Szalom /A/
192. Sapancer Szaja /L/
193. Sarnak Jerzyk /L/
194. Simson Zygfryda /L/
195. Szwarcfus Janek /L/

196. Barenka /Sz/
197. Suskienik Icchak /Kora/ /Sz/
198. Szajngot Tuwia /Tadek/ /Sz/
199. Szafirsztajn Rebeka /Jelir /Sz/
200. Szarfsztajn Moszek /D/
201. Sobol Szmul /D/
202. Szulman Genia /D/
203. Szerman Majorek /D/
204. Skulska Chana /D/
205. Szuster Szlamek /D/
206. Sylman Batia /D/
207. Szklar Ruth /D/
208. Szyfman Leja /D/
209. Troks Lejb /D/
210. Tenenbaum Szlamek /L/
211. Tajchler Guta /L/
212. Wortman Zef /Sz/
213. Wincgron Szloma /Sz/
214. Wald Benjamin /B/
215. Bartowicz Moniek /L/
216. Waksfeld Mojsze /L/
217. Wartowicz Olek /L/
218. Wichter Icchak /TL/
219. Wilner Arje /Jurek /Sz/
220. Wengrowicz Jehuda /Sz/
221. Zajfman Aron /TP/
222. Żimak Naftali /D/
223. Zając Herman /D/
224. Zyberberg Moniek /L/
225. Zagiel Wara /L/
227. Rimak Lilka /D/
228. Zylbersztejn Moszek /L/
229. Zelcer Israel /D/
230. Stolak Abram /TL/
231. Szolotow /L/
232. Rapierdowa /TL/
233. Zylberman Israel /D/

Lista niniejsza nie jest kompletna z powodu braku informacji o pozostałych członkach ŻOB.

List of Those Who Fell in the Defense of the Warsaw Ghetto*

Organizational affiliation is indicated by the following initials or abbreviations: "Sz" – Haszomer Hacair, "D" – Dror, "A" – Akiba, "G" – Gordonia, "B" – Bund, "PR" – Poalej Syjon Right, "PL" – Poalej Syjon Left, "HH" – Hanoar Hacyjoni, "L" – the Left.

Anielewicz, Mordchaj /Sz/
Altman, Tosia /Sz/
Aleksandrowicz, Jakób /Sz/
Asz, Eliezer /HH/
Arsztajn, Zachariasz /D/
Altenberg, Estera /D/
Alterman, Szlomo /D/
Arbuz, Chaim /Sz/
Bresler, Szmul /Sz/
Błones, Mejlach /Sz/
Berman, Franka /L/
Baum, Mosze /HH/
Błones, Icchak /HH/
Brojde, Berl /D/
Biegelman, Menachem /D/
Blausztajn, Icchak /D/
Bartmesser, Nute /D/
Baran, Dwora /D/
Błones, Jurek /B/
Błones, Guta /B/

Błones, Lusiek /B/
Brylantsztejn, Stasiek /B/
Brzezińska, Zocha /L/
Blank, Marek /G/
Baczyński, Szloma /Sz/
Chadasz, Icchak /Sz/
Chmielnicki, Nachum /B/
Cukier, Nesia /D/
Cygler, Mosze /D/
Chrzanowicz, Icchak /D/
Cebularz, Tosia /L/
Libeskind, Dolek /A/
Drenger, Szymek /A/
Drajer, Abram /D/
Drezner, Abram /D/
Dobuchno, Szaul /D/
Dawidowicz, Tauba /B/
Duński, Sewek /B/
Dembiński, Icchak /L/
Dembińska, Dorka /L/

---

* This list, which I call the London list, was compiled in November 1943 by the leaders of the ŻOB who had survived the April uprising, and sent to the Polish government-in-exile. The reproduction is taken from the collections of Studium Polski Podziemnej in London. Below, I copy the list from the original, including all errors and inconsistencies.

Diamant, Abram /PL/
Elek /Sz/
Edelsztejn, Cwi /D/
Erlichman, Sujka /G/
Einsdorf, Miriam /Sz/
Eiger, Abram /B/
Fajner, Abram /B/
Finkelsztejn, Majorek /D/
Fass, Józef /L/
Frenkiel, Toba /Sz/
Farber, Józef /Sz/
Finkelsztejn, Motek /D/
Furmanowicz, Pesia /D/
Folman, Marek /D/
Futerman, Ignac /B/
Finkelsztajn, Cyla /D/
Frydrych, Zalman /B/
Fajgenblat, Jakób
Blum, Abram [Abrasza] /B/
Finkelsztejn, Abram /D/
Fidelzajd, Symcha /PR/
Fidelzajd, Pola /PR/
Goldsztejn, Izaak /B/
Granatsztejn, Sara /D/
Gutrajman, Kuba /L/
Gold, Wulf /L/
Grauman, Chana /Sz/
Guterman /D/
Grynbaum, Icchak /D/
Gutsztat, Cypora /D/
Gutman, Henoch /D/
Gerszuni, Gedalia /D/
Grauzalc Lejb /B/
Grynszpan, Jurek /L/
Gertner, Israel /B/
Górny, Jechiel /PL/
Gertner, Aba /Sz/
Grzęda, Szoszana /D/
Holand, Zalman /A/

Hajman, Ruth /Sz/
Heller, Szymon /Sz/
Halzband, Aron /D/
Hochberg, Adolf /D/
Hochberg, Dawid /D/
Hejman, Itka /L/
Himelfarb, Adek /G/
Icuś /A/
Izbicka, Mira /Sz/
Jasiński, Lejb /B/
Jankielewicz, Adek /B/
Juszkiewicz, Efraim /B/
Igła, Zygmunt /B/
Jakubowicz, Szoszana /D/
Kapłan, Josef /Sz/
Kamień, Salka /L/
Karliner, Arje /Sz/
Kerenbrum, Alma /Sz/
Kirszner, Sigi /D/
Klepfisz, Icchak /D/
Kirszenbaum, Rachel /D/
Kac, Jankiel /D/
Koziebrodzka, Lońka /D/
Klepfisz, Michał /B/
Klejnman, Ziuta /L/
Kawa, Heniek /L/
Klajnman, Sara /L/
Koński, Jehuda /G/
Korn, Lea /G/
Kleynwajs, Heniek /G/
Katowicz, Szoszana /D/
Kacenelson, Cwi /D/
Kożuch, Hela /D/
Landau, Margalith /Sz/
Lejbowicz, Lejb [Laban] /D/
Liteski /PR/
Lerer, Cypora /D/
Lewental, Szymon /G/
Litman, Josef /PL/

Lewin, Gina /D/
Liliensztejn, Moniek /B/
Lewski, Izio /L/
Lent, Szanan /PL/
Libert, Chaim /D/
Lewender, Jaffa /D/
Mordkowicz, Basia /D/
Manfred /D/
Mittelman, Izrael /B/
Maselman, Rysiek /L/
Manulak, Bronka /PL/
Morgenlender, Icek /Sz/
Morgensztern, Jochanan /PR/
Majufes /L/
Meirowicz, Marek /PR/
Nulman, Sewek /L/
Nowodworski, Dawid /Sz/
Nożyce, Icchak /D/
Niemiecka, Renia /L/
Ochron, Wanda /L/
Oszerowski, Michał /Sz/
Obersztyn, Josef /D/
Orwacz, Abraham /Sz/
Pelc, Boruch /B/
Perelsztajn, Leja /D/
Pachoł, Chawa /D/
Pasamanik, Rebeka /A/
Praszkier /HH/
Perelman, Mejlech /B/
Putermilch, Jakób /G/
Papier, Zygmunt /PL/
Płotnicka, Chańcia /D/
Rozowski, Izrael-Wolf /B/
Rozental, Chaim /D/
Romanowicz, Israel /B/
Rozowski, Israel /B/
Rozowski, Lejb /B/
Rudnicki, Lew /L/
Rozenfeld, Różka /L/

Rozen, Stefa /PL/
Rotman, Cwi /Sz/
Rysia /D/
Rutman, Gedalia /A/
Rotblat, Lutek /A/
Rotblit, Chil /Sz/
Rozenberg, Jardena /Sz/
Rubin, Mosze /D/
Rozencweig, Rachel /D/
Rapoport, Lejb /D/
Rabow, Fejcze /D/
Rajngewirc, Moniek /D/
Rubeńczyk, Mosze /D/
Szlubowska, Sara /D/
Szwarc, Szlomo /B/
Sznajdmil, Abram /Berek/ /B/
Szyfman, Miriam /B/
Szwarc, Meir /B/
Szuszkowska, Szulamith /Sz/
Szwarcsztejn, Faek /D/
Sztengel, Moniek /D/
Sznaderman, Tema [Wanda] /D/
Sylman, Suja /D/
Szulman, Dawid /D/
Symplak, Icchak /D/
Sufit, Szalom /A/
Szpancer, Szaja /L/
Sarnak, Jerzyk /L/
Simson, Zygfryda /L/
Szwarcfus, Janek /L/
Sarenka /Sz/
Sukienik, Icchak [Koza] /Sz/
Shajngot, Tuwia [Tadek] /Sz/
Szafirsztejn, Rebeka [Julia] /Sz/
Szarfsztajn, Moszek /D/
Sobol, Szmul /D/
Szulman, Gienia /D/
Szerman, Majorek /D/
Skulska, Chana /D/

Szuster, Szlamek /D/
Sylman, Batia /D/
Szklar, Ruth /D/
Szyfman, Lea /D/
Troks, Lejb /D/
Tenenbaum, Szlamek /L/
Tajchler, Guta /L/
Wortman, Zef /Sz/
Winogron, Shloma /Sz/
Wald, Beniamin /B/
Bartowicz, Heniek /L/
Waksfeld, Mojsze /L/
Wartowicz, Olek /L/
Wichter, Icchak /PL/

Wilner, Arje [Jurek] /Sz/
Wengrowicz, Jehuda /Sz/
Zajfman, Aron /PR/
Zimak, Naftali /D/
Zając, Herman /D/
Zylberberg, Heniek /L/
Zagiel, Sara /L/
Zimak, Lilka /D/
Zylbersztajn, Moszek /L/
Zelcer, Israel /G/
Stolak, Abram /PL/
Zolotow /L/
Papierówna /PL/
Zylberman, Izrael /D/

This list is incomplete owing to the lack of information on the remaining members of the ŻOB.

A Rereading of the List

The staff company of the Jewish Fighting Organization in the April uprising
29 Miła, 18 Miła

Mordechaj Anielewicz, commander-in-chief of the ŻOB, Haszomer Hacair
Hersz Berliński—Poalej Syjon Left
Icchak Cukierman—Dror
Marek Edelman—Bund
Jochanan Morgensztern—Poalej Syjon Right
Michał Rozenfeld—PPR

Commanders in the field

Izrael Kanał—Akiba	Nine groups of insurgents in the central ghetto: Nalewki, Gęsia, Zamenhofa, and Miła Streets
Eliezer Geller—Gordonia	Eight groups of insurgents in the Toebbens-Schultz 'shop yards: Leszno, Nowolipie, and Smocza Streets
Marek Edelman—Bund	Five groups of insurgents on the brushmakers' premises: Franciszkańska, Wałowa, Świętojerska, and Bonifraterska Streets

ŻOB fighting groups

Central ghetto: Nalewki, Gęsia, Zamenhofa, Miła

Nalewki/Gęsia*
Artsztajn, Zachariasz—Dror

Borzykowski, Tuwia
Cygler, Mosze
Drejer, Abraham
Finkelsztajn, Cyla
Finkelsztajn, Motek
Grynbojm, Icchak
Guterman, Jakub
Jakubowicz, Szoszana

Lubetkin, Celina
Manfred
Rozencwajg, Rachela
Rubin, Mosze
Salka
Szlomo
Szwarcsztajn, Fajwel
Zając, Herman

Miła, Zamenhofa/Gęsia
Braude Berl—Dror

Bigielman, Menachem
Błones, Melach
Cukier, Nacha
Frymer, Chaim
Halzband, Aron
Lawender, Jaffa
Pasamonik, Rywka

Rajzband, Aron
Sobol, Szmuel
Szarfsztajn, Moszek
Szulman, Dawid
Zimak, Lilka
Zimak, Naftali

Miła, Zamenhofa/Gęsia
Bryskin, Aron—PPR

Akerman, Chaim
Berman, Franka
Berman, Tosia
Kamień, Salke
Ochron, Wanda

Sarnak, Jerzyk
Simson, Zygfryda
Szpancer, Szyja
Szwarcfus, Janek

Farber, Josek—Haszomer Hacair
[Wengrower, Juda]**   [Zylberberg, Rachel]

---

* Street on which the group was stationed on April 19, and, wherever it was possible to establish them, the subsequent addresses of the insurrectionists' bases.

** Names given in square brackets are those of insurrectionists who may have belonged to this group or another one.

Zamenhofa/Gęsia
Growas, Mordechaj—Haszomer Hacair
Hejman, Rut
Jechiel
Natek or Jurek
Suknik, Icchok
Szuszkowska, Szulamit
[Wengrower, Juda]
[Zylberberg, Rachel]

29 Zamenhofa, 29 Miła, 18 Miła
Gruzalc, Lejb—Bund
Glajtman, Masza
Jankielewicz, Adek
Liliensztajn, Mosze
Mittelman, Srulek
Perelman, Majloch
Puterman, Ignacy
Szerman, Majorek
Szyfman, Lea
Tasenkrojt, Berl

29 Zamenhofa
Hochberg, Dawid—Bund

Nalewki/Gęsia
Rotblat, Lutek—Akiba

Nalewki/Gęsia
Nulman, Sewek
Tamara
Zylberberg, Heniek—PPR

Toebbens-Schultz 'shops: Leszno, Nowolipie, Smocza

Blaustein, Icchak—Dror
[Kirszner, Sigi]
Mordkowicz, Basia
Sztengiel, Moniek

Leszno 76, fourth floor
Fajgenblat, Jakub—Gordonia

Blank, Marek***
Chmielnicki, Aron
Fingerhut, Gienek
Himelfarb, Adek
Kawenoki, Guta
Klajnwajs, Heniek
Korn, Lea
Korngold, Lea
Lewski, Izio
Putermilch, Jakub
Tajchler, Guta
Tenenbojm, Szlamek
Wajs, Kuba

74 Leszno
Kawe, Heniek—PPR

Alter, Aron
Bonder, Chawa
Borg, Bernard
Brzezińska, Zocha
Cebularz, Tosia
Czerniakower, Lejb
Hejman, Itkie
Klajnman, Sara
Rochman, Halinka
Rozenfeld, Adek
Rozenfeld, Rόżka
Rudnicki, Lew
Ryba
Szmutke, Rywa

31 Nowolipie
Majerowicz, Marek—Poalej Syjon Right

Fidelzajt, Pola
Fidelzajt, Simcha
Litewski, Josef
Zajfman, Mosze

67 Nowolipie Street
Nowodworski, Dawid—Haszomer Hacair

Aleksandrowicz, Jakub Chaim
[Gertner, Aba]
[Grauman, Chana]
Heller, Szymon
Holand, Zalman
Horowic, Abram
Kornblum, Elma
Morgenlender, Icchak
[Putermilch, Hagit]
Rotman, Cwi
Sufit, Szlomo
Szafirsztajn, Rywka
Sztajn, Dawid
[Zandman, Abraham]
[Zandman, Pnina]

*** Marek Blank fought in one of the groups on the brushmakers' premises, because that was where he happened to be when the uprising broke out.

8–10 Smocza, 56 Nowolipie
Rozowski, Welwł—Bund

Bełchatowska, Chajka
Dawidowicz, Tobcia
Einstein, Cypora
Fryszdorf, Gabryś
Igła, Zygmunt
Juszkiewicz, Efraim
Juszkiewicz, Samuel
Kryształ, Chana
Szpigiel, Boruch
Szwarc, Meir
Szwarc, Szlomo

36 Leszno
Wald, Beniamin—Dror

Altenberg, Estera
Biederman, Sara
Chrzanowicz, Icchak
Edelsztajn, Cwi****
Icuś
[Kirszner, Sigi]
Rapaport, Lejb
Rutman, Gedalia
Skulska, Chana

Nowolipki 40
Winogron, Szlomo—Haszomer Hacair

Arbuz, Chaim
Baczyński, Szlomo
[Gertner, Aba]
[Grauman, Chana]
Hajnsdorf, Miriam
Karliner, Ari
[Putermilch, Hagit]
Rotblit, Jechiel
[Zandman, Abraham]
[Zandman, Pnina]

The brushmakers' premises: Franciszkańska, Wałowa, Świętojerska, Bonifraterska

38 Świętojerska
Grynszpan, Jurek—PPR

Korensztajn, Aron
Lewita, Jerzy
Mirski, Sławek
Niemiecka, Renia
Żogel, Sara

****Cwi Edelsztajn was in Henoch Gutman's group on the brushmakers' premises, but he happened to be in the central ghetto when the uprising broke out. (He fought in Beniamin Wald's group.)

30 Świętojerska
Praszkier, Jakub—Hanoar Hacyjoni

Asz, Eliezer
Błones, Icchak
Bojm, Mosze Izrael
Goldsztejn, Izaak
Mastbojm, Szoszana

Berliński, Hersz—Poalej Syjon Left

Diamant, Abraham
Erlich, Eliahu
Frojnd, Emus
Górny, Jechiel
Lent, Szaanan
Litman, Josef
Manulak, Bronka
Papier, Pinia
Papier, Zysie
Rozen, Stefa
Stolak, Abram
Wichter, Icchak
Wroński, Hirsz

30 Świętojerska / 6 Wałowa
Gutman, Henoch—Dror

Alterman, Szlomo
Baran, Dwora
Ejgier, Abraham
Gutsztat, Cypora
Hochberg, Adolf
Jaszyński, Lejb
Lerer, Cypora
Obersztyn, Josef
Rabow, Fejcze
Ratajzer, Kazik
Sylman, Basia
Szuster, Szlamek

34 Świętojerska
Błones, Jurek—Bund

Bilak, Janek
Błones, Guta
Błones, Lusiek
Blum, Abrasza
Brylantsztajn, Staszek
Duński, Sewek
Frydrych, Zygmunt
Junghajzer, Julek
Klepfisz, Michał
Romanowicz, Izrael
Rozowski, Lejb
Sznajdmil, Berek
Szyfman, Miriam

April insurgents whose group could not be established

Aleksander—PPR
Bartmesser, Nate—Dror
Bartowicz, Heniek—PPR
Born-Bornstein, Roman
Chadasz, Icchak—Haszomer Hacair
Dembińska, Dorka—PPR
Dembiński, Icchak—PPR
Drezner, Abraham—Dror
Fass, Józef—PPR
Fondamińska, Ala—PPR
Fondamiński, Efraim—PPR
Frenkel, Towa—Haszomer Hacair
Fuchrer, Mira—Haszomer Hacair
Gold, Wolf—PPR
Gutrajman, Kuba—PPR
Halina—Haszomer Hacair
Izbicka, Mira—Haszomer Hacair
Jaworski, Michał—PPR
Jeremiasz—Haszomer Hacair
Joel—Haszomer Hacair
Kirszenbojm, Rachela—Dror
Klajnman, Ziuta—PPR
Klepfisz, Icchak—Dror
Kożuch, Hela—Dror
Krótki, Izrael—Haszomer Hacair
Lolek—Haszomer Hacair
Orwacz, Abraham—Haszomer Hacair
Oszerowski, Michał—Haszomer Hacair
Rozenberg, Jardena—Haszomer Hacair
Siekierski, Mieczysław—PPR
Szejntal, Szymon—Haszomer Hacair
Szlubowska, Sara—Dror
Szniper, Dow—Haszomer Hacair
Szulman, Genia—Dror
Tamar—Haszomer Hacair
Wachenhojzer, Chedwa—Haszomer Hacair
Waksfeld, Mojsze—PPR
Wartowicz, Olek—PPR
Wilner, Arie—Haszomer Hacair
Wortman, Zeew—Haszomer Hacair
Zylbersztajn, Moszek—PPR

Jewish ŻOB couriers inside and outside the ghetto

Alterman, Malke—Poalej Syjon Left
Altman, Tosia—Haszomer Hacair
Beatus, Frania
Blady-Szwajgier, Adina—Bund
Blumenfeld, Tola—PPR
Celemeński, Jakub—Bund
Feinmesser, Bronka—Bund
Frydman, Renia
Frydrych, Zygmunt—Bund
Fudem, Regina—Haszomer Hacair
Gelblum, Irka
Goldkorn, Dorka—PPR
Grasberg, Jurek—Boy Scout
Jarost, Józiek—PPR
Klepfisz, Michał—Bund
Margolis, Ala
Maselman, Rysiek—PPR
Moszkowicz, Rywka
Natek
Pekier, Rebeka
Peltel, Władka—Bund
Płotnicka, Chańcia—Frajhajt

Schüpper, Hela—Akiba
Szajngut, Tadek—PPR
Tajtelbaum, Niuta—GL

Wilner, Arie—Haszomer Hacair
Zołotow, Jurek—PPR
Zylberg, Luba

Polish couriers for the ŻOB outside the ghetto walls

Adamowicz, Irena—scouting leader
Grabowski, Henryk—Boy Scout
Krzaczek, Władysław Gaik—GL
Legiec, Stanisława—PPR
Legiec, Władysław—PPR
Pokropek, Stefan—PPS
Rajszczak, Felek

Sawicka, Marysia—PPS
Siewierski, Stefan
Świętochowski, Władek—PPS
Wąchalska, Anna—PPS
Wanda—PPS?
Wąsowska-Leszczyńska, Eugenia

ŻOB soldiers murdered in the January 1943 operation

Chmielnicki, Nachum—Bund
Czarny, Mietek—PPR
Fajner, Awram—Bund
Finkelsztajn, Majorek—Dror
Gertner, Izrael—Bund
Goldsztajn, Icchok—Bund
Granatsztajn, Sara—Dror
Landau, Margalit—Haszomer Hacair
Lejbgot, Beniamin—GL
Libert, Chaim—Dror
Pachoł, Chawa—Dror

Pelc, Boruch—Bund
Perelsztajn, Lea—Dror
Różański, Elek—Haszomer Hacair
Rysia—courier
Stach—PPR
Sylman, Sara—Dror
Symplak, Icchak—courier
Sznajderman, Tema—Dror, courier
Troks, Lejb—Dror
Zilberman, Izrael—Dror

ŻOB soldiers murdered before April 1943[1]

Koński, Juda—Gordonia
Lewental, Szymon—Gordonia
Sztern, Mietek—PPR

---

1 The stories of these ŻOB soldiers murdered before April 1943 are included in this book.

ŻOB soldiers murdered or arrested before January 1943

Bresław, Szmuel—Haszomer Hacair
Erlichman, Sujka—Gordonia
Justman, Reginka—Haszomer Hacair
Kapłan, Josef—Haszomer Hacair
Koziebrodzka, Lońka—Dror
Zelcer, Izrael—Gordonia

Other names from the London List[2]

Members of Dror murdered in Werbkowice and the woods in the Hrubieszów region in the summer of 1942

Dobuchno, Saul
Finkielsztajn, Abram
Furmanowicz, Pesia
Gerszuni, Gedalia
Kac, Jankiel
Katowicz, Szoszana
Lewin, Gina
Nożyce, Icchok
Rajngewirc, Moniek
Rozental, Chaim
Rubenczyk, Mosze
Szklar, Rut

ŻOB soldiers in Krakow

Drenger, Szymek—Akiba
Lejbowicz, Lejb—Dror
Liebeskind, Dolek—Akiba

Others

Folman, Marek—was in the partisan forces in 1943
Grzęda, Szoszana—a Dror courier; shot and wounded in 1942, she survived Pawiak prison and Majdanek concentration camp; died in Israel in 2003

---

2 None of those listed below took part in the January operation or fought in the April uprising. Nonetheless, their names are recorded on the "London list" of the defenders who fell in the defense of the Warsaw ghetto.

Kacenelson, Cwi—the son of the poet Icchak Kacenelson, arrested in January 1943; not a member of the ŻOB

Majufes—an employee of the Judenrat; not a member of the ŻOB

Rozowski, Izrael-Wolf—the father of Welwł Rozowski; not a member of the ŻOB (listed a second time as Rozowski Israel)

A Cemetery of Letters, a Cemetery of Words

The cult of death in the Mediterranean Basin has been in existence for a very long time. The Egyptian pyramids, the Roman sarcophagi, beautiful green cemeteries with stones carved with the surname and forename of the dead person. Often with a brief sentence about their life added. The more the person had done, the longer the inscription, the more magnificent the monument, the fuller the story.

In Poland we live in a cult of independence—we pay homage to those who fought for our Country. And each of them has their own surname, their own forename; they live on in our memory. The Warsaw rising: a vast body of birch crosses. Monte Cassino: where the soldiers fell in the bright sunlight, they now have light-coloured stones bearing their names, military ranks, and date of death. And then Katyń, and Starobielsk. In Powązki more names and military ranks. And each one of them exists. Every name is recorded.

The Warsaw ghetto has no cemetery. The bones of the Jewish soldiers lie in among the bricks of the razed city. The ashes of their burnt bodies are mixed with earth. There are no graves, no stone tablets. And those people are absent, their forenames and surnames; there are not even the briefest of stories telling who they were and how they lived.

Hanka Grupińska is creating a monument. She is building a monument to each one of them, to each soldier of the Warsaw ghetto. And this is the cemetery of the Jewish Fighting Organization. A cemetery not of greenery, flowers, or stones. It is a cemetery of letters, a cemetery of words about those people. This cemetery will stand on shelves, and every day it will remind us of those who have no graves of stone.

Marek Edelman, July 2002

Glossary

Akiba (Hanoar Hacyjoni "Akiba"). A Zionist youth organization, an arm of the Ikhud party, that raised young people to respect the Jewish tradition and religion, and in opposition to the assimilatory movement. Like the Halutz movement, Akiba prepared its young adherents for life in Palestine. Unlike the members of Cukunft or Dror, however, the young people in Akiba did not join any party. During the occupation, Akiba had about three hundred young followers, chiefly in Warsaw and Krakow. (In the 1930s, Jewish youth organizations in Poland together had over one hundred thousand members.) In the Warsaw ghetto, Akiba members had a kibbutz of their own at 10 Nalewki Street, where twenty-five people lived until the *große Aktion*. From September 1942, they met at Mariańska Street. In the April uprising there was one Akiba group, which fought under Lutek Rotblat.

Aktion (Ger.: campaign, operation; Pol. akcja). Colloquial term used by both Jews and Poles in occupied Poland. After mid-1942 it came to refer specifically to operations mounted with the aim of deporting those apprehended to extermination camps. The efficacy of the various deportation methods was founded on the element of surprise, efficiency of execution, and keeping the victims unaware of their real destination and the purpose of their deportation. The standard official explanation was "resettlement to the East," ostensibly for employment in workplaces there. The euphemistic expression "to the East" rapidly caught on among both Jews and Poles as a synonym for the Holocaust. In smaller ghettos, such campaigns usually took one day, in larger ones several, even many weeks.

In the Warsaw ghetto, the first major deportation came to be known as the *große Aktion* (and in Polish as *Wielka Akcja*). It was carried out between July 22 and September 12, 1942, and was preceded, like most other similar campaigns, by increased isolation of the Jews, a reduction in the size of the ghetto, restrictions in postal connections, a disorienting rumor campaign, and terror; several hundred people were killed in executions. On July 21, 1942, sixty hostages were taken, including members of the Judenrat. The following day, the Germans entered the ghetto, which was surrounded by detachments of Polish police and auxiliary units of Ukrainians and Lithuanians. The Judenrat was forced to sign a public announcement informing residents of the deportation; the daily contingent of deportees was six thousand to ten thousand people. The only exemptions were for those employed in German businesses and ghetto institutions, and members of their families. The baggage allowance was fifteen kilograms plus unlimited valuables. On the second day of the campaign, the community chairman, Adam Czerniaków, committed suicide. Throughout the first week, Jews reported for the transports voluntarily (in all, approx. 20 percent of the ghetto population); thereafter they were rounded up by the Jewish Order Police and the Germans. The collection point was the Umschlagplatz, from where they were then deported by rail to the extermination camp in Treblinka. An estimated two hundred sixty thousand Jews were deported from Warsaw during the *große Aktion*; a further ten thousand were murdered in the ghetto in the same period.

American Jewish Distribution Committee (colloquially "the Joint"). An American charitable organization, founded in 1914, that supported Jewish community institutions outside the USA. The Joint was particularly active in Europe during World War II. Until 1941 it operated legally, and from February 1941 it carried out its work in the General Government through the Jewish Social Welfare (Pol. Żydowska Samopomoc Społeczna). After the USA entered the war, Joint activists continued their work gathering funds underground. Among the directors of the Joint were Icchak Giterman, Leon Neustadt, and Dawid Guzik, a member of the underground.

Arsenał operation. On March 26, 1943, a group from the underground paramilitary scouting organization codenamed "the Gray Ranks" (Pol. Szare Szeregi) mounted a successful operation to free their comrade Janek "Rudy" Bytnar from the Gestapo prison at the intersection of Długa and Bielańska Streets in Warsaw, near the Arsenał building. 28 members of the Gray Ranks' Storm Groups took part in the operation. They managed to spring 21 Gestapo prisoners. On the German side, there were four dead and nine wounded. The day after the operation, March 27, the Germans executed one hundred forty Poles and Jews by firing squad in the Pawiak prison courtyard in revenge. "Rudy" himself and two other underground soldiers died a few days after the operation.

Aryan side, the. The colloquial wartime name for all the parts of a city (esp. Warsaw) outside the ghetto, that is, anywhere Jews were officially prohibited from spending time after the ghettos were sealed (in Warsaw this was on November 18, 1940).

Befehlsstelle. From September 1942, the SS command center for the ghetto was at 103 Żelazna Street. During the liquidation (July–September 1942), the Befehlsstelle was in the building of the Jewish Order Service headquarters at 17 Ogrodowa Street.

Betar, Beitar. The colloquial name for the Trumpeldor Association of Jewish Youth, a right-wing Zionist youth organization founded in 1923 by Vladimir Jabotinsky (1880–1940) in Riga, with links to the New Zionist Organization. Betar was also active in other countries in Europe, though it was strongest in Poland: in 1936, 75 percent of its fifty-two thousand members lived there. Like He-Halutz, Betar prepared its youth for life in Palestine on *hakhsharas*, ideological camps, and vocational courses. Betar organized illegal emigration to Eretz Israel because its aim was to build a Jewish state. It was a paramilitary organization; its members wore uniforms and underwent military training. Some members sympathized with Italian fascism, and their gangs broke up Jewish left-wing youth meetings. During the occupation, Betar managed to get many of its people out of Warsaw. Some of them went into hiding on a farm and in woods near Hrubieszów; most of them were killed. Betar was also instrumental in creating the Jewish Military Union (ŻZW), the second armed formation alongside the Jewish Fighting Organization (ŻOB) in the Warsaw ghetto.

Brushmakers' yard. The brushmakers' yard was a huge block between Bonifraterska, Franciszkańska, Wałowa, and Świętojerska Streets (at the northeastern tip of the ghetto). These workshops ("shops") employed brushmakers, metalworkers, and electrotechnicians.

Bund (Yid.: Union), **the General Jewish Labor Bund.** A Jewish socialist party founded in Vilnius in 1897, active in Lithuania, Russia, and Poland until World War I, and from 1919 a legal party in Poland, Lithuania, Latvia, and Estonia. In interwar Poland, the Bund collaborated with the Polish Socialist Party (PPS) but had no deputies of its own in the Polish parliament. The Bund was social-democratic, anti-Zionist, and anti-religious in its orientation. It advocated cultural autonomy for Jews in the diaspora, and propagated the Yiddish language and secular schooling, while encouraging a strong bond on the part of Jews with their place of residence. In the 1930s it had some fifty thousand members in Poland. Before the war, the Warsaw Bund committee was at 26 Długa Street. The Bund incorporated the women's organization JAF (Yid. Yidishe Arbeter Froy, Jewish Working Women; Pol.: JAF); the children's group Skif; a youth arm Cukunft [Tsukunft, Zukunft]; the sports club Morgensztern; and the academic union Ring. It published its own press in Polish and Yiddish. Within the Jewish community, the Bund cooperated with Poalej Syjon Left. During the occupation, it organized civilian and armed resistance in the ghettos. In the Warsaw ghetto, it joined the ŻOB, with four fighting groups under Marek Edelman's command. The Bund in the Polish People's Republic was dissolved in 1949. Its headquarters were moved to the USA. In Israel, the Bund ceased to exist in 2017, with the death of the 95-year-old Itzhak Luden, the last editor of the Bundist newspaper.

CENTOS (Pol. Centralne Towarzystwo Opieki nad Sierotami i Dziećmi Opuszczonymi, the Central Society for Care of Orphans and Abandoned Children). A Jewish welfare institution founded in 1924 that organized aid for children: canteens, summer camps, medical care, and orphanages across interwar Poland. It was also active in the ghettos in occupied Poland. From 1942 it ran around a hundred welfare points in the Warsaw ghetto: orphanages, school boarding houses, out-of-school care, and a library. It was based at 56 Zamenhofa Street. The orphanage run by Janusz Korczak was also a CENTOS establishment.

Cukunft, or the Yugnt-Bund "Cukunft" (Yid. Tsukunft, the "Future" Youth Organization). An organization for working-class youth. In the mid-1930s it had ten thousand members. From 1916 Cukunft was the youth arm of the Bund. Its equivalent for schoolchildren was the organization called Skif. Cukunft members printed and distributed the illegal literature of the SDKPiL and the Bund, organized self-education courses, published the *Jugnt Weker*, and ran the Morgensztern [Morning Star] sports club, which had its Warsaw seat at 2a Nalewki Street. In the ghetto they published the *Jugnt Sztime*, the *Junge Gwardie*, and the Polish-language *Nowa Młodzież*. In Poland, Cukunft was dissolved along with the Bund in 1949. The official Polish socialist youth organization ZMP was willing to accept Cukunft members on an individual basis without further checks, but the young Jewish socialists refused this offer.

Czerniaków, Adam (b. 1880 in Warsaw). Chairman of the Jewish Community Organization in the Warsaw ghetto. Studied chemistry at the Warsaw Polytechnic, and qualified as an engineer in Dresden. A well-known social and political activist, journalist, and pedagogue. He supported the association of Jewish craftspeople, organized Jewish vocational training, and cooperated with the Joint. In 1931 he was elected to the Senate of the Republic of Poland. He was also a city councilor, and deputy chairman of the Interim Community Board. When in September 1939 Maurycy Meisel, the Jewish community chairman, fled Warsaw, Czerniaków was appointed by the city's mayor to assume his office. He was the chairman of the Warsaw Judenrat until his suicide on July 23, 1942.

Death March (Yid. Toyte Marsh). In January 1945, with the Soviet troops about to invade, the evacuation of the extermination and concentration camps in Eastern Europe began. Of the around seven hundred thousand prisoners marched toward Germany, over two hundred thousand perished on the marches. The Yiddish name *Toyte Marsh* usually refers to the evacuation of prisoners from the Auschwitz-Birkenau extermination complex.

Dror (Heb.: Freedom). An organization formally founded in Poland in 1922 by Jewish émigrés from Ukraine, where it had been in existence since 1917; it was ideologically close to Poalej Syjon Right, like Frajhajt. It encouraged young people to work toward building a socialist Jewish state in Palestine and called for national and cultural autonomy in the diaspora. Before the war, Dror had around a thousand members.

In the Warsaw ghetto, Antek Cukierman and Celina Lubetkin, the Dror leaders, voiced their support for an armed resistance movement in July 1942. The Dror youth lived or met up to study in the kibbutzes at 34 Dzielna, 58 Zamenhofa, and 34 Miła. Apartment no. 8 on Dzielna Street, on the top floor, was the home of Antek, Celina, and the organization's other instructors. Officially, Dzielna was a soup kitchen, and the first contact point for people resettled from other cities.

It was also the base of the clandestine seminar program for members of the organization. Cukierman wrote that in the Warsaw ghetto, Dror had eight hundred young members. In the April uprising, Dror fielded four fighting groups.

Einsatzgruppen (Ger.: operation groups). Police operations squads active from 1938 until 1945 in the rear guard of the Wehrmacht in German-occupied territory. Initially, their primary task was to murder enemies of the Third Reich; later, they were tasked with the mass extermination of the Jews in the eastern territories.

Expropriation operations ("exes"). The tradition of "exes" dated back to the days of the PPS under Józef Piłsudski. Both Jewish combat organizations, the ŻOB and the ŻZW, used various methods of persuading or forcing wealthy Jews to supply material support to the underground. The most resistant were sometimes held by young soldiers in a cellar or bunker known as a prison and "persuaded" to contribute by the use of force.

Jews expelled from Germany. Term used to refer to Jews with Polish citizenship resident in the German Reich, whom the Germans expelled from their territory in October 1938. The Germans were taking advantage of a Polish act of parliament permitting Polish citizens living abroad for upwards of five years to be stripped of their citizenship; around seventeen thousand Polish Jews were deposited in the Polish border town of Zbąszyń, where they remained camped in limbo for several days. After that, the Polish authorities took six thousand of these refugees at random and incarcerated them with no legal grounds in a camp constructed especially for them in army barracks in Zbąszyń. The Polish foreign affairs ministry orchestrated the whole situation to facilitate negotiations with the Germans regarding the expellees' property. From spring 1939 until the end of that August, only those intending to emigrate were allowed to leave the camp. On the eve of the war, the camp was liquidated, and its internees shared the fate of the Polish Jews.

First news of the extermination camps. The first information about systematic murders of Jews in extermination camps came from fugitives who had escaped from Chełmno nad Nerem. The testimony of Szlamek (Jakub Grojnowski, real name Szlama Ber Winer), who reached Warsaw in February 1942, was recorded and handed over to the Ringelblum Archive. A copy of the Oneg Shabbat report compiled on the basis of this testimony was sent to the Polish Underground State. In the ghetto, this information, like later accounts from extermination camps, was received with disbelief. The first news about Treblinka probably reached the Warsaw ghetto in early August 1942.

Frajhajt (Yid. Yidishe Arbeter Yugnt "Fraihait", "Freedom" Jewish Socialist Working Youth). A Halutz organization for working-class youth affiliated to the party Poalej Syjon Right, Frajhajt operated in Poland from 1925 till 1938. With around twenty thousand members in 1935, it was the largest and most dominant Zionist youth movement in the country. In 1938, it merged with Hehaluc Pionier. Frajhajt published the monthly paper *Jugnt-Frajhajt*. It sponsored the sporting organization Hapoel [Worker], which in 1933 had ninety clubs and seven thousand members. In the Warsaw ghetto, Frajhajt members usually belonged to Poalej Syjon or Dror ŻOB groups (hence Ron Szmuel's expression "Dror Frajhajt").

Gas chamber. An enclosed space used by the Germans during World War II to commit mass murders using gas. This method was initially introduced as more productive and less problematic than mass executions. From the summer of

1941 until the end of the war, gas chambers were used above all to murder Jews as part of the campaign known as the "final solution of the Jewish question," first in the extermination center in Chełmno, and later in Bełżec, Sobibór, Treblinka, and Auschwitz II Birkenau and Majdanek. Gas chambers were also installed and used in five concentration camps: Mauthausen, Neuengamme, Sachsenhausen, Stutthof, and Ravensbrück. The poisonous substances used were carbon monoxide, carbon dioxide, and Zyklon B. The first gas chambers were specially constructed trucks; later, stationary chambers connected with crematoria were used.

Gomułka, Władysław (1905–1982). Polish communist politician, for many years the leader of the Central Committee of the ruling Polish United Workers' Party. Generally held up as the initiator of the 1956 political thaw. In 1970 accused of causing strikes and anti-government revolts.

Gordonia. Youth organization founded in Poland in 1923 based on the legacy of the writer and worker Aaron David Gordon. It drew its support largely from among the Jewish intelligentsia and propagated the idea of a socialist state in Palestine. Before and after the war, it prepared young people for emigration in kibbutzes. In the Warsaw ghetto, Gordonia had its seat, the "commune," at the intersection of Dzika and Stawki, and a clandestine office at 23 Nalewki, on the second floor. There were one hundred to two hundred Gordonians, though Marek Edelman says that there were no more than twenty of them. In the ghetto, they published the Polish-language *Słowo Młodych* [Word of the Young]. Like all other Jewish organizations, Gordonia was dissolved in 1949.

Halutz movement (*Halutz* [Heb.]—pioneer). An umbrella organization of Zionist youth movements: Frajhajt, Hehaluc Hacair, Akiba, Gordonia, and Dror, all of which prepared young people for life in Palestine. The Halutz movement did not participate in public or political life in Poland, which it treated as a staging-post on the journey to Eretz Israel. The world He-Halutz movement accepted volunteers from the age of eighteen. Pioneers were sent on *hakhshara* to learn and work. After completing these courses, they could obtain emigration certificates from the British authorities. In the years 1925–1926, twenty-six thousand pioneers emigrated from Poland. Like the Shomerim, the Halutzim established agrarian kibbutzes in Palestine. At the beginning of the war, many members of Halutz organizations attempted to cross the German-Soviet border. Antek Cukierman, a Dror activist, wrote that Akiba and Gordonia joined forces with the Halutzim in Soviet-occupied territory at the turn of 1939 and 1940 to "protect young people from the Soviet regime," and that "in those days, the movement did not concern itself with either Marxism or Borochowism; we merely hoped to survive."

Hanoar Hacyjoni (Heb. Ha-Noar Ha-Tsioni, Zionist Youth). An organization established in Poland in the early 1930s. Its statutory aims were propagation of Zionism among young people, running sporting activities, teaching Polish and Yiddish, as well as history and literature, and preparing young people for emigration to Palestine. In the Warsaw ghetto, Hanoar Hacyjoni had its own kibbutz on Leszno Street. In the April uprising it fielded one fighting group.

Haszomer Hadati (Heb. Ha-Shomer Ha-Dati, The Religious Guard). A religious youth organization which, along with Hehaluc Hamizrachi, Hanoar Hadati, and Brit Halucim Datiim, formed Bnei Akiba. In 1954 these groups united to form World Bnei Akiva.

Haszomer Hacair (Heb. Ha-Shomer Ha-Tsair, Young Guard). The Jewish scouting movement, Zionist and socialist in orientation, founded in 1913 in Galicia, and from 1918 operating throughout Poland. (Like all Jewish political representations in Poland, it was closed down in 1949). Shomer instructors prepared young people spiritually and physically for emigration to Palestine; indeed, many members of the movement emigrated to Palestine and founded a kibbutz organization there. Until World War II, however, Haszomer Hacair operated chiefly in eastern and central Europe. In 1931, the organization had over twenty-two thousand members in 262 cells. Haszomer Hacair, like Akiba, had its own ideology, and had no party affiliation. Haszomer Hacair members did not want to merge with the Halutz movement, because they felt that the Halutzim were too nationalistic; the Shomerim were far closer to Soviet Marxists than to Zionist Jews. (The views of the Shomerim were akin to those of Poalej Syjon Left.)

In the Warsaw ghetto, Haszomer Hacair had some five hundred members. The Shomerim were probably closest to the communists from the PPR. They had communes at 23 Nalewki, 61 and 63 Miła, and 63 Gęsia. 23 Nalewki—where there was a soup kitchen, a reception point for resettled people, run by the Judenrat, and a Shomer kibbutz called Gal On—was the organization's central hub in the ghetto, where its members met until the *große Aktion*. There was also a Shomer library there, concealed inside a wall (built by Josek Kapłan, because he was a good carpenter). In the ghetto, the Shomerim published a Hebrew language paper, *Neged Ha-Zerem*, and *Der Ojfbrojz* (Der Oyfbroyz) in Yiddish. Four Haszomer Hacair groups fought in the April uprising.

Home Army (Pol. Armia Krajowa, AK). Clandestine armed forces operating during World War II in both German-occupied and Soviet-occupied Poland; subordinate to the Polish government-in-exile in Great Britain. The biggest military campaign undertaken by the AK was the Warsaw rising of 1944.

Hotel Polski. In the spring of 1943, there were still several thousand Jews—perhaps even more than twenty thousand—in hiding on the Polish side of the city, living among the Polish Varsovians. In May 1943, rumors began to circulate about the Hotel Polski: that there was a chance of rescue. All one had to do was come out of hiding and report to the Hotel Polski at 29 Długa Street. Word was that Jews who were citizens of neutral states would be able to emigrate from the General Government. People therefore came out of their safe houses, and for many spring days in 1943 there were crowds on the streets outside the Hotel Polski and the Royal Hotel on Chmielna Street. People put their names down to emigrate using documents from diplomatic missions of neutral states. (Many of these passports and certificates were counterfeit, probably issued for profit.) Some people also bought documents from Jewish Gestapo agents (these were bona fide, left by people murdered in the ghettos or camps).

The Polish underground press was somewhat suspicious, and rather ill-disposed towards the entire notion: it held the Jews to be in a privileged situation. The Jewish underground, for its part, was disoriented: the experience of the liquidation of the ghettos and the existence of the extermination camps suggested that any chance of survival offered openly and above board by the Germans was not to be trusted.

And indeed: several transports left from both hotels to the camps in Bergen-Belsen and Vittel. Moreover, on July 18, four hundred twenty Jews holding passports from South American countries were shot in Pawiak prison. At that point, the Polish underground began to call the Hotel Polski operation a provocation, and to write that it was simply another means of rounding up and plundering the Jews. Nonetheless, in November 1943 and February 1944, an exchange was carried out of Jews interned in Vittel for Germans interned in Palestine. Furthermore, the governments of the South American countries called the authenticity of the internees' passports into question, probably under pressure from the Allies. Some two thousand five hundred Jews were sent to Auschwitz-Birkenau, and barely a few hundred of the Hotel Polski's "guests" survived the war.

January operation. On January 18, 1943, the Germans relaunched their deportation campaign in the ghetto. The poorly armed ŻOB decided to mount an impromptu resistance operation (also known as the January self-defense) and there were a number of street skirmishes. All those who could, used weapons—Cukierman, Geller, Wilner, Artsztajn, Wald, Henoch Gutman . . . Others assumed moral leadership, organizing hideouts for those in danger, and calling for unarmed resistance at the Umschlagplatz. The ghetto residents defended themselves against the attacking German, Ukrainian, and Lithuanian units until January 22, when the Germans abandoned their deportation plans. In all, around one thousand people were killed in that January operation, and six thousand deported.

Many of those who were rounded up were murdered on the Umschlagplatz because they refused to board the trains. For the ŻOB, the January resistance operation was a rehearsal for the April uprising. It showed the other ghetto residents that there was sense in resisting. And it gave the Polish underground at least a modicum of confidence in the operations of its Jewish counterpart. (Hirsz Berliński noted that the ŻOB actually had an act of resistance planned for January 22, 1943. Marek Edelman was to have been its commandant, on Muranowski Square. Their plan was this: between 6 p.m. and 7 p.m. they would display wreaths and slogans on the fencing along Muranowska Street and light a bonfire on Muranowski Square. Groups under Berliński would lie in wait along Miła and Muranowska Streets, while Anielewicz would have groups ready on Nalewki, Zamenhofa and Gęsia, and they would ambush the attending Jewish police officers, beat them up, and steal their caps.)

Jewish Fighting Organization (Pol. Żydowska Organizacja Bojowa, ŻOB). The armed underground of the Warsaw ghetto (it also had a presence in Częstochowa, Krakow, Białystok, and Będzin and Sosnowiec in the Dąbrowa Basin). It was created in July 1942, expanding and strengthening rapidly from the days of the *große Aktion* in the Warsaw ghetto until the very end, that is, until the outbreak of the uprising in April 1943. In the July the Halutzim and the Shomerim held talks about the need to fight, and it was they who founded the "first"—sometimes called the "July"—ŻOB. Then, in the October, they were joined by the non-Zionist Bund. (Marek Edelman believed that they could in fact only be called the ŻOB from the point at which the future insurgents were barracked together, that is, from the end of January 1943. Because then, after the "January campaign," they knew for certain that they would be defending the ghetto residents.) The ŻOB comprised young people from a range of political organizations. (The only ones who did not join them were the young Betarists, who belonged to the ŻZW, and the religious youth, for whom an armed defense was an inadmissible solution.) The ŻOB was poorly armed: the Polish underground organizations, the AK and the GL, passed on few arms to them, and fewer still could be bought or manufactured. The ŻOB fighters lived in groups affiliated to their organizations in barrack arrangements on the premises of German factories in the ghetto. They learned to handle weapons and manufactured incendiary bottles. They were strong through the support of the ghetto residents, both those living there "legally" and those in hiding in bunkers. They were resolved not to allow themselves to be deported, and to defend others from deportation. The Germans scheduled the final deportation campaign for April 19, and it was then that the ŻOB launched its armed defense operation. Those weeks of fighting later became known as the Warsaw ghetto uprising. The commanders of the ŻOB included Mordechaj Anielewicz, Icchak Cukierman, and Marek Edelman. In all, some two hundred to three hundred Jewish soldiers fought in twenty-two groups from April 19 till May 8.

Jewish Military Union (Pol. Żydowski Związek Wojskowy, ŻZW). An organization established in the Warsaw ghetto that was military in both name and ideals. The exact date of its foundation is not known, because no pertinent documents have survived. It was probably established during or after the *große Aktion* (in summer or early fall 1942). It is surrounded by several, often contradictory accounts. Some of these stories are more reminiscent of legends than testimonies. (Most of these are accounts by Poles, whose value is questioned by contemporary historians.) It was founded by members of right-wing Zionist organizations (Betar and the Zionist Revisionists). Most of the soldiers of the ŻZW were killed in the first days of the uprising or shortly thereafter on the Polish side. The few who survived did not tell their stories, partly because for years after the war the Holocaust was taboo, and partly because in both Poland and Israel, Betar, the party from which the ŻZW drew most of its members, was in the shadow of other parties and organizations. Thus, very little is known about it at all. (There are two accounts written by members of the formation: one dated June 1943 and signed only with the forename Paweł, the other, from 1946, by Adam Halperin. The text by "Paweł" was not published until the 1980s.) The commander of the ŻZW was Paweł Frenkiel, and the Kielce journalist Leon Rodal a member of its staff. The ŻZW had its base at 7 Muranowska; many records, citing Emanuel Ringelblum, who went there, reported that the rebels had a sizable arsenal there. No one ever counted how many soldiers the ŻZW numbered (though the figures one hundred and two hundred sixty are mentioned in accounts). They are known to have dug a tunnel used to smuggle food, medicines, and arms into the ghetto. Shortly ahead of the uprising, the leaders of the ŻZW and the ŻOB met, but the two organizations did not join forces: there were too many differences between the young people, who probably had divergent conceptions of their role. After heavy fighting on Muranowski Square on April 19, 20, and possibly also 21, most of the surviving ŻZW soldiers left the ghetto via the tunnel. Many of them were killed on Muranowska, on the other side of the wall; others near Michalin. Very few survived the war.

Jewish National Committee (Pol. Żydowski Komitet Narodowy, ŻKN). An underground political body in the Warsaw ghetto that was founded after the *große Aktion*, in November 1942. It comprised representatives from the Zionist parties, youth organizations, and the communist PPR, and was established in order to exert a political influence on the ŻOB. The only significant party in the ghetto that did not join the ŻKN was the Bund. This prevented the organization from being able to cooperate with the Polish underground, because the AK was only willing to negotiate with an entity representing the whole ghetto community. In December 1942, therefore, a second body was established, the Coordinating Committee (Pol. Komisja Koordynacyjna, KK), which did include representatives from the Bund. The role of the KK was to manage the fighting organization. It maintained contact with the Polish government-in-exile in London, sending communiques and appeals for aid for the ghetto. After the April uprising, it was partly funds raised by the ŻKN and the network of contacts it had built up that enabled Jews in hiding to help each other. There were also Poles working for the ŻKN.

Jewish Order Service (Ger. Jüdischer Ordnungsdienst; Pol. Żydowska Służba Porządkowa). A formation commonly known in the ghetto as the "Order Service" or "Ghetto Police," and outside of it as the "Jewish Police" (its members were referred to derisively as "Dachshunds"; those on duty at guardposts were known as "players" [Pol. *grajki*] because whenever they accepted a bribe to let someone out of the ghetto, they were wont to say "The jukebox is now playing" [Pol. *szafa gra*]). It was established on Gestapo orders on the eve of the creation of the ghettos, and open only to Jews. It numbered one thousand seven hundred police officers after its first recruitment drive, and two thousand five hundred in July 1942. It was formally subordinate to the Judenrat but answered in practice to the German police authorities. The service stood guard at the ghetto gates, directed ghetto traffic, escorted people who had been resettled, combatted smuggling, and oversaw the ghetto prisons. Jewish police officers were often lawyers, doctors, or former Polish Army or state police officers.

One such prewar professional policeman (in the rank of colonel) was the first chief of the Jewish Order Service, Józef Andrzej Szeryński (Szynkman). It was an unpaid service, but its members received larger food rations, and—for a certain period—the policeman and his family enjoyed a relative sense of security. Jewish police officers did not command respect among the ghetto residents. They were demoralized and corrupt; many were known for their ruthlessness and cruelty. During the *große Aktion*, the Jewish Order Service snatched and marched some two hundred sixty-five thousand Jews to the Umschlagplatz. Then, on September 6, the Germans issued the service with just five hundred "numbers for life." After that campaign, it numbered only two hundred men. In the January operation the following year, its members (by then just eighty in number) were no longer so zealous. On April 19, 1943, the Jewish police officers were ordered to gather at the Nalewki Street gate. The majority were deported to Treblinka or Majdanek; around twenty were killed in Pawiak prison.

Jewish partisans. From late 1941, there were Jewish partisans, fugitives from the ghettos, in hiding in woods and forests all over Poland. Jews who wanted to fight and those who simply wanted to hide out in the woods often formed independent groups; only rarely were they accepted into Polish partisan units. The local peasants tended to be ill-disposed toward the Jewish partisans, and often treated them like gangs of looters. Sometimes, Polish forest units eliminated Jewish groups that had been more or less truthfully accused of attacks on and looting of nearby houses and farmsteads. There were around thirty Jewish partisan units operating in the General Government.

One Jewish partisan, Bauman, reported meeting in the Białowieża Forest some Jews from a unit of the AL that had been smashed. Those "Lasockis" (as the Jews codenamed their partisans [from the Polish word for forest, *las*]) were from Warsaw. Many of them had been smuggled out of the ghetto. Their leader was Ignacy Podolski, a metalworker from Żelazna Street. Bauman recorded that Podolski had been shot dead by the commander of another forest group, and his group, of around thirty, had been murdered in April 1944 somewhere near Ostrów Mazowiecka.

Some Jews returned from the forests to Warsaw, to go into hiding in the city. Many perished because they were denounced by local peasants. Yet others were killed in action or by Polish partisans.

Jewish Social Welfare Society (Pol. Żydowskie Towarzystwo Opieki Społecznej, Żytos, ŻTOS). A welfare institution in Warsaw founded in October

1941. The ŻTOS concentrated its support on specific groups of ghetto society: party and public activists, and members of youth movements, the intelligentsia, and religious institutions. It hosted clandestine meetings between activists of various political alliances. It was based at 25 Nowolipki.

Jewish soldiers released from POW camps. Jewish soldiers in the Polish Army (WP) who had fought in the September 1939 defense campaign were interned, like their Polish comrades, in prisoner-of-war camps in the German Reich. They were separated from the Polish POWs, however, and held in much worse conditions. Somewhat unexpectedly, at the turn of 1939 and 1940, Jewish soldiers in the ranks of private and NCO began to be released from these camps. (The Germans probably took this decision as one element of the campaign to "purge" the Reich of Jews.) The liberated Jewish soldiers were sent to major cities in the General Government. On February 18, 1940, historian Emanuel Ringelblum recorded that two thousand POWs had returned from Germany to Warsaw. On March 6, he wrote that thousands more Jews were returning every day. One major problem with which this presented the Judenrats was finding food and clothing for the new returnees; many of them died of starvation and cold during that harsh winter. Jewish WP officers, who were protected by international conventions, remained in the Oflags until the end of the war.

Judenrat (Ger.: Jewish Council). The German name usually used to denote the administrative bodies set up by the Germans to manage the Jewish communities. After the creation of the ghettos, they acted as executive bodies in respect of the Jewish population, but above all played the role of liaison between the ghetto population and the German authorities. Among the Judenrat employees' duties were assigning people for forced labor; evacuating apartments and making them over to the Germans; paying fines, ransoms, and tribute payments; confiscating valuables; organizing resettlement operations; preventing smuggling; distributing food, coal, and other wares; guaranteeing appropriate sanitary conditions; preventing epidemics; organizing welfare; and above all, implementing the various ordinances of the occupying authorities. In the final period of the ghettos' existence, Judenrats were required to participate in the deportations of their populations to the death camps. Most councils were ill-disposed to any form of activity that represented opposition to the occupying authorities.

Kamiński, Aleksander, Hubert, Kazimierz (1903–1978). Polish pedagogue, scouting activist, and historian. During the German occupation he was the co-founder of the Gray Ranks, the underground paramilitary scouting organization;

editor-in-chief of the news bulletin *Biuletyn Informacyjny*, the leading press organ of the Polish underground; counter-intelligence officer for Division II of the AK High Command; an organizer of small-scale sabotage operations; and author of flyers and of the best-known book about occupied Warsaw, *Kamienie na szaniec*, first published in 1943.

Kapłan, Josef (Josek, Józef). Born in Kalisz in 1913, from the age of thirteen he was a member of Haszomer Hacair, and later became an activist at the organization's headquarters in Warsaw. At the turn of 1939 and 1940, he organized its underground activity in eastern Poland. From December 1940 he was active in the Warsaw ghetto. He worked in the Joint's offices, established the Maapilim kibbutz, and was then sent to Częstochowa in Silesia to help set up a kibbutz there, in the village of Żarki. He kept Jewish organizations abroad informed on the situation of the Jewish community in occupied Poland. In 1941, he completed his book documenting the work of Haszomer Hacair; it was published in Palestine in 1942. He was active in the ŻKN and was elected to the ŻOB's staff company. On September 3, 1942, he was arrested by the Gestapo in Landau's 'shop, where he worked (probably betrayed by one of the movement's other members, who had been arrested a few days previously). Kapłan was murdered in Pawiak prison on September 11, 1942.

Karski, Jan (real name Jan Kozielewski, 1914–2000). Courier and political envoy of the Polish underground; historian. In spring 1940, he drew up a report for the Polish government-in-exile in which he gave a chilling account of the dramatic situation of the Jews and the attitudes of Poles toward the Holocaust. In the fall of 1942, he smuggled to London materials obtained from Polish and Jewish underground activists, and his own reports, describing the annihilation of the Warsaw ghetto and the extermination campaign underway throughout Poland. These showed unequivocally that the Nazis' aim was to annihilate the Jews. The Polish government-in-exile issued a diplomatic memorandum on the matter, and the Allied governments condemned the German crimes and announced that the criminals would be brought to justice. No action was taken, however. Karski reiterated his information on the fate of the Jews in Poland repeatedly in interviews with Polish, British, and American journalists and politicians (in the summer of 1943 he was received by Franklin D. Roosevelt). In his book *The Story of the Secret State*, published in 1944, he wrote extensively about the Holocaust. After the war, he settled in the USA; he was a professor at Georgetown University, Washington, D.C. In 1982, he was decorated with the Righteous Among the Nations medal.

Kennkarte (Ger.: identity card). Only in the first half of 1942 did the German authorities start to issue identity documents in the General Government (GG, the name given to occupied Poland). *Kennkarten* were compulsory for all non-German residents of the GG. Their introduction gave many Jews in hiding the chance to obtain "Aryan papers."

Kettle on Miła Street. This is the name given to the final phase of the liquidation of the Warsaw ghetto that had begun on July 22, 1942. On September 6, 1942, the registration was ordered of all ghetto residents who were still alive. A selection was carried out in the sector of the streets adjoining the Umschlagplatz: on Niska, Gęsia, Smocza, Miła, Zamenhofa, and Lubeckiego Streets, and Parysowski and Stawki Squares. Tens of thousands of people were herded into this "kettle," which remained in place until September 12. In the first few days, some sixty thousand people were "deported," that is, taken to Treblinka, from the Umschlagplatz. The "numbers for life" issued in the kettle were given to people including Judenrat employees, and some hospital personnel and German factory workers.

Kielce pogrom. After the war, some Jews, a very few, returned to their hometowns and villages. In Kielce, many of them went to live at 7 Planty Street. There may have been one hundred fifty to one hundred sixty of them living there—in any case, the majority of those who had returned to the town. Together, they established a Jewish Committee, an orphanage, and a kibbutz—a sort of neighborhood community, a community of survivors. On July 3, 1946, a Polish man reported to the local police precinct that his son, eight-year-old Henryk Błaszczyk, had been kidnapped by the Jews and was being held in the cellars of the house at Planty Street. (Not until 1998 did Henryk Błaszczyk himself admit in an interview that he had never been kidnapped, and that he had remained silent out of fear.) On July 4, 1946, an avalanche of crimes engulfed the city. Soldiers, police officers, military secret agents, and civilians all joined the carnival of violence. People were beaten and killed both inside the building on Planty Street and on the streets, and even on trains passing through the city. Military personnel used firearms, and civilians rocks, metal bars, and clubs. On that day, forty-two Jews were murdered, and over forty more wounded, several of whom died in hospital. (The figures are not entirely accurate, since the documentation of the crimes is incomplete.) A number of Poles were also killed in the tumult. That same month, a highly publicized military court in emergency session sentenced nine people to death, and the sentences were carried out the following day. Three people were handed prison sentences, which ranged from three years to life. The crimes committed in Kielce were a watershed for many Jewish survivors: over the next year or so, around one hundred fifty thousand Jews left Poland. By the spring of 1947, barely ninety thousand remained in the country.

Korczak, Janusz (real name Henryk Goldszmit, 1878/1879–1942). Writer, pedagogue, social activist, and physician. Came from a non-religious Jewish family. In the years 1912–1942 he was the director of the Jewish orphanage in Warsaw. Despite having the chance to leave the ghetto, he remained with his charges. Deported to Treblinka death camp with the children and their carers on August 5 or 6, 1942.

Koziebrodzka, Lea (Lońka). Born in Pruszków in 1917. During the war she was a courier for Dror and traveled to ghettos all over Poland (on the "Aryan side" she operated under the name Krystyna Kosowska), convoying documents and money, running arms, and escorting members of her organization from city to city. In April 1942, on her way back from Vilnius to Warsaw, she was arrested at the railroad station in Małkinia. Four pistols and some clandestine newspapers were found on her person. During interrogations at the Gestapo headquarters at Szucha Avenue and in the Pawiak prison, she did not confess to possession of counterfeit documents. On November 11, 1942, she was deported to Auschwitz, where she died on March 18, 1943, of typhus.

Landau's 'shop. A carpentry factory in the Warsaw ghetto. Before the war it had been co-owned by Aleksander Lejb Landau. When it was confiscated from him during the war, he became its manager. Landau's factory was a place where many ŻOB members found refuge. For a while it was also the home of the ŻOB command. Landau's daughter, Emilka, was a ŻOB member herself.

League for Aid to Workers in Israel or League for Aid to Workers in Palestine. A multi-party bloc of socialist Zionist groups in Poland. Poalej Syjon Left joined the movement in 1937; Haszomer Hacair and Poalej Syjon Right had been members since 1927.

Lejzer (Eliezer) **Lewin.** Born in 1891. After the outbreak of World War II, he moved from Łódź to Warsaw, where he was one of the organizers of Poalej Syjon Left in the underground. He left the ghetto during the April uprising via the sewers, from the Toebbens-Schultz yard, and managed to reach Łomianki with some other insurgents. After the war, he emigrated to Palestine, where he lived on the Yagur kibbutz. He died in 1967.

"Life" Socialist Youth Organization (Pol. Organizacja Młodzieży Socjalistycznej "Życie"). Popularly known as the "Academic Left," this was a student organization for communist and pro-communist young people, which operated between 1923 and 1938 in Warsaw, Krakow, Lwów, and other cities. Its members were active in politics and education: they protested against the "bench ghetto" at universities and cooperated with other groups including the Bundist Academic Union Ring.

Lohamei Ha-Getaot (Heb.: the Ghetto Fighters' Kibbutz). Kibbutz founded in Galilee in 1948 by Holocaust survivors from Poland, most of them from the Warsaw ghetto. Beit Lohamei Ha-Getaot is also an education center, with a museum, gallery, archives, and its own publishing house.

Makkabi. A Jewish sporting movement with a presence in Poland from the early twentieth century; it was supported by the Zionist parties. Before the war it numbered around one hundred fifty thousand members in Poland, in almost two hundred fifty sports clubs. Makkabi sports activists organized Jewish sporting events in both summer and winter, which were known as the Makkabi Games. (They are still held today in Israel, and the Jewish youth in Poland reactivated their national club in 1990.)

March 1968. March 1968 (sometimes simply "March" or "1968") is shorthand for the socio-political crisis that erupted at that time in Poland. Anti-communist protests were deflected by the authorities of the People's Republic of Poland with anti-Jewish speeches and rulings. That year, as a result of or in response to the repressions, over twenty thousand Jews emigrated from Poland.

Medem Sanatorium. The Włodzimierz Medem Memorial Child Sanatorium Association for Jewish children in Miedzeszyn near Warsaw was founded in 1926. It was a Bundist residential treatment center for children with tuberculosis. In the years 1926–1939, some eight thousand children received treatment and attended school in the Miedzeszyn sanatorium. During World War II, the sanatorium was incorporated into the Falenica ghetto. On August 20, 1942, the Jewish population of Falenica and Miedzeszyn was deported to Treblinka extermination camp. Those deported included two hundred children and sanatorium personnel. The architectural sanatorium complex remained standing for just over two decades after the war; it was demolished in 1970, probably in connection with the 1968 purges and the drive to erase traces of the past.

Mizrachi. A religious Zionist party founded in Vilnius in 1902. It agitated in many countries for the creation of a seat of orthodox Judaism in Palestine. In Poland, Mizrachi was largely present in Warsaw, Krakow, and Lwów, among the orthodox middle classes. It conducted educational activity in Hebrew and Polish through the Tarbut organization. Its youth arm, Cejre Mizrachi, provided religious education, propagated a new, Hebrew-based culture, and prepared young people for emigration to Palestine. It had no fighting groups in the April 1943 uprising in the Warsaw ghetto.

National Armed Forces (Pol. Narodowe Siły Zbrojne, NSZ). An underground military organization (1942–1947) that formed one element of the Polish armed underground during the war, when it fought against both the Germans and Polish left-wing formations (the People's Guard and the People's Army). After the war it conducted partisan warfare against the Russian and Polish communist state structures. Accused, not groundlessly, of antipathy toward the Jews.

National Democracy (Pol. Narodowa Demokracja, ND, "Endecja"). A nationalist movement founded in Poland under the partitions, in the nineteenth century. Its founder and ideologue was Roman Dmowski. After the restitution of Poland's independence in 1918, until the outbreak of World War II in 1939, the ND was an oppositional force; the first president of the new republic, Gabriel Narutowicz, was assassinated by a member of the movement who was also operating as an agent for the USSR. The National-Radical Camp (ONR), known for its fascist views and antisemitic activity, was born out of the nationalist movement in the 1930s.

National-Radical Camp (Pol. Obóz Narodowo-Radykalny, ONR). An extreme right-wing, nationalist political organization, founded in 1934 following a split in the National Alliance (Stronnictwo Narodowe). The ONR propagated anti-Semitic slogans, called for the expropriation of Jewish capital, organized economic boycotts of Jewish businesses, and instigated anti-Jewish violence. An overtly fascist splinter group of the ONR, Falanga, which operated in the years 1935–1939, fielded gangs that carried out pogroms of Jews and other racist violence on an extensive scale: commercial boycotts, damage to Jewish stores, homes, and other premises, and implementing "bench ghettos" by force at universities.

Number for life. At the beginning of the *große Aktion*, the population of the Warsaw ghetto was divided into two categories: the majority were taken to Treblinka straight away, while a minority (members and employees of Jewish institutions, employees of German companies, and ghetto medical personnel, along with members of their families) were temporarily released. In the final phase of the liquidation of the ghetto, after September 6, the thirty-five thousand people permitted to remain there were issued with special authorizations, known as "numbers for life."

People's Army (Pol. Armia Ludowa, AL). Clandestine armed formation in occupied Poland, subordinate to the underground Polish Workers' Party (PPR).

People's Guard (Pol. Gwardia Ludowa, GL). Partisan military formation in occupied Poland, founded in March 1942 by the underground Polish Workers' Party (PPR) to carry out assassinations and revenge attacks on the German occupying forces. It collaborated with the Red Army. In early 1944 it was subsumed into the People's Army.

Pionier (Pol.: Pioneer). An illegal communist children's organization modeled on its Soviet namesake. It came into existence in 1925 and was active largely in Warsaw. Its motto was "The Pionier is the younger brother of the communist." In 1930, there were two thousand five hundred Pioneers in Poland. Pionier ceased to exist when the Communist International dissolved the Polish Communist Party and the Communist Union of Polish Youth in 1938.

Poalej Syjon (Heb. Poalei Zion, Workers of Zion). A socialist Zionist organization founded as an underground movement in 1905 during a congress of Jewish socialist Zionists in the Polish spa town of Ciechocinek. Its chief ideologists were Dow Ber Borochow and Nachman Syrkin. In 1920, the party split into two: Poalej Syjon Right (Heb. Poalei Zion Yemin) and Poalej Syjon Left (Heb. Poalei Zion Smol). Poalej Syjon Right reconciled Zionist ideals with the interests of Jewish workers in the diaspora, and its adherents tended to be members of the intelligentsia and craftspeople. Like other Jewish parties, Poalej Syjon had its own sports club, Sztern [Star]. While it continued to advocate emigration to Palestine, Poalej Syjon Left refuted the religious Zionism of Poalej Syjon, openly sympathized with the Bolsheviks, and began to stress the socialist and internationalist obligations of the Jewish proletariat. It also stressed the need for regulation of the Jewish question in Poland and advocated the use of Yiddish as the national language of the

Polish Jews. (In Israel, advocates of Poalej Syjonist ideals are members of the Labor Party.) In 1937, Poalej Syjon Left numbered five thousand members. The children's arm was called Jungbor. In the April uprising there was one Poalej Syjon Left fighting group.

Poalej Syjon Right, the continuator of the original Poalej Syjon ideology, propagated a Zionism infused with tradition and religion among craftspeople and the intelligentsia. In 1923 the left-leaning youth from Cejre Syjon joined Poalej Syjon Right, and in 1925 they were joined by the young people from Dror. In 1933, Poalej Syjon Right merged with Hitachdut, a socialist-Zionist party. Like other Jewish parties, Poalej Syjon Right had defense units, which were known as Frajhajt Szuc, and its own sports club, Hapoel. In the Warsaw ghetto, Poalej Syjon Right ran a soup kitchen at 12 Dzielna Street. In July 1942, during the *große Aktion*, when the first combat organization in the Warsaw ghetto was being formed, Poalej Syjon Right was still opposed to armed resistance, but the young people from Dror came out strongly against their elders, and in the April 1943 uprising, Poalej Syjon Right was represented by one fighting group. In 1947 the two fractions reunited, becoming the strongest Jewish party in Poland, and were active in the cause of Holocaust survivors. Poalej Syjon was dissolved in 1950.

Polish police (Ger. Polnische Polizei). This force was made up entirely of Poles. It had its own command system but was essentially subordinate to the German order police (Ger. Ordnungspolizei, Orpo). Outside the ghetto walls it was colloquially known as the dark-blue police (Pol. *granatowa policja*). It was generally used for secondary interventions, usually those more involved with keeping order than of a political nature. Although it did not operate inside the ghetto, its officers did serve at the guardhouses, the ghetto gates, on the outside. During the deportations, the Polish police took part in roundups of Jews in hiding outside the ghetto walls. Many officers were corrupt and took a cut from smuggling operations (Ringelblum wrote that sixty percent of all bribes paid to facilitate smuggling went to the Polish police), and actively engaged in blackmail and denunciation of Jews outside the ghetto. There were, however, also a few who supported the ghetto residents, by passing on underground press and sometimes "Aryan" papers or assisting in smuggling operations or escapes from the ghetto. During the uprising in the Warsaw ghetto, a unit numbering several hundred Polish policemen stood guard around the fighting ghetto.

Polish Socialist Party (Pol. Polska Partia Socjalistyczna, PPS). A social democratic party with a long tradition of advocating Polish independence. Founded in 1892, it had often worked with Jewish parties and organizations before the war. In the ghetto, it extended its support to the Jewish underground and maintained contact with the socialist Bund. No closer cooperation developed between the two parties, however, largely due to their differing stances on the USSR. The PPS's working-class sports club, Skra, was based at 43–47 Okopowa Street. (Marysia Sawicka of the PPS and Gina Klepfisz from the Bund's sports club Morgensztern ran the eight hundred meters together in Skra. Later, during the occupation, friendships such as these were the pillars of the safest underground contacts.) The bodies of Jews murdered in the ghetto were taken to the Skra stadium.

Polish United Workers' Party (Pol. Polska Zjednoczona Partia Robotnicza, PZPR). Founded in 1948, the PZPR held power in the Polish People's Republic. It was dependent on and obedient toward the Communist Party of the Soviet Union. The PZPR was dissolved following the political transformations in Poland in 1990.

Polish Workers' Party (Pol. Polska Partia Robotnicza, PPR). A communist party founded in 1942 by envoys from the Soviet Union. In the Warsaw ghetto, it formed part of the Anti-Fascist Bloc, an alliance of left-wing Zionists and communists. The socialist Bund did not join the bloc. Groups of young communists, communist sympathizers, and other left-wingers from the PPR joined the ŻOB and fought in the Warsaw ghetto uprising. From July 1944, the PPR was a dependent party in Poland, ruling in line with USSR politics. In 1948, the PPR, by then a mass movement with over a million members, and the PPS (with five hundred thousand members) merged to form the hegemonic PZPR, which held power in Poland until 1989.

Political relations in the Warsaw ghetto. The prewar division into right- and left-wing had no bearing on the ghetto reality. Warsaw ghetto historian Ruta Sakowska says that there was a broad leftward shift (engulfing even the religious parties Agudat Israel and Mizrachi), with moves to tax the rich to feed the hungry, and support for civil disobedience. In 1942, when young people began to plan their armed resistance, some parties and party leaders were opposed to the idea. In time, however, even those differences faded. There was space for political options of almost all colors in the ŻOB. The Jewish underground was known in the ghetto as "the Party." Ghetto residents trusted, respected, and supported "the Party," which held sway in the ghetto from January 1943 until the sealed district ceased to exist. When in March 1943 the proprietor of the Toebbens 'shops demanded action in some matter from the head of the Judenrat, the latter is said to have responded: "I no longer hold the authority in the ghetto; others rule here."

Prewar antisemitism in Poland. In the years 1935–1939, Polish anti-Jewish propaganda, waged an increasingly energetic campaign, undoubtedly under the influence of Nazi ideology, to encourage Jews to emigrate. There were calls for the removal of Jews from political, social, and cultural life, and economic boycotts. From June 1935 a wave of pogroms engulfed over a dozen towns, lasting until 1937. The Catholic Church played a significant role in this violence, disseminating anti-Semitic flyers calling for economic boycotts of Jewish businesses and the removal of Jewish teachers and students from public schools. The Church stigmatized the Jews as a "hotbed of communism," and some advocated stripping them of their citizens' rights. One Polish diplomat, in a memorandum filed with the Vatican in 1938, spoke of a "zoological anti-Semitism among the Polish clergy." There is an indisputable connection between the views disseminated by the Catholic Church in Poland and attitudes towards Jews in Polish society both before and during the war. Many ordinary Poles participated actively in the anti-Semitic violence orchestrated by the Germans at Easter 1940 in Warsaw.

Prewar antisemitism in Polish higher education. There were two main forms of antisemitism that were to a greater or lesser extent sanctioned in higher education in Poland in the 1930s. The first was the "bench ghetto." This involved the designation of separate seats in lecture halls for Jewish students, who were identified on the basis of the religious criterion. (At the University of Warsaw, Jewish students had their grade record books stamped with the words "Seat in odd-numbered benches.") On the pretext of preventing the annual antisemitic violence perpetrated every year by nationalist organizations, in 1937 the minister for religious confessions and public enlightenment gave university rectors a free hand in selecting the segregation methods they wished to use. Some rectors decided to implement a "bench ghetto" (which provoked protests by many leading scholars), but this failed to produce results. Jewish students themselves protested against this form of discrimination by not sitting down at all; lecturers demonstrated solidarity with them by also delivering their lectures standing up. Discrimination at universities affected medical students above all, perhaps in view of the high percentage of Jews in that profession. The second took the form of calls for the introduction of limits on numbers of Jews accepted to universities (*numerus clausus*), or for total bans on Jews studying (*numerus nullus*). In fact, no such principles were ever introduced on any scale (the *numerus nullus* was only ever implemented at the Catholic University of Lublin). Nonetheless, the *numerus clausus* was a constant element of antisemitic propaganda at universities.

Ringelblum Archive. An underground ghetto institution, known in Hebrew as Oneg Shabat ("the joy of the Sabbath," because that was the day the archive members met). It was founded in 1940 by the historian and Zionist Emanuel Ringelblum. Two of the three parts of the archive's collections buried for safekeeping during the Holocaust survived the destruction of Warsaw and were rediscovered after the war; today, these are a primary source of knowledge about the lives of the Jews in the Warsaw ghetto and other places in occupied Poland. The thousands of documents (manuscripts, printed matter, and photographs—in all, twenty-eight thousand sheets) amassed by Oneg Shabat are collectively known as the Underground Archive of the Warsaw Ghetto. The collection is now held in the Emanuel Ringelblum Jewish Historical Institute in Warsaw.

Schools. The CISzO (Polish acronym of Yid. Tsentrale Yidishe Shul Organizatsye, Central Organization of Jewish Schools), Szul-Kult (Association for Schooling and Culture), Tarbut (the Jewish Educational and Cultural Association), and Chorew, Beit Jaakow, and Jawne (organizers of religious girls' and boys' schools) were all founded in the 1920s. The CISzO offered modern, secular (anti-Hebrew and anti-Zionist) Jewish schools with Yiddish, under the patronage of the Bund and Poalej Syjon Left. Its day and evening schools were attended by the children of workers and craftspeople—some twenty-five thousand in the late 1920s. Szul-Kult ran elementary schools, night schools, kindergartens, and libraries. Its main language of instruction was Hebrew. It won the support of Poalej Syjon Right, which had previously worked with the Bund to run the CISzO. Tarbut propagated Hebrew and modern Jewish culture. Its schools were run under the patronage of the Zionist parties, and also offered subjects taught in Polish. In the 1930s, around fifty thousand students attended Tarbut schools at several different levels.

On October 1, 1941, six schools were officially opened in the Warsaw ghetto. That was the only year when education was legal in the ghetto. Children were taught in soup kitchens, where clandestine lessons had previously been held. In that school year, 1941/1942, among the schools that operated were three run by the CISzO, one by Shul-Kult, four by Tarbut, and six belonging to religious organizations. Over those few months, those schools were able to teach just seven thousand of the almost fifty thousand children in the ghetto. In all, six thousand seven hundred children completed the school year in nineteen schools. In parallel, however, and later, underground schools were also active, in children's centers, resettlement centers, childminders' rooms, residential accommodation, and above all community soup kitchens. For the kitchens were schools. Many of them were in former school buildings—on Nowolipki, Krochmalna, and Karmelicka, for instance. Clandestine teaching was also conducted in private homes. Zosia Frydman recalls lessons preparing her for her high school finals in the home of the principal of her prewar Jewish high school, for instance.

'**Shop** (Pol. *szop*, Ger. *Schuppen*). A ghetto slang term (taken in Polish and Yiddish directly from the English) to mean a large German-owned workshop (hence the apostrophe in this rendering) or factory/manufactory operating in the ghetto and built up around pre-existing smaller-scale Jewish workshops or ateliers. Their production output was reserved for the needs of the German economy and brought their owners vast profits. Cobblers', tailors', carpenters' and other workshops started to spring up in the Warsaw ghetto from January 1941. The first was the carpentry workshop of Bernard Hallman, an entrepreneur from Danzig (now Gdańsk, Poland). The second, opened in September 1941, was a furrier's workshop, owned by Fritz Schultz, also from Danzig. The next was that of Walter Toebbens, a textile manufacturer from Bremen. The Jews employed there worked eleven to twelve hours a day for a few coppers, a mug of coffee, and a plate of soup. At the beginning of the *große Aktion*, employment in a 'shop was highly prized, because it was believed to offer protection from deportation to Treblinka. Before long, however, it transpired that 'shop employees were not exempt from roundups. During the kettle on Miła Street, which lasted from September 6 to 12, 1942, those "selected" to continue working were issued with stamped slips of paper, known as "numbers for life" (Pol. *numerki życia*). And thereafter, only holders of these "numbers," registered to work in the 'shops, were legal ghetto residents. When the *große Aktion* came to an end, after September 21, 1942, there were just thirty-five thousand people left with the right to live in the ghetto: the last "legal" employees of the 'shops and their families.

Smuggling (Pol. *szmugiel*). The smuggling of goods (for example, ritually slaughtered meat) both into and out of the Warsaw ghetto, and between the ghettos in various cities was a necessity due to the drastic shortages. It was practiced by thousands of people: both individuals supplying themselves and their families, and groups of Polish and Jewish smugglers, which usually collaborated, and operated on a large scale and in an organized fashion. Prices inside the ghetto were 10–70 percent higher than on the "Aryan side." Small quantities of goods might be carried in and out by Jews employed in work details outside the ghetto, or by Poles with passes authorizing them to enter the ghetto, for example, public services employees. Jewish women also engaged in smuggling, but children were prized above all, as they could slip through holes in the wall, or exploit momentary distractions of the guards at the guardpost. Larger quantities of goods were exchanged using all manner of more refined methods. Food would be passed into the ghetto over the wall, via tunnels and holes dug under it, through disguised holes made in it, through adjoining houses, or by being thrown out of streetcars passing through the ghetto.

Spartakus (Pol. Związek Niezależnej Młodzieży Socjalistycznej "Spartakus," the Spartacus Union of Independent Socialist Youth). A youth organization for high school students that operated semi-legally in Warsaw from 1934 under the aegis of the PPS. In 1937 it had around two hundred members. In 1939 it aligned itself more closely with the radical left and operated in clandestine groups of five. It launched the paper *Strzały* [Shots]. Its leading activists were Leszek Raabe and Hanka Szapiro (Krystyna Sawicka). In 1941 it disbanded, and many of its members later joined the PPR and the GL.

In the ghetto, young people from this organization kept together. From July 1942 they began to think about fighting and made preparations with the PPR.

Socialist Revolutionary Party (SR). Its members and supporters were known as SRs. Founded in Russia in 1901, it advocated the establishment of a democratic republic and increased privileges for the peasant class, hence its largest support base was among the peasantry. Until the February Revolution (1917) and the overthrow of the tsarist system, it was illegal; after the October revolution, it was once again delegalized by the Bolsheviks. In 1922, the SR leaders were arrested and sentenced to death or lengthy imprisonment. Those who survived the great terror of the 1930s were murdered by the NKVD in executions at the beginning of the German-Soviet war in the fall of 1941.

Society for the Propagation of Labor among the Jews (Pol. Organizacja Rozwoju Twórczości Przemysłowej, Rzemieślniczej i Rolniczej wśród Ludności Żydowskiej, ORT). Founded in Russia in 1880 with the aim of equipping Jews for work in crafts and farming. From 1921, when an office of the organization was opened in Berlin, the ORT evolved from a philanthropic institution into an international social movement.

In prewar Poland, the ORT operated many schools for young people, a range of vocational courses for adults, and summer camps. It pursued some of its work in semi-legal conditions in the Warsaw ghetto. In postwar Poland, ORT schools, vocational courses, and farms continued to operate until 1950.

SS-Werterfassungsstelle. This was an enterprise established to work alongside the SS and police in the Warsaw ghetto, at 4–20 Niska Street. Its function was to seek out, confiscate, store, and ship back to the Reich property left behind by Jews transported to Treblinka. It was run by Fritz Konrad. In the summer of 1942, the Werterfassungsstelle employed some five thousand people.

Stigmatization of the Jews. External marks to be worn by Jews, such as a special color (yellow) and/or cut of their clothes, footwear, or hats, were employed from the seventh century until the early modern age. Sometimes the purpose of this was to render them easier to identify; in other cases, it was simply to humiliate them. In the Third Reich, and countries occupied by it, dependent upon it, or allied to it, the obligation for Jews to wear armbands or marks sewn onto their clothing was intended for identification. From December 1, 1939, pursuant to an ordinance issued by General Governor Hans Frank, it was compulsory for all Jews in the General Government aged over twelve (including those who had been baptized) to wear an armband on their right arm. This order, rigorously executed (on pain of arrest or a fine) and hence dutifully obeyed, remained in force even after the ghettos were sealed. Some, among them Janusz Korczak, consistently refused to wear the armband. (Korczak paid for his decision with incarceration; he was released thanks to the efforts of his Polish friends, who claimed that he was of unsound mind.) These armbands were of various colors and sizes (usually white and ten centimeters wide), but always displayed a star of David (usually blue). In some areas of Poland subsumed into the Reich, yellow stars of David usually made from two triangles of material, usually around ten centimeters across and sometimes with the word "*Jude*" (Ger.: Jew) in the middle, were used instead of armbands, sewn onto clothes on the left side of the chest and at shoulder-blade height on the back. In the Warsaw ghetto there were as many as nineteen types of armbands.

Suicide at 18 Miła Street. The Central Command of the ŻOB was at 18 Miła Street. This was a large bunker with five entrances, part of the ghetto "*unterwelt*," or "underworld." In the final days of the uprising, it sheltered around two hundred people, including about a hundred insurrectionists. Of these, fourteen people are reported to have survived the assault on the bunker on May 8, 1943.

Szeryński, Col. Józef Andrzej (1892/1893–1943). Prewar Polish police inspector, commander of the Jewish Order Service in the Warsaw ghetto. During the *große Aktion* in 1942, he became known as a cruel and over-zealous executor of German orders, for which he was sentenced to death by the Jewish underground. On August 25, 1942, he was shot and wounded by Izrael Kanał, a ŻOB member disguised as a member of the Jewish Order Service. Szeryński is thought to have committed suicide by swallowing cyanide after the battles in the ghetto in January 1943.

Szmalcownictwo (or: szmalec [Pol.], from the word meaning lard, or tallow). The practice of extorting payment from Jews outside the ghetto, above all fugitives from enclosed districts, under threat of handing them over to the Germans. After October 1941, Jews caught on the "Aryan side" without passes were subject to death, as were Poles who gave them shelter or helped them in any way. This meant that Jews could be robbed in public with impunity (on the streets, in particular in the vicinity of the ghetto walls, or on public transport) and blackmailed (under threat of denunciation to the German or Polish police) with the aim of extorting money from them. Those who engaged in such practices were known as "*szmalcownicy*" (sg. "*szmalcownik*").

Toebbens-Schultz. In the Toebbens-Schultz yard there were tailors' workshops ("'shops"). The factory owned by W.C. Toebbens was one of the biggest factories in the ghetto; it produced uniforms for the German army. The factory buildings were at 74 Leszno and in the small ghetto at 14 Prosta. During the deportation in the summer of 1942, ten thousand people were registered as employed in the Toebbens 'shop. The 'shops owned by Fritz Schultz and Karl Georg Schultz ("the small Schultz") were in the area of Leszno and Nowolipie Streets.

Umschlagplatz (Ger.: reloading yard). The yard known by this name, with a railway siding leading to the Gdańsk Railway Station, was on the northern edge of the ghetto, bounded by Stawki, Niska, and Zamenhofa Streets. In the years 1940–1942 it was used as a hub for the reloading, under German supervision, of goods being brought into and out of the ghetto. During the *große Aktion* and thereafter, this area and the hospital at 6 Stawki Street adjacent to it served as the collection point for the Jews being deported to Treblinka. There were days when ten thousand people might be packed into the yard.

Uprising in the Warsaw ghetto. Armed struggle waged against the Germans from April 19, 1943, by the combat organizations in the Warsaw ghetto: the ŻOB and the ŻZW, and other informal groups, known as "wildcat" groups. It was the biggest armed campaign in the Polish lands since the September campaign in 1939, the biggest act of Jewish armed resistance in World War II, and the first urban insurrection in occupied Europe. In April 1943, there were around seventy thousand people living in the Warsaw ghetto. On April 19, German units numbering some two thousand troops in all, with reinforcements including tanks and artillery, attacked the ghetto, which was defended by a few hundred poorly armed insurgents; the Polish police was also drafted in to fight the rebels. The insurrectionists' leaders were Mordechaj Anielewicz, Marek Edelman, Izrael Kanał, and Eliezer Geller of the ŻOB, and Paweł Frenkiel and Leon Rodal of the ŻZW. The Germans adopted a tactic of setting fire to street after street, house by house, and liquidating the bunkers in which the insurgents and civilians alike took shelter. Jews caught in the course of this campaign were deported to the extermination camp in Treblinka or the forced labor camps in Trawniki, Poniatowa, and Majdanek. On the first day of the uprising, a unit of the AK made an unsuccessful attempt to blow up part of the ghetto wall. Around seven thousand Jews perished during the battles in the ghetto. Some of the fighters retreated from the ghetto via the sewers—most of them perished either on the "Aryan side" or in partisan units. Those who survived also later fought in the Polish Warsaw rising. The Germans pronounced the ghetto campaign over on May 15, 1943; the symbol of this was the razing of the Great Synagogue on Tłomackie Street. Further isolated skirmishes on the site of the razed Jewish quarter continued to erupt into June 1943.

Volksdeutsche. A person of German descent living outside the 1937 borders of Germany, without German or Austrian citizenship.

Warsaw ghetto. A sealed district for Jews established in October 1940 pursuant to the division of Warsaw into three districts—German, Polish, and Jewish—by the occupying authorities. The population of the ghetto and its exact area were constantly changing and fluctuating. In the period after its creation, it covered an area of 307 hectares (2.4 percent of the city's overall area) and concentrated nigh-on four hundred thousand people. Between January and March 1941, Jews from smaller towns elsewhere in Distrikt Warschau (the Warsaw region) were resettled into the ghetto, and in April 1942 several thousand Jews from the Reich were also deported there. In March 1941, there were four hundred forty-five thousand people enclosed within the ghetto walls. The area of the sealed district was repeatedly reduced, and in December 1941 the exclusion from it of further streets produced a division into two ghettos, the large and the small, which were connected via a wooden bridge over Chłodna Street in the Polish part of Warsaw. At that point, the streets were so crowded that residents could barely cross the roads. Thereafter, there were fewer and fewer people in the enclosed district, due to both the high death rate and deportations. The ghetto continued to be cut down in size, as better houses were excluded, with moves to improve measures against smuggling, and ultimately because there were fewer and fewer people there. After the *große Aktion* (in the summer of 1942) some sixty thousand Jews remained in the Warsaw ghetto, which was now known as the "remnant ghetto," something over thirty thousand employed in the 'shops and a similar number in hiding in abandoned houses (these were known as "wildcat" residents). After that, the enclosed district was reduced in size yet again, and divided into isolated sectors, each of which comprised labor camps: they were, respectively, the brushmakers' yard, the central ghetto (where the Judenrat and further 'shops were situated), the main 'shop yards (where 'shops including the Toebbens-Schultz workshops were), and the small ghetto (known as "the large Toebbens"). The 'shops where the Jews worked, their homes, and the last remaining stores were all enclosed by wooden fences or walls. The remaining territory, where nobody lived, was a kind of no-man's land (Pol. *międzygetcie*, "interghetto"), not to be entered, on pain of death. After the January operation (in January 1943), the streets were completely empty. The April uprising played out across three areas: in the central ghetto (Gęsia, Smocza, Szczęśliwa, Stawki, Pokorna, Franciszkańska Streets and Muranowski Square), in the Toebbens-Schultz 'shop yards (on Leszno, Żelazna, Smocza, and Karmelicka Streets), and on the brushmakers' premises (Franciszkańska, Wałowa, Świętojerska, and Bonifraterska Streets). In the fourth area, the small ghetto (on Pańska, Żelazna, Waliców, Prosta, Ciepła, and Twarda Streets), there were no battles during the uprising. After the defeat of the insurrection in May 1943, the ghetto as the official living space for Jews ceased to exist, and its last residents hid out in the ruins. On Gęsia Street, between Zamenhofa and Okopowa, a camp known colloquially as "Gęsiówka", and more officially as KL Warschau, was established, in which Jewish prisoners searched through what was left of the houses and blew them up. The district was finally razed in September 1943.

Warsaw rising. The name given to the armed operations carried out by the Polish underground Home Army (with the support of the People's Army) in Warsaw from August 1 until October 3, 1944, targeting the Germans in military terms and the USSR in political terms. The Jewish survivors of the uprising in the Warsaw ghetto joined ranks with the AL, because members of the AK were often ill-disposed toward Jews. In the course of the two months of fighting, sixty thousand Varsovians were killed, twenty thousand wounded, and fifteen thousand taken prisoner.

Werbkowice. During the *große Aktion* (July and August 1942), Celina Lubetkin and Antek Cukierman sent several groups of Dror members into the forests around Hrubieszów (Lublin province); in all, around one hundred people managed to leave the Warsaw ghetto on that mission. In the woods, the young people were commanded by Mosze Rubenczyk. One of the groups was caught on a train during a document spot-check; all eighteen in that group were shot dead on the spot. Almost all the other would-be partisans were murdered at their base in Werbkowice (a village west of Hrubieszów). Moniek Sztengiel was the only one of that group who managed to return to Warsaw; two or three others are thought to have survived that attack. Only a few names of those in Rubenczyk's group were recorded: Gedalia Gerszuni, Moniek Rajngewirc and his girlfriend Pesia Furmanowicz, Gina Lewin, Jakub Kac, Ruth Szklar, Szaul Dobuchno, and Icchok Nożyce.

Werkschutz (Ger.: factory guard). A formation that had police authorization in the German businesses ('shops) in the ghetto. It comprised units staffed by Germans (Volksdeutsche), Ukrainians, and Jews. The latter included former ghetto policemen, smugglers, but also Jewish underground activists. The polonized version of the word, *werkszuc* (pl. *werkszuce*), was used in the ghetto to refer to individual members of the formation. Many *werkszuce* oppressed the ghetto residents and demanded protection money from the owners of production operations, traders, and unregistered, "wildcat" ghetto residents. The underground organizations executed several death sentences on particularly zealous *werkszuce* (for example, on March 12, 1943, ŻOB soldiers shot dead two *werkszuce* on Miła Street).

Workers on detail (Pol. placówkarze). Jews who worked outside the ghetto, on "details" (Pol. *placówki*): at stations and in armaments factories.

Workers' University Society Youth Organization (Pol. Organizacja Młodzieży Towarzystwa Uniwersytetu Robotniczego, OMTUR). The youth arm of the PPS, which worked through self-education groups, art clubs, and sports teams to educate and shape young people. It was founded in 1926. Its members took part in demonstrations and strikes alongside the PPS. They also cooperated with Cukunft and other Jewish youth organizations. After the war, OMTUR lost its autonomy and was subsumed into the state communist organization ZMP (Związek Młodzieży Polskiej), the Union of Polish Youth.

Yugnt (Yid. Yidishe Sotsialistishe Arbeter Yugnt "Yugnt," the "Youth" Jewish Socialist Working-class Youth). Operated in Poland between 1922 and 1939 under the aegis of the party Poalej Syjon Left. Several thousand young people identified with the movement, which issued its own paper, *Di Fraje Jugnt* (Di Fraye Yugnt). The partner organization in schools of higher education was the "Jugnt" Academic Socialist Group.

Zygielbojm, Szmuel (1895–1943). The leader of the Bund, an activist in Warsaw and Łódź. After the outbreak of the war, he organized the party's underground activity. Appointed the Bund delegate to the Warsaw Judenrat but resigned soon afterwards because he refused to collaborate with the Germans. In December 1939, he travelled illegally to Belgium via France, and in September 1940, he reached New York. There he worked as a glovemaker, and remained active in the Bund, publishing articles on the situation of the Jews in Poland. In late 1941 the Bund started putting pressure on the Polish authorities in London to have a delegate appointed to the National Council of the government-in-exile, in which the only Jewish representative was Ignacy Schwartzbart, a Zionist. In March 1942, Zygielbojm was sent to London as that member, the second representative of the Jewish community. He was the first to learn about the situation in the Warsaw ghetto and other ghettos, via a Bund report on the fate of the Warsaw Jews sent from Poland by Leon Feiner. Zygielbojm petitioned the Polish government in vain for financial aid for the Jews. In July and August 1942, during the *große Aktion*, he called on the Polish government to make Jewish issues one of its priorities, again in vain. He accused the government and its delegates of indifference and ill will. In October 1942 he met Jan Karski, the courier of the Polish Underground State, who had smuggled extensive information out of Poland, including much from the leaders of the Jewish underground. Mindful that time was running out, Zygielbojm appealed to politicians' consciences, and called on leaders including Churchill and Roosevelt for assistance. On May 12, 1943, when he learned that the last Warsaw Jews had been murdered (among them his own wife and sixteen-year-old son), he committed suicide. He left two letters: to the Polish president, Władysław Raczkiewicz, and to the Polish prime minister, Władysław Sikorski, in which he explained his decision: "Let my death be a cry of protest against the indifference with which the world looks upon the extermination of the Jews; looks, yet does nothing to halt it."

The author is grateful to Alina Skibińska for her assistance in compiling the footnotes.

Bibliography

In-person, telephone, and correspondence conversations

Reuven Aloni, Hedera 2002
Hela Balicka-Kozłowska, Warsaw 2000–2001
Kazimiera Bergman, Ramat Efal 2002–2003
Adina Blady-Szwajgier, Warsaw and Israel 1990–1993
Awiwa Blum-Wachs, October 2021
Jarek Dulewicz, 2021
Marek Edelman, Łódź and Warsaw 1985–2009
Chawka Folman-Raban, Lohamei Ha-Getaot kibbutz and Warsaw 1988–2000
Leon Fudem, Wrocław 2004
Luba Gawisar, Tel Aviv, 1988–2009
Masza Glajtman-Putermilch, Tel Aviv 1988–2006
Pnina Grynszpan-Frymer, Tel Aviv 1988–2006
Prof. Israel Gutman, Jerusalem and Warsaw 1988–2001
Irena Jaszuńska, Warsaw 2000–2002
Eryk Kamieniecki, 2016
Aron Karmi, Tel Aviv 1988–1998
Wacek Kornblum, Warsaw 2021
Ewa Legiec, Warsaw 2012
Alina Margolis-Edelman, Paris, Warsaw, and Podkowa Leśna 1999–2007
Wojtek Mazan, 2021
Mayus/Marek Nowogrodzki, 2015
Bronisław Mirski (Sławek Friedman), Warsaw 2013–2015
Eugenia Pocalun, 2018
Jacek Podsiadło, 2021
Kazik Ratajzer (Simcha Rotem), Jerusalem, Warsaw 1988–2013
Izchar Regev, 2021
Szmuel Ron, Jerusalem 1988–1999
Itay Rotem, 2021
Hela Rufeisen-Schüpper, Bustan Ha-Galil Moshav 2001
Julian Rutkowski (formerly Fiszgrund), Warsaw 2000
Tzvi Schacham, 2020
Lodzia Silverstein, Washington, D.C. 2000–2002
Dawid Stein, Haifa 2003
Jerzy Szapiro, Warsaw 2000
Bronek Szpigiel, Toronto, Warsaw 1999–2006
Bronek Szpigiel and Chajka Bełchatowska, Montreal and Warsaw 1999–2005

Hela Szuster-Kron, Tel Aviv 2003
Alina Świdowska, Warsaw 2021
Jerzy Warman, 2021

Depositions, testimonies, documents, studies

Adamowicz, Irena. [no title]. *Mosty* 168, no. 46 (19 IV 1948).
Assuntino, Rudi, and Włodek Goldkorn. *Strażnik. Marek Edelman opowiada*. Krakow: Znak, 1999.
Balicka-Kozłowska, Helena. *Mur miał dwie strony*. Warsaw: Bellona, 2002.
Bartoszewski, Władysław, and Zofia Lewinówna, eds. *Ten jest z ojczyzny mojej. Polacy z pomocą Żydom 1939–1945*. 2nd edition. Cracow: Znak, 1969.
Berg, Mary. "Pamiętnik pisany w getcie w maju i czerwcu 1943." *Mosty* 168, no. 46 (19 IV 1948).
Berland, Marian. *Dni długie jak wieki*. Warsaw: Nowa, 1992.
Berliński, Hersz. "Z dziennika członka komendy ŻOB." *Biuletyn ŻIH*, no. 50 (1964).
Blady-Szwajger, Adina. *I więcej nic nie pamiętam*. 2nd edition. Warsaw: Znak, 1994.
Borg, Bernard. "Powstanie na terenie 'shopów.'" *Biuletyn ŻIH*, no. 5 (1953).
Borzykowski, Tuwia. *Between Tumbling Walls*. Translated by Mendel Kohański. Tel Aviv: Hakibbutz Hameuchad, 1976.
Celemeński, Jakub. *Mitn farshnitenem folk*. New York: Unzer Tsayt, 1963.
Cukierman, Icchak ("Antek"). *A Surplus of Memory: Chronicle of the Warsaw Ghetto Uprising*. Translated and edited by Barbara Harshav. Berkeley: University of California Press, 1993.
Datner, Szymon. *Zbrodnie Wehrmachtu na jeńcach wojennych w II wojnie światowej*. Warsaw: Wydawnictwo MON, 1961.
Dunin-Wąsowicz, Krzysztof, ed. *Warszawa lat wojny i okupacji 1939–1944*, books 1–4. Warsaw: Wydawnictwo Warszawa, 1971–1975.
Edelman, Marek. *The Ghetto Fights*. writing.upenn.edu/~afilreis/Holocaust/warsaw-uprising.html. Translation anon. (original: Edelman, Marek. *Getto walczy*. Łódź: CK Bund, 1945).
[Edelman, Marek]. "Obrona ghetta." *Za Waszą i Naszą Wolność*, April 1946. Reprinted after: *Głos Ludu* no. 97 (19 IV 1945).
Engelking, Barbara. "Rozmowa z prof. Israelem Gutmanem." *Zagłada Żydów. Studia i materiały* 2013, no. 9.
Engelking, Barbara, and Jacek Leociak. *Getto warszawskie. Przewodnik po nieistniejącym mieście*. Warsaw: Stowarzyszenie Centrum Badań nad Zagładą Żydów, 2013.
Engelking, Barbara, and Dariusz Libionka. *Żydzi w powstańczej Warszawie*. Warsaw: Centrum Badań nad Zagładą Żydów, 2009.
Folman-Raban, Chawka. *Nie rozstałam się z nimi* . . . Translated by Inka Wajsbrot and Dora Sternberg. Warsaw: Żydowski Instytut Historyczny, 2000.
Friedman, Philip. *Their Brothers' Keepers*. New York: Crown Publishers, 1957.
Fuks, Marian, ed. *Adama Czerniakowa dziennik getta warszawskiego. 6 IX 1939–23 VII 1942*. Warsaw: Państwowe Wydawnictwo Naukowe, 1983.
Goldkorn, Dorka. *Wspomnienia uczestniczki powstania w getcie warszawskim*. Warsaw: Żydowski Instytut Historyczny, 1951.
Goldstein, Bernard. *Five Years in the Warsaw Ghetto*. New York: Nabat Books, 1961.

Grabski, August. *Żydowski ruch kombatancki w Polsce w latach 1944–1949*. Warsaw: Trio, 2002.

Grupińska, Hanka. *Ciągle po kole. Rozmowy z żołnierzami getta warszawskiego*. 4th edition, Warsaw: Wielka Litera, 2022.

———. *Odczytanie Listy*. 3rd edition, Warsaw: Wielka Litera, 2022.

Grynberg, Michał. *Księga sprawiedliwych*. Warsaw: Państwowe Wydawnictwo Naukowe, 1993.

Gutman, Israel. *Fighters Among the Ruins: The Story of Jewish Heroism During the World War II*. Washington, D.C.: B'nai B'rith Books, 1988.

———. *Resistance: The Warsaw Ghetto Uprising*. Boston: Mariner Books, 1998.

———. *The Jews of Warsaw, 1939–1943: Ghetto, Underground, Revolt*. Translated from the Hebrew by Ina Friedman. Bloomington: Indiana University Press, 1982.

———. "Eliahu Różański." *Mosty* no. 7–8 (1947).

Herz, J.S. *Doyres Bundistn*. New York: Farlag Unzer Tsayt, 1956.

———. *Der Bund in Bilder*. New York: Farlag Unzer Tsayt, 1958.

———. *Di Geshikhte fun a Yugnt*. New York: Farlag Unzer Tsayt, 1946.

Holzer, Jerzy. *Mozaika polityczna Drugiej Rzeczypospolitej*. Warsaw: Książka i Wiedza, 1974.

Iranek-Osmecki, Kazimierz. *Kto ratuje jedno życie . . . Polacy i Żydzi 1939–1945*. London: Księgarnia Polska Orbis, 1968.

Jaworski, Michał. "Plac Muranowski 7," *Biuletyn ŻIH* no. 2/3 (1974).

Karmi, Aron, and Chaim Frymer. *Min hadlika haesh*. Tel Aviv: ???, 1961.

Kermisz, Józef. *Powstanie w getcie warszawskim (19 IV–16 V 1943)*. Łódź. Centralna Żydowska Komisja Historyczna, 1946.

———. "Z historii dni kwietniowych." *Mosty* 168, no. 46 (19 IV 1948).

———. "Chalucowe powstanie styczniowe." *Mosty* (24 I 1948).

Krall, Hanna. *Shielding the Flame: An Intimate Conversation with Dr. Marek Edelman, the Last Surviving Leader of the Warsaw Ghetto Uprising*. Translated by Joanna Stasinska and Lawrence Weschler. New York: Henry Holt and Co., 1977.

Księgi urodzeń wyznania mojżeszowego z lat 30. XX wieku [Records of Jewish births from the 1930s], USC [Registry Office], Ostrowiec Świętokrzyski.

Kurzman, Dan. *The Bravest Battle: 28 Days of the Warsaw Ghetto Uprising*. New York: Da Capo Press, 1993.

Legec, Władysław i Stanisława. "Żołnierze ŻOB-u i ich przyjaciele." *Biuletyn ŻIH* no. 5 (1953).

Leociak, Jacek. *Biografie ulic. O żydowskich ulicach Warszawy: od narodzin po Zagładę*. Warsaw: Dom Spotkań z Historią, 2017.

Lewin, Abraham. *A Cup of Tears: A Diary of the Warsaw Ghetto*. Translated by Christopher Hutton. London: Fontana, 1990.

Liber, Brener. *Umkum un vidershtand in chenstokhover getto*. Warsaw, 1951.

Libionka, Dariusz, and Laurence Weinbaum. *Bohaterowie, hochsztaplerzy, opisywacze. Wokół Żydowskiego Związku Wojskowego*. Warsaw: Oficyna Wydawnicza, 2012.

Lubetkin, Zivia. *In the Days of Destruction and Revolt*. Translated from the Hebrew by Ishai Tubbin. Tel Aviv: Hakibbutz Hameuchad/Am Oved Publishing House, 1981.

Majerczak, Beniamin. *Żydzi – żołnierze Wojsk Polskich polegli na frontach II wojny światowej*. Warsaw: Bellona, 2001.

Margolis-Edelman, Ala. *Ala z elementarza*. London: Aneks, 1994.

Mark, Bernard. *Powstanie w getcie warszawskim*. Warsaw: Żydowski Instytut Historyczny, 1954.

———. *Powstanie w getcie warszawskim na tle ruchu oporu w Polsce. Geneza i przebieg*. 2nd edition. Warsaw: Żydowski Instytut Historyczny, 1954.

———. *W XV rocznicę powstania w getcie warszawskim*. Warsaw: Komitet obchodu 15-tej rocznicy powstania w getcie warszawskim, 1958.

———. *Życie i walka młodzieży w gettach w okresie okupacji hitlerowskiej (1939–1944)*. Warsaw: Iskry, 1961.

Meed, Vladka. *On Both Sides of the Wall. Memoirs of the Warsaw Ghetto*. Translated by Steven Meed. New York: Random House Inc., 1979.

Melamed, Aliza. "Z pamiętnika gniazda w getcie warszawskim." *Mosty* 168 no. 46 (19 IV 1948).

Mirski, Bronisław. "Przygotowania do powstania i pierwsze boje na terenie szczotkarzy." *Biuletyn ŻIH* no. 5 (1953).

Moczarski, Kazimierz. *Rozmowy z katem*. 2nd edition. Warsaw: Znak, 1983.

Najberg, Leon. *Ostatni powstańcy getta*. Warsaw: Żydowski Instytut Historyczny, 1993.

Neustadt, Melekh. *Khurbn un oyfshtand fun di yidn in Varshe. Eydes-bleter un azkores*. Translated by D.B. Malkin. Tel Aviv: Executive Committee of the General Federation of Jewish Labour in Palestine and the Jewish National Workers' Alliance in U.S.A., 1948.

Płotnitskah, Hants'ah. *Mikhtavim veDivrei Zikaron*. Tel Aviv: ha-Ḳibuts ha-me'uḥad, 1945.

Powstanie w ghetcie warszawskim 1943 r. Zbiór dokumentów. Warsaw: Państwowe Wydawnictwo Literatury Politycznej, 1945.

Prekerowa, Teresa. *Konspiracyjna Rada Pomocy Żydom w Warszawie 1942–1945*. Warsaw: Państwowy Instytut Wydawniczy, 1982.

[Ratajzer, Kazik], "Jak walczyło getto. Ze wspomnień powstańca żydowskiego." *Robotnik* no. 95 (19 IV 1945).

"Reminiscence of Sara Biederman" [Hebrew original]. *Dapim* no. 301 (21 VII 1972).

Ringelblum, Emanuel. *Kronika getta warszawskiego. Wrzesień 1939–styczeń 1949*. Translated by Adam Rutkowski. Warsaw: Czytelnik, 1983.

Rotem, Simha ("Kazik"). *Memoirs of a Warsaw Ghetto Fighter*. Translated from the Hebrew and edited by Barbara Harshav. New Haven: Yale University Press, 1994.

Rudnicki, Henryk. *Martyrologia i zagłada Żydów warszawskich*. Łódź: n.p., 1946.

Rufeisen-Schüpper, Hela. *Pożegnanie Miłej 18. Wspomnienia łączniczki Żydowskiej Organizacji Bojowej*. Cracow: Beseder, 1996.

Sakowska, Ruta, ed. *Archiwum Ringelbluma – getto warszawskie. Lipiec 1942–styczeń 1943*. Warsaw: Żydowski Instytut Historyczny, 1980.

———. *Dwa etapy. Hitlerowska polityka eksterminacji Żydów w oczach ofiar*. Wrocław: Ossolineum, 1986.

———. *Ludzie z dzielnicy zamkniętej. Żydzi w Warszawie w okresie hitlerowskiej okupacji październik 1939–marzec 1943*. 2nd edition. Warsaw: PWN, 1993.

Silverstein, Leokadia. *Tak właśnie było*. Translated by Hanna Sochacka-Kozłowska. Warsaw: Żydowski Instytut Historyczny, 2002.

Stein, Dawid. "Ostatnia Wielkanoc w getcie warszawskim." *Mosty* 168 no. 46 (19 IV 1948).

Shulman, Abraham. *The Case of Hotel Polski: An Account of One of the Most Enigmatic Episodes of World War II*. New York: Holocaust Library, 1982.

Temkin-Bermanowa, Basia. *Dziennik z podziemia*. Warsaw: Twój Styl, 2000.

Tych, Feliks ed. *Słownik biograficzny działaczy polskiego ruchu robotniczego*. Warsaw: Książka i Wiedza, 1987.

Tokarska-Bakir, Joanna. *Społeczny portret pogromu kieleckiego*, vols. 1 and 2. Warsaw: Czarna Owca, 2008.
Wala [Marek Edelman]. *Nasi bohaterowie, "Za waszą i naszą wolność."* April 1946.
Zeznanie dr. Ryszarda Walewskiego [Statement of Dr. Ryszard Walewski], AIPN, GK, 317/874, vol. 1. Protokół rozprawy głównej Jürgena Stroopa [Transcript of the main hearing of Jürgen Stroop], box 15 (19 VII 1951).
Ziemian, Józef. *Papierosiarze z placu Trzech Krzyży*. Warsaw: Niezależna Oficyna Wydawnicza, 1989.

Unpublished reports from the archives of the Jewish Historical Institute

1678, Alef, B.
5042, Bauman, Eliasz
1683, Cukierman, Icchak
5002, Edelman, Marek
5064, Flamenbaum, Mojżesz
302/186, Goldman, B.
5016, Jaworski, Michał
5039, Lehman, Józef
659, Lista powstańców napisana przez Bernarda Marka [List of insurgents written by Bernard Mark]
5006, Mirski, Bronisław (Frydman)
302/206, Motyl, Binem
5061, Polisiuk, A.
5011, Popower, Karl
5010, Reich-Ranicki, Marcel
4423, Świętochowski, Władysław
6467, Świętochowski, Władysław
5009, Teller
318, zespół [fonds] ZWZ, Siekierski, Mieczysław
5021, Zymler, J.J.
Związek Walki Zbrojnej fonds, file no. 10, pp. I–XVII, spis członków związków żydowskich – uczestników walki zbrojnej z faszyzmem, sporządzony przez Zarząd Wojewódzki w Łodzi 5 IV 48 [list of members of Jewish associations who participated in military combat against fascism, drawn up by the Provincial Executive in Łódź on April 5, 1948], signed by B. Majerczak.

Photographic sources

The photographs of the ŻOB fighters that accompany their biographies are taken from the following sources: J. Celemeński, *Mitn farshnitenem folk*, New York 1963; J.S. Herz, *Doyres Bundistn*, New York 1956; *Der Bund in Bilder*, New York 1958; *Die Geshikhte fun a Yugnt*, New York 1946;

B. Mark, *Powstanie w getcie warszawskim na tle ruchu oporu w Polsce. Geneza i przebieg*, Warsaw 1954; M. Neustadt, *Khurbn un oyfshtand fun di yidn in Varshe. Eydes-bleter un azkores*, Tel Aviv 1948; L. Silverstein, *Tak właśnie było*, Warsaw 2002; and private collections.

The contemporary portraits of my interlocutors in the first section of the book are by Adam Rozenman.

The presumed provenance of the photographs from the Collection of Łukasz Biedka is discussed in the introduction.

Index

Adamowicz, Irena, 331, 362, 387, 462, 486
Agudat Israel, 261, 512
Africa, 42
AK (Armia Krajowa), 23–27, 31n51, 47, 80, 112, 160n50, 168n5, 174–75, 195n29, 209n47, 234–35, 236n4, 239, 250–51, 253, 272–73, 277–78, 292n6, 295–96, 320–21, 331, 346, 362, 366, 377, 384, 387–89, 396, 402, 421, 426, 430–31, 433, 499, 501–2, 505, 519–20
Akiba, 245, 248, 302, 343, 351, 353, 367, 378, 395, 400, 425, 434–35, 441, 445, 475–77, 479, 481, 486–87, 491, 497–98
AL (Armia Ludowa), 24, 27, 47, 112, 197, 216n49, 235–37, 250, 252n31, 278, 280, 282, 302n23, 344, 346, 353, 362, 384, 408, 414, 424, 429, 433, 503, 510, 520
Allies, 242n14, 499, 525
Aloni, Reuven, 470
Alter, Aron, 333, 401–2, 482
Alter, Wiktor, 320n34
Alterman, Ewa, 64
Alterman, Szlojme (Szlomo), 75, 79, 334, 391, 475, 484
Altman, Tosia, 47, 49, 98n24, 107, 304, 334–35, 341, 353, 392, 428n9, 435, 475, 485
America, 3, 18, 37, 153, 195, 239, 288, 293–94, 310, 312, 314, 320, 355, 363, 394, 408, 459, 499. *See also* USA
American Jewish Distribution Committee. *See* Joint

Anders' Army, 371
Aneks, journal, 221
Anielewicz, Mordechaj, 4, 27, 41, 49n16, 66–68, 98n24, 166, 170, 248, 255, 262, 264, 289, 290–91, 295–96, 301, 303, 307–8, 323, 328, 336–37, 357, 361–62, 370, 380, 388, 392, 401, 414, 427, 439, 442, 446, 451–52, 466, 468, 470, 475, 479, 500–1, 519
Antisemitism, 16, 21n23, 22n25, 29, 31n50, 36, 182, 187–95, 288n2, 508–9, 513–14
April uprising, 5–8, 65, 74, 80, 101, 103, 140–42, 146–51, 153–55, 170n8, 219, 245, 257–58, 262, 270–71, 308, 317, 321, 331, 333–35, 337–44, 346–47, 349–54, 357–60, 362–66, 368–74, 376–80, 382–463, 466–70, 475, 479, 486, 487n2, 491, 495, 498–503, 507, 509, 511, 518–20
Argentina, 174
Arsenał operation, 24–25, 328, 492
Artsztajn, Zachariasz, 9, 338–39, 347, 352–53, 362, 364, 370, 372–73, 390–91, 397, 406, 416, 436, 439–40, 448, 455, 457, 467, 480, 500
Aryan papers, 125, 506, 511. *See also* Kennkarte
Aryan side, 23–25, 27, 48–49, 75, 78, 80, 82, 90, 93, 102n33, 106–8, 110, 133, 143, 146–47, 152–53, 155, 166–68, 172n11, 183n9, 183n12, 192n25, 204, 207–8, 216n49, 218, 226–27, 250–51, 253–55, 268, 298, 308, 310, 315n28, 347, 381, 465, 492, 507, 515, 518–19

Ashkelon, 49n16
assimilated family, 163, 180–83, 194, 370, 393, 403, 411, 434, 449, 470, 491
Association of Jewish Medical Students, 189
Auschwitz, 16n12, 21, 26, 46–48, 51, 64, 88n2, 96, 100n28, 121, 177n1, 191, 202, 203n38, 210n47, 322n39, 323n40, 335, 346, 352, 371, 382, 386, 401, 409, 412, 448, 507
Auschwitz-Birkenau, 495, 497, 499

Bafrajung Arbeter Sztyme, journal, 419
Baginen, newspaper, 385
Balicka-Kozłowska, Helena, 252, 344
Baran, Dwora, 254–56, 258, 340, 475, 484
Baranowicze, 335, 398, 428
Bartoszewski, Władysław, 209–10
Bauman, Zygmunt, 221–22
Beatus, Frania, 268–69, 340–41, 454, 485
Będzin, 41, 43–44, 51, 149, 308, 335, 337, 358, 372, 420, 428, 500
Befehlsstelle, 147, 151, 399, 405, 411, 493
Beit Borochow, 372
Beit Jaakow, 514
Belarus, 13, 15, 25n37, 356
Bełchatowska, Halina (Chajka), 3, 81–82, 113n52, 225–231, 341–42, 349, 379, 451–52, 458, 483
Belgium, 204n39, 445, 522
Bełżec, 42, 497
Bemowo, 31n49
Ben Gurion, David, 296
bench ghetto, 187–88, 360, 459, 508–9, 513. *See also* Black Hundreds
Bednarczyk, Józef. *See* Grynblatt, Józef
Bergen-Belsen, 382, 386, 401, 442, 499
Bergman, Kazimiera, 342, 436, 460
Berlin, 194, 439, 464, 516
Berliński, Hirsz (Hersz), 77, 98–102, 104–6, 230, 307, 342, 350, 364, 369, 376, 384, 387, 410, 413, 416, 423–24, 432, 467, 479, 484, 500
Berman, Adolf Abraham, 170n8, 295
Bermanowa, Basia, 342
Betar, 50, 291, 336, 361, 383, 470, 493, 501
Bielecki, Czesław, 36
Białowieża, 503
Biały, Michał. *See* Rozenfeld, Michał
Białystok, 331, 335, 345, 356, 360, 386–87, 398, 402, 409, 427–28, 430, 449, 451, 467, 500
Biederman, Sara (Serafin, Krysia), 171, 341, 343–44, 483
Biedka, Łukasz, vii, 4, 528
Bilak, Janek, 75, 106, 110, 274, 305, 345, 424, 450, 484
Biuletyn Informacyjny, journal, 168, 388, 505
Bielsko, 46, 431
Blady-Szwajgier, Adina (Inka), 3, 175–222, 236, 276, 279–80, 301–2, 310–12, 315–17, 319, 345–48, 358, 367, 371, 376, 417, 485
Black Hundreds, 16
Black Panthers, 20
Blank, Marek, 145, 347, 475, 482
Blaustein (Blausztajn), Icchak, 339, 347, 352, 370, 373, 419, 435, 453, 475, 481
Błones, Guta, 107, 141–42, 226–27, 274, 312, 349–50, 378, 475, 484
Błones, Jurek, 7, 100, 106–8, 226, 312, 341, 345, 349–50, 354, 356, 365, 378, 400, 405, 424, 426, 432, 434, 437, 475, 484
Błones, Eliezer (Lusiek), 77, 107, 226, 274, 305, 312, 349–51, 378, 475, 484
Błoński, Jan, 221
Blum, Abram, 107, 207, 215, 274, 347–48, 352, 354, 366, 426, 443, 450, 476, 484

Blum-Bielicka, Luba, 347, 416–17
Bnei Akiba, 498
Boernerowo, 31–32, 241, 280, 354, 371
Borg, Bernard, 351–52, 392, 482
Borochow kibbutz, 333, 340, 342, 355, 360, 369, 390, 410, 416–17, 444, 498
Borochow, Dow Ber, 353, 498, 510
Borzykowski, Tuwia (Tadek), 6, 31n49, 78, 171, 175, 177, 262, 310, 353–55, 362, 372, 385, 392, 399, 414, 417, 431, 440, 448, 471, 480
Boy Scout, 48, 116, 292, 301, 304, 420, 485–86
Brandt, Karl, 134–36
Brańsk, 467
Bratniak, medics' association, 189
Braude, Berl (Brojde), 62, 344, 351, 355, 360, 368, 378, 392, 394, 411, 425, 431, 444, 448, 454, 468–69, 480
Braude-Hellerowa, Anna, 205, 412
Breslov, 18n19
Brezhnev, Leonid, 30
Brzozowska, Helena. *See* Goldkorn, Dorka
brushmakers' yard, 64, 77, 100–3, 105n36, 139–40, 146–47, 151, 207, 230, 248n25, 252, 255, 257–58, 261, 287–88, 302, 334, 339–40, 342, 345, 347, 349–51, 359, 364, 366, 368–69, 377, 386–87, 390–91, 394, 398, 400, 402, 405–6, 410–12, 416, 418, 421, 423, 429, 431–32, 434–36, 446, 450, 455, 458, 461, 469, 479, 483, 493, 520
Brünnlitz, 375
Brylantsztajn, Stasiek (Staszek), 75, 105, 340, 355–56, 484
Bryskin, Paweł (Aron), 62, 67, 331, 343, 356–57, 389, 400, 411, 423, 440, 442, 444, 446, 468, 480
Bucharest, 82, 161

Budzyń, 375
Bug, river, 334, 384, 391, 397, 400, 413, 435, 445, 456, 468
Bujak, Zbigniew (Zbyszek), 25–26, 35–36, 38, 225
Bund (General Jewish Labor Bund), 6, 15, 22–23, 24n31, 53–54, 60, 71, 74, 101, 103n36, 105–7, 110, 149, 181, 208n44, 225–26, 230, 239, 245, 262–63, 267, 279, 283, 294–95, 296n14, 301, 303, 315n28, 320n34, 341–42, 345, 347–50, 356, 358, 360–61, 363, 365–66, 368, 370–71, 374, 377, 379, 382–83, 385–86, 389, 393–94, 396–97, 399–400, 402, 404–5, 407, 412, 416, 418, 424–27, 429–30, 433–34, 437–38, 441, 448, 450–51, 455–58, 461–62, 464, 467, 475–79, 481, 483–86, 493–94, 500, 502, 508, 512, 514, 522

Canada, 64, 81, 342, 452
Casimir III, the Great, king of Poland, 29
Catholic Church, 16, 20, 29, 34–35, 189, 265n43, 513
Celemeński, Jakub (Celek), 270, 350, 358, 378–79, 485
CENTOS, 291, 436, 494. *See also* ŻTOS
Central Committee of Polish Jews. *See* CKŻP
Chagall, Marc, 37
cheder, 116, 334, 342, 355, 359, 378, 419, 432, 449, 463
Chełmno nad Nerem, 42, 496–97
China, 37, 322
Chmielnicki, Aron. *See* Karmi, Aron
Chmielnicki, Icchak, 118
Chmielnocki, Nachum, 360, 475, 486
Chorew, 514
Chorzów, 258n35
Chruściel, Antoni, 292
Churchill, Winston, 522

Ciechanów, 360
Ciechocinek, 360, 510
CISzO, 53, 208n44, 345, 349–50, 356, 360, 363, 377–78, 383, 394, 407, 422, 426, 457, 514
CKŻP (Centralny Komitet Żydów Polskich), 183, 412, 424
Collection of Studium Polski Podziemnej, 475
Communism, 15, 20, 33–35, 373, 370, 513
Communist Union of Polish Youth, 459, 510
Constanța, 82, 453
Coordinating Committee, 308, 348, 420, 426, 450, 502. See also ŻKN
Crimea, 357
Crystal Night, 22–23
Cukierman, Icchak (Antek), 6, 8–9, 31n49, 31n51, 78, 82–83, 106, 113, 155, 170n8, 171n10, 174–75n13, 237n10, 291, 300n21, 302n23, 339, 341, 344, 350, 355, 357, 361–62, 377, 382, 389, 393, 408, 414, 417–18, 420, 429, 433, 442, 447, 449, 454, 463, 471, 479, 495, 497, 500–501, 520
Cukierman, Ilana, 135
Cukunft, 54, 225, 342, 345, 348–50, 356, 363, 377–78, 383, 389, 407, 427, 434, 437–38, 448, 491, 493–94, 521
Cukunft-Szturm, 365, 368, 382, 396, 400, 412, 450
curfew, 49, 59, 263, 346, 438
Cyprus, 242n13
Cyrankiewicz, Józef, 33, 320
Czas, magazine, 3, 13
Czechoslovakia, 20n20, 113, 384
Czerniaków, Adam, 27, 41, 192n25, 215–17, 322–23, 492, 494–95
Czerniaków farm, 245–46, 250, 301, 331, 338–40, 343, 353, 357, 362, 365, 372, 390, 396, 398, 402–3, 406, 414, 424–25, 427, 430–32, 439, 444, 448, 455, 457, 469
Czerwińsk, 88n2
Czerwony Bór, 402–3
Częstochowa, 121, 175, 236n7, 271, 282, 333–34, 342, 346, 382, 408, 420, 426, 433, 437, 440, 446–47, 465, 469, 500, 505
Czyżyk, Cipora, 242

Dąbrowa, 160n50
Dąbrowa Basin, 419, 500
Danzig. See Gdańsk
Dawidowicz, Tobcia (Tauba), 231, 363, 368, 379, 388, 406, 475, 483
Dead Sea, 296
Death March, 64, 323, 495
deportation from the ghetto. See *große Aktion*
Diamant, Abraham (Awram), 100, 102n33, 340, 364, 476, 484
Diaspora, 18, 194, 493, 495, 510
Dmowski, Roman, 509
Dziennik Ludowy, newspaper, 294n8
Dnieper, river, 37
Dobuchno, Szaul, 475, 487, 521
Domb, engineer, 172, 174
Donetsk, 404
Dresden, 382, 494
Dror, 6, 48, 67, 101, 103n36, 171n10, 236n7, 313, 333–34, 338, 340, 343, 347, 353, 355, 360–62, 365, 368, 372, 387, 390–92, 394, 397–98, 403–4, 406–7, 410–11, 414, 416, 419, 422–23, 428, 430–31, 436, 440, 444, 446–48, 453–55, 462–63, 467, 469, 475–78, 479–81, 483–87, 491, 495–97, 507, 511, 520
Dubiński, Dawid, 293n7, 294
Duński, Cwi (Sewek), 47, 344, 365, 475, 484

Edelman, Marek, 3, 5–10, 13, 14n3, 24n31, 31n49, 31n51, 34n59, 35n60, 38, 53–54, 60, 74, 100, 105, 146, 166, 178n2, 196, 217, 228n3, 234, 248n25, 259n36, 270n47, 272n49, 283n55, 287, 296n12, 300n21, 312, 316n29, 320, 327n41, 328, 332, 335, 337, 339, 342, 344, 346–50, 353, 356, 360–61, 363, 365–67, 373, 377–78, 380, 383, 390, 393–94, 396, 410, 412–15, 417, 421, 423, 427, 432, 438, 441–42, 451, 456, 458, 463, 471, 479, 489, 494, 497, 500–1, 519

Egypt, 37, 193n28

Einsatzgruppen, 58, 122, 495

Einstein, Brucha, 226, 368

Einstein, Cypora, 226, 368, 483

Ejgier, Abraham (Eiger, Awram / Josek), 105, 254, 256, 332, 340, 368, 476, 484

Engelking, Barbara, 318–19

England, 37, 202, 371

Eretz Israel, 7, 46–47, 50, 60, 81–82, 101, 106, 113, 242–43, 338, 342, 355, 360, 391, 396, 403, 416, 420, 441, 465, 493, 497

Erlich, Eliahu (Alek / Elek), 100n27, 102n33, 342, 369, 484

Estonia, 493

Ethiopia, 37

expropriation activity ("exes"), 102, 252–54, 287, 293, 359, 383, 390, 401, 412, 421, 456, 495

extermination camps, 23n27, 88n2, 91n8, 146, 149n41, 169n6, 170n7, 177n1, 209n47, 213n48, 233n1, 387, 428n10, 491–92, 495–97, 499, 505, 508, 519

Europe, 16n13, 37, 179, 241, 260, 296–97, 300, 392, 492–93, 495, 498, 518

Fajgenblat, Jakub (Jakób, Jacek), 145–46, 359, 369, 388, 393, 396, 402, 411, 421, 430, 476, 482

Fajner (Feiner), Abram (Awram), 230, 370, 410, 457, 476, 486

Falanga, 17, 27, 31, 509

Falenica, 369, 393, 508

Farber, Józef (Josek), 97–99, 339, 352, 370, 373, 423, 476, 480

Feiner, Leon, 6, 9, 358, 426, 522

Feinmesser, Bronka (Fajnmesser).
    See Warman, Bronisława

Filipek, Włodzimierz, 13

Fingerhut, Genek, 145, 372, 388, 482

Fiszgrund, Julek, 31n49, 234, 417

Fiszgrund, Salo, 315–16, 438

Fliederbaum, Julian, 213n48

Folkscajtung, newspaper, 377, 450

Folman, Chawka, 8, 313, 339, 344, 355, 387–88, 390, 448, 462

Folman, Marek, 388, 405, 476, 487

Forward, newspaper, 294n8

Frajhajt, 48, 333–34, 338, 340, 347, 355, 360, 362, 364–65, 367, 372, 387, 390–92, 396, 398, 410, 413, 419–20, 428, 436, 439, 444, 454, 457, 461, 463, 468–69, 486, 495–97, 511

Frajhajt Szuc, 444, 511

France, 3, 37, 194, 218, 243, 398, 417, 522

Frank, Hans, 517

Frankfurt am Main, 377

Frasyniuk, Bogdan, 38

Freje Jugnt, Di, newspaper, 521–22

Frenkiel, Izio, 63

Frenkiel, Paweł, 289, 501, 519

Friedman, Sławek. *See* Mirski, Bronisław

Friedman, Zysie, 260–61

Frydman, Renia (Zosia), 197, 205, 234, 346, 371, 376–77, 417, 485, 515

Frydrych, Elżunia, 319–21, 377

Frydrych, Zygmunt (Zalman), 7, 57, 262, 271, 309, 319, 341, 349–50, 362,

377–78, 413, 433, 441, 462, 464, 476, 484–85
Frymer, Chaim, 60, 71–72, 81, 101, 105, 378, 384, 399, 424, 480
Fryszdorf, Gabriel (Gabryś), 231, 345, 378–79, 400, 407, 450–51, 468, 483
Fryszdorf, Hanka. *See* Krysztal-Fryszdorf, Chana
Fudem, Leon, 380
Fudem, Regina (Lilit), 141, 149, 339, 380, 395–96, 453, 485

Gąbin, 358
Gaik, Władysław (Krzaczek), 108, 159, 272, 274–76, 282–83, 309, 349, 359, 408–9, 453, 486
Galicia, 335, 419, 498
Gal On, 498
gathering funds, 172n11, 252, 294, 492, 502
Gawisar, Luba (Zielona Marysia), 163–75, 239, 242, 248, 300–1, 344, 371, 381, 388, 470–71, 486
Gdańsk, 34, 515, 518
Gefen, Lejb, 138, 359
Gelblum, Irena (Irka), 81–82, 166, 169, 171, 239, 243, 252, 265, 300, 302, 344, 381, 388, 471, 485
Geller, Eliezer, 120, 130, 136, 139–40, 146, 149, 155, 336, 347, 359, 381–82, 385, 391, 393, 402, 406, 438, 449, 479, 500, 519
General Government, 91n8, 335, 358, 433, 492, 499, 503–4, 506, 517
Geneva, 382, 413, 420
Gepner, Abraham, 77n54
German occupation, 20n20, 31n49, 209n47, 331, 351, 358, 381–82, 413, 426, 428, 433–34, 437, 458–59, 464, 491, 493–95, 499, 504–6, 510, 512, 514, 517–19

Germany, 22nn25–26, 118–19, 125, 208n44, 242–44, 377, 403, 415, 439, 442, 459, 464, 467, 495–96, 504, 519. *See also* Reich
Gerszuni, Gedalia, 476, 487, 521
Gestapo, 42, 46–47, 49, 90, 97–98, 111–12, 120–21, 131, 134n15, 135, 141, 144, 166–67, 169, 171, 201, 278, 283, 294, 331n1, 338, 348, 355, 364, 372, 387, 396, 402, 407, 409, 421, 429, 439, 443, 447–48, 451, 454, 460, 466, 492, 499, 502, 505, 507
Gęsiówka, prison, 192, 520
Gibraltar, 18
Giliński, Motl, 322
Giterman, Icchak, 492
Givat Olga, 412
GL (Gwardia Ludowa), 236n5, 357, 371, 375, 385, 408, 410, 460–61, 485–86, 501, 509–10
Glajtman–Putermilch, Masza, 9, 52–53, 58n17, 59n19, 83, 113, 145, 161, 295, 303, 307, 334, 342, 356, 365, 383–84, 394, 397, 418, 420, 422, 424, 427, 430, 445, 448, 451, 458, 461
Gniezno, 29n47
Goliborska, Teodozja (Tosia), 31n49, 311, 317, 415, 417
Goldman, Baruch, 351
Goldkorn, Dorka, 354, 385, 409, 421, 444, 485
Gomel, 13–15, 365
Gomułka, Władysław, 24, 280, 293, 390, 497
Gorbachev, Mikhail, 30
Gordonia, 48, 115–16, 120–21, 139, 144, 347, 353, 359, 364, 369, 372, 381–82, 388, 393, 402–3, 405–6, 411, 430, 475–79, 482, 486–87, 497
Górny, Jechiel (Jur), 100n27, 344, 386–87, 476, 484

Grabowski, Henryk (Heniek), 251–52, 308, 387, 466, 486
Grajek, Stefan, 150, 153, 155, 157–59, 175, 236, 310, 431
Grasberg, Jurek, 166–71, 174–75, 235, 236n4, 239, 279, 299, 301, 344, 388, 420, 470–71, 485
Gray Ranks, 29n46, 492, 504
Great Britain, 24т30, 499
Grobelna, 121
Grochów, 184, 308, 361, 364, 376, 394, 416, 428, 444, 463
Grodno, 120n7, 387, 427
Grodzisk, 31, 172, 174–75, 415
Gross-Rosen, 375
große Aktion, 4, 8, 54, 57, 93–94, 136n17, 167, 192n25, 244, 319, 332, 337, 341, 343, 345–46, 349, 361, 365, 368, 370, 373–75, 377, 379, 383, 388, 393, 395–96, 400, 416, 423–24, 427, 432, 434–35, 436n11, 438, 440, 445, 456, 460, 466, 469–70, 491–92, 498, 500–3, 510–11, 515, 517–18, 520, 522. *See also* kettle on Miła Street
Growas, Mordechaj, 74–75, 231, 337–38, 352, 354, 389, 392, 399–400, 407, 411, 421, 430, 439, 446, 455, 461, 468, 481
Gruzalc, Lejb, 60, 72, 345, 363, 389, 394–95, 397, 412, 418, 427, 429, 448, 457, 461, 481
Grynberg, Michał, 92n8
Grynblatt, Józef (Bednarczyk), 289, 291
Grynszpan, Jurek, 125, 340, 350, 390, 405, 411, 421, 432, 469, 476, 483
Grynszpan-Frymer, Pnina (Pinia), 60, 77, 81, 85, 90n3, 92n9, 93n13, 93n15, 98nn23–24, 100nn27–28, 102n33, 106n42, 113, 242, 274, 345, 354, 367, 378, 384, 423–24, 452, 458

Gutman, Hanoch (Henoch), 74–75, 77, 79, 101, 103, 105, 252–55, 257, 302, 334, 338, 340, 350, 368, 375, 390–91, 394, 398, 410, 422, 431–32, 446, 455, 476, 484, 500
Gutman, Israel, 248n25, 261, 287, 301
Guzik, Dawid Daniel, 172, 492

Haifa, 242–43, 412, 452–53
Hajnsdorf, Miriam, 97, 391, 483
hakhshara, 333, 403, 405, 410–11, 413, 419, 428–30, 441, 465, 467, 493, 497
Hallman, Bernard, 515
Hallman workshop, 338, 379, 388, 439, 451, 453, 466, 468, 515
Halperin, Adam, 501
Halutz movement, 7, 245–46, 301, 331, 333, 335, 338 39, 343–44, 347, 353, 355, 360–62, 372, 390–91, 402–3, 406–7, 410, 413, 416, 425, 427–31, 436, 441, 444, 446–49, 453–55, 457, 462, 467–68, 491, 493, 496–98, 500
Hamersztajn, Lodzia, 6, 337, 406, 446, 458
Hannover, 17
Hanoar Hadati, 498
Hanoar Hacyjoni, 104n36, 245, 248n25, 339, 349, 351, 386, 418, 429, 432, 434, 439, 445, 475, 477, 484, 491, 498
Hapoel, sports club, 334, 444, 457, 496, 511
Hasidim, 18, 394
Haszomer Hacair, 6, 41–42, 44, 75n49, 96–99, 141, 159, 242n15, 331–32, 334–37, 339–40, 354, 358, 370, 374, 380, 382, 385, 389, 391–93, 395–96, 399, 406–7, 409, 413, 419, 421–23, 425, 429, 435, 438, 446–48, 450, 452, 461–62, 465–68, 470, 475–83, 485–87, 498–99, 505, 507

536 | Index

Haszomer Hadati, 48, 498
Hebrew, 3–4, 10, 37n64, 86, 116, 120, 170n8, 181, 241, 242n15, 258, 261n38, 334–35, 339, 351, 355, 359, 361, 370, 380, 405, 412, 427–28, 432, 452, 454, 467, 498, 509, 514
Hedera, 242n13
Hehaluc Hacair, 344, 497
Hehaluc Hamizrachi, 498
Hehaluc Pionier, 496
Held, Adolf, 293n7, 294
Heller, Szymon, 141, 151–53, 363, 476, 482
Himelfarb, Adek, 145, 393, 476, 482
Hirszfeld, Ludwik, 183–85, 371
Hitler, Adolf, 17, 21, 23, 31–32, 149
Hitlerjugend, 22n25
Hlond, August, Cardinal, 29
Hochberg, Adolf, 79, 254, 263, 274, 281, 284, 306, 344, 352, 354, 394, 413, 433, 437, 476, 484
Hochberg, Dawid, 72, 313, 394–95, 457, 461, 476, 481
Holocaust, 3–5, 10, 22, 24, 42, 115, 190, 215, 216n50, 221–22, 242, 328, 335, 365, 376, 381, 491, 501, 505, 508, 511, 514
Holon, 47
Home Army. *See* AK
Hrubieszów, 7, 391, 487, 493, 521
Hungary, 48, 50, 113, 404, 422

Igła, Zygmunt, 231, 396, 402, 421, 476, 483
Ikhud, party, 491
intelligentsia, 181, 194, 497, 504, 510–11
Iran, 194
Israel, 3, 17–18, 35, 37, 51, 82, 115, 128, 130, 149n43, 174, 177–79, 193–95, 231, 233–34, 236n7, 243nn15–16, 251n30, 258, 260, 295–98, 300, 315n28, 331, 335, 344, 355, 358, 360, 378, 381, 412, 419–20, 433, 436, 441, 443, 453, 470–71, 487, 494, 501, 507–8, 511. *See also* Eretz Israel
Italy, 252, 381
Iwińska, Estera, 320

Jabotinsky, Vladimir, 493
JAF (Yidishe Arbeter Froy), 15, 383, 493
Jankielewicz, Adek, 60, 363, 397, 457, 476, 481
January operation, 5, 7–8, 24–25, 60–64, 77, 97–100, 125, 146, 169, 185n18, 216n49, 244–45, 250–51, 290, 308, 321, 337–38, 341, 343, 346, 353, 355, 359–61, 363–64, 366, 370, 372, 375, 381–83, 385–87, 390–91, 393, 399, 401, 405, 409–12, 414, 417, 423, 425, 428, 430, 432, 439–40, 443–47, 449, 451, 460, 462–63, 466, 468–69, 486–87, 500, 503, 518, 520
Jaruzelski, Wojciech, 20–21, 30
Jaszyński, Lejb (Jasiński), 398, 411, 476, 484
Jawne, 382, 461, 514
Jaworski, Michał (Najkrug), 398–99, 437, 485
Jaworski, Seweryn, 38
Jehudija, school, 181–82, 216, 345, 376, 387, 435, 469–70
Jelenkiewicz, Jasia (Ostaszewska), 195–96
Jerusalem, 51, 251n30, 258n35, 284, 298, 300, 361, 433
Jewish Community Organization, 65, 196n30, 348, 436, 492, 494, 505, 522
Jewish Educational and Cultural Association. *See* Tarbut
Jewish Fighting Organization. *See* ŻOB
Jewish Military Union. *See* ŻZW
Jewish Museum, 20n20

Jewish National Committee. *See* ŻKN
Jewish Order Service, 50–51, 56, 120, 122–23, 144, 152–53, 167, 169, 185n18, 185n20, 192n25, 253, 291, 364, 366, 389, 400–1, 409, 439, 444, 457, 460n12, 492–93, 500, 502–3, 517–18, 521
Jewish Police *See* Jewish Order Service
Jewish Social Welfare. *See* ŻSS
Jewish Social Welfare Society. *See* ŻTOS
Jewish Socialist Working-class Youth. *See* Jugnt
Jewish Working Women. *See* JAF
JHI (Jewish Historical Institute), 8, 514, 527
John Paul II, Pope, 34n59
Joint, 172, 261n38, 492, 494, 505
Jóźwiak, Franciszek (Witold), 236, 272n49, 298
Judaism, 29nn46–47, 180–81, 509
Judenrat, 4, 42, 46, 92, 100n28, 118–19, 123, 213, 216–17, 319, 322n39, 375, 401, 449, 460n12, 488, 491–92, 495, 498, 502, 504, 506, 513, 520, 522
Jugnt, 369, 416, 467, 521–22
Jugnt-Frajhajt, newspaper, 496
Jugnt Sztime, newspaper, 494
Jugnt Weker, newspaper, 363, 494
Junge Gwardie, newspaper, 494
Jungbor, 369, 467, 511
Justman, Reginka, 9, 487
Jutrznia, sports club, 363, 441, 448

Kac, Jakub, 476, 487, 521
Kac, Mania, 322, 394
Kacenelebogen, Mosze, 118
Kacenelson, Icchak, 338, 361, 488
Kajszczak, Bronisław, 160
Kalisz, 505
Kalwaria, Góra, 87, 297–98, 467
Kamieniecki, Eryk, 357

Kamiński, Aleksander (Hubert), 27, 166–68, 174–75, 234, 239, 248, 299, 388, 420, 470, 504–5
Kanał, Izrael, 276, 354, 382, 400–1, 468, 479, 518–19
Kapłan, Josef (Josek), 41, 47, 96–98, 331, 391–92, 476, 487, 505
Karmi, Aron (Chmielnicki), 80, 115, 139, 145, 161, 242, 254, 258, 359–60, 363, 388, 393, 399, 404, 406, 452–53, 462, 482
Karski, Jan (Kozielewski), 48, 297, 505, 522
Katowice, 41, 44, 46, 51
Katyń, 121n7, 489
Kaunas, 294n8, 331
Kawe, Herszl (Heniek, Hesiek), 149, 333, 351–52, 357, 363, 392, 401–3, 436–37, 439–40, 419, 482
Kawęczyn, 387, 435, 442, 466
Kawenoki, Guta, 145, 154, 369, 396, 402, 421, 482
Kedyw, 292
Kennkarte, 27, 111, 506
kettle on Miła Street, 57–59, 96, 208–9, 210–11, 506, 515
kibbutz, 6, 49n16, 171, 174, 177, 242–43, 245n19, 296, 298, 308, 313–14, 333, 335n3, 336, 339, 344, 353, 355, 360–62, 364–65, 372, 382, 390, 394, 400, 406, 410–11, 415–16, 418, 420, 425, 428n10, 429, 430, 435–36, 444–46, 448, 454–55, 465, 470–71, 491, 495, 497–98, 505–6, 508
Kielce, 36, 115, 175, 193, 320, 333, 360, 382, 419–20, 423, 436, 501, 506–7
Kielson, Hela, 208n45, 211, 317
King, Martin Luther, 21
Kiszczak, Czesław, 36
KK (Komisja Koordynacyjna). *See* Coordinating Committee

Klajnwajs, Henoch (Heniek / Michałek), 142, 145, 149–50, 155, 160, 403–4, 422, 428, 455, 482
Klepfisz, Gina, 441, 512
Klepfisz, Michał, 7, 54, 103, 251, 258–59, 302, 309, 321, 350, 358, 379, 399, 404–5, 426, 441, 447, 476, 484–85
Klog, Blima, 318, 365, 438
Knesset, 260
Kojfman, Mosze (Mojszele), 226–28, 341
Kolbe, Maksymilian Maria (Rajmund), 21
Kolomyia, 294, 336
Koluszki, 125, 127–28
Komorowski, Tadeusz, (Bór-Komorowski), 23–24, 389
Koniecpol, 426, 433
Konin, 340, 440
Konrad, Fritz, 517
Koński, Jehuda (Juda), 143, 145, 405–6, 411, 476, 486
KOR (Komitet Obrony Robotników), 29n46, 35
Korczak, Janusz, 21, 183n12, 204–7, 215, 338, 410, 466, 494, 507, 517
Korczak, Różka, 331
Korn, Leja (Lea), 145, 154, 402, 405–6, 445, 476, 482
Kornblum, Alma (Kerenbrum), 406, 476, 482
Korngold, Lea, 149, 406, 482
Kościuszko, Tadeusz, 328
Kossak-Szczucka, Zofia, 199
Kossower, Róża, 218n50
Kotarbiński, Tadeusz, 44
Kowner, Aba, 242–43, 331, 433
Kowner, Witka Kempner, 243
Koziebrodzka, Lea (Lońka), 335, 476, 487, 507
Koziebrodzki, Abraham, 338
Krakow, 7, 9, 315n28, 175, 241, 316n29, 346, 358, 361, 377, 393, 433, 440–42, 447, 462, 468–69, 487, 491, 500, 508–9
Krall, Hanna, 3, 26, 32, 36, 195, 198, 296n12, 314, 328
Kripo (Kriminalpolizei), 202, 282, 408
Krupnik, engineer, 172
Krzaczek. *See* Gaik, Władysław
Kryształ-Fryszdorf, Chana, 110–11, 231, 345, 378, 400, 407–8, 424, 450, 483
Kuroń, Jacek, 38
Kutno, 140, 381, 412
Kyiv, 17

Landau, Margalit (Emilka), 74, 96, 98–99, 337, 389, 409, 438–39, 476, 486, 507
Lanzmann, Claude, 177n1
Latvia, 169n6, 493
League for Aid to Workers in Israel, 419–20, 436, 507
Lebendiger, Aba, 121
Łęczyca, 459
Leipzig, 394
Legiec, Stanisława and Władysław, 373, 386, 397, 408–10, 417–18, 447, 449, 469, 486
Legionowo, 91–92
Lejkin, Jakub, 389, 409, 439, 454
Lenin, Vladimir, 15
Lent, Szanaan (Hersz), 100n27, 106, 230, 340, 410, 435, 451, 477, 484
Lerer, Cypora, 254, 340, 368, 410, 476, 484
Lewental, Szymon, 143, 405, 411, 476, 486
Lewin, Gina, 477, 487, 521
Lewin, Lejzer (Eliezer), 150, 154, 431, 507
Lifszyc, Pola, 322
Lis, Bogdan, 38
Litman, Josef (Josek), 96, 98–100, 102n33, 104–6, 109, 413, 423, 476, 484

Lithuania, 42, 120–21n7, 169n6, 194, 294n8, 356, 361, 449–50, 470, 493

Łódź, 32–33, 38, 100n27, 101, 115, 119, 122, 127–28, 130, 145, 185n18, 196, 217, 226, 252, 322n39, 323n40, 328, 333, 339, 342, 347, 351, 353–55, 360, 367, 371–72, 381, 386, 390, 402, 405, 408, 410–12, 416–19, 422, 427, 428n10, 429–30, 440–41, 444, 449, 459–60, 464–65, 467, 507, 522, 527

Lohamei Ha-Getaot, 82, 177, 308, 314, 344, 355, 471, 508

Łomianki, 80, 107, 109–10, 159–61, 178, 269–70, 272, 276, 281, 335, 338, 342, 345, 349–51, 359, 362–63, 370, 378–79, 384, 389, 400, 408, 417, 420, 422, 424, 434, 443–44, 447–48, 453, 455–56, 459, 462, 465, 469, 507

London, 24n31, 217, 221n57, 227n2, 259, 294, 296, 475, 502, 505, 522

London List, 6–8, 10, 475, 487

Łopata, Chaim, 261, 287–88

Loth, Felek, 188, 191–92, 198

Lubetkin, Celina (Cywia), 6, 31n49, 78–79, 83, 104, 171n10, 177, 192, 227n2, 235, 242, 244–45, 281, 294, 297–98, 301, 306, 310, 317, 337, 344, 348, 355, 361–62, 367, 413–15, 417, 420, 431, 455, 469, 471, 480, 495, 520

Lublin, 113, 183n13, 216n49, 261n38, 280, 358, 375, 378, 384, 391, 409, 415, 418, 514, 521

Luden, Itzhak, 494

Lustiger, Jean-Marie (Aron), 183

Lwów, 188, 374, 398, 404, 415, 436, 441, 460, 465, 508–9

Maapilim, 505

Machtyngier, Leon, 164

Mądry, Polish policeman, 271, 277–78, 433

Majdanek, 64, 352, 371, 377, 420, 487, 497, 503, 519

Majerowicz, Marek (Meirowicz, Meir), 336, 372, 412, 415, 482

Makkabi, sports movement, 115, 404, 508

Makower, Henryk, 185, 187

Małkinia, 128, 355, 377, 409, 456–57, 507

Manulak, Bronka, 100n27, 107, 274, 344, 416, 423, 477, 484

March 1968, socio-political crisis, 33–36, 177, 190, 193–95, 221n57, 347, 371, 375, 399, 429, 459, 508

Margolis-Edelman, Ala (Alina), 9, 33–34, 175, 196–98, 208, 320, 346, 366, 371, 376, 415–17, 485

Mark, Bernard, 8, 103n34, 108n47

Marseilles, 242

Martial Law, 21n21, 25n38, 29–30n48, 34n58, 36n63

Maselman, Rysiek (Moselman), 108, 268, 276, 281–83, 409, 417, 469

Matywiecki, Anastazy (Nastek), 237, 257

Mauthausen, 26, 51, 358, 497

Medem Sanatorium, 53–54, 225, 322, 383, 393, 508

Meed, Vladka (Międzyrzecka). *See* Peltel, Fajgele

Meisel, Maurycy, 494

Merchants' Congregation school, 16, 182, 374

Michalin, 399, 437, 502

Michnik, Adam, 38

Midrasz, journal, 196n30

Miedzeszyn, 53, 383, 508

Międzyrzec Podlaski, 333

Milanówek, 197–98, 346, 421, 428

Milejkowski, Izrael, 213n48

Miłosz, Czesław, 170n7

Minsk, 13, 356

Mińsk Mazowiecki, 89, 400

Mirski, Bronisław, 8, 347, 374–76, 390, 405, 411, 469, 483
Mischling, 133–34, 359
Mitterrand, François, 30
Mizrachi, 395, 413, 419, 509, 512
Modlin, 90–91, 112, 423, 450
Monte Cassino, 489
Montreal, 64, 231, 342, 452
Moravia, 375
Morgen Frei, newspaper, 331
Morgensztern, Jochanan, 150, 154, 419–20, 477, 479
Morgensztern, sports club, 404, 493–94, 512
Moscow, 318n31
Mosdorf, Jan, 16n12
Mostowicz, Arnold, 322–23
Mubarak, Hosni Muhammad, 18
Munich, 17
Mussolini, Benito, 297
Mysłowice, 46, 51

Nachman of Breslov, rabbi, 18n19
Najberg, Leon, 261
Nakam, group, 242–44
Nansen, Fridtjöf, 79n5
Nansen passport, 179
Narew, river, 91n8, 402–3
Narutowicz, Gabriel, 29, 509
Nasz Przegląd, newspaper, 164n3
National Alliance (Stronnictwo Narodowe), 509
National Armed Forces. *See* NSZ
National Democracy. *See* ND
National-Radical Camp. *See* ONR
ND (Narodowa Demokracja), 16n12, 187–89, 191, 509
Neged Ha-Zerem, newspaper, 336, 466, 499
Neuengamme, 497
Neustadt, Leon, 492
Neustadt, Melekh, 6, 74n44, 75n49, 301–2, 309, 355, 449–50, 466n15

Neveh Sha'anan, 410
New York, 7, 208n44, 358, 371, 393, 405, 408, 426, 493, 522
New Zionist Organization, 493
Niewiadomski, Eligiusz, 29
NKVD, 516
Norway, 42
Nowa Młodzież, newspaper, 494
Nowodworski, Dawid, 144, 147, 152, 157, 159–60, 333, 359, 363, 395, 404, 406, 413, 421–22, 430, 434–35, 445, 447–48, 453, 477, 482
Nowogrodzki, Majus, 7, 360, 405, 450
Nowy Dwór Mazowiecki, 85–86, 88, 90–94, 96, 100–1, 112, 396, 413, 423–24
NSDAP, 50, 408
NSZ (Narodowe Siły Zbrojne), 234n2, 338, 389, 509
number for life, 57, 136, 146, 166, 210–12, 366, 503, 506, 510, 515
Nuremberg, 242n14

occupied territory. *See* German occupation
Ochota, 219, 434
Odessa, 37
Ogórek, Chana, 184
Ojfbrojz, Der, newspaper, 499
OMTUR (Organizacja Młodzieży Towarzystwa Uniwersytetu Robotniczego), 443, 521
Oneg Shabbat, 216n50, 386–87, 496, 514
ONR (Obóz Narodowo-Radykalny), 16–17, 27, 31, 202, 509
Opolion, factory owner, 141–42, 453, 462
Opoczno, 115–16, 118–20, 123, 125, 130, 134–36, 139, 359, 381
ORT (Organizacja Rozwoju Twórczości Przemysłowej, Rzemieślniczej i Rolniczej wśród

Ludności Żydowskiej), 53, 64, 333, 339, 349, 383, 407, 410, 516
Orzech, Maurycy, 294
Osęka, Janusz, 32
Ostrów Mazowiecka, 413, 503
Ostrowiec Kielecki (nad Kamienną / Świętokrzyski), 332, 338, 340, 355, 368, 382, 395, 419, 431, 440, 446–47, 452–54, 462, 468
Oświęcim. *See* Auschwitz
Otwock, 89, 117, 183n12, 208n45, 360

Pajewski, Tadeusz, 216n50
Palestine, 6, 74n44, 116, 125–26, 128, 142, 161, 172n11, 179, 230, 241, 242n13, 280, 296–98, 333, 338, 344–45, 360, 362, 367, 378, 384, 391, 394, 397, 404–5, 415, 418–19, 422, 424, 428–29, 433–36, 447–48, 453, 463, 468, 470, 491, 493, 495, 497–99, 505, 507, 509–10
Papier, Pnina. *See* Grynszpan-Frymer, Pnina
Papier, Zygmunt (Zysiek), 92–93, 98–99, 100n27, 102n33, 104, 106n42, 340, 423–24, 435, 477, 484
Paris, 178, 183n11, 191, 417
partisan units, 42, 74, 80, 107, 110–12, 153–54, 159, 161, 234, 242n15, 270, 334, 336, 338, 342–43, 345, 349, 363, 372, 378, 384, 386, 389, 391, 396–97, 400–1, 411, 424, 426, 430, 435, 437, 441, 443, 445, 451–53, 456–59, 461, 487, 503, 509, 519–21
Pasamonik, Rebeka (Rywka), 245, 353, 378, 424–25, 432, 480
Pat, Jakub, 226, 293n7, 294
Pawiak, prison, 16n12, 172, 191, 216n50, 371, 373, 396, 461, 466, 487, 492, 499, 503, 505, 507
Peltel, Fajgele (Władka) 107, 141n19, 301, 348, 350, 358, 378, 426, 438, 443, 447, 458, 464, 485

People's Army. *See* AL
People's Guard. *See* GL
People's Republic of Poland, 14n3, 29n45, 33n55, 35n60, 36n63, 188, 195n29, 209n47, 320n37, 494, 508–9, 521
Perelman, Mejlach, 65–72, 302–3, 418, 426, 477, 481
Peretz, Yitzhak Leib, 37, 407
Perlstein, Leon, 428n9
Petakh Tikva, 241
Piaseczno, 240, 410, 432
Piłsudski, Józef, 23n29, 495
Pinkiert, Mordechaj, 144n27, 170n8
Pińsk, 25, 428
Piwnik, Jan (Ponury), 25n37
Pionier (Pioneer), 163, 459, 496, 510
Piotrków, 323, 358, 366, 417, 436
Płaszów, 375
Plewczyńska, Janina, 202
Płock, 119, 131, 374
Płotnicka, Chańcia (Chana), 149–50, 404, 428, 455, 477, 485
Płudy, 349–51, 378, 462
Poalej Syjon Left (Poalei Zion Smol), 104n36, 216n50, 226, 230, 334, 342, 369, 376, 386, 394, 410–11, 413, 416–17, 435, 439, 445, 451, 465, 467, 475–79, 484–85, 494, 498, 507, 510–11, 514, 521
Poalej Syjon Right (Poalei Zion Yemin, 98, 150, 154, 159, 278, 333, 340, 371–72, 412, 415, 419–20, 467, 475–79, 482, 495–96, 507, 510–11, 514
Podkowa Leśna, 131
Pocalun, Eugenia, 7
Podolski, Ignacy, 503
pogrom, 16, 22n25, 23, 29, 36, 182, 193, 320, 382, 506, 509, 513
Poland, 3, 5–6, 13, 16–18, 20, 22–23, 25n38, 27, 29n44, 29n47, 34–37,

44, 47, 51, 71, 81–82, 86, 101, 113, 161, 172, 175, 177–78, 180, 183, 190–94, 196, 209n47, 221, 233n1, 243, 250n27, 252, 255, 258, 261n38, 279–80, 287, 296, 298n16, 314–15, 319–20, 331n1, 335–36, 342, 346, 351–52, 358, 367, 370–71, 378, 381–82, 403, 412, 415, 417, 424, 426–27, 428n10, 433, 438, 442, 445, 449–50, 452, 456, 459, 464, 471, 489, 491, 493–99, 501, 503, 505–17, 521–22

Poleszuk, Włodzimierz, 399
Polish Army (WP), 24n30, 29n46, 289n4, 292, 445, 450, 502, 504
Polish Communist Party, 236n5, 351, 373, 410, 510
Polish government-in-exile, 227n2, 475, 499, 502, 505, 522
Polish People's Army (LWP), 353, 399. *See also* AL
Polish police (dark-blue police), 121, 125, 131, 134, 192n25, 271, 277, 336, 354, 357, 359, 378, 385, 399, 413, 426, 433, 436, 442, 491, 511, 517–19
Polish Socialist Party. *See* PPS
Polish Underground State, 24n31, 496, 522
Polish United Workers' Party. *See* PZPR
Polish Warsaw rising, 14, 23–24n30, 27, 29n46, 31–32, 80, 110–11, 172, 192, 197–98, 208n44, 234n2, 241, 252n31, 254, 259n36, 265n44, 319, 342, 344–46, 353–54, 358, 362, 367, 369, 371, 384, 388, 407, 409, 414, 417, 424, 426, 431, 433, 441, 450–51, 459, 464, 471, 489, 499, 519–20
Polish Workers' Party. *See* PPR
Polityka, journal, 196n31
Pomiechówek, 88n2, 90n3, 91–93, 424

Ponary, 120–21, 387
Poniatowa, 346, 454, 519
Popiełuszko, Jerzy, 34
Posner, rabbi, 179
Powązki, 489
POWs (prisoners of war), 24n30, 25, 121n7, 198, 242n14, 370, 375, 378, 381, 460, 504
Poznań, 13, 38, 189, 368
PPR (Polska Partia Robotnicza), 8, 62, 67, 105, 153, 159–60, 236n5, 272n49, 293, 331, 333, 339–40, 343, 351–52, 354, 357, 363, 370, 373, 375, 384–86, 390, 392, 397–98, 400–1, 403, 405, 411, 421–22, 436, 440, 443–44, 448, 451, 460–61, 463, 469–71, 479–83, 485–86, 498, 502, 510, 512, 516
PPS (Polska Partia Socjalistyczna), 15, 23, 216, 230, 236n5, 252n31, 267n45, 294n8, 318n31, 342, 374, 401, 428, 441, 443, 464, 486, 493, 495, 511–12, 516, 521
PPS-WRN (Wolność, Równość, Niepodległość), 318n31
Praga, Rafał, 318yf
Prague, 20
Praszkier (Praszker), Jakub, 104, 248n25, 349, 351, 386, 418, 429, 477, 484
Provisioning Authority, 77n54, 256, 390, 433
Pruszków, 198, 208n44, 265, 319, 338, 406, 433, 454–55, 507
Przegląd Powszechny, newspaper, 34
Przełom, newspaper, 46
Przemyk, Grzegorz, 29
Przemyśl, 319
Przytyk, 23, 29n47
Putermilch, Jakub, 62, 81–82, 113, 145, 384, 424, 430, 451, 458, 477, 482
Pużak, Kazimierz (Bazyli), 318
PWN, publishing house, 371, 376

PZPR (Polska Zjednoczona Partia
    Robotnicza), 8, 33, 236n5, 314n28,
    497, 512

Raczkiewicz, Władysław, 522
Radom, 23, 121, 364, 398
Radomsko, 353, 440
Radomyśl, 179
Rajszczak, Feliks (Felek), 278, 354, 421,
    431, 486
Rajszczak, Tadeusz (Tadek), 101, 252,
    431
Rakowski, Mieczysław, 33
Rappaport, Natan, 49
Ratajzer, Kazik (Rotem, Simcha), 3, 8, 75,
    86, 108, 170, 233, 248n25, 258n35,
    284, 298, 340–41, 343–44, 349, 352,
    354, 362, 377, 381, 405, 408, 413–
    14, 417, 420–21, 424, 429, 432–33,
    441, 444, 447, 464, 471, 484
Ravensbrück, 386, 497
Rawa Mazowiecka, 342
Rawicz, 318n31
Reagan, Ronald, 30
Red Cross, 197, 384, 464
Reich, 22, 495–96, 504, 517, 519
Rembertów, 343, 387, 442, 466
Riga, 493
Righteous Among the Nations, medal,
    44n6, 210n47, 251, 252n31, 331,
    387, 410, 429, 431, 441, 444, 459,
    464, 505
Ring, union, 360, 494, 508
Ringelblum, Emanuel, 216–17, 289, 422,
    501, 504, 511, 514. *See also* Oneg
    Shabbat
Rodal, Leon, 289, 501, 519
Romania, 81, 113, 161, 336, 360, 424,
    453
Rome, 29n47
Ron, Szmuel (Rozencwajg), 4, 41, 49n16,
    51, 335, 396

Roosevelt, Franklin D., 294, 505, 522
Rotblat, Lutek (Lejb), 245, 248n25, 353,
    357, 389, 434–35, 441, 446, 466,
    477, 481, 491
Rotszajn, Heniek, 94
Rotem, Gina, 258
Rotem, Simcha. *See* Ratajzer, Kazik
Rowecki, Stefan (Grot), 23–24
Różański, Eliahu (Elek), 337, 389, 409,
    423, 438, 486
Rozenfeld, Michał, 436–37, 357, 422,
    456, 479
Rozenfeld, Różka, 352, 362, 385, 434,
    436–37, 477, 482
Rozenman, Adam, vii
Rozensztajn, Rywka (Stasia), 208, 228,
    236, 265, 310, 312–14, 318, 365,
    367, 383, 438
Rozental, Mordechaj, 119–20
Rozowski, Lejb (Lejbl), 306, 344, 416,
    437, 477, 484
Rozowski, Welwł (Wolf), 4, 207, 226–28,
    231, 306, 310, 313, 315–16, 342,
    363, 365, 368, 379, 396, 400, 407,
    438, 451, 455–56, 458, 483, 488
Rubeńczyk, Mosze, 477, 488, 521
Rybicki, Józef, 292
Rudnicki, Lew, 402, 439, 477, 482
Rufeisen-Schüpper, Hela, 154n47, 336,
    341, 343, 357, 401, 435, 441–42,
    444–45, 466, 486
Rumkowski, Chaim Mordechaj, 322–23
Russia, 13–14, 54, 128, 180, 190, 293n7,
    345, 356–57, 371, 407, 411, 493, 516

SA (Sturmabteilung), 23n25
Sachsenhausen, 24n30, 497
Sadowska, Barbara, 29n48
Sak, Józef, 6, 236, 265, 338
Sakowska, Ruta, 512
Samsonowicz, Ignacy (Leszczyński,
    Tadeusz), 6, 366, 464

Saska Kępa, 163, 172, 174, 239, 388, 470–71
Sawicka, Krystyna, 516
Sawicka, Marysia, 208n44, 236, 265, 271, 371, 441, 443, 458, 463, 486, 512
Sawicka, Paula, 314
SB (Służba Bezpieczeństwa). *See* UB
Schüpper, Hela. *See* Rufeisen-Schüpper
Schwarzbart, Ignacy, 6, 296, 298
SDKPiL, 494
Security Service. *See* UB
Sejm, 29, 36n63, 260
Shaulists, 169
Sherer, Emanuel, 6
Shoah, 177
Shomer, 303, 334–38, 350, 361, 370, 380, 385, 388–89, 392–93, 401, 406, 409, 422, 425, 430, 435, 445–47, 455, 462, 465–66, 470, 497–99, 500
Shulman, Victor, 294n9
Siauliai, 331
Siberia, 408, 429, 463
Siekierski, Mieczysław, 442–43, 485
Siewierski, Stefan, 252, 443–44, 463, 486
Sikorski, Władysław, 259n36, 522
Siła-Nowicki, Władysław, 221
Silesia, 466, 505
Silverstein, Leokadia (Hamersztajn, Lodzia), 110, 175, 337, 362
Six-Day War, 193n28
Skała, 121
Skarżysko-Kamienna, 408, 433
Skif, 54, 312, 322, 345, 349–50, 356, 363, 365, 378, 383, 394, 399, 407, 418, 426, 437–38, 493–94
Skra, sports club, 267n45, 441, 512
Skrzeszewska-Wysocka, Zosia.
  See Frydman, Renia
Słonim, 355, 391, 398
Słowacki, Juliusz, 317, 361n7
Slovakia, 42
Słowo Młodych, newspaper, 120, 497

Sobibór, 197n1, 497
Socialist Youth Organization Life.
  See Życie
Society for the Propagation of Labor among the Jews. *See* ORT
Sokółka, 386, 427
Sokółka, Szyfra (Stenia), 336
Solidarity, movement, 21n21, 34n58, 35–36
Sokołów, 333, 360, 377
Sorbonne, 180
Sosnkowski, Kazimierz, 259n36
Sosnowiec, 41–44, 46n8, 337, 358, 500
Soviet Army, 31, 456, 395, 510
Soviet occupation, 120n7, 398, 497, 499
Soviet Union, 385, 512. *See also* USSR
Spartakus, Union of Independent Socialist Youth, 362, 385, 421, 434, 437, 459, 516
Spasowski, Władysław, 44
SR (Socialist Revolutionary Party), 14–15, 179, 516
Środula, 44
SS (Schutzstaffel), 22n25, 91n8, 120, 121n7, 125, 127, 133, 242n14, 265, 315, 332, 375, 410, 460, 466, 493, 517
SS-Werterfassungstelle, 99, 136, 138, 166, 372, 517
Stalin, Joseph, 21, 30, 190, 352
Starobielsk, 489
Starzyński, Stefan, 320n34
Stein, Dawid. *See* Sztajn
Sterdyń, 333, 360
stigmatization of the Jews, 29n47, 88, 90, 118, 164, 167, 373, 517. *See also* number for life
Stolak, Abram, 64, 100n27, 102, 107, 274, 423–24, 445, 478, 484
Stroop, Jürgen, 103n34
Strzały, newspaper, 385, 516
Strzelecka, Jadwiga, 174, 471

Stutthof, 497
Suknik, Icchok (Koza), 64, 357, 442, 444–46, 477, 481
Sweden, 208n45, 320, 353, 408, 429
Świdowska, Inka. *See* Blady-Szwajger, Adina
Święcicki, Tytus, 31
Śwital, Stanisław, 31–32, 371
Świętochowski, Władysław (Władek), 316, 342, 430, 451, 458–59, 486
Switzerland, 126
Sword and the Plow, The, movement (Miecz i Pług), 288–89
synagogue, 20, 22n25, 86, 115, 120, 180–81, 360, 398, 441, 519
Syrkin, Nachman, 510
Szajngut, Tuwia (Tadek), 159, 169, 272, 275–76, 282, 359, 409, 429, 447–48, 453, 471, 486
Szapiro, Hanka. *See* Sawicka, Krystyna
Szczecin, 195–96, 346
Szeryński, Józef Andrzej (Szynkman), 217, 401, 503, 517–18
Sznajdmil, Berek, 75, 105, 292, 302, 340, 366, 449–50, 477, 484
Szniper, Dow, 110, 345, 450, 458, 485
Szpigiel, Baruch (Bronek), 81, 113n52, 225–231, 316, 342, 368, 379, 451–52, 458, 468, 483
Szpigielman, Stefan, 179, 208, 345
Sztajn, Dawid, 332, 395, 452–53, 482
Sztengiel, Moniek, 453, 481, 521
Sztern, sports club, 369, 510
Szul-Kult, association, 415, 514
Szulman, Meir, 47
Szuster, Szlamek, 77–78, 108, 254–56, 258, 264, 274, 281, 284, 306, 352, 354, 367, 394, 414, 437, 454–55, 478, 484
Szuster-Kron, Hela, 331, 338, 340, 406, 427, 454–55
Szwarc, Meir, 149–50, 154, 336, 362, 379, 404, 428, 455–56, 477, 483

Szwarc, Szlomo (Szlojme), 231, 456, 477, 483
Szymańska, Zofia (Rozenblum), 183–84
Szyfman, Leja, 60, 72, 363, 457, 478, 481
Szyfman, Miriam, 60, 368, 370, 457–58, 477, 484

Tabaczyński, Beniamin, 293n7, 294
Tajtelbaum, Niuta (Witwicka, Wanda / Rywa), 7, 459–61, 486
Tarbut, association, 116, 334, 339, 359, 367, 405, 429, 454, 465, 509, 514–15
Tatra, mountains, 450
Tel Aviv, 83, 113, 115n1, 150n42, 161, 175, 241n12, 243, 360, 370, 378, 384, 410, 412, 424, 430, 454, 471
Teller, Motek. *See* Siekierski, Mieczysław
Tomaszów Mazowiecki, 120–22, 125, 405
Torah, 49
TOZ (Towarzystwo Opieki Zdrowotnej), 394
Trawniki, 42, 148–49, 216n50, 346, 454, 519
Treblinka, 42, 56n12, 57, 59, 96, 115, 127–28, 130, 150–51, 160, 177n1, 202, 204nn39–40, 205n42, 209, 213n48, 225, 227, 343, 346, 349, 352, 355, 358–59, 368, 374, 377, 387, 393, 399, 403–4, 412, 416, 422, 425, 438, 440, 442, 449, 452, 492, 496–97, 503, 506–8, 510, 515, 517–19
Troki, 120
Trupianski, Yankl, 322
Trzeciak, Stanisław, 16, 29
TSKŻ (Towarzystwo Społeczno-Kulturalne Żydów w Polsce), 315n28
Tygodnik Powszechny, newspaper, 34, 221

UB (Urząd Bezpieczeństwa), 34n58, 35–36
Ujazd, 125–26

Ukraine, 42, 182, 294n8, 495
Umschlagplatz, 54, 56, 96, 98–99, 149, 212, 219, 221, 225, 227, 233, 308, 313, 337, 341, 343, 346, 349, 352, 355, 361, 364, 366, 371, 375–76, 379, 386, 391, 399–400, 409, 425, 438–40, 449, 451, 492, 500, 503, 506, 518
Union. *See* Bund
Union of Armed Combat. *See* ZWZ
Union of Polish Youth. *See* ZMP
Unzer Vort, newspaper, 354
Uppsala, 221n57
USA, 293n7, 320n34, 371, 492, 494, 505. *See also* America
USSR, 17n17, 183n13, 509, 512, 520. *See also* Soviet Union

Vatican, 513
Vienna, 15
Vilnius, 47, 120–21n7, 242n15, 243n16, 294n8, 331, 335–36, 347, 361, 363, 385, 387, 419, 427, 447, 449, 465, 470, 493, 507, 509
Virtuti Militari, Order, 7, 259, 405
Vistula, river, 34n58, 37, 49, 77, 90n3, 91, 110, 121, 135, 174, 350, 471
Vittel, 409, 499
Volksdeutsche, 50, 119, 167, 246, 316, 422, 519, 521

Wąchalska, Anna, 263, 267, 271, 341, 354, 426, 441, 443–44, 463–64, 486
Wajs, Kuba, 145, 462, 482
Wajsgruz, Minia, 226, 342
Wald, Beniamin, 149, 250, 252, 254, 333, 343, 360, 368, 393, 395, 432, 439, 444, 463, 478, 483, 500
Walewski, Ryszard, 339
Walka Młodych, newspaper, 386
Warman, Bronisława (Feinmesser, Marysia), 202, 236, 279, 302, 321, 358, 370–71, 376, 396, 471, 485

Warman, Zygmunt, 31n49, 216, 236, 371, 417
Warsaw ghetto uprising, 3–4, 6–9, 22, 25–27, 70–71, 97, 112, 146, 205n41, 234, 244, 260–61, 287, 310, 343, 346, 363, 379, 401, 409–10, 417–18, 447, 461, 501, 509, 511–12, 518–20
Warsaw rising. *See* Polish Warsaw rising
Warsaw Polytechnic, 343, 370, 373
Warszawski, Dawid (Gebert), 196
Wasilewska, Wanda, 322
Wasser, Hirsz (Hersz), 102n33, 342
Wdowiński, Dawid, 288
Werbkowice, 391, 453, 487, 520–21
Wehrmacht, 495
Weil, Simone, 328
Wengrower, Jehuda, 70, 74–75, 78, 107, 160–61, 304, 384, 392, 464, 480, 481
Wiązowna, 117, 240
Wieliczka, 375
Wielun, 119
Wiernik, Jakub, 227n2
Wiernik, Lola, 226–27, 341
Więź, newspaper, 34
Wilchelmów, 131
Wilczyńska, Stefania, 204–5, 338
wildcat residents, 5, 135, 210, 212, 276, 339, 518, 520–21
Wilner, Izrael (Jurek / Arie), 4, 47, 170–71, 250–51, 295, 308, 312, 335, 361, 377, 387, 392, 428n10, 435, 442, 446, 465–66, 478, 485–86, 500
Windman, Icchak (Lalo / Lala), 282, 408
Winogron, Esterka, 204–6, 466
Winogron, Jehoszua (Szlomo), 338–39, 379, 392, 401, 430, 435, 466, 478, 483
Włodzimierz, 367, 508
Wola, 167, 265, 267, 463–64
Wolf, Helena, 189
Workers' Defense Committee. *See* KOR

Workers' University Society Youth Organization. *See* OMTUR
World War I, 179, 342, 493
World War II, 29n47, 242n13, 492, 496, 498–99, 507–9, 518
Wort, Dos, newspaper, 419
Wrocław, 183n9, 185
Wyszków, 74n44, 80, 110, 270, 333, 336, 338, 342, 349, 350–51, 358–59, 363, 369, 372, 378–79, 384, 389, 391, 396–97, 399–400, 402–4, 407, 411, 413, 422–24, 427, 430, 434–35, 437, 444–45, 447, 450–51, 456, 459, 461
Wyszogród, 88n2, 451

Yad Vashem, 251n30
Yagur, 344, 507
Yiddish, 4, 9–10, 37n64, 70, 72, 86, 116, 163, 167, 170n8, 241, 258, 317, 321, 332, 339, 354, 359, 361, 376, 383, 385, 394, 422, 430, 454, 493–95, 498–99, 510–11, 514–15
YIVO, 7, 405, 408
Yugnt. *See* Jugnt
Yugoslavia, 42

Za Naszą i Waszą Wolność, newspaper, 450
Żagiel, Sara, 8, 375, 469, 478
Zakroczym, 88n2
Zalcman, Baruch (Bruch), 226, 342
Zamość, 36n64, 419
Zamoszczer Sztyme, newspaper, 419
Zandman, Pnina, 76n49, 344, 430, 468, 482–83
Zarchi, Alik, 208
Żarki, 446, 505
Zawiercie, 44, 446
Zbąszyń, 22–23, 194, 496
Żegota Council for Aid to Jews, 209n47, 295n11, 421, 464
Żelechów, 333–34

Zieja, Jan, 29
Zielisławice, 426
Ziemian, Józef (Józek), 321
Zionism, 17–18, 194, 298, 301, 498, 510–11
Zionist Revisionists, movement, 413, 501
ŻKN (Żydowski Komitet Narodowy), 308, 315n28, 342, 348, 373, 392, 420, 502
ZMP (Związek Młodzieży Polskiej), 494, 521
Znak, periodical, 34
ŻOB (Żydowska Organizacja Bojowa), 5–10, 13, 31n49, 98n22, 100n27, 136n17, 139–40, 166–68, 170n8, 171n10, 172n11, 207, 215, 216n49, 228, 235n3, 236–37, 244–46, 248, 257, 264, 268–69, 282n54, 290, 292, 294–95, 301–2, 317, 322, 331–33, 335–37, 339–40, 343–44, 346, 348–49, 353–54, 356–59, 361–62, 366, 369–72, 378–79, 381–84, 386–92, 394–96, 399–405, 407–411, 414–17, 419–20, 423–26, 428, 431–36, 438, 440–43, 448–53, 455, 458, 462–69, 470–71, 475, 478–80, 485–89, 493–96, 500–2, 505, 507, 512, 517–19, 521, 527
Żoliborz, 31, 171, 175, 197, 236–37, 241, 342, 354, 362, 367, 369, 371, 414, 417, 433, 438
ŻSS (Żydowska Samopomoc Społeczna), 150n43, 492
ŻTOS (Żydowskie Towarzystwo Opieki Społecznej), 54, 291, 393, 503–4
Zurich Polytechnic, 29n45
Zweibaum, Juliusz, 185
ZWZ (Związek Walki Zbrojnej), 24n30. *See also* AK
Życie, socialist youth organization, 189, 373, 436, 459, 508

Zygielbojm, Szmuel, 217, 296n14, 323, 450, 522

Zylberberg, Heniek, 422, 461, 470, 478, 481

Zylberberg, Rachela, 374, 380, 470, 479, 481

Zylberg, Luba. *See* Gawisar, Luba

Żyrardów, 89, 319–21, 347, 362, 390, 392, 411, 457

ŻZW (Żydowski Związek Wojskowy), 5–6, 136n17, 248, 261, 287–92, 327n41, 339, 398, 493, 495, 501–2, 518–19